WE ARE AMERICA

A THEMATIC READER AND GUIDE TO WRITING

SIXTH EDITION

ANNA JOY
Sacramento City College

THOMSON

WADSWORTH

Australia • Brazil • Canada • Mexico • Singapore
Spain • United Kingdom • United States

THOMSON

WADSWORTH

We Are America
A Thematic Reader and Guide to Writing
Sixth Edition
Anna Joy

Editor in Chief: *PJ Boardman*
Publisher: *Lyn Uhl*
Director of Developmental English and College
  Success: *Annie Todd*
Development Editor: *Cathy Richard Dodson*
Editorial Assistant: *Daniel DeBonis*
Managing Technology Project Manager:
  Stephanie Gregoire
Associate Technology Project Manager: *Marla Nasser*
Marketing Assistant: *Kathleen Remsberg*
Marketing Communications Manager: *Darlene
  Amidon-Brent*
Content Project Manager: *Jennifer Kostka*
Senior Art Director: *Cate Rickard Barr*

Senior Print Buyer: *Betsy Donaghey*
Permissions Manager, Text: *Ron Montgomery*
Rights Acquisition Account Manager: *Mardell
  Glinski Schultz*
Permissions Freelancer: *Writer's Research Group*
Senior Permissions Manager, Images: *Sheri Blaney*
Photo Researcher: *Jill Engebretson*
Production Service/Compositor:
  ICC Macmillan Inc.
Text Designer: *Cyndy Patrick*
Cover Designer: *Hiroko Chastain/Cuttriss &
  Hambleton*
Text/Cover Printer: *Thomson West*
Cover Photos: © *Jamie Tanaka Photography*

Printed in the United States of America
1 2 3 4 5 6 7 11 10 09 08 07

Library of Congress Control Number: 2006941026

Thomson Higher Education
25 Thomson Place
Boston, MA 02210-1202
USA

For more information about our products,
contact us at:
Thomson Learning Academic Resource Center
1-800-423-0563

For permission to use material from this text or
product, submit a request online at
http://www.thomsonrights.com
Any additional questions about permissions can
be submitted by e-mail to
thomsonrights@thomson.com

ISBN-13: 978-1-4130-3037-2
ISBN-10: 1-4130-3037-8

Contents

Part IV Guidelines for Writing a Research Paper 387

Part V   Editing Your Writing   415

Preface

We Are America: A Thematic Reader and Guide to Writing introduces beginning writers to the writing process, basic reading skills, and the essential elements of effective writing—unity, coherence, completeness, and sentence skills. This textbook includes a thematic reader whose selections reflect culturally and ethnically diverse points of view. Readings, discussion questions, and topics for writing are designed to mirror students' backgrounds and concerns, and to increase students' sensitivity to experiences and cultural perspectives different from their own. In addition, this edition comes with cross-cultural thematic readings, practice exercises, a grammar handbook, and references to online explanations and exercises. Ideally, students will see themselves, their ideas, and their cultural or ethnic group as an important part of the larger, and increasingly more complex, American experience.

ORGANIZATION

The selection and organization of material in this book reflect the goals just outlined. Part I is an introduction to the writing process and a guide to active reading. Journal and freewriting exercises in Chapter 1 give students writing practice they need to gain confidence in their writing. Models of marginal notes and sample summaries in Chapter 2 illustrate active reading techniques, which students apply in a series of exercises. The second chapter also prepares students to write a critical response to a reading and provides a sample student response to a reading in the chapter. Chapter 3 and parts of Chapters 4 and 5 introduce the writing process and explain how the steps in writing can be used to compose paragraphs and essays. Chapters 4 and 5 also present the principles behind well-written paragraphs and essays, and ask students to revise sample papers for unity, development, and coherence.

Part II, Strategies for Writing, is a guide to writing designed to help students master several writing modes. Chapters in this section feature discussions of nine writing strategies, including narrating, describing, defining, process analysis, classification, causal analysis, comparing/contrasting, evaluating, and taking a stand. The discussions of model professional and student essays in each chapter support the premise that students can become better writers if they learn to identify key features, and rhetorical and organizational patterns, in the writing of others. Chapters include additional suggestions for applying the writing strategies featured in the chapter to student essays.

Part III is a cross-cultural reader that features readings by professional writers with themes such as the family, education, gender issues, culture and identity, and stereotypes.

Part IV introduces the process of writing research papers using the Modern Language Association's guidelines for writing research papers. Chapter 15 presents basic research techniques, such as time management, finding a topic, locating sources, taking notes, and planning and drafting the essay. The chapter also addresses proper citation of sources and includes suggestions for revising the essay. Chapter 16 provides sample bibliographical listings and models for citing sources in students' papers.

Part V focuses on sentence skills and is aimed at improving students' mastery of standard, academic English. Exercises show students how to find and correct errors that may appear in their own work. In addition, sentence-combining exercises target sentence fluency and encourage students to proofread and revise their writing. References to online explanations and exercises provide additional help for students who need more practice on their sentence skills.

As a whole, the five parts of this textbook offer students a complete writing program, the elements of which form a coherent whole. In Chapter 2, for example, instructions for active reading and for writing summaries give students information they need to analyze reading selections in Parts II and III. Instructions on the writing process in Chapters 3, 4, and 5 prepare students to write paragraphs and essays in response to topics that follow readings in Parts II and III. Topics for Writing make connections between two or more writers' approaches to a subject. Exercises in Parts I and V help students practice revising for essay coherence and development as well as for sentence correctness.

FEATURES

Clear explanations followed by practice exercises characterize the material in Part I. Basic writing and active reading techniques introduced in this section prepare students for more demanding tasks in Parts II and III.

Chapters 6, 7, and 8 in Part II introduce nine strategies or modes of writing and are arranged by the level of complexity of the strategy they introduce. Students study models of each writing strategy and practice using these strategies in their own work. In Chapter 9 students learn techniques for reading and responding to poetry.

The reading selections in Parts II and III address a wide range of student reading abilities and interests, giving instructors a great deal of flexibility in designing courses to fit their students' needs. The readings include first-person narratives as well as more complex models of writing, making the textbook appropriate for several levels of developmental writing and composition. The *Instructor's Manual* offers several sample syllabi for designing courses.

Practice exercises in Parts I, II, and III; the freewriting exercises in Questions for Discussion; and Topics for Writing that accompany the readings in Parts I, II, and III help students connect what they have read to their own experience. These exercises also encourage students to develop critical thinking and writing skills as they move beyond their experience and observations to deeper analysis.

Like the professional selections in this textbook, the examples of student writing reflect a broad spectrum of personal and cultural issues, and address many of the concerns of student writers. In Part I, student samples illustrate journal writing (Chapter 1), techniques for writing summaries and critical response papers (Chapter 2), and the process of writing paragraphs and essays (Chapters 3, 4, and 5). In Part II, student papers illustrate particular writing strategies and reinforce the modes featured in each chapter. In addition, many of the sample citations and bibliographic entries in Part IV and exercises in Part V are taken from students' writing.

Vocabulary lists and explanations of word usage follow readings in Parts I, II, and III. These vocabulary sections build students' word-recognition skills.

Four appendices provide students with questions for generating ideas and evaluating papers. An index of key terms, authors' names, and titles of reading selections makes the text easy to use.

NEW IN THIS EDITION

The sixth edition retains the original vision of *We Are America* as a text that provides the elements of an effective writing program—an introduction to rhetoric, a reader, and a handbook of sentence skills.

While the vision of the text remains unchanged, several features have been added, augmented, or improved. Part I of this edition has an updated discussion of paragraphs and an expanded guide to writing essays. The addition of Part II, Strategies for Writing, provides students with models and detailed explanations of several writing modes—narrating, describing, defining, process analysis, classification, causal analysis, comparing/contrasting, evaluating, and taking a stand. Part III offers students additional readings on contemporary themes. New, updated readings in Parts II and III continue to reflect culturally and ethnically diverse points of view.

Parts II and III also feature five new readings by professional writers, one new student selection and updated versions of several other student samples. "How Urban Legends Work," by Tom Harris, provides the professional model of process analysis in Chapter 7, Making Connections. In Chapter 8, "MySpace Nation: The Controversy," written by Bill Hewitt and several other writers, offers students a published example of evaluating. Barbara Ehrenreich's "Oh, Those Family Values," Nathan Thornburgh's "Dropout Nation," and Abigail McCarthy's "The New Immigrants" expand the choices for discussion in Chapters 10, The Family; 11, Getting an Education; and 13, Culture and Identity. The new student essay in Chapter 7, Making Connections, entitled "Americans' Obsession with Celebrities," by Misty Kent, provides students with a sample essay that employs causal analysis.

In Part V, Editing Your Writing, chapters on grammar and parts of speech have been folded into the general skills chapter, now Chapter 23, Sentence Types, Grammar, and Mechanics. Chapters 17 through 22 emphasize strategies for correcting sentences and achieving sentence variety through sentence combining, tense consistency, and sentence logic. New to this section are references to online grammar explanations and exercises for students who require additional practice.

ACKNOWLEDGMENTS

This textbook is the product of many years of work with sensitive, conscientious students in my developmental writing and composition classes. Many of them contributed their ideas and writings to this textbook. I would also like to thank the following reviewers, who took the time to offer valuable comments on this revision: Jeff Calkins, *Tacoma Community College;* Fran Canterbury, *University of Cincinnati;* and Esther Sampol, *Barry University*.

Finally, a special thanks to my husband Chuck and daughters Sarah and Rachel for their continuing love and patience.

Anna Joy

Part I
An Overview of the Writing Process

First Steps

Writing probably plays some part in your life already, whether you write a memo to fellow workers, take a phone message for a roommate or family member, jot down items for a grocery list, or write to a relative who is having a birthday. As a student, of course, you can expect your instructors to give you writing assignments that require a great deal of planning and critical thinking.

Part I of this book prepares you for the formal writing assignments required in your college courses. The explanations and exercises in each chapter are designed to help you improve your reading and writing skills. After you have worked through assignments that ask you to read and respond to readings, you should find that you've become a more efficient, careful, and confident writer.

In this first chapter, you will examine your feelings about writing. You'll see how doing freewriting exercises and keeping a journal makes writing a little easier.

TAKING STOCK

The following survey helps you take stock of the kinds of writing you do and explore some of your ideas about writing.

1. What writing have you done for personal reasons during the past few weeks?

_____

_____

_____

_____

2. What kinds of writing do you like to do? _____

_____

_____

_____

3. Write about a time when you felt good about something you wrote. Briefly

describe what you wrote and why you were proud of it. _____

_____

_____

_____

_____

4. What do you find most difficult about writing for class assignments? _____

_____

_____

_____

5. If you were giving advice to a friend, what would you say are the most impor-

tant things to remember when writing a paper for a class? _____

_____

_____

_____

_____

_____

There are lots of good suggestions to make about writing, and your collective answers to and discussion of question 5 will give you a class list of ideas for successful writing. Here are two suggestions from professional writers that you may find useful when beginning a writing task.

1. *"Meaning is not what you start out with but what you end up with. . . . Think of writing then not as a way to transmit a message but as a way to grow and cook a message."*—Peter Elbow

Don't think you must know exactly what you want to say *before* you begin writing. As Peter Elbow points out, it takes time to "grow and cook" your ideas. Writer's block, the feeling that you have nothing to say, often comes from having the mistaken idea that something is wrong with you if you can't dash off perfect paragraphs, or if ideas don't flow effortlessly from your pen or computer the first time you sit down to work. The truth is that writing takes work, and it is work for *everybody* who writes.

2. *"There are days when the result is so bad that no fewer than five revisions are required. In contrast, when I'm greatly inspired, only four revisions are needed."*—John Kenneth Galbraith

Instead of worrying when the words don't come easily or you aren't happy with what you have written, accept the fact that you probably won't be satisfied with your earliest efforts. Expect to do quite a bit of preliminary writing, drafting, and revising before you write something that you genuinely like.

GATHERING YOUR THOUGHTS

If you are like many writers, getting started is your most difficult task. Freewriting and keeping a journal are two methods you can use to start writing and keep writing.

FREEWRITING

What Is Freewriting?
Freewriting means writing continuously about whatever comes to mind without worrying about how it sounds or stopping to check wording and spelling. Initially you might feel as if you have nothing to write, but because your mind is constantly processing sounds, smells, sights, memories, and ideas, you can always record what is going on inside your head. Chapter 3 shows how these thoughts provide the raw material for writing essays.

How Does It Work?
When freewriting, write *anything* to keep yourself going. If, for example, you are thinking, "I hate to write, and I hate this stupid assignment," write *that*. If you get stuck and can't think of anything to write, try writing about how hard it is to get

started. Regardless of where you begin, you will soon find yourself following your own thoughts and having plenty to say. It doesn't really matter *what* you write as long as you keep writing.

Sample of Freewriting

Tamara Baumann wrote this freewriting exercise on a day when she thought she didn't have anything to write.

> I hate having to write what's on my mind without thinking about it. My mind grabs onto a total blank, and I can't find a thing. I don't like writing much because it takes me too long to find something to write about. If I'm listening to music, then I can write about something. The music relaxes me, and I can find all kinds of things to write about. My ceramics teacher said the right side of the brain starts to work when music is playing. Maybe that is true. I don't know. Someday I'll try an experiment on it. I have a lot of things on my mind, but when I have to write something, I go blank. Maybe if I didn't think so much and wrote more, this wouldn't happen.

Although she thought she didn't have anything to say, Tamara wrote about 130 words. In the process, she made the important discovery that it might be easier to write if she didn't worry so much about it—at least while she is getting started.

FOR PRACTICE

Practice 1a. Now you try it. Take out a piece of paper or, if your class uses computers, get ready to type. Record the date, note the time, and begin writing. Write steadily for ten minutes. Keep your pen moving across the page (or your fingers moving on the keyboard), and record your thoughts as they come to you. Whatever you do, don't stop to look back; don't correct anything. Just let the words flow out of you.

KEEPING A JOURNAL

Reserve a section of your loose-leaf notebook, or buy a separate binder, and begin keeping a **journal**. Writing regularly in this journal is an excellent way to explore ideas, record observations, and experiment with language. The word *journal* comes from the French word meaning "daily." Occasionally you may feel like writing every day. Most of us should write as often as we exercise—about three times a week. Like regular running or swimming, frequent writing can become a familiar, even comfortable, exercise.

Sample Journal Entries

Journal entries are as diverse as the people who write them. The following samples illustrate a few ways to use your journal for comments and sketches. For a list of other possible topics, see "Ideas for Journal Entries" at the end of this chapter.

Recording Incidents and Making Observations

2/13

What happens in a child's world? About four months ago, I was standing in the kitchen cooking dinner. All of a sudden my youngest son came running in the door. His shirt was torn, he had red marks on his face and neck. I immediately ran after him to try to find out what had happened. He told me six boys had started hitting him. They chased him home, took his coat from him. I ran immediately to the school, which is only a block away, and explained to the principal what had happened. The next day we were all in the office. I asked them why this happened and got the old standard answer, "I don't know." When I looked at the boys, I couldn't help but wonder what kind of home life they had. They were so young yet so hard. That's one of the many reasons I decided to become a counselor. I feel if we can help children in some way, no matter how small, maybe, just maybe, we can keep a few out of prison or off drugs. Maybe I can help them to love themselves as human beings.

—Norma Davis

Responding to a Movie, Concert, or Other Activity

4/3

I'm at home, thinking about the movie Fatal Attraction. Why? Why did Michael Douglas fall for Glenn Close? He had it all—marriage, a beautiful little girl, money, a wonderful life. Why? Michael Douglas' wife was far more beautiful than Glenn Close—so it can't be that his wife was letting herself go or anything because he was still attracted to her. Was it just convenience or maybe just another "roll in the hay"? Now I'll tell you what I think—Glenn Close (MiMi) knew what she wanted the first time they met. She was a sick woman, as they disclosed later in the movie. Michael Douglas was, by all means, attracted to her (she wasn't ugly). But remember, his wife was out of town, and before you knew it he was having dinner with this semi-attractive woman, and he was probably feeling pretty good after a couple of drinks. Too bad for him because she ends up nearly killing him and his wife later in the movie. And all it was for, especially to him, was a "fatal attraction."

—Doug Gonzales

Reflecting on Your Writing

10/5

Today I don't feel very good. I still have a cold, but it seems as though my cold is getting worse. I don't even want to go to school, but I hate missing school because you get behind when you miss. I don't know what to write about today. I haven't been writing in my journal three times a week, but this week I am determined to do so. You know sometimes just picking up my journal and writing makes me feel better—especially when I'm lonely. Writing in my journal is like talking to someone. It kind of helps me to say things that I would not usually say. I think I'm starting to like this journal writing exercise. I'm beginning to see writing as a way of expressing myself, not just in journals, but in the assignments I have done on subjects that interest me, like drug babies.

—Renita Phillips

Responding to Something You Have Read

2/1

    I read the essay "Freewriting" by Peter Elbow this week. He writes like he has been in the same shoes as many of us would-be writers. I can relate to one statement he made: "schooling makes us obsessed with the 'mistakes' we make in writing." I would have to add that I sometimes can't write anything at all because I'm so worried about spelling and grammar. I just get writer's block and feel helpless. I appreciate Elbow's encouraging statement that having nothing to say happens to the best of writers. This is great because if they struggle to write, I can too. He is right about editing too much, too. I always write something, erase it, and then forget what I was going to write afterwards. Then it takes forever to squeeze out a sentence and I get discouraged with the whole thing. Elbow also says that you can stop over-editing if you keep on writing even when you have nothing to say, and if you get stuck just keep on going. I like that. It is very inspiring. I always thought I couldn't write much, but Elbow is telling me that I can write a lot, write more, and just keep going. That way the words will pour out of me. Eventually I may get to something I like.

—Wendy Luu

MAKE A COMMITMENT TO WRITING

Here are a few additional techniques that experienced writers have used to help them write. Practice them a few times and see if they make writing a little easier for you.

1. Write at the same time every day or every other day. When you do, you are keeping a promise to yourself to write regularly.
2. Make your writing sessions brief so that you don't feel overwhelmed by the task. Start by writing for five minutes and work up to ten or fifteen. On some days you will not want to stop, so you may occasionally write for twenty minutes.
3. Write in the same place several days in a row to associate the habit of writing with a particular spot. Start anywhere—your bedroom, the cafeteria, or the library at school.
4. Sneak up on yourself. Get up a few minutes early, and before you have a chance to think, "Oh, no, I'm trying to write something," pick up a pencil or pen and begin writing in your journal or on a notepad that you keep beside your bed. Another good time to write is just before going to bed. You might also try jotting down journal entries while waiting for class to begin.

Practice 1b. Journal entries are often reflections on topics like those listed here. Choose one of these topics, and take about ten minutes to write a one-page entry in your journal, or open a new file on your computer and begin freewriting. Share your writing with classmates.

- An event in your life
- Observations you have made
- A recent controversy at school, at work, or in the news
- An issue in a reading for one of your classes
- Something startling you have heard about, seen, or experienced
- Issues about your own writing
- Problems in your community
- Your search for the right career
- Fast food

IDEAS FOR JOURNAL ENTRIES

1. Describe your surroundings. Where are you right now? What does the place look like, smell like, and feel like? Who usually goes there? Why?
2. Write about how your classes are going.
3. Describe a few of the people you have met this semester.
4. Write a letter to a friend explaining what has been on your mind lately.
5. Discuss your plans for the near future.
6. If you are working, describe the kind of work you do. What do you like or dislike about your job? If you know of a conflict or problem, describe it and explain what you would do to resolve it.
7. Describe what it is like to get up in the morning.
8. Think about a family member or friend you haven't seen for a while. Write that person a letter.
9. Discuss what you and your friends have been doing lately.
10. Describe activities or sports that you enjoy.
11. List any special skills that you have. Describe a few in detail.
12. Write about an interesting article you have read or a good movie you have seen.
13. Write about a time when you couldn't stop laughing.
14. Describe something you did that got you into trouble.

LOOKING AHEAD

In college you are often asked to write about something you have read. The next chapter suggests several techniques for understanding, remembering, and responding to what you read. Parts II and III, the rhetoric and reading sections in this book, give you additional practice in writing about reading and generating papers based on what you have read.

Writing about Reading

CHAPTER

2

Most college writing assignments require you to read about a subject before you write. For example, your sociology instructor might have you read several articles that describe the facts and myths about AIDS and write an analysis of your findings. You also might see a question on a biology exam that asks you to write about characteristics of the seed-producing plants covered in your textbook. Your English teacher might ask you to find articles on a subject of interest to you or to identify and describe a problem and offer solutions. To help you prepare for such assignments, this chapter gives you practice reading actively—locating important ideas, summarizing main points, and writing a response to what you have read.

ACTIVE READING

Successful students are attentive, active learners. That means they take notes in class, ask questions, and make appointments with instructors to go over ideas that they don't understand. Learning to be an alert, active reader is also important for college success.

You may have had the experience of reading a textbook or newspaper article and suddenly realizing that even though your eyes have been scanning the words, you have not really *read* anything on the page. This is an example of passive reading—you read words but don't think about what they mean. **Active reading,** on the other hand, involves thinking on paper—making notes in the margins of your books, jotting down journal entries as you read, drawing pictures, and making diagrams of what you think the writer is saying—in short, doing anything that helps you visualize what you are reading and keeps you alert and responsive to the author's ideas.

STRATEGIES FOR ACTIVE READING

Preview for Main Ideas

The first time you read an assignment, preview or skim the material in a systematic way. This initial view of the reading serves as an introduction to the writer's ideas and to the organization of those ideas. Keep a pen or pencil handy for underlining central points and for taking notes in response to the reading.

- Read the title to see what the reading will cover. The title is usually connected to the thesis or the writer's main argument.
- Skim the introduction (usually the first paragraph or two) looking for a thesis.
- Notice headings the writer might use—they indicate central ideas and "map" the information in the text.
- Make a note of words whose meaning you don't know.
- Also read topic sentences (usually the first sentence or two of each paragraph, but sometimes the last sentence) to find the smaller units of meaning.
- Read the conclusion to see how the writer ties together the points in his or her essay.

FOR PRACTICE

Practice 2a. Preview one of your textbooks for this term by scanning the table of contents, which is essentially a list of the topic ideas covered in the book. Without looking back at what you have read, write a paragraph explaining what you think the text will be about.

Reread Carefully and Respond to What You Read

After previewing for main ideas, reread the text more slowly, this time looking for evidence that supports the main points and for indications of the writer's tone or attitude toward the topic, the purpose for writing, and a strategy for organizing ideas. As you read a second time, remember to keep yourself active.

- Underline the thesis or main idea, and the topic sentences. (Be careful not to mark everything that seems important. Too much underlining makes it difficult to identify the writer's central points.)
- Consult a dictionary if you aren't sure about the meaning of a word.
- If the essay is long, section off groups of paragraphs that focus on the same point, and note in the margin what each section is about.

Rereading also means responding to material in the text. When ideas in reading assignments stir memories, cause emotional responses, or raise questions in your mind, note these reactions in the margins. These notes are important when writing a critical response to an assigned reading.

- Use the book's margins or your journal to record experiences that relate to ideas you are reading about.
- Mark portions of the text where you have questions about the writer's meaning, or disagree with his or her ideas and assumptions.

WHY USE THE ACTIVE READING METHOD?

1. Previewing, or viewing in advance, gives you an overview of the material and prepares you to do a more careful reading later.
2. Your comprehension and reading speed should increase with your second reading because you have some familiarity with the subject.
3. Active reading also prepares you to take objective tests, to summarize what you have read, and to generate ideas for writing assignments.

Sample of Active Reading

Here is a sample of one student's active reading notes on "The Civil Rights Movement Was the Sum of Many People." She first previewed the article and then reread it more carefully, underlining key ideas and writing notes in the margin. Her personal responses appear in parentheses.

The Civil Rights Movement Was the Sum of Many People

Paul Rogat Loeb

Paul Loeb is a scholar at Seattle's Center for Ethical Leadership and has appeared in over 1,000 television and radio interviews including CNN, NPR, and CSPAN. His comments on social activism have been published in the New York Times, *the* Washington Post, Psychology Today, *and* New Age Journal. *Loeb is the author of five books, including* Nuclear Culture, Hope in Hard Times, Generation at the Crossroads, On the American Campus, *and* Soul of a Citizen: Living with Conviction in a Cynical Time. *His most recent book,* The Impossible Will Take a Little While, *published in 2004, received the Nautilus Award for the best book on social change published that year.*

1   We learn much from how we present our heroes. A few years ago, on the Rev. Martin Luther King Jr. Day, I was interviewed on CNN. So was Rosa Parks, by phone, from Los Angeles.

Author interviewed (his importance, authority)

2   "We're very honored to have her," said the host. "Rosa Parks was the woman who wouldn't go to the back of the bus. She wouldn't get up and give her seat in the white section to a white person. That set in motion the yearlong boycott of city buses in Montgomery. It earned Rosa Parks the title of 'mother of the civil rights movement.'"

About Rosa Parks' interview; summary of her role in civil rights movement

3   I was excited to hear Parks' voice and to be part of the same show, but it occurred to me that the host's description—the story's familiar rendition—stripped the Montgomery boycott of its most important context.

Loeb's thesis: larger meaning of bus boycott

4   Before the fateful December day in 1955 when Parks refused to obey a law designating segregated seating on public buses, she had spent 12 years helping lead the local NAACP chapter, along with union activist E. D. Nixon, from the Brotherhood of Sleeping Car Porters; teachers from the local Negro college, and a variety of members of Montgomery's African American community. Parks allowed her arrest to be used to spark a boycott, which was led by King. That 382-day boycott ended on Dec. 20, 1956, when the U.S. Supreme Court declared segregated seating on the city's buses unconstitutional.

Parks' activism (I didn't know about her background.)

Realities of bus boycott

5   The summer of 1954, Parks had attended a 10-day training session at Tennessee's labor and civil rights organizing school, the Highlander Center, where she'd met an older generation of civil rights activists and discussed the Supreme Court's Brown decision banning "separate but equal" schools.

Parks' civil rights training

(Boycott occurred after Brown v. Board of Education)

6   Parks didn't make a spur-of-the-moment decision that gave birth to the civil rights

movement. She was part of an existing force for change when success was far from certain. Her tremendously consequential act might never have occurred without all the humble and frustrating work she and others had been doing. Her initial step of involvement 12 years before was just as courageous and critical as the moment she refused to move further back in the bus.

Parks—part of larger movement

7   People such as Parks shape our models of social commitment. Yet the conventional retelling of her story creates a standard so impossible to meet, it may actually make it harder for us to get involved.

Problem knowing part of story ordinary people discouraged from taking action (good point)

8   This portrayal suggests that social activists come out of nowhere to make sudden, dramatic stands. It implies that we act with the greatest impact when we act alone, or at least alone initially; that anyone who takes a committed public stand, or at least an effective one, has to be a larger-than-life figure—someone with more time, energy, courage, vision or knowledge than any normal person could ever possess. These beliefs pervade our society, in part because the media rarely represent historical change as the work of ordinary human beings.

9   Parks' real story conveys a far more empowering moral. In the 1940s, she goes to a meeting and then another. Hesitant at first, she gains confidence as she speaks out. She keeps on despite a profoundly uncertain context as she and others act as best they can to challenge deeply entrenched injustices with little certainty of results. Had she and others given up after her 10th or 11th year of commitment, we might never have heard of Montgomery.

Lesson: change is never certain—heroes are ordinary people who keep going.

10   Once we enshrine our heroes on pedestals, it's difficult for mere mortals to measure up. When individuals speak out, we're tempted to dismiss their motives, knowledge and tactics as insufficiently grand. We fault them for not being in command of every fact and figure. We fault ourselves as well for not knowing every detail, or for harboring uncertainties and doubts. We find it hard to

Restates the lesson: heroes are "mere mortals" who can make change happen

imagine that <u>flawed human beings</u> might make a <u>critical difference</u> in worthy <u>social causes.</u>

11   Our culture's <u>misreading of</u> Parks' story hints at a <u>collective amnesia</u> in which we forget the examples that might most inspire our courage and conscience. Most of us know next to nothing of the <u>grass-roots movements</u> in which ordinary men and women fought to preserve <u>freedom,</u> expand the sphere of <u>democracy</u> and create a more <u>just</u> society: abolitionists, the populists, the women's suffrage campaigns, the union movements that ended 80-hour workweeks at near-starvation wages. These movements <u>could teach us</u> how their participants successfully shifted public sentiment, challenged entrenched institutional power and found the strength to persevere. But their stories are buried.

Important grass-roots movements in U.S. history

(Most I haven't heard of)

what they teach us

12   In the <u>prevailing myth,</u> Parks decides to act almost on a whim, in isolation. She's a political innocent. The lesson seems to be that if any of us suddenly got the urge to do something equally heroic, that would be great. Of course most of us don't, so we wait our entire lives to find the ideal moment.

Returns to "misreading" of Parks' action

Repeats for effect?

13   Parks' journey suggests that change is the product of <u>deliberate, incremental action,</u> whereby we join together to try to shape a better world. <u>Sometimes our struggles will fail,</u> as did many earlier efforts of Parks, her peers and her predecessors. Other times they <u>may bear modest fruits.</u> And at times they will trigger a <u>miraculous outpouring of courage and heart</u>—as happened with her arrest on the bus and all that followed. <u>Only when we act despite all our uncertainties and doubts do we have the chance to shape history.</u>

Concluding summary of Parks' significance

Her lesson for us again

FOR PRACTICE

Practice 2b. Apply the techniques for active reading to one chapter of a textbook you are using this term. First skim it for main ideas; then reread more carefully, writing marginal notes as you go.

WRITING SUMMARIES

You can apply your active reading skills to writing summaries. **Summaries** are paragraphs or outlines in which you paraphrase (state in your own words) the main ideas in something you have read. Summaries may consist of a short paragraph or a more detailed paper, depending on your purpose for writing.

The first few sentences of a summary refer to the author and title of the writing, and state the author's thesis or "big idea." The rest of the summary includes important points the author makes in support of the thesis. Because the purpose of a summary is to record *main points,* you should omit minor details that support the writer's ideas. You should also omit personal observations or reactions to what you have read. You may occasionally quote a word or phrase if it helps you clarify the writer's point, but try to keep quotations to a minimum. In general, it is easier to remember the ideas you have restated in your own words.

Summaries are extremely useful in preparing for essay examinations and other writing assignments. For example, if you write summaries for chapters in your textbook on cultural anthropology, you will find it much easier to study for a midterm or final exam. Instead of rereading all the chapters, you can review the main points, additional comments of your own, and any notes you have from lectures. Writing summaries also prepares you to write analytical essays, essays that ask you to make a point or respond critically to a reading. When you can paraphrase the writer's points in a summary, you are more likely to have the understanding you need to develop a critical response to the writer's text. In addition, research essays are built from summaries and an analysis of several readings.

After previewing and rereading "The Civil Rights Movement Was the Sum of Many People" and writing notes in the margins, one student wrote the following one-paragraph summary of Paul Loeb's main ideas.

Summary of "The Civil Rights Movement Was the Sum of Many People"

In "The Civil Rights Movement Was the Sum of Many People," Paul Rogat Loeb argues for a broader view of Rosa Parks and social activists in general than the limited one we get from the media. The interview with Rosa Parks that sparked Loeb's article praises her for refusing to sit in the black section of a city bus in Montgomery, Alabama in December 1955. This action, the reporter notes, started the famous bus boycott and gave Parks the title of the "mother of the civil rights movement." According to Loeb, this way of looking at history as a series of heroic acts by lone individuals is likely to discourage ordinary people from getting involved in movements for social justice because they think only heroes acting alone on the spur of the moment can effect change. Loeb advises us to look at the "real story" of Rosa Parks and at other historical movements for social justice. We will find, he says, that Rosa Parks had been involved with the civil rights movement for 12 years. Loeb points out that social change in general requires years of hard work during times when success is not

---

guaranteed. When we view social activism in these larger terms, Loeb argues, we are more likely to understand that people just like us can be instrumental in effecting social change.

Another student's more detailed summary of Loeb's article mentions additional topic ideas and key supporting details.

Summary of "The Civil Rights Movement Was the Sum of Many People"

In "The Civil Rights Movement Was the Sum of Many People," Paul Rogat Loeb argues that focusing solely on Rosa Parks' refusal to sit at the back of a city bus, the incident that made her famous, does an injustice to the ordinary citizens whose hard work over many years makes social change possible.

Loeb discusses the narrow view of Rosa Parks' role in the civil rights movement typical of media reporting. Interviewed with Parks for a CNN program, Loeb quotes the reporter's summary of Parks' actions in December 1955. Her refusal to move to the black section of the bus so a white person could take her seat led to the bus boycott in Montgomery, Alabama. The reporter pointed out that her courageous act "earned [her] the title of 'mother of the civil rights movement.'" Loeb adds that the boycott, organized by Martin Luther King Jr., ended on December 20, 1956, with the Supreme Court's ruling that segregated seating on public buses is unconstitutional. In Loeb's opinion, by ignoring the long, difficult struggle that brought about this decision, reporters like the one who interviewed Rosa Parks perpetuate the myth that activists are extraordinary beings who act spontaneously and alone. In the end, ordinary people like us may decide not to work for social causes because we think that only heroes can effect change.

Paul Loeb insists that we see Parks' actions in a larger context. For one thing, Parks was trained by older activists and "was part of an existing force for change." She became involved in the civil rights movement twelve long years before she refused to sit at the back of the bus. This story, the "real story" of Rosa Parks, Loeb argues, contains an "empowering moral." The persistent efforts of Parks and many other activists throughout U.S. history produced few results for many years. In short, real courage comes from speaking out against injustice when change is far from certain.

Loeb's conclusion contrasts the media's view of Parks' heroic act with his own view of Parks' actions as part of a long, difficult struggle led by average citizens whose courage changed history.

WRITING BEFORE READING

The following assignment, and similar assignments that precede reading selections throughout this book, are designed to help you explore ideas you already have about the author's themes and main points before you begin reading.

Freewrite about a time when you had difficulty completing a writing task. This task may have required you to write a personal letter, complete a project at work, or finish an assignment for a class. Describe the steps you took to overcome writer's block.

READING AND RESPONDING

Read the following essay by Gail Godwin, entitled "The Watcher at the Gates." Use this essay to practice reading actively, and review the student's response to the text. The strategies for active reading on pages 11–12 show you how to preview for main ideas and to read carefully and critically. Marginal notes, questions, and comments you make as you read are also useful in writing a response to Godwin's essay.

The Watcher at the Gates

Gail Godwin

Gail Godwin is the author of fifteen books, including eleven novels and two collections of short stories. Her novel, A Mother and Two Daughters *(1982) was a best seller. Three of her best-known novels are* The Good Husband *(1994),* Evensong *(1999), and* Evenings at Five *(2003).* Heart: A Personal Journey through Its Myths and Meanings *(2001) is a nonfiction work. Godwin's novels have been nominated for the National Book Award three times; she has also received a Guggenheim Fellowship and other awards for literature. Godwin coauthored ten musical compositions, including an opera. The following article about writer's block was published in the* New York Times Book Review *on January 9, 1977.*

1   I first realized I was not the only writer who had a restraining critic who lived inside me and sapped the juice from green inspirations when I was leafing through Freud's "Interpretation of Dreams" a few years ago. Ironically, it was my "inner critic" who had sent me to Freud. I was writing a novel, and my heroine was in the middle of a dream, and then I lost faith in my own invention and rushed to "an authority" to check whether she could have such a dream. In the chapter on dream interpretation, I came upon the following passage that has helped me free myself, in some measure, from my critic and has led to many pleasant and interesting exchanges with other writers.

2   Freud quotes Schiller,[1] who is writing a letter to a friend. The friend complains of his lack of creative power. Schiller replies with an allegory. He says it is not good if the intellect examines too closely the ideas pouring in at the gates. "In isolation, an idea may be quite insignificant, and venturesome in the extreme, but it may acquire importance from an idea which follows it. . . . In the case of a creative mind, it seems to me,

---

[1] Johann Friedrich von Schiller (1759–1805) was an eighteenth-century German poet, dramatist, and philosopher.

the intellect has withdrawn its watchers from the gates, and the ideas rush in pell-mell, and only then does it review and inspect the multitude. You are ashamed or afraid of the momentary and passing madness which is found in all real creators, the longer or shorter duration of which distinguishes the thinking artist from the dreamer . . . you reject too soon and discriminate too severely."

So that's what I had: a Watcher at the Gates. I decided to get to know him better. I discussed him with other writers, who told me some of the quirks and habits of their Watchers, each of whom was as individual as his host, and all of whom seemed passionately dedicated to one goal: rejecting too soon and discriminating too severely.

It is amazing the lengths a Watcher will go to keep you from pursuing the flow of your imagination. Watchers are notorious pencil sharpeners, ribbon changers, plant waterers, home repairers and abhorrers of messy rooms or messy pages. They are compulsive looker-uppers. They are superstitious scaredy-cats. They cultivate self-important eccentricities they think are suitable for "writers." And they'd rather die (and kill your inspiration with them) than risk making a fool of themselves.

My Watcher has a wasteful penchant for 20-pound bond paper above and below the carbon of the first draft. "What's the good of writing out a whole page," he whispers begrudgingly, "if you just have to write it over again later? Get it perfect the first time!" My Watcher adores stopping in the middle of a morning's work to drive down to the library to check on the name of a flower or a World War II battle or a line of metaphysical poetry. "You can't possibly go on till you've got this right!" he admonishes. I go and get the car keys.

Other Watchers have informed their writers that:

"Whenever you get a really good sentence you should stop in the middle of it and go on tomorrow. Otherwise you might run dry."

"Don't try and continue with your book till your dental appointment is over. When you're worried about your teeth, you can't think about art."

Another Watcher makes his owner pin his finished pages to a clothesline and read them through binoculars "to see how they look from a distance." Countless other Watchers demand "bribes" for taking the day off: lethal doses of caffeine, alcoholic doses of Scotch or vodka or wine.

There are various ways to outsmart, pacify, or coexist with your Watcher. Here are some I have tried, or my writer friends have tried, with success:

Look for situations when he's likely to be off-guard. Write too fast for him in an unexpected place, at an unexpected time. (Virginia Woolf[2] captured the "diamonds in the dustheap" by writing at a "rapid haphazard gallop" in her diary.) Write when very tired. Write in purple ink on the back of a Master Charge statement. Write whatever comes into your mind while the kettle is boiling and make the steam whistle your deadline. (Deadlines are a great way to outdistance the Watcher.)

---

[2] English novelist and essayist (1882–1941). Woolf is best known for her discussion of women writers in the essay "A Room of One's Own."

12   Disguise what you are writing. If your Watcher refuses to let you get on with your story or novel, write a "letter" instead, telling your "correspondent" what you are going to write in your story or next chapter. Dash off a "review" of your own unfinished opus. It will stand up like a bully to your Watcher the next time he throws obstacles in your path. If you write yourself a good one.

13   Get to know your Watcher. He's yours. Do a drawing of him (or her). Pin it to the wall of your study and turn it gently to the wall when necessary. Let your Watcher feel needed. Watchers are excellent critics after inspiration has been captured; they are dependable, sharp-eyed readers of things already set down. Keep your Watcher in shape and he'll have less time to keep you from shaping. If he's really ruining your whole working day, sit down, as Jung did with his personal demons, and write him a letter. On a very bad day I once wrote my Watcher a letter. "Dear Watcher," I wrote, "What is it you're so afraid I'll do?" Then I held his pen for him, and he replied instantly with a candor that has kept me from truly despising him.

14   "Fail," he wrote back.

RESPONDING TO THE READING

Summarizing ideas is an important part of understanding what you have read. But active reading also means *responding* in some way to what the writer has said. Your response may take the form of notes in the margin or journal entries. In either case, as you write your response, try imagining you are talking directly to the writer; this tactic will help you become more actively involved with what you read.

As you respond to the reading, record the initial satisfaction, surprise, anger, or sadness you felt as you were reading; you might question the author's ideas, assumptions, tone, or purpose. If the reading reminds you of experiences you have had that are similar to or different from the writer's, you can test the validity of the reading against your experience. The more you question and analyze a reading, the more supporting evidence you will have for your response paper.

FOR PRACTICE

Practice 2c. Write a journal entry in which you respond in some way to the ideas in Gail Godwin's "The Watcher at the Gates." You can record feelings, experiences, or questions you have in response to particular passages. Share your entries with classmates. Here is a sample response.

After reading Gail Godwin's "The Watcher at the Gates," I began to understand why it seems so difficult for me to commit my ideas to paper, why I find it hard to develop the ideas I get, and why I waste so much paper.

I too have a "watcher." A very egocentric one, at that. He always has to have it his way. He's a perfectionist and has the ability to influence things and people around me, creating every possible distraction. If I try to write outside, for instance, he calls for a car whose muffler has a hole in it. If I'm inside the house, he'll let in a fly to pester me until I give up. Of course, I have some control over his actions. When I put myself in a public place, I invite distractions. When I stay up late and listen to my old punk tapes, however, I can drive him off (as well as most of my family) and get some work done. In the end, writing is a tug-of-war.

—Christian Cinder

—Richard Hansard

Responding to the Reading **21**

Practice 2d. Freewrite about one of Godwin's ideas that you think is helpful or encouraging.

Practice 2e. Freewrite about why you disliked or disagreed with something Godwin said.

BUILDING YOUR VOCABULARY

Your teacher may ask you to set aside a section of your notebook for keeping a vocabulary list that includes definitions of words that you had difficulty understanding. Before consulting your dictionary, look for clues from the **context** in which the word appears—the other words near the word you want to find and the ideas in the paragraph—to help you figure out the most likely meaning for a word. For example, *allegory* is a word that may be unfamiliar to you. But Godwin gives you suggestions about its meaning when she quotes Schiller's interpretation of what happens when we have writer's block. Unlike "the case of a creative mind" whose "intellect has withdrawn its watchers from the gates," writers who feel they have lost their "creative power" will "reject too soon and discriminate too severely." An allegory, then, draws conclusions about human experience and includes symbolic figures like the "watchers at the gates." *The American Heritage Dictionary* defines allegory as "a literary, dramatic, or pictorial device in which characters and events stand for abstract ideas, principles, or forces, so that the literal sense has . . . a deeper symbolic sense." In other words, an allegory is a story given symbolic significance. This definition supports the educated guess we made based on contextual clues.

Another good technique for decoding a word is to break it apart and see if it is composed of other words that are more familiar. If, for example, you see the word *abhorrer,* you might remember that the word *abhorrent* means repulsive or detestable. An abhorrer, then, is someone who is repulsed by something; the abhorrers Godwin mentions in paragraph 4 loathe "messy rooms or messy pages."

The beginnings and endings of words also offer clues to meaning. Here are a few common suffixes and prefixes with sample words.

COMMON PREFIXES AND EXAMPLES

Prefix	Meaning	Sample Word
bi-	two	**bi**sect (cut in two)
de-	take away from	**de**grade (cut in rank, diminish)
ex-	out of, from	**ex**claim (to cry out)
mis-	bad, wrong	**mis**behave (behave badly)
post-/pre-	after/before	**post**war (after a war)/**pre**war (before a war)
sub-	beneath	**sub**marine (beneath the ocean)

Suffix	Meaning	Sample Word
-able	worthy of	depend**able** (worthy of trust)
-ant	person	defend**ant** (person defending himself/herself)
-less	without	hope**less** (without hope)
-ness	quality or state	happi**ness** (state of being happy)

Consulting a Dictionary

You should look up all unfamiliar words in a dictionary. When you record a definition, don't forget to look at the etymology of the word. The etymology gives the history of the word—its original form, language, and meaning. Under *penchant,* for example, you will find an entry similar to this one from *The American Heritage Dictionary:*

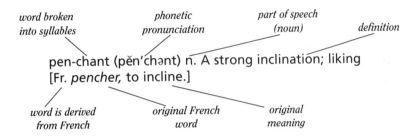

word broken into syllables   phonetic pronunciation   part of speech (noun)   definition

pen-chant (pĕn′chənt) n. A strong inclination; liking [Fr. *pencher,* to incline.]

word is derived from French   original French word   original meaning

Knowing that the original French word, *pencher,* means "to incline" may help you remember the meaning for the English *penchant,* "a strong inclination" or "definite liking."

FOR PRACTICE

Practice 2f. Make a vocabulary list of all the words Gail Godwin used in "The Watcher at the Gates" that were unfamiliar to you. Look them up in the dictionary; try to write two or three sentences with each new word to help you remember it.

DEEPENING YOUR RESPONSE

When we write a response to a text, we isolate certain of its elements—such as the thesis, the writer's point of view, the organization of ideas, the tone or style of writing, or the audience and purpose for writing—in order to discuss the text and come to some conclusion about how it works.

The meaning of a text has much to do with the **perspective** or "stance" the writer takes toward his or her subject, and toward the reader. **Tone** and style help the writer convey this "stance." *Tone* refers to tone of voice, the attitude (defensive, playful, sad, judgmental, etc.) that we convey about a subject when we speak. The concept of tone also applies to the attitude a writer conveys through his or her choice of words and phrasing. Reading for tone helps us discover the emotional shadings of a text. In "The Watcher at the Gates," for example, Godwin changes her attitude toward her "inner critic" as she discovers more about it. At first she is cautious, even fearful; after all, the watcher caused her to lose faith in her creativity. She is more playful when she offers advice for fooling the watcher, suggesting at one point to write "on the back of a Master Charge statement" or "while the kettle is boiling." Finally, she sympathizes with her watcher's fear of failure and realizes how helpful her inner critic can be when the time comes to revise what she has written.

Style, an idea related to tone, is the collection of features an author uses that constitutes his or her unique way of writing. Novelist Kurt Vonnegut calls style "revelations, accidental or intentional," that writers make about themselves. In other words, authors assume a "writing personality" that they reveal, either unintentionally or by design, through the words they use. A writer's words disclose a "cultural" personality as well—a point of view, an attitude, or assumptions that have to do with the cultural environment in which he or she lives and writes. Learning to "read" clues about this context helps readers appreciate ways that culture informs a writer's ideas and opinions. At the same time, interpretations of a text depend on the reader's own perspective and cultural assumptions.

Let's look at Godwin's text again for indications of stylistic flair. For one thing, she is adept at using metaphors to convey ideas as she does in the phrase describing the inner critic who "sapped the juice from green inspirations." In this comparison, creativity becomes a plant that her predatory watcher sucks dry. The watcher itself is a personification of writer's block, and the personified version of a positive review confronts her stubborn watcher "like a bully." Godwin also brings "authorities" into her essay, relying on Freud and Schiller for an understanding of writer's block, and Virginia Woolf to propose a way to get around it. She also includes examples of other writers' inner critics rather than rely solely on her own experience with the watcher.

A writer's **purpose** has to do with what he or she hopes to accomplish by writing the essay, and the intended **audience** influences the author's organization of ideas, as well as the writer's particular tone and style of writing. The most likely audience for "The Watcher at the Gates" are writers who occasionally suffer from writer's block. The fact that this essay appears in a number of English readers for college students suggests that Godwin has found a receptive audience among novice writers and college composition students. Her tone and style of writing not only acknowledge the watcher's threat but also give power to the writer, whether a professional or a student author, first by personifying writer's block as something that can be talked to and manipulated, and then by proposing several solutions for tricking the beast.

The organization of ideas moves from identifying a problem—her inability to continue writing—to solutions proposed by Godwin and other writers, and, finally, to her picture of a mutually beneficial partnership with her inner critic. Arrangement of ideas, purpose, audience, tone, and style work together to present her central idea that although watchers can be intimidating, writers can outsmart them and eventually make good use of them.

Writing a Response

Writing a critical response to a text involves an awareness of the words, phrases, ideas, tone, point of view, structure, and other considerations that make up the content and texture of a reading. Initially, your response might be that you find an essay either interesting or disagreeable. Such reactions are valid and may lead to a deeper analysis if you can explain exactly what you appreciate or dislike about the text. For a critical response to convey something about the reading or the way it is put together, it must include support for the conclusions you have reached. In other words, you need to communicate an understanding of what the writer says, his or her purpose for writing, how well the writer achieves that purpose, the writer's assumptions, or how those ideas and assumptions correspond to or contradict your own. Your purpose for writing should be to deepen your own and your reader's understanding of the text.

QUESTIONS FOR DISCUSSION

The following questions, and similar questions in the chapters in Parts II and III, are designed to improve your comprehension and your ability to draw conclusions by helping you evaluate what you read. Such critical thinking exercises may give you ideas you'll want to explore further in more formal writing assignments.

1. Make a note of any sections of "The Watcher at the Gates" that you thought were difficult to understand. Explain what confused you or what you think Godwin might have meant.
2. Why do you think it was important for Godwin to get to know her watcher? Does this concept of getting to know the watcher make sense to you?
3. Why do you think Godwin includes examples of what watchers will do to interrupt writers? How do these examples contribute to her central argument or thesis?
4. How effective is the final line of Godwin's essay? Explain your answer.
5. What are the most important ideas in Godwin's essay? Choose one of them and evaluate her support for this idea.

TOPICS FOR WRITING

Topic 1. Write a summary of Gail Godwin's "The Watcher at the Gates." Before you begin writing, section off groups of paragraphs that illustrate the same point. Make a note of what each section is about; shape these notes into sentences and include them in your summary. Be sure to state the author, title, and thesis or "big idea" of the essay in your opening sentence.

Topic 2. Pick a passage from "The Watcher at the Gates," and write a letter to the author in which you explain what you appreciated about her essay.

Topic 3. Write a paragraph or two describing your own solutions for overcoming writer's block.

Topic 4. Review the notes printed in the margins, and write comments of your own on Paul Rogat Loeb's "The Civil Rights Movement Was the Sum of Many People" (pages 12–15). Refer to these notes as you write a critical-response paper that interprets or evaluates his essay. For an explanation of how to write a critical response to a reading, see pages 20–25.

Topic 5. Take careful notes as you read "The Watcher at the Gates," and use these notes to write a critical response to Godwin's essay. Organize your notes and develop a thesis that states the main point and the direction of your essay. Write a draft and revise it carefully for paragraph focus and specific support for your ideas. (See the following sample student writing.)

Student Writing

Shenice Jamison wrote the following critical response to "The Watcher at the Gates" by Gail Godwin.

Critical Response to "The Watcher at the Gates"

Gail Godwin's "The Watcher at the Gates" presents an entertaining and useful essay on writer's block. Godwin divides her essay into three main sections. She first consults experts and discovers by accident that she has a "watcher at the gates" of creativity. Next she explores other writers' experiences with their watchers and then illustrates ways to live with these "inner critics." The essay's clear sequence of ideas and funny, original perspectives on writer's block keep her readers focused on a dilemma they have probably experienced themselves.

The image of the watcher controls Godwin's essay from the opening line when she recalls discovering that she has a "watcher" that likes to close the gates of creativity. In the first few paragraphs of her essay, Godwin introduces the "watcher" as she discovers that this self-critical voice has caused her to doubt her own creativity. A creative writer who has published over a dozen books, Godwin suddenly doubts that the dream she has given one of her characters is believable. By writing so specifically about her doubts and her later "consultation" with Sigmund Freud, the famous expert on dreams, Godwin lends realism to her situation. She also helps students and other writers who have struggled with writing projects realize that they are not the only ones who have an overactive inner critic. Freud leads Godwin to the dramatist, Johann Friedrich Schiller, and to the realization that her loss of confidence in herself and not the quality of her character's dream is the real problem with her writing. Godwin's long quotation from Schiller adds an authority's definition of the "inner critic" as a "watcher at the gates." After defining this term, Godwin develops examples of how the watcher works and suggests ways to control a hypercritical "watcher."

Godwin livens up the discussion of writer's block with colorful descriptions of the trouble watchers have caused her and other professional writers. At this point her essay includes a list of possible tricks the watcher in the mind can play on an unsuspecting writer. This list of distractions includes the need to sharpen pencils, clean house, look up information, and do whatever else watchers can imagine. Godwin gives life to the general list of distracting activities by including her watcher's crazy demands to buy a certain grade of paper or to look up a quotation that may have little to do with what she is writing.

The best source of humor and the most entertaining section of her essay have to do with other writers' experiences. There's something wonderfully illogical about having to wait until after a dental appointment to start working on a writing project. The funniest and most ridiculous demand that a watcher makes on a writer is to post the pages he has written on a clothesline and view them with binoculars to get the proper "distance" on the work.

Godwin does not end her essay with this funny image; instead, she offers entertaining suggestions for freeing oneself from those nagging inner voices, and she also helps the reader see the watcher in a new light. Her advice about how to pretend not to write while writing includes a funny description of writing "in purple ink on the back of a Master Charge statement." Moreover, she can tell the watcher that demands "20-pound bond paper" before letting ideas flow that this isn't really writing. Her advice to write letters to the "watcher" or draw pictures of him sounds like a kind of writer's therapy. In the process she and the reader are getting to know why they put such roadblocks in their own way. Godwin proposes making friends with the detractor who has given her such trouble and acknowledging that her critic is essential to the last phase of the writing process. In the end she and the reader have sympathy for the once harsh critic who ultimately is afraid of failure.

Godwin's way of organizing and imagining new ways of looking at writer's block gives hope to novice writers. If a writer as prolific as Godwin can have trouble with writer's block, students can see their own struggles as a normal part of the creative process. Godwin gives all writers a model for digging themselves out of a self-critical hole.

—Shenice Jamison

LOOKING AHEAD

Chapter 3 explains the process for writing essays in clear, manageable steps. The chapter also illustrates how one student used the writing process to compose an essay.

The Writing Process

CHAPTER

3

This chapter introduces the writing process, a step-by-step approach to writing that takes you from initial ideas to a finished paper. The opening discussion compares the structures of paragraphs and essays. The rest of the chapter shows how one student used the writing process to compose an essay. Exercises and directions in this chapter invite you to follow the writing steps in composing your own essay. Additional exercises give you practice with each of the writing steps. Part II of this book shows you how to apply the writing process to specific writing tasks that require narrating, describing, defining, explaining, classifying, explaining causes and effects, comparing/contrasting, evaluating, or taking a stand.

WHAT IS A PARAGRAPH?

A **paragraph** is a group of closely related sentences that support one point or main idea. Like the one-paragraph summaries you wrote in Chapter 2, paragraphs may be written to stand alone. Paragraphs are usually part of the body of an essay, and they support the larger idea or the essay's thesis.

WHAT IS AN ESSAY?

Just as sentences in paragraphs support a main idea with details, the closely related paragraphs in an essay develop *one idea,* which is stated in a **thesis.** The thesis is usually the last sentence of your **introduction.** The paragraphs that follow the introduction, called **body paragraphs,** contain topic sentences, subtopics, and supporting information that expand, support, and substantiate the thesis. The **conclusion,** the last paragraph or last few sentences of an essay, returns to the thesis idea. Whereas the introduction states the writer's approach to a subject, the conclusion provides a satisfying sense of completion.

The diagram on page 30 illustrates the relationship between a paragraph and an essay. The sample student paragraph, "A Sports Fanatic," illustrates basic paragraph structure. The essay, "The Life of a Sports Fanatic" (pages 31–32), shows the student's essay written on the same topic. Read the paragraph and essay carefully, and answer the questions for discussion that follow the two papers. Topic sentences, subtopics, and supporting details are labeled for you in the student's paragraph and in the first several paragraphs of his essay.

A Sports Fanatic

Most leisure time in the life of a sports fanatic involves some kind of sporting activity. A fanatic will ⟶ *Topic sentence*

surround himself with sports paraphernalia like wall ⟶ *Subtopic: sports paraphernalia*

posters, baseball cards, and bumper stickers. He probably has T-shirts that say "Go Raiders" or "Celtics ⟶ *Examples*

Rule." If he takes time to watch television or read, he watches a program about sports or reads an article ⟶ *Subtopic: television, reading*

from <u>Sports Illustrated</u>. In his more active moments, ⟶ *Examples*

the sportsaholic, who is usually a pretty good athlete himself, plays some sort of sport. You may find him at ⟶ *Subtopic: plays sports*

the local YMCA shooting baskets with his friends, or

he may have joined a baseball league through his ⟶ *Examples*

job. No matter what he does, the sports fanatic finds

some way to express his dedication to sports. ⟶ *Concluding point*

The Essay

Thesis (main idea of the essay)	*Introduction*

The Paragraph

Topic Sentence (main idea of paragraph)

Supporting ideas or subtopics

Details, examples, and explanations that support subtopics

Concluding point

Topic Sentence (main idea of paragraph)

Supporting ideas or subtopics

Details, examples, and explanations that support subtopics

Topic Sentence (main idea of paragraph)

Supporting ideas or subtopics

Details, examples, and explanations that support subtopics

Topic Sentence (main idea of paragraph)

Supporting ideas or subtopics

Details, examples, and explanations that support subtopics

—*Body paragraphs*

Return to idea stated in thesis

Concluding point

Conclusion

The Life of a Sports Fanatic

Most of us have known a sports fanatic at some time in our lives. They are the kids with collections of baseball caps and team pennants. As adults, they pull the sports section out of the paper before anyone else can grab it. They are also the husbands whose love of football makes Monday night widows of their wives. If they are tennis buffs, they play several sets every evening and compete in tournaments on weekends. Sports fanatics usually find ways to fill their lives with sporting activities.

— Introduces subject

Examples of paraphernalia

Examples of reading about sports

Examples of television watching

Example of playing sports

— Thesis

The dedicated sports fan places sports-related items around him. He probably has a favorite team's bumper sticker on his car or a superstar's poster on the wall in his room. A friend of mine, for example, has a Cowboys bumper sticker on his 4 x 4 Bronco and a life-sized poster of Kobe Bryant in his room. The avid sports fan also wears clothes with the team logo of his favorite football or baseball clubs. Take me for example; I wear my Dodgers baseball cap every day during the season and also enjoy wearing my Lakers sweats.

— Topic sentence

Subtopic: paraphernalia (implied)

Examples of paraphernalia

— Subtopic: clothes

— Examples

Now label the last three paragraphs on your own.

A sports fanatic fills his relaxing and lounging around time watching a sports program or reading an article about an athlete or a local team he admires. If he reads a book, it is usually a superstar's biography or a couple of pages from a sports magazine. I love to read about sports myself and just finished a biography on Brian Bosworth called <u>The Boz.</u> I also subscribe to <u>Sports Illustrated</u> and have been known to read it cover to cover in one sitting. When watching television, the sports enthusiast watches the baseball game of the week, Monday Night Football, or a Lakers game. Just last month I watched more television than usual because of the World Series.

Not only does a sportsaholic love to watch games and read about sports, but he also loves to play. He never gets tired of one sport because he can play several sports well. Some afternoons you may find him shooting baskets at the local park, playing catch with his friends, or joining a neighborhood pick-up game. My friends and I are the perfect examples of athletic sports fans. We love to take a whole Saturday and devote it to playing many different sports. We often play volleyball at the YMCA in the morning and basketball at the local high school in the afternoon. Then we do a little swimming and try batting cages later in the evening.

Most people have run across a sports fanatic at some time in their lives, but if you are still having trouble recognizing one, here's a final rundown. He is in good physical condition from year-round sports activities and is usually decked out in sweats with "Raiders" across his chest. His sports car will have a Lakers or Jets bumper sticker, and his room will have a poster of James Worthy on the wall. He has subscriptions to both <u>Sports Illustrated</u> and <u>The Sporting News</u>, as well as videos of all the professional golf tours. Last, but not least, the sports fanatic will be the easiest person on your Christmas list to buy for. You just have to get him tickets to see the Reds or Dolphins, a new pair of Champion sweats, or a subscription to <u>Baseball Digest</u>.

QUESTIONS FOR DISCUSSION

1. What are similarities between the paragraph titled "A Sports Fanatic" and the essay titled "The Life of a Sports Fanatic"?
2. What differences did you notice?
3. Why do you think this writer focused on male sports enthusiasts?

Although the topics and supporting information in the papers you write for college classes may be quite diverse, the structure for most body paragraphs and essays is pretty standard:

1. Begin with the main idea (topic sentence or thesis).
2. Add specific examples and explanations that support your topic ideas.

By learning this pattern, completing the exercises in this book, and writing paragraphs and essays for practice, you will become a more confident, proficient writer.

WHAT IS THE WRITING PROCESS?

Most experienced writers look at writing as a *process*—a series of steps they can take to generate, arrange, refine, expand, and revise their ideas. If you look at writing as a series of small steps, it isn't nearly as frightening as it is if you think you must produce a perfect, error-free paper the first time you sit down to write.

As you practice using the writing techniques described in this chapter, keep in mind the following:

1. You probably won't know exactly what you want to say before you begin writing. In the process of writing, however, you will create new approaches to your subject that you hadn't thought of before you began.
2. Don't start revising too soon. Your initial goal is to get ideas on paper before you begin correcting grammar, spelling, and sentence errors. If you stop every few lines in order to make corrections, you might lose the flow of ideas and personal "voice" that make your writing unique.
3. You will need to add, cross out, and rearrange ideas once you have a draft to work with. Remember: neatness counts only at the end of the writing process.

As you become familiar with the steps in the writing process, you will develop a procedure for writing that works for you. That may mean completing a step out of order, repeating it at different stages, or choosing one writing technique over another. At this stage it is important for you to learn what your choices are, experiment with steps that are new to you, and, above all, *keep writing*.

THE PROCESS FOR WRITING ESSAYS

As you follow the steps in the writing process and examine student samples of each step, you will develop your topic, consider the audience for whom you are writing, do some preliminary writing to gather supporting ideas, organize your ideas, write a draft of your essay, consult with other students, and revise the essay several times. The following explanations and practice exercises are designed to help you focus, organize, write, and revise your essays.

This chapter shows how one student, Doug Gonzales, used the steps in the writing process to generate and arrange ideas in response to a topic, to draft an essay, and to revise it. The exercises and explanations that accompany each of Doug's tasks are designed to help you develop your own essay.

STEP 1: DEVELOPING A TOPIC

In many college classes, instructors will ask you to respond to assignments they have given you. When you get such assignments, be sure to spend some time thinking about what your instructor is asking you to do. In particular, underline key words that identify the subject and tell you how to approach it. For example, if you were asked to write a portrait of someone you knew well, you would look for key words in the topic that will help you focus your writing. Key words in this topic include the subject, an important person, and the request to describe that person. A description might include details of the person's appearance as well as typical or quirky behavior. Understanding what you need to write about can help you decide what specifics you want to include in the paragraph. A description of a person you know might include details of the person's appearance—for instance, a tall, angular woman with thick, black hair—as well as typical or quirky behavior—a generous soul who takes in wayward children, or perhaps a neatnik who spends hours cleaning countertops and arranging the clothes and shoes in his closet.

Sample Assigned Topics

For the topics listed here, key words are underlined for you in the left-hand column and explained in the column on the right. Studying the important words in these sentences can make it easier for you to determine what to write about when faced with an assigned topic.

Topic	Explanation
Explain why you decided to go to college.	Subject: Your decision to go to college Task: Explain, which means to make clear by telling reasons why people, events, or circumstances influenced your decision to go to college.

Sometimes topics appear as questions. Here is an example:

Topic	Explanation
In what situations could you justify lying to someone?	Subject: Lying Task: Give examples and explain why lying might be acceptable in certain situations.

FOR PRACTICE

Practice 3a. Underline the key words in these topics. Use the lines in the second column to explain your strategy for responding to the topic.

1. Describe someone you know well.

   Subject: _____

   Task: _____

   _____

2. What are the advantages of living alone?   Subject: _____

   Task: _____

   _____

3. Explain to a friend why he or she should   Subject: _____
   vote in the next election.

   Task: _____

   _____

4. Compare your study habits with those   Subject: _____
   of a close friend.

   Task: _____

   _____

5. Your boss has just asked you to work   Subject: _____
   more hours. Write her a letter
   explaining why you need to keep your   Task: _____
   current schedule.

   _____

Choosing Your Own Topic

Sometimes you will be asked to develop your own topic for a paragraph or paper. In this case, you might focus on a subject that has been discussed in class. If the topic is open, you could write about your interests, something that has happened to you, or people you have observed. Another alternative is to find a journal entry that mentions a subject you want to explore. With your writing task in mind, reread your journal entries, and circle words and phrases that suggest a topic. Freewrite in your journal again to gather more information on this topic. (See the list of ideas for journal entries at the end of Chapter 1.)

Student Writing

For an assignment in his English class, Doug Gonzales was asked to write on one of several topics. A topic about stresses placed on students caught his eye, but he wasn't sure what he had to say about it. He decided to write a journal entry and record whatever he could think of about the stress in his life.

3/3

     I saw a bumper sticker today that said, "Have you hugged your kids today?" I haven't seen my parents in weeks because I'm so busy, and I know they get really busy, too. Who has time for anything??? I have no time at all for myself, and I bet lots of students are like me. I mean, it's 9 PM and I've been up since 6 AM. STRESS!!! I wake up, still tired. At school I get stressed. My girlfriend threatens to break up with me if I don't spend more time with her. My mom gets on my case about yard work. My boss says I have to work harder. I have to find some way to relax, right? We all cope with stress in different ways. I used to smoke. Now I exercise to escape stress. Some people take drugs, others drink beer. Not me, that's just another kind of stress. Gotta go now—I've got math homework and more STRESS!!!

Doug reviewed the ideas he had underlined and saw that he had several possible topics for his paper. He drew up the following list of possible topics.

1. We cope with stress in different ways.
2. I give up a lot to go to school. (This topic came from Doug's journal entry statement that he had no time at all for himself.)
3. The stress in my life comes from school, my girlfriend, my mom, and my boss.
4. I have several ways of coping with stress. (This topic idea came to Doug when he read his entry notes about smoking and exercise.)

Work with the next step, "Thinking about Your Audience," helped Doug chose a focus for his essay.

FOR PRACTICE

Practice 3b. Spend ten minutes writing whatever comes to mind about one of the following topics. When the time is up, reread what you have written and underline possible ideas for essay topics. Then list several topics you could discuss in an essay.

- The importance of exercise
- Parking problems on campus
- Choosing the right roommate
- Benefits of wearing contact lenses
- Overcoming computer fears
- Air pollution

Practice 3c. Reread several journal entries you have written this semester. Pick one that interests you, and list possible topics for a paragraph or essay.

STEP 2: THINKING ABOUT YOUR AUDIENCE

Often in your life you are aware of an "audience." When you talk to a relative on the telephone or send a text message to a friend, you probably picture the person you're addressing. You might imagine that person's surroundings and how his or her facial expressions change in response to what you say. You also choose your words according to the way your audience expects you to sound. Similarly, when you write, your audience helps you decide the tone or attitude to take toward your subject, the style of writing to use (slang or more formal English), and the kind of information to include. If, for example, you are writing an email to a close friend or tapping out a text message to a roommate, you are more likely to use a personal, informal style and to state your message briefly. An assignment for an English class, however, requires that you use a writing style free of slang and that you explain your ideas in some depth. In general, when you write for a college class, assume that you have an educated, sympathetic reader who wants to learn more about your subject and who takes an interest in what you have to say. Imagining your audience in this way helps you think of your writing as a communication between you and your reader, and is one of the most effective tools for narrowing your topic.

Student Writing

To help him generate ideas and a focus for his essay, Doug Gonzales asked himself two questions about his audience and purpose for writing.

Who am I writing for?

I am writing for students who, like me, may experience some of the same kinds of stress that I do.

What am I trying to communicate to this audience?

I want students to see that they are not alone. I also want to explore ways people cope with stress.

After answering questions about his audience, Doug reread the four topics he had written for Step 1: Developing a topic, and selected the first one, "We cope with stress in different ways" as the most promising topic for his audience and purpose for writing.

FOR PRACTICE

Practice 3d. Choose one of the topics you listed in Practice 3b or 3c on page 36, and answer these two questions about audience and purpose: "Who am I writing for?" and "What am I trying to communicate to this audience?"

Practice 3e. Read the following paragraphs carefully, noting the differences in writing styles and in the kind of information presented. Then identify a possible audience for each paragraph.

1. I have had it with Omar. I really wanted to go to that dance last night. I was wearing the nicest, slinkiest dress I own. I had fixed my hair and put on my makeup and was ready at 9:30, but I waited and waited—9:30, 10:00—no Omar. I called his apartment, his mother's house, and the printing company where he works—still no Omar. I was really mad at that jerk! My friend Lana happened to be home watching a movie with Patrice. They didn't feel like going out, so I changed clothes and went over there. This morning Omar called and said he just couldn't make it. Ha! I flat out told him to forget it and hung up. I got so hot about it I couldn't even talk to that creep. I'm better off without him.

   Possible audience: _____

   _____

2. Last night I decided to break up with Omar. He usually picks me up half an hour late. Sometimes he has been drinking and I end up driving myself and having a miserable time. But last night he didn't show up at all. He had told me he would come by at 9:30, and we would go dancing, but he never bothered to call when

he found out he couldn't make it. It isn't as though I didn't try to find him, either. I called his apartment, his mother's house, and even the printing company where he works to see if he might have been working late. He wasn't at any of those places, and no one knew where he was. Instead of feeling depressed and rejected, I decided to break up with him. I called my friend, Lana, and joined her and her cousin, Patrice, for a DVD party. Lana had rented three films she thought Patrice might like, so we ate popcorn and watched movies until 3:00 in the morning. The good time I had with my friend and her cousin convinced me that my decision to break up with Omar was the right one; I can have much more fun without him.

Possible audience: _____

_____

Practice 3f. Choose a subject from the following list. Write two responses, each for a different audience.

1. Think about your ideal vacation—either real or imagined.
   a. Write a letter to your parents describing this vacation.
   b. Describe the same event in a letter to a close friend.
2. Think of an argument you witnessed that did not involve you directly.
   a. Explain to a friend who was not there what was being argued and your position on the issue.
   b. Explain your view of the argument to one of the people involved.
3. Give reasons why teenagers should not drink and drive.
   a. Write to convince the parents of teenagers why their children and their children's friends should not drink and drive.
   b. Write a plea to teenagers themselves, explaining why they should not drink and drive.

STEP 3: DEVELOPING IDEAS

This is an extremely important step in the writing process because it helps you figure out what you want to say and how to say it. This step also prepares you to write a detailed outline of your essay and, eventually, to compose your first draft. This stage of your writing can be most frightening and exciting as you begin to discover that you have interesting things to say.

If you have trouble figuring out what to write during this stage of the process, or if you find that just getting started is sometimes hard to do, try using the following strategies: ask yourself questions to help you start writing and keep writing, draw a diagram or idea wheel, or list ideas as though you were composing a list of the day's activities. Eventually, as you become more confident about your writing, you will probably favor one of these methods over the other two.

Strategies for Developing Ideas

1. Ask Yourself Questions. This first strategy is something like interviewing yourself and recording what you know and how you feel about your subject. You have already seen how Doug Gonzales used a question-and-answer technique to explore ideas about his audience and purpose for writing (Step 2). In addition, the journalist's questions (who, what, when, where, why, and how) provide a good starting point for exploring your topic. By turning these one-word questions into longer ones related to your topic, you can dig deeply into the topic and think of examples, ideas, and explanations that you might be able to use in your essay. Often the best question you can ask yourself is "What am I trying to say?" Asking this question periodically helps you to be precise about what you want to say, and if you suffer from writer's block, answering questions will help you keep writing. (If you have difficulty coming up with questions on your own, consult "Questions for Expanding Ideas," Appendix B at the back of this book.)

Student Writing

When Doug Gonzales reached this point in his writing, he reviewed his topic and purpose for writing and asked himself what his readers needed to know about ways to cope with stress.

Topic: Explore ways to cope with stress
Purpose: To describe some of the pressures I face as a student and to show others ways to deal with these stresses.

To help him focus on causes of stress in his own life and ways to relieve such pressures, Doug asked himself additional questions, which he then tried to answer.

What pressures do I have in my life that other students might share?

Deadlines at school, family demands, stress at work.

How can people cope with stress?

I use exercise. My family watches TV to relax. I used to smoke, and I know people who drink or use drugs to calm down.

2. Draw an Idea Wheel. Your next response to a topic might be to draw an idea wheel—a cluster of ideas connected to one another like spokes on a wheel. This strategy is also called *clustering* or *branching*. It is one way to visualize your ideas and make connections between them. To put this strategy into practice, use your subject as the hub or center of the wheel. Then put general ideas related to that subject in bubbles and draw spokes connecting them to the hub. Place details and examples in additional bubbles that connect to the general points they illustrate.

Student Writing

Doug Gonzales drew an idea wheel to help him visualize his general points about stress and supporting ideas and details. Not only was he able to see his ideas better, but the resulting picture helped him gather more details about a few points, thereby giving him a greater choice of ideas for his essay.

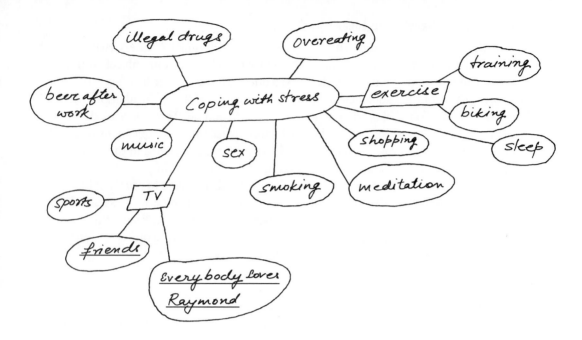

Practice 3g. To practice this strategy for generating ideas, complete the following idea wheels by filling in details and examples for subtopics. Add spokes as needed. If you need more room, copy the idea wheels on separate sheets of paper.

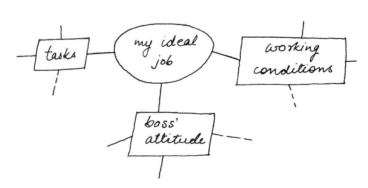

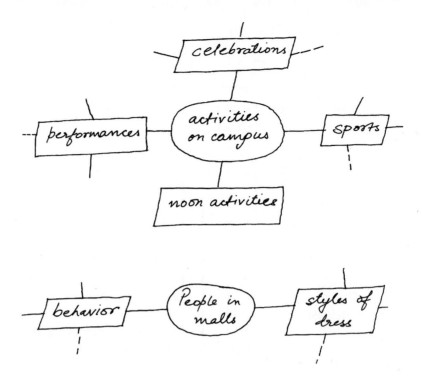

Practice 3h. Fill in subtopics and details for the following topics.

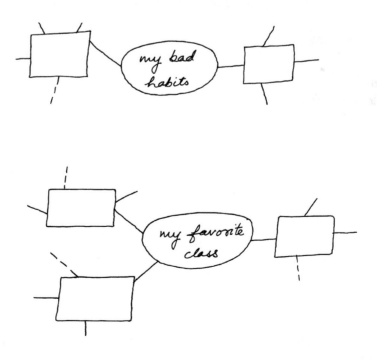

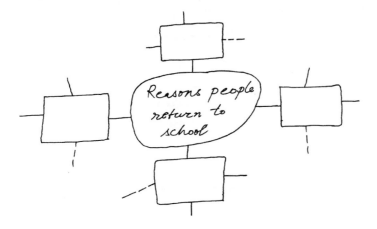

3. Make a List of Ideas. The strategy of listing ideas should be familiar to you because of lists you have made of household chores, groceries, or homework assignments. The lists you make for writing are just as practical as these other lists; you can use them to generate ideas and details about your topic, and to select, group, and arrange those ideas before you move to Step 4: Organizing Ideas: Writing a Thesis and an Outline. You might want to make several lists, each more specific than the last, as you work toward composing a brief outline of the essay.

The difficult part is that you will not be able to use all the information you gather in your idea wheels or lists of ideas. The ideas that don't quite fit are probably the ones you need to drop. Record these extra ideas in your journal or in a computer file; you might be able to use them in another writing assignment.

Student Writing

When Doug Gonzales made a list of ideas, he saw that he could group some of them according to several subtopics.

Coping with Stress
    exercise
        training
        biking
    shopping
    music
    TV
        sitcoms
    sports
    sleep
    overeating
    meditation
    using illegal drugs
        cocaine
        smoking
        drinking beer
  sex

Doug was able to expand his original list of ideas by adding complete sentences that expressed his thoughts about each item.

Coping with Stress—ways we do it

Exercise is a good way to fight stress.

– Biking long distances helps me sleep well.

Sleep lets some people work off tension.

Meditation and yoga work for other people.

Using legal drugs isn't too risky but can cause problems later on.

– Cigarettes—nicotine may increase anxiety.

– Alcohol is a temporary solution.

Using illegal drugs is a risky way to cope.

– Cocaine is a very short-term solution.

Overeating is a popular reaction to stress.

Shopping works for some people I know.

Music can be a soothing escape.

– Mom and Dad listen to salsa. Ray uses hip hop to escape stress.

Watching TV lets you think about other people's problems.

– <u>Friends</u> and <u>Everybody Loves Raymond</u> work well for me.

– Talk shows and trash TV occupy some viewers.

Sports is like exercise.

Sex?

FOR PRACTICE

Practice 3i. Choose one of the topics from Practice 3b (listed here) and apply at least one of the preliminary writing strategies to develop ideas for an essay: (1) ask yourself questions, (2) draw an idea wheel, and (3) make a list of whatever comes to mind about the topic you selected.

- The importance of exercise
- Parking problems on campus
- Choosing the right roommate
- Benefits of wearing contact lenses
- Overcoming computer fears
- Air pollution

STEP 4: ORGANIZING IDEAS: WRITING A THESIS AND AN OUTLINE

When ideas are clearly organized, another reader can easily follow and make sense of them. To create a clear organization for your paper, first gather the information from your responses to questions, idea wheels, and any lists you have made. Then group ideas and details that are similar if you haven't already done so. With this step, you are identifying two, three, or four points for your topic sentences and selecting details and examples that support them. The thesis or main idea for your paper comes from the strategies you have used to gather ideas.

Writing a Thesis and Topic Sentences

The thesis states the main idea of your essay and is usually summed up in a single sentence. You might also look at the thesis as a promise you make to yourself and your readers about the subject you will discuss and the way you will discuss it. Because it determines what will appear in the rest of your paper, the thesis is the most important sentence in the essay.

Once you know some of the points you want to make in your essay, it is a good idea to create at least a preliminary thesis to help you stay on track as you generate and arrange ideas. This beginning thesis provides a direction for your essay and allows you to see what organizational pattern you might use when arranging paragraphs. Although it is easy to understand the importance of developing a working thesis, it takes some effort to come up with a good one.

Student Writing

Let's look at Doug Gonzales's plans for writing his paper. To create a working thesis, Doug reviewed the list of ideas he had created earlier. He saw that his thesis could include healthy and unhealthy ways of relieving stress. He then wrote the following preliminary thesis: "People have different ways of relieving stress, but some are healthier than others." Once Doug had a tentative thesis, he grouped his ideas as either harmful or healthy ways to relieve stress, and wrote the following thesis and brief outline.

Thesis: People have different ways of relieving stress, but some are healthier than others.

Unhealthy, even harmful, ways of dealing with stress include:
– Taking drugs
– Drinking beer, either alone or in a bar
– Smoking
Healthy ways to relieve stress:
– Watch television shows
– Listen to music
– Have sex
– Do exercise

Once he saw a pattern he liked, Doug was able to narrow his list of ideas to those he could discuss in some detail.

FOR PRACTICE

Practice 3j. To help you distinguish general topic ideas from details and examples that support them, read the following groups of sentences and put a check mark (✓) beside the sentence that states the main point, the most general idea of the whole paragraph. The topic sentence in the first group is identified for you.

1. _____ a. Players shift the ball constantly and pass frequently to confuse their opponents.

   _____ b. Unlike most men's games, women's basketball is team-based rather than hero-based.

   _____ c. Constant motion is the rule in women's basketball.

   _✓_ d. Women's basketball is often very exciting to watch.

   _____ e. Women will sometimes forgo the chance to make a spectacular play to avoid throwing away the ball.

2. _____ a. But something always came up; I had to cancel, Joe had to go out of town, or Frank got sick.

   _____ b. Soon we stopped trying to make lunch dates.

   _____ c. I also made several attempts to have lunch with them.

   _____ d. At first, I called Frank and Joe frequently—at least once a month.

   _____ e. When I graduated from high school, I had every intention of keeping in touch with my friends.

   _____ f. And before we knew it, we stopped calling each other.

   _____ g. As our lives filled with obligations of family and work, we simply had no time for each other.

3. _____ a. He figured he might as well try it; he had been through just about everything else.

   _____ b. Then one day Marvin heard about acupuncture.

   _____ c. Now Marvin has been smoke-free for six months, the longest time he has gone without a cigarette since he started smoking at the age of fourteen.

   _____ d. Patches, antismoking tablets, hypnosis—nothing seemed to work.

   _____ e. My brother worked hard to stop smoking and was finally able to quit.

   _____ f. He tried everything.

4. _____ a. I always take them and place well below my real level.

   _____ b. Midterms and final exams are almost as bad as assessment tests.

   _____ c. Assessment tests are the worst.

   _____ d. I wish I knew what to do about this test anxiety I have.

   _____ e. I can study all week long, go into an exam, and forget my own name.

   _____ f. Tests make me so nervous I panic and can't think straight.

   _____ g. I have a terrible time taking tests.

5. _____ a. For one thing, it is a highly competitive field.

   _____ b. I have always wanted to be an architect, but now I am not sure.

   _____ c. And I hate to give up the prestige that being an architect would bring.

   _____ d. The money an architect makes used to intrigue me.

   _____ e. An architect can spend a long time between jobs.

6. _____ a. They often have a lot of energy, especially if they are exercising.

   _____ b. People should not be forced to retire just because they are old.

   _____ c. They often make hardworking, reliable employees.

   _____ d. The elderly have a lot of experience to give their employers.

Practice 3k. The topic sentences for several essays are grouped together in the exercises below. Write a thesis for an essay that develops these ideas.

Example:
Competing in sports helps children set goals.
Children who play sports learn to make decisions.
Team involvement is another important benefit for children who play organized sports.
Possible thesis: Children who play organized sports learn to set goals, make their own decisions, and cooperate with others.
Possible thesis: Playing organized sports helps children develop self confidence and teaches them valuable social skills.

1. The store owners and waitresses in Malberg are hostile to servicemen.
   It is difficult to get on a bus or hail a cab without being either ignored or insulted.
   When servicemen go to nightclubs in Malberg, they must sit in a segregated section in the bar.

   Possible thesis: _____

   _____

2. Football players must be in excellent physical shape.
   Members of a football team must also be mentally prepared for the games.
   Most important of all, players must learn to work together.

   Possible thesis: _____

   _____

3. Friends may begin asking "When are you getting married?" after a man and woman have been dating for only a few months.
   Family members often add to the couple's discomfort by assuming that because they enjoy spending time together they'll eventually marry.

   Possible thesis: _____

   _____

4. Tobacco use makes a person very unappealing.
   Not only is smoking a socially obnoxious habit, it is considered the number one cause of heart and lung disease in the United States.
   Smoking endangers other people's health as well.

   Possible thesis: _____

   _____

5. Sioux Falls, South Dakota, has fewer opportunities for entertainment than does San Francisco.
   San Francisco also has Sioux Falls beat in terms of job opportunities.

The crime rate is a major problem in San Francisco and a minor consideration in Sioux Falls.

The costs of housing, food, clothing, and utilities make it much more difficult to live in San Francisco than in Sioux Falls.

Possible thesis: _____

_____

Writing a Detailed Outline

Your instructor may ask you to write a detailed outline of your essay. This might be an expanded list of ideas similar to Doug's first outline or a longer sentence outline. The sentence outline for Doug's essay includes five main points or topic ideas.

Outline for Coping with Stress

I. A portrait of my personal stress to open the essay
   A. Mom's orders cause stress at home.
       1. She demands I do the yard work.
   B. My teacher says I'm not passing.
       1. I have to do more homework.
   C. My boss is unhappy.
       1. He tells me I must work harder at my job.
          a. He wants to see more sales.
   D. My girlfriend wants time.
       1. She calls me at work.
       2. She says, "Pay more attention to me!"

Thesis: People have different ways of relieving stress, but some are healthier than others.

II. There are unhealthy, even harmful ways to deal with stress
   A. Using drugs is unwise.
       1. My friend Ricky used drugs to relieve his stress.
          a. He had a positive drug test at work.
       2. Drinking beer is a solution for some people.
          a. People at work drink to relieve stress.
       3. Smoking is another way to cope.
          a. My experience with smoking is one example.
   B. Healthy ways to relieve stress
       1. Watching television shows can help people relax.
          a. Mom and Dad watch TV for this reason.
             i. Mexican soaps are their favorite.
          b. I watch my own programs.
             i. Sports are my main interest.
             ii. My brother and I also like <u>Friends</u> and <u>Everybody loves Raymond</u>.

2. Music is another healthy stress-reliever.
   a. Mom and Dad listen to Mexican music like mariachis.
   b. My little brother listens to hip hop.
   c. I like salsa.
3. Exercise is the most positive way to cope with stress.
   a. Jogging works for some.
   b. I have an exercise plan called the Basic Training Workout.
      i. I do aerobics and lift weights.
   c. Playing racquetball, swimming, and biking are other ways to keep stress away.
4. Sex can be another way to relax.

Patterns of Organization

In the discussion of thesis statements earlier in this chapter, we saw how a thesis helps a writer arrange ideas in the body of an essay. There are several patterns of organization you may use to help you craft the best structure for your essay. Which one you choose depends on your subject and purpose for writing. If, for example, you are writing about something that happened to you or an event you witnessed, you will probably put those events in **chronological** order—the order in which they occurred. The student paragraph "Moving On" illustrates this pattern of organization.

Student Writing

Moving On

I remember my childhood in bits and pieces, a blur of different houses and new neighborhoods. In my earliest memory I see the giant gray porch at my grandfather's house in Ohio. I recall lying on the front porch in the summer waiting for the ice-cream truck. Then one day my father received orders to leave for Oklahoma, and we moved for the first time, leaving our relatives behind. I remember one Halloween in Oklahoma when I was in the second grade. The neighbor kids decided to visit the haunted house just down the block from where I lived. We were sure that a doll haunted the house, and when someone yelled that the doll was com- ing down from the second floor to get us, we all

Topic sentence— childhood memories

Earliest memory

Move to Oklahoma

screamed and ran home. In the middle of the third grade, my father left for Vietnam; I didn't see him again for three and a half years. We packed up and left Oklahoma, this time for Sacramento, California. There I made friends with the kids on the block—Harold, Westly, and Bill—and started life all over again. This life lasted until I finished tenth grade and my father came home from Vietnam. My mother and father discovered that they were virtual strangers and decided to separate. I finished the eleventh and twelfth grades in Syracuse, New York; Paul, Gary, and Chris were my best friends. Once we made the news as the four crazies who ran wild on the airport runway late one night. The pattern of my life hasn't changed much over the years. I usually stay a few years in one place, make friends, and then move on.

Move to Sacramento, California

Parents' separation and move to Syracuse, New York

Current lifestyle

If you are writing a description of a room, a painting, or a photograph, you will probably use **spatial** organization to describe details from top to bottom, foreground to background, or left to right.

Student Writing

Pictures of Grandmother

In the photograph of my grandmother taken in 1945 sits a woman whom I can barely recognize. In that forty-five-year-old picture, my grandmother is sitting on the steps of her house in Old Land Park with my mother on her lap. A huge camellia bush hangs gracefully over the porch. She is dressed like a little girl, wearing penny loafers, a plaid skirt, and matching blue sweater. In the photograph, the wind is blowing her curly, dark brown hair away from her face as she leans over to put her thinner

Topic sentence

Background—location, pose

Clothing

Hair

face next to my mother's little fat one. Grandmother's skin looks slightly tanned next to my
mother's rosy cheeks. She smiles radiantly as she
looks at the camera, her face quite youthful and — *Face*
free of the deep lines near the corners of her mouth
and under her eyes with which I am familiar. In spite
of how much she has aged since this picture was
taken, the youthful happiness I see in the photo- — *Eyes*
                                                        (central feature)
graph is there, even now, in her eyes.

If you want to explain causes or effects, or argue a point, you might use **order-of-importance** organization or **emphatic** order, saving your strongest point for the end of the discussion. One student used this pattern to develop her paragraph about students who drop out of college.

Student Writing

Why Students Drop Out

There are several reasons why students drop — *Topic sentence*
out of college. A few leave school because they lack
patience. My friend Serita, for example, attended
City last semester but ended up dropping her classes
and enrolling in a trade school. She felt she was   *A few lack patience*
wasting her time getting a general education. In-   *(least frequent cause)*
stead, she decided to get a skill and find a job
quickly rather than take five or six years to complete a degree.

Other students are also parents and find it hard — *Topic sentence*
to play both roles. My friend Serita eventually left
school because her daughter, Erin, was always getting colds from taking buses so early in the morning. Serita found it impossible to care for her sick
child, change her diapers, and feed her while trying *Difficulties for*
to attend school and study for classes. She hopes to *parents*
return to school when Erin is a little older.

Most students quit college for economic reasons. Even in a community college, students pay at least fifty dollars in fees every semester, buy several hundred dollars' worth of books, and either purchase a bus pass or pay expenses on a car. Two of my best friends had to drop out this semester because they ran out of money. They couldn't work enough hours to pay their living expenses, yet increasing their hours at work meant they had no time for homework. It isn't easy to stay in college, but luckily, most of us find a way.

— Topic sentence

— Most cannot afford to go (most frequent cause)

FOR PRACTICE

Practice 3l. Which of the three organizational patterns does the writer use in the essay, "The Life of a Sports Fanatic," pages 31–32?

Practice 3m. Select a possible pattern for organizing topic ideas you developed in Practice 3i.

Practice 3n. Write an outline based on one of the idea wheels you drew for either Practice 3g or 3h. Note in the margin the pattern of organization you used.

STEP 5: DRAFTING AND REVISING ESSAYS

Writing a Fast Draft

This all-important step marks the first time you write your ideas in essay form. If you have followed the steps in the writing process, you have a pretty good idea of what you want to say and the details that will help you say it.

The purpose of writing your draft is to get ideas on paper in sentence, paragraph, and essay form. At this point the plan for your essay might be a list of ideas, an idea wheel, a detailed outline, or a combination of these. Regardless of the method you use, keep your plan next to you as you write, but be flexible. If you think of ideas and examples that are not in your plan, write them down even if they don't follow your original thoughts about the paper. The plan is meant to guide your writing efforts, not to limit them; it simply gives you the courage to begin writing. To keep the flow of ideas going, don't stop to correct awkward-sounding sentences or to look up words in the dictionary until you have completed your draft.

Your work with gathering information, using a thesis to focus your essay, and organizing and developing ideas is designed to help you draft your paper.

Student Writing

After writing an outline for his essay on stress, Doug Gonzales wrote the following fast draft.

Stress!!!

I just got home from work its 9 p.m. and I've been up since 6 a.m. I am stressed out!! I think I have good reasons for feeling this way. This was my day. I wake up, and I'm still tired from the day before. I go to school, and my teacher told me I have to work just a little harder if I want to pass the class (STRESS!!). I went to work and my boss says he has some complaints about me (STRESS!!). Finally, at 9 p.m. I get to go home after a long, stressful day. I walk in the door and the first thing my mom says is that the yard looks terrible. When do I have time to clean the yard? (STRESS!!) This is just an example of my very stressful day. With all these "highs" going on in my life, how do I come back down? What are some ways other people come back down? People have different ways of relieving stress, but some are healthier than others.

Some ways of relieving stress are unhealthy, even harmful. Take drugs, for example. My friend Ricky is a perfect example of someone who used cocaine and eventually lost his job. One day his employer make him take a drug test. Ricky got fired. I also have a stressful job. When 5 p.m. rolls around, most people I work with say "It's beer time." That is just another way people cope with stress they drink beer. I think stress is one of the big reasons people start smoking. I used to smoke. A cigarette always seemed to calm me right down. It will also kill you.

My whole family watches television to relax and forget about work. Mom and Dad watch Mexican soaps. I watch my own programs—sports is my favorite, but I also like "Friends" and "Everybody Loves Raymond." Music is another way my family has of relaxing. Mom and Dad listen to Mexican music like mariachi bands, my little brother, Ray, likes hip hop, and I listen to salsa.

The best way to handle stress, I have found, is through exercise. I found a workout system that works for me. I like to play racquetball and do what's called "Basic Training Workout." A complete workout system that deals with everything from aerobics to weight training. I take long bike rides. Especially in the evening. And sometimes I swim at the Y.

I wasn't going to mention sex, but sex is one of the most common ways people relieve stress. Its good exercise, too, you feel good, and its a healthy activity that relieves stress. I guess we all have our own ways of coping.

Revising Essays

Editing and Proofreading. The process of revising marks the second time that you will need to stop and think seriously about your audience's needs. Early in our discussion of the writing process (Step 2), you saw how considering his audience's interests helped Doug Gonzales narrow the topic for his essay on stress. By the time you reach this step in the writing process, you are ready to concentrate on whether the ideas in your paragraph are arranged and supported in such a way that your readers can understand and appreciate the points you want to make. These considerations about organization and support are **editing** considerations. A thorough editing might involve the following procedures:

1. Write a second outline to see if your ideas follow a distinct chronological or spatial order, or if you have arranged them clearly according to their order of importance.
2. Move sentences, add examples, and delete information when such changes make your ideas clearer to your reader.
3. Rewrite sentences that don't make sense when read out loud or that do not say exactly what you mean. If you have a particular problem with your writing, your instructor might refer you to specific discussions and exercises in Part V of this book, "Editing Your Writing."

When **proofreading,** you are concentrating on individual words, phrases, and sentences in your writing. Your goal when you proofread is to find and correct errors in sentence structure, grammar, and mechanics—spelling, punctuation, and capitalization. You might also refer to the rules for punctuation, spelling, and capitalization in Chapter 23, "Grammar and Mechanics," as you proofread your paper. In addition, it is useful to keep the following suggestions in mind while proofreading a paragraph or an essay:

1. Proofread your paper several times. Check for words and phrases you may have omitted in your fast draft.
2. Keep a list of mistakes that recur in your writing, and when you proofread, go through your draft several times, each time looking for a different type of error. If, for example, you frequently drop the past tense (-*ed*) endings from verbs and you also tend to write fragments, read your paragraph once to check your verb forms; then read it a second time to find any fragments you may have written. (You might also want to check the explanations in Chapter 20, "Correcting Fragments and Run-on Sentences.")
3. Read your paper aloud and, if you can, tape-record it. This procedure usually makes writers look more carefully at what they have written.
4. After proofreading your essay on your own, your instructor might ask you to share your writing with another student. Like most people, you may not be able to catch all the errors in your own writing; that's why having someone else look at your work is another good way of finding mistakes.

Sharing Your Writing

At first, the idea of sharing what you have written with other students may make you uncomfortable or may even seem frightening. But once you have done it a few times, you will find that your fellow students can give you support and encouragement as well as good suggestions for clarifying your ideas. Sharing your writing is also beneficial because you can see how other students write. As a result, you may discover ways of organizing and developing ideas that you can use in future papers.

Begin the peer review process by dividing into small groups with three or four students in each. When sharing writing, read your paper aloud to classmates—or better yet, have a classmate read it aloud to you. When a classmate reads it, he or she is less likely to fill in missing words or reconstruct sentences for you. One member of the group or the author of the paper being discussed can act as recorder and write down the group's ideas. Discuss each paper as thoroughly as you can before going on to the next one.

Your group may wish to use the questions given here to help focus your discussion. These questions are also listed in Appendix C, "Questions for Peer Review," at the back of this textbook.

1. What did you like about the essay?
2. Does the opening paragraph get you interested in the subject? Explain why or why not.
3. Does the introduction include the main point of the paper—its thesis—either stated or implied? Write the thesis.
4. Would you like more information about any of the general ideas in the body paragraphs? If so, which ones?
5. Were there paragraphs that seemed off the topic and unrelated to the thesis?
6. Did you have any difficulty following the writer's ideas or reading some of the sentences? Explain.
7. Does the essay come to a logical end?
8. Would you like to ask the writer any questions about the topic, or do you have additional points you would like to make about the essay?

FOR PRACTICE

Practice 3o. In a group of three students, use the questions for peer review to evaluate Doug Gonzales's fast draft.

Student Writing

Doug shared the draft of his essay with two of his classmates. His group used the questions for peer review to discuss their essays. A student recorder wrote the following observations that Doug's group made about his essay.

1. What did you like about the essay?

We liked the opening of his essay. We got stressed out just reading it. We liked seeing some of the ways that people relax. Doug had a pretty good list . . . it was good to put drugs in there, too because so many people use alcohol and illegal drugs to escape, and those can be dangerous. We also liked the way that he organized his paragraphs.

2. Does the opening paragraph get you interested in the subject? Explain why or why not.

Yes. It put us in a mood to read about stress.

3. Does the introduction include the main point of the paper—its thesis— either stated or implied?

He could write a more specific thesis mentioning ways of coping with stress that he discusses in the essay. He asked so many questions near the end of the introduction that we couldn't be sure which he was going to answer.

> *4. Would you like more information about any of the general ideas in the body paragraphs? If so, which ones?*

We didn't know whether the workout system was Doug's own creation or it if was part of the "basic training workout" at a gym, and how do all these ideas reduce stress?

> *5. Were there paragraphs that seemed off the topic and unrelated to the thesis?*

No. The paragraphs were about either unhealthy or healthy ways to reduce stress.

> *6. Did you have any difficulty following the writer's ideas or reading some of the sentences? Explain.*

The essay jumped around too much—from drugs to drinking to smoking, then from TV to music. We found a few fragments, too.

> *7. Does the essay come to a logical conclusion?*

No. It just seems to stop. He could bring in the ideas in his thesis.

> *8. Would you like to ask the writer any questions about the topic, or do you have additional points you would like to make about the essay?*

We had trouble with the topic in the last paragraph. We agree that sex can be relaxing, but it's not always that healthy.

In response to the peer review, Doug wrote the following entry in his journal to figure out how he might revise his draft.

4/7

My group was really encouraging. I was glad they noticed the details I included in the paragraphs. They made some good suggestions. I plan to take out the questions in the introduction and rewrite the thesis to give it a more specific focus. I also need to explain how exercise, music, and television relieve stress. I wasn't that comfortable discussing sex, so I'll leave it out. I also need to proofread for fragments.

FOR PRACTICE

Practice 3p. Compare your responses in Practice 3o (using questions on page 54) to the responses Doug got from his fellow students. Did you anticipate any of their responses? Did you make suggestions they overlooked?

Practice 3q. If your instructor conducts a peer review workshop for an essay assignment, examine student comments carefully. Then write a journal entry explaining which of the student suggestions you will incorporate in your revision and which ones you rejected. Explain your choices.

Making Final Revisions

After working with a piece of writing for a while, it is often difficult to complete your final, careful reading and make last-minute corrections. A checklist may keep you on track. You might also use this checklist for peer review in the classroom or in a computer lab.

- ❑ Does my essay have a thesis that includes my subject and what I will say about it?
- ❑ Did I include enough details and examples to give a vivid picture of my subject?
- ❑ Are there gaps in any paragraphs that may confuse the reader?
- ❑ Have I provided smooth connections between sentences and ideas and between paragraphs?
- ❑ Have I used my computer's spell-check function and proofread this paragraph well enough to catch spelling mistakes I may have made and words I may have omitted?
- ❑ Have I checked carefully for sentence errors like fragments and run-ons?

Most writers will tell you that no piece of writing is ever "finished." In other words, there is usually something else you could change or another detail you might add. But at some point, after careful editing and proofreading, you have to stop writing and turn in your paper.

Student Writing

After considering students' comments and reworking the focus of his essay, Doug Gonzales wrote his final essay.

Coping with Stress

I just got home from work. It's 9 p.m., and I've been up since 6 a.m. I am stressed out!! I think I have good reasons for feeling this way. When I woke up, I was still tired from the day before. I went to school, and my math teacher told me I have to work just a little harder if I want to pass the class (STRESS!!). I arrived at work, and my boss said he'd had some complaints about me last week (STRESS!!). Finally, at 9 p.m. I went home after a long, stressful day. I walked in the door, and the first thing my mom said was, "The yard looks terrible. When do you have time to clean it?" (STRESS!!). If you are a student, you probably have some of the same pressures in your life, and, like me, you must find ways to cope with stress. The trick is to avoid the more harmful methods of relieving stress, like taking drugs, and to find healthier outlets, like music and exercise, to relieve stress.

Some ways of relieving stress are unhealthy, even harmful. I think stress is one of the main reasons why people smoke. I was a heavy smoker until recently. I work for an insurance agency and spend most of my day dealing with angry claimants. Smoking a cigarette after work used to calm me down after a long, stressful day. Because of the risk of lung cancer and heart disease, I quit smoking

---

a few months ago. Most people I work with drink after work to relieve stress. When 5:00 rolls around, I will hear someone say, "It's beer time." Drinking becomes a problem for everyone on the road if an intoxicated person tries to drive. My co-workers are smart enough to take public transportation or appoint someone as the "designated driver." He or she stays liquor-free and drives everyone else home. But that arrangement doesn't solve the health problems people may develop because they drink.

Illegal drugs can be even more damaging. My friend Ricky is a perfect example of someone who misused drugs and eventually lost his job because of them. He had a very stressful job and used cocaine to escape. At work he spent eight hours a day loading trucks as fast as he could. By the time he got home, he was dead tired. To feel better, he started using cocaine. At first no one knew, not even his friends. Then he got careless and began using it at work to keep himself going. One day his employer made him take a drug test, and Ricky got fired. He not only lost his job but also changed his life for the worse. Recently I heard he was in jail on a drugs charge.

My family and I have found healthier ways to relieve stress. We often watch television to relax and forget about work. Mom and Dad, for instance, watch Mexican soaps. My mom, especially, gets very involved with the characters' lives and forgets about her own aches and pains. I watch my own programs—sports is my favorite. I love to watch golf games because the players aren't like football players who try to knock each other down. Instead, golf is a slow-moving sport that requires a lot of thinking and concentration. Besides, the setting is always beautiful and makes me feel at ease. I also enjoy watching baseball because even though it is exciting when your team gets a double play or the opponents score a home run, there are still long stretches in between where the manager, pitcher, and catcher are figuring out what to do.

Music is another way my family has of relaxing. Mom, Dad, and my sister listen to Mexican music. Dad likes Carlos Guardel, who sings love songs and ballads that remind him of Mexico. Mom and my sister, Ida, enjoy listening to mariachi, that wonderful music from the Mexican Revolution. My little brother, Ray, likes hip hop. I have no idea how he is able to relax while that is on, but he just loves it and seems to be in a world of his own as he listens to his headphones. I am a little older than Ray, and I am happiest listening to salsa, especially the music of Ruben Blades. Music is a great way of taking your mind off your troubles.

The best way to handle stress, I have found, is through exercise. My family joined the YMCA a few years ago, and I have been going regularly since I stopped smoking. In the winter months I swim at the Y, play racquetball on weekends, and do a "Basic Training Workout" during the week. The program at the Y offers a complete workout with everything from aerobics to weight training, and it always ends with a long period of stretching. When summer comes and the weather is right, I also like to take long bike rides, especially in the evening. When I ride on those warm nights, the summer breeze is very soothing, and my body always feels better for the exercise.

> With the stress most of us have in our lives, we must find ways to calm down without threatening our health. My family and I find that watching television and listening to music are effective ways to forget about our problems. Exercise, however, offers the best alternative for me because it makes me feel equal to my tasks at work and school.
>
> —Doug Gonzales

FOR PRACTICE

Practice 3r. Write a paragraph explaining the two or three most important changes Doug made in his essay. Briefly explain how these changes improved the paper. What other improvements might he make?

TOPICS FOR WRITING

Topic 1. Pick a topic from the following list. Use the steps in the writing process to narrow the topic, identify your audience, gather details and information, organize, write, and revise a short paper.

- Write a detailed description of the worst or best restaurant in town.
- Explain how you establish friendships.
- Write an essay about a problem in your life and ways to solve it.
- Discuss the two or three reasons why you became angry with someone recently.

Topic 2. Write a paper explaining why you are attending college at this time in your life. Be sure to mention the two or three reasons in your thesis. Use the writing process to narrow your topic, do preliminary writing, organize, draft, and revise.

Topic 3. Write a draft for an essay based on the outline you completed for Practice 3n. After consulting with your instructor and/or participating in a peer review, revise your draft.

LOOKING AHEAD

Chapter 4 provides additional information about basic essay structure, and it gives you practice writing thesis statements, topic sentences, titles, and introductions and conclusions.

Revising
Paragraphs

This chapter reviews basic paragraph structure—topic
sentences, supporting details and examples, and
concluding or transitional sentences. Exercises in this
chapter give you practice editing paragraphs for unity,
development, and coherence—crucial elements in
well-written paragraphs.

BASIC PARAGRAPH STRUCTURE

The **topic sentence** states the main idea you want to discuss in any paragraph that you write. It also links the paragraph to the thesis statement in an essay and usually begins a paragraph. **Key words** in your topic sentence announce the subject you will discuss and predict how you will discuss it. In published writing, you may find the main idea in the second or third sentence, or at the end of a paragraph. Occasionally it is not stated at all but merely implied by the discussion. Until you gain confidence in your writing skills, it is best to begin your body paragraphs with a topic sentence to make the point of the paragraph clear.

Supporting sentences of the paragraph provide subtopics, facts, details, examples, and explanations to support the main idea stated in your topic sentence. Think of these supporting sentences as links in a chain; each sentence you write has a logical connection to the one before it and anticipates those that follow it. Most body paragraphs must be six to ten sentences long to provide adequate support for the main idea.

The **concluding sentence** (or two) brings the paragraph to a satisfying close and sometimes suggests a connection to the paragraph that follows.

Student Writing

In the following paragraph, Gary Gilbert promises to discuss how difficult it is for him to go to school. The rest of the paragraph discusses how distractions at home and concern about his relationship with his son make it hard for him to attend school. Transitional phrases connect ideas, which are organized by order of importance; Gary's relationship with his son is his last subtopic. In his conclusion, Gary acknowledges his family's patience and looks forward to graduation. The topic sentence and words that link sentences and ideas are underlined for you.

Getting through School

indent about 1/2 inch   *transition*

    It is difficult for me to go to school. For one thing,   ]– *Topic sentence*

the distractions at home make it hard for me to con-   ]– *Subtopic*

centrate on homework. Just as I'm about to solve a

math problem, my son runs screaming through the
                          transition
house with my wife in hot pursuit. Then there are the   ]– *Examples*

phone calls from family, friends, and solicitors that in-

terrupt my thoughts and make me wonder if I will
                    transition
ever get my work done. I also worry that my relation-   ]– *Subtopic*

ship with my son will suffer because I'm not with him
                    transition
as much as I want to be. I feel especially guilty if I   ]– *Examples*

don't get home in time for dinner, or I have to rush off

to the library on a Sunday afternoon instead of playing catch with him. I can always tell when he thinks
I have been neglecting him. Sometimes he refuses to   ⎤—*Examples*
give me a goodnight kiss, or he flips on the television ⎦
while I'm trying to hold a family discussion. It won't ⎤
be easy on my family but with the commitment and   ⎬ *Concluding*
patience of us all, I'll get through school.   ⎦ *sentences*

—Gary Gilbert

ELEMENTS OF A STRONG PARAGRAPH

When you revise paragraphs, it is important to check for *unity, development,* and *coherence*—three characteristics of a well-written paragraph.

WRITING UNIFIED PARAGRAPHS

Strong paragraphs are *unified.* For a paragraph to be unified, sentences in the body should stick to the idea stated in the topic sentence. In freewriting, you may wander from one idea to another, but this freedom is characteristic of preliminary writing, not revised, polished paragraphs. In the preceding sample paragraph, for example, all sentences either explain or illustrate the topic idea that it is difficult to work and go to school. The writer is careful not to include irrelevant ideas.

If you are writing a paragraph and find yourself straying from your topic, take out your journal and freewrite until the irrelevant ideas have played themselves out. Then return to your writing and continue developing your support for the main idea. After you have finished writing, check the paragraph to make sure that ideas and examples support the topic sentence.

Topic Sentences

A topic sentence whose focus is clear enough to develop in the paragraph is one of the keys to writing unified paragraphs. As the most general idea in your paragraph, the topic sentence states the point that prepares your reader for all other ideas, details, and examples in the rest of the paragraph.

The following exercises give you practice identifying and developing topic sentences and writing unified paragraphs.

FOR PRACTICE

Practice 4a. Read the following paragraphs carefully. Then underline the topic sentences. Remember that the topic sentence is the general idea supported by the rest of the discussion.

1. For transportation around town, I prefer riding my bike to driving my truck. I look forward to the workout I get on the mornings when I ride my 18-speed mountain bike. By the time I have cycled the five miles to school, I can feel the muscles in my legs. On the other hand, it takes very little energy to drive my truck because the machine moves and stops when I apply the slightest pressure to the accelerator or brake. Another thing I enjoy about my bike is the way it hums like a bee as I move freely and gracefully through quiet residential streets. In contrast, when I drive my truck, I feel trapped inside the cab like a crab in its shell. With traffic all around me, I seem to crawl along the crowded thoroughfares. Every time I drive my truck, I am reminded of how much more sense it makes to take my bike across town.

2. When you live alone, yours is the only mess you have to clean up. No roommate lets his dishes pile up in the sink because he is too busy working overtime to wash them. If there are dirty clothes left in the bathroom, they are yours and not someone else's greasy jeans. In addition, you have much more privacy living by yourself. Fewer phone calls come in, and, unless you turn them on yourself, no television programs prevent you from doing your homework. Furthermore, you needn't worry about someone else's friends dropping over unexpectedly while you are taking a bath. There is nothing like settling down in the tub, a good book in hand, without fear of interruptions. Living alone certainly has its advantages.

3. News reporting on the air and in print feeds on sensationalism. The latest multiple-car crash, burn victim, or drive-by murder is sure to make the morning headlines or the evening news. It could be argued that viewers and readers are eager for negative news, and they get what they want. But I think there is more to it than that. We suffocate people with the grim, the horrible, and the pessimistic because we have forgotten that people who are helping and saving others are even more newsworthy than the legion of killers, rapists, and child abusers who march across the news columns and fill the tube. What we need is nothing less than a revolution in the way we define journalism.

4. When I worked for Union Carbide Chemical Plant, I had a foreman who always gave my partner and me all the worst jobs. We lifted heavy boxes, dismantled scaffoldings, and did other heavy labor. The foreman would come around and watch us as if he thought we didn't know what we were doing. He told us that he gave us the menial jobs because we were the best people in his crew. I figure that if we were the best people he had, he should have stopped wasting us on such mindless tasks. The foreman also had the habit of yelling at us for no particular reason. One day when he was screaming about a welding job I had done, I threatened to report him to the general manager. Even though the manager usually took our side, that foreman always managed to find ways to make our lives miserable.

KEY WORDS IN TOPIC SENTENCES

Key words tell the reader the subject you will discuss in the paragraph and what you will say about that subject. In the following sentences, study the subject and the words that clarify or limit what the writer will say about the subject.

subject   *words that limit the subject*

<u>Using a computer</u> can be a <u>frustrating</u> experience.

subject   *words that limit the subject*

<u>Exercise</u> is an important way of <u>relieving stress</u>.

subject   *words that limit the subject*

<u>Shoplifting costs</u> store <u>owners</u> a great deal.

subject   *words that limit the subject*

<u>Older Americans</u> should <u>not be forced</u> to <u>retire</u>.

FOR PRACTICE

Practice 4b. Underline the key words in the following topic sentences.

Example: <u>John McEnroe</u> was famous for his <u>outbursts</u> on the tennis court.

1. Shy people sometimes have difficulty showing emotion in public.
2. My parents were too strict when I was growing up.
3. I look forward to the day when we have a metal detector at Winthrop Stadium.
4. Lassen is my favorite national park.
5. Peer pressure is a major cause of drug and alcohol addiction.
6. Hardly a day goes by that I don't remember the good times I have had with Amy.
7. Encouragement from their families helps students stay in school.
8. Child development specialists think communication between mother and baby begins even before the child is born.
9. Children often feel terribly guilty when parents divorce.
10. Coaches have a very good reason for being hard on their players.

Practice 4c. To practice revising for unity, read the following paragraphs carefully. Pick out the topic sentence, and underline key words that identify the subject and give it focus. Cross out any sentences that wander from that topic.

1. I was very close to my father when I was a child because he paid so much attention to me. Whenever he went into town, he always brought me something from the store. I once admired a stuffed cocker spaniel that looked just like Rowdy, my brother's dog, and the very next week Dad bought it for me. We had a lot of pets when I was a child and still do to this day. We must have had over a dozen pets including cats, dogs, birds, and hamsters. My father always encouraged me to try new things to see what I could do. He put me on our neighbor's pony when I was three and-a-half years old and entered me in a horse show at the age of four. I took second place. He was so proud of me that he bought me a horse of my own. I still have lots of pictures of my Dad with his arms around me.
2. Before I went to college, I worked at the Crystal Theater. Frank, a chronic repeater, was a customer I remember well. Every time he asked for popcorn, he

repeated it four times in four different ways: "I'd like a popcorn." "Gimme a popcorn, please." "One large popcorn." "I'll take a big box of popcorn." I think he did it just to see if I would get so nervous that I'd forget to ask for his money. I usually brought a magazine to work with me in case things got dull. Thelma the Inquisitor came every time we had a new movie—usually on Thursday nights. She would catch me at the ticket window and hold up the line to ask, "What do you know about this film? What other movies has the director made? Does it have a happy ending? Is it worth seeing?" I never had to worry about answering Thelma's questions because she barked them out, one after another, without pausing for a reply. Rudy was my favorite. He was about twenty years old, used a walking stick, and acted like an old man on a long hike. He usually arrived about half an hour before the movie started, but rather than sit in the theater and wait for the film to start, he paced back and forth in the lobby as though he were waiting for someone. When the credits started to roll, he went in alone. On reflection, I think the people that came to the Crystal were more interesting than anything I saw on the screen.

3. Ten years ago computer nuts rarely strayed from their habitat on New York's Wall Street or on Wilshire Boulevard in Los Angeles. Their sunken eyes and fixed stares make them easy to identify. You will find them sitting at their computers with their heads thrust forward as if they are about to dive into the screen. They own a variety of computers, including Macintosh, IBM personal computers, Commodores, and Hewlett-Packards, to name a few. It is not unusual for computer nuts to work sixteen to twenty hours straight. To keep themselves going, they eat and drink for quick energy, preferring foods and beverages that have sugar or caffeine, like coffee, strong tea, cola, and chocolate candy. The best candy bars for staying awake have sugar listed first in the description of ingredients. Sometimes computer nuts are so intent on their work that it is difficult to distinguish them from their machines.

4. My grandfather loves to tell me stories about the old days in Mexico. In most of the stories he is young, likes to gamble, and travels around Mexico looking for work. He tells one story about meeting and falling in love with my grandmother. There wasn't much law and order in their small town, so thieves were often apprehended and sentenced by townspeople. In those days, couples married young and once a girl turned fifteen she was considered old enough to marry in the Catholic Church. On my grandmother's fifteenth birthday, he simply kidnapped and married her. When he advises me to do the same thing with my girlfriends, I tell him I can't do that at this time in this country.

WRITING A WELL-FOCUSED TOPIC SENTENCE

It is important to write topic sentences that are specific enough to give your paragraphs a clear direction, yet broad enough that you can add supporting ideas and examples. If a topic is too broad, you will not have a clear idea of how to discuss it.

You may need a bit of practice in limiting the topics of your paragraphs. The following topic, for example, is too broad: Relationships can be difficult. First, the subject, "relationships," is so broad that the paragraph could be about relationships between family members, intimate partners, or casual friends. A more focused topic sentence would mention the specific relationship the writer will discuss and what is "difficult" about it. To narrow this topic and give it a more specific focus, the writer can ask a question: What kind of relationships do I want to discuss: male–female, mother–son, high school friendships? The answer to this question helps the author replace the generalized subject "relationships" with key words that give the paragraph a clearer direction. By asking what is difficult about this relationship, the writer will be able to focus on the way the paragraph will discuss that relationship.

Possible topic sentences:

The relationship   the difficulty
        ↓   ↓
1. Marriage can be confining.

   The relationship   the difficulty
           ↓   ↓
2. Being a parent often means you have very little time for yourself.

To narrow the topic sentence "Music brings back memories," the writer might ask, What music will I discuss, and whose memories do I want to use?

Possible topic sentence: Songs by the Pointer Sisters remind me of the years I was living a bachelor's life in San Francisco.

Is this topic sentence specific enough? Why or why not?

_____

FOR PRACTICE

Practice 4d. Write more focused topic sentences for "Classes can be challenging."

1. _____

   _____

2. _____

   _____

Practice 4e. Here are several topic sentences. Underline the word or words that predict what the writer will say. If the topic sentence is too broad, write a more focused topic sentence below it.

Example: I always look forward to holidays.
Focused alternative: I love <u>Thanksgiving</u> because that's the one time of year when my whole <u>family gets together.</u>

1. People always seem to do the wrong thing. _____

_____

2. Professionals work very hard at what they do. _____

_____

3. The life of a lawyer involves more hard work than glamour. _____

_____

4. I am happy to be in school. _____

_____

5. Wonderful things happen when you start playing sports. _____

_____

6. It's not easy staying in school. _____

_____

7. My classes are so difficult this semester. _____

_____

8. Alcoholism is a terrible problem. _____

_____

9. Driving is more dangerous than we realize. _____

_____

10. I have no patience with anything. _____

_____

STATEMENTS OF FACT

Statements of fact do not usually make good topic sentences because they may leave you with nothing else to say about the topic. "My mother is more than six feet tall" is a statement of fact. If it were used as a topic sentence, it would leave the writer little to discuss in the rest of the paragraph. "My mother is an imposing woman" is a better topic sentence because it points to a discussion of the ways the mother is imposing. Her height, her strength, and her assertiveness are possible subtopics that explain why she is imposing.

"I registered for school last week" is another statement of fact. A topic sentence on the subject of registering for school should mention something about the experience that the writer can discuss in a paragraph.

Now think about this topic sentence: "Trying to register for classes was a frustrating experience." Is this a good topic sentence? Why or why not?

Practice 4f. In each of the following topic sentences, underline the subject and words that clarify it. If the ideas are too broad or too narrow, write an alternative topic sentence.

Example: The divorce rate has been climbing steadily since 1975. (too narrow)
Alternative: Many <u>women who get divorced</u> find that they are much <u>worse off financially.</u>

1. Mount Everest is more than 29,000 feet high. _____

_____

2. The Beatles' songs remind me of the years when my oldest sister was still dating. _____

_____

3. Cats can have as many as seven kittens. _____

_____

4. Television can harm our minds. _____

_____

5. When I was in high school, I had the mistaken idea that college classes would be much too hard for me. _____

_____

6. Thrill seeking runs in my family. _____

_____

7. I have no luck with men. _____

_____

8. I had a pretty easy time in high school. _____

_____

9. My algebra teacher is very demanding. _____

_____

10. As many as one-fourth of all homeless people have had some training or have taken college classes. _____

_____

Practice 4g. The topic sentences are missing in the following paragraphs. Read each group of sentences carefully; then write a topic sentence that expresses the main idea in each paragraph.

1. _____

_____

It is often difficult just to get seated. After waiting thirty to forty minutes, a waiter may show you to a table that has not been cleared of dishes and crumbs. Eventually a different waiter brings you a menu that you will have difficulty opening because the pages are stuck together with catsup. Finally, a waitress, chewing gum, asks you rudely if you are ready to order. By this time you should know what to expect. Your hamburger will arrive at the table nearly as cold as it was when it was taken from the refrigerator and slapped on the grill. Your partner's burger may be warmer, but it will be smaller than yours because the heat lamps have dried out the bun. By the time your drinks arrive, you are just about finished with your meal. That's the Skyburger Restaurant—at your service!

2. _____

_____

Whether he was conscious of it or not, he passed his love of working with students on to me. My father, who taught high school art classes, would come home every afternoon and tell me about the accomplishments of students in his art classes. Sometimes he brought home samples of their work and displayed them in the den. It didn't take much to get him to tell me how each student was improving: Melissa was developing a stronger brush stroke; Gabriel's recent compositions showed greater depth than did any of his earlier drawings. In addition to my father's love of teaching, his love of art came to me through the splendid paintings I saw in books in his library. His shelves were filled with books about mural art in Mexico, Italian Renaissance painting, and traditional African masks.

3. _____

_____

When my grandmother was a teenager, premarital sex was the farthest thing from her mind. Not only did she blush if anyone asked to hold her hand, she didn't have the slightest idea how babies were conceived. Now, of course, people often talk about having sex before they are married, and many young women have had intercourse before turning twenty. In my grandmother's day, a woman married the man she "loved," and she married him for life. The current statistics on divorce in this country would probably make her think we have given up trying to keep families together.

4. _____

_____

In one supermarket, a display on aisle three said, "Please don't squeeze the Charmin." An elderly woman approached the sign, read it carefully, walked over to squeeze a package, then dropped it in her basket. Behind her, a ten-year-old boy read the sign out loud, picked up a package, and hugged it to his chest. When his mother caught up with him, he tossed the toilet paper into her cart. A little further down the aisle, a twelve-foot sign pictured a mountain of soap; its caption read, "Want to make your hands look younger while you do the dishes?" The words framed the picture of a mother and daughter comparing their equally young-looking hands. Sure enough, only women with their teenage daughters were selecting bars of soap from this display.

5. Most parents lecture their children about something. _____

_____

They believe that in America education is the key to success. "Without an education," they would say, "you probably will work at McDonald's all your life." When they weren't trying to scare me about the kind of job I'd have to take, they were comparing me to my older brother. "Look at your brother John. He is so smart and does so well in school that he got a scholarship to UC–Berkeley." My parents convinced me that if I didn't do well in school, I would pay heavily afterward. "Study and work hard now, and it will pay off later," they assured me. I hope they are right.

Practice 4h. The next two sample paragraphs are not unified. Study them carefully, and decide whether the topic sentence prepares the ideas developed in the paragraph. Then compare your findings with the explanations that follow.

1. From the moment I heard about college, I knew it would be a great place for me to go. My counselor encouraged me to go to college. After talking to me about majors that might interest me, she gave me a list of colleges to visit. On her recommendation, I visited several of those campuses and became enthusiastic about applying to three of them. My friends were also helpful when I was deciding whether or not to go to college. Gloria and Federico were in their first year at City College when I graduated high school. They told me how much they were learning and how motivated they were. They were impressed by the motivation of other college students as well who are more interested in studying than their high school counterparts are. I owe the most thanks to my parents, however, who drove me to eight different colleges, offered to help me pay for my student fees and books, and told me I should continue my education and make use of my intelligence.

In this paragraph, the topic sentence is not related to the rest of the paragraph. Although the first sentence asserts that college is a great place to go, the sentences that follow are not about the reasons why college is such a good choice. Because the rest of the paragraph is about the people who helped the student decide to attend college, we can write that idea in a new topic sentence, and the paragraph will be unified: *I am in college now because my counselor, friends, and parents encouraged me to go.*

2. Homeless children have little sense of self-worth. They have difficulty concentrating. Homeless children rarely have enough food to eat. They also show signs of total helplessness. They have little privacy and no sense of safety. They are

anxious, nervous, lonely, and depressed. They attend school sporadically. They are ashamed of their lifestyle. Often, homeless children are abused, some become drug addicted, and others are forced into prostitution.

This paragraph is not unified because it is a collection of ideas about homeless children. A more unified paragraph, like the next one, might focus on one point and discuss it in some detail.

Homelessness can be emotionally devastating for children. Children who are homeless have no room to go to, no door where they can hang their name, no wall where they can display their drawings or photographs. There is no place they can call their own. Without a room, privacy is nearly impossible. These children cannot feel entirely safe, either, without the security and protective shelter of a house. Because they don't live like other, more fortunate children, homeless children are often ashamed of their lifestyle. They feel powerless to change their circumstances and anxious because their lives are filled with uncertainty and risk.

Practice 4i. Use your journal to freewrite and ask yourself questions about one of the following topics. Then write a topic sentence whose key words make it specific and give the paragraph a clear focus.

- a bad habit
- an athletic event
- dating
- a family tradition
- an unfair situation
- an important change

Practice 4j. Write a paragraph that develops the topic sentence that you wrote for Practice 4i.

WRITING WELL-DEVELOPED PARAGRAPHS

Strong paragraphs *develop* the topic idea; effective essays are composed of several such strong body paragraphs. Your topic sentences have strong support when you include enough details, examples, and explanations that the reader can *see* and *understand* the point you want to make about your subject. Most paragraphs have several levels of support—the general idea (topic sentence), ideas that help focus the topic sentence (subtopics), and examples that support it. To help you visualize how a paragraph moves from a general idea to supporting explanations and examples, the sentences in the following paragraph on the difficulties of going to school are numbered for you. The general point in the paragraph, the topic sentence, is number 1; subtopics are number 2; and details and examples are numbers 3 and 4.

(1) It is difficult for me to go to school.
    (2) For one thing, the distractions at home make it hard for me to concentrate on homework.
        (3) Just as I'm about to solve a math problem, my son runs screaming through the house with my wife in hot pursuit.
        (3) Then there are the phone calls from family, friends, and solicitors that interrupt my thoughts and make me wonder if I will ever get my work done.

(2) I also worry that my relationship with my son will suffer because I'm not with him as much as I want to be.

(3) I feel especially guilty if I don't get home in time for dinner, or I have to rush off to the library on a Sunday afternoon instead of playing catch with him.

(3) I can always tell when he thinks I have been neglecting him.

(4) Sometimes he gets so angry with me that he refuses to give me a goodnight kiss, or he flips on the television while I'm trying to hold a family discussion.

(2) It won't be easy on my family, but with the commitment and patience of us all, I'll get through school.

Try numbering sentences in your own paragraphs to determine whether you have adequate development for your ideas. This process will also tell you when you have sentences that do not belong in the paragraph because they don't clearly support the main idea. Keep in mind that the topic sentence, the sentence you will label number one, is not always the first sentence in the paragraph.

FOR PRACTICE

Practice 4k. Use the numbering system discussed here to chart three paragraphs from Practice 4a, page 62. Use your own paper for this exercise. As an alternative, number the sentences in the paragraph you wrote for Practice 4j.

Add Supporting Details and Examples

Supporting details personalize your writing and make it interesting to read. In Chapter 3 you saw how Step 3 in the writing process includes strategies that will help you think of details and examples to support your points. To understand the difference that details can make in your writing, compare the following paragraphs.

Changing our habits just a little can go a long way toward helping the environment. One obvious thing we should do is stop littering. We can also fight air pollution by taking public transportation whenever possible. Recycling is another important way to conserve resources. It makes good sense to be more conscious about the environment.

Here is the revised paragraph with supporting examples and explanations. Take a minute to underline the additions.

Changing our habits just a little should go a long way toward helping the environment. One obvious thing we should do is stop littering. Instead of tossing aluminum cans and plastic cups out the car window when we are through with them, we should put them in a sack and take them home. We can also fight air pollution by taking public transportation whenever possible. By learning the schedule of subways and busses, we can leave our cars at home when we go to work or school. With a little bit of planning, we can ride the bus rather than drive to a doctor's appointment. Recycling is another important way to conserve resources. It takes little effort to keep separate containers for aluminum cans, bottles, and newspapers. A trip to the recycling center every other week takes just a few minutes of our time, but saves trees and conserves areas that might otherwise be used as landfills. It makes good sense to be more conscious about the environment.

FOR PRACTICE

Practice 4l. After a careful reading of the preceding sample paragraphs, use your own experience, observations, and imagination to fill in at least three details or examples that support the following general ideas.

1. My cousin loves to take risks.

_____

_____

_____

2. There are several things students can do to improve their scores on tests.

_____

_____

_____

3. Looking for a job can be rewarding as long as you take it one step at a time.

_____

_____

_____

4. Living with your parents while attending college isn't as bad as some people imagine. _____

_____

_____

5. My brother's car is totally unreliable.

_____

_____

_____

Practice 4m. To prepare for this exercise, review the sample paragraphs about changing our habits to help the environment on pages 71–72. Then add your own supporting details to the paragraphs that follow. Use the spaces provided.

1. The clothes I wear reflect the different roles I play during the day. In the morning I am the student, casual and comfortable in my going-to-school clothes.

_____

_____

In the afternoon I must look professional to please the travel agency I work for.

_____

_____

In the evening I might have a PTA meeting, school play, or teacher's conference to attend, so I must look responsible and parental. _____

_____

2. There are several ways to fight writer's block. First, be sure you have all the tools you need to write. _____

_____

Next, find a place where you will be comfortable. _____

_____ You should also take steps to be sure you will not be distracted. _____

_____

3. Just because a person is old doesn't mean he or she is debilitated or feebleminded. Many elderly people travel. _____

_____ They do volunteer work in the community. _____

_____ They may even go back to school and take subjects they are interested in but never had time for.

_____

_____

4. It's difficult to make love relationships work. Sometimes partners aren't sure what they want out of the relationship. _____

_____ Even when they are, they may discover that what they want doesn't have much to do with what their partner wants.

_____

_____

5. College classes are difficult for me because I have such trouble taking tests. For one thing, I have a strong physical reaction every time one of my teachers hands out an exam. _____

_____

What's worse, my mind won't cooperate any better than my body. _____

_____ If things don't improve, I'll have to ask my teachers if I can take oral exams instead. _____

_____

Practice 4n. On a separate sheet of paper, write unified, well-developed paragraphs for two of the following topic sentences. Make sure you include enough details and examples to support your points.

1. Finding time to do homework requires good planning.
2. The best teachers present their subjects clearly and encourage students to ask questions.
3. The characters in my favorite movie are very believable.
4. There are a few things you should think about when buying a used car.
5. It takes a lot of discipline to become a good college football player.
6. For many people the idea of commitment makes *love* a four-letter word.

REVISING FOR COHERENCE

Strong paragraphs are *coherent*. In a coherent paragraph, sentences follow one another logically; each sentence looks forward to the next and at the same time is logically linked to the one preceding. Writers commonly achieve coherence in paragraphs in two ways. First, the order of ideas gives a paragraph its coherence. As we saw in Chapter 3, ideas may follow a chronological, spatial, or emphatic order. Second, transitional words and phrases create a logical sequence of ideas.

Transitional Words and Phrases
The following chart lists commonly used transitions and their functions. Use them when you complete the exercises on the next few pages, and refer to them when writing your own essays.

Function	Transitional Words and Phrases
To add ideas	above all, also, and, another, besides, in addition, furthermore, for one thing, too
To order ideas in time	after, before, briefly, by this time, currently, during, eventually, finally, first, now, later, meanwhile, next, presently, recently, second, so far, soon, then, third, when, while
To order ideas in space	above, behind, below, beside, next to, in front of, inside, on top of, in the foreground/background, to the right, to the left, under
To introduce examples	especially, for example, for instance, namely, for one thing, in particular, the most, one of the most
To show contrast	although, but, however, in contrast, more than, nevertheless, on the other hand, than, unlike
To show similarity	as, like, likewise, in both cases, in comparison, in the same way, similarly, too
To draw conclusions or show results	as a result, because, because of, consequently, for, for this reason, in fact, therefore, thus, unfortunately

Student Writing

The following paragraph about chemical weaponry follows an emphatic order from a discussion of the handling of chemical weapons to detailed descriptions of the deadly effects of these chemicals. Moreover, transitions and phrases that repeat ideas allow the writer to move skillfully from theoretical to practical training. Transitional phrases and repeated ideas are underlined to show you how they move the reader from one idea to the next.

Using Chemical Weapons

My military training taught me contradictory things about chemical weapons. My drill instructors trained me to use chemical weapons. In contrast, the medical courses I took showed me how inhumane these weapons really are. In tactical training, we were told that we had to learn how to conduct chemical warfare because the enemy was training 20 percent harder than we were. Consequently, we learned the parts of the missiles used to carry these deadly weapons and how to clean and care for them. Later we practiced loading and firing the missiles. Proper handling of chemical agents was another part of our training. While I was learning how to use chemical weapons, I was also finding out what they are capable of doing to human beings. The instructors in my medical classes showed me how nerve agents enter the body through the skin and cause such damage that the victims lose all control of their internal organs. As a result, convulsions, urination, defecation, vomiting, and crying precede death. In addition, I learned that some chemical agents prevent the blood from carrying oxygen. One medic said that death would come slowly; like a fish out of water, the victim might flop around for two or three days. Then I learned that the blister agents are the most painful of all. If a droplet gets on your skin, it will swell up to the size of a fat apple. The only good thing about this agent is that if it is inhaled, death is immediate. As my training intensified, it became harder and harder to reconcile the technical and inhumane sides of chemical warfare.

Practice 4o. Underline the transitional words and phrases in the following paragraphs.

1. Competition brings out the best in all of us. If we feel someone is doing better in math or is faster in track than we are, we will probably try to do better. Take me, for example. When I was younger, particularly in high school, I was always competing with my niece. She got A's and B's in English and math while I would get by with a C. Then I noticed that everyone in my family praised her for every little thing she did. Eventually I decided I should do something to get more attention at home. From then on, I tried harder in school and raised my grades. My attitude toward schoolwork improved too. By the time we graduated from high school, there was only five points difference in our grade point averages.

2. City College has one of the best college athletic programs in the country. Specifically, the football program here at City ranked fifth in the nation last year and is again in the top twenty this season. These rankings are excellent, especially since over three hundred junior colleges participate in the football program. Most of our athletes are strong players who try out but can't quite compete for an athletic scholarship to a university. On the other hand, some players do receive scholarships but can't adjust to university life and flunk out. In both cases, the alternative is to go back home and attend City College.

Practice 4p. Read the following sentences carefully. Then add a transition that links ideas logically. Try to find transitions on your own before consulting the list.

1. According to Mollie Stevenson Neely, one-third of all cowboys were black

    _____ you'd never know it from watching TV westerns.

2. Some were slaves who migrated west with their owners. _____, when

    they were freed, they stayed on in the area.

3. Many black cowboys lived in Texas. Bill Pickett, _____, was a famous

    black Texas cowboy of the late 1800s.

4. Pickett is said to have originated the rodeo technique of bulldogging — a

    method of wrestling a steer to the ground. _____ most cowboys, who

    simply grab the steer's neck or horns with their hands, Pickett used to bring the

    beast down by biting its nose with his teeth.

5. Another famous black cowboy was Nat Love. _____ competing in a shooting contest in Deadwood, South Dakota, in 1876, he was given the name Deadwood Dick.

6. Black women like Stagecoach Mary _____ were part of the western cowboy tradition.

7. Mary was very tall and heavy. _____ she was about six feet tall and weighed over three hundred pounds.

8. Mary always carried a shotgun; _____, she looked dangerous.

Practice 4q. In the following example, several sentences are part of a paragraph whose topic sentence is listed first. The sample paragraph here uses transitional phrases to compose a coherent paragraph using the original list of ideas. Refer to this sample when completing the practice exercises that follow it.

Example: Success means different things to different people.

Some people are materialistic.

Success means having an expensive car, living in a $300,000 house, and earning $100,000 a year.

They may not consider themselves wealthy enough to be truly "successful."

Other people see healthy, happy children as the measure of their success.

They consider themselves successful when their sons and daughters do well in sports, become class president, or get a 3.0 on their report cards.

Here is one possible combination with the transitional words and phrases underlined for you.

Success means different things to different people. <u>For instance</u>, some people are materialistic. <u>Consequently, they</u> think success means having an expensive car, living in a $300,000 house, and earning $100,000 a year. <u>In spite of having all that money</u>, they <u>still</u> may not consider themselves wealthy enough to be truly "successful." <u>In contrast</u>, other people see healthy, happy children as the measure of their success. <u>For this reason</u>, they value their children's achievements and consider themselves successful when their sons and daughters do well in sports, become class president, or get a 3.0 on their report cards.

Use transitional phrases to compose a coherent paragraph that includes the list of ideas you are given. You may need to change the original wording slightly, but stay as close as you can to the original.

1. Mollie Neely and her foreman, Howard "Cowboy" Beauchamo, are spreading the word about the black cowboy.
   They have attracted attention not only in Houston but also across the country.
   Beauchamo teaches horseback riding.

He lectures on cowboy history.

He made a 2,500-mile journey on horseback from Houston to Newark, New Jersey, to call attention to the black cowboy's contribution to settling the Old West.

An article about Neely appeared in *Essence* magazine.

She was bombarded with mail from all over the country.

One writer, noting the picture of Neely on horseback, said she had never seen a black woman riding before.

Neely and Beauchamo have done a great deal to inform people about black participation in the settlement of the American West.

2. It is important to prepare yourself well before going to a job interview. You should think carefully about what you want to wear.

If the job involves labor or a technical skill, you might come dressed to work.

You might be asked to demonstrate a welding technique or safety procedure.

If you are applying for an office job, you'll probably want to wear a suit or a dress that makes you look professional.

Take examples of your work.

Carpenters might bring photographs of kitchens and bathrooms they have remodeled.

Analysts can bring examples of proposals, handbooks, or regulations they have written.

It is important to show that you can do the job.

3. When I think of my Salvadorean heritage, oppression comes to mind. The Spanish conquered Central America.

They subjugated my ancestors.

In the name of Christianity, they destroyed a rich culture.

I am very proud of my ancestry.

My people, the Pipiles, were part of the great Mayan civilization.

The Spanish mixed with the "Indians," as they were incorrectly called.

From that mixture comes the ethnicity of most Salvadorans.

I always have a question in my mind: What would have happened if our original culture had been left alone?

Practice 4r. Chose a topic from the following list and write your own paragraph. Refer to the steps in the writing process discussed in Chapter 3 to help you generate ideas. When you revise, check for unity, development, and coherence.

- A portrait of a family member or someone who means a lot to you
- An adventure you had

- A family problem
- Reasons you decided to enroll in college
- Why the country, the city, or the suburbs is the best place to live

LOOKING AHEAD

Chapter 5 reviews basic essay structure and shows you how to revise your essays to improve introductions, thesis statements, body paragraphs, and conclusions—the basic components of an essay. Exercises in that chapter give you practice writing focused thesis statements, using several patterns of development, and composing introductions and conclusions.

Revising Essays

This chapter reviews basic essay structure—
introduction, thesis, body paragraphs, and conclusion.
Exercises in this chapter give you practice editing
essays for unity, development, and coherence—crucial
elements in well-written essays. In preparation for
writing your own essays, you will compose thesis
statements, use several patterns of development to
support ideas in body paragraphs, explore strategies for
writing introductions and conclusions, and practice
writing titles for essays.

BASIC ESSAY STRUCTURE

An essay is composed of several paragraphs that present a focused, coherent, well-supported discussion of a central idea. The **introduction,** the first paragraph of an essay, introduces your audience to your subject and catches their interest. The **thesis,** usually the last sentence of your introduction, states the main point of the essay and how you plan to develop that point. The thesis makes the most general statement in your essay just as the topic sentence makes the most general statement in your paragraph. The **body** of the essay consists of several **paragraphs** that contain topic sentences, subtopics, and supporting details and examples that expand or develop the thesis statement. The **conclusion** is usually the last paragraph or last few sentences of an essay. Whereas the introduction anticipates the writer's approach to a subject, the conclusion provides a satisfying sense of an ending.

ELEMENTS OF A STRONG ESSAY

Strong essays communicate the writer's ideas to an audience. When revising your own essays, be sure that the topic sentences develop ideas in the thesis, topic sentences are well supported, and ideas make sense and follow one another logically and coherently.

WRITING UNIFIED ESSAYS

Essays are unified when the focus of each body paragraph is clearly connected to the ideas expressed in the essay's **thesis.** The thesis makes the most general statement in your essay just as the topic sentence makes the most general statement in your paragraph. In the sample student essay on stress on pages 56–58, for example, all topic sentences illustrate the thesis that harmful ways of relieving stress, such as taking drugs, should be avoided in favor of the healthier ways of coping, such as music and exercise. The writer is careful not to include ideas that are not relevant to the stated thesis.

Four Suggestions for Writing an Effective Thesis

1. Always write your thesis statement as a complete sentence. Your title can be a phrase rather than a sentence, but the thesis must clearly state the topic and your approach to it.

   Incomplete: How school changed my life
   Complete: When I started going to college, I changed my friends, my attitude toward learning, and even the way I think.

2. Write your thesis as a statement rather than a question. Starting your essay with a question is confusing for your reader because the essay should be answering questions rather than asking them. If you find yourself writing a

question for your thesis, simply answer the question, and you'll probably have the thesis statement you need.

> **Question:** Should children be encouraged to play organized sports?
> **Answer:** Playing organized sports helps children develop self-confidence and teaches them valuable social skills.

3. Avoid using the thesis to announce what you intend to discuss in your essay. Phrases like "I will now discuss . . ." or "I think that . . ." or "In my opinion . . ." call attention to yourself and actually suggest that you are uncertain about your opinion or your approach to the topic. Such phrases also distract the reader from the point you want to make.

> **Announcement:** It is my belief that we are trashing America with our garbage.
> **Clear:** There are signs everywhere that we are trashing America—in our parks, on our campus, and in our own neighborhoods.

4. State your thesis in clear, crisp language that is easy to follow. A thesis that is weighed down with vague phrases and clauses obscures rather than clarifies the ideas you want to communicate.

> **Incoherent:** People who follow celebrities are often found to be unsure in the ways of their own identities and obsessed to the extreme with an appetite for curiosity about the overall lives of these famous people due to merchandising campaigns and media gossip.
> **Clear:** Americans' obsession with the lives of celebrities may come from a need to fill a personal void, but most often the media and the advertising industry feed our insatiable curiosity about celebrities.

Placing the Thesis Statement

You learned in Chapter 3 that the thesis is usually the last sentence in the introduction. It pulls your readers into the essay and tells them what to expect. Experienced writers sometimes put the thesis at the beginning of the introduction or in the conclusion. If the essay is particularly long, the writer may restate the thesis part way through the essay. As a beginning writer, you will have an easier time sticking to your subject if you state your thesis at the end of the introduction.

Writers sometimes place a thesis at the beginning or middle of an introduction. For novice writers, however, it's a good idea to end the introduction with your thesis as a way of pulling the reader into the essay and giving the rest of the paper a clear direction. The thesis statements in the following paragraphs are underlined for you.

1. <u>I was six when my mother taught me the art of invisible strength</u>. It was a strategy for winning arguments, respect from others, and eventually, though neither of us knew it at the time, chess games. (Amy Tan, "Rules of the Game")

2. Since my sophomore year at UCLA, I have become convinced that <u>we blacks spend too much time on the playing fields and too little time in the libraries.</u> Consider these facts: for the major professional sports of hockey, football, basketball, baseball, golf, tennis and boxing, there are roughly only 3170 major league positions available (attributing 200 positions to golf, 300 to tennis and 100 to boxing). And the annual turnover is small. (Arthur Ashe, "An Open Letter to Black Parents: Send Your Children to the Libraries")

3. This is a story about what went wrong while we were all so busy doing what was right: marrying and having families and working the long days that would get us a home and get us ahead. I'll try to tell you what I know about the loss of friendship. <u>I'll put the different ways in which I have lost friends into three categories.</u> The first, category A, of the ABCs of lost friends, is neglect. The second, category B, is letting go, cutting bait. The third, category C, is betrayal. (Art Jahnke, "What Ever Happened to Friendship?")

Key Words in Thesis Statements

Key words in your thesis, like the key words in your topic sentences, announce the subject you will discuss and predict how you will discuss it. To become more familiar with the way a thesis works, study the following thesis sentences and the explanations that accompany them.

subject

Example: I become a <u>compulsive</u> shopper whenever I get unbearably

causes

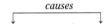

<u>bored</u> or feel <u>pressured</u> to take on more work than I can possibly complete.

In this thesis, the writer promises to discuss why she becomes a compulsive shopper—it happens because she gets bored or feels pressured at work. Like all strong thesis sentences, this one predicts the topic sentences the writer will use in later paragraphs. If she fulfills her promise, her paragraphs will focus on one of the two causes for her compulsive shopping—boredom and pressure.

Topic sentences for her paragraphs might be the following:

Sometimes I can cure my boredom by going on a shopping binge.

Nothing makes me itch to go shopping like the stress I feel when my boss gives me too much work.

Notice how the thesis anticipates the number of ideas she'll discuss in the essay and an order for her paragraphs—boredom first, then pressure. Her body paragraphs will offer supporting examples and explanations to show how each cause triggers her compulsive desire to go shopping.

Example: Training for a marathon takes both physical and mental energy.

Here the writer's subject is the training required to run a marathon. Specifically, he will discuss both the physical and mental stamina the devoted runner must possess. Possible topic sentences for this thesis are as follows:

> The physical endurance required to run in a 26-mile marathon must be built up over time.

> Physical strength is important, but a runner must have the will to train and to run a grueling 26-mile race.

Example: There aren't many children as creative as my daughter.

For this thesis, the writer's subject is "daughter." Unlike the other two examples, this thesis doesn't state the ideas for body paragraphs explicitly. Instead, the general creative quality of the daughter is mentioned. This idea will have to be broken down into more specific, manageable pieces in the essay's topic sentences.
A few possibilities are listed here:

> The images in my daughter's paintings and drawings are unique and unrepeated.

> My daughter's everyday play shows how imaginative she is.

> At eight years of age, my daughter is already writing stories and poems.

FOR PRACTICE

Practice 5a. Read this thesis statement carefully: *People decide to return to college for several reasons.* Think about this statement for a moment before answering the following questions.

What is the subject of the thesis?
What will the writer say about this subject?
What specific reasons might the writer discuss?

Practice 5b. Underline the subject and words that narrow it in the following thesis statements.

1. There are a few practical steps women can take to protect themselves from assault.
2. Our newest immigrants contribute more dollars to the economy than they take in public benefits.
3. Too high a percentage of young black males are dying in America, not from natural causes but from gang-related violence.
4. Once I became a working mother, I was torn between my desire for independence and the traditional role of woman-as-homemaker that I had known all my life.

5. Members of a band who are struggling to be discovered sacrifice a great deal of time and money.
6. Uncle Rupert has several bad habits that drive my mother crazy.
7. Soccer games are fast-moving and require a great deal of concentration.
8. The Briggsmore School of Design has very strict entrance requirements.
9. Maui has the most to offer the family on vacation.
10. The Wind River Mountains in Wyoming offer the backpacker intimate views of wildlife, challenging hikes, and spectacular views of waterfalls and mountain peaks.

Writing a Well-Focused Thesis

Like topic sentences, thesis statements must be narrow enough that you can support them in body paragraphs. If the thesis is not sufficiently narrow, you will not have a clear guide for the essay, and you will be more likely to wander from topic to topic without a sense of logical progression or purpose.

Here is a thesis that is not narrow enough to produce a well-focused paper: *My family is very wasteful.* This sentence has a subject—the writer's family—and includes the general point the writer intends to make about that family—they are wasteful. This thesis statement lacks a clear direction, however, because the subject is so general that the essay could be about anything vaguely related to being wasteful. The writer's family might, for example, waste water, paper, food, electricity, or time. To help narrow this thesis statement the writer asked several questions:

Exactly *how* is my family wasteful?

What do they waste?

Who is wasteful in my family?

The answers led to the following thesis and topic sentences for a well-focused essay.

Revised Thesis:
My family wastes water, electricity, and paper products.

Topic Sentences:
My brother and sister waste gallons of water every day.
My father is no better—he always forgets to turn off the lights and unplug small appliances.
Every week we throw away several feet of newspapers and computer paper.

FOR PRACTICE

Practice 5c. Compare these thesis statements:
a. My trip to Mexico was very interesting.
b. My trip to Mexico was an interesting adventure that led us to several of the beaches along the western coast, the Aztec ruins in Mexico City, and the badlands of central Mexico.

Which would make the best thesis for an essay? _____

Explain your answer: _____

_____

Practice 5d. Narrow each of the following sentences to create a well-focused thesis statement. Use the journalistic questions to help you.

1. It is difficult to be an athlete.

Narrowed: _____

_____

2. Some people make me angry.

Narrowed: _____

_____

3. Addicts are not all alike.

Narrowed: _____

_____

4. Divorce can be an awful experience.

Narrowed: _____

_____

5. Americans shouldn't watch so much television.

Narrowed: _____

_____

6. I am proud of myself.

Narrowed: _____

_____

7. It isn't easy to get rid of bad habits.

Narrowed: _____

_____

8. Not all movies are entertaining.

Narrowed: _____

_____

9. Technology has really changed in the last 5 years.

Narrowed: _____

_____

10. Travel can add a lot to a student's education.

Narrowed: _____

_____

Practice 5e. Develop topic sentences for two of the thesis statements you wrote for Practice 5d. (You may have two, three, or four topic sentences.) Use the example here to help you complete this practice. If you have difficulty, check to see if your thesis is narrow enough.

Example:

Thesis:
I am proud of the study skills I have developed in college.

Topic sentences:
Before leaving class, I check carefully to make sure I understand each assignment.
I find quiet places to study.
When I am confused about a problem or an assignment, I jot down questions to ask my instructors.
Finally, I leave enough time to complete my homework assignments.

1. Thesis: _____

_____

Topic sentence: _____

_____

Topic sentence: _____

_____

Topic sentence: _____

_____

Topic sentence: _____

_____

2. Thesis: _____

_____

Topic sentence: _____

_____

Topic sentence: _____

_____

Topic sentence: _____

_____

Topic sentence: _____

_____

3. Thesis: _____

_____

Topic sentence: _____

_____

Topic sentence: _____

_____

Topic sentence: _____

_____

Topic sentence: _____

_____

Statements of Fact

Like topic sentences, thesis statements must be general enough to give you something to discuss in your essay. The following sentence states a fact and does not make a good thesis because it leaves you with nothing else to say:

> I got divorced last year.

A better thesis states what the writer will say about getting divorced. For example, the following revised thesis suggests ideas for several body paragraphs:

> I gained independence but lost companionship and financial security when I got divorced last year.

This expanded version suggests one advantage of getting divorced (gaining independence) and two disadvantages (the losses of companionship and financial security). These points will develop into topic ideas for the paragraphs in this essay.

FOR PRACTICE

Practice 5f. Each of the following thesis sentences is a statement of fact that is too narrow to provide topic ideas for an essay. Write a well-focused thesis statement for each by creating a specific approach to the topic implied in each statement. This exercise requires a major revision of each sentence.

1. Smoking gets on my nerves.

Narrowed: _____

_____

2. I have a terrible job.

Narrowed: _____

_____

3. My parents have a successful marriage.

Narrowed: _____

_____

4. My sister is taking Spanish in high school.

Narrowed: _____

_____

5. Jeremy is training to be on the Junior Olympic Ski Team.

Narrowed: _____

_____

6. I still live at home with my parents.

Narrowed: _____

_____

7. My friend Brianna created a website using MySpace.

Narrowed: _____

_____

8. I must babysit my two little cousins once a month.

Narrowed: _____

_____

9. The latest version of *Pirates of the Caribbean* came out last week.

Narrowed: _____

_____

10. The World Cup is played every four years to determine the best soccer team in the world.

Narrowed: _____

_____

WRITING WELL-DEVELOPED ESSAYS

Strong paragraphs *develop* the topic idea; effective essays are composed of several such strong body paragraphs. The supporting information in an essay usually comes from examples, details, and case histories based on the writer's experience and observations. Occasionally writers conduct interviews and do other kinds of research to gather information for an essay.

Depending on your subject and the information you wish to discuss, you may use one of several strategies for developing your ideas:

1. **Narrating.** When you narrate events, you are telling about something that happened. The event may have happened to you or to other people; in either case, you will usually follow a chronological sequence when organizing a narrative essay. Occasionally the entire essay may narrate or tell the story of something that happened. In that case, it is important to use the writing process (Chapter 3), especially the questions in Steps 1 and 2, to determine what central idea or impression you wish your narrative to convey.

2. **Describing/Illustrating.** In descriptions, you record the details, sensual impressions, and observations you have made about an object, place, person, or event. Well-written descriptions convey one important idea about the subject or create a dominant impression.

3. **Analyzing.** When you analyze something, you essentially break it apart into smaller ideas to show how it works. Here are some examples of things you might write about using analysis:

   the importance of an event in your life (analyzing)

   a complex task you perform at work or the steps involved in forming a friendship (process analysis)

   four different kinds of students in your math class (classifying)

   how two things, people, places, or events are similar or different (compare/contrast)

   factors that made you decide to attend a particular college or choose a specific major (causal analysis)

   several learning disabilities (defining)

   assaults on campus free speech (identifying a problem, posing solutions)

   critical response to a reading (analyzing)

   images and double meanings in a poem (analyzing)

4. **Evaluating.** When you evaluate a subject, you judge it on the basis of criteria you have identified. You might, for example, evaluate the performance of your favorite baseball team based on examples of individual players and overall teamwork. Perhaps you will evaluate a concert you went to, a restaurant you tried, or an essay in this book. Each of these subjects implies different criteria for evaluation.

5. **Taking a stand.** In essays that persuade or take a stand on an issue, you are trying to use enough evidence and common-sense arguments to convince your audience that your position is valid. Here are two sample topics for a persuasive essay:

Persuade the nonvoting population in your state to vote in the next election.

Persuade your reader that although the structure of the family is changing, family ties are still strong in the United States.

The following excerpt from Elizabeth Stone's "Stories Make a Family" illustrates how writers combine these writing strategies in their essays.

Stories Make a Family

Many families build self-esteem through stories about money and self-made men. But in my family there wasn't a single story like that. What the Bongiornos substituted was a sense that they came from a long line of people with talent, a talent that was innate, nearly genetic. Their celebration of the artist and their conviction that art was in their blood dated back to an unnamed (and probably apocryphal) court musician who had lived before the beginning of family time. And of course this talent was invoked again in the story in which my great-grandmother, the tale's moral center, fell in love with that poor but talented musical postman.

— Contrasts

— Explains family identity

The motif of art and talent was too important and too powerful a symbol to live in those two stories alone, and so it flourished in many. One of the oldest stories in our family was about my great-grandfather long after his elopement. He could play any instrument he laid eyes on, it was said. And so could his sons who, like my grandmother, inherited his musical genes. In the evenings after dinner, he and his sons would go into the courtyard, each with his instrument, and play music together for several hours. People would come "from miles around" just to listen.

— Explains importance

— Narrates

FOR PRACTICE

Practice 5g. Add marginal notes to identify strategies for developing ideas in the last four paragraphs of "Stories Make a Family."

My grandmother, the youngest of his children, had a lovely singing voice, and this was the subject of one very important family story set during her childhood in Sicily. One day she was at home with her mother, singing as she did some chore around the house. Suddenly, her mother looked out the window and saw the parish priest ambling up the road. "Be quiet! Be quiet!" she hissed to my grandmother. "The *padre* will hear you singing, and he will again tell us that we must send you to Rome for singing lessons, and you know we don't have the money for that."

My grandmother never did have voice lessons, but thirty years later she was still singing. By then, she and her six children were living on Vanderbilt Street in a second-floor apartment over a grocery store run by a man named Mr. Peterson. Every Friday morning, my grandmother would get down on her hands and knees and wash the tile floor in the first-floor entry hall. She loved opera, and as she scrubbed the floor, she would sing one aria or another. As the story goes, Mr. Peterson would invariably stop whatever he was doing and hush his customers in order to listen to her without interruption.

I wonder about these stories now. How could a man with a postman's income afford to buy all those instruments? And would a nineteenth-century parish priest in a small Sicilian village really encourage a family to send their preadolescent daughter hundreds of miles away to Rome? And would he do it for as secular an undertaking as singing lessons? And did Mr. Peterson really stop everything to listen?

No one ever noticed the oddities in these stories. In part, it was because they inhabited a strangely protected realm, half real, half fanciful; they were too useful for us to question whether they were true or not. But literal truth was never the point. What all these stories did was give us something strong and important to hold onto for as long as we needed it—a sense of belonging in the world. When I was growing up, my sense of what the future might hold was shaped by the stories I'd heard about our past.

REVISING FOR COHERENCE

Coherence in essays depends on both clear connections between ideas in paragraphs, usually provided by transitional words and phrases, and a logical sequence of ideas that provides clear connections between paragraphs. Here is a brief list of strategies for achieving coherence between paragraphs in an essay:

Refer to an idea in the thesis.

Use transitional words and phrases.

Refer to an idea expressed earlier in the paragraph.

Refer to an idea in a preceding paragraph.

In the discussion of thesis statements on pages 81–85, we saw how a thesis helps a writer arrange ideas in the body of an essay. Like paragraphs, effective essays have a clear organizational pattern. The patterns of organization for paragraphs discussed in Chapter 3 on pages 48–51—**chronological, spatial,** or **emphatic order** (order-of-importance)—apply to essays as well.

FOR PRACTICE

Practice 5h. Thesis statements and topic sentences for three essays follow. Number the topic sentences in the space provided to give them a clearer, more logical order. In each case, be ready to explain the pattern of organization you have chosen.

1. Thesis statement: College classes are much more difficult than I thought they would be.

   _____ I soon found out how demanding instructors could be.
   _____ My math class in particular requires three hours of homework a night.
   _____ With all the papers I have to write, English isn't much easier.
   _____ When I was still in high school, I imagined I would join campus clubs, spend my time talking in coffee houses, and go to parties all week long.

2. Thesis statement: Sally and I had to stop dating because we never agreed on anything.

   _____ Occasionally we argued about more serious things, like whether we wanted to get married or have children.
   _____ Little things like what to order in a restaurant or who would drive home were frequently sources of arguments.
   _____ Sally didn't like my parents, and that was a sore spot as well.

3. Thesis statement: My grandparents endured many hardships before coming to this country.

   _____ Even though they came legally, border guards took money and other valuables from them.
   _____ War and persecution drove them from Eastern Europe.
   _____ Trains were often overcrowded and soldiers searched the cars continually, looking for illegal immigrants.
   _____ It wasn't easy finding ways to travel across Europe.
   _____ They waited in London for three years before booking passage on a steamship to New York.

4. Thesis statement: My room contains a curious combination of items.

_____ The pennants on the wall came from teams like the Milwaukee Braves and the Brooklyn Dodgers, teams that have long since changed cities.

_____ The hardwood floor is covered with a bright red Turkish carpet that my aunt gave me.

_____ My ceiling is covered with a foil-like wallpaper that reflects the light.

_____ My desk and chair occupy a modest position in one corner of the room, but the black globs I fashioned out of papier-mâché and stuck on the legs make the furniture anything but invisible.

5. Thesis statement: Although it lacks any true cultural or historical significance, body piercing in the United States is a legitimate way to express oneself.

_____ Other countries' views of body modification offer helpful contrasts to our own.

_____ Unfortunately, masses of people in the United States have embraced this antisocial activity and are turning it into a meaningless fad.

_____ If the spirituality displayed in other societies is not the driving force behind piercing in the United States, then why are we following these trends?

_____ Despite its seeming superficiality, body modification can be a legitimate, unique form of self-expression.

Transitional Words and Phrases

Writers use connecting or transitional words and phrases to create a logical sequence of ideas within paragraphs and between paragraphs in their essays. The chart of commonly used transitions and their function from Chapter 4 is reprinted here.

Function	Transitional Words and Phrases
To add ideas	above all, also, and, another, besides, in addition, furthermore, for one thing, too
To order ideas in time	after, before, briefly, by this time, currently, during, eventually, finally, first, now, later, meanwhile, next, presently, recently, second, so far, soon, then, third, when, while
To order ideas in space	above, behind, below, beside, next to, in front of, inside, on top of, in the foreground/background, to the right, to the left, under
To introduce examples	especially, for example, for instance, namely, for one thing, in particular, the most, one of the most
To show contrast	although, but, however, in contrast, more than, nevertheless, on the other hand, than, unlike
To show similarity	as, like, likewise, in both cases, in comparison, in the same way, similarly, too
To draw conclusions or show results	as a result, because, because of, consequently, for, for this reason, in fact, therefore, thus, unfortunately

Practice 5i. The thesis and topic sentences from Doug Gonzales's essay, "Coping with Stress," are reprinted here. Underline the words that Doug used to make logical connections between his paragraphs. The thesis and first topic sentence are done for you.

Coping with Stress

If you are a student, you probably have some of the same pressures in your life, and, like me, you must find <u>ways</u> to <u>cope with stress</u>. The trick is to avoid the more <u>harmful methods</u> of <u>relieving stress</u>, like taking <u>drugs</u>, and to find <u>healthier</u> outlets, like <u>music</u> and <u>exercise</u>, to <u>relieve stress</u>.

Some <u>ways</u> of <u>relieving stress</u> are <u>unhealthy</u>, even <u>harmful</u>.

Illegal drugs can be even more damaging.

My family and I have found healthier ways to relieve stress. We often watch television to relax and forget about work.

Music is another way my family has of relaxing.

The best way to handle stress, I have found, is through exercise.

With the stress most of us have in our lives, we must find ways to calm down without threatening our health.

Practice 5j. Create topic sentences for paragraphs 2 through 6 in the following essay. State the main point discussed in the paragraph, and use transitional words and phrases to connect the paragraph logically with ideas in the thesis and in preceding paragraphs.

Starting the Day

1. I am a creature of habit. There is no better proof of this than the morning ritual I have been following since I left my parents' house many years ago. My multiple alarms, morning bath, carefully paced cups of coffee, and the final rituals of dressing, putting on makeup, and fixing my hair are as much a part of my morning as breathing.

2. (Topic sentence) _____

_____

The first alarm goes off at 6:00, though I have no intention of getting up then. Instead, it's a signal for my little dog, Frito, to jump onto the bed and snuggle with me. I relax with Frito until the second alarm sounds at 6:18; some days I get up, but I know a third alarm will go off at 6:30. The 6:30 alarm has the ring of authority; it is the loudest and the most obnoxious of the three. I respond immediately by making the bed as I am getting out of it. Where I acquired that habit is a mystery.

3. (Topic sentence) _____

_____

I have a huge, claw-foot tub and every morning I climb in and settle down while it is filling. I built a wooden rack on the side of the tub for my coffee. I relax in water hot enough to turn my skin a rosy pink while I read the morning paper—first the front-page news, then local stories, the travel section, and the comics. I can usually hear my three dogs romping outside the door while I enjoy my coffee, newspaper, and hot bath. Then I take a few minutes to look over my daily calendar. Generally I'm out of the tub before 6:55 as yet a fourth alarm warns me that it's time to pull the plug.

4. (Topic sentence) _____

_____

On the way back to my bedroom I pour myself a second cup of coffee. I choose a suit or dress from my closet that fits my mood—dark colors for somber professional meetings, bright prints for times when I wish the sun were shining. I iron-as-I-wear, so next I iron my choice for the day. If I were following the advice of cosmetics companies, I would coordinate the color of my foundation and blush with the clothes I wear. But that sort of nonsense would take too much time, disrupt my schedule, and confuse me. I brush my hair a vigorous sixty strokes and arrange it swept to one side or falling evenly around my face. A rather stubborn hair spray completes my preparations.

5. (Topic sentence) _____

_____

By the time I pull on my shoes, grab my purse, and flick off the bedroom light, the 7:25 alarm has gone off. I have just ten minutes to straighten up the bathroom—hang up wet towels, wipe out the tub, and put away my nightclothes while I brush my teeth—before the final 7:35 alarm goes off.

6. (Topic sentence) _____

_____

In the old days I would get up late, rush around in a panic, forget my shoes, put on my makeup while driving, or drive recklessly in an attempt to make up ten or fifteen minutes, and arrive late anyway. Now I have time for a leisurely drive to work. The best part is that when I say "Good morning" to fellow workers, I mean it.

SPECIAL PARAGRAPHS

INTRODUCTIONS

Students sometimes have difficulty writing papers because they try to write the introduction before they are ready. If you find yourself having this sort of difficulty, write the body paragraphs first; then write the introduction. That way you will know what the essay actually says before writing the opening paragraph.

Remember that the introduction is *not* the place to write a detailed explanation of a point you want to make. Because its purpose is to ease the reader into the essay, the introduction is one of the most general paragraphs in the essay. Support, explanations, details, and examples belong in the body paragraphs.

Effective Patterns for Introductions

There is no single "right way" to write introductory paragraphs. However, some of the more common patterns are presented here. Notice that each ends with the thesis.

1. Begin with a general statement of the subject.

I guess it is always difficult for immigrants to adjust to life in a new culture. That was certainly true for me. When I first came to the United States, I found learning English to be very difficult. I had trouble orienting myself to the physical layout of this city, and I had problems socializing with American students in school and people in general.

2. Begin with a specific scene.

I can still remember the distinct smell of cow manure that filled our van as my boyfriend and I crossed the border into Mexico. That smell stayed with us as we drove through Mexicali. The roads in Mexicali were like mazes and dogs were everywhere. Dented buses that belched smoke passed us on the shoulder; trucks cut us off. At first I was afraid of this chaotic place, but eventually I came to appreciate the warmth, humor, and pride of the people.

3. Begin with a question that you answer in the introduction.

Have you ever envied popular musicians their wealth and fame? If you have, you may not realize how much time, work, and dedication it takes to succeed in this highly competitive business. Members of bands like the local Smokin' Jax must sacrifice much of their personal lives and abandon other potential careers as they struggle to compete for auditions, bookings, and recording contracts.

4. Begin with facts or statistics.

According to the American Cancer Society, smoking is responsible for 83 percent of all cases of lung cancer in the United States. People who smoke two packs of cigarettes a day are 15–25 percent more likely to die of lung cancer than nonsmokers. The American Heart Association has found that smokers die of heart attacks two to four times more often than nonsmokers do. With such overwhelming evidence of the health risks related to smoking, why do thousands of Americans continue to smoke? Some people see smoking as a way to relax. Others smoke socially. Most smokers continue to smoke because they believe their habit is too hard to break.

5. Begin with a quotation.

In the sixties, John Lennon told us, "All you need is love." He made life sound so simple, as though it would be easy to be happy. Now that I have reached forty and have been through a divorce and the death of a child, I know that you need more than love to survive—you also need strength to get through the bad times and determination to grow from your experiences.

6. **Begin with a contrast.**

Images we see on television and at the movies suggest that the life of a lawyer is filled with exciting cases and jurors who are easily impressed. When television lawyers aren't driving around in their Porsches, they are impressing the jury with their uncanny insights. But the truth is much different. Lawyers, particularly new ones, are chained to a desk most of the day, writing briefs and motions. When they do appear in court, the opposing lawyer may convince the judge to postpone their trial. If the trial proceeds, it is likely to be quite routine, even boring. Lawyers are frequently "in it for the money," and greed can take the heart out of the work.

FOR PRACTICE

Practice 5k. Use several of the six patterns of organization listed previously to create introductions for each of the following thesis statements. Write your introductions so they end with the thesis.

1. People who experiment with drugs think they can control their habit, but eventually the habit controls them.
2. Friendships can be lost because friends grow apart or simply neglect one another.
3. Many high school freshmen think their future college classmates will be much smarter than they are and teachers will be indifferent to students' problems with course material.
4. Music puts us in the right mood to study, takes our minds off our troubles, and helps us remember the past.
5. Computers are wonderful tools for writing because there is such a variety of programs for word processing, learning grammar skills, and composing papers.

From Topic to Introduction
The following student sample illustrates how to narrow a topic, write a thesis, and draft introductory paragraphs.

1. One student wrote on the topic "teachers."
2. To narrow her subject, this student used the idea wheel, list of ideas, and questions to help her gather information about her topic. Notice that as she listed her ideas about teachers, she thought of questions that helped her narrow her topic.

I've had good and bad teachers.

Some teachers encourage students to talk in class.

Some care about students, but others don't.

Some will insult you rather than explain things.

Some teachers talk to themselves and not to students.

Am I being too general? Which teachers have I seen acting in these ways?

math teachers I had

Riley and Jackson in high school

completely different styles

One liked his job; the other didn't.

Riley came in late, took out her notes, and read every word even if we weren't listening.

no questions in her class Jackson explained everything, sometimes more than once.

What am I trying to show in this paper?

The difference between the teaching styles of two high school math teachers—Ms. Riley and Mr. Jackson

To arrange her ideas more clearly, she drew this idea wheel:

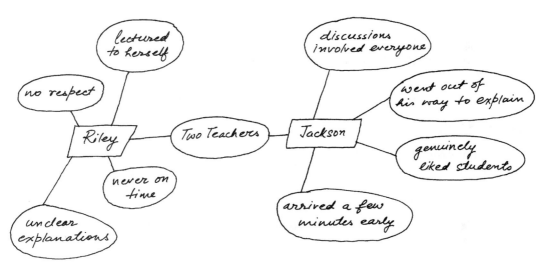

3. Next, the student wrote the following thesis: *The difference in teaching styles and attitude toward students made Mr. Jackson the better teacher.*
4. The student then wrote two introductions. One began with a general statement of the subject. The other began with a specific scene.

   (1) The math teachers I have had over the years have been as different as night and day. Ms. Riley and Mr. Jackson illustrate the extreme differences between the two types of teachers. The difference in teaching styles and attitude toward students made Mr. Jackson the better teacher.

   (2) Students in Ms. Riley's Math 1 class stir restlessly in their seats. Splat! Someone throws a spit wad and hits Letitia Briggs in the neck. Ms. Riley keeps writing examples from her notes on the chalkboard. Next door the teacher sits among the students and listens as one of his pupils explains how he solved one

of the math problems he did for homework. Several students have their hands raised, waiting to ask questions. I was in both of these classes in high school and saw for myself why the difference in teaching styles and attitude toward students made Mr. Jackson the better teacher.

FOR PRACTICE

Practice 5l. Pick one of the following topics; narrow the topic by drawing an idea wheel, making a list of ideas, or asking yourself questions. Then create a working thesis. Once you have your thesis, write two different introductions using the previous sample introductions as models.

- teachers
- a movie
- commuting to school
- student athletes
- family problems
- the dating game
- your writing
- parents

CONCLUSIONS

Effective Patterns for Conclusions

A good conclusion gives the audience the feeling that the writer has brought ideas to a logical end and has said what he or she wanted to say. The best conclusions leave readers with an interesting or thought-provoking idea. Like the introduction, the conclusion is usually a general paragraph; its purpose is to ease the reader out of the essay.

Students sometimes have difficulty deciding what to say in their conclusions. If you find yourself in this situation, reread your essay to remind yourself of what you actually wrote. Your general goal is to write a conclusion that is closely related to the ideas you presented in the paper.

As with introductions, writers commonly rely on one of several patterns for writing conclusions. See if you can match the conclusions here with the appropriate introductions on pages 97–98.

1. End with a summary of the main ideas.

I hope to do a lot of traveling in my life, but I will probably be tempted to measure my new destinations by the experiences I had in Mexicali. Whenever I arrive as a stranger in a new country, I will remember the people who welcomed us at hotels as though we were long-lost relatives. If I have trouble making myself understood in another culture, I will remember the kind waitress who made good-humored jokes about my poor Spanish. In countries with much older cultures than that of the

United States, I will look for people like the elderly man in the National Museum of Anthropology who wasn't rich enough to travel to other countries, but who took great pride in the art and culture of ancient Mexico.

2. End with a discussion of the outcome or consequences.

As the years went by, I overcame most of my difficulties with English. I learned the areas of the city pretty well by traveling around every day. In addition, I improved my understanding of English by reading books by Mark Twain, Helen Keller, and other writers. The most important step for me was learning to speak English well enough to communicate with American students, teachers, and people off campus.

3. End with a prediction about what will happen.

Musicians give up a great deal for the chance to become well-known performers. But in spite of the tremendous pressures and hard economic times, the results can really be rewarding when the recording contracts start coming in and the band plays to capacity crowds. At first it may not seem possible, but occasionally the self-sacrifices do lead to recognition. As for Smokin' Jax, the crowds are coming earlier and staying later, and agents are more interested than they were a few years ago. In short, their future looks bright.

4. Ask the reader to take action.

No amount of relaxation can make up for the shortness of breath, chest pains, and fatal diseases caused by smoking. And if smoking seems to be an impossible habit to break, smokers should remember what they are doing to their health and their family's peace of mind. The relatives of smokers suffer because they have to watch their husband, wife, child, or parent get sick and die. If smokers can't think of themselves, they should consider the agony they cause their families and stop smoking today.

5. End with a question.

Who could have guessed that life would be so much more complex and painful than John Lennon predicted? I have learned that it takes more than love to survive this life. It takes the strength to go on when you are alone and grieving, or when it seems as though you can't face another day. Learning to survive despite the difficulties makes you a stronger person than you ever imagined you could be.

FOR PRACTICE

Practice 5m. Use one of the patterns for writing conclusions to create concluding paragraphs for two of the introductions you wrote in Practice 5l.

Practice 5n. Locate an essay that you have written recently. First, identify the kind of conclusion you have written; then write a different conclusion using another of the five patterns suggested earlier.

WRITING A TITLE

The title of your essay introduces your subject. Because it is usually the first thing your readers see, it should be interesting enough that they will want to keep reading.

A title is usually a phrase (not a complete sentence) containing words that are closely related to those in the thesis. Here are a few possible titles matched with their thesis statements:

Title: Making Adjustments
Thesis: When I got married, I had to adjust my social life, household responsibilities, and financial goals.

Title: Trashing America
Thesis: I see garbage everywhere these days—on campus, in parks, and in my own neighborhood.

Title: Defensive Moves
Thesis: Using a few practical techniques helps women to protect themselves from assault.

FOR PRACTICE

Practice 5o. Write a title for each of the following thesis statements.

1. Thesis: Playing organized sports helps children develop self-confidence and teaches them valuable social skills.

Title: _____

_____

2. Thesis: Members of a band who are struggling to be discovered sacrifice a great deal of time and money.

Title: _____

_____

3. Thesis: A large percentage of young, black males are dying in America, not from natural causes but from gang-related violence.

Title: _____

_____

4. Thesis: Once I became a working mother, I was torn between my desire for independence and the traditional role of woman-as-homemaker that I had known all my life.

Title: _____

_____

5. Thesis: Our newest immigrants contribute more dollars to the economy than they take in public benefits.

Title: _____

_____

Practice 5p. Write two alternate titles for the most recent essay you have written or an essay that you are currently writing.

_____

_____

Which title do you prefer?

_____

Why? _____

_____

Practice 5q. Choose a topic from the following list and write your own essay.

- benefits of playing a particular sport
- the meaning of success
- ways of dealing with misunderstandings between partners
- reasons why you chose a specific career
- ways your hometown might become a more appealing place for people your age to live
- something you experienced that you felt was unfair

Use the techniques discussed in Chapter 3 to help you generate ideas. When you revise, check for unity, development, and coherence. You instructor might use the peer review process or a computer exercise for sharing your writing. Make sure the introduction has a clear thesis statement, paragraphs have topic sentences that connect each paragraph to the thesis, details and examples provide support for your paragraphs, and the conclusion provides a satisfying finish for the essay.

LOOKING AHEAD

Part II, "Strategies for Writing," analyzes patterns of development in essays written by professional writers. Explanations of each reading show you how these writers use narrating, describing, analyzing, comparing, evaluating, and taking a stand to make their essays interesting and convincing. Discussions of the writing process follow the analysis of each strategy.

Part II
Strategies for Writing

Writing and Observing

The chapters in Part II focus on writing strategies that you will use to develop essays—narrating, describing, explaining, defining, classifying, causal analysis, compare/contrast, evaluating, and taking a stand. The analysis of each writing strategy includes (1) essays written by professional writers that illustrate the writing strategies featured in the chapter, (2) an analysis of the authors' use of those strategies, (3) additional considerations for applying steps in the writing process to the writing strategy introduced in the chapter, and (4) student samples.

Each reading selection in Part II is accompanied by several sets of questions and topics asking you to respond to the reading in several ways. Practices in "Writing before Reading" ask you to explore what you already know about ideas in the selections you are about to read. "Freewriting" contains practices that help you formulate a response to what you have read. The "Questions for Discussion" ask you to think critically about the reading and to discuss your ideas with classmates. "Topics for Writing," which closes each reading selection, may ask you to employ the writing strategies discussed in the chapter or in other chapters.

The prominent writing strategies in this chapter—narrating, describing, defining, and classifying—introduce ways to write about observations and experiences. Examples from "Mother," an excerpt from the first chapter of Russell Baker's autobiography, *Growing Up*, illustrate writing techniques typical of narratives. "Border Culture" presents several definitions of life along the U.S.-Mexican border. Art Jahnke's "What Ever Happened to Friendship?" shows how one writer used classification to explain the ways we can lose friendships.

CHAPTER 6

We lived in San Francisco's Chinatown. Like most of the other Chinese children who played in the back alleys of restaurants and curio shops, I didn't think we were poor. My bowl was always full, three five-course meals every day, beginning with a soup full of mysterious things I didn't want to know the names of.
—Amy Tan

It is in these remote border cities, far from national capitals, that the United States and Mexico not only meet but [also] merge to form a new society.
—Marjorie Miller and
     Ricardo Chavira

Probably it happened little by little, year by year, as we grew up and as we did all the things that adults do. And one day we woke up and realized that this wasn't the way we thought it would be. Our friends were gone. And we wondered what ever happened to those guys and girls, those friends who didn't stay friends forever.
—Art Jahnke

NARRATING

Human beings are natural storytellers. Think about the conversations that take place in your classroom before the teacher arrives. In a typical classroom scene, one student might tell another what happened after her car broke down on the highway the previous afternoon. Another might reply with an account of an annoying series of events that happened in an auto repair shop a few months earlier. A few seats away one student might be telling another about the agonies he went through before his math test that morning. In a third conversation, a student might be recounting a funny story about his son's first attempt to eat a cheese pizza. Such conversations show you that everyone has stories to tell, and these stories come out naturally. Russell Baker's well-crafted story about his mother offers an excellent example of a compelling narrative.

WRITING BEFORE READING

Write steadily for 20 minutes about your earliest memories of your mother, father, or an important person in your life. Then record your memories of that person when you were a teenager, and add a few more details to describe your most recent memories. Write a few closing sentences to summarize the changes you have noticed in that person or in your relationship.

Mother

Russell Baker

Russell Baker was a writer and columnist for the New York Times *for over forty years. In 1979 Baker won a Pulitzer Prize for commentaries published in "Observer," the longest-running column in the* Times' *history (1962–1998). Collections of Baker's columns include* An American in Washington *(1961) and* Poor Russell's Almanac *(1971). The first volume of his memoir,* Growing Up, *also earned him a Pulitzer in 1983. In volume two,* The Good Times *(1989), Baker writes about his life as a reporter. He has written over a dozen other books, including* Work in Corporate America *(1971), an examination of the country's move from a manufacturing to a service economy, and* Looking Back *(2002), the latest installment of his autobiography. In addition to his literary accomplishments, Baker was host of the PBS series* Masterpiece Theater *from 1992 to 2004. In "Mother," an excerpt from* Growing Up, *Baker writes an entertaining and poignant account of his mother at several stages in her life. He contends that her history, like that of all parents, offers an important personal connection to the past.*

1   At the age of eighty my mother had her last bad fall, and after that her mind wandered free through time. Some days she went to weddings and funerals that had taken

place half a century earlier. On others she presided over family dinners cooked on Sunday afternoons for children who were now gray with age. Through all this she lay in bed but moved across time, traveling among the dead decades with a speed and ease beyond the gift of physical science.

"Where's Russell?" she asked one day when I came to visit at the nursing home. 2

"I'm Russell," I said. 3

She gazed at this improbably overgrown figure out of an inconceivable future and 4 promptly dismissed it.

"Russell's only this big," she said, holding her hand, palm down, two feet from the 5 floor. That day she was a young country wife with chickens in the backyard and a view of hazy blue Virginia mountains behind the apple orchard, and I was a stranger old enough to be her father.

Early one morning she phoned me in New York. "Are you coming to my funeral 6 today?" she asked.

It was an awkward question with which to be awakened. "What are you talking 7 about, for God's sake?" was the best reply I could manage.

"I'm being buried today," she declared briskly, as though announcing an important 8 social event.

"I'll phone you back," I said and hung up, and when I did phone back she was all 9 right, although she wasn't all right, of course, and we all knew she wasn't.

She had always been a small woman—short, light-boned, delicately structured—but 10 now, under the white hospital-sheet, she was becoming tiny. I thought of a doll with huge, fierce eyes. There had always been fierceness in her. It showed in that angry, challenging thrust of the chin when she issued an opinion, and a great one she had always been for issuing opinions.

"I tell people exactly what's on my mind," she had been fond of boasting. "I tell them 11 what I think, whether they like it or not." Often they had not liked it. She could be sarcastic to people in whom she detected evidence of the ignoramus or the fool.

"It's not always good policy to tell people exactly what's on your mind," I used to 12 caution her.

"If they don't like it, that's too bad," was her customary reply, "because that's the 13 way I am."

And so she was. A formidable woman. Determined to speak her mind, determined 14 to have her way, determined to bend those who opposed her. In that time when I had known her best, my mother had hurled herself at life with chin thrust forward, eyes blazing, and an energy that made her seem always on the run.

She ran after squawking chickens, an axe in her hand, determined on a beheading 15 that would put dinner in the pot. She ran when she made the beds, ran when she set the table. One Thanksgiving she burned herself badly when, running up from the cellar oven with the ceremonial turkey, she tripped on the stairs and tumbled back down, ending at the bottom in the debris of giblets, hot gravy, and battered turkey. Life was combat, and victory was not to the lazy, the timid, the slugabed, the drugstore cowboy, the libertine, the mushmouth afraid to tell people exactly what was on his mind whether people liked it or not. She ran.

16   But now the running was over. For a time I could not accept the inevitable. As I sat by her bed, my impulse was to argue her back to reality. On my first visit to the hospital in Baltimore, she asked who I was.

17   "Russell," I said.

18   "Russell's way out west," she advised me.

19   "No, I'm right here."

20   "Guess where I came from today?" was her response.

21   "Where?"

22   "All the way from New Jersey."

23   "When?"

24   "Tonight."

25   "No. You've been in the hospital for three days," I insisted.

26   "I suggest the thing to do is calm down a little bit," she replied. "Go over to the house and shut the door."

27   Now she was years deep into the past, living in the neighborhood where she had settled forty years earlier, and she had just been talking with Mrs. Hoffman, a neighbor across the street.

28   "It's like Mrs. Hoffman said today: The children always wander back to where they come from," she remarked.

29   "Mrs. Hoffman has been dead for fifteen years."

30   "Russ got married today," she replied.

31   "I got married in 1950," I said, which was the fact.

32   "The house is unlocked," she said. . . .

33   The doctors diagnosed a hopeless senility. Not unusual, they said. "Hardening of the arteries" was the explanation for laymen. I thought it was more complicated than that. For ten years or more the ferocity with which she had once attacked life had been turning to a rage against the weakness, the boredom, and the absence of love that too much age had brought her. Now, after the last bad fall, she seemed to have broken chains that imprisoned her in a life she had come to hate and to return to a time inhabited by people who loved her, a time in which she was needed. Gradually I understood. It was the first time in years I had seen her happy. . . .

34   After the last bad fall, she had managed to forget the fatigue and loneliness and, in these free-wheeling excursions back through time, to recapture happiness. I soon stopped trying to wrest her back to what I considered the real world and tried to travel along with her on those fantastic swoops into the past. One day when I arrived at her bedside she was radiant.

35   "Feeling good today," I said.

36   "Why shouldn't I feel good?" she asked. "Papa's going to take me up to Baltimore on the boat today."

37   At that moment she was a young girl standing on a wharf at Merry Point, Virginia, waiting for the Chesapeake Bay steamer with her father, who had been dead sixty-one years. William Howard Taft was in the White House, Europe still drowsed in the dusk of the great century of peace, America was a young country, and the future stretched before it in beams of crystal sunlight. "The greatest country on God's green earth," her

father might have said, if I had been able to step into my mother's time machine and join him on the wharf with the satchels packed for Baltimore.

I could imagine her there quite clearly. She was wearing a blue dress with big puffy 38 sleeves and long black stockings. There was a ribbon in her hair and a big bow tied on the side of her head. There had been a childhood photograph in her bedroom which showed all this, although the colors of course had been added years later by a restorer who tinted the picture.

About her father, my grandfather, I could only guess, and indeed, about the girl on 39 the wharf with the bow in her hair, I was merely sentimentalizing. Of my mother's childhood and her people, of their time and place, I knew very little. A world had lived and died, and though it was part of my blood and bone, I knew little more about it than I knew of the world of the pharaohs. It was useless now to ask for help from my mother. The orbits of her mind rarely touched present interrogators for more than a moment.

Sitting at her bedside, forever out of touch with her, I wondered about my own chil- 40 dren, and their children, and children in general, and about the disconnections between children and parents that prevent them from knowing each other. Children rarely want to know who their parents were before they were parents, and when age finally stirs their curiosity there is no parent left to tell them. If a parent does lift the curtain a bit, it is often only to stun the young with some exemplary tale of how much harder life was in the old days. I had been guilty of this when my children were small in the early 1960s and living the affluent life. It galled me that their childhoods should be, as I thought, so easy when my own had been, as I thought, so hard. I had developed the habit, when they complained about the steak being overcooked or the television being cut off, of lecturing them on the harshness of life in my day.

"In my day all we got for dinner was macaroni and cheese, and we were glad to 41 get it."

"In my day we didn't have any television." 42

"In my day . . . " 43

"In my day . . . " 44

At dinner one evening a son had offended me with an inadequate report card, and 45 as I leaned back and cleared my throat to lecture, he gazed at me with an expression of unutterable resignation and said, "Tell me how it was in your days, Dad."

I was angry with him for that, but angrier with myself for having become one of 46 those ancient bores whose highly selective memories of the past become transparently dishonest even to small children. I tried to break the habit, but must have failed. A few years later my son was referring to me when I was out of earshot as "the old-timer." Between us there was a dispute about time. He looked upon the time that had been my future in a disturbing way. My future was his past, and being young, he was indifferent to the past.

As I hovered over my mother's bed listening for muffled signals from her childhood, 47 I realized that this same dispute had existed between her and me. When she was young, with life ahead of her, I had been her future and resented it. Instinctively, I wanted to break free, cease being a creature defined by her time, consign her future to the past, and create my own. Well, I had finally done that, and then with my own children I had seen my exciting future become their boring past.

48   These hopeless end-of-the-line visits with my mother made me wish I had not thrown off my own past so carelessly. We all come from the past, and children ought to know what it was that went into their making, to know that life is a braided cord of humanity stretching up from time long gone, and that it cannot be defined by the span of a single journey from diaper to shroud.

RESPONDING TO THE READING

FREEWRITING

Chapter 1 explains "freewriting" as writing quickly without pausing to correct mistakes. In freewriting practices your goal is to write as much as you can in ten to fifteen minutes. (See pages 5–6 for a more detailed explanation of freewriting.)

FOR PRACTICE

Practice 6a. Freewrite about the most vivid images, phrases, or ideas that you remember from Russell Baker's essay. What is the main impression these images create?

Practice 6b. In a section of your notebook or journal, record any unfamiliar words and their definitions that you find in reading selections. Vocabulary lists in this book identify words you might add to your personal list.

BUILDING YOUR VOCABULARY

presided (1)[1]	formidable (14)	impulse (16)
improbably (4)	debris (15)	diagnosed (33)
inconceivable (4)	slugabed (15)	senility (33)
briskly (8)	libertine (15)	layman (33)
ignoramus (11)	inevitable (16)	

THINKING ABOUT WORDS

Chapter 2 introduced several techniques for recognizing unfamiliar words: read for context clues, break words apart, and learn prefixes and suffixes. You will find these techniques quite helpful as you read the essays in this and other chapters in Parts II and III.

---

[1] Parenthetical numbers refer to paragraphs in Russell Baker's narrative.

Looking for context clues works especially well, and you will find that authors often either define a word for you or suggest a word's meaning. For example, Russell Baker tells you that a "mushmouth" is someone who is "afraid to tell people exactly what [is] on his mind."

Many words in English are formed from other words, and breaking them apart will often help you figure out the meaning of the reassembled word. A composite word like *slugabed* carries the idea of *slug* (the slimy wormlike creature found eating our plants) and *abed,* which contains the word *bed.* Put them together and you have a lazy, slow-moving person who stays abed (in bed)—a sort of pretelevision "couch potato."

QUESTIONS FOR DISCUSSION

1. How does Russell Baker feel about his mother? Identify sentences in the reading that convey his feelings.
2. The discussion of purpose following "Mother" (page 115) points out that writers may write for a variety of reasons: to entertain, inform, explain, explore causes or effects, interpret, or persuade. What is Baker's purpose for writing his narrative? What phrases or passages support that purpose?
3. Baker describes his mother at various stages of her life. Identify specific details that create a dominant impression of his mother.
4. Why does Baker think it is important to remember the past? What are your feelings about this subject with regard to your own family?

TOPICS FOR WRITING

Topic 1. Using the techniques for writing summaries discussed in Chapter 2, write a one-paragraph summary of Russell Baker's "Mother."

Topic 2. Using Baker's vivid descriptions of his mother as a model, write your own portrait of someone you remember well. Include dialogue that lets the reader "hear" this person's voice. Follow the steps in the writing process discussed in Chapter 3 and later in this chapter (pages 119–121) to gather details, organize, and revise your paper.

Topic 3. Russell Baker's narration connects his own childhood to his mother's and to that of his own children, thereby illustrating his point that "we all come from the past, and children ought to know what it was that went into their making." Often, the most compelling narratives illustrate an idea that the writer wishes to convey. Write an essay in which you use narration to convey the meaning of one of the five common phrases listed here.

- There's a light at the end of the tunnel.
- It's a time for thinking outside the box.
- What goes around comes around.

- The more things change, the more they stay the same.
- If at first you don't succeed, redefine success.

Topic 4. Baker explains that he is writing to help his own children understand their family history because he realizes that, like him, they may not become curious about their own history until he is no longer capable of explaining it. Think of an important event in your life, one that you feel would tell your children the most about who you are or what it was like growing up when you did. Write a letter to real or imaginary children in which you recreate that experience for them. (See the guidelines for writing about an event on pages 131–132.)

Topic 5. Choose a scene from "Mother" and rewrite it from the point of view of Russell Baker's mother. Then write a paragraph explaining how her perspective changes the story.

Topic 6. Write about a time when you had a misunderstanding with a parent or guardian. Be sure to include a vivid, detailed description of one or more of the following: (1) what you saw as you lived through this misunderstanding, (2) the meaning of the experience, or (3) your parent's interpretation of what happened.

NARRATING: AN ANALYSIS OF "MOTHER"

When we tell our stories to others or write privately for ourselves, we are organizing experiences in coherent patterns that help us understand what people, places, and events really mean to us. At times, we may be explaining what an experience taught us; at other times, we may be presenting ideas we hope can teach others. We also may be attempting to preserve details and feelings that are important to us. When we wish to convey such meanings to an audience, it is helpful to know how other writers have made their stories interesting and meaningful. The following discussion uses passages from Russell Baker's "Mother" to illustrate characteristics common to well-written narratives.

CHARACTERISTICS OF NARRATING

A Distinct Point of View

Narratives are usually told from a single point of view with an author or character using the first person, "I," to tell what happened. The writer frequently establishes point of view, time, and place in the opening paragraphs of an article or essay. For example, in his autobiographical portrait of his mother, Russell Baker introduces himself, his subject, and his perspective on that subject in the first paragraph.

> At the age of eighty my mother had her last bad fall, and after that her mind wandered free through time. Some days she went to weddings and funerals that had taken place half a century earlier. On others she presided over family dinners cooked on Sunday afternoons for children who were now gray with age. Through all this she lay in bed but moved across time, traveling among the dead decades with a speed and ease beyond the gift of physical science.

Because he is writing an autobiography, Baker uses his own "voice," identifying himself as a grown man who speaks from the bedside of his declining mother. His perspective is important because he can make sense of his mother's mental "travels" in a way that she cannot. As recorder and interpreter, he places each event that she imagines in its proper place in the past, sometimes as much as "half a century earlier" than the moment of his writing.

A Sense of Audience and Purpose

Writers can choose from among several reasons for writing. They may wish *to inform* their audiences of a particular subject, as the author of "The Life of a Sports Fanatic" did when he wrote to inform readers about the things that sports lovers enjoy doing (see pages 31–32). Writers may have other purposes as well. They may, for example, write *to entertain* their readers. In this case they may use humor or an unusual approach to their subject. Another common purpose in writing is *to explain* something that happened, a condition that exists, or the expected result of a situation. Writers may also explain why something happened, what it meant, how something works, or why it is important. In other instances, authors may write *to persuade* their readers to change their minds about an issue, or they may urge them to take action. Authors often write for several of these reasons.

In writing about his mother, Baker includes lively descriptions to entertain us and to illustrate her strong-willed personality. Here is one passage from paragraphs 14 and 15 that suggests these purposes:

> In that time when I had known her best, my mother had hurled herself at life with chin thrust forward, eyes blazing, and an energy that made her seem always on the run.
>
> She ran after squawking chickens, an axe in her hand, determined on a beheading that would put dinner in the pot. She ran when she made the beds, ran when she set the table. One Thanksgiving she burned herself badly when, running up from the cellar oven with the ceremonial turkey, she tripped on the stairs and tumbled back down, ending at the bottom in the debris of giblets, hot gravy, and battered turkey.

Baker also writes for himself in order to capture his own memories of his mother and to speculate about her memories of times before he was born. In yet another passage from "Mother," he complains about how much of his mother's past he has lost:

> Of my mother's childhood and her people, of their time and place, I knew very little. A world had lived and died, and though it was part of my blood and bone, I knew little more about it than I knew of the world of the pharaohs. It was useless now to ask for help from my mother. The orbits of her mind rarely touched present interrogators for more than a moment.

If Baker hopes to preserve anything from the past, he must write down what he remembers about his mother and his own childhood before he himself is beyond remembering.

Conflict or Complexity

A well-written narrative usually has some edge, some conflict, or uncertainty that may remind us of conflicts in our own lives. In Russell Baker's narrative, his insistence that his mother stop imagining herself as a younger, more vital woman living in a completely different time and place conflicts with her inability to stay in the present "for more than a moment." Controlled by her illness, his mother ignores her son's objections and seems to go wherever she wishes.

Baker writes:

> For a time I could not accept the inevitable. As I sat by her bed, my impulse was to argue her back to reality. On my first visit to the hospital in Baltimore, she asked who I was.
>
> "Russell," I said.
>
> "Russell's way out west," she advised me.
>
> "No, I'm right here."
>
> "Guess where I came from today?" was her response.
>
> "Where?"
>
> "All the way from New Jersey."
>
> "When?"
>
> "Tonight."
>
> "No. You've been in the hospital for three days," I insisted.
>
> "I suggest the thing to do is calm down a little bit," she replied. "Go over to the house and shut the door."

Baker's conflict with his mother is resolved when he finally stops trying to bring her back to the present. He realizes that "after the last bad fall, she seemed to have broken chains that imprisoned her in a life she had come to hate and to return to a time inhabited by people who loved her, a time in which she was needed." He concludes that it is best to let her relive the times when she was truly happy.

Chronological Organization

In the word *chronological, chron-* is derived from the Greek word *khronos,* meaning *time.* Hence, *chronological* refers to the arrangement of events as they occur in time. Many professional writers like Russell Baker change this order by using **flashback,** a technique you are probably familiar with from watching movies that interrupt the chronological order to show events that took place before the story started. As you have seen, Baker begins his narration as an adult describing his eighty-year-old mother and, through a series of flashbacks, he remembers her as a young woman who "hurled herself at life."

Use of Transitions to Connect Events

It is important to separate scenes, events, and reflections so that the reader can tell where one ends and another begins. This is especially true of narratives that use flashbacks. Writers use transitional words and phrases to link events in a steady, even stream without gaps or abrupt stops. The opening paragraph of Baker's "Mother" is repeated here with transitions underlined to show how several memories can be linked effectively with the help of transitions.

At the age of eighty my mother had her last bad fall, and <u>after that</u> her mind wandered free through time. <u>Some days</u> she went to weddings and funerals that had taken place half a century earlier. On others she presided over family dinners cooked on Sunday afternoons for children who were <u>now</u> gray with age. <u>Through all this</u> she lay in bed but moved across time, traveling among the dead decades with a speed and ease beyond the gift of physical science.

The connecting words that are most useful for linking scenes and events in narratives are reprinted here from the list of transitional words and phrases in Chapter 4.

To order ideas in time	after, before, briefly, by this time, currently, during, eventually, finally, first, now, later, meanwhile, next, presently, recently, second, so far, soon, then, third, when, while

Describing and Explaining

Writers may include two other writing strategies—describing and explaining—in their narratives in order to clarify what was meaningful about a person or scene. When using description, writers appeal to the senses (sight, hearing, smell, touch, and taste) to create vivid descriptions of people, places, objects, and events. Explaining allows writers to interpret what an experience means to them. As Amy Tan's "Rules of the Game," discussed later in this chapter, shows, describing may be the prominent writing strategy in an essay. Authors also may choose one of several forms of analysis as their principal writing strategy.[2] In the discussion that follows, you can see how strategies of describing and explaining can supplement narratives.

In the descriptive writing in this chapter, the writers use the senses to record vivid memories of their families. In Russell Baker's description of his mother, for example, we not only see her but also hear her voice—strong, uncompromising, and full of self-assurance. (In the passage excerpted here, sense impressions are underlined for you.)

She had always been a small woman—<u>short, light-boned, delicately structured</u>—but now, under the <u>white hospital sheet,</u> she was becoming tiny. I thought of a <u>doll</u> with <u>huge, fierce eyes.</u> There had always been a fierceness in her. It showed in that angry, challenging <u>thrust of the chin</u> when she issued an opinion, and a great one she had always been for issuing opinions.

"<u>I tell people exactly what's on my mind,</u>" she had been fond of boasting.

"<u>I tell them what I think whether they like it or not.</u>" Often they had not liked it. She could be sarcastic to people in whom she detected evidence of the ignoramus or the fool.

"It's not always good policy to tell people exactly what's on your mind," I used to caution her.

---

[2] Various strategies that analyze or explain ideas include process analysis (Chapter 6), classifying (Chapter 7), comparing and contrasting (Chapter 7), explaining causes and effects (Chapter 7), evaluating (Chapter 8), and taking a stand (Chapter 8).

"If they don't like it, that's too bad," was her customary reply, "because that's the way I am."

And so she was. A formidable woman.

In addition to the more obvious visual and auditory details that Baker uses to describe his mother, he also uses an analogy or comparison: "under the white hospital-sheet, she was becoming tiny. I thought of a doll with huge, fierce eyes." This comparison between the woman who is wasting away and a child's doll helps us see the rather startling contrast between her tiny size, which would make her seem harmless, and her fighting spirit—a spirit reflected in her eyes.

CHARACTERISTICS OF DESCRIBING AND EXPLAINING

A Dominant Impression or Idea

Descriptions offer a single, dominant impression of the person, place, object, or event being described. In addition, writers frequently explain the larger meaning of impressions they provide. For example, after using many sense impressions to describe his mother, Russell Baker tells the reader what they suggest about the sort of person she was. After describing her "huge, fierce eyes," he tells us, "There had always been a fierceness in her." He adds, "a great one she had always been for issuing opinions. . . . She could be sarcastic to people in whom she detected evidence of the ignoramus or the fool." He concludes this passage by stating this dominant impression: "And so she was. A formidable woman."

Clarify Connections

Writers also use explanations to show how events in the past are somehow meaningful to the present. Baker makes this point clear by using his memories of his mother to explain the connections between his experiences and those of all children:

> Sitting at her bedside, forever out of touch with her, I wondered about my own children, and their children, and children in general, and about the disconnections between children and parents that prevent them from knowing each other. . . .
>
> These hopeless end-of-the-line visits with my mother made me wish I had not thrown off my own past so carelessly. We all come from the past, and children ought to know what it was that went into their making; to know that life is a braided cord of humanity stretching up from time long gone, and that it cannot be defined by the span of a single journey from diaper to shroud.[3]

In drawing this conclusion, Baker speaks not only to his children but to "children in general" about the importance of knowing that there is more to their lives than can be understood by the relatively short time allotted us from birth to death. We are each part of a family history, he implies, and heritage is important because it tells us who we are and something of the history of which we are a part. It is interesting to note that Baker's autobiography, *Growing Up,* from which these passages are taken, has sold about 22 million copies and was on the *New York Times'* best-seller list. It appears that he has reached a very broad audience.

---

[3] A sheet used to wrap a body for burial.

Practice 6f. Use examples from one or two readings in this book to illustrate several elements of a strong narrative. You may wish to use evidence from "Fathers Playing Catch with Sons" (Chapter 10, page 280), "I Just Wanna Be Average" (Chapter 11, page 303), "Complexion" (Chapter 13, page 350), or "The Myth of the Latin Woman" (Chapter 14, page 376).

THE WRITING PROCESS: NARRATING

Chapter 3 applied the steps in the writing process to the tasks of writing an essay. (To review the steps, see the inside cover of this book.) This section gives you additional suggestions for applying the writing process to narration and the other idea development patterns that were introduced in Chapter 3.

Remember that the steps in the writing process are meant to provide a manageable progression from the inception of an idea to the final draft of a paragraph or essay. They need not, however, be followed in order. Instead, you should use them so that they enhance your own methods of writing. If, for example, you work best by writing a fast draft shortly after thinking of a topic, your sequence of steps might be 1: Developing a Topic, 2: Thinking about Your Audience, 5a: Writing a Fast Draft, 4: Organizing Ideas, 3: Developing Ideas, 5b: Editing and Proofreading, 5c: Sharing Your Writing, and 5d: Making Final Revisions. Moreover, your writing strategy will probably change from one paper to the next. You may find, for example, that for one paper you will follow the sequence outlined here, but for the next, you might follow the steps in numerical order from your initial idea to your final revision.

The discussion on the next few pages gives you additional considerations for applying the writing process to writing narratives about a person you want to remember. These considerations will help you produce well-written narratives with a distinct point of view, a sense of your audience, a well-defined purpose for writing, chronological organization with clear transitions between events, and elements of conflict or complexity—the characteristics of narrating illustrated earlier in this chapter.

DEVELOPING A TOPIC

If you have difficulty developing a topic for a paper about someone you wish to remember, try answering a few of these questions that interest you most:

What are some of the earliest memories you have of people, family members, or close friends?

Which of your teachers made an impression on you?

Who was your first boss, or the boss who made the biggest impression on you?

What person do you remember when you listen to a particular song?

Who has had a major influence on your life?

THINKING ABOUT YOUR AUDIENCE

Before you gather subtopics and details for your narrative, it is a good idea to clarify your topic, purpose, audience, and dominant impression. Put these concerns in the form of questions, too:

Who am I writing about?

Why am I writing about this topic?

Who am I writing for?

What is the main idea or dominant impression I want to convey?

DEVELOPING IDEAS

When you develop your writing, you may find that some memories are easier to write about than others. Journal writing is valuable for recording memories because the more you rely on your journal, the easier it will be to retrieve specific details and events. You may find it helpful to write several entries about the memory you want to recapture, especially if it seems to be coming back to you a little at a time.

The following questions may prove helpful as you gather details about a person you wish to remember.

What did this person look like?

How did he or she dress?

What distinctive characteristics do you remember?

How did he or she walk and talk?

What was his or her general pace in life—slow, moderate, fast?

What did this person enjoy doing? What did he or she hate doing?

What was his or her role in life?

Did he or she work in the home or have an outside job? What was it?

What conversations do you remember that illustrate something about this person?

How have other people described him or her?

Who were this person's other friends? What were they like?

How close were you to this person? How did the two of you display closeness or separation?

Did you do things together? If so, what? When? Where?

What sort of person was he or she? What did this person do or say to illustrate this trait?

What caused the person to be the way he or she was?

Did you have a different view of this person at different times?

Has anything about this person changed?

In addition to asking yourself questions, you might list ideas or draw an idea wheel to record details and associations as they come to you. Speaking into a tape recorder, recounting incidents orally to a friend or classmate, or talking to someone who shares the memory can also revive details. If you like to doodle or draw, you might try sketching this person to illustrate some behavior, conversation, or situation that you remember.

ORGANIZING IDEAS

Several patterns can help you organize material for your narrative. Put the events, descriptions, or explanations about the person you are discussing in chronological order, at least at first. That will help you determine whether you have all the details you need or if you should omit some that don't seem appropriate.

Your thesis should state the dominant impression you wish to create in your essay. This impression will prepare your reader for the descriptions and explanations in supporting paragraphs.

If you wish to experiment with the order of events, you might try using the flashback technique, as Russell Baker does, to make your ideas more vivid or to add interest to the sequence of events you are narrating. Regardless of whether you use straight chronological order or flashbacks, write an outline of the sequence of events you plan to follow.

WRITING A FAST DRAFT

Reread your answers to the questions about subject and purpose before you begin writing your fast draft. Use your outline for guidance and include plenty of descriptions, details, and dialogue in this draft.

SHARING AND REVISING

You may use the general questions in Appendix C at the end of this book for responding to paragraphs or essays. The following checklist is especially useful for writing narratives. Check each question as you complete it.

Checklist

- ❑ Is it clear to the reader *who* I am writing about and *why* I am writing?
- ❑ Have I given the reader a clear impression of the person, place, or event I'm describing?
- ❑ Are there any additional details in the descriptions or examples that would make the memory more vivid?
- ❑ Will adding explanations clarify the meaning of these details?
- ❑ Overall, have I successfully recreated what I remember?
- ❑ Have I proofread this description carefully enough to catch spelling mistakes I may have made and words I may have omitted?
- ❑ Have I checked my sentences for errors like fragments and run-ons?

When you write your revised draft, keep in mind that your goal is to recreate this person, place, or event for someone who does not know what you know and has no way of imagining or understanding the subject without your help.

Student Writing: Narrating

As a student in a college composition class, Sam Masuno wrote the following tribute to his mother and grandmother, survivors of the atomic bomb dropped on Hiroshima on August 6, 1945.

To Be Thankful

My mother, Naoko Uemitsu, was born in war-ravaged Japan on February 22, 1943. World War II roared in her ears as she lay in a crib in the ship-building city of Kure.

Naoko lived in a nice Japanese home with her father, mother, two older brothers, and one older sister. Sadly, the bombs kept beating on the city of Kure, angrier day by day. The time arrived when it was too dangerous to stay, and the Uemitsu family moved. Naoko's mother ran with Naoko strapped on her back, bundled in lots of blankets. Naoko's father placed all of the family's most prized possessions in a wheelbarrow and led the family to safety.

The Uemitsu family arrived in the peaceful countryside of Kurose many days later. They were tired, hungry, and scared but very happy to be alive. Naoko's father's parents lived on a farm in Kurose, and the family stayed there. This was a life Naoko had never experienced before—a lull in a raging storm. Her father (oto–san) began a job as a high school principal, and Naoko's brothers and sister began to attend school once more.

Naoko's mother (oka–san) was a faithful Japanese wife and mother and worked hard at raising the children. Life during wartime was very harsh even in Kurose. Distant bombings could be felt all day long. Food was very scarce and drinking water even scarcer, yet oka–san taught the Uemitsu children to be very humble and appreciate all of the little things in life. "Kansha, kansha," oka–san would say gently. "Be thankful, be thankful." Oka–san was very religious and repeatedly thanked God for blessing them with the incredible good fortune of living so well in the midst of a horrible war. "Our whole family is eating together," oka–san would say with tears in her eyes. "Kansha, kansha."

On August 6, 1945, the atomic bomb was dropped on the city of Hiroshima, fifty miles away from Kurose. Oto–san saw the nightmarish mushroom cloud that darkened the sky and was burdened with grief. That day was full of tears cried for friends and relatives who perished in Hiroshima. Naoko, who was only two-years-old, cried in her sleep.

After much confusion and devastation, the war finally ended and the Uemitsu family decided to move once more. Naoko was now six-years-old and she wanted to go to school. When the A-bomb was dropped, the city of Hiroshima was not destroyed entirely. In the middle of Hiroshima was Higeyama (little hill). To one side of the hill was utter destruction, but the other side, thanks to Higeyama, survived with only minor damage.

The Uemitsu family moved in with an aunt who lived on the habitable side of Hiroshima. At such a young age, Naoko was shocked to see the hibakusha, the people who were deformed from the effects of the bomb. She was at first disgusted and frightened of their hideously melted faces and bodies. But oka–san taught her otherwise. "You appreciate people for how they look on the inside, not on the outside. These, too, are beautiful." Naoko took this to heart and overcame her fear of the hibakusha. In fact, Naoko began to help them in any way she could. She held their hands when they stumbled. She gave them water when they were thirsty. She would soothe them when they cried out in pain and loneliness. Naoko helped the hibakusha to momentarily forget the pain and smile. She was eager to let them know that people still listened and cared.

Naoko Uemitsu was born during World War II, an era of full of pain, confusion, and anger. But Naoko did not succumb to the bitterness of her surroundings. She learned to appreciate the little things in life—to always look at the brighter side. "Kansha, kansha," my mother says to this day. "Be thankful, be thankful."

—Sam Masuno

QUESTIONS FOR DISCUSSION

1. What is the dominant impression in "To Be Thankful"? How does Masuno convey this impression?
2. What do you think his purpose was in writing this narrative? How well did he achieve it?
3. What do you remember reading about the U.S. attack on Hiroshima and Nagasaki, the bombings that ended World War II? What did Masuno's narrative add to your understanding of those events?
4. Describe the point of view Masuno uses in this narrative. How does he include Naoko's perspective?

DESCRIBING

Whether re-creating an experience for their readers or providing support for a definition or argument, writers rely on vivid sense impressions to make their ideas compelling. Writers often try to capture the sights, sounds, smells, feel, and even taste of an experience, in order to recreate it for their reader. As you will see, Amy Tan is an expert at drawing the reader into vividly written scenes of her childhood.

WRITING BEFORE READING

Freewrite about the street where you grew up or the neighborhood where you live now. Don't worry about the order of details or events; just record as much as you can remember.

Rules of the Game

Amy Tan

Amy Tan was born in Oakland, California, in 1952, just two years after her parents emigrated from China to the United States. She is the author of four novels, numerous essays, and two children's books. Her latest novel, Saving Fish from Drowning: A Novel, *was published in 2006. It explores the hardships endured by several travelers on an art expedition in the Burmese jungle. Tan's first novel,* The Joy Luck Club, *was a finalist for the National Book Award and the National Book Critics Circle Award in 1989. The novel has been translated into seventeen languages and was made into a motion picture. The following excerpt is taken from a chapter in* The Joy Luck Club.

1   I was six when my mother taught me the art of invisible strength. It was a strategy for winning arguments, respect from others, and eventually, though neither of us knew it at the time, chess games.

2   "Bite back your tongue," scolded my mother when I cried loudly, yanking her hand toward the store that sold bags of salted plums. At home, she said, "Wise guy, he not go against wind. In Chinese we say, Come from South, blow with wind—poom!—North will follow. Strongest wind cannot be seen."

3   The next week I bit back my tongue as we entered the store with the forbidden candies. When my mother finished her shopping, she quietly plucked a small bag of plums from the rack and put it on the counter with the rest of the items.

4   My mother imparted her daily truths so she could help my older brothers and me rise above our circumstances. We lived in San Francisco's Chinatown. Like most of the other Chinese children who played in the back alleys of restaurants and curio shops, I didn't think we were poor. My bowl was always full, three five-course meals every day, beginning with a soup full of mysterious things I didn't want to know the names of.

5   We lived on Waverly Place, in a warm, clean two-bedroom flat that sat above a small Chinese bakery specializing in steamed pastries and dim sum. In the early morning, when the alley was still quiet, I could smell fragrant red beans as they were cooked down to a pasty sweetness. By daybreak, our flat was heavy with the odor of fried sesame balls and sweet curried chicken crescents. From my bed, I would listen as my father got ready for work, then locked the door behind him, one-two-three clicks.

6   At the end of our two-block alley was a small sandlot playground with swings and slides well-shined down the middle with use. The play area was bordered by wood-slat benches where old-country people sat cracking roasted watermelon seeds with their golden teeth and scattering the husks to an impatient gathering of gurgling pigeons. The best playground, however, was the dark alley itself. It was crammed with daily

mysteries and adventures. My brothers and I would peer into the medicinal herb shop, watching old Li dole out onto a stiff sheet of white paper the right amount of insect shells, saffron-colored seeds, and pungent leaves for his ailing customers. It was said that he once cured a woman dying of an ancestral curse that had eluded the best of American doctors. Next to the pharmacy was a printer who specialized in gold-embossed wedding invitations and festive red banners.

Farther down the street was Ping Yuen Fish Market. The front window displayed a tank crowded with doomed fish and turtles struggling to gain footing on the slimy green-tiled sides. A hand-written sign informed tourists, "Within this store, is all for food, not for pet." Inside, the butchers with their bloodstained white smocks deftly gutted the fish while customers cried out their orders and shouted, "Give me your freshest," to which the butchers always protested, "All are freshest." On less crowded market days, we would inspect the crates of live frogs and crabs which we were warned not to poke, boxes of dried cuttlefish, and row upon row of iced prawns, squid, and slippery fish. The sanddabs made me shiver each time; their eyes lay on one flattened side and reminded me of my mother's story of a careless girl who ran into a crowded street and was crushed by a cab. "Was smash flat," reported my mother.   7

At the corner of the alley was Hong Sing's, a four-table café with a recessed stair-well in front that led to a door marked "Tradesmen." My brothers and I believed the bad people emerged from this door at night. Tourists never went to Hong Sing's since the menu was printed only in Chinese. A Caucasian man with a big camera once posed me and my playmates in front of the restaurant. He had us move to the side of the picture window so the photo would capture the roasted duck with its head dangling from a juice-covered rope. After he took the picture, I told him he should go into Hong Sing's and eat dinner. When he smiled and asked me what they served, I shouted, "Guts and duck's feet and octopus gizzards!" Then I ran off with my friends, shrieking with laughter as we scampered across the alley and hid in the entryway grotto of the China Gem Company, my heart pounding with hope that he would chase us.   8

My mother named me after the street that we lived on: Waverly Place Jong, my official name for important American documents. But my family called me Meimei, "Little Sister." I was the youngest, the only daughter. Each morning before school, my mother would twist and yank on my thick black hair until she had formed two tightly wound pig-tails. One day, as she struggled to weave a hard-toothed comb through my disobedient hair, I had a sly thought.   9

I asked her, "Ma, what is Chinese torture?" My mother shook her head. A bobby pin was wedged between her lips. She wetted her palm and smoothed the hair above my ear, then pushed the pin in so that it nicked sharply against my scalp.   10

"Who say this word?" she asked without a trace of knowing how wicked I was being. I shrugged my shoulders and said, "Some boy in my class said Chinese people do Chinese torture."   11

"Chinese people do many things," she said simply. "Chinese people do business, do medicine, do painting. Not lazy like American people. We do torture. Best torture."   12

RESPONDING TO THE READING

FREEWRITING

Practice 6c. Use sense impressions in Amy Tan's description of the neighborhood where she grew up to write about similar sights, sounds, and smells you have experienced in urban neighborhoods.

Practice 6d. How do the sights, sounds, and smells of Waverly's neighborhood compare to a neighborhood that you remember?

BUILDING YOUR VOCABULARY

imparted (4)	pungent (6)	sanddabs (7)
curio (4)	deftly (7)	grotto (8)
saffron (6)	cuttlefish (7)	

QUESTIONS FOR DISCUSSION

1. Choose a few favorite scenes from "Rules of the Game." What makes these scenes effective? Compare your responses with those of your classmates.
2. Waverly's mother is an important force in her life. What is the dominant impression conveyed by her behavior and speech?
3. Locate passages that include speech or dialog between characters. Discuss why Tan might have included these passages.
4. In paragraph 2, Waverly's mother advises her daughter: "'Wise guy, he not go against wind.'" Then she quotes a Chinese proverb: "'In Chinese we say, Come from South, blow with wind—poom!—North will follow. Strongest wind cannot be seen.'" Examine paragraphs 1 through 4 carefully and decide how this advice applies to Waverly. Explain how this scene and the passage in paragraph 2 contribute to our understanding of the relationship between mother and daughter.
5. Reread the last exchange between Waverly and her mother at the end of paragraph 9, beginning with the sentence "One day, as she struggled to weave a hard-toothed comb through my disobedient hair, I had a sly thought. . . ." Write a one-sentence summary of what happens next. What does the dialogue imply that is not stated directly?
6. If you have read Russell Baker's "Mother," discuss similarities or differences between his mother and Waverly's mother.

TOPICS FOR WRITING

Topic 1. Reread your freewriting notes for the Writing before Reading exercise on page 123. Use the questions for remembering places on page 130 to help you add new details to the memories of the street where you grew up. Then take your reader on a walk through your neighborhood. Be sure to use transitions to move the reader from one spot to another as Amy Tan does. Make sure your descriptions are vivid and consistent enough to convey a dominant impression of that street.

Topic 2. Write a letter to a friend in which you describe an event that occurred in your neighborhood or community when you were a child. Write the letter quickly to catch as much about the place, people, circumstances, and details as you can remember. Treat this letter as a freewriting practice, adding details that you may have omitted. Then group similar details and arrange them in the order you would like to follow for a class assignment. Finally, rewrite the letter, using clear topic sentences and vivid details to recreate the event for your friend.

Topic 3. Describe an event that taught you something important about your parents or another adult authority. In writing this paper you might explain the "rules of the game" you learned in this encounter with the adult world.

Topic 4. Write an essay in which you use narration and description to recreate a time and place when you felt like an outsider or felt threatened in some way. Ai Vang's "The Quilt" is a good example of an essay that uses narration and description to convey a life-threatening experience (page 135).

Topic 5. Compare Waverly's attitude toward her neighborhood with the perspective Elizabeth Wong offers on her Chinese upbringing in "The Struggle to Be an All-American Girl" (page 300). Locate descriptions and comments that identify the speaker's attitude; use these passages as evidence to support your thesis about the differences that you identify.

DESCRIBING: AN ANALYSIS OF "RULES OF THE GAME"

Techniques for writing narration—attention to point of view, purpose, and organization—are also useful for writing descriptions of places, objects, and events. Writers who record their observations rely primarily on detailed descriptions and explanations to recreate a particular place, object, or event, and to interpret its significance.

CHARACTERISTICS OF DESCRIBING

A Distinct Point of View

In the discussion of "Mother" earlier in this chapter, we saw that point of view plays an important part in shaping narratives (page 114). Russell Baker's point of view as an adult determined which incidents he used to illustrate his mother's slow retreat into the past. Point of view is equally important when describing places, objects, and events. Here, too, writers must clarify their stance and their relationship to their subject. In the case of fiction, writers do not speak in their own voice. Instead, like Amy Tan, they write through the voice of their characters.

In the opening paragraphs of "Rules of the Game," for example, Tan's character, Waverly, describes an event from her childhood and introduces herself and her mother.

> I was six when my mother taught me the art of invisible strength. It was a strategy for winning arguments, respect from others, and eventually, though neither of us knew it at the time, chess games.
>
> "Bite back your tongue," scolded my mother when I cried loudly, yanking her hand toward the store that sold bags of salted plums. At home, she said, "Wise guy, he not go against wind. In Chinese we say, Come from South, blow with wind—poom!—North will follow. Strongest wind cannot be seen."
>
> The next week I bit back my tongue as we entered the store with the forbidden candies. When my mother finished her shopping, she quietly plucked a small bag of plums from the rack and put it on the counter with the rest of the items.

Tan has her character speak in the first person and writes from the perspective of an adult remembering herself as a six-year-old when her mother taught her "the art of invisible strength." Waverly describes two trips to the store, one before the lesson and one after, in order to help the reader understand her mother's prominence in her life.

Reliance on Details and Sense Impressions

To recreate an experience for the reader, a writer might describe sights, sounds, smells, tastes, and tactile sensations. The paragraph that follows illustrates Amy Tan's use of sense impressions to describe the apartment in Chinatown where Waverly lived with her family:

> We lived on Waverly Place, in a warm, clean, two-bedroom flat that sat above a small Chinese bakery specializing in steamed pastries and dim sum. In the early morning, when the alley was still quiet, I could smell fragrant red beans as they were cooked down to a pasty sweetness. By daybreak, our flat was heavy with the odor of fried sesame balls and sweet curried chicken crescents. From my bed, I would listen as my father got ready for work, then locked the door behind him, one-two-three clicks.

Tan has her character describe the "clean, two-bedroom flat" and helps us imagine its location "above a small Chinese bakery." Next, we smell the "fragrant red beans," and she suggests that if we were to taste them, we would notice a "pasty sweetness." She also recalls the "odor of fried sesame balls and sweet curried chicken crescents." The last sense impressions are the sounds of her father getting ready for work and his locking the door behind him—"one-two-three clicks."

A Dominant Impression or Idea

As you saw at the beginning of this chapter, a writer uses particular details to create a dominant impression or idea. In the preceding passage, the description of Waverly's room in the early morning conveys the impression of a comforting home, rich with sights, sounds, and smells.

Spatial Arrangement

In contrast to narratives, descriptions are arrangements in space rather than time. Here, Waverly describes the alley behind her family's apartment:

> At the end of our two-block alley was a small sandlot playground with swings and slides well-shined down the middle with use. The play area was bordered by wood-slat benches where old-country people sat cracking roasted watermelon seeds with their golden teeth and scattering the husks to an impatient gathering of gurgling pigeons. The best playground, however, was the dark alley itself. It was crammed with daily mysteries and adventures. My brothers and I would peer into the medicinal herb shop, watching old Li dole out onto a stiff sheet of white paper the right amount of insect shells, saffron-colored seeds, and pungent leaves for his ailing customers. . . . Next to the pharmacy was a printer who specialized in gold-embossed wedding invitations and festive red banners.
>
> Farther down the street was Ping Yuen Fish Market. The front window displayed a tank crowded with doomed fish and turtles struggling to gain footing on the slimy green-tiled sides. A handwritten sign informed tourists, "Within this store, is all for food, not for pet." Inside, the butchers with their blood-stained white smocks deftly gutted the fish while customers cried out their orders and shouted, "Give me your freshest," to which the butchers always protested, "All are freshest."

This detailed description moves us down the block from the playground to its border of "wood-slat benches" and on "to the dark alley itself." There we follow Waverly and her brothers first to the pharmacy, then to the printer next door, and finally to the fish market where we progress from the window display to the interior, each location rich with sense impressions.

FOR PRACTICE

Practice 6e. Underline sense impressions in the description of Waverly's neighborhood. Label the sense to which each impression appeals. What is the overall effect that these details create?

Use of Transitions to Link Details

To organize details in their descriptions, writers use directional cues to move readers from one point to another. The list of transitional words and phrases most useful for writing descriptions is reprinted from Chapter 4:

To order ideas in space	above, behind, below, beside, next to, in front of, inside, on top of, in the foreground/background, to the right, to the left, under

Reliance on Explaining

Writers often use explanations to clarify meaning for their readers. Tan frequently interprets a description for her readers by simply telling them what the description means. For example, after Waverly describes the trips with her mother to the grocery store, she explains the importance of her mother's lesson and how well her mother protected her from knowledge of the family's "circumstances":

> My mother imparted her daily truths so she could help my older brothers and me rise above our circumstances. We lived in San Francisco's Chinatown. Like most of the other Chinese children who played in the back alleys of restaurants and curio shops, I didn't think we were poor. My bowl was always full, three five-course meals every day, beginning with a soup full of mysterious things I didn't want to know the names of.

THE WRITING PROCESS: DESCRIBING

In general, the steps in the writing process are useful for writing any kind of paragraph or essay. The suggestions and questions below offer more specific help in writing descriptions.

DEVELOPING A TOPIC

The Topics for Writing that follow the first two reading selections in this chapter give you ample opportunity to use your memories and observations to write about a person, place, object, event, or idea. Journal entries and freewriting practices in this chapter and class discussions may suggest additional topics. The following questions are designed to help you explore your topic and shape details and subtopics into a paper.

Questions for Remembering Places

What are some of your earliest memories of a neighborhood and home?

Make a list of the places you have lived. Which do you remember most vividly? Why?

Have you been anywhere that made you feel out of place, as though you were clearly an outsider?

What schools have you attended? Which did you like or dislike most?

If you have taken trips to the mountains, desert, or seashore, what were your impressions?

What was your first job like?

How would you describe the most attractive place or the least attractive place you have worked?

What place was special to you as a child or teenager?

Is there a place that has special meaning to you as an adult?

Where do you go to have fun?

Where did you go to have fun when you were a child?

Questions for Remembering Objects

What have you owned that has meant something to you?

Is there a particular feature in your home, like a fireplace or wall hanging, that interests you?

Is there a special object you remember from the house or apartment where you lived as a child?

Is there something that terrified you when you were little?

Do you own something now that you can't live without? How long have you had it? Why is it important to you?

Questions for Remembering Events

What was it like to do something for the first time—drive a car, attend your first college class, fly in an airplane, hike, or camp?

Think of a song that has special meaning for you. What events come to mind when you hear it?

What embarrassing, rewarding, or maddening things happened at your first job?

Which school year do you remember best? What do you remember about it?

What have you done especially well in your life?

What have you found particularly difficult to do?

What is the worst conflict you have ever experienced? Who was involved?

What happened? How was it resolved—or has it?

THINKING ABOUT YOUR AUDIENCE

When you write a description, your goal is to recreate an experience as vividly as you can. Some students find it easier to write if they have a particular audience in mind that has never seen the place or object they are describing. Then the writer must be the reader's eyes and ears.

The following questions will help you narrow your topic and decide what you want your description to accomplish:

What do I want to describe?

Who is my intended audience?

What point of view will I adopt?

What is the dominant impression I want to create?

DEVELOPING IDEAS

Once you discover the topic you'd like to develop, you may wish to use these additional questions to generate details, examples, ideas, and explanations for your essays:

Questions for Describing Places

What did this place look like from the inside or outside?

What distinctive characteristics do you remember about it?

What was your relationship to this place?

What generally happened here?

Were any people involved with the place? How were they involved? What were they like? What conversations do you remember?

How did other people describe this place?

Has this place changed over the years? If so, how?

Have you had different impressions of this place at different times in your life? Describe these perspectives. How do you explain the differences?

Questions for Describing Objects

What did this object look like from the inside or outside?

What distinctive characteristics do you remember about it?

How did other people describe it?

Were other people involved with the object? How? What were they like?

Did you have a different view of this object at different times?

What was your relationship to it? Did you observe it, buy it, or have it given to you?

Has anything about this object changed over the years? What might have caused these changes?

Questions for Describing Events

What was important about the event you want to describe?

What have other people said about this event?

What sights, smells, sounds, tastes, or feelings are associated with this event?

How were you involved in what happened?

Were any other people involved? How?

What conversations took place at the time?

Why might things have happened the way they did? What was the result?

What long-term effects do you foresee as a result of this event?

Have you had a different perspective on this event at different times or in different moods?

How close were you to this event? What did it mean to you?

You might arrange your answers to the questions you select by drawing an idea wheel or listing ideas. Speaking your memories into a tape recorder or talking to a friend or classmate might also prove fruitful as you recall and shape events. Sketching significant details might also help you recreate your experience.

ORGANIZING IDEAS

Most descriptions follow a spatial order; left to right, top to bottom, or inside to outside are a few possible arrangements. If you are writing about the place where you grew up, it might be helpful to imagine yourself walking through the neighborhood, much as Waverly remembers walking through her Chinatown neighborhood, and to describe what you are seeing on this walk. If possible, visit the place you want to describe before you write about it. You might actually take a walk there, jotting down what you see, smell, hear, taste, and touch.

MAKING FINAL REVISIONS

Once you have written a few drafts of your paper, try underlining your dominant impression or thesis, and the topic sentences in your paragraphs to ensure that your descriptions and ideas are linked coherently. Then circle the supporting details to see if your paragraphs are fully developed. Finally, use the following checklist to make revisions. Check each question as you complete it.

Checklist

- ❑ Will the object I am describing and my purpose for writing be clear to a reader?
- ❑ Does this description have a dominant impression or a point I want to make?
- ❑ Would additional details, examples, dialogue, or comparisons make this description more vivid?
- ❑ Should I add explanations to clarify the importance of what I'm discussing?
- ❑ In general, have I recreated this place or experience successfully?

Student Writing: Describing a Place
In this essay, Norman Ferguson describes his garage, the objects in it, and the memories that some of those objects hold for him.

Garage

My garage has always been a special place to me. It is the place where I go when I want to work on my projects. But more than that, it is like a museum that contains things that I have taken up but since discarded and objects to which memories have attached like barnacles.

My garage is located in the backyard separated from the house by the lawn and a huge tree that shades the whole yard from the hot summer sun. The garage, built in 1936, is old but in good condition. It has a double-car door that faces an alley and has a single-car door that faces the backyard so I can bring cars into the backyard and wash them or work on them in the shade of the tree. Crunching and grinding sounds of cars driving on the gravel road in the alley behind my garage let me know that a car is coming long before it gets to my garage. Clouds of dust and the smell of dirt fill the air for quite a while after the car drives by. All of this gives me a feeling of days gone by. Once in a while when I'm in my garage I remember how it felt when I used to go into my father's garage and work on my first car with him.

My garage is a place where nothing is touched or moved unless I say so. Everything is where I want it—comfortable reminders of things I like to think about. I see one of my major projects as I walk into the garage. It is an old black 1956 Ford T-bird with a porthole top and a continental spare tire on the back bumper. The car hasn't been driven in at least a year and has a layer of dust all over it. When I look at the car, I always smile because someone has written on the trunk in the dust, "Wash me" and under that "fix me," and I will someday. Next to the back door is a lawnmower and other garden tools that remind me of how long it has been since I have done any yard work. Along the same wall there is the sporting section where I keep the camping gear and fishing equipment. When I see it I always remember the last fishing or camping trip we took, or I dream about the next one.

Across from that wall is my workbench with an old girlie calendar hanging on the wall above it; the calendar is at least ten years old. The girl is wearing a skimpy swimsuit and holding a tool that nobody knows a use for. On the workbench is a clock radio that my wife was going to throw away because the clock doesn't work, but the radio works well, and what do I need a clock for in my garage? Also on the workbench is a pile of tools and car parts that have been there so long I don't even remember where they go or what they are for. Best of all is my old chair next to the workbench where I spend most of my time smoking cigars and making plans to get started on one of many projects. It always happens that when I'm about ready to get started on one, my wife calls from the back door telling me that dinner is ready, or it's time to go someplace.

She always calls me when I am in the middle of something important, or at least it seems important to me.

—Norman Ferguson

QUESTIONS FOR DISCUSSION

1. What was Ferguson's purpose for writing this description?
2. What overall impression of the garage do the details of the essay convey?
3. What organizational pattern does Ferguson use? If you think the essay is organized clearly, explain what contributes to its organization. Make suggestions if you think the organization needs work.
4. Imagine that you have read this paragraph for an in-class workshop. What are its strengths? Do you have suggestions for expanding the descriptions? Are there other improvements the student might make?

The Quilt

I have a quilt that is special to me because it is a constant reminder of who I am and where I came from. I feel this need to be reminded of where I came from because I can't remember it very well. My family and I immigrated to the United States when I was about five years old, and I can only remember bits and pieces of the past. This quilt reminds me of what life must have been like for me, my parents, grandparents, and many other Hmong families. My quilt was hand made by a Hmong woman who may still be living in one of the refugee camps in Thailand where my family and I once lived. A lot goes into the making of a Hmong quilt, and although the quilt depicts the Green tribe (I am from the White tribe), our stories and history are the same.

The styles of dress, patterns of clothing, and the artistry of Hmong quilts reflect the uniqueness of the tribe that produced it. The three major groups of Hmong, the White Hmong, the Green Hmong, and the Stripe Hmong, are distinguished by the style and color of clothes they wear and the dialects they speak. The quilts sewn by women artists from each tribe reflect that tribe's unique dress. The men in my quilt wear clothing typical of the Green Hmong. Their pants are loose and baggy, and the crotch of the pants falls below the knees. The pants are held up by a long piece of folded red cloth tied around the men's waist several times with half a foot left from each end forming a covering for the crotch. The women wear black blouses with colorful designs along the collars and sleeves. Attached to the collar behind the neck are pieces of cloth with intricate designs. The artistry that goes into the quilts is different for each tribe. When the women sew their embroidery, the White and Stripe Hmong concentrate on the side they will display, and the women from the Green tribe concentrate on both sides of the cloth. To them, perfecting both sides makes their embroidery unique because, they say, anyone can make one side look beautiful, but not everyone can make both sides look beautiful at the same time.

The quilt itself tells two distinct stories. The upper portion depicts the daily lives of Hmong villagers. One scene shows several people feeding hogs and chickens. Other villagers are harvesting corn, pumpkins, and other fruits and vegetables. A little further down is a small section depicting the rice harvest; there are no modern tools, so the harvesting of rice takes a long time. The quilt shows a man and woman gathering rice into a pile, then beating a few handfuls at a time to separate the grains from the stems. There is a huge grinder in the scene with a long pole made like a swing to help turn the grinder. The woman is pushing the grinding arm around while the man slowly drops grains of rice into the mill. The quilt shows another piece of equipment that looks like half a seesaw attached to a big ax head. This machine takes a considerable amount of strength to operate, so the man uses all his weight to push it up and down while the woman scoops cooked rice into the wooden bowl on the ground. He continues to pound until the rice gets really sticky before he replaces that batch of rice with the next. My mother once told me that it took the weight of both her and her friend to accomplish the task of mashing the rice. A little further down from this scene is a group of men and women walking on a trail with wicker baskets on their backs. I assume they must be heading for their farm or perhaps they are gathering firewood.

The lower panel of the quilt depicts a sad story shared by many Hmong people. It marks the end of the calm village life shown in the upper section of the quilt. One scene shows men, women, and children fleeing their homes with what little they can carry with them. Soldiers are shooting on the ground and planes are firing bullets and dropping toxic chemicals into the village from above. People are fleeing from Laos into Thailand for safety. The quilt shows the crossing of the Mekong River with soldiers shooting at those who are trying to swim over; many are killed. The lucky few make their way into Thailand.

The story on the quilt is a story shared by my family and thousands of other Hmong. I was just a baby when my entire family sneaked out of their homes at night and fled into the jungles. My parents often tell stories about the cruelty of those times. They say that sometimes when families were on the run, young children who wouldn't stop crying were left behind while the others would run ahead to find new hiding places. I told my parents that it was cruel for parents to do such a thing to their children. My parents tried to explain that in those days it was crucial that everyone remain silent because soldiers were roaming everywhere looking for refugees. One loud sound could cause the death of an entire family, so it was necessary to sacrifice one life for the sake of everyone else. I often wonder if my parents were tempted to leave me behind, but I never had the courage to ask.

When I was younger I often thought that my parents were ignorant people because they were just farmers and had no formal education, and I wished they were more like parents of my American friends. Now when I look at the quilt I don't envy anyone else because I know that my parents struggled for a better life for my brother and me. They wanted to make sure we got the education they could never have because the farm depended on all able bodies to work it. I also realize that my parents, grandparents, and thousands like them are brave and courageous people. It takes courage and strength to move an entire family in time of war to settle in an unknown territory. I am grateful to have the quilt as a reminder of the life they left and horrors of war that my family and I survived.

—Ai Vang

QUESTIONS FOR DISCUSSION

1. Ai Vang combines a description of the quilt with family history and memories. How well does she integrate the story of the quilt and the story of her family?
2. Vang includes one story about families who must abandon their crying children as they flee into Thailand. What is the effect of this story on the essay as a whole?

DEFINING

When writers rely on definitions to develop their essays, they convey the precise meaning or significance of their subject. Definition involves not only a clear statement of the meaning of an idea but also involves setting it apart from what it isn't. For this reason, comparison/contrast is a useful writing strategy for clarifying what something means. In "Border Culture," Marjorie Miller and Ricardo Chavira demonstrate important characteristics of essays that rely on defining as their principal writing strategy.

WRITING BEFORE READING

What cultural, ethnic, or religious groups are familiar to you? What mixing of cultures have you observed?

Border Culture

Marjorie Miller and Ricardo Chavira

Marjorie Miller is currently foreign editor for the Los Angeles Times. *Ricardo Chavira was a correspondent for* Time *from 1983 to 1992 and now reports on international news for the* Dallas Morning News. *Miller and Chavira were staff writers for the* San Diego Union *newspaper when they wrote this article about the mixing of Mexican and U.S. cultures along their common border. Their article appeared in the* San Diego Union *on December 26, 1983, under the title "A Unique Culture Grows in the Desert."*

Highway 80, a blacktop ribbon of road through scrub brush and hill after rugged hill, unfolds to the south toward Douglas. The windswept Arizona highway leads to the 1,900-mile border where Mexico and the United States stand face to face in a barren land. At the border, the highway joins a trio of narrow Mexican highways that also traverse the arid geography. But there are more than lonesome roads among the scrub brush. These Mexican and American highways form a network that connects far-apart towns and cities from San Diego to Brownsville, Texas; from Tijuana to Matamoros, Tamaulipas. It is in these remote border cities, far from national capitals, that the United States and Mexico not only meet but merge to form a new society. 1

It is a society of people like Elsa Vega and Celia Díaz, both of whom grew up south of the border, but now live north. It is people like Barney Thompson and William Arens, who married women from Tijuana but live in San Diego. It is Robert Bracker, whose father built a store in Nogales, Arizona, to serve Mexican customers, or Pablo Hourani, who lives in Bonita and commutes south daily to run his family clothing business. Or Leobardo Estrada of Los Angeles, the grandson of Mexican immigrants whose family still extends south to Tijuana. At the border, a wealthy technological superpower meets a developing agricultural nation; a predominantly Anglo-Protestant people encounters a 2 society of *mestizos,* Indians, and Spanish Catholics. Here on the border a 200-year-old, upstart culture meets one with roots that predate Christ. Together they meld into a new, third culture of the borderlands that blurs the very border from which it was born.

3   This barren land has been fertile ground after all, fertile for a culture that has flourished in part because of its isolation. The border culture has had room to grow in the desert. It has grown in Mexican cities like Mexicali, where the land once belonged to American developers, and in Tijuana, which was so isolated that until the 1940s Tijuanans had to pass through the United States to visit their mainland. It has grown in American cities like Laredo and Calexico, where the mainstream is a Hispanic majority.

4   The culture of the borderlands is a binational world where Mexicans are becoming more Americanized and where Americans are becoming more Mexicanized. It is an area, sometimes hundreds of miles wide, where families, businesses, languages, and values from the two countries often are entwined as tightly as the chain link fence that attempts to separate them. While not all of the cities and the 7 million people who live along the U.S.–Mexico boundary belong to the binational culture, there is a border society that is distinct from Mexico and the United States. In parts, the border culture reaches as far north as Santa Barbara and San Antonio, Texas, as far south as La Paz in Baja California Sur, and Chihuahua City, Chihuahua. In a few instances, the borderlands culture crops up like an island far from the international boundary, such as in Chicago—where Mexican immigrants have converted old neighborhoods into replicas of border communities. By and large, the culture clings to the area along the U.S.–Mexico border, where people might live in one country and work or go to school in another. It is where Americans and Mexicans intermarry and have children who are dual citizens for the first 18 years of their lives, until they must choose one country or the other. It is a region where the people speak English and Spanish and often a third language, Spanglish, that is a hybrid of the two. And it is a society where certain businesses exist simply because the border exists—businesses like currency exchange houses, import–export brokerage firms, and drive-through Mexican car insurance agencies—and where businessmen must learn to operate in two cultures so that after years of doing so they become bicultural.

5   The border society is made up of towns and cities that experience international issues, like illegal immigration, as local problems. Pollution, sewage, and natural disasters affect Mexican and American border cities equally, because such problems do not respect an international boundary. Society on the border is united by footbridge, ferry and bus; by bilingual radio and television; by millions of people who legally cross the border hundreds of times each year, and by countless others who cross illegally. It is a society in which the local economies on each side of the border often are more attached to one another than to the mother country's. It is a society that is slightly scorned by both Mexico and the United States for its unconventional behavior.

6   Even some of the cities have blended. Take Calexico and Mexicali—on opposite sides of the border, but both named by the Colorado Land River Co. from the words California and Mexico. And cities such as Columbus, New Mexico, and its neighbor Palomas, Chihuahua, that have merged in other ways, helping to sustain each other. Many Columbus residents have family in Palomas, while nearly half of Columbus'

schoolchildren are from the border's other side. Columbus provides the Mexican town with ambulance and fire services. Mexicans commonly use the hospital on the U.S. side, the only one in the area. On the other hand, Palomas is still the place where Columbus residents go to eat bargain-priced steak dinners and drink hearty Mexican beer. And despite Mexico's ailing economy, Columbus still relies on Mexican shoppers to spend money in the U.S. town.

But this binational blend is not spread evenly along the boundary. The border society is not homogeneous. The border region is the wealthiest in Mexico, but one of the poorest regions of the United States. Its people are a mix of pioneers who have called the frontier home for generations, and a generation of new settlers who arrived yesterday from Ohio or Oaxaca, from Michigan or Michoacan. There are people living along the boundary line who are so oblivious to the new, third culture that they might be nearer the Canadian border. There are fourth, fifth, sixth cultures, such as that of the Kickapoo Indians in Texas, the Chinese of Mexicali, the Filipinos of San Ysidro, that exist under the umbrella of the border society. And there are differences between urban and rural people, the rich and poor, Texans and Californians. In fact, those who are totally immersed in the border culture are a minority. Far greater are the numbers who dip in and out, whose cross-border experience might be limited to occasional shopping or dining in the other country, whose cross-cultural experience might be limited to Mexicans seeing an American movie or to San Diegans living next door to a family whose mother tongue is Spanish. Some might be touched by the border only because they work with Americans or employ a Mexican. But inevitably, bits and pieces of the culture rub off—exposure to another language or lifestyle, a conversion from dollars to pesos or kilometers to miles, a sketchy knowledge of the history of another country, a familiarity with its holidays and traditions. **7**

While some people who live in the border culture embrace it as a positive and inevitable change, others are hostile toward it for fear it will degrade their own culture. The history of the border begins with such antagonism. After a two-year war between Mexico and the United States, the present-day border was drawn up, which cost Mexico nearly half its territory. Mutual hate and distrust poisoned relations, and for years after the conquest Americans and Mexicans launched cross-border raids against each other. Mexico later decided to put up the only barrier it had—people—to prevent Americans from capturing more land by simply moving onto it. The government in the 1930s made it a national policy to entice Mexicans to move north—ironically, by offering them access to cheap American goods. More recently, Mexicans in the interior have chastised those northern Mexicans for becoming too Americanized and too dependent on American goods. Today, many Mexicans see the cultural encroachment of the United States in Mexico as a further "occupation" of their country. Many Americans, on the other hand, fear that Mexicans are slowly reconquering the Southwest with *their* cultural encroachment. **8**

Just as the border is not homogeneous, neither is it completely unified. Conflicts, clashes, and contradictions have developed out of the interaction between two such diverse peoples: Mexicans and Americans. On both sides of the border, there is the **9** necessary mutual dependence of neighbors. But respect and friendship often have combined with resentment and racism to form a love–hate relationship.

10   There is suspicion and scorn on both sides. Americans who value speed and efficiency often huff if Mexican goods break down or service is slow; Mexicans, on the other hand, sometimes turn up their noses at Americans whom they feel are rushing through life too fast to appreciate living it. Many Mexicans are envious of American wealth while, at the same time, they are put off by the individualism, egotism, and selfishness that they believe goes with it. They are offended by American haughtiness and bluntness. A mythology has evolved on both sides that leads Americans to believe all Mexican police will demand a bribe or throw them in jail, and Mexicans to believe that U.S. businessmen always are honest and that U.S. authorities always will deal with them fairly. U.S. police along the border patrol America's underbelly. It is 1,900 miles of largely unprotected boundary that is vulnerable to anyone determined enough to enter or to bring something into the country. Even in an era of sophisticated electronic surveillance, millions of people and billions of dollars of narcotics find their way north, while stolen cars, high-tech equipment, and top-secret defense documents flow south. It is that permeability that scares Americans. Mexicans, meanwhile, have heard horror stories about discrimination in the United States and for that reason some are wary of going north. Americans continue to picture the Mexican border as replete with goodtime towns of sleazy honky-tonk bars where anything is for sale for the right price. Some of that does exist, yet Americans played a large role in the creation of that Mexico in the '20s and '30s during Prohibition. While spending their dollars for fun, Americans developed a double standard, frowning on Mexico for being "that kind of place." Mexicans invoked their own double standard, profiting from the indulgence while disapproving of Americans for acting as they would not act at home. Misconceptions and misunderstandings about border life still exist, but they are not unique to the border. They exist away from the border— in Mexico City and Washington, D.C., among other places.

11   For all that border residents criticize each other, however, they are becoming more tolerant of each other and more alike. U.S. border residents who do business in Mexico learn to temper some of their American straightforwardness with a little Mexican graciousness. Mexican businessmen learn to speed up their timetables to meet Americans' habits, so that a 2 PM lunch in Tijuana becomes a noon lunch in San Diego. American hostesses who invite guests from south of the border learn to time their evenings accordingly, because one never knows how long it will take to cross the border. Many border Mexicans want their children schooled in the United States to learn English, but send them to Catholic schools to make sure they preserve traditional values of family, religion, and respect. A few Americans send their children south to learn proper Spanish.

12   Tastes have changed along the U.S. border. From California to Texas, tacos and burritos have become as American as apple pie—so American, in fact, that the way they are prepared is foreign to many Mexicans from the interior. While Mexican restaurants are just now becoming an expensive fad in New York, rare is the shopping mall or hotel center along the border without at least one Mexican restaurant—fast-food or fancy.

And products from both countries intermingle easily on supermarket shelves for people whose tastes include chilies and Idaho potatoes, tortillas and grits. Some holidays are heartily celebrated on both sides of the border. In the United States, Cinco de Mayo has become the St. Patrick's Day of the Southwest. Border Mexicans have become attuned to American holidays such as July Fourth, Labor Day, and Memorial Day, if only because they mean added business over long weekends. U.S. sports teams in the borderlands are vigorously supported by thousands of Mexican fans. While Mexicans head north to see football and baseball, Americans head south for bullfights, cockfights, and jai alai. For residents of the binational society, the border is united by cooperation among peoples through charity and neighborliness, among businesses through joint ventures, and governments through joint projects.

Despite the rugged terrain of scrub brush and fear, the border is not a barrier but   13
a network of relationships and opportunities: The people who straddle the boundary guarantee that the border society will continue to grow in the desert.

RESPONDING TO THE READING

FREEWRITING

Practice 6f. Freewrite about the attitudes toward cultural mixing that the authors discuss in "Border Culture." What are a few misconceptions as well as happy results of the meeting of cultures at the U.S.-Mexican border?

Practice 6g. Freewrite about differences between the culture of the United States that Miller and Chavira describe and another culture with which you are familiar.

BUILDING YOUR VOCABULARY

traverse (1)	arid (1)

QUESTIONS FOR DISCUSSION

1. Why do you think the authors wrote this article? What tone or attitude do they adopt toward their topic? Cite evidence of this tone in their article.
2. What is unique about the region Miller and Chavira describe?
3. Which examples are most effective in depicting the blending of cultures and communities along the border? What makes them effective?
4. Are there hostile reactions to this blending of cultures? How do the authors explain this resistance? Can you think of other areas in the United States or elsewhere in the world where cultures are mixing? What are the sources of tension in those places?
5. Describe a peaceful or antagonistic meeting of two cultures that you have observed.

TOPICS FOR WRITING

Topic 1. Freewrite about the neighborhood where you live or one you know well. Where do your neighbors come from? What culture do they seem to belong to? How do they get along with one another? When you have thought of lots of examples, incidents, and descriptions concerning the people in your neighborhood, write a paper explaining how different people with different styles, values, and perhaps different cultures live together there.

Topic 2. Pick two or three other essays from a chapter in Part III that illustrate a blending of cultures. You might, for example, choose "The Struggle to Be an All-American Girl" in Chapter 11, "Pursuit of Happiness" or "Complexion," readings in Chapter 13, or "The Good Daughter" in Chapter 10. Once you have selected the readings you will use, identify the cultures involved; then examine how each article depicts a peaceful blending of cultures, an antagonistic meeting, or something in between.

DEFINING: AN ANALYSIS OF "BORDER CULTURE"

Most writers who use definition, whether as the principal writing strategy or for a small but important explanation of terms, answer one or more of these questions:

What is _____? (Fill in the blank.)

Why is it important?

Does it have historical significance?

How does it affect our lives; how might it change our lives in the future?

In "Border Culture," for instance, the authors' definitions answer these questions: "What is this border culture?" "What does it mean to the people who live there?" "How is it affecting people's lives?"

CHARACTERISTICS OF DEFINING

A Purpose and Point of View

Usually the purpose of an essay that relies principally on defining is to explain what something means and why it is important. As with other writing strategies, authors choose either a first-person point of view or the more objective third-person perspective. In the essay "Border Culture," Miller and Chavira write objectively in order to inform the reader about the uniqueness of the culture along the border between the United States and Mexico.

Use of Other Writing Strategies

In most cases, writers whose main purpose is to define a subject rely on other writing strategies to make that definition clear to the reader. Describing, giving examples, explaining, comparing and contrasting, or discussing causes and effects are common ways that writers use to define their subjects. Miller and Chavira's article, "Border Culture," illustrates each of these strategies.

Using Describing to Define. Writers may choose to describe the characteristics of their topic; these descriptions may include qualities, behavior, size, or shape, depending on whether a commercial product, person, or object is being defined. In "Border Culture," because the authors are defining a place, they devote their opening paragraph to a description of that place—the borderland between Mexico and the United States.

> Highway 80, a blacktop ribbon of road through scrub brush and hill after rugged hill, unfolds to the south toward Douglas. The windswept Arizona highway leads to the 1,900-mile border where Mexico and the United States stand face to face in a barren land. At the border, the highway joins a trio of narrow Mexican highways that also traverse the arid geography. But there are more than lonesome roads among the scrub brush. These Mexican and American highways form a network that connects far-apart towns and cities from San Diego to Brownsville, Texas; from Tijuana to Matamoros, Tamaulipas.

Here the authors describe the physical characteristics of the borderlands; they are mostly barren and arid wastelands stretching between the towns and cities that comprise the border culture. As this description makes clear, the highways that form the boundaries of this area have all but invented the border culture in the sense that it could not exist without this vital network.

Once Miller and Chavira have described the landscape of the border for the reader, they write their thesis: "It is in these remote border cities, far from national capitals, that the United States and Mexico not only meet but merge to form a new society." Two paragraphs later the authors restate the thesis in more specific terms: "Here on the border a 200-year-old, upstart culture meets one with roots that predate Christ. Together they meld into a new, third culture of the borderlands that blurs the very border from which it was born" (paragraph 2).

Using Examples to Define. Case studies and examples show the reader specific instances that clarify the meaning of a particular term or concept. In our sample essay, Miller and Chavira define the border culture by offering cross-cultural examples of the people who live there.

> It [the border culture] is a society of people like Elsa Vega and Celia Díaz, both of whom grew up south of the border, but now live north. It is people like Barney Thompson and William Arens, who married women from Tijuana but live in San Diego. It is Robert Bracker, whose father built a store in Nogales, Arizona, to serve Mexican customers, or Pablo Hourani, who lives in Bonita and commutes south daily to run his family clothing business. Or Leobardo Estrada of Los Angeles, the grandson of Mexican immigrants whose family still extends south to Tijuana.

Using Explanations to Define. Effective writing usually requires that authors explain or interpret their examples for the reader. In paragraphs following their examples of the people who live along the border, Miller and Chavira offer the following observations:

> At the border, a wealthy technological superpower meets a developing agricultural nation; a predominantly Anglo-Protestant people encounters a society of *mestizos,* Indians, and Spanish Catholics. . . .

The culture of the borderlands is a binational world where Mexicans are becoming more Americanized and where Americans are becoming more Mexicanized. It is an area, sometimes hundreds of miles wide, where families, businesses, languages, and values from the two countries often are entwined as tightly as the chain link fence that attempts to separate them.

Using Comparing and Contrasting to Define. Writers sometimes explain how something is like or unlike the topic being defined. In "Border Culture," for example, the authors use this strategy when contrasting the diverse culture along the border with its opposite—a homogeneous culture.

> Just as the border is not homogeneous, neither is it completely unified. Conflicts, clashes and contradictions have developed out of the interaction between two such diverse peoples: Mexicans and Americans. On both sides of the border, there is the necessary mutual dependence of neighbors. But respect and friendship often have combined with resentment and racism to form a love–hate relationship.
>
> There is suspicion and scorn on both sides. Americans who value speed and efficiency often huff if Mexican goods break down or service is slow; Mexicans, on the other hand, sometimes turn up their noses at Americans whom they feel are rushing through life too fast to appreciate living it. Many Mexicans are envious of American wealth while, at the same time, they are put off by the individualism, egotism, and selfishness that they believe goes with it. They are offended by American haughtiness and bluntness. A mythology has evolved on both sides that leads Americans to believe all Mexican police will demand a bribe or throw them in jail, and Mexicans to believe that U.S. businessmen always are honest and that U.S. authorities always will deal with them fairly.

By using examples of people who are not part of the border culture, Miller and Chavira suggest what the border culture *is* by showing the reader what it is *not*. Furthermore, their illustrations of the antagonism between Mexicans and citizens of the United States also show that the culture is not harmonious.

Using Causal Analysis to Define. Sometimes examining causes and effects helps writers define their subject. Examining the history that produced the border culture, for example, clarifies not only what it is, but why it exists in its present form.

> While some people who live in the border culture embrace it as a positive and inevitable change, others are hostile toward it for fear it will degrade their own culture. The history of the border begins with such antagonism. After a two-year war between Mexico and the United States, the present-day border was drawn up, which cost Mexico nearly half its territory. Mutual hate and distrust poisoned relations, and for years after the conquest Americans and Mexicans launched cross-border raids against each other. Mexico later decided to put up the only barrier it had—people—to prevent Americans from capturing more land by simply moving onto it. The government in the 1930s made it a national policy to entice Mexicans to move north—ironically, by offering them access to cheap American goods. More recently, Mexicans in the interior have chastised those northern Mexicans for becoming too Americanized and too dependent on American goods. Today, many Mexicans see the

cultural encroachment of the United States in Mexico as a further "occupation" of their country. Many Americans, on the other hand, fear that Mexicans are slowly reconquering the Southwest with *their* cultural encroachment.

Notice, too, that this look at history employs narration to tell what happened along the border in years past. Transitions in each topic sentence ("after a two-year war," "Mexico later decided," "more recently," and "today") link events in this chronological arrangement smoothly.

THE WRITING PROCESS: DEFINING

The steps in the writing process will prove useful if defining is the dominant writing strategy for a paper you wish to write. The following considerations will help you apply the writing process to the task of defining a subject.

DEVELOPING A TOPIC

If you write an essay that relies principally on defining to develop ideas, it is best to choose a topic for which you can find specific examples to illustrate your points. The topic you choose should hold some interest for you so that it will keep your attention; this way you will be less likely to put off writing your paper.

DEVELOPING IDEAS

To generate ideas for your definition, you might ask yourself the following questions. They will also help you explore other possible writing strategies for writing your definition.

What parts, sections, or categories will you describe?

What examples illustrate your subject?

How might discussing causes or effects help you define your subject?

Does your subject serve a purpose or have a particular function that might help you define it?

What else does it resemble?

What is its opposite and how might the contrast help define the topic?

As you generate ideas and information for your essay, keep in mind that you should use dictionary definitions sparingly and only if you refer to them directly in your paper. Edit these definitions carefully to avoid introducing unnecessary ideas or ideas that are too abstract to illustrate your points.

ORGANIZING IDEAS

Order of importance and chronological arrangement are common ways to organize ideas in an essay whose purpose is to define. In the student essay "Emergency Room," for example, Ernesto Morales arranges his topic ideas in the order of their importance. He first define the kind of work he does and the function of the emergency room where he works. He then examine the positive (paragraph 3) and negative sides (paragraph 4) of his experience in the emergency room, concluding with an illustration of the overall value of working in the ER.

SHARING AND REVISING

The following checklist will help you revise your essay for effective focus, organization, and development. Put a check mark beside each question as you revise.

Checklist

- ☐ Do I have a thesis that announces my topic and purpose for writing?
- ☐ Is my point of view subjective (first person) or objective (third person)?
- ☐ Have I provided enough background information for the reader?
- ☐ Is the point I am making in each paragraph expressed in a topic sentence or implied by the details and examples I have given?
- ☐ What other writing strategies do I use (examples, explanation, comparison, contrast, cause/effect)? How have these strategies helped clarify my subject?
- ☐ Do any paragraphs need additional examples or explanations?
- ☐ How have I organized the essay? Do some ideas or paragraphs seem out of order and need rearranging?
- ☐ Have I proofread my sentences carefully enough to catch spelling and punctuation errors and words I may have omitted by mistake, and to find sentence errors I sometimes make (such as fragments or run-on sentences)?

Student Writing: Defining

Emergency Room

I work at Mercy General Hospital as an emergency room technician. The emergency room is an in- and out-patient clinic for people who feel they cannot wait for an appointment with their regular doctor, and for trauma patients brought by ambulance to the emergency room. My duties consist of assessing the patient's life history and chief complaint of illness; documenting blood pressure, temperature, and pulse rate; and assisting the doctors and nurses in resuscitating patients who have suffered cardiac arrest—a heart attack in layman's terms. As you might imagine, I have become more intensely involved with the lives of strangers than most people who work with the public. In the emergency room, I have been exposed to many situations that challenged my knowledge of the human body, and as a result, I have developed exceptional skills. I have also suffered unimaginable insults that tested my patience and desire to care for sick people. At other times my experiences have overwhelmed me with feelings of gratitude for being in such an occupation, and I have emerged with a deeper understanding of human emotions than I could have ever had otherwise.

Being an emergency room technician means learning what to do and how to react during emergency situations. All emergency personnel must learn to act quickly when a patient is wheeled in. For instance, if a patient cannot be stabilized at our level of emergency care, we cannot transport him to surgery but must perform an operation in the ER itself. If that proves necessary, the attending cardiac surgeon prepares for open heart surgery in the emergency room. He starts by cutting the epidermis, or outer layer of skin, with a scalpel, and then while I suction away blood and bits of loose skin with a long, plastic tube, he cuts the exposed subdermal part of the skin. He then carves the fat away while cutting his way into the sternum and rib cage with a long-nosed tool that resembles a pair of bolt cutters. Shaping and twisting his way through the exposed sternum, the surgeon reveals the thin lining of the pleural sac, which covers the heart and lungs. After cutting the thin sack, he grasps the unoxygenated, bluish gray heart and starts to massage the flaccid organ while searching for the right location to insert a pacemaker. Wiring and twisting in the pacemaker, the surgeon carefully sutures in the pacer like a mechanic tightening a spark plug into a motor. After setting a rhythm for the pacer, he sutures in long hooked tubings and attaches the patient to a life-support machine until further surgery can be done. Situations like this have given me a good understanding of the structure of the human body and what goes into repairing it.

My work as an ER technician usually requires that I work with patients who are conscious and, very often, in pain. When I work with patients in the emergency room who are conscious, I have to be compassionate toward each one. However, I find it very difficult to maintain my professionalism with especially difficult patients. For example, I once had to deal with a patient who was brought in for care because he had fallen on broken glass while being arrested for public drunkenness. It must have been 3:30 in the morning—my time for feeling grouchy—when the nurse asked me to help her draw blood for an alcohol-level exam. The patient—an irritable alcoholic—was being very uncooperative, and while he resisted, he called me every filthy racial name he could think of. I patiently explained that if he didn't cooperate, we would have no choice but to restrain him with force. He then proceeded to spit on me, so I forced him onto a gurney and stuffed a towel in his mouth while the nurses tied his hands to the rail. I was later angry at myself, but I had no other alternative because we had no time to waste. Those sorts of incidents make me want to get out of this work altogether.

Fortunately, the rewarding experiences outweigh the unpleasant ones. Special holidays really touch me when I see patients having to be hospitalized; I think of who might be in the waiting room anticipating good or bad news when they should be at home celebrating and rejoicing. For instance, a patient had stopped breathing at 11:30 PM one Christmas Eve. As I ran past the waiting room toward the patient who had gone into cardiac arrest, I saw the family members pounding on the closed door, demanding to know what was wrong. One of the sobbing members of the family grabbed me, but I shrugged away and entered the room, committed to saving the woman's life. While assisting with artificial resuscitation, I looked down and noticed that this comatose woman was as old as my own grandmother. I felt a sense of sadness come over me as I repeated over and over in my head, "You have to make it! You have to make it!" I felt so helpless, knowing that this was all we could do for her and that at this point her survival would be determined by fate alone. By 11:59 we had no rhythm and at 12:00 AM the physician called off the artificial support and drugs that were being pumped into her heart. Several seconds later, she miraculously produced a rhythm on her own and at that moment the puzzled doctor ordered the drugs and life support to be continued and asked the surgery room to prepare for an emergency bypass. While washing up, I wondered if I had just witnessed an act of God; after all, it was Christmas morning. Why couldn't it have been?

Throughout the emotional stress and thankless moments that define my work in the emergency room, the true meaning of gratitude comes at the end of a shift when I go home with more knowledge and understanding of the human body, or when the alcoholic nods a thank you on his way out the door, or when I see the smiles and dried tears of the family that was able to enjoy life with their grandmother through one more Christmas.

—Ernesto Morales

QUESTIONS FOR DISCUSSION

1. What experiences of working in a hospital does Morales emphasize? How do they compare to your own ideas about hospitals?
2. Identify the writing techniques that Morales uses. How effective are these techniques in communicating the job of an ER technician?

CLASSIFYING

One of the ways we organize our lives is to put things into categories. We might, for example, color-code our electronic planner to distinguish assignments for math, English, and history. We can organize our e-mails into projects for school, home, and work. This method for making sense of our lives also works as a strategy for organizing essays. In the essay "How Urban Legends Work" in Chapter 7, for example, Tom Harris divides his topic into two categories: urban legends that provide us with cautionary tales, and those that are simply entertaining. Art Jahnke's essay, "What Ever Happened to Friendship?" illustrates important characteristics of essays that use classification as the dominant writing strategy.

WRITING BEFORE READING

Write a definition of friendship based on your own experience. Use examples of friends you have had to illustrate the qualities of a good friend.

What Ever Happened to Friendship?

Art Jahnke

Art Jahnke writes a weekly column for the Internet newsletter "Sound Off." He also writes articles about health management and Internet technology for other Internet publications. Jahnke has taught journalism for Harvard University's summer program, and his essays have appeared in many magazines and newspapers. At the time he wrote "What Ever Happened to Friendship?" in 1989, Jahnke was an editor for Boston *magazine.*

Once there were friends who were friends forever. Once there were lots of guys who were always there to shoot a few hoops, give us a lift downtown, or loan us a few bucks. And once there were lots of girls who would listen all night and never laugh, no matter how goofy or self-indulgent our complaints. We never worried about whether they would be there for us. What was there to worry about? There were lots of friends, and friends, true friends, were friends forever.

But something happened. Maybe it happened when we went away to college. Maybe it happened when we got married. Or when we started working 40, 50, and 60 hours a week. Or had kids. Or got divorced, changed jobs, and moved to another town.

Probably it happened little by little, year by year, as we grew up and as we did all the things that adults do. And one day we woke up and realized that this wasn't the way we thought it would be. Our friends were gone. And we wondered what ever happened to those guys and girls, those friends who didn't stay friends forever.

This is a story about what went wrong while we were all so busy doing what was right: marrying and having families and working the long days that would get us a home and get us ahead. . . . I'll try to tell you . . . what I know about the loss of friendship. . . . I'll put the different ways in which I have lost friends into three categories. The first, category A, of the ABCs of lost friends, is neglect. Here's how it works:

My oldest friend lives in eastern Connecticut, about an hour and 15 minutes from Boston. I've known this man since we were in the first grade, since we used to play with blocks together. In high school we caroused together: I remember my mother chastening him as he drove away from my house late one night, leaving me reeling in the driveway from too much beer.

After college we worked together as landscapers—sweating together, taking down trees and putting up stone walls, pissing together, and talking about the weirdness of John Milton, whose works we had studied with the same professor. When I left that job and headed south, for Mexico, I quoted to him from a poem written by the Chinese poet Li Po to a friend about 1,200 years ago:

> And if you ask how I regret that parting:
> It is like flowers falling at Spring's end
> Confused, whirled in a tangle.
> What is the use of talking, and there is no end of talking,
> There is no end of things in the heart.

7   Is it true that there is no end of things in the heart? I don't know. But I haven't seen my friend in five years. Because I moved? No. Because I got divorced? No. Because I re-married? No. It's because I haven't called him. Because I neglected to call.

8   Most of the people to whom I talked while researching this story were men and women whom I had met in either social or professional settings and who had impressed me as thoughtful, articulate, and sane. One of the first was David D'Alessandro, 38, pres-ident of the corporate sector at John Hancock. D'Alessandro is an interesting guy. Around town, he has the reputation of being a tough wheeler-dealer who knows his mind and speaks it. Hancock hired him five years ago to move the company's image out of colonial times and into the modern age. He is credited with Hancock's decision to spend $10 million on the Boston Marathon and $7 million on TV spots during football bowl games. He took over Michael Dukakis's advertising campaign in the last months of the Duke's doomed quest. When I told him I wanted to talk about the importance of friends, he chuckled.

9   "It's funny you should ask about that," he said. "It's something that has been on my mind a lot lately. Two years ago I realized that I had virtually no friends in Boston, yet male friendship is extremely important to me. I had just moved up here, and Boston is kind of a hard town to make friends in. I realized that the only people I really trusted were the people I grew up with in the old neighborhood."

10   When you're working 70 hours a week and have two young kids at home, D'Alessandro said, it's hard to find the time it takes to nourish friendships. And it's easy to neglect old friends.

11   I talked to a lawyer in Cambridge, a friend of a friend, an introspective guy with a preference for keeping his name out of print.

12   "I've got about three good friends," he told me. "Maybe a couple more. A half dozen, and they are primarily from the old neighborhood."

13   His friends are, he said, the people he would turn to at the time of a personal calamity: when a marriage is in trouble or when a parent dies. The trouble with those re-lationships, he said, is that marriages don't go bad very often and a parent dies only once. So there are many gaps between meaningful exchanges with his friends. If he turned to friends only when he or they were in need, how could he be sure that they would always be there?

14   "There is an understanding that they will be there," he told me, "and that I will be there for them. I don't know how implicit it is, maybe it's an adolescent notion, but I think it's fairly clear."

15   "When I think about what I'm going to do this weekend, it usually involves the kids," says this friend of a friend. "And if I'm not with the kids, then I want to be with my wife. As is, we never have enough time together. I seldom see my friends. I take my friends for granted, and when I think about that, I regret it."

16   Regret is a harsh word. It's a reminder of just how easily things go bad, of how we miss what shouldn't be missed, how we fail to see the obvious. It is also a subtle theme in a book I read: *Just Friends: The Role of Friendship in Our Lives,* by Lillian B. Rubin. I tracked Rubin to Berkeley, where she is working at the Institute for the Study of Social Change.

"One of the tragedies in our lives is that friendship is so undervalued as a relationship of permanence," she told me. "Love relationships are so overvalued. Despite all of the evidence in our lives that it doesn't work, people are still looking for that magical salvation from a love relationship, and they are ignoring the relationship that could offer them ongoing sustenance: friendship. One of the sad things about friendship is that it often gets put on hold when we get married or find a loved other."

"In childhood and in adolescence, friends are the people we turn to help us out of the family. That's what adolescent peer groups are about. They provide a transition and give us the support that enables us to leave the family. It's ironic that it is those very relationships that become the cause for our search for a new family. When you start a family, you are supported by a sense that everybody is doing it, and it is part of living—that it is disruptive not to do it. When the mating time comes, those close relationships tend to go by the boards."

My second category in the ABCs of lost friends may be less lamentable than the first but no less saddening. It is letting go, cutting bait—deliberately blowing off a relationship. Here's how it works:

I went back to my hometown a couple of years ago and looked up an old friend, a neighborhood kid with whom I used to shoot baskets after school. My idea was to relive old times. Maybe to revive the friendship.

We met at another friend's house, and he drove up in a car that was fast and Italian and worth about 10 times what my car was worth. On his arm was a woman who was approximately half his age. My old friend strolled in, sat down, and set about laying down lines of cocaine. He talked for an hour or two about how he had made his money, and when he was done I knew that I was not his friend anymore. I didn't want him for a friend.

Was I callous? Was I unduly judgmental? Was I being a prig? Should I have made an allowance and exempted my old (former) friend from the value system to which I now subscribed? I think not.

I talked to David Ross, a kind of middle-ground friend, who is the director of the Institute of Contemporary Art, and he told a similar story about an old friend of his who evolved into what Ross believes to be a less-than-respectable PR guy in New York. Ross no longer sees him, no longer wishes to.

Then a colleague at the office told me a story about an old friend of his who, after divorcing his wife, turned into a first-class cad. Like me, and like Ross, my colleague blew off his old friend and believed he did the right thing. But it wasn't an easy decision. Friendship may not get the kind of fawning press that we heap on romantic love, but its virtues have been celebrated for thousands of years. A simple glance at the literature of Western civilization reveals centuries of reverence for friendship, from the Greek tale of Damon and Pythias to the biblical story of David and Jonathan to television's "Cagney and Lacey."

And still, despite its history, friendship—that voluntary, nonsexual love affair between two people—perplexes social scientists no end. . . . Most of the social scientists I talked to couldn't even offer a definition of friendship.

26   I started with the psychology department at Harvard and was told that the university has no professors whose expertise is friendship. I called Tufts, where the psychology department chairman, Walter Swap, told me that the best person in the Boston area to talk to about friendship was Zick Rubin, who, Swap said, was teaching at Brandeis. . . . But when I called Brandeis, I was told that Rubin had quit studying friendship to go to law school.

27   I tracked down Rubin's home number and called him anyway. He was helpful and polite, but he didn't want to talk about friendship, he explained, because he had been away from his research for so long. Instead of giving me a definition of friendship, Rubin gave me a half dozen names and a few telephone numbers of academics who could help. The best, he said, may be Robert Weiss, a research professor at the University of Massachusetts and the author of *Loneliness: The Experience of Emotional and Social Isolation.* . . .

28   "It's very tough to say what a friend is," Weiss told me. "Essentially, it is someone we maintain a relationship with when there is no reason for doing so except for the relationship. There is no kinship obligation. It is not someone we work with, so there is no work obligation. It is not necessarily a neighbor, so there is no neighborhood obligation. That is an enormous opportunity to define a relationship."

29   I asked Weiss if there were certain kinds of people who became friends with each other. He said there were. "One recipe for friendship is the right mixture of commonality and difference," he said. "You've got to have enough in common so that you understand each other and enough difference so that there is something to exchange."

30   When I asked several people what friends do for friends, they gave me one of two answers: nothing or everything. What they meant is that friends lack . . . specific responsibilities. They don't even have unspoken, understood roles, as the members of most families do. In friendship, experts and most of the people I spoke with insisted, there are no obligations. But there are expectations, enormous expectations—tougher, deeper, and longer lasting than in any . . . relationships except perhaps those with family members. In fact, when those relationships crack—when a parent dies or when a marriage falls apart—a friend is expected to be there for emotional support.

31   "If I were seeking some feedback on a possible career change, or marital issues, or worrying about a father's failing health, I would turn to a friend," a 40-year-old Cambridge businessman told me.

32   "I use friends to play back events in my life that I want to understand better," Zella Luria, a psychologist at Tufts, told me. "Friendship is a way of comparing life's notes."

33   Luria said that she was not an expert on friendship but that she had read a few books about it, and the thing that fascinated her was the alleged difference between friendships among men and friendships among women.

34   "I think men have been given a bum rap," Luria said. "But if what I read about men's relationships is true, if there is really nothing more going on than meets the eye, then it's very sad. Men are truly bereft."

35   I asked psychologist Lillian Rubin about that.

36   "Can you imagine a man telling a friend that his wife was leaving him because she was dissatisfied with his sexual performance?" Rubin asked me.

"I doubt it," she said, answering her own question. "Not even in Cambridge. But a woman would talk to a friend about that kind of thing. The central difference between men friends and women friends is that men tend to *do* things together, women tend just to *be* together. It isn't that they don't do things, but in the process of just being together there is for women some kind of intimate exchange. With men, relationships are based on a kind of nonverbal bonding, the bonding that goes on while shooting baskets or watching a football game. One of those guys might have had some very bitter pill to swallow the day before—maybe with his wife or at work—but he is not likely to mention it. Yet this is exactly what women will talk about. 37

"Women will turn to women for that kind of talk because it is something that men do not do well," Rubin said. "Just look at the difference in the way men and women use the telephone. If a man wants to make a tennis date, he'll call up and say what time he wants to play and say, 'Meet you at the court.' If a woman wants to do the same thing, she will call up and say, 'Hi, how are you?' and talk for 20 minutes before making the date. Professional women will go to great lengths to maintain friendships, even when it means calling somebody up at 11 o'clock, when both of them should be asleep." 38

"I'm living through a threat to my friendships right now," Rubin told me. "I just got a job in New York, and it is playing havoc with my friends here, who are feeling abandoned. I can hear their pain and their anger and their envy because it's the idea that I'm leaving them for a new life. All that gets talked about." 39

"What is interesting about that is that for the woman, the one-on-one intimate friendships become very important and they remain very important for the rest of their lives. But the men will remain dependent on the women in their lives for their emotional needs, so for the men friendships will never really regain that kind of ascendancy." 40

There is a third category, the C in the ABCs of lost friends. It's the fastest, dirtiest, and most painful way to go. Psychologist Paul Wright calls it "a negation or a denial of a friend's personalized interest." David D'Alessandro calls it betrayal, a violation of the rules. 41

"The rules of my friendships are very simple," said D'Alessandro. "They are based on Italian tradition. Unless I tell you otherwise, assume that anything I tell you is confidential. When I lived in New York, I had a very good friend, a roommate who broke a confidence and told another friend something I did not want known. I moved out, and I haven't talked about it since." 42

It wasn't only macho Italian men who told me that they have no patience with friends who break the rules. A professional woman in her forties, call her woman A, told me this story. Her best friend, woman B, whom she had known for 10 years, betrayed confidences about woman A's future plans to a third person they both knew. When woman A found out, she didn't speak to woman B for five months, and then only after they had reaffirmed the rules of their relationship. 43

I heard stories about a different kind of betrayal: the betrayal that results from a failure to follow the rules of mutual aid. A friend told me that he had suffered months of shame because he wasn't there to help a friend weather an emotional breakdown. I know that scenario well. For years I watched from afar while a friend crept more deeply 44 into drugs, from recreational use to finally being a junkie. I watched as his wife left him. I watched as he lost his job, and I watched as they took him away to prison for writing bad checks. Did my friend feel betrayed? He should have.

45   A businessman I know said that he felt betrayed when a friend steadfastly refused to discuss his own divorce. "He walked out on his wife," the businessman said. "Because of the close relationship I have had with him for 20 years, I tried repeatedly to reach out. There was no acknowledgment on his part of responsibility for his action or for the damage. I felt that he wasn't playing by the ground rules of the friendship. I had expectations that certain things would happen. It was his failure even to talk about it that bugged me, and now the relationship has been soured."

46   One thing that I heard over and over again from the men and women I talked to was that it is easier to lose old friends than to make new ones—a sad formula for loneliness. . . .

47   The beginnings of my own friendships, I learned from psychologist Robert Weiss, are dishearteningly typical. They start in the office or on one of the racquetball or squash courts at the YMCA.

48   "A man will have a tennis friend," Weiss said. "A friendship will start with a small sense of reciprocity. There is almost always a sense of linkage that goes with it. *You* bring the balls this time, and *I'll* bring them next time. Soon you get a sense of the other person as a person, and you start to feel loyalties."

49   I know that. I see how a relationship grows. I learn that my partner is getting divorced. He learns that I have been through a divorce. It's a sadness that we share, our knowledge that love doesn't last forever. We both try to make it easy on the kids, and sometimes we succeed. But are we friends yet, as in "friends forever"? Maybe. I don't know. Both of us hardly have time to play ball, let alone hang out and talk.

50   Is he someone I'll call late at night when something is troubling me? Probably not. Probably, I'll do something else typical of men my age: I'll talk to my wife. Will he call me? And if he does, will I listen? Do I really have the time and energy to invest in a brand-new friendship? Does anyone?

51   After all, we're not kids anymore.

RESPONDING TO THE READING

FREEWRITING

Practice 6h. Freewrite about the passages you found most like your own experiences of friendship. What about them seemed familiar?

Practice 6i. What does Jahnke assume will happen to most friendships? Does your experience support or contradict his assumption?

Practice 6j. Are there additional categories you would like to add to Jahnke's list of the ways in which we lose friendships?

self-indulgent (1)	permanence (17)	colleague (24)
caroused (5)	sustenance (17)	fawning (24)
chastening (5)	by the boards (18)	expertise (26)
colonial (8)	disruptive (18)	alleged (33)
wheeler-dealer (8)	lamentable (19)	bereft (34)
introspective (11)	callous (22)	ascendancy (40)
calamity (13)	prig (22)	scenario (44)
implicit (14)	cad (24)	reciprocity (48)

QUESTIONS FOR DISCUSSION

1. Write a one-page summary of the main and supporting points in Art Jahnke's article. Which sections do you find most convincing? What writing strategies does he use most effectively?
2. What sources did Jahnke consult in his research for this article? Which of his sources gave you the most valuable information?
3. Notice that Jahnke does more than just list the categories of lost friendships. What subtopics does he explore for each? How do they add interest to his essay? How is each relevant to his overall discussion?
4. Which of the categories of lost friendships contains relationships that are most worth saving? Reread the examples in this section and suggest what might be done to save these friendships.

TOPICS FOR WRITING

Topic 1. Think about Robert Weiss's definition of friendship as "someone we maintain a relationship with when there is no reason for doing so except for the relationship." Write a paper in which you classify the friendships you have had or have still. Freewrite to gather details about the characteristics of those friendships. Ask yourself these questions:

Why were you friends?

What did you see in each other?

What did you do together?

What did you talk about?

What qualities about the other person made you his or her friend?

In what interesting ways were you different?

What common ground did you share?

What did your friend add to your life, and you to his or hers, that made this friendship work?

Once you have lots of information, organize it by grouping similar elements among the friendships and developing a topic idea that characterizes each group—steadfast friends and friends who betrayed you are two examples. Focus on "non-sexual love affairs" you have had with friends.

Topic 2. Jahnke quotes writer Lillian Rubin, who argues that "friendship is so undervalued as a relationship of permanence," while "love relationships are so overvalued." Write a paper in which you offer evidence from your own experience that either supports or contradicts Rubin's evaluation of friendship and love relationships.

Topic 3. Write a paper in which you analyze how well Art Jahnke's depiction of the loss of friends parallels your own experience. Which instances correspond to your experience and observations? Which contradict them? Consider using a T-graph to help you generate and organize ideas. On the left side list incidents from Jahnke's article, and on the right list your own experiences, observations, and reactions. (See page 213 for an explanation of the T-graph as a tool for organizing comparisons.)

Topic 4. Certain friends are good for certain things. Examine your own life and the lives of people you know to write about the different needs we have for different kinds of friends. Give numerous examples of each to establish your categories clearly.

CLASSIFYING: AN ANALYSIS OF "WHAT EVER HAPPENED TO FRIENDSHIP?"

Writers who use classification in their essays organize their ideas into parts or categories, which they then analyze in ways that distinguish each piece from other pieces or from other parts of a larger experience. For example, in the student sample of classification (page 161), Donald Inn separates the lion dance into three parts: the head, the tail, and the teaser. His analysis of the actors in each section clarifies the responsibilities and importance of their movements in the dance. In Art Jahnke's article, "What Ever Happened to Friendship," he identifies three ways we lose friends. In his analysis of each category of lost friendship, he describes these losses and explains why they happen.

CHARACTERISTICS OF CLASSIFYING

Purpose, Audience, and Point of View

Like essays that define or describe, classification essays need a purpose—a reason for grouping people, places, events, or objects into categories—and that purpose is usually stated in a thesis or implied in the body of the essay.

In the opening paragraphs of his essay, Art Jahnke establishes his point of view, audience, and purpose for writing "What Ever Happened to Friendship?"

Once there were friends who were friends forever. Once there were lots of guys who were always there to shoot a few hoops, give us a lift downtown, or loan us a few bucks. And once there were lots of girls who would listen all night and never laugh, no matter how goofy or self-indulgent our complaints. We never worried about whether they would be there for us. What was there to worry about? There were lots of friends, and friends, true friends, were friends forever.

But something happened. Maybe it happened when we went away to college. Maybe it happened when we got married. Or when we started working 40, 50, and 60 hours a week. Or had kids. Or got divorced, changed jobs, and moved to another town.

Probably it happened little by little, year by year, as we grew up and as we did all the things that adults do. And one day we woke up and realized that this wasn't the way we thought it would be. Our friends were gone. And we wondered what ever happened to those guys and girls, those friends who didn't stay friends forever.

This is a story about what went wrong while we were all so busy doing what was right: marrying and having families and working the long days that would get us a home and get us ahead. . . . I'll try to tell you . . . what I know about the loss of friendship. . . . I'll put the different ways in which I have lost friends into three categories. The first, category A, of the ABCs of lost friends, is neglect. Here's how it works.

Jahnke writes in the first person about his experiences with losing friends. By using the pronoun *we,* Jahnke makes a personal appeal to his readers and suggests that their experiences are probably similar to his own. Jahnke enhances this connection by explaining exactly what he intends to do: "I'll try to tell you . . . what I know about the loss of friendship." In addition, his examples identify the audience as anyone who has gone to college, married, divorced, had kids, worked long hours, moved, or changed jobs. In other words, he appeals to a broad reading population.

Jahnke's purpose is to explain what can go wrong with friendships. His thesis states how he will discuss these losses: "I'll put the different ways in which I have lost friends into three categories." He mentions the first category—neglect—in the introduction. The other two categories, rejection of someone no longer liked, and violation of personal rules, come up later in the essay.

Not all essays are as straightforward as Jahnke's, and in some essays, Jahnke's style of addressing the reader personally might not be appropriate. His style does, however, illustrate how audience, purpose, and point of view can work together in an essay.

Strong Support for Each Category

Experienced writers who discuss categories take care to provide adequate details, examples, definitions, and explanations for their categories. Not all categories will have equal importance in an essay, but each should have enough support to give readers a clear understanding of it.

Jahnke's discussion of his categories is lengthy and thorough. His explanations include personal experiences with the loss of friends and excerpts from interviews with experts and acquaintances. The following segment from his article illustrates the variety of sources he uses as evidence for the third category of lost friends.

Those sources include quotes from authorities on the subject of friendship, information gathered during interviews, the experience of a friend, his own experience, and an incident in the life of an acquaintance.

There is a third category, the C in the ABCs of lost friends. It's the fastest, dirtiest, and most painful way to go. Psychologist Paul Wright calls it "a negation or a denial of a friend's personalized interest." David D'Alessandro calls it betrayal, a violation of the rules.

"The rules of my friendships are very simple," said D'Alessandro. "They are based on Italian tradition. Unless I tell you otherwise, assume that anything I tell you is confidential. When I lived in New York, I had a very good friend, a roommate who broke a confidence and told another friend something I did not want known. I moved out, and I haven't talked about it since."

It wasn't only macho Italian men who told me that they have no patience with friends who break the rules. A professional woman in her forties, call her woman A, told me this story. Her best friend, woman B, whom she had known for 10 years, betrayed confidences about woman A's future plans to a third person they both knew. When woman A found out, she didn't speak to woman B for five months, and then only after they had reaffirmed the rules of their relationship.

I heard stories about a different kind of betrayal: the betrayal that results from a failure to follow the rules of mutual aid. A friend told me that he had suffered months of shame because he wasn't there to help a friend weather an emotional breakdown. I know that scenario well. For years I watched from afar while a friend crept more deeply into drugs, from recreational use to finally being a junkie. I watched as his wife left him. I watched as he lost his job, and I watched as they took him away to prison for writing bad checks. Did my friend feel betrayed? He should have.

A businessman I know said he felt betrayed when a friend steadfastly refused to discuss his own divorce. "He walked out on his wife," the business man said. "Because of the close relationship I have had with him for 20 years, I tried repeatedly to reach out. There was no acknowledgment on his part of responsibility for his action or for the damage. I felt that he wasn't playing by the ground rules of the friendship. I had expectations that certain things would happen. It was his failure even to talk about it that bugged me, and now the relationship has been soured."

In his discussion of the second category of lost friendships—letting go of a friend—Jahnke *defines* friendship for the reader. Here again, he offers his definition as well as the definitions of experts who have written books on the subject of human relations. Jahnke defines friendship as "that voluntary, nonsexual love affair between two people." Robert Weiss, professor at the University of Massachusetts, offers this definition of a friend: "Essentially, it is someone we maintain a friendship with when there is no reason for doing so except for the relationship. There is no kinship obligation. It is not someone we work with, so there is no work obligation. It's not necessarily a neighbor, so there is no neighborhood obligation." In other words, the relationship is an end in itself. Jahnke uses these definitions in later discussions of what makes a good friendship and in interviews in which he asks people what they think friends do for each other.

Clear Organization

In most essays organized by categories of experience, writers save the most important point for the end of their paper. The logic behind this arrangement is that people are more likely to remember the last thing they read. The organization also adds drama to the paper because it builds to its strongest point.

Jahnke makes the order of his discussion clear in topic sentences. He says, "The first, category A, of the ABCs of lost friends, is neglect." For the next thirteen paragraphs he explains how this particular abandonment occurs. He announces his second category with this topic sentence: "My second category in the ABCs of lost friends may be less lamentable than the first but no less saddening. It is letting go, cutting bait—deliberately blowing off a relationship." Twenty-two paragraphs later, and after much detailed support, he says, "There is a third category, the C in the ABCs of lost friends. It's the fastest, dirtiest, and most painful way to go. Psychologist Paul Wright calls it 'a negation or a denial of a friend's personalized interest.' David D'Alessandro calls it betrayal, a violation of the rules."

FOR PRACTICE

Practice 6k. What transitional words and phrases link the three topic sentences discussed above? What pattern of organization do they suggest?

THE WRITING PROCESS: CLASSIFYING

When you use classifying in your essay, you break a subject into categories or parts of experience and analyze each in detail. The following steps are designed to help you write an effective classification essay.

DEVELOPING A TOPIC

When you have a topic that asks you to classify experiences, people, or objects by category, think of specific details and events that you can group according to similar and contrasting qualities. Writing assignments in college sometimes ask you to analyze particular categories of experience. You might, for example, be asked to write a paper about different kinds of homeless people in the United States or effective strategies for solving math problems. If you must choose your own topic, the questions here and some of the topics that follow the readings in this chapter may help you find a good one.

What subjects have you read about in magazines, newspapers, or books that interest you? Are there subject areas your instructors have covered that you would like to investigate?

How can you break a subject into smaller categories?

What kinds of teachers, students, partners, pets, doctors, or politicians are there?

THINKING ABOUT YOUR AUDIENCE

After shaping a topic, ask yourself what you want to tell your readers about the topic. You might want to inform your audience about your topic—the kinds of bosses you have had, for example—to warn them what to watch for, or how to handle certain people and situations. On the other hand, you might want to entertain your readers with humorous descriptions of the ridiculous people you have met at work or the boring jobs you have held in the last few years. Yet another purpose might be to evaluate your categories. You might, for example, categorize the types of colleges you are considering for transfer or those you investigated before making your present choice. In this case, your purpose might be to advise fellow students which colleges offer the greatest number of courses for a particular major or the most well-qualified faculty.

Regardless of your purpose, you must offer enough details to develop your categories and make them distinct from one another.

DEVELOPING IDEAS

Once you have given some thought to your audience and know your purpose for writing, break your topic into categories; use the techniques for developing ideas—drawing an idea wheel, listing ideas, and asking questions—to help you gather information and evidence for discussing your categories. Don't overlook the possibility of interviewing experts or friends to gather additional material. The following questions may help you generate ideas:

What are the characteristics of each category?

What examples from your own experience or from interviews illustrate each?

What details, features, actions, or experiences are unique to any particular category?

What differences do you find among these categories that make them distinct?

When setting up categories and gathering details for discussion, consider drawing a graph to help you visualize your categories. Here is a three-column graph suggested by the three categories in Jahnke's essay:

Neglect	Letting Go	Betrayal

FOR PRACTICE

Practice 6l. Use a separate sheet of paper to add the details from Art Jahnke's essay in the appropriate columns here.

ORGANIZING IDEAS

If you are comparing categories or evaluating which is the most advantageous, important, or interesting, organize your ideas by their importance, saving the category you want to emphasize until the end. Arranging categories from most to least familiar is another possible arrangement.

Some of the transitional words and phrases that should be useful for writing classification papers are listed here:

To order ideas in time or according to importance	after, before, briefly, by this time, currently, during, eventually, finally, first, now, later, meanwhile, next, presently, recently, second, so far, soon, then, third, when, while
To introduce examples	especially, for example, for instance, namely, for one thing, in particular, the most, one of the most
To show contrast	although, but, however, in contrast, more than, nevertheless, on the other hand, than, unlike

SHARING AND REVISING

When revising your essay, you may wish to add the following questions to the checklist for revising found in Appendix C. Your instructor may ask that you share your draft during a peer review session. If you are in a computer-assisted class, you might participate in a workshop using a computer program that allows you to make comments and suggestions on essays written by fellow students.

Checklist

- ❑ Does the thesis anticipate a classification essay?
- ❑ Is the reason for writing the essay clear?
- ❑ Are categories distinct from one another?
- ❑ Are categories developed adequately?
- ❑ Would additional examples and explanations help to make one or more of the categories more convincing?
- ❑ How are the categories organized?
- ❑ Does the essay need transitions and topic sentences to provide smooth connections between categories?
- ❑ Is the organization effective, or should a category or two be rearranged?

Student Writing: Classifying

Donald Inn wrote this essay as a college freshman. He now holds a graduate degree in civil engineering.

The Art of Lion Dancing

For centuries, the Chinese people have practiced the art of lion dancing to celebrate the new year. This custom still goes on even in America to show respect for the gods and to symbolize the chasing away of evil and bad luck. Most Americans have seen the lion costume in magazines and may have watched part of the dance on the news. But very few who are not Chinese know much about the head, the tail, and the teaser—the three different roles played in lion dancing.

The lion's head, the most obvious and fearsome part of the beast, is supported on the shoulders of the man inside. His most important task is to learn how to bow. Bowing with the lion's head on your shoulders isn't just a simple matter of bending over. Rather, the bow is part of an elaborate, well-choreographed dance the lion must perform. First, he takes three steps forward with the head raised, lowers and raises the head gracefully, then walks backwards four or five steps, swinging the head from side to side. This movement creates the feeling that the lion is being courteous while keeping a watchful eye for anything evil. Next, he does several leg kicks while simultaneously positioning the lion's head to look up in the direction of the kicking leg. At the same time, the person operating the head must open and close the eyes and mouth and flap the ears. His hands operate the lion's mouth while his own mouth pulls on a string controlling the lion's eyes and ears. After about ten minutes, he is free to do any leg movements he chooses and to raise the head, turn, and shake it. The rest of the dance consists of improvisations created by the person in the head as he maintains the interest of the crowd.

Operating the tail does not require as many intricate movements as does working with the head. Three people work underneath the flowing, velvet tail connected to the back of the head. Their hands grasp the outer edge of the material; they lean forward, bringing their backs parallel to the ground, and point their arms at the ground. They flap their arms in coordination with each other to create a smooth, rippling effect up and down the length of the tail. Their eyes must look forward at all times to anticipate which direction the head will move so they can keep the head and tail looking united. Although their footwork needn't be as exact as the little ballet performed by the dancer inside the lion's head, they have the important job of keeping the tail looking alive, not dragging along behind the head. Also keep in mind that they must continue dancing with their backs bent uncomfortably toward the ground.

The teaser, although not part of the lion-body itself, is an essential player in the lion dance. He wears a painted, Mardi Gras-type mask and represents the evil being who torments the lion until it strikes back and chases the evil one away. The teaser carries a little paper lantern, and he makes his appearance ten minutes after the lion completes his bow. He waves the lantern in front of the lion's face, challenging him to give chase. Once the lion charges, the teaser must travel, on a path of his choice, down the streets of Chinatown. The teaser does not have any set rules or footwork. He randomly runs and jumps in front of the lion, zigzags through the street, and occasionally pauses to playfully tease some of the small children watching from the sidewalk.

Though performing the lion dance might seem to be just for fun, there are rewards that many people are unaware of. While the lion moves through Chinatown, shop owners hang traditional red envelopes with money inside on a stick outside their shops. As the lion passes the shops, someone comes out and waves the money in front of the lion to attract its attention. The beast grabs their money with its mouth, offers a bow of thanks, and moves on. At the end of the day, the lion dancers divide the well-earned money equally among themselves. Lion dancing takes a lot of hard work, but with practice and persistence, the dancers can reap monetary rewards and be proud of their part in this important seasonal dance.

—Donald Inn

RESPONDING TO THE READING

QUESTIONS FOR DISCUSSION

1. What are your impressions of the lion dance now that you have read Donald Inn's essay?
2. Who is Donald Inn's intended audience? What clues in the essay suggest that he is writing for this audience?
3. How effectively does Inn explain the art of lion dancing? Is there anything else you would like to know about the dance?

Making Connections

CHAPTER
7

The prominent writing strategies in this chapter—
process analysis, causal analysis, and comparing/
contrasting—introduce ways to make connections
between ideas. Tom Harris's essay, "How Urban Legends
Work," analyzes the process by which stories develop
into pop culture legends. The authors of "Immigrants:
How They're Helping to Revitalize the U.S. Economy"
analyze the effects that recent waves of immigrants
from Asia, Latin America, and Eastern Europe are
having on the economy. "Why Can't He Hear What I'm
Saying?", an article by Deborah Tannen, provides a
model for writing about differences between two
subjects—in this case, between the ways that men and
women communicate.

*Urban legends are simply the modern
version of traditional folklore.*
 —Tom Harris

*Studying the way people talk convinced
me that male-female conversation is
cross-cultural communication.*
 —Deborah Tannen

PROCESS ANALYSIS

Process analysis, the writing strategy for explaining how something works, involves breaking a subject into parts, stages, or categories to define or explain something about the parts you have identified. Tom Harris's essay, "How Urban Legends Work" explores how urban legends are created, how they are passed on, and what they mean.

WRITING BEFORE READING

Freewrite about stories you have gotten by e-mail, through the Internet, or by word of mouth that would qualify as "urban legends." Are there elements of these stories that you think are true?

How Urban Legends Work

Tom Harris

Tom Harris is the vice president of editorial and site production for the innovative website HowStuffWorks. *He holds a bachelor's degree in English from the University of North Carolina at Chapel Hill. Since Harris wrote the essay "How Urban Legends Work," his article has been republished in English textbooks.*

1   In 1994, the Las Vegas police reported a disturbing series of crimes along the Vegas strip. The first victim in this wave was an Ohio man in town for a sales convention. At the bar in his hotel, the man happened to strike up a conversation with an attractive young woman. According to the man, the two hit it off, sharing several drinks over the course of a couple hours. At some point, the man blacked out, and when he came to, he found himself lying in a hotel bathtub, covered in ice. There was a phone resting on the floor beside the tub, with an attached note that said, "Call 911 or you will die." He called an ambulance and was rushed to the hospital, where the doctors informed him that he had undergone massive surgery. One of his kidneys had been removed, apparently by a gang selling human organs on the black market. Following this occurrence, many similar crimes were reported, leading Las Vegas police to issue warnings to travelers visiting the city.

2   There's a good chance that you've heard this story, or some variation of it. News of the Vegas "organ harvesters" has been passed on by thousands and thousands of people over the course of 10 years. It has been relayed by word of mouth, e-mail and even printed fliers. But there is absolutely no evidence that any such thing ever occurred, in Las Vegas or anywhere else. This fictional story is a quintessential **urban legend,** an incredible tale passed from one person to another as truth.

3   In this article, we'll look at urban legends to see what they are, where they come from and why they spread so quickly. We'll also explore some ideas regarding the social significance of urban legends, as well as take a look at how the stories have changed over the years.

Generally speaking, an urban legend is any modern, fictional story, told as truth, that reaches a wide audience by being passed from person to person. Urban legends are often false, but not always. A few turn out to be largely true, and a lot of them were inspired by an actual event but evolved into something different in their passage from person to person. More often than not, it isn't possible to trace an urban legend back to its original source—they seem to come from nowhere.

While these "facts" don't always have the narrative elements of traditional legend, they are passed from person to person and frequently have the elements of caution, horror or humor found in legends. Particular urban legends may be spread either as fact or as a story. For example, someone could tell you that there are giant alligators in New York's sewers, or he could tell you a riveting story about a group of kids who stumbled upon such an animal.

Thematically, urban legends are all over the map, but several persistent elements do show up again and again. Typically, urban legends are characterized by some combination of humor, horror, warning, embarrassment, morality or appeal to empathy. They often have some unexpected twist that is outlandish but just plausible enough to be taken as truth.

In the story of the organ harvesters, you can see how some of these elements come together. The most outstanding feature of the story is its sense of horror: The image of a man waking up lying in a bathtub full of ice, with one less kidney, is a lurid one indeed. But the real hook is the cautionary element. Most people travel to unfamiliar cities from time to time, and Las Vegas is one of the most popular tourist spots in the world. The story also includes a moral lesson, in that the businessman ended up in the unpleasant predicament only after going to drink at a bar and then flirting with a mysterious woman.

This is what's called a cautionary tale. A variation of the cautionary tale is the contamination story, which has played out recently in the spate of reports about human body fluids being found in restaurant food. One of the most widespread contamination stories is the long-standing rumor of rats and mice showing up in soda bottles or other prepackaged food.

There are also a lot of contamination stories that have to do with the unintentional injection of drugs. One particularly pervasive legend reports that drug dealers have been coating temporary tattoos with LSD. The dealers give these tattoos to children, who put them on and absorb the LSD through their skin. Supposedly, this is a scheme to get the kids addicted to LSD so they become regular customers (a particularly doubtful notion, since LSD does not seem to be physically addictive). Despite repeated public announcements that this story is not true, concerned people continue to spread the word about these drug-laced tattoos, posting warnings in police stations, schools and other public places.

Not all urban legends deal with such morbid, weighty issues. Many of them have no cautionary or moral element at all: They are simply amusing stories or ordinary jokes told as if they really occurred. One common "news story" reports that a man took out an insurance policy on an expensive box of cigars, smoked them all and then tried to collect a claim, saying that they had been damaged in a fire. Another tale tells of a drunk driver who is pulled over by the police. The officer asks the man to step out of the car for a

4

5

6

7

8

9

10

sobriety test, but just as the test is about to begin, a car veers into a ditch up the road. The officer runs to help the other driver, and the drunk man takes the opportunity to flee the scene. When he gets home, he falls fast asleep on the couch. In the morning, he hears a loud knocking on his door and opens it to find the police officer from the night before. The man swears up and down he was home all night, until the officer asks to have a look in his garage. When he opens the door, he's shocked to see the officer's police cruiser parked there instead of his own car.

11   This story about the police car, in various forms, has spread all over the world. It even made it into the movie "Good Will Hunting," relayed by one of the characters as if it had happened to one of his friends. In the next section, we'll look at how urban legends like this one spread, and explore why so many people believe them.

Friend of a Friend

12   In the last section, we saw that urban legends are unusual, funny or shocking stories, relayed from person to person as absolute truth. The most remarkable thing about urban legends is that so many people believe them and pass them on. What is it about these stories that makes people want to spread the word?

13   A lot of it has to do with the particular elements of the story. As we saw in the last section, many urban legends are about particularly heinous crimes, contaminated foods or any number of occurrences that could affect a lot of people if they were true. If you hear such a story, and you believe it, you feel compelled to warn your friends and family.

14   A person might pass on non-cautionary information simply because it is funny or interesting. When you first hear the story, you are completely amazed that such a thing has occurred. When told correctly, a good urban legend will have you on the edge of your seat. It's human nature to want to spread this feeling to others, and be the one who's got everyone waiting to hear how the story turns out. Even if you hear it as a made-up joke, you might be tempted to personalize the tale by claiming it happened to a friend. Basically, people love to tell a good story.

15   But why does an audience take this at face value, instead of recognizing it is a tall tale or unsubstantiated rumor? In most cases, it has to do with how the story is told. If a friend (let's call her Jane) tells you an urban legend, chances are she will say it happened to a friend of somebody she knows. You trust Jane to tell you the truth, and you know she trusts the person who told her the story. It seems pretty close to second-hand information, so you treat it as such. Why would Jane lie?

16   Of course, Jane isn't really lying, and her friend wasn't lying to her—both of them believe the story. They are, however, probably abbreviating the story somewhat, and you will probably abbreviate it yourself when you pass it on. In this situation, the story happened to a friend of one of your friend's friends, but to simplify things, you'll probably just say it happened to a friend of Jane's, or even to Jane herself. In this way, every person who relays the story gives the impression that he or she is only two people away from one of the characters in the story, when in reality, there are probably hundreds of people between them.

The original source of an urban legend can be any number of things. In the case of   17
the LSD-coated temporary tattoos, the story most likely came from a misinterpretation
of an actual occurrence. While there is little evidence of LSD stickers being distributed
to kids, it is common practice for drug-dealers to sell acid on small pieces of blotter
paper, which dealers often stamp with a trademark cartoon character. It's a good bet
that somebody read about these "acid tabs," or saw a picture of one, and thought they
were temporary tattoos aimed at kids.

It's not clear who originally started the Las Vegas organ thief story. Most likely, it   18
was just somebody pulling one over on a friend. But we do know something about how
the legend really took off. A writer for the show "Law and Order" heard the story somewhere and worked it into an early episode. The show is well known for its "ripped from
the headlines" stories, so many viewers may have gotten the impression that the episode
depicted a real event.

Popular culture and urban legends are often closely related. Old legends end up as   19
plot points in movies, and fictional elements from movies are circulated as real-life
tales. In the latter case, somebody might start the legend because it's more exciting to
say that an event really happened than that it happened in a movie. Or maybe the person simply forgot where he or she actually heard the story.

Many people believe an urban legend must be true because it is reported by a news-   20
paper, or other "authoritative source." The persistence of Halloween stories (razors in
apples, needles in candy) is an example of this. There are no documented cases of contamination of Halloween candy, but the media and police issue warnings year after year.
Journalists, police officers and other authorities do get things wrong from time to time,
and most of them openly admit this. There is no infallible source of information.

Just about anybody can be duped into believing an urban legend because very few peo-   21
ple distrust everything and everybody. Most of us don't investigate every single piece of
information we hear—for efficiency's sake, we accept a lot of information as truth without
looking into it ourselves. Psychologically, we need to trust people, just for our own sense of
comfort. And if you trust somebody, you'll believe almost anything that person tells you.

In many cases, this trust runs so deep that a person will insist that an urban legend   22
actually occurred, even when confronted with evidence to the contrary. Urban-legend
Web sites like Snopes.com get a lot of e-mail from readers who are outraged because the
site is calling their friend a liar.

Another reason such stories get passed on is because the details make them seem real.   23
You may have heard stories of children being kidnapped from a specific location of a local
department store, or you may have heard about various gang initiations (more on this later)
that occurred in a specific part of your town. Since you are familiar with the setting—you
know it's a real place—the story sounds real. This level of specificity also plays into your
own fears and anxieties about what could happen to you in the places you visit regularly.

Urban legends are spread in cultures all over the world. In these diverse regions,   24
the familiar elements of horror, humor and caution show up again and again, though the
specific themes vary. In the next section, we'll explore the significance of urban legends
to find out what these persistent themes might say about the societies we live in.

What Do Legends Mean?

25 On the Internet and in universities all over the world, you'll find a lot of people interested in the role of urban legends in modern society. Many folklorists argue that the more gruesome legends embody basic human fears, providing a cautionary note or moral lesson telling us how to protect ourselves from danger.

26   The most famous cautionary urban legend is the "Hook-hand killer" tale. In this story, a young couple on a date drive off to a remote spot to "park." Over the radio, they hear that a psychopath with a hooked hand has escaped from a local mental institution. The girl wants to leave, but her boyfriend insists there's nothing to worry about. After a while, the girl thinks she hears a scratching or tapping sound outside the car. The boyfriend assures her it's nothing, but at her insistence, they eventually drive off. When they get to the girl's house, the boyfriend goes around to the passenger side to open her door. To his horror, there is a bloody hook hanging from the door handle.

27   The warning and moral lesson of this story are clear: Don't go off by yourself, and don't engage in premarital intimacy! If you do, something horrific could happen. When the story first circulated in the 1950s, parking was a relatively new phenomenon, and parents were terrified of what might happen to their kids. Most people who tell the story today don't take it very seriously. Like the tale of the vanishing hitchhiker, it has graduated from urban legend to "campfire ghost story," a tale passed on to others for amusement, not told as gospel truth.

28   As gang violence increased in the 1990s, cautionary tales began to focus more on criminal groups, rather than lone lunatics. In many cities around the United States, concerned citizens have been spreading a report of a gang initiation rite in which gang members drive at night with their headlights turned off. When another driver flashes his or her headlights to signal that their car's lights are out, the gang pursues and kills them. Even people who don't believe this wholeheartedly may err on the side of caution. After all, with so much gang violence going on, why take a chance by flashing your lights?

29   The rash of stories circulating about food contamination are a logical extension of the way Americans eat these days. More often than not, we are fed by faceless corporations and nameless restaurant employees. We're aware that we are putting a lot of trust in people we know nothing about, and this fear is played out in our urban legends. As a general rule, if an urban legend touches on something many people are afraid of, it'll spread like wildfire. Urban legends also express something about the individual who believes them. You are much more likely to believe and pass on legends that have some resonance with your personal fears or experience.

30   In this way, urban legends provide valuable insight into the cultures that create them. Legends evolve as cultures evolve, so new themes and variations pop up all the time.

31   People didn't begin talking about "urban legends" until the 1930s and 1940s, but they have existed in some form for thousands of years. Urban legends are simply the modern version of traditional folklore. In most cultures of the world, folklore has always existed alongside, or in place of, recorded history. Where history is obsessed with accurately writing down the details of events, traditional folklore is characterized by the "oral tradition," the passing of stories by word of mouth.

In this tradition, the storyteller will usually add new twists and turns to a story related by another storyteller. Unlike mythology, these stories are about real people in believable situations. Just as with modern legends, old folk tales often focus on the things a society found frightening. Many of the "fairy tales" we read today began life as believable stories, passed from person to person. Instead of warning against organ thieves and gang members, these tales relayed the dangers of the forest. In old Europe, the deep woods was a mysterious place to people, and there were indeed creatures that might attack you there. We do have a lot of fears in common with our ancestors, of course. As is clear in "Snow White and the Seven Dwarves," the fear of food contamination has been around for quite a while. 32

The methods of passing urban legends have also evolved over time. In the past 10 years, there has been a huge surge of urban legends on the Internet. The most common venue is forwarded e-mail. This storytelling method is unique because usually the story is not re-interpreted by each person who passes it on. A person simply clicks the "Forward" icon in their e-mail, and types in all his friend's e-mail addresses. Having the original story gives e-mail legends a feeling of legitimacy. You don't know the original author, but they are speaking directly to you. 33

Forwarded e-mail legends are often the work of one or more pranksters, not the product of many different storytellers. For these authors, the thrill is seeing how far a legend will spread. As with word-of-mouth legends, there are all sorts of e-mail hoaxes. Cautionary legends are very common in e-mail forwards, often focusing on made-up computer viruses or Internet scams. Even a skeptical person might forward this sort of message, just in case it's true. A similar sort of e-mail legend is the charity or petition appeal, which outlines a good cause or a horrible miscarriage of justice and then instructs you to add your name to a petition and send it on to everybody you know. There are real e-mail petitions, of course, and these do help out good causes. It can be tricky to spot a hoax, but one indicator is that the e-mail includes no address to send the list to when it is completed. Additionally, if a message begins with "This is not a hoax or urban legend," it probably is. 34

One of the most famous e-mail legends, the Neiman Marcus cookie recipe, combines a great story with an appeal to fight injustice. The e-mail is a personal account of a mother and her daughter eating at a Neiman Marcus store. After their meal, they order a couple of Neiman Marcus chocolate cookies, which they enjoy immensely. The mother asks the waitress for the recipe, and is told that she can buy it for "two-fifty." Later, when she sees the Neiman Marcus charge on her credit card, she realizes that she has been charged $250, rather than $2.50. The customer-service representative refuses to refund her money, because the company's recipe is so valuable that it cannot be distributed cheaply. In order to exact revenge on the company, the mother claims in the e-mail, she has decided to distribute the recipe freely over the Internet, and she encourages you to send it to everyone you know. 35

The recipe in the message does make delicious cookies, but they are not the sort sold at Neiman Marcus, and there is no $250 Neiman Marcus cookie recipe. In fact, when the message was first circulated, Neiman Marcus didn't even make such a chocolate chip 36 cookie. Amazingly, this story has been around in various forms since the 1940s. In the 1980s, the overcharging company was Mrs. Fields. Years before that, it was the Waldorf Astoria hotel in New York, and the recipe was for a "Red Velvet Cake."

37   These sorts of e-mail stories demonstrate just how deep-rooted urban legends are. No matter how much "information technology" we develop, human beings will always be drawn in by the unsubstantiated rumor. In fact, information technology actually accelerates the spread of tall tales. By definition, urban legends seem to have a life of their own, creeping through a society one person at a time. And like a real life form, they adapt to changing conditions. It will always be human nature to tell bizarre stories, and there will always be an audience waiting to believe them. The urban legend is part of our make-up.

RESPONDING TO THE READING

FREEWRITING

Practice 7a. Which of the urban legends that Harris recounts are familiar to you? What qualifies them as typical urban legends?

Practice 7b. Which of the categories of urban legends do you find most believable? What do you think accounts for their apparent truthfulness?

BUILDING YOUR VOCABULARY

quintessential (2)	pervasive (7)	heinous (12)	infallible (19)
empathy (5)	spate (7)	unsubstantiated (14)	gruesome (24)
persistent (5)	unintentional (8)	duped (15)	resonance (28)
plausible (5)			

QUESTIONS FOR DISCUSSION

1. How does Harris explain people's fascination with urban legends? What do you think these stories reveal about our interests and fears?
2. What roles do trust and distrust play in the making of an urban legend?
3. What effect might urban legends have on choices we make and the way we behave?
4. Summarize the most interesting or surprising point Harris makes in his essay. Explain your choice.

TOPICS FOR WRITING

Topic 1. Write a summary of the main points in Harris's essay, "How Urban Legends Work."

Topic 2. Interview several students and teachers on campus, and ask them to discuss urban legends they know and what they think makes them appealing stories. Then write an analysis of the most popular urban legends based on these interviews. Make sure to discuss elements in the stories that make them appealing.

Topic 3. Describe a story that you have heard lately that might make a good urban legend. Examine the elements that would make it believable.

Topic 4. Use the Internet on your home computer or one in your library or classroom to find examples of urban legends. Analyze at least two or three of the stories you find, and write an essay in which you discuss their origins, why you think people are interested enough to pass them on to their friends, or characteristics that make theses tales part of our culture's folklore.

PROCESS ANALYSIS: AN ANALYSIS OF "HOW URBAN LEGENDS WORK"

CHARACTERISTICS OF PROCESS ANALYSIS

Purpose, Audience, and Point of View

A process analysis may be written from the perspective of an observer, as a personal experience, or a mixture of the two. Each point of view conveys the writer's tone or attitude toward the subject. In "How Urban Legends Work," Tom Harris writes an objective, third-person analysis of what he has discovered about urban legends.

With process analysis, as with most writing strategies, the writer's approach to the subject, as well as the purpose for writing, is often stated in the introductory paragraphs. Harris draws the reader into his essay by retelling a shocking tale about a man who blacked out during a conversation with a woman in a bar and awoke to discover that his kidney had been removed. In paragraph 2, Harris reveals his attitude toward such urban legends: "But there is absolutely no evidence that any such thing ever occurred, in Las Vegas or anywhere else. This fictional story is a quintessential urban legend, an incredible tale passed from one person to another as truth." Harris lets us know that he is skeptical about such tales, and in revealing his opinion of these tales, he is also promising to take a reliable, reasonable look at them.

The second paragraph also establishes his audience. Harris notes that the legend of the "organ harvesters" "has been relayed by word of mouth, e-mail, and even printed fliers." In this statement and elsewhere in his essay, Harris makes it clear that he writes for a broad audience that includes anyone who uses the Internet, receives e-mails, watches television programs that are likely to incorporate urban legends in their scripts, or listens to friends and acquaintances recount stories they have heard.

Purpose, audience, and point of view are further clarified in paragraph 3, the thesis paragraph of Harris's essay.

> In this article, we'll look at urban legends to see what they are, where they come from and why they spread so quickly. We'll also explore some ideas regarding the social significance of urban legends, as well as take a look at how the stories have changed over the years.

Harris promises to take a clear-eyed look at what goes into the making and retelling of urban legends and what they say about the society that perpetuates them. Although his essay takes a no-nonsense, objective look at urban legends, Harris uses the pronoun *we* in his thesis paragraph and *you* in the second paragraph when he assures the reader, "There's a good chance that you've heard this story . . .". The use of *we* and *you* establishes an intimacy, a partnership with the reader as though the author and the reader are exploring the process that goes into the making of urban legends together.

A Clear Sequence

Like narration, a process analysis may be organized chronologically, that is, according to the order in which things occur during the process. In the student sample of process analysis, "Relationships in My Life" (pages 180–181), the author analyzes each of the stages in love relationships he has had. To organize this kind of analysis, writers divide their topic into parts or stages and explain each in turn. They may organize these divisions according to importance, ending with the most significant or, for emphasis, closing with a category they wish to stress.

Harris builds his ideas using order of importance to reveal successive stages of what goes into the making of urban legends. In the progression of ideas, he begins with a discussion of what an urban legend is, explains the categories of urban legends, discusses how urban legends get started, what makes them appealing enough to be passed on, how television programs and newspapers perpetuate these stories, and ends with the most profound side of urban legends—their significance as folk tales. In each stage of his discussion, Harris uses examples and analysis of the stories themselves to illustrate his points.

Transitional Words and Phrases

One of the challenges in writing a process analysis is to make smooth transitions between each part of the process. Harris achieves coherence in his essay not only by organizing his discussion as a clear sequence of ideas but also by using words and phrases that link one idea to another and tie paragraphs together logically. Because "How Urban Legends Work" presents several complex topics, Harris occasionally restates a point he promised to cover in the thesis to make the progression of ideas clear to the reader. For example, he occasionally stops his analysis to state the next topic for discussion, as he does in the transition from paragraphs 10 to 11: "In the next section, we'll look at how urban legends like this one spread, and explore why so many people believe them." He uses the same technique to move the reader from paragraph 23 to 24: "In the next section, we'll explore the significance of urban legends to find out what these persistent themes might say about the societies we live in."

Most of time, Harris's transitions are subtler. For example, following his discussion of why we need to trust people and how that leads us to accept stories we hear (20), Harris starts the next paragraph with the phrase: "<u>In many cases, this trust</u> runs so deep that a person will insist that an urban legend actually occurred . . ." (21). Notice how the underlined phrases move the reader smoothly from the discussion in one paragraph to further exploration of the subject in the next. Paragraph 22 connects seamlessly with the other two by the use of this phrase: "Another reason such stories get passed on . . ." Phrases that begin other paragraphs in Harris's essay also illustrate his effective use of transitions: "Generally speaking" (4), "This is what's called" (7), "In the last section" (11), "In this way" (29), "In this tradition" (31), "One of the most famous" (39), and "These sorts of e-mail stories" (36).

Writing Strategies

To help explain a particular process and to add interest to their process analysis, writers may use other writing strategies, such as narrating, defining, classifying, explaining a process, or comparing/contrasting.

Narrating. Tom Harris's essay, for example, uses an anecdote or story about a terrifying urban legend to pull the reader into his essay. He prefaces the story with this intriguing sentence: "In 1994, the Las Vegas police reported a disturbing series of crimes along the Vegas strip." His tale about "the first victim" includes a description of the man blacking out and waking up "in a hotel bathtub, covered in ice." Beside the tub, Harris tells us, the man found a note warning, "Call 911 or you will die." This story, which illustrates the tale of the "organ harvesters," not only gets his reader interested in the topic but also provides Harris with an excellent definition of an "urban legend."

Defining. Writers rely on definitions to clarify the meanings of their topic and the terms they will use in their discussion. In addition to the anecdote that begins "How Urban Legends Work," Harris provides a clear definition of his topic in paragraph 4 of his essay: "an urban legend is any modern, fictional story, told as truth, that reaches a wide audience by being passed from person to person." The tales themselves, he suggests, contain "some combination of humor, horror, warning, embarrassment, morality or appeal to empathy." In addition, "they often have some unexpected twist that is outlandish but just plausible enough to be taken as truth." With these elements of the urban legends clarified for the reader, Harris is now ready to discuss several categories of such tales to make them more understandable for the reader.

Classifying. To his initial, straightforward definition, Harris adds an analysis of two kinds of urban legends to help the reader appreciate the complexity and variety of these stories. The focus for this section of the essay (paragraphs 5 through 9) appears in Harris's mention of "several persistent elements" that "show up again and again in urban legends." He then analyzes the story of the organ harvesters for its "sense of horror," ultimately classifying this kind of tale as "cautionary," a tale that contains the "moral lesson" that drinking in bars and flirting with women you don't know can get you into serious trouble. Harris illustrates the category of the cautionary tale with another variety of urban legend, "contamination stories," which may involve rodents or human fluids appearing in packaged and bottled foods, or the unintentional intake of drugs.

A second category of urban legends is the "amusing story," told simply because it's entertaining. In one such story illustrating this type of urban legend, a man who has been drinking and driving mistakenly drives home in the police car of the officer who stopped him on suspicion of drunk driving.

Explaining a Process. In explaining how something works, writers may focus on the stages or steps involved in the task or situation. The most common use of process analysis is in cooking—we follow a series of chronological steps from the gathering of ingredients to the presentation of the dish we're preparing. Essays based on process analysis usually describe the parts or stages involved in a more abstract situation. For instance, Dan Krum, the author of the student essay that follows this discussion of process analysis, breaks the pattern his love relationships usually take into stages, from the initial infatuation to the final "indifference, mutual respect and friendship, or eventual commitment."

Harris's essay explores what goes into the making of urban legends, how they get started, how they are passed from person to person, and how that process has changed over time. Harris theorizes that most stories probably begin with a "misinterpretation of an actual occurrence" as did the rumor that drug dealers were distributing LSD to kids who thought the tabs were temporary tattoos. Actually, the dealers were using cartoon characters as trademarks for their drugs. He speculates that the organ story was probably intended as a joke that was passed on as truth. Regardless of how they began, urban legends appeal to our inherent love of storytelling, Harris explains. The cautionary tale travels from person to person because the teller may have some personal interest in the story or "feel compelled to warn [his or her] friends and family." Harris also provides psychological insight in to the making of urban legends when he points out that these stories often reflect what we most fear—that our children, and we ourselves, are in danger from enemies we don't know and can't identify.

Harris credits the media with accelerating the passing on of urban legends, another clue about how such stories are perpetuated. To support his point, he cites the television series *Law and Order,* which worked the organ theft story into one of its early episodes. Newspapers, he suggests, are responsible for keeping alive the tales of razors or needles hidden in Halloween candy in spite of the fact that no such stories of contaminated candy have ever been substantiated.

Comparing/Contrasting. By using comparison and contrast, writers introduce parallel or differing elements of a topic that are likely to be familiar to the reader. Sometimes, as in the case of Harris's essay, a comparison or contrast presents a topic in a larger context, broadening its meaning historically or culturally. In this way, Harris deepens his analysis of how urban legends work by concluding that these stories are a form of folklore, and, therefore, part of a tradition as old as human civilization. Like all folktales, ancient and modern, he argues, urban legends are part of the "oral tradition" of a culture. He supports this argument with a convincing look at the parallels between the traditional folktales and urban legends. For example, each storyteller adds his or her own personal flavor to the tale, and, unlike fairy tales and myths, these urban tales are about real people, and the stories are realistic enough that they could be about any of us.

Harris's discussion of how urban legends have evolved illustrates his use of comparative analysis to explain another way that urban legends are kept alive.

What was once communicated by word of mouth is now posted on the Internet or sent by e-mail to hundreds of people. He further demonstrates how things have changed but also stayed the same in his account of the "Neiman Marcus cookie recipe," a fabricated story that circulated in the 1940s as a recipe for "Red Velvet Cake" baked at the Waldorf Astoria and, forty years later, reappeared as a Mrs. Fields recipe.

THE WRITING PROCESS: PROCESS ANALYSIS

When you give directions to a lost motorist, explain to a fellow student how to write an effective essay, or recite a recipe for chocolate mousse, you are analyzing how something works. That is, you are breaking down a larger process in order to explain how to get the desired results or, as in the case of Harris's essay, how urban legends were developed and how they are perpetuated. Your ability to explain a process will help you write papers for a variety of subjects. You might, for example, describe the process of photosynthesis for a biology class, explain in a political science exam how to pass a bill in the state legislature, or, in a paper for an English class, advise fellow students about the procedures and pitfalls involved in registering for college classes. Writing assignments listed later in this chapter ask you to apply your skills to explain how something works.

DEVELOPING A TOPIC

An instructor may give you an assignment to write a process analysis that demonstrates your understanding of course material. If you must generate a topic of your own, it is best to pick one with which you are familiar or one in which you have a genuine interest. From the reader's point of view, the most interesting papers explore unfamiliar subjects or introduce a perspective that most people overlook.

If you have difficulty thinking of a topic, the following questions can also help you identify an interesting topic:

Have you taken part in a holiday or celebration lately? What happened?

How does the ceremony work?

Do you have any hobbies or talents that might make for interesting reading?

Are any tasks where you work engaging or dangerous?

What stages do you or people you know seem to go through when they apply for a job, fall in love, or purchase an automobile?

How does the selection process work at your school for making the football team, the debate squad, or some other competitive group on campus?

What steps must people go through to become citizens?

THINKING ABOUT YOUR AUDIENCE

As with descriptive writing, your task is to be interesting and specific as you analyze the workings of your subject. Before gathering details for your process analysis, it is important to have a good idea about your purpose, audience, and point of view. The following questions will help you make these decisions:

What process am I describing?

What are the major stages, parts, or categories in this process?

What is my purpose in explaining this process?

Who is my audience?

Am I writing an objective, third-person essay, or will I use my own voice (first person) to analyze my topic?

DEVELOPING IDEAS

When drawing an idea wheel or listing ideas, try separating your topic into parts and generating details for each part. Dan Krum, for example, might have drawn the following idea wheel to collect details for his analysis of the stages in a love relationship.

To generate details and explanations about your points, ask yourself a few of the following questions. Although the word *part* is used in these questions, you might wish to substitute *stage, step, category,* or *procedure,* depending on your topic.

What details can I use to describe each part?

Do any of these parts need defining?

What is the function of each part?

What does it contribute to the overall process?

How do the parts of this process work together?

Are there problems that should be avoided?

What are the consequences of not avoiding them?

Will a comparison with another topic or activity clarify my point?

ORGANIZING IDEAS

Make an outline from your list of ideas or idea wheel that represents the order of ideas you will follow in your paper. Try several different arrangements until you find one that makes the most sense to you. You may choose to follow a chronological order, as does Dan Krum, author of the student sample that follows. You might also emphasize the most important or dramatic stage in the process by discussing it last.

WRITING A FAST DRAFT

Using your outline as a pattern for the essay, write a fast draft to record as much detail as you can about the process you are discussing. Revise the essay several times; fill in details that add to your descriptions and explain the importance of each part. Be sure to proofread for omissions, and correct sentence structure, spelling, and punctuation.

SHARING AND REVISING

Use the following checklist to revise your paper either in a peer review or as part of an online forum.

Checklist

❑ Do I have a main point that clarifies my approach to the topic?

❑ What point of view have I used?

❑ Is the point of view consistent throughout the paper? (In other words, if the paper begins in the first person, does it maintain that perspective throughout?)

❑ Are parts of the process distinct from one another?

❑ Are descriptions clear enough for my readers to follow?

❑ Do any sections of the paper appear to be jumbled or out of order?

❑ Are discussions detailed enough or would some benefit from a more detailed description?

Student Writing: Process Analysis

Dan Krum writes this personal account of what happens in various stages of a love relationship.

Relationships in My Life

I have met many people, and out of these interactions I have found a few women that I wanted to get to know better. Although I don't do much conscious planning, I seem to go through certain stages in my progress from mild interest to love.

The first thing I do when entering a new relationship is to decide whether or not this woman makes me happy. Usually I make my decision very quickly without giving it much thought. One evening, for example, I may discover that my date is wearing a brightly colored dress that makes her look like Madonna or the gorgeous little sister of my last girlfriend. Suddenly I am convinced that this resemblance is the answer to my prayers. On one occasion in particular, I became deliriously happy because my date started staring at me for no reason, and when I turned to look back at her, she gave me a smile that could make roses bloom.

What follows this initial burst of happiness is a sickness that I call the "New Person Syndrome." This syndrome is like a disease that undermines my objectivity and makes me act like a love-sick puppy. During this phase, I make every attempt to find out where my new love works, where she is likely to eat lunch, what she does in her spare time. Whenever possible, I manage to "run into her" as if by accident, although I've actually planned the meeting. I have been known to sit outside a girl's house in my car, waiting for a glimpse of her. If she happens to appear, I'm instantly embarrassed by my own lack of control and slink down in my seat, hoping she doesn't see me. Basically this is the infatuation state, and it is needed to keep me interested in my partner long enough to get through the other two characteristics of "New Person Syndrome"—the insecurity and testiness. Whenever I'm not with the girl I love, I worry that she is seeing someone else. If I go through a weekend without being able to reach her, I convince myself that I have lost her. I'm irritable with my friends and roommate, and can't abide my parents. If an old girlfriend should have the bad luck to call me, I fly into a rage and accuse her of ruining a perfectly good relationship. My infatuation with a new person has its charm, but I'm always happy to move onto the next phase—"self-sacrifice."

Once the initial infatuation and uneasiness wear off, I volunteer to give up whatever freedom I have left because I am convinced that I'm in love. I rationalize giving up my independence by thinking romantic thoughts about

---

my gal and I sitting on a hilltop, speaking in low voices, unable to take our eyes off each other. Since I am so in love, I give up time I would ordinarily spend with friends to become totally faithful to my girlfriend. Monday night football with the guys, predatory weekends going from club to club—everything goes out the window for the sake of my own true love. Even though I may realize that I am in love with an ideal and not the person I am with, I still willingly sacrifice my independence in the name of love.

At this point in the relationship all the major sacrifices have been made and all that is left to deal with are a few difficulties like parental disapproval, quarrels over money, and disputes about seemingly insignificant things like who sleeps on which side of the bed. By parental disapproval, I am talking about trying to convince a pair of doting parents that I am a nice, responsible young man who is worthy of dating their daughter. On occasion I have worn my older brother's suit and tie, taken my girlfriend's whole family to dinner, or rented a limousine for the senior prom in order to impress her and her family. Money is always a problem, especially when I am trying to impress my girlfriend's parents. Finding someone who will loan me enough money to make a lasting impression on doubting parents requires a fair amount of conniving. The little things in a relationship are also important when you are adjusting to living with someone else. Figuring out which side of the bed belongs to whom sounds simple enough, but it's the kind of issue that reveals the first signs of conflict. How a couple works out the problem of perceived rights to an accustomed sleeping space will determine how other problems get solved later on. This phase of a relationship can be exciting as well as stressful. In my experience it is characterized by euphoria interspersed with headaches and sleepless nights.

Relationships that go beyond the "New Person Syndrome" usually go in one of several directions: toward indifference, mutual respect and friendship, or eventual commitment. I have avoided making too firm a commitment in any relationship because I have a lot of hard work ahead of me before I finish school. However, I have been lucky enough to develop one very strong friendship with a woman with whom I was once quite infatuated. Now we like to get together and talk about old times as well as more current issues in our lives. The remaining possibility—indifference—always takes me by surprise. I rarely see it coming, nor do I usually detect it in a partner. It can happen quite suddenly—one of us simply stops caring. If a relationship is headed for it, sooner or later deadly indifference will surface. When it does, I find it best not to question it but rather to pack my bags and leave my key at the door.

Any relationship is a lot of work because no two people are exactly alike, and we are all unpredictable. At times the whole business of relationships seems to be just one big hassle, but the times that I have weathered this storm, I have developed a very close and caring relationship with someone whom I love and who loves me.

—Dan Krum

QUESTIONS FOR DISCUSSION

1. What do you think are strong points of Krum's essay?
2. What suggestions do you have for revising it?
3. Write a letter advising Krum what he might do differently at each of the stages of love he identifies. Be sure to explain why he should follow your advice.
4. What tone does Krum adopt toward his subject and toward himself in this essay?
5. In what ways are Krum's descriptions of his relationships intensely personal? Are there times the essay approaches more universal themes? Do the personal and the universal ever converge?
6. Do you agree with Krum that relationships take "a lot of hard work"? How does your own experience support this claim? Are there concerns that Krum has omitted from his analysis of love's progress?

CAUSAL ANALYSIS

The discussions of process analysis and comparing and contrasting in this chapter, as well as the discussion of classifying in Chapter 6, will help you write about the causes of a certain event or the results of a particular action. At this point, drawing distinctions among these strategies might be helpful. Process analysis describes *how* things happen; causal analysis explains *why* they happen or what the *results* will be. Classifying involves grouping similar experiences, ideas, or behavior, and discussing characteristics common to each category. Similarly, discussing causes or effects requires grouping events or behavior that *caused* something to happen, or that *resulted* from a particular action or circumstance. Comparing and contrasting involve discussing similarities and differences. Causal analysis employs these skills when *causes are weighed against effects* or important reasons and results are *compared* to those of lesser importance. Characteristics of comparative essays are discussed later in this chapter. "The Immigrants: How They're Helping to Revitalize the U.S. Economy" illustrates some of the characteristics of essays that use causal analysis as the dominant writing strategy.

WRITING BEFORE READING

Freewrite about a controversy over immigration that has been in the news lately either in your state or in a state with a high percentage of immigrants—New York, California, or Florida, for example. What are your impressions of the controversy you chose? What might have influenced your opinion of immigrants?

The Immigrants: How They Are Helping to Revitalize the U.S. Economy

Michael J. Mandel and Christopher Farrell

Christopher Farrell is a contributing editor for Business Week. *His radio commentary,* Sound and Money, *is produced by Minnesota Public Radio and broadcast to 200 stations in the United States.* Business Week *also publishes the* Sound and Money *commentaries online. Michael J. Mandel is chief economist at* Business Week *and the author of* High Risk Society: Peril and Promise in the New Economy *(1996). He received the Gerald Loeb award in 1998 for his defining work on the "new economy." In this essay on effects of immigrants on the U.S. economy, Mandel and Farrell address the controversial question of whether the United States should reject its traditional role as a haven for immigrants or embrace the new arrivals. Their analysis of the positive effects of immigrant populations on the U.S. economy supports their position that the United States should preserve its identity as an immigrant nation. This article first appeared in the July 13, 1992, issue of* Business Week.

> *Give me your tired, your poor,*
> *Your huddled masses yearning to breathe free. . . .*

These words carved into the base of the Statue of Liberty speak to America's vision of itself. We were, and still are, a nation of immigrants. In the 1980s alone, a stunning 8.7 million people poured into the U.S., matching the great immigration decade of 1900–10. But with the country facing difficult economic and social problems, is it time to put aside our romantic past and kick away the immigrant welcome mat? 1

A lot of Americans feel the answer is "yes." In a *Business Week*/Harris poll, 68% of respondents said today's immigration is bad for the country, even though most thought it was good in the past. [Former] President Bush found it politically expedient to refuse refugees from Haiti.[1] And in areas like recession-weary Southern California, immigrants are being blamed for everything from rising unemployment to a rocketing state budget deficit. "I understand, in the past, 'give me your tired, your poor.' Today, the U.S. has to look at our own huddled masses first," says former Colorado Governor Richard D. Lamm,[2] who ran for the U.S. Senate. 2

This rising resentment against immigrants is no surprise. The million or so immigrants—including 200,000 illegals—that will arrive in the U.S. this year are coming at a time when unemployment is high and social services strained. Unlike past waves of immigration, the new immigrants are mainly from Asia and Latin America. And just like the American work force, these immigrants are split between the highly skilled and well educated and those with minimal skills and little education. Hungry for work, the 3

---

[1] In his first term as president, Bill Clinton also denied Haitian refugees entry into the United States.
[2] Richard D. Lamm, director for the Center for Public Policy and Contemporary Issues, University of Denver, and former governor of Colorado, challenged Ross Perot for the Reform Party's nomination for president in 1996.

newcomers compete for jobs with Americans, particularly with the less skilled. The large number of untrained immigrants, especially those from Mexico, are finding it harder to move up the employment ladder than did past generations of newcomers. And in the cities, the new immigrants seem to inflame racial and ethnic conflicts.

4   But on balance, the economic benefits of being an open-door society far outweigh the costs. For one thing, the U.S. is reaping a bonanza of highly educated foreigners. In the 1980s alone, an unprecedented 1.5 million college-educated immigrants joined the U.S. work force. More and more, America's high-tech industries, from semiconductors to biotechnology, are depending on immigrant scientists, engineers, and entrepreneurs to remain competitive. And the immigrants' links to their old countries are boosting U.S. exports to such fast-growing regions as Asia and Latin America.

5   Even immigrants with less education are contributing to the economy as workers, consumers, business owners, and taxpayers. Some 11 million immigrants are working, and they earn at least $240 billion a year, paying more than $90 billion in taxes.[3] That's a lot more than the estimated $5 billion immigrants receive in welfare. Immigrant entre-preneurs, from the corner grocer to the local builder, are creating jobs—and not only for other immigrants. Vibrant immigrant communities are revitalizing cities and older sub-urbs that would otherwise be suffering from a shrinking tax base. Says John D. Kasarda, a sociologist at the University of North Carolina at Chapel Hill: "There is substantial evidence that immigrants are a powerful benefit to the economy, and very little evi-dence that they are negative."

6   In 1965, when Congress overhauled the immigration laws, nobody expected this great tide of new immigrants. But that law made it easier to bring close relatives into the country and, influenced by the civil rights movement, eliminated racially based barriers to immigration. Prior to that, it was difficult for anyone who was not European or Canadian to settle here. The result: a surge of immigrants from Asia and Latin America, especially from countries like South Korea and the Philippines that had close economic and military ties to the U.S. And once a group got a foothold in the U.S., it would con-tinue to expand by bringing over more family members.

New Wave

7   The aftermath of the Vietnam War provided the second powerful source of immigrants. Over the last 10 years, the U.S. granted permanent-resident status to about 1 million refugees, mostly from Vietnam, Cambodia, and Laos. And now the end of the Cold War is tapping another immigrant stream: Over the last three years, the fastest growing group of new settlers has been refugees from Eastern Europe and the former Soviet Union.

8   Throughout the 1970s and 1980s, a total of some 5 million illegal immigrants from Mexico and other countries settled in the U.S., drawn by opportunity here and fleeing economic troubles at home. Many settled in Southern California and Texas. In 1986, Congress passed the Immigration Reform & Control Act (IRCA), which imposed penalties

---

[3] In a more recent report, the American Immigration Law Foundation estimates that "immigrant households and businesses pay more than $162 billion in direct taxes to federal, state, and local govern-ments each year" (2002).

on employers who hired illegal immigrants but also gave amnesty to many illegal immigrants. About 2.5 million people have become permanent residents under the amnesty program. And the pending North American Free Trade Agreement, by strengthening economic ties between Mexico and the U.S., might very well increase illegal immigration in the short run rather than diminish it.

Opening the gates to Asians and Latin Americans dramatically altered the face of immigration. In the 1950s, 68% of legal immigrants came from Europe or Canada. In the 1980s, that percentage fell to only 13%. Conversely, the proportion of legal immigrants coming from Latin America and Asia rose from 31% to 84%, including illegal aliens granted amnesty under the 1986 law.   9

As the ethnic mix of the new immigrants changed, so did their levels of skill. At the low end, the plethora of low-wage service-sector jobs drew in a large number of unskilled, illiterate newcomers. About one-third of immigrant workers are high school dropouts, and one-third of those entered the U.S. illegally.   10

But the number of skilled immigrants has been increasing as well. "The level of education of recent immigrants has definitely increased over the last 10 years," says Elaine Sorensen, an immigration expert at the Urban Institute. About one-quarter of immigrant workers are college graduates, slightly higher than for native-born Americans. Some groups, such as Indians, are on average much better educated than today's Americans. Observes Steven Newman, an executive at the New York Association for New Americans, which will resettle about 20000 immigrants from the former Soviet Union this year, including many engineers, computer programmers, and other skilled workers: "The only thing they lack is English skills."   11

Talent Base

Even immigrants who were doing well in their home countries are being drawn to the U.S. Take Subramonian Shankar, the 43-year-old president of American Megatrends Inc., a maker of personal-computer motherboards and software based in Norcross, Ga. He was director of personal computer R&D[4] at one of India's largest conglomerates. Then in 1980, he came to the U.S. In 1985, he and a partner founded AMI, which last year had sales of $70 million and employed 130 workers, both immigrants and native-born Americans. "I couldn't have done this in India," says Shankar. "That's one good thing about America. If you're determined to succeed, there are ways to get it done."   12

And U.S. industry has been eager to take advantage of the influx. About 40% of the 200 researchers in the Communications Sciences Research wing at AT&T Bell Laboratories were born outside the U.S. In Silicon Valley, the jewel of America's high-tech centers, much of the technical work force is foreign-born. At Du Pont Merck Pharmaceutical Co., an $800 million-a-year joint venture based in Wilmington, Del., losartan, an antihypertensive drug now in clinical trials, was invented by a team that included two immigrants from Hong Kong and a scientist whose parents migrated from Lithuania. People from different backgrounds bring a richness of outlook, says Joseph A. Mollica, chief executive   13

---

[4] Research and development.

of Du Pont Merck, "which lets you look at both problems and opportunities from a slightly different point of view."

14   The next generation of scientists and engineers at U.S. high-tech companies will be dominated by immigrants. While about the same number of Americans are getting science PhDs, the number of foreign-born students receiving science doctorates more than doubled between 1981 and 1991, to 37% of the total. In biology, the hot field of the 1990s, the number of non-U.S. citizens getting doctorates tripled over the last 10 years. And about 51% of computer-science doctorates in 1991 went to foreign-born students. "We are getting really good students—very, very smart people," says Victor L. Thacker, director of the office of international education at Carnegie Mellon University, which has doubled its foreign enrollment since 1985.

Up the Ladder

15   Attracted by the research opportunities and the chance to use what they know, about half of them stay in the U.S. after graduation, estimates Angel G. Jordan, a professor and former provost at Carnegie Mellon, who himself emigrated from Spain in 1956. And the 1990 changes to the immigration law, by increasing the number of visas for skilled immigrants, will increase the number of foreign graduates who remain in the U.S.

16   Besides boosting the nation's science and engineering know-how, the latest wave of immigrants is loaded with entrepreneurs. Korean greengrocers and other immigrant merchants are familiar sights in many cities, but the entrepreneurial spirit goes far beyond any one ethnic group or single line of business. Almost by definition, anyone who moves to a new country has a lot of initiative and desire to do well. Says Dan Danilov, an immigration lawyer based in Seattle: "They're willing to put in more hours and more hard work."

17   And do they work. Paul Yuan, for example, left Taiwan with his wife in 1975, seven days after their marriage, eventually settling in Seattle with several thousand dollars in life savings and no work visas. For two years Yuan, a college graduate, worked in Chinese restaurants. Then, in 1978, he became a legal resident and opened his own travel agency while working nights as a hotel dishwasher. Today, at age 43, Yuan owns a thriving Seattle travel business, and he and his family live in a $4 million house. In 1965, 21-year-old Humberto Galvez left Mexico City for Los Angeles. He started pumping gas and busing tables, working his way up the ladder, with a lot of bumps along the way. After starting, then selling, the chain of 19 "El Pollo Loco" charbroiled chicken restaurants in the Los Angeles area, he now owns six Pescado Mojado (wet fish) seafood diners, employing 100 workers.

18   Immigrant entrepreneurs have also made big contributions to the U.S. export boom. Businesses run by immigrants from Asia, for example, have ready-made connections overseas. Immigrants bring a global perspective and international contacts to insular American businesses. And it is not just Asians. From Poles to Mexicans, "the utility of the immigrant groups is that they bring their fearless spirit of competing globally," observes Michael Goldberg, dean of the University of British Columbia's business school.

That's certainly true for Benjamin and Victor Acevedo, two brothers whose family   19
moved from Tijuana, Mexico, to California in 1960, when they were 3 and 8. In 1984, the
Acevedos started up a wood-products company in the south San Diego community of
San Ysidro, just across the U.S.–Mexico border. CalState Lumber Sales Inc. now commands 10% of the architectural molding market in the U.S. and had 110 employees and
$147 million in sales last year [1991] . And as long-term trade barriers with Mexico crum-
bled over the past few years, the Acevedos have been able to take advantage of their
bicultural heritage. "My brother and I started shipping all over Mexico, and our export
business boomed," says Ben Acevedo.

Urban Boosters

Perhaps the least-appreciated economic benefit from the new immigrants is the contri-   20
bution they are making to American cities. Immigrants have been drawn to the major
metropolitan areas. They are invigorating the cities and older suburbs by setting up
businesses, buying homes, paying taxes, and shopping at the corner grocery. In the past
decade [1980–1990], population in the nation's 10 largest cities grew by 4.7%, but without
new immigrants it would have shrunk by 6.8%, according to calculations done by *Business Week* based on the 1990 census. Almost a million immigrants came to New York
City in the 1980s, more than offsetting the 750,000 decline in the rest of the city's population. Indeed, about a third of adults in New York, 44% of adults in Los Angeles, and 70%
of adults in Miami are now foreign-born, according to the 1990 census.

Immigrants have turned around many a decaying neighborhood. Ten years ago,   21
Jefferson Boulevard in south Dallas was a dying inner-city business district filled with
vacant storefronts. Today, there are almost 800 businesses there and on neighboring
streets, and about three-quarters of them are owned by Hispanics, many of them first-
and second-generation immigrants. "They were hungry enough to start their own businesses," says Leonel Ramos, president of the Jefferson Area Assn. And sociologist
Kasarda adds: "There is a whole multiplier effect throughout the community."

Moreover, immigrants provide a hardworking labor force to fill the low-paid jobs   22
that make a modern service economy run. In many cities, industries such as hotels,
restaurants, and child care would be hard-pressed without immigrant labor. At the
Seattle Sheraton, 28% of the hotel's staff of 650 is foreign-born, and most work in
housekeeping, dish-washing, and other low-paying jobs. "We don't have American-born
people apply for those positions," says Carla Murray, hotel manager for the Seattle
Sheraton.

Margin Dwellers

But all the economic vitality immigrants add comes at a price. While economists and em-   23
ployers may celebrate industrious immigrants, many barely survive on the economy's
margins. "They don't go to the doctor, don't buy insurance, don't buy glasses, don't buy
anything you or I are used to," says Hannah Hsiao, head of the Employment Program at
the Chinese Information & Service Center in Seattle. A firing, unpaid wages, a deporta-
tion, or some other calamity is always threatening. And racial discrimination makes

their lot even harder, especially those who don't speak English. Some, like economist George J. Borjas of the University of California at San Diego, worry that these poor and unskilled immigrants are condemned to years of poverty.

24   In many cities, newcomers and long-time residents struggle over jobs and access to scarce government resources. Immigrants are straining health and education services in some cities and suburbs. And many African-Americans believe the apparent success of immigrants is coming at their expense. In New York City, blacks picketed a number of Korean greengrocers. According to the *Business Week*/Harris poll, 73% of blacks said businesses would rather hire immigrants than black Americans.

25   The people hurt worst by immigrants are native-born high school dropouts, who already face a tough time. They compete for jobs against a large number of unskilled immigrants, including illegals from Mexico and the Caribbean who are poorly educated, unable to start their own businesses, and willing to work harder for lower wages than most longtime residents.

26   For Americans who have at least a high school education, however, the influx of immigrants hasn't had much negative impact. High school graduates, for example, saw their real wages decline by 10% in the 1980s. But almost all of that drop came from import competition and rising skill requirements of many jobs, and only a fraction from immigrant competition, according to a study by Borjas of UC, San Diego, and Richard Freeman and Lawrence Katz of Harvard University. "It is extremely convenient to point a finger at immigrants," says Muzaffar Chishti, director of the Immigration Project for the International Ladies' Garment Workers' Union in New York. "But the problems of black employment are outside the immigrant domain."

27   Moreover, for all their struggles, most immigrants are hardly wards of the state. Illegals are not eligible for welfare,[5] and even many legal immigrants shun it, fearing that it will make it harder to become a citizen in the future. A study by Borjas shows that in 1980—the latest national data available—only 8.8% of immigrant households received welfare, compared to 7.9% of all native-born Americans.[6] And with the education and skill levels of immigrants rising in the 1980s, the expectations are that the spread between the two hasn't worsened and may have even narrowed. In Los Angeles County, for example, immigrants amount to 16% of the 722,000 people on Aid to Families with Dependent Children, the government's main welfare program. Yet immigrants are more than 30% of the county's population. "Immigrants benefit natives through the public coffers by using less than their share of services and paying more than their share of taxes," says Julian L. Simon, a University of Maryland economist.

School Daze

28   One real concern is whether urban school systems can handle the surge of immigrant children. "The public school is the vehicle through which the child of immigrants

---

[5] Since the 1996 Welfare Reform Act, undocumented immigrants are not eligible for most welfare benefits.
[6] According to the PBS report "The New Americans" (2003), immigrants earn $240 billion a year, pay $90 billion in taxes, and collect $5 billion in welfare.

becomes Americanized," says Jeffrey S. Passel, a demographer for the Washington-based Urban Institute. But in many cities, the task of educating immigrant students has become an enormous burden. In Los Angeles, 39% of the city's students don't speak English well, and in Seattle, 21% come from homes where English is not the family's first language. In the nation's capital, the school system is nearly overwhelmed by a huge number of Vietnamese, Haitian, and Salvadorean children. "If the school system is inadequate, then it's much more difficult to help immigrants move up the economic ladder," says Robert D. Hormats, vice-chairman of Goldman, Sachs International and head of the Trilateral Commission's working group on immigration.

City schools, despite the constraint of tight resources, are finding innovative ways   29 to reach immigrant children. In Seattle, about half the immigrant students speak such limited English that they qualify for a program where they are taught subjects in simplified English. The Los Angeles schools offer dual language classes in Spanish, Korean, Armenian, Cantonese, Filipino, Farsi, and Japanese. Other organizations, such as unions, are also teaching immigrants English. In New York, the Garment Workers Union, often called the immigrant union, offers English classes to its members and their families.

In the coming decade, it won't be easy to assimilate the new immigrants, whether   30 they come from Laos or Russia. But the positives far outweigh any short-term negatives. In today's white-hot international competition, the U.S. profits from the ideas and innovations of immigrants. And by any economic calculus, their hard work adds far more to the nation's wealth than the resources they drain. It is still those "huddled masses yearning to breathe free" who will keep the American dream burning bright for most of us.

RESPONDING TO THE READING

FREEWRITING

Practice 7c. Freewrite about immigrants you have known or have read about. Compare these examples to the profiles in "The Immigrants."

BUILDING YOUR VOCABULARY

stunning (1)	vibrant (5)	insular (18)
respondent (2)	sociologist (5)	molding (19)
expedient (2)	substantial (5)	invigorate (20)
minimal (3)	amnesty (8)	vitality (23)
inflame (3)	conversely (9)	deportation (23)
bonanza (4)	plethora (10)	calamity (23)
unprecedented (4)	conglomerate (12)	wards (27)
semiconductors (4)	influx (13)	coffers (27)
biotechnology (4)	doctorate (14)	demographer (28)
entrepreneurs (5)	initiative (16)	assimilate (30)

QUESTIONS FOR DISCUSSION

1. Describe the writing strategy that the authors of "The Immigrants" use in the first three paragraphs. Why do you think they waited until the fourth paragraph to state the thesis? Explain why you think this tactic is effective or ineffective.

2. Carefully reread the sequence of ideas from "The Immigrants" that are listed on pages 192–193. Why do you think the writers chose this particular order? Rearrange sections of the article so paragraphs that discuss causes and effects appear in a different order. Is this new order more or less effective than the original arrangement of ideas? Explain your answer.

3. What reasons do the authors give in support of their position that immigrants have a positive effect on the American economy? Which reasons do you find most convincing and why? What examples of these or other effects have you seen?

4. What solutions to the negative effects of immigration do the writers discuss? How effective do you think they would be in answering critics' objections to immigration? Offer evidence in support of your answer.

5. Who might be the audience for the magazine *Business Week,* the periodical in which this article first appeared? Refer to evidence from the article to help you describe these readers. How might the interests of this audience explain the writers' positive view of immigration?

TOPICS FOR WRITING

Topic 1. Conduct your own survey of a dozen friends, relatives, or classmates to examine their views of immigrants' effects on the economy. In the course of your interview, you might ask them (1) whether they think of immigrants as mostly skilled or unskilled, (2) whether immigrants contribute to or deplete the economy, and (3) whether the respondents or someone they know has had to compete with immigrants for jobs. Once you discover your interviewees' attitudes toward immigrants, ask them to explain what experiences or observations contributed to that attitude. Spend some time organizing the data you gathered, and write an essay in which you categorize the attitudes you uncovered and explain two or three reasons why the respondents developed these attitudes.

Topic 2. Interview fellow students or other people you know who have immigrated to the United States to discover the reasons why people emigrate from their home countries. Write an essay in which you explain these reasons using the experiences of people you interviewed as support for your ideas.

Topic 3. Write an essay in which you provide updated research for two or three points Mandel and Farrell make about the role of immigrants in the United States. Analyze the economic effects of documented and/or undocumented immigrants on the U.S. economy.

EXPLAINING CAUSES AND EFFECTS: AN ANALYSIS OF "THE IMMIGRANTS: HOW THEY ARE HELPING TO REVITALIZE THE U.S. ECONOMY"

Writers who choose causal analysis may choose to discuss causes, effects, or both. For example, researchers battling the AIDS epidemic in the 1980s were most interested in finding the causes of AIDS in order to develop an effective cure. For their article in *Business Week,* Michael J. Mandel and Christopher Farrell are primarily concerned with the effects that immigrants have had on the U.S. economy in the last few decades. Many scientific papers on global warming are concerned with both the causes and the effects of the changes in the Earth's weather patterns. Because the analysis of causes and/or effects can be quite complex, writers must have a clear focus and direction for their essays. The discussion that follows illustrates how Mandel and Farrell achieve focus, support, and coherence for their essay on the economic role of immigrants in the United States.

CHARACTERISTICS OF CAUSAL ANALYSIS

Point of View

Writers who wish to analyze why a situation exists or to examine its results may adopt a subjective (first person) or an objective (third person) point of view, depending on their topic. Dympna Ugwu-Oju, author of "Pursuit of Happiness" (pages 358–360) writes about how she balances her Ibo values with what she considers the more self-centered concerns of her American cohorts. The authors of "The Immigrants: How They Are Helping to Revitalize the U.S. Economy," on the other hand, choose an objective point of view when discussing reasons U.S. citizens may feel that it is not in the best interests of this country to accept more immigrants. They maintain that perspective as they counter with an analysis of the positive economic effects that the influx of immigrants has had on the American economy.

The writers make their point of view and the purpose of their essay clear in the opening paragraphs of "The Immigrants":

> *Give me your tired, your poor,*
> *Your huddled masses yearning to breathe free. . . .*

These words carved into the base of the Statue of Liberty speak to America's vision of itself. We were, and still are, a nation of immigrants. In the 1980s alone, a stunning 8.7 million people poured into the U.S., matching the great immigration decade of 1900–10. But with the country facing difficult economic and social problems, is it time to put aside our romantic past and kick away the immigrant welcome mat?

A lot of Americans feel the answer is "yes." In a *Business Week*/Harris poll, 68% of respondents said today's immigration is bad for the country, even though most thought it was good in the past. [Former] President Bush . . . found it politically expedient to refuse refugees from Haiti. And in areas like recession-weary Southern California, immigrants are being blamed for everything from rising unemployment to a rocketing state budget deficit. "I understand, in the past, 'give me your tired, your poor.' Today, the U.S. has to look at our own huddled masses first," says former Colorado Governor Richard D. Lamm, who is running for the U.S. Senate.

In addition to establishing an objective point of view, these paragraphs clarify the kind of information the authors will use to support their discussion. In the opening paragraphs, they do not draw on their own experience to support their analysis. Instead, they rely on statistics, an example (former president Bush's refusal of asylum to Haitian refugees), and testimony—in this case the testimony of a former governor who represents one perspective on immigration. At other places in the article, the authors quote experts in a particular field.

A Main Point or Thesis

Authors of causal analysis need to identify clearly the causes or effects they will discuss. The first two paragraphs of "The Immigrants" introduce ideas that the writers address near the end of their article. The thesis or main point of the article appears at the beginning of paragraph 3: "But on balance, the economic benefits of being an open-door society far outweigh the costs." This statement prepares the reader for an analysis of the positive effects that immigrants' entry into the United States have on the economy. We might also note that the authors use the thesis to answer the question raised at the end of the first paragraph: "is it time to put aside our romantic past and kick away the immigrant welcome mat?" Their answer is "the economic benefits of being an open-door society far outweigh the costs."

FOR PRACTICE

Practice 7d. Why do you think the authors of "The Immigrants" began their essay with a question? What effect does the question have on the essay's opening?

A Clear Sequence of Ideas

Clear organization is important in any paper, but it is imperative with writing strategies as complex as causal analysis. "The Immigrants" is a good example of how effective an analysis can be when the writers are able to make clear distinctions between effects and causes, arrange them logically, and address critics' concerns. Most of this article addresses the causes of current immigration patterns, skill levels of recent immigrants, and the effects of their presence on job competition and education. Transitional phrases signal movement from one topic to another. The following list shows the order in which the writers discuss their points.

Refer to American tradition reflected in Emma Lazarus's famous poem (paragraph 1).

Acknowledge opposition to immigration (paragraphs 2–3).

Discuss *effects* of immigration in immigrants' contributions to high-tech industries and to the tax base (paragraphs 4–5).

Discuss historical *causes* of recent immigration from Asia, Latin America, and Eastern Europe (paragraphs 6–9).

Discuss varied skill levels of the new immigrants (paragraphs 10–12).

Discuss *effects* of these workers' entry into the labor force (paragraphs 13–19).

Discuss immigrants' positive *effects* on inner cities (paragraphs 21–22).

Address the negative *effects* of immigrants who compete for low-skilled jobs (paragraphs 23–27).

Discuss the *effects* immigrant children have on schools (paragraphs 28–29).

Conclusion rephrases the thesis (paragraph 30).

Information Mapping

Another organizational technique deserves mention. Writers whose articles are several pages long often use a technique called information mapping, which involves the use of headings to guide the reader from one point to another. The authors of "The Immigrants" use six headings: "New Wave," "Talent Base," "Up the Ladder," "Urban Boosters," "Margin Dwellers," and "School Daze" to announce major topic breaks. Furthermore, these headings break up large blocks of writing and help the reader identify important points discussed in the article.

Clear Reasoning

Several techniques are involved when a writer presents a convincing, well-reasoned analysis of causes and effects. For one thing, ideas must have detailed support. As we saw in the opening paragraphs of "The Immigrants," evidence for causes and effects comes from statistics, examples, and testimony. In paragraph 5, statistics illustrate the amount of taxes collected from working immigrants; at the end of that paragraph, the authors quote sociologist John D. Kasarda to make their final point about the immigrants' contribution to the U.S. economy. The authors also rely on examples from the lives of immigrants, as in the discussion of the Indian entrepreneur in paragraph 12. Surveys conducted by *Business Week* (paragraph 2) and research done at universities (paragraphs 26 and 27) provide additional evidence.

Causal analysis examines more than one cause or effect. Few events in life have only one cause or produce a single effect. Writers of causal analysis recognize that to do justice to the complexity of most topics they must discuss multiple causes and effects. In "The Immigrants," for example, the writers examine several reasons why American citizens might feel threatened by these newcomers. Some are afraid that immigrants will compete for scarce jobs. Others fear they will place a tremendous burden on limited resources or exacerbate ethnic conflicts, especially in the inner cities. The authors also discuss causes of the current influx of Asian, Latin American, and Eastern European immigrants: the 1965 revision of the immigration laws and the passage of the Immigration Reform and Control Act, the end of the Vietnam War, the collapse of the Soviet Union, and economic problems in Latin America. The numerous effects of the government's accepting the numbers and kinds of immigrants it does are also examined in detail. These effects, both positive and negative, include the impact of immigrant workers on businesses, job competition, the tax base, the condition of inner cities, and the costs of social services like welfare and education.

For a causal analysis to be convincing, it must show the reader that the author has examined not only possible causes and effects but has also looked at the issue from several points of view. The authors of "The Immigrants" begin their article by acknowledging legitimate objections to the open-access attitude toward immigration that they feel is part of our heritage (paragraphs 1–3). They address these concerns in greater detail in paragraphs 23–29. At the end of the article they reach the conclusion that despite the costs of accommodating the new arrivals, "the positives far outweigh any short-term negatives."

THE WRITING PROCESS: CAUSAL ANALYSIS

DEVELOPING A TOPIC

The topics for writing in this chapter suggest several assignments for practicing causal analysis. To develop a topic of your own, you might examine journal entries that would lead to a discussion of causes or effects. Think of major events in your life or the lives of people you know. Pick one of these events and examine its causes or effects. If, for example, gas prices have gone up in your area, or schools have had to eliminate some teachers, leading to increased class size, you might interview people to see how these changes are affecting their lives. Newspaper articles will also give you information about the effects of such events.

Perhaps a local or national issue has piqued your curiosity recently. You might write about how it became an issue or what its effects have been. If you decide, for example, to investigate how immigrants might be contributing to the revitalization of an inner city, research databases that collect news articles to find information on this topic. You might also contact the Chamber of Commerce of an urban area near you to see if they are aware of immigrant-owned businesses that have started up in the past five to ten years. Once you have gathered information from three to five sources, write a paper with an introduction that states your thesis and paragraphs that provide supporting evidence from your sources. For help planning your research paper and citing sources, see Chapters 15 and 16. For a review of paraphrasing, see pages 16–17 on writing summaries.

THINKING ABOUT YOUR AUDIENCE

It is helpful if you think about purpose, point of view, and thesis as you gather information and write your paper. Your purpose may change as you develop and organize your ideas; that's normal in writing. To keep your main point clear in your own mind, try answering the following questions before you begin writing, and revise them as your paper develops.

What causes or effects will I examine?
What is my purpose for writing about these causes or effects?
Who is my audience?
What point of view will I adopt?

DEVELOPING IDEAS

Use any of the preliminary writing techniques that work best for you. These additional questions may be useful:

> What situation will you discuss?
>
> What are some immediate causes or effects?
>
> What do you think will be long-term or lasting causes or results?
>
> Which cause is most important? Why?
>
> How might physical conditions, events, behavior, attitudes, assumptions, laws, values, or regulations cause a situation to exist? How might one or more of these be the effects of a situation?
>
> Are there other points of view you should consider when discussing causes or effects for this topic?
>
> What additional causes or effects might these points of view suggest?
>
> Do causes or effects follow one another in time, or, as in "The Immigrants," do some occur simultaneously?

ORGANIZING IDEAS

There are several ways to organize a causal analysis. If the causes or results follow one another in time, you will probably want to use chronological order to arrange them. If, on the other hand, causes or effects occur simultaneously, as they do in "The Immigrants," then order of emphasis or importance works well. Here are a few possible patterns for cause–effect essays.

Pattern 1

1. Identify problem or event
   Thesis
2. Discuss causes of that problem or event
3. Conclusion

Pattern 2

1. Identify problem or event
   Thesis
2. Discuss effects of that problem or event
3. Conclusion

Pattern 3

1. Identify problem or event
   Thesis
2. Discuss effects of that problem or event
3. Discuss solutions
4. Conclusion

Pattern 4

1. Identify problem or event
   Thesis
2. Discuss effects of that problem or event
3. Discuss the causes of that problem or event
4. Discuss solutions
5. Conclusion

WRITING A FAST DRAFT

As you write your essay, be careful not to settle for *one* cause or result. Only the simplest, and usually the least interesting, situation has merely one cause or effect. Even something that may seem straightforward may not really be so simple on closer examination.

Let's say, for example, that your cousin Max tripped on a skateboard left on a landing and fell down the stairs. What are the possible causes of his fall? The most immediate is the skateboard itself, but his own behavior might have contributed to the fall. Perhaps he was reading a book, thinking about something else, or simply not watching where he was going. He might, on the other hand, have been running to get somewhere and may not have seen the skateboard in time to avoid the accident. It's good practice when writing a causal analysis to consider as many possible causes or outcomes as you can. Once you have a list of these, choose the most important and most plausible for your essay.

When you are examining more serious issues, it is even more important to look at several causes before drawing your conclusions. For example, if you are analyzing a decrease in the rate of unemployment in the United States, you need to look at several things. First, it is important to understand that unemployment rates measure the percentage of people who recently lost their jobs and are collecting unemployment insurance. This means that a decrease in the rate of unemployment may be caused by a possible increase in job opportunities, which means people have gone back to work. Another possibility is that some people may no longer be looking for work; they may have become homeless, or even if they are still trying to find a job, their allotted time to collect unemployment insurance may have expired. These kinds of causes and effects are important to think about when examining statistical information.

SHARING AND REVISING

Use the following checklist when revising your paper. You might also complete a peer review or online commentary using these questions.

Checklist

- ❑ Does the introduction present the essay's point of view and topic?
- ❑ Does the thesis state the causes or effects discussed?

- Is the point of view objective or subjective? Is this point of view maintained throughout the essay?
- Do paragraphs discuss a sufficient number of causes or effects, or are there others that might be included?
- Does the essay include adequate support for the causes or effects discussed?
- Is the paper organized clearly enough that the reader can follow the ideas presented?
- Do transitions make it clear when the essay moves from one cause or effect to another?
- If the writer includes source information, is that information documented correctly? Is the list of works cited accurate?
- Does the conclusion follow logically from the discussion of causes and effects?
- Has the essay been proofread carefully for sentence correctness, spelling, and punctuation?

Student Writing: Causal Analysis

Misty Kent's research led her to some startling discoveries about America's obsession with celebrities. Her essay presents her analysis of the topic. The sources she refers to in her paper are cited by author's last name or a brief title of the article if the author's name isn't stated. Numbers in parentheses refer to the page of the citation in printed sources. For detailed guidelines about writing a research paper, see Part IV.

Americans' Obsession with Celebrities

Celebrity culture hits Americans from every angle, saturating every aspect of the media, from the Internet and television, and to the headlines in newspapers. Americans appear more interested in celebrity divorces and wardrobes than the war in Iraq or the actions of the president. One star-crazed student referred to keeping up with serious news events as something "like eating Brussels sprouts" (Jaffe). She, like many others, prefers to follow the lives of the rich and famous, who appear to have a "real" life, rather than follow the depressing headlines that might possibly affect her. Americans follow celebrity life at least in part because the media create an interest in celebrities. The media splatter intimate details of stars' personal lives in every possible way, and the advertising industry uses them to sell merchandise. For some people, this information may be just a passing interest, for others it represents an attempt to fill a personal void, but for some this can become an extreme obsession. Whether the media, personal insecurity, or pure self-gratification is to blame, Americans have a long-standing curiosity about the lives of celebrities.

America's love affair with celebrities began in the 1930s when "real" life was extremely stressful and the movies were a refreshing escape from reality. According to David McNair, a writer for <u>Oldspeak</u> magazine, "celebrity worship took

---

hold in America during the Depression" when Americans welcomed the distraction. Hollywood "offered a seductive, larger-than-life representation of reality" in the movies and on the radio, creating a make-believe world that provided Americans with an escape. This fantasy life drew "eighty million people a week" to the theatres and increased record sales by 600% in the 1930s (McNair). This increased exposure to celebrities no doubt contributed to Americans' interest in them and helped shape the celebrity culture of today.

The media continue to bear the primary responsibility for creating and feeding our craving for knowledge of celebrities. Tabloid magazines and TV gossip shows keep us updated on celebrities' every move. We hear about everything from where they just had lunch to how many parking tickets they received in a month. Who doesn't know that Brad Pitt and Jennifer Aniston, or the newest high-profile couple, just broke up? Our frequent exposure to these stars' personal lives intensifies our obsession with them. According to Carlin Flora in "Seeing by Starlight: Celebrity Obsession," "we're built to view anyone we recognize as an acquaintance ripe for gossip or for romance" (36). This false feeling can cause us to believe that we actually know these people and need to follow up on their mundane affairs. If we hear that Gwyneth Paltrow is pregnant, then we will naturally want to know the sex of the baby and learn about any difficulties during the birth. Sometimes we may know more details about famous people's lives than about the lives of our own friends. According to McNair, "In many ways, we get to "know" these famous people in a more intense, intimate way than we do the people we work with or see on a daily basis." In some cases, there's a question as to whether these "stars" are really worth knowing.

Clearly, the attention the media give these celebrities fuels our obsession and more and more celebrities are considered famous only because of their exposure in the media, not for their talents. Mick Hume, editor for The Times in London, wrote, "fame was once seen as recognition for your accomplishments in the world. Now, it just means being recognized in public." Celebrities in the past may have worked harder to achieve their status. An actress like Audrey Hepburn started acting as a young woman on Broadway, then worked her way into movies. Her hard work coupled with her unique style and grace resulted in her receiving five Oscars, a testimony to her true acting ability. Today, "pop singers and soft porn stars can all be lumped together and feted as celebrities" (Hume). Today it takes only wealthy parents to ensure the celebrity of an Evana Trump, or outrageous behavior, like that of the Hilton sisters, to make you famous. Paris Hilton, heiress of the hotel fortune, became famous after her personal sex tape was published; she enjoys fame and recognition because of her willingness to participate in a pornographic film. Her notoriety suggests that if you can get media attention, good or bad, chances are you will become famous. With the attention shifting from true talent to raw publicity, the former requirements for becoming well-known, or for that matter, for becoming the next role model for our children, have disappeared.

One reason for the relentless presence of celebrities in the media is the increasing use of such figures to sell products. Advertisers market their goods by giving celebrities on their payroll "an artificial importance" (Wikipedia). Everywhere we look we find faces we recognize as "famous" selling everything from cosmetics and hair products to motor oil. George Foreman, a former heavyweight champion boxer, retired his boxing gloves for the "Lean Mean Fat-Reducing Grilling Machine." The Salton brand grill had poor sales until Foreman brought attention to its potential as a low-fat cooker and, with his help, the manufacturer sold over "375 million grills in 2002" (Cabell). The majority of modern day celebrities advertise for several companies; hence, Foreman is also a spokesperson for Meineke and McDonald's. Pepsi has used celebrities such as Michael Jackson and Britney Spears to sell its popular soft drink, and for years Nike has used Michael Jordan to sell shoes. Americans are easily persuaded to purchase merchandise that celebrities are endorsing in hopes of being a little more like "them." Famous people can sell us just about anything because, we reason, if "it works for [them], it will work for me, too" (Cabell). Such frequent, persuasive advertising not only gets Americans to buy whatever celebrities are selling but it also contributes to our familiarity with the stars, and thus provides another way of fostering our obsession with them.

The familiarity, undoubtedly, keeps us tuned into the lives of famous people, but is the real reason we follow celebrity culture because we need to feel good about ourselves? In his article published in Psychology Today Carlin Flora reveals that "catching sight of a beautiful face bathes the brain in pleasing chemicals," which shows a personal payoff for this guilty pleasure (Flora 36). If we are getting a rush of feel-good chemicals each time we read a tabloid, then we could be drawn to these shallow magazines subconsciously, hoping for another "fix." Flora himself admitted to being personally star-struck after being introduced to Britney Spears: " I confess, I felt dizzy." Although he admits that he wasn't even a fan of Spears, he still felt a "contact high" and reported their meeting to his associates. After analyzing his reaction, Flora explains that "they [celebrities] live in a parallel universe—one that looks and feels just like ours yet is light-years beyond our reach" (36). This fascination with the beautiful people who appear to live in fairy tales affects the old as well as the young. Flora concludes that "It wasn't just that I saw Britney; it was that Britney saw me" (87). The admiration and "contact high" we feel when we meet someone famous may be more about us and the gratification we get than about them.

Another possible reason for following celebrities, one more dangerous and potentially unhealthy than the others, could be a desire to fill a spiritual need or personal void. An article in Wikipedia compared modern-day celebrity fame "to that of royalty or gods in the past" ("Celebrity Culture"). Americans have put these celebrities on a pedestal and made them worthy of their worship and admiration. It makes sense that one of the most popular television programs is titled "American Idol." Psychologist James Houran points out that people who lack religion in their lives are "more interested in celebrity culture" than those involved with religion (qtd. in Flora 37). It makes sense that a religious person who is focused on a clear set of moral and spiritual values, and who is active in programs associated with a religious community, will not need to follow every detail in the lives of media celebrities. Mick Hume reports that Americans in general are experiencing "a collective loss of faith, which has left behind the void now being filled with an overblown celebrity culture." This "overblown celebrity culture" leaves people feeling empty and all too eager to shift attention from meaningful relationships to the "false intimacy" they crave with these celebrities. The problem is that this false relationship "creates unrealistic expectations and makes disappointment and self-loathing all but inevitable" (McNair). People are left feeling "alone in the relationship," realizing that they have created a bond with someone they don't even know. This "unhealthy fascination," which has been identified in the <u>Journal of Nervous and Mental Disease</u> as "Celebrity Worship Syndrome," can leave people feeling that their own lives are devoid of meaning, and they may even develop severe depression (McNair).

Such extreme cases are evident in our society. With celebrities replacing real role models in our culture, young Americans often become overly concerned with physical looks and go too far in their quest to look like their favorite idols. A popular MTV show called "I Want a Famous Face" films young people who are obsessed with their favorite celebrities and follows them through the long, painful process of getting plastic surgery to make their own features resemble those of their celebrity icon. MTV followed a set of 10-year-old twins, Mike and Matt, who appeared on the show. The brothers went through surgery to look like their favorite celebrity, Brad Pitt, in hopes of attracting girls and possibly making it in Hollywood ("I Want"). When asked why he picked Brad Pitt's face, Mike responded, "I knew that if I imitated Brad Pitt's appearance, I would be happy with mine". Since the surgery, the boys "have not been mistaken for Brad Pitt," but they did report overall satisfaction with the results and bragged that "girls tell us all the time that we really look good." The sad thing is that when asked what advice they would give other teens wanting plastic surgery to look like their favorite stars, they said, "If you know that surgery will make you happy, go for it." Encouraging this risky, intrusive medical procedure for teens with low self esteem is not only an example of how celebrity worship is affecting young people but is also a frightening reminder of just how self-destructive and superficial the obsession with celebrity really is. As film critic Richard Schickel points out, "our obsession with celebrity has given the power of personality authority over the power of ideas, ideologies, and even authentic human connections" (qtd. in McNair).

Celebrity worship continues to haunt American culture and invade our lives. A local writer, Michael Santore, gave his opinion on celebrity obsession in a recent feature article: "Celebrity worship is probably the biggest tragedy in journalism and news reporting" (6). It is a tragedy that affects television, movies, and radio as well, and it is an affliction suffered by far too many Americans.

Works Cited

Cabell, A. K. "Celebrity Endorsements Reach for the Stars." <u>Brandhome</u> 5 May 2006. <http:www.brandchannel.com/features_effect>.

"Celebrity." <u>Wikipedia.</u> 12 April 2006. <http://en.wikipedia.org/wiki/Celebrity>.

"Celebrity Culture." <u>Wikipedia</u> 27 April 2006.
    <http://en.wikipedia.org/wiki/Celebrity_culture>.
Flora, Carlin. "Seeing by Starlight: Celebrity Obsession." <u>Psychology Today</u>.
    12 April 2006: 36–40, 87.
Hume, Mick. "The Fame Game." <u>Spiked Life</u>. 1 May 2006. <http://www.spiked-
    online.com>.
"I Want a Famous Face." <u>MTV News</u>. 8 May 2006.
    <http://www.mtv.com/onair/i_want_a_famous_face.com>.
Jaffe, Dana. "Celebrity Obsession Becomes Extreme." <u>The Auburn Plainsman</u>
    30 March 2006. <http://www.theplainsman.com>.
McNair, David. "Celebrity Culture in America." <u>Oldspeak</u>. 27 April 2006.
    <http://www.rutherford.org/oldspeak/articles/culture.com>.
Santore, Michael. "Street Talk." <u>Sacramento News and Review</u>. 27 April 2006:6.

—Misty Kent

QUESTIONS FOR DISCUSSION

1. What was Misty Kent's purpose for writing "Americans' Obsession with Celebrities"? Who was her intended audience?
2. Identify the primary reasons Kent gives to explain why Americans are fascinated with celebrity culture. Which of these discussions do you think is most convincing? Explain what makes it so compelling.
3. In a small-group discussion or a forum online, analyze any additional aspects of celebrity culture that you have observed.

COMPARING AND CONTRASTING

The author of *Gulliver's Travels,* Jonathan Swift, wrote, "Undoubtedly philosophers are in the right when they tell us that nothing is great or little otherwise than by comparison." Swift was saying that we can judge the true size of a thing only by comparing and contrasting it with other things. If, for example, we ask a man who is six feet tall to stand beside a California redwood that measures ten feet in diameter and is three hundred feet tall, we get a much better idea of just how large the redwoods are. Similarly, to appreciate a certain condition, attitude, or event, we might compare it with something like or very unlike it.

Comparative analysis is another important writing strategy that writers use to make connections between similar or dissimilar things. It is important, however, that the comparison has a specific purpose, a clear reason for making such connections. For example, in "Becoming an American," the student essay at the end of this chapter, Tony Nuñez compares his experiences as an English-language learner to the stories Elizabeth Wong tells about her assimilation into American culture. Deborah Tannen's essay, "Why Can't He Hear What I'm Saying?" provides examples of how to organize and develop a comparison that illustrates why men and women have difficulty understanding each other.

Even in the best of relationships couples must learn to listen to one another and understand what each is saying. Freewrite about difficulties people you know have had when communicating with a partner. How have these difficulties been resolved?

Why Can't He Hear What I'm Saying?

Deborah Tannen

Deborah Tannen is a professor of linguistics at Georgetown University. Tannen has made numerous guest appearances as an expert in linguistics on television news and information shows such as The News Hour with Jim Lehrer, 20/20, Larry King Live!, *and National Public Radio programs. Tannen has also taught at Princeton and Stanford universities. She is the author of ten nonfiction books and has edited ten other books in linguistic studies. She has also written over 100 essays and articles and has received numerous awards for her work. In addition to her linguistic research and writing, Tannen has published poetry, short stories, and personal essays and is the author of several plays. Her nonfiction works include* The Argument Culture: Stopping America's War of Words *(1999), winner of the Common Ground Book Award, and* I Only Say This Because I Love You: Talking to Your Parents, Partner, Sibs, and Kids When You're All Adults *(2002), which won the Books for a Better Life Award. Her most recent work is* You're Wearing That? Mothers and Daughters in Conversation *(2006). In the following excerpt from* That's Not What I Meant! How Conversational Style Makes or Breaks Relationships, *published in 1986, Tannen examines the reasons why men and women may have difficulty communicating.*

1   You know the feeling: You meet someone for the first time and it's as if you've known each other all your lives. The conversation goes smoothly. You each know what the other means. You laugh at the same time. Your sentences are in perfect rhythm. You're doing everything right.

2   But you also know the other feeling: You meet someone, you try to be friendly, but everything goes wrong. There are uncomfortable silences. You fish for topics. You both start talking at the same time and then both stop. Whatever you do to make things better only makes them worse.

3   Most talk falls somewhere between these two patterns. And, if sometimes people say things that sound a little odd or if someone doesn't quite get our point, we let it go, the talk continues, and no one pays much attention. But, when the conversation is with the most important person in your life, the little hitches can become big ones, and you can end up in a dialogue of the second sort without knowing quite how you got there. Sometimes strains in a conversation reflect real differences between people—they are

angry or at cross-purposes with each other. But at other times trouble develops when there really are no basic differences of opinion, when everyone is sincerely trying to get along. To say something and see it taken to mean something else; to try to be helpful and be thought pushy; to try to be considerate and be called cold—this is the type of miscommunication that drives people crazy. And it is usually caused by differences in conversational style.

I got hooked on linguistics, the study of language, the year my marriage broke up. 4 Seven years of living with the man I had just separated from had left me dizzy with questions about communication. What went wrong? Why did this wonderful, lovable man turn into a cruel lunatic when we tried to talk to each other? I remember one argument near the end of our marriage. It stuck in my mind because it was so painfully typical and because my frustration reached a new height. It was one of our frequent conversations about plans—in this case, about whether or not to accept an invitation to visit my sister.

Cozy in the setting of our home and willing to do whatever my husband wished, I 5 asked, "Do you want to go to my sister's?" He answered, "Okay." To me, "okay" didn't sound like a real answer; it seemed to indicate he was going along with something. So I said, "Do you really want to go?" He blew up. "You're driving me crazy! Why don't you make up your mind what you want?"

That explosion sent me into a tailspin. I was incredulous and outraged at his seem- 6 ing irrationality. "*My* mind? I haven't even said what I want. I'm willing to do whatever you want, and this is what I get?" I felt trapped in a theater of the absurd. I thought my husband was crazy and that I was crazy for having married him. He was always getting angry at me for saying things I'd never said or for not paying attention to things I was sure *he* had never said.

I had given up trying to solve these communication impasses but was still trying to 7 understand how they developed when I heard Professor Robin Lakoff lecture about indirectness at a linguistic institute at the University of Michigan. Lakoff explained that people prefer not to say exactly what they mean because they're concerned not only with the ideas they're expressing but also with the effect their words will have on those they're talking to. They want to maintain camaraderie, avoid imposing, and give (or at least appear to give) the other person some choice in the matter being discussed. And different people have different ways of achieving these potentially conflicting goals.

Suddenly I understood what had been going on in my marriage. I had taken it for 8 granted that I could say what I wanted and that I could ask my husband what he wanted and that he would tell me. When I asked if he wanted to visit my sister, I was seeking information about his preferences so I could accommodate them. *He* wanted to be accommodating, too, but he assumed that people don't just blurt out what they want. To him, that would be coercive because he found it hard to deny a direct request. So he assumed that talkers hint at what they want and listeners pick up on those hints.

A good way to hint is to ask a question. When I asked my husband if he wanted to 9 go to my sister's, he assumed I was letting him know, indirectly, that *I* wanted to go. Since he agreed to give me what I wanted, I should have gracefully—and gratefully—accepted. When I then asked, "Are you sure you want to go?" he heard that I didn't really want to go and was asking him to let me off the hook. From my husband's point of view, I was being capricious while he was trying to be agreeable—exactly my impression, but with our roles reversed. The intensity of his explosion (and of my reaction) came from the cumulative effect of repeated frustrations like this.

10   Although these differences in attitudes toward questions and hints could arise between any two people, perhaps it was not a coincidence that we were man and woman. Studying the way people talk convinced me that male–female conversation is cross-cultural communication. Culture, after all, is simply a network of habits and patterns based on past experience—and women and men have very different past experiences. Between the ages of five and fifteen, young girls and young boys are learning—mainly from their playmates—how to have conversations, and during those years they play mostly with friends of their own sex. So it's not surprising that they learn different ways of having and using conversations.

11   Little girls tend to play in small groups or, even more common, in pairs. Their social life usually centers around a best friend, and friendships are made, maintained, and broken by talk, especially "secrets." The secrets themselves may or may not be important, but the fact of telling them is all-important. It's hard for newcomers to get into these tight groups, but anyone who is admitted is treated as an equal. Girls like to play cooperatively; if they can't cooperate, the group breaks up.

12   Little boys tend to play in larger groups, often outdoors, and they spend more time doing than talking. It's easy for boys to get into a group, but once in they must jockey for status. One of the ways they do so is through talk—telling stories and jokes, arguing about who is best at what, challenging and sidetracking the talk of other boys and withstanding the others' challenges in order to maintain their own story and, consequently, their status.

13   When these boys and girls grow up into men and women, they keep the divergent attitudes and habits they learned as children—which they don't recognize as such but simply take for granted as the way people talk. Women want their partners to be a new and improved version of a best friend. This gives them a soft spot for men who tell them secrets. As Jack Nicholson once advised a guy in a movie: "Tell her about your troubled childhood—that always gets 'em." Men, on the other hand, expect to *do* things together and don't feel anything is missing if they don't have heart-to-heart talks all the time.

14   If they do have heart-to-hearts, the meaning of those talks may be opposite for men and women. To many women, the relationship is working as long as they can talk things out. To many men, the relationship *isn't* working out if they have to keep talking it over. If she keeps trying to get things going to save the relationship and he keeps trying to avoid them because he sees them as weakening it, then each one's efforts to preserve the relationship appear to the other as reckless endangerment.

15   If talks (of any kind) do get going, men's and women's ideas about how to conduct them may be very different. For example, Dora is feeling comfortable and close to Tom. She settles into a chair after dinner and begins to tell him about a problem at work. She expects him to reassure her that he understands and that what she feels is normal and to return the intimacy by, perhaps, telling her a problem of his. Instead, Tom sidetracks

her story, cracks jokes about it, questions her interpretation of the problem, and gives her advice about how to solve it and avoid such problems in the future.

All these responses, natural to men, are unexpected to women, who see them in terms of their own habits—negatively. When Tom comments on side issues or cracks jokes, Dora thinks he doesn't care about what she's saying and isn't really listening. If he challenges her interpretation of what went on, she feels he is criticizing her. If he tells her how to solve the problem, it makes her feel as if she's the patient to his doctor and that he's condescending. And, because he doesn't volunteer information about his problems, she feels he's implying he doesn't have any. [16]

Her bid for intimacy ends up making her feel distant from him; she tries harder to regain intimacy the only way she knows how—by revealing more and more about herself; he tries harder by giving more insistent advice. The more problems she exposes, the more incompetent she feels, until they both see her as emotionally draining and problem-ridden. He wonders why she asks for his advice if she doesn't want to take it. [17]

In a long-term relationship, a woman often feels, "After all this time, you should know what I want without my telling you," whereas a man feels, "After all this time, we should be able to tell each other what we want." These incongruent expectations pinpoint one of the key differences between men and women. Communication is always a matter of balancing conflicting needs for involvement and independence. Though everyone has both these needs, women often have a relatively greater need for involvement and men a relatively greater need for independence. Being understood without saying what you mean is the payoff of involvement; that's why women value it so highly. [18]

Harriet complains to Morton, "Why don't you ask me how my day was?" He replies, "If you have something to tell me, tell me. Why do you have to be invited?" What he doesn't understand is that she wants an expression of interest, evidence that he cares how her day was, regardless of whether or not she has something to tell. [19]

A lot of trouble is caused between women and men by, of all things, pronouns. Women often feel hurt when their partners use "I" or "me" in a situation in which they would use "we" or "us." When Morton announces, "I think I'll go for a walk," Harriet feels specifically uninvited, though Morton later claims she would have been welcome to join him. She feels locked out by his use of "I" and his omission of an invitation: "Would you like to come?" [20]

It's difficult to straighten out such misunderstandings because each person feels convinced of the logic of his or her position and the illogic—or irresponsibility—of the other's. Harriet knows that she always asks Morton how his day was and that she'd never announce, "I'm going for a walk," without inviting him to join her. If he talks differently to her, it must mean that he feels differently. But Morton wouldn't feel unloved if Harriet didn't ask about his day, and he would feel free to ask, "Can I come along?" if she announced she was taking a walk. So he can't believe she is justified in having reactions he knows he wouldn't have. [21]

One of the commonest complaints wives have about their husbands is, "He doesn't listen to me any more!" And a second is, "He doesn't talk to me any more!" Since couples are parties to the same conversations, why are women more dissatisfied with them than men? [22]

23   The silent father was a presence common to the childhoods of many women, and that image often becomes the model for the lover or husband. But what attracts us can become flypaper to which we are unhappily stuck, and many women who were lured to the strong, silent type as a lover find he's turned into a lug as a husband. To a woman in a long-term relationship, male silence may begin to feel like a brick wall against which she is banging her head. These wives may be right in thinking that their husbands aren't listening if the men don't value the telling of problems and secrets to establish rapport. But some of the time men feel unjustly accused: "I *was* listening." And, some of the time, they're right. They were.

24   Anthropologists Daniel Maltz and Ruth Borker report that women and men have different ways of showing that they're listening. Women make—and expect—more listening noises, such as "mhm" and "uh-huh." So, when a man is listening to a woman telling him something, he's not likely to make enough such noises to convince her he's really hearing her. And, when a woman is listening to a man, making more "mhms" and "uh-huhs" than he expects or would use himself, he may get the impression she's impatient for him to finish or exaggerating her interest in what he's saying.

25   To complicate matters further, what women and men mean by such noises may be different. Maltz and Borker contend that women tend to use these noises just to show they're listening and understanding, while men, in keeping with their different focus in communication, use them to show they agree. Women use the noises to indicate "I'm listening: go on," which serves the relationship level of talk; men use them to show what they think of what is being said, a response to the content of talk. So, when a man sits through his wife's talk, follows it, but doesn't agree with all she says, he's not going to shower her with "uh-huhs," and she's going to think he's not paying attention.

26   Sometimes, when men and women feel the other isn't paying attention, they're right. And this may be because their assumptions about what's interesting are different. Muriel gets bored when Daniel goes on and on about the stock market. He gets bored when she goes on and on about the details of her day or the lives of people he doesn't even know.

27   It seems natural to women to tell and hear about what happened today, who turned up at the bus stop, who called and what she said, not because these details are important in themselves but because the telling of them proves involvement—that you care about each other, that you have a best friend. Since men don't use talk for this purpose, they focus on the inherent insignificance of the details. What they find worth telling are facts about such topics as sports, politics, history, or how things work, and a woman listening to this kind of talk feels the man is lecturing her or being slightly condescending.

28   Women describing an experience often include reports of conversations. Tone of voice, timing, intonation and wording are all re-created in the telling in order to explain—dramatize, really—the experience that is being reported. But most men aren't in the habit of reporting on conversations and are thus less likely to pay as much

attention at the time they're going on. If men tell about an incident, they are more likely to give a brief summary instead of recreating what was said and how, and, if the woman asks, "What exactly did he say?" and "How did he say it?," the man probably can't remember.

These different habits have repercussions when a man and woman are talking about their own relationship. She claims to recall exactly what he said, and she wants him to account for it. He can hardly do so because he has forgotten exactly what was said—if not the whole conversation. She secretly suspects he's only pretending not to remember; he secretly suspects that she's making up the details. So women's conversations with their women friends keep them in training for talking about their relationships with men, but many men come to such conversations with no training at all—and an uncomfortable sense that this really isn't their event.

Most of us expect our partners to be both lovers and best friends. Though women and men may share fairly similar romantic expectations, they have very different ideas about how to be friends, and these are the differences that mount over time and can keep two people stewing in the juice of accumulated minor misunderstandings. Ironically, the big issues—values, interests, philosophies of life—can be talked about and agreed on. It is far harder to achieve harmony in the nuances of talk regarding simple day-to-day matters.

If you and your mate fight constantly about insignificant matters, it's natural to assume something's wrong with him—or with you for having chosen him. But, when you begin to recognize the different ways men and women talk, you can begin to accept the differences between you in habits and assumptions about how to have a conversation, show interest, be considerate, and so on. And you can start to make the small, steady changes that will accommodate two conflicting conversational styles.

Sometimes explaining assumptions can help. If a man starts to tell a woman what to do to solve her problem, she may say, "Thanks for the advice, but I really don't want to be told what to do. I just want you to listen and say you understand." A man might want to explain, "If I challenge you, it's not to prove you wrong; it's just my way of paying attention to what you're telling me." Maybe you won't always correctly interpret your partner's intentions immediately, but you can remind yourself that, if you get a negative impression, it may not be what was intended.

Most of all, we have to give up our conviction that, as linguist Robin Lakoff put it, "Love means never having to say 'What do you mean?'"

RESPONDING TO THE READING

FREEWRITING

Practice 7e. Freewrite about your own experiences or observations that support or contradict Tannen's discussion of male/female communication.

hitches (3)	coercive (8)	incongruent (18)
cross-purposes (3)	capricious (9)	rapport (23)
incredulous (6)	cross-cultural (10)	repercussions (29)
camaraderie (7)	divergent (13)	accumulated (30)
preferences (8)	endangerment (14)	nuances (30)
accommodate (8)	condescending (16)	

QUESTIONS FOR DISCUSSION

1. What is Deborah Tannen's purpose in writing this article? Which passages best communicate that purpose?
2. Tannen uses the pronoun *you* in addressing the reader. Who is Tannen's intended audience?
3. Tannen argues that "differences in conversational style" between men and women cause miscommunication. What examples does she offer in support of this idea? Do you agree with her position?
4. What have you observed as the most important difference between men and women, a difference that sometimes makes communication difficult?
5. Paraphrase Tannen's definition of culture in paragraph 10. Find another definition of culture in a dictionary or encyclopedia. How does it compare with Tannen's? How does Tannen's definition fit her purpose?
6. What connections does Tannen make between the "culture" learned as children and the adult behavior of men and women? What behavior does this early patterning cause? What evidence does she provide, and is the evidence sufficient to make this connection between childhood and adult behavior plausible?

TOPICS FOR WRITING

Topic 1. Write an essay in which you explain how well Tannen's analysis of male and female differences matches your own experiences. In preparation for writing your essay, review the techniques for writing a comparison on pages 213–214.

Topic 2. Choose a spot for people watching—an airport, a train station, a bus stop, a library, a shopping mall, a movie theater lobby, a restaurant, a bar, or a coffee shop. Observe people carefully, and record in your journal exactly what you see. Try to get more than just superficial descriptions. Look at the whole person and how he or she communicates. Examine such things as gestures, body movement, speech, and dress. Choose one or two of the people you observed. Then write an explanation of what they communicate to others and how they convey this message.

Topic 3. Tannen's research shows that men and women (1) place different emphasis on involvement and independence, (2) learn different cultural patterns and habits as children, (3) have different ways to show they're listening, (4) make different assumptions about what is interesting, and (5) can learn to communicate.

Choose one of these ideas and write a paper about your own experience and observations on the subject.

Topic 4. Interview half a dozen men and women, and ask them to discuss what they think are the four or five most common problems that occur when people try to communicate with their partner. Ask your interviewees to give you examples of the problems they mention and possible solutions. After gathering your information, write an essay in which you analyze the two or three problems that seemed most important to the people you interviewed. Include a description of each problem, a discussion of what causes the problem, and what might be done about it.

COMPARING AND CONTRASTING: AN ANALYSIS OF "WHY CAN'T HE HEAR WHAT I'M SAYING?"

If you have read the discussion of "Defining" in Chapter 6 and "Process Analysis" in this chapter, you already have some idea of how comparisons work. You may recall that in their effort to provide the reader with a detailed understanding of the "Border Culture," Marjorie Miller and Ricardo Chavira compare the hostile attitudes displayed by some Mexicans and Americans living along the border. Tom Harris uses comparison in discussing the historical development of urban legends as part of American folklore. The following analysis of "Why Can't He Hear What I'm Saying?" provides an in-depth discussion of the comparative elements in Tannen's discussion of men and women.

CHARACTERISTICS OF COMPARING AND CONTRASTING

Point of View

For his essay, "Becoming an American," the student sample at the end of this chapter, Tony Nuñez writes in the first person as he compares his experiences as an immigrant in an American school to Elizabeth Wong's conflicting feelings about her education in "The Struggle to Be an All-American Girl" (pages 300–301). Deborah Tannen writes about male and female ways of communicating from an objective point of view, although she does mention personal experiences when they clarify her ideas. She also addresses the audience directly because her purpose is to explain and explore. Here are the first three paragraphs of "Why Can't He Hear What I'm Saying?"

> You know the feeling: You meet someone for the first time, and it's as if you've known each other all your lives. The conversation goes smoothly. You each know what the other means. You laugh at the same time. Your sentences are in perfect rhythm. You're doing everything right.

> But you also know the other feeling: You meet someone, you try to be friendly, but everything goes wrong. There are uncomfortable silences. You fish for topics. You both start talking at the same time and then both stop. Whatever you do to make things better only makes them worse.

> Most talk falls somewhere between these two patterns. And, if sometimes people say things that sound a little odd or if someone doesn't quite get our point, we let it go, the talk continues, and no one pays much attention. But, when the

conversation is with the most important person in your life, the little hitches can become big ones, and you can end up in a dialogue of the second sort without knowing quite how you got there.

In the first two paragraphs, Tannen addresses the reader directly as "you" and describes two situations—one in which people are completely comfortable, the other in which absolutely everything goes wrong—likely to be familiar to her reader. In the third paragraph, she adopts the point of view of the examiner who will analyze situations where partners who care about each other show signs that they are not quite communicating.

A Clear Purpose

It is extremely important that writers make clear, probably in an introductory paragraph, why they are making their comparison or contrast. They must communicate that purpose to the reader to prevent their essay from appearing random or unfocused.

In nonfiction works, authors often explain their purpose for writing. Tannen, for example, explains that she became interested in the problems of how men and women communicate—or fail to communicate—because of a misunderstanding that arose between her and her ex-husband. Her purpose in writing "Why Can't He Hear What I'm Saying?" was to get couples to understand one another and be more tolerant of their differences. In her concluding paragraphs she makes that purpose clear:

> If you and your mate fight constantly about insignificant matters, it's natural to assume something's wrong with him—or with you for having chosen him. But, when you begin to recognize the different ways men and women talk, you can begin to accept the differences between you in habits and assumptions about how to have a conversation, show interest, be considerate, and so on. And you can start to make the small, steady changes that will accommodate two conflicting conversational styles.

In addition to a purpose, writers usually tell their readers not only what subjects they plan to compare or contrast but also the way they will draw those comparisons or contrasts. The plan or *thesis* that controls Tannen's essay is contained in paragraph 10.

> Studying the way people talk convinced me that male–female conversation is cross-cultural communication. Culture, after all, is simply a network of habits and patterns based on past experience—and women and men have very different past experiences. Between the ages of five and fifteen, young girls and young boys are learning—mainly from their playmates—how to have conversations, and during those years they play mostly with friends of their own sex. So it's not surprising that they learn different ways of having and using conversations.

Tannen explains that her essay will show that "male–female conversation" is based on very different assumptions about the way people communicate—assumptions that are so different that men and women might as well be from different cultures. Furthermore, she will show that these differences are caused by contrasting expectations that boys and girls develop in their gender-segregated play.

Supporting Details

Detailed writing is important for any writing strategy. One element that makes comparisons and contrasts different from other kinds of writing is that topics being compared or contrasted have matching subtopics, details, and examples that develop their similarities or differences. In objective writing—when the author's task is to explain similarities and differences—such matches are exact, and contrasts are stated clearly as we see in the following paragraphs from "Why Can't He Hear What I'm Saying?"

> Little girls tend to play in small groups or, even more common, in pairs. Their social life usually centers around a best friend, and friendships are made, maintained, and broken by talk, especially "secrets." The secrets themselves may or may not be important, but the fact of telling them is all-important. It's hard for newcomers to get into these tight groups, but anyone who is admitted is treated as an equal. Girls like to play cooperatively; if they can't cooperate, the group breaks up.
>
> Little boys tend to play in larger groups, often outdoors, and they spend more time doing than talking. It's easy for boys to get into a group, but once in they must jockey for status. One of the ways they do so is through talk—telling stories and jokes, arguing about who is best at what, challenging and sidetracking the talk of other boys and withstanding the others' challenges in order to maintain their own story and, consequently, their status.

The following T-graph illustrates the contrasts Tannen makes between the play of little boys and little girls.

Little Girls	Little Boys
Play in small groups, have a "best friend"	Play in large groups
Use talk and secrets to keep friendships together	Spend more time doing than talking
Make it difficult to be admitted to the group	Make it easy to be admitted to the group
View those admitted as equal	Don't see members as equal
Play cooperatively	Compete with each other for status

Organization by Subject or Point by Point

Tannen's article illustrates the two main patterns writers use to organize comparisons: they may discuss one subject first, mentioning all its points and examples before going on to the second subject; or they may discuss one point about their first subject and then the same point about their second subject, and so forth. The two paragraphs cited earlier about the differences between the play of little girls and little boys illustrate the first pattern; Tannen discusses all the points about girls' play first and then all the opposing points typical of boys' play. The following paragraph from Tannen's article illustrates the second organizational pattern:

> When these boys and girls grow up into men and women, they keep the divergent attitudes and habits they learned as children—which they don't recognize as such but simply take for granted as the way people talk. Women want their partners

to be a new and improved version of a best friend. This gives them a soft spot for men who tell them secrets. As Jack Nicholson once advised a guy in a movie: "Tell her about your troubled childhood—that always gets 'em." Men, on the other hand, expect to *do* things together and don't feel anything is missing if they don't have heart-to-heart talks all the time.

In this paragraph Tannen first discusses one point about women—how they carry childhood expectations of their close friends into relationships with men—and then apply the same point to men, explaining that in contrast to women, they expect to "do" things and don't need intimate talk. This point-by-point or alternating pattern is useful when writers have a lot of information to convey because that way the reader doesn't have to remember the points the writer made about the first topic before going on to the second.

Regardless of the pattern of organization the writer chooses, the subtopics mentioned for one topic should have a matching or contrasting point in the discussion of the second topic.

Using Transitions

Like causal analysis, comparisons can be quite complex, so it is essential that writers be clear about when they are discussing one subject and when they have moved to the other. In the paragraph in which Tannen discusses both male and female expectations, she uses a transitional phrase to signal the shift from women to men: "men, on the other hand, expect to *do* things together." Here are a few additional transitional words and phrases that you will find useful when discussing similarities or differences.

To Show Similarity	To Show Difference or Exception
similarly	in contrast
in the same way	on the other hand
at the same time	but
likewise	yet
too, also	however
equally	not as . . . as
furthermore	nevertheless
much in common	in spite of
much alike	although

FOR PRACTICE

Practice 7f. The excerpt from Deborah Tannen's book is reprinted on pages 202–207. After reading it carefully, reread paragraphs 14 through 18, and underline transitional words that signal contrasts between what men and women expect of each other.

THE WRITING PROCESS: COMPARING AND CONTRASTING

Comparing and contrasting are familiar activities to anyone who has shopped for clothing, an automobile, or gifts for someone's birthday. More important decisions, such as what classes to take, which of two careers to pursue, or what school to attend, also involve making comparisons; for decisions such as these, it is usually best to list what you know about your alternatives and then compare them to see which is the best choice. Comparison is also an important writing strategy. As we have seen in discussions of readings in Chapter 6 and in this chapter, comparing and contrasting is useful in developing essays that define or those that use process analysis to structure ideas.

In general, follow the steps in the writing process when making comparisons or drawing contrasts. Writing techniques especially useful for comparing and contrasting are discussed next.

DEVELOPING A TOPIC

An important part of getting started on your comparison or contrast involves making sure that you can think of enough interesting points that the two people, events, situations, objects, movies, paintings, or readings you will analyze have in common. The best way to see if you can gather enough details about your two subjects is to do some preliminary writing before you decide on a topic.

DEVELOPING IDEAS

To determine whether you can generate the details you will need for your comparison or contrast, freewrite, draw an idea wheel, make a list, and ask yourself questions. Another useful tool for exploring similarities and differences is the T-graph, which allows you to visualize the similarities or differences between your subjects. One student who wanted to write about the contrast between her grandmother's shopping habits and her own drew the following T-graph:

Grandmother's Shopping Habits	My Shopping Habits
Arrives early to avoid crowds	Shop at noon because I like the crowds
Goes to lots of stores to look for sales and get the best bargains	Usually buy the first thing I see
Never buys more than one of anything	Own identical pairs of shoes in different colors

By drawing a T-graph like this one, you can quickly discover whether or not you have matching or contrasting points for your topics.

THINKING ABOUT YOUR AUDIENCE

You should ask yourself early in the writing process why you are writing your paper and what the point is that you want your comparison or contrast to make. You must communicate your purpose to your audience so they will know what they should be looking for in the comparison or contrast they are reading.

The student who wrote the preceding T-graph decided that her purpose was to describe how whimsical her shopping habits are when compared with those of her more conservative grandmother. Her next step was to turn that statement of purpose into a thesis: "My whimsical shopping habits are quite different from those of my conservative grandmother."

ORGANIZING IDEAS

The two organizational patterns you may choose for your comparison are (1) arrangement by subject or (2) point-by-point discussion. When details are arranged by subject, writers discuss all the points or ideas about one subject and then all the similar or contrasting points about the second subject. Writers who organize their papers using the point-by-point method make one point, comparing or contrasting both subjects together, and then a second, and perhaps a third point about the two subjects. The following essays contrasting the student's shopping habits with her grandmother's illustrate these two arrangements.

Arranged by Subject

The gap between generations has no better example in my family than the one between my grandmother and me. In particular, my whimsical shopping habits are quite different from those of my conservative grandmother.

For one thing, Grandmother likes to shop early on weekdays to avoid the crowds. She is a frail woman who is deathly afraid of being knocked down by customers so intent on their shopping that they don't see her. By noon, Grandma has been to half a dozen stores, shopping for one particular article of clothing that she has seen on sale. As far as I know, she has never bought more than one of anything, regardless of the fact that it is on sale.

My shopping habits look thoughtless in comparison. I get up at about 10:30 AM on weekends and arrive at my first store by noon. Unlike Grandmother, I shop during peak hours because I enjoy being in the middle of a crowd of eager shoppers; in their excitement I feel a kind of camaraderie. I let my enthusiasm carry me along and never bother planning what to buy. I usually pick up the first thing I see that appeals to me without giving much thought to whether I need it or not. Moreover, I usually have no idea what is on sale. If I happen to find a dress or pair of jeans I like that is marked down, I buy them instantly and consider myself lucky. In addition, I have none of Grandmother's reservations about buying several similar items. If I find something I really like, I will buy two or three if I can afford them. I have two pairs of the same style shoes, for example, because they fit me so well.

Family photographs show that my grandmother looked just like me when she was in her twenties. But if I were to judge by our shopping habits, I might question whether she and I are related at all.

Practice 7g. Underline the points this student made in her essay about her grandmother's methods of shopping and then those about her own method of shopping. What do you notice about the sequence of ideas in the paragraphs on each subject?

Discussed Point by Point

> The gap between generations has no better example in my family than the one between my grandmother and me. In particular, my whimsical shopping habits are quite different from those of my conservative grandmother.
>
> For one thing, Grandmother likes to shop early on weekdays to avoid the crowds. She is a frail woman who is deathly afraid of being knocked down by customers so intent on their shopping that they don't see her. In contrast, I get up at about 10:30 AM on weekends, the time I do most of my shopping, and arrive at my first store by noon, about the time my grandmother is ready to go home. Unlike Grandmother, I shop during peak hours because I enjoy being in the middle of a crowd of eager shoppers; in their excitement I feel a kind of camaraderie.
>
> Grandmother is a very methodical shopper who knows exactly what she came to buy. By noon, Grandma has been to half a dozen stores, shopping for one particular article of clothing that she probably saw on sale. When I shop, I let my enthusiasm carry me along and never bother planning what to buy. As a result, I usually buy the first thing I see that appeals to me without giving much thought to whether I need it or not. Moreover, I usually have no idea what is on sale. If I happen to find a dress or pair of jeans I like that is marked down, I buy them instantly and consider myself lucky.
>
> My grandmother and I differ in one other area as well. As far as I know, Grandmother has never bought more than one kind of anything, regardless of the fact that it is on sale. I am just the opposite. If I find something I really like, I will buy two or three if I can afford them. I have two pairs of the same style shoes, for example, because they fit so well.
>
> Family photographs show that my grandmother looked just like me when she was in her twenties. But if I were to judge by our shopping habits, I might question whether she and I are related at all.

Practice 7h. Underline the points in the second example that the student makes about her grandmother and herself; then compare this point-by-point discussion with the arrangement by subject that you read earlier. Which method of organization do you think is most effective and why?

The Writing Process: Comparing and Contrasting **215**

SHARING AND REVISING

You may find the following checklist helpful when revising your essay. As with other checklists in this book, you may be asked to use these questions in peer review or for an online writing workshop. Put a check mark beside each question as you complete it.

Checklist

- ☐ Is the purpose for comparing or contrasting points about subjects stated clearly in the introduction?
- ☐ What point of view has the writer adopted (first person or third person)?
- ☐ Is that perspective maintained throughout the paper?
- ☐ Would additional details, examples, or explanations make any of the ideas being compared or contrasted more convincing?
- ☐ Is the paper's organizational pattern (arrangement of ideas by subject or point-by-point discussion) used consistently and clearly?
- ☐ Is each point made about one subject matched by a corresponding point of comparison or contrast for the second subject?
- ☐ Do transitional words and phrases make it clear when the writer moves from one point of comparison or contrast to another?
- ☐ Has the writer proofread carefully for sentence correctness, spelling, and punctuation?
- ☐ Overall, does the essay achieve its original purpose in comparing or contrasting two subjects?

Student Writing: Comparing and Contrasting

Can You Go Home Again?

I was born in Georgia and raised in South Carolina. I was a country girl much of my young life. When my family moved to the city, I had to learn a whole new way of life, but the biggest change was in the way I talked.

In Georgia, my family lived a very simple life, but in the city, nothing was simple. On the farm, everybody pitched in and helped because we had to. I learned to grow vegetables, milk cows, and gather eggs when I was three or four years old. These were basic skills for survival on a farm. There was nothing fancy about the way we lived—we had outdoor toilets and wood-burning stoves to cook on. Coming from such a basic life, I found the city overwhelming. At the age of eleven, I learned to use an indoor toilet. I saw my first escalator and wondered if the thing would just keep going straight up through the ceiling. The biggest department store I had ever seen in my life was Woolworth's five-and-dime. Talk about home sweet home—you could just turn me loose in that place. Every sidewalk was paved and jammed with people, or so it seemed to me. In this new world, I knew I would have to speed up to keep from being run over.

When I started school, I discovered that it wasn't just my pace of life I would have to correct. I have one big problem: no one could understand anything I said. My speech sounded like something out of Huckleberry Finn; phrases like "taters," "maters," "that-there," "shornuff," and "pert near" littered my half of any conversation. I remember someone asking me what time it was, and I said, "It's pert near four o'clock." I took speech classes and just about drove my teacher mad. It took about three years for me to get proper English down. I still slip up now and then.

I was grown and married when I went back home. It was such a shock. The house seemed smaller. The old dirt road we used to pedal the vegetable cart down was paved. Even my grandparents seemed shorter. The old water well out back was covered and water was now being piped into the house. Grandpa said, "Girl, what happen to ya! Ya sound like a damn Yankee!" I just started laughing and said, "No, Grandpa, it's called schooling. I went to school and learned the proper way to speak English." He just looked at me with those eyes. "Twerent nothing wrong with the way ya spoke before, girl. Just sound high fluten now is all." As I looked around, I could see the slow pace of this life and reflect on my new life. I had such an easy going, laid back kind of feeling now that I was back home. There sat Grandpa under the shade of a tree, leaning back in his chair, with his shoes off. The crops were in, and the sun was going down. It was time to rest before starting the new day. Here, it seemed like there was all the time in the world. Then I thought about my new life and how different things were in town. Everyone there was always in such a hurry. In town, everyone was chasing the dollar while in the country, people kept scratching a living out of the ground.

I took a good look at my grandfather. He couldn't read; he could barely sign his name. I thought how blessed I am to be able to read. As I sat down beside my grandfather and read him some poems, he looked at me and smiled. "You can give the city your head, girl, but don't let it take your heart." I didn't know what he meant then, but I think I do now.

—Norma Davis

QUESTIONS FOR DISCUSSION

1. What is Davis's main point in this essay?
2. What is the most effective section of her narrative for you? Explain your reasons for selecting this passage. Can you think of ways that Davis might strengthen her essay?
3. Explain the effect of using her family's speech in her narrative. Do you think this technique enhances or detracts from the essay? Explain your answer.

Student Writing: Comparing and Contrasting

Tony Nuñez wrote the following essay as a response to Elizabeth Wong's narrative "The Struggle to Be an All-American Girl" (Chapter 11). In his essay, he establishes important differences between their experiences.

Becoming an American

Elizabeth Wong's "The Struggle to Be an All-American Girl" struck a sensitive chord with me. It wasn't that I struggled against my native culture the way she did. Instead, my struggle had more to do with trying to understand what was going on around me and make myself understood because my English was so limited. Wong embraced the English language and was embarrassed by the sounds of her native tongue while my lack of comprehension and difficulties learning were constant embarrassments when I was growing up.

While Elizabeth Wong had little difficulty speaking and writing in English, I struggled to figure out what people were saying. Wong boasted that at ten years old she not only could read children's classics like Little Women and Black Beauty, she could also "write reports" on those books. In contrast, even classroom lessons were difficult for me to follow. I remember my fourth grade teacher giving instructions for a spelling test. I was still trying to understand her instructions when she started dictating the first spelling word. I was the last one prepared to take any test because I first had to take in what she was saying in English, then translate it into Spanish so I could really understand it.

In addition, Wong found it easy to understand English, but for me, the language barrier made it difficult, if not impossible, to understand other people. When Wong spoke English, "people nodded at me, smiled sweetly, said encouraging words." Even the people in her community recognized that because of her skills in English, she would "be able to keep up with the world outside Chinatown." The responses to my English were anything but pleasant. For example, one of my classmates would be telling a joke, and after he was finished, everyone else would laugh while I was still translating what he had said from English to Spanish. It often happened that the joke wasn't that funny in translation, so I wouldn't understand why everyone else thought it was. Not understanding my plight, my classmates made fun of me because I could never follow their jokes and conversations. They called me "clueless" and worse names. Other things I missed were more important than jokes. I remember the days when we would have assemblies, and the principal would speak about current issues on campus. Those assemblies confused me the most because I could never understand what he was talking about; my system for translating couldn't keep up with the principal's speech. The frustrating thing was that the school could be under attack, and I wouldn't know anything about it.

For Elizabeth Wong, it was her native Chinese that embarrassed her, but for me my limited English was a constant source of shame. Wong tried to "dissociate" herself from the "nagging, loud voice" of her grandmother and the sounds of the street vendors in Chinatown. She complained that Chinese was "quick . . . loud, . . . and unbeautiful." She preferred speaking English because she "did not want to be thought of as mad, as talking gibberish." My "gibberish" was limited to the English I tried to speak. My trouble with English was bad enough that I was separated from the "native" speakers until I could learn to communicate in the language of my adopted country. It seemed like every school year I was in some type of special education class. Whether it was reading comprehension, pronunciation, or spelling, I always needed extra attention. My elementary school had a system where the students who were average and above average came to school at 8:30 AM. Those of us with learning difficulties came an hour earlier for "special tutoring." It was a source of shame to me that I had already been in school an hour when most of my friends arrived on campus. My classroom performance was another source of embarrassment. When it came time to read out loud in class, for instance, I would shrink in my seat, hoping my teacher would skip me that time. Unfortunately, I was often the first one she called on to read. Every time that happened, my voice would crack and I would turn bright red with embarrassment. I knew she would recognize the sounds I made as horrible mispronunciations. Spelling was another subject I dreaded. When I had spelling tests, I would usually get the lowest grade in the class. That didn't stop me from trying, though. Every year our school held a spelling bee, and I used to dream about taking first place and showing everyone how smart I really was.

Even though Elizabeth Wong's story is different than mine, I understand what she means when she writes about "The Struggle to Be an All-American Girl." My struggle was different because I am an immigrant and had not mastered English as well as she had. She was admired by people in her community because she could "keep up with the world outside Chinatown" while I was all alone and struggling to translate everything into Spanish. My story has a happy ending, though. Every once in a while, when I drive by my old elementary school and think about how horribly isolated and clueless I felt, I remind myself how much more confident I am now about my abilities to use English and about my own intelligence. It took me a long time to realize that there was nothing wrong with me, and after years of struggle, I am proud that I stayed in school and eventually did well enough that I am now taking college classes.

—Tony Nuñez

QUESTIONS FOR DISCUSSION

1. Discuss the organization of "Becoming an American." How well does Nuñez connect examples and explanations in his essay?
2. What tone or attitude does Nuñez adopt toward his subject? How might his attitude help explain what he has been able to accomplish?
3. How does Nuñez's story compare to Mike Rose's experiences in "I Just Wanna Be Average" in Chapter 11?

Interpreting

The writing strategies discussed in this chapter, evaluating and taking a stand, are useful tools when interpreting everyday experiences, as well as social, cultural, and political issues. A team of writers at *People* magazine examine the security issues surrounding the popular website MySpace.com. in the essay "MySpace Nation: The Controversy." Excerpts from their essay illustrate some of the techniques that writers use when evaluating a subject. The "Letter from the Birmingham Jail" by Martin Luther King, Jr. serves as a model for essays that take a position on a subject and argue that position persuasively.

Injustice anywhere is a threat to justice everywhere.
—Martin Luther King, Jr.

An online playground for kids—an astounding 16 million have their own Web pages—MySpace.com also attracts creeps and [perverts].
—Bill Hewitt et al.

EVALUATING

To *evaluate* literally means "to judge the value or worth of something." People use evaluation techniques every day. To make decisions about whether to take a particular class, buy one car instead of another, or recycle newspapers, people must evaluate their choices. When writers evaluate an experience, they usually discuss either the value that experience had for them or ways that it proved harmful. Writers frequently use evaluation to analyze social, cultural, or political issues.

WRITING BEFORE READING

Based on your experience, observations, or reading, what dangers does the Internet currently pose for children and teens?

MySpace Nation: The Controversy

An online playground for kids—an astounding 16 million have their own Web pages—
MySpace.com also attracts creeps and pervs

**Bill Hewitt, Johnny Dodd, Michelle York, Eileen Finan,
Margaret Nelson, Alexandra Rockey Fleming, and David Searls**

A team of journalists based in six major American cities worked together to produce the following essay, which was published June 5, 2006, in People *magazine.*

1   When it comes to using MySpace, the explosively popular Web site for kids and young adults, Niki Martin and her 12-year-old daughter Ashley have a deal. "She only talks to her friends from school," says Niki. But on Feb. 26 Ashley happened to be visiting a neighbor in Vancouver, Wash., when she logged onto her MySpace page, which was decorated with pictures of herself playing softball, and noticed an e-mail from a stranger that said, "Hey, beautiful, we should get together sometime."

2   What unfolded next was a chilling object lesson in how children are now closer than ever to the dark alleys of the Web. Alerted by Ashley to the message, the neighbor, 26-year-old Adrienne Sylvester, slid in front of the keyboard and pretended to be the 12-year-old. Within minutes the man was asking what kind of underwear the girl had on and soon afterward was streaming video to her MySpace page of himself performing a sexual act—footage that Sylvester had the presence of mind to capture on a camcorder pointed at the monitor. Sylvester, who meanwhile had summoned police, made arrangements to meet the man nearby. An hour later when Jeramie Ray Eidem, 26, pulled into the parking lot of a fast-food restaurant, he was arrested. (He is now being held on charges of attempted rape of a child, to which he has pleaded not guilty.) And while he never laid a finger on Ashley, that does not mean she was untouched by the episode. "She knew what was going on," says her mother, Niki, "and she was shocked."

And she is not alone. Launched two years ago, MySpace has swiftly become one of the biggest hits in the history of the Internet. A social networking site meant to share music, foster new friendships and a sense of community, it now boasts 80 million members and is second only to Yahoo in the number of page views per day—making it by far the biggest player in the Web's networking niche, which also includes such sites as Facebook and Xanga. Geared for teens and young adults—20 percent of the site's visitors are between 14 and 17—MySpace owes much of its popularity to the fact that, unlike old-fashioned chat rooms, it allows members to upload photographs and video clips to their own pages and include information about themselves.

But along with success MySpace has also generated considerable controversy. Crimes as serious as murder and rape have been linked to teens using the site, which has also become a preferred venue for cyber-bullies and online pedophiles. Kids have posted tales—and photos—of their alleged drinking and drug use. Even a casual visitor can quickly encounter raunchy, explicit sexual advice or memoirs. As a result, a growing number of schools around the country have blocked access to the site. "Everywhere I go, parents and teachers are very concerned about MySpace," says Dr. David Walsh, a psychologist who heads the Minneapolis-based National Institute on Media and the Family. "In the past two months it's been on everyone's radar."

MySpace cofounder Chris DeWolfe insists the company takes its responsibility for preventing misuse of the site very seriously. He points out that nearly a third of its 300 employees are assigned to review content and take down anything objectionable, and that the company offers a 24-hour hotline to work with law enforcement on catching online predators. "Much of what we do revolves around user policing and deputizing users to report abuse," says DeWolfe, 40. "From a policing standpoint we put a lot of effort into this site." On April 10 the company announced that it had hired a former federal prosecutor to oversee security on the site.

There is no denying the enormous power and appeal of MySpace among teens. It is not uncommon for kids to log on repeatedly to their pages to check for new postings from friends. C.J. Freeman, 16, of LaOtto, Ind., admits that she goes three times a day to her page, which contains photos, snippets from her favorite music, comments from her boyfriend and bits of trivia about herself (she's lactose intolerant, loves sports, hates health food). "It's a great way to keep in touch and to meet new friends," she says. "You can really personalize your space." Says psychologist Walsh: "Kids have always congregated with other kids. Two generations ago, it was at the corner candy store. Now, in this high-tech age, MySpace is the candy store on steroids."

Freeman's mother, Teresa, takes some basic precautions. For example, she insists that the computer be in the family room so that she can keep tabs on her daughter's computer activity. But ultimately, she trusts her daughter's judgment. "There are probably some things on the site that would make me uncomfortable," she says. "But if I sat in the backseat of her car on one of her dates I would probably be uncomfortable too."

Parents who visit the site can come away shaken all the same. "It's totally blowing their minds," says John Shehan, manager of the CyberTipline of the National Center for Missing and Exploited Children. "They think of the diaries they kept when they were younger and can't imagine anyone reading what they've written[,] and it's the same stuff their kids are putting out there." Shellee Davies, 42, of Centerville, Utah, who has two daughters, Lindsay, 17, and Whitney, 14, who have been using the site for about six months, concluded that even more innocuous material could pose a threat. Prompted by a local news report about MySpace, she decided to have a look at her kids' sites for herself. "Until then," she says, "I was just clueless." What she found disturbed her, including entries on her daughters' MySpace pages that mentioned the schools they attended and their birthdays. She told the girls to delete anything that could make them targets, which Lindsay and Whitney were almost relieved to do. "It was okay with me because it can sometimes be kind of creepy," says Lindsay. "People will write and say, 'You're hot. Let's hang out.' And it turns out the person who wrote it is some 40-year-old guy with kids."

9   With younger kids, the risks are even greater. MySpace is supposedly restricted to users 14 and over. But there is nothing to prevent a younger child with an e-mail address from lying about his or her age and signing up as a member. And when they, as well as anyone else, venture on the site they can quickly be exposed to raw content. In New Hampshire, Det. James McLaughlin of the Keene Police Dept., who specializes in catching Internet predators, is astonished by some of what he stumbles upon. "Some kids perform sexual acts on Web cams," he says. "We'd like to think it's from socially isolated kids, but some of them are high-achieving kids who are sound socially. Parents can't believe it." Det. Ali Bartley, 30, of the Boulder County Sheriff's office got her first taste of MySpace in February, when she began investigating an alleged rape of an 18-year-old woman who said she met her attacker through a mutual friend on the site. "I'm not a prude," says Bartley. "But I was shocked when I started looking through MySpace."

10   Yet pornography may not be the most troubling issue. As with any place popular with kids in the brick-and-mortar world, MySpace attracts more than its share of pedophiles, who comb through entries looking for clues to vulnerability. Scarcely a week goes by without news of a predator nabbed on MySpace. In March five teenage boys in Fontana, Calif., went on MySpace and created a profile of a 15-year-old girl as a prank. Instead they drew the attention of a 48-year-old man who agreed to meet the "girl" in a local park. The boys went to the park and when the man showed up summoned police, who arrested the suspect. While praising the kids, police caution against civilians using such ruses. "This isn't something I'd suggest that other people try to reel in sexual predators," says Sgt. William Megenney of the Fontana police. "This could have turned ugly real quick."

11   Not surprisingly some experts have concluded that parents should simply discourage kids from going on MySpace at all. "Get off of it," says Det. Dan Jackman of the Louisville, Ky., police's Crimes Against Children Unit. "There's no way to tell who is a pedophile and who is not." But that is far from a unanimous opinion. Debbie Beach, a therapist in northern Virginia who specializes in treating adolescents, points out that MySpace can offer some distinct benefits to teens. "MySpace and other sites open up a world where they can test out who they are and who they want to be," maintains Beach. "They can write uncensored, they can test out identities anonymously."

12   As for Niki Martin, she stifled her impulse to pull Ashley off the Web altogether. "That would have been like I was punishing her for doing the right thing," says Niki. Instead Ashley's Internet time is down to 15 minutes a day. To MySpace cofounder

DeWolfe, that sort of measured response makes perfect sense. "The problems of the off-line world are the same problems of the online world," he says. "When you grow up the first thing your parents teach you is to look both ways before you cross the street and to not get in cars with strangers. It's very similar for the Internet."

Caught in the Web
Advice for Kids and Parents

Girls should always use a boy's name as their alias. "Most of the predators want females, and they'll use the browser tool to search for female names," says [Detective] Dan Jackman of the Louisville, Ky., police's child unit.

Check for postings about drinking and sex. But be aware teens also often make up wild exploits that aren't true, cautions Aftab: "They think that is cooler than explaining that they were home coloring with their 5-year-old cousin."

Make sure you have your child's password for MySpace to check on postings. If they refuse to turn it over, says Parry Aftab of WiredSafety.org, there is software, from SpectorSoft.com and others, that can be used to uncover it.

Make sure that friends are not giving away clues about you on their MySpace sites. "Predators are able to link to their friends and deduce specifics about a child from one site to another," says John Shehan of the National Center for Missing and Exploited Children.

How It Works

Once you sign up for MySpace, which is free, you are given a Web page, where you can post photos and blogs. You also fill out an "About Me" form that covers personal details such as name (though many members don't give their real one), school, sexual orientation and the like. From then on MySpace acts something like a high-tech chain letter. Members get requests by e-mail from people wanting to be "friends." This is the heart of the MySpace culture—meeting new people and then communicating with their friends. As an added security feature the Web pages of any members who list their age as between 14 and 15 can only be viewed by approved people on their "friends" list.

RESPONDING TO THE READING

FREEWRITING

Practice 8a. If you or people you know have a MySpace webpage, try to determine, either by visiting those web pages or interviewing the authors, whether Hewitt's description of typical pages is accurate or not.

BUILDING YOUR VOCABULARY

niche (3)	pedophiles (4)	objectionable (5)
controversy (4)	venue (4)	vulnerability (10)

QUESTIONS FOR DISCUSSION

1. Describe in your own words the "controversy" over the use of MySpace by teens.
2. "MySpace Nation: The Controversy" presents a unique opportunity to examine point of view in an essay. A team of seven journalists contributed information to the article, yet the point of view is consistently objective and the arguments are easy to follow. Describe what you think might have been the process for writing "MySpace" to ensure that the point of view, level of language, and style would appear to have been written by a single author?
3. How well do you think the essay explains the dangers that websites such as MySpace pose for teens? Which sections of the essay did you find most convincing? What made them so compelling?
4. Does the article seem to you to be one-sided, or do the authors achieve a balanced view of the "controversy"? Use examples from the essay to support your position.

TOPICS FOR WRITING

Topic 1. Based on information you gather about web pages published on MySpace, write an essay in which you analyze the legitimate and/or objectionable uses of the website.

Topic 2. Write an evaluation of the essay "MySpace Nation." Consider how convincing you find the evidence used to support arguments, the completeness and accuracy of the information in comparison with your knowledge of the website, or other considerations of tone, point of view, coherence, and interest.

Topic 3. Using "MySpace Nation: A Controversy," "Internet Censorship Will Solve Nothing" (pages 258–263), and one additional source, write your own analysis of why the Internet is both attractive and dangerous for its users.

EVALUATING: AN ANALYSIS OF "MYSPACE NATION: THE CONTROVERSY"

To evaluate a subject (such as a painting, a movie, a restaurant, or a car), it is important to identify strengths or weaknesses of that subject based on standards that help the writer judge the subject's effectiveness, quality, or value. "MySpace Nation" illustrates characteristics of essays that evaluate or make judgments about a topic. In this case, the authors explore the controversy surrounding MySpace, a website that has become an Internet phenomenon.

CHARACTERISTICS OF EVALUATING

A Distinct Point of View and Purpose
As with other strategies for writing, evaluating demands that the writer establish a clear point of view. Jaime Myers's "Hypocrisy," a student essay, adopts a first-person

point of view in order to evaluate the extent to which her mother is actually "religious." In "Love and War: An Evaluation of *Dr. Zhivago*" and "Body Piercing in America: Legitimate Form of Self-Expression?", also student essays, the writers assume an objective point of view to evaluate a movie ("Love and War") and to examine the authentic and inauthentic aspects of body piercing ("Body Piercing in America").

The writing of "MySpace: The Controversy" involved a team of journalists whose efforts resulted in an objective look at the problems created by the overwhelmingly successful website. The writers take the objective, third-person point of view in describing the incident that opens their essay, as well as three additional examples of MySpace use discussed in the essay. The essay begins: "When it comes to using MySpace, the explosively popular Web site for kids and young adults, Niki Martin and her 12-year-old daughter Ashley have a deal." Their journalistic style presents information gathered in interviews in developing their judgments about MySpace. They introduce other examples using this objective, journalistic perspective:

> "C.J. Freeman, 16, of Lotto, Indiana, admits that she goes three times a day to her page . . . ."

> "Shellee Davies, 42, of Centerville, Utah, who has two daughters, Lindsay, 17, and Whitney, 14, . . . concluded that even more innocuous material could pose a threat."

> "In March, five teenage boys in Fontana, California, went on MySpace and created a profile of a 15-year-old girl as a prank."

Clear Criteria or Standards

Identifying distinct, believable criteria for evaluating a subject is one key to writing effective evaluations. Bill Hewitt and the other authors of "MySpace: The Controversy" evaluate the security of the website based on the number of people, especially teens, who use it, the accessibility of personal web pages posted on MySpace, and the analysis of adult authorities.

EVALUATION

Evaluative Judgment	Criteria for Judgment	Supporting Evidence
MySpace has some benefits but poses real dangers for the teens who use it.	MySpace serves as "a social networking site."	Teens "share music, foster new friendships," and enjoy "a sense of community." One Internet user, C.J. Freeman, 16, says, "It's a great way to keep in touch and to meet new friends." Therapist Debbie Beach, Virginia, sees MySpace as a positive place where teens can "test out identities."

(Continued)

Evaluative Judgment	Criteria for Judgment	Supporting Evidence
	Its attractiveness, coupled with the sheer number of users, suggests the potential for abuse.	Teens who have web pages were attracted to MySpace because they can personalize their space by posting photos and personal information about themselves.
		MySpace attracts millions of teens and young adults; 20 percent of those who visit the site are 14 to 17 years old.
		Eighty million people are members of MySpace, and sixteen million children under 18 "have their own Web pages."
	Web pages on MySpace are generally accessible to anyone who registers and logs on.	The site is now the "preferred venue for cyber-bullies and online pedophiles."
		MySpace monitors the content of web pages and investigates complaints of abuse, but nothing prevents cyber-stalkers from visiting random sites.
		Children younger than 14, the required age to register, simply lie about their age and obtain access to the site.
	Both psychologists and law enforcement officers see the potential for abuse.	Psychologist Dr. David Walsh expresses the concern of parents and teachers about potential abuse.
		John Shehan, who manages a center for missing and exploited children, reports that parents are horrified at what youngsters are posting on MySpace.
		Detectives James McLaughlin, Keene, New Hampshire, and Ali Bartley, Boulder County, Colorado, are equally disturbed at the content of some web pages.

Detailed Support for Criteria

Depending on their topic, writers may rely on the detailed information typical of describing, narrating, comparing, process or causal analysis, explaining, or classifying as long as such information contributes to the evaluation they are making.

Using Narration and Description to Evaluate. The writers of "MySpace" rely heavily on narrative descriptions that involve teens being contacted by predators who have seen their websites on MySpace. They begin with "12-year-old Ashley" who was contacted by a 26-year-old, Jeramie Ray Eidem. The writers continue with a story about Lindsay, 17, who was solicited by "some 40-year-old guy with kids," and add the anecdote about the five boys who posed as a 15-year-old girl and were contacted by a middle-aged man who arranged a meeting "in a local park." The number of stories helps the authors convince us that such stalking happens with enough frequency that we should exercise caution when using MySpace ourselves or when allowing our children to log on to the website.

Using Comparing/Contrasting to Evaluate. Comparisons provide useful tools for helping readers understand a subject in a larger context. For example, we can better understand the attraction of MySpace when the authors compare its advantages to the "old-fashioned chat rooms" that consisted of nothing but text. MySpace, on the other hand, allows users to upload photos, videos, and personal information that were formerly confined to diaries. Psychologist David Walsh compares the exchanges teens have in cyberspace to conversations kids had "two generations ago" as they hung out with friends at "the corner candy store."

Using Process Analysis to Evaluate. In a boxed section of their essay, the authors of "MySpace" describe the process for obtaining a web page. They describe four basic steps involved in signing up, obtaining a site, posting information, and communicating with friends. They add a fifth point that MySpace has a security feature allowing access to approved "friends."

Organizing Ideas by Order of Importance
When evaluating a subject, writers sometimes rely on chronological order, but more frequently they arrange criteria by order of importance in a logical progression of ideas. You can see this second pattern in topic sentences from "MySpace." The authors present a logical progression from a description of MySpace and its popularity, to general objections, specific abuses (pornographic use and haven for predators) to possible resolutions (disallowing use or monitored use).

"Launched two years ago, MySpace has swiftly become one of the biggest hits in the history of the Internet." (attractiveness)

"But along with success MySpace has also generated considerable controversy." (potential objections)

"MySpace cofounder Chris DeWolfe insists the company takes its responsibility for preventing misuse of the site very seriously." (defense of MySpace)

"There is no denying the enormous power and appeal of MySpace among teens." (attractiveness)

"Freeman's mother, Teresa, takes some basic precautions." (combating dangers)

"Parents who visit the site can come away shaken all the same." (potential abuse)

"With younger kids, the risks are even greater." (pornographic use)

"Yet pornography may not be the most troubling issue." (predatory abuse)

"Not surprisingly some experts have concluded that parents should simply discourage kids from going on MySpace at all." (reactions to abuse)

"As for Niki Martin, she stifled her impulse to pull Ashley off the Web altogether." (conclusion, reaction to abuse)

FOR PRACTICE

Practice 8b. Identify transitions in the preceding topic sentences that signal a shift from one topic to the next.

THE WRITING PROCESS: EVALUATING

The steps in the writing process are useful for completing any writing assignment, including one that requires you to evaluate a subject. The following discussion presents particular considerations for adapting the writing process to the task of evaluating.

DEVELOPING A TOPIC

If you have difficulty finding a subject to evaluate, the following suggestions may prove helpful.

Think of policies, procedures, or attitudes at work or school that you think need changing.

Ask yourself what hobbies, goals, or jobs you have judged harshly or favorably.

Consider writing about a law passed by Congress or your state legislature that you disagree with or applaud.

Try to recall a performance, movie, or piece of music that affected you either positively or negatively.

Study the strengths and weaknesses of several colleges you considered attending.

Write an evaluative analysis of one of the readings in this book. You might discuss writing techniques, support for ideas, tone, or purpose in your evaluation.

DEVELOPING IDEAS

Once you have picked a topic, use the steps in the writing process to gather information, organize your ideas, and revise your paper. The preliminary writing questions listed here should prove helpful as you evaluate your topic.

Who or what is your topic? What background will the reader need to have in order to understand this topic?

What are the characteristics—both positive and negative—of your topic?

Is there anything you might compare it with that would help you show the positive or negative side of your topic?

What is your main criticism or praise of this topic?

If witnesses or experts can provide information on your topic, contact such people for an interview. If, for example, you are evaluating programs at a particular college, you might interview counselors at your school or call a professor in a department or program that interests you. If you use ideas or information from people you interview, be sure to acknowledge them with lead-ins like "According to Stephanie Brophie, advisor at the University of Colorado . . ." or "Jacqueline McKnight, a nurse-practitioner at the University Medical Center, says . . . ."

ORGANIZING IDEAS

Arranging ideas by importance or putting them in chronological order are common ways to organize details when you are evaluating. But before you choose your organizational pattern, you must have a clear idea of the criteria you will use to evaluate your topic. Following are criteria commonly used to evaluate places, events, people's behavior, movies and other forms of entertainment, and political, cultural, or social issues.

Criteria for Evaluating Places

Quality of the location
Who is there and what they are doing
What goes on in that place
What is positive or negative about being there
How it is better or worse than other places

Criteria for Evaluating Events

Details about what happened
The people involved and their motives
The circumstances surrounding the event
How this event compares with other events
The positive or negative outcome of the event
The effects of this event on other events or on the people involved

Criteria for Evaluating Movies or Television Shows

The nature of the subject and theme
Who the characters are
What they are like
The speech or dialog they use
Whether they are realistic, appealing, and convincing
How setting or special effects are used

A student essay evaluating a movie appears later in this chapter under "Student Writing."

Criteria for Evaluating Music or Live Performances

The audience for the music or performance

The appropriateness of the music or performance for that audience

The effectiveness of words and instrumentation or other aspects of performance

How this music or performance is like or unlike others you have seen

Whether or not the performance is what you expected

Positive or negative effects of the music or the acting

Criteria for Evaluating People's Behavior

Performance

Actions

Attitude toward certain events or other people

Taste or preferences

Similarities or differences when compared with other people

If you decide to evaluate people, avoid taking a point of view that is too personal, that sounds petty, or that offers a stereotypical or narrow view of your subject. Instead, evaluate your subject's performance, attitude, or other behavior using appropriate examples as evidence of what this person does.

For an example of an essay that evaluates a person's behavior, examine Jamie Myers's essay "Hypocrisy" at the end of this discussion.

Criteria for Evaluating Political, Cultural, or Social Issues

The people or other entities this issue affects

Positive and/or negative values implicit in this issue

Consequences resulting from this issue

Motivations of people on different sides of the issue

What other steps the issue calls for

Bobby Whitright's essay, "Body Piercing in America: Legitimate Form of Self-Expression?" (pages 237–239) provides a sample evaluation of a cultural issue.

SHARING AND REVISING

When revising essays, the questions for sharing essays in Appendix C are always helpful. The following checklist provides guidelines you can use when revising or participating in evaluation.

Checklist

❏ Is the point of view clearly expressed?

❏ Does the thesis predict the criteria the writer uses?

❏ Are the criteria and supporting ideas developed adequately?

- ❏ Has the author made it clear to the reader where one criterion ends and another begins?
- ❏ Does he or she need to add transitional words or phrases to clarify the essay's organization?

Student Writing: Evaluating Behavior

Hypocrisy

My mother feels that she is securely in God's hands. She goes to church three times a week and gives ten percent of her income to church work. In her mind, that is what a good Christian does. However, I see major differences between what my mother does and what Christian values teach. For one thing, she narrow-mindedly thinks that whether or not a person goes to church on Sunday is the most important measure of a true Christian. Nor does it seem to me at all Christian that my mother is prejudiced against people who happen to belong to ethnic groups different from her own. Finally, if she is such a good Christian, why is it so hard for her to show respect and love to her own children? To me, a good Christian thinks and behaves a little differently.

I object to my mother's insistence that people can't be truly religious unless they attend church every Sunday. I once pointed out that it takes more than church attendance to make a good Christian. I told my mother about one of my classmates at school who spends two days a month working as a volunteer in a local soup kitchen that, on an average, feeds 400 homeless people each day. I also mentioned a friend of mine who volunteers for the county's literacy program. My friend has worked with six people in the last two years and has enabled them to read for the first time in their lives. Although my mother admitted that these two people were doing good work, she refused to accept the idea that they could be fully authentic Christians because they don't go to church. I have been around some of the people who are in their pews every Sunday morning. Several of them spend their time talking about how much other people need to reform. One woman in particular who is my mother's good friend gossips continually about what other members of the church are or are not doing. It saddens me to think that my mother has been so influenced by these hypocrites that she cannot recognize true Christian charity.

Along with my mother's dogmatic insistence on church attendance, I cannot accept her prejudice against people from non-European cultures who don't share her beliefs or whose skin color is darker than hers. I find her attitude toward some of her own family members particularly disgusting. One of my stepsisters is married to a Mexican-American. My mother and her husband are always making racist jokes about "stupid Mexicans," in spite of the fact that they have grandchildren whose heritage is part Mexican. One of my other sister's sons lives with my mother, and he complains that she does not like his friends because one is Chinese-American and the other racially mixed. She keeps telling him to "pick better friends." I would think that Christians aren't supposed to judge their friends or neighbors, especially for such superficial reasons, if they truly follow the teaching "Judge not lest ye be judged."

My mother's dogmatism and prejudice are very hard for me to take, but worst of all is her inability to show respect and love to her own children. It seems to me that loving one's children should be just as Christian a value as honoring one's father and mother. But where my mother is concerned, she dreads rather than loves being with us. In order for her to maintain her composure when her children are present, she takes tranquilizers. Without drugs she becomes hysterical. Even cooking dinner with her daughters is a major ordeal for her. Last Christmas my sister Jeannie and I were helping her prepare dinner. My mother was going to cook some hard-boiled eggs. Jeannie made several suggestions that she felt would help make the eggs come out perfect, but my mother became insulted and stormed off to the bathroom to cry. This year she said very little to any of us because she was too high on tranquilizers to carry on a conversation.

I always thought of God as love and light, but when people tell me they are in God's hands, or they are walking in God's light, I expect to see God in their interactions with other people. There is a feeling—call it peace or concern for others—that I feel when God is present in a person, and if this feeling is not present, spirituality isn't there either. It has been a long time since I have gotten that feeling from my mother. She says she has God in her heart, but I don't see Him in her actions. She would have to do a lot of changing before I could believe in her brand of Christianity.

—Jamie Myers

RESPONDING TO THE READING

FREEWRITING

Practice 8c. If the author of "Hypocrisy" were to ask for your advice, what would you tell her?

QUESTIONS FOR DISCUSSION

1. How does Myers defend her position that her mother's actions are hypocritical? Which of her arguments is most or least convincing? Explain your response.
2. Can you offer wholehearted support for Myers's critique of her mother's behavior, or are there points with which you disagree? Explain the basis for your disagreement.

Student Writing: Evaluating a Movie

Love and War: An Evaluation of <u>Dr. Zhivago</u>

<u>Dr. Zhivago</u>, the movie based on a novel by Boris Pasternak, is a well-made movie. It is artistically filmed and makes good use of shots of the Russian countryside during different seasons. The handling of the movie's complex

plot, however, stands out as its greatest achievement. The director, David Lean, uses his main characters, Dr. Zhivago, played by Omar Sharif, and Lara, played by Julie Christie, to effectively tell two stories. The first is a rich-boy, poor-girl love story. The second follows the Bolshevik Revolution. Lean sometimes gets too heavy-handed, and he occasionally overstates his point, but as a whole, <u>Dr. Zhivago</u> is an entertaining movie that tells both of its stories well.

The audience follows the movie's double plot mainly through the eyes of the main character—Dr. Zhivago himself. We see the love between Lara and Zhivago develop at the same time as the revolution is brewing. The relationship and the revolution seem to be born together and develop together; Zhivago's first indication that an insurrection might be possible and his first view of Lara happen almost simultaneously. On the same evening he discovers this beautiful woman who will haunt his dreams, he walks into the street and is nearly trampled by horses ridden by the Czar's troops who are chasing a band of rebels. The stories are constantly intertwined in this fashion. Later, one of Lara's shy, seemingly inconsequential suitors becomes a general in the Bolshevik Army and is instrumental in persecuting the lovers. Then, too, as the rebels struggle for control of the countryside and the revolution slowly gains momentum, Zhivago and Lara struggle and grow in their love. Certainly the revolution shapes the lives of these two lovers who are eventually swept up in the general chaos. They are torn apart, then brought back together several times by the jealous general and other forces of the revolution.

The director also brings the two plots together when he uses the characters to show the feelings of the common people during the revolution. Like most Russians under the cruel Czar Nicholas II, Zhivago starts out believing that a change might be good for his country, and for this reason, he is not initially opposed to the revolt. But through his eyes we see the ugliness that develops. The Bolsheviks first take over Zhivago's house, then steal his possessions. Through his eyes we see the fear and despair of people swept up in something they don't understand and cannot control. As Zhivago loses control over his life, the entire Russian population experiences homelessness, exile, and starvation to one degree or another.

Another tactic successfully used by the director is the filming of beautiful scenes with Zhivago and Lara in the Russian countryside as a commentary on the contrasting ugliness of the war. At one point in the movie, Zhivago and Lara retreat to a house in the Caucasus Mountains. It is snowing as Zhivago arrives for the rendezvous with his lover; they enjoy each other for several days in that glorious world full of glittering snow and bright sunshine until the war tears them apart once more. In another, even more pointed, scene, the Czarist troops battle with the Bolsheviks in a field of golden wheat. As the wheat blows gently and peacefully in the wind, the grisly battle claims hundreds of lives. At one point a group of young boys are mistaken for soldiers and massacred by the Red Army. As they lie bleeding in the field, the camera shows acres and acres of beautiful, moving wheat, a sad commentary on their tragedy.

The negative points of the movie are few, but they do detract from its over-all effectiveness. The first is the overuse of the theme music, "Lara's Song." It is a lovely, haunting tune, but it is just used too often. Whenever Zhivago sees Lara or even thinks of her, we hear this music. After a while, it becomes intrusive. A little more restraint would have made it a little easier to listen to. Second, the director sometimes feels compelled to hit the audience over the head with his point about the evils of the Russian Revolution. For one thing, he portrays Lara's ex-lover as one of the coldest, most evil men I have seen in movies. One scene in particular typifies him; he is standing in the locomotive of a fast-moving train (symbolic of the revolution itself?) staring straight ahead, jaw set, arms at his sides, as though he had turned into a robot. In another scene, a group of soldiers in the Red Army attack a group of peasants who are marching to protest the lack of food in their village. The Bolshevik soldiers run them down in the street, killing unarmed women and children. We see their deaths through Zhivago's eyes, which register the disgust and horror of the doctor—a man whose duty is to save lives. True, the director wants to make his point that the people have become the innocent victims in this brutal, wrong-headed revolution. However, most people and situations are not all evil or all good, and a little subtlety would still have made the point, and perhaps been more true to life.

Putting these few flaws aside, this movie is very enjoyable. The love story is moving, and the characters are generally believable. You really care what hap-pens to them because they are warm, troubled, and suffering people. Who can watch the end where Zhivago dies before reaching Lara after so many years of separation without crying? If a love story can make you cry like that, it must be a success.

—Sheryl Little

QUESTIONS FOR DISCUSSION

1. What criteria does Sheryl Little use to evaluate *Dr. Zhivago*? How does she organize her discussion?
2. Which of her arguments do you find most convincing? Explain your choice.

Student Writing: Evaluating a Cultural Issue

Bobby Whitright wrote the following essay after gathering information about body piercing from articles in magazines and journals. The articles he refers to in his essay are listed under "Works Cited" at the end of his paper. After each piece of in-formation he used, Whitright enclosed in parentheses the name of the author of the article and the page number where he found the information. When he men-tioned the author elsewhere in his paragraph, he put only the page number in parentheses. For additional help on writing a research paper, see Part IV: Guide-lines for Writing a Research Paper.

Body Piercing in America: Legitimate Form of Self-Expression?

Within the past few years, body piercing in the United States—once an underground activity—has found its way into the cultural mainstream. It is now commonplace to turn on the television and see popular athletes or young actresses adorned with body jewelry and showing off fresh tattoos. What is more, tattoos and piercings are no longer hidden behind clothing or confined to ears, eyebrows, or nostrils. As one commentator put it, "What started innocently enough with multiple ear piercings and the odd hole in a nostril, has taken off and traveled southward to include nipples, navels, and even genitals" (Rogers 65). This current trend, which some view as mere self-mutilation, leads to much speculation as to the legitimacy of body piercing as a form of self-expression in America. Although perhaps superficial and lacking in any true cultural or historical significance, body piercing in the U.S. can still be used as a way to express one's self.

Other countries' views and approaches to body modification offer helpful comparisons to our own. Some non-Western societies have a rich history of tradition in which body alterations, such as "tongue piercing by the Mayans, Ubangi lip stretching, or Tiv scarification," are an integral part of life, and are practiced and applied by successive generations (Myers 268). The same cannot be said for people in the United States. Even though nose rings now scarcely get a second glance, it wasn't until fairly recently that earrings were deemed acceptable, particularly on men. In other cultures, "the decorated body may become a shrine, a canvas with religious and moral meaning" (Quarcoopome 56). For the Maisin women of Papua New Guinea, "tattooing is a secular ritual that marks the transition of girls into strong, sexually active, beautiful women" (Barker 226). In the trendy and impulsive U.S., however, the women whom our society admires as symbols of strength and beauty, such as pop stars and models, can offer no better explanation for getting marked than, "Why not? I just wanted to try it" (Betts 406). Americans often think of self-gratification first, and if any spirituality or moral can be applied to it afterward so be it. For us, the physical body has always been a source of fear and vessel of sin, and it is difficult to comprehend the idea of it being painted, tattooed, or scarred in praise of a god (Quarcoopome 56).

While the spiritual and religious reasons for body modification are far less evident in American culture, it should be noted that they're not altogether non-existent. Sixty-two-year-old Fakil Musafar, a guru of sorts, has achieved high recognition among piercing enthusiasts and practitioners, and has been credited with bringing a higher sense of spirituality and mysticism to the act. While Musafar claims that he is "preserving rituals that are otherwise dying out," some critics question the motives of his "weekend shamanistic seminars and performances in trendy nightclubs" (Caniglia 31). *Bay Guardian* reporter and skeptic Shoshana Marchand suggests that Musafar's act is intended for "modern primitives seeking to fill our own cultural void with rituals imported like luxury automobiles" (31).

If the spirituality displayed in other societies is not the driving force behind the motives of so many Americans, then why are we following these trends? There are actually a wide variety of reasons. The hurried pace of our lives has left many with a feeling of helplessness or of being overworked. As one piercer explains, "In chaotic times, your body's the one thing you control. And being pierced is a symbolic way of taking control of your body" ("The Holes in Some of the Parts" 70). Whether this sort of reasoning can be applied to everybody is hard to say. Other motives range from sexual enhancement to the anticipation and desire for pain, from wanting to fit in with a particular group to just plain wanting to shock people. After receiving a genital piercing, one individual expressed his "enjoyment at being separated from the despicable norm." This smugness runs parallel to those who become involved "because of the attendant disaffiliation from mainstream society" (Myers 292). In other words, these individuals are proud that their piercings set them apart from a society they consider alien and place them in a much smaller group whose ideas they can relate to. This is how "a single body modification may announce that its possessor is in harmony with an entire system of beliefs and values" (298).

Unfortunately, the masses of people are starting to embrace this antisocial activity and turn it into a meaningless fad. What was once the sign of a twisted mind and accepted by few, the idea of piercing and tattooing has now become a million dollar industry. As though there weren't enough money to go around, some practitioners have begun discrediting each other in order to legitimize themselves. In describing his studio, one tattoo artist claims, "It's not a freaky atmosphere and there's none of that piercing going on here; that stuff's just for shock value" (Betts 406). But since shock value is what makes money, more people are turning to it, even if in an artificial way. Popular fashion designer Jean Paul Gaultier has taken to using "supermodels wearing clip-on face jewelry and sheer T-shirts to look like tattoos" in some of his runway shows, all in an effort to cash in on a trend (406). Entrepreneur Jonathan Wayne has profited as well, to the tune of $14 million. His business marketing fake tattoos has provided people with "a cheap and painless way to be hip. Unlike real tattoos, these are the perfect impulse buy" (Gubernick 66).

Despite its seeming superficiality, body modification can be a legitimate, unique form of self-expression. Rather than generalize about the practice, we need to wade through all the hype created by the herd mentality of our society in order to grasp anything real. Though what this message would say about us is anyone's guess, especially when comparing the genital piercing of an American with the practice of the "Suya of central Brazil, who highlight the importance of hearing by wearing large wooden discs in their earlobes" (Myers 298). Perhaps we, too, are simply highlighting what is important to us. It's also ironic that while other cultures have slowly abandoned some of their customs and adopted Christianity and a Westernized system (Barker 218), some Americans have countered by participating in more tribal-inspired rituals and less organized religion (Caniglia 32). One study concludes that "whether the alteration was a piercing, branding, or tattoo, everyone involved in the process regarded the new decoration as art" (Myers 292). And art is, indeed, self-expression.

Works Cited

Barker, John, and Anne Marie Tietjen. "Women's Facial Tattooing among the Maisin of Oro Province, Papua New Guinea: The Changing Significance of an Ancient Custom." Oceania March 1990: 217–34.

Betts, Katherine. "Body Language." Vogue April 1994: 344–50.

Caniglia, Julie. "Making Body Art." Utne Reader January/February 1993: 30–32.

Gubernick, Lisa. "The King of Tattoos." Forbes 28 March, 1994: 66–67.

"The Holes in Some of the Parts." The New Yorker 4 October, 1993: 70–71.

Myers, James. "Nonmainstream Body Modification: Genital Piercing, Branding, Burning, and Cutting." Journal of Contemporary Ethnography October 1992: 267–306.

Quarcoopome, E. Nii. "Self-Decoration and Religious Power in Dangme Culture." African Arts July 1991: 56–65.

Rogers, Patrick, and Rebecca Crandall. "Think of It As Therapy." Newsweek 31 May, 1993: 65.

—Bobby Whitright

QUESTIONS FOR DISCUSSION

1. What might have been Whitright's purpose for writing his essay on body piercing? Who might be his intended audience?
2. In paragraph 2 Whitright discusses tattooing and other body modifications common in other cultures. Why did he include this discussion in his paper?
3. What position does Whitright take in this paper? How well does his essay support that stand?
4. Identify several strategies for writing Whitright uses to help him evaluate the cultural practice of tattooing.
5. Do you agree that tattooing and piercing are legitimate forms of self-expression for Americans?

TAKING A STAND

When writers take a stand on an issue or argue for or against it, they are asking readers to listen to their side of an issue. That means presenting a reasonable, commonsense approach to the topic, and providing information about opposing viewpoints as well as detailed, appropriate examples that clearly justify the writer's position. For example, the student essay "Internet Censorship Will Accomplish Nothing" evaluates attempts to censor material on the Internet and presents several arguments that show the problems with promoting such censorship. Passages from Martin Luther King Jr.'s "Letter from the Birmingham Jail" illustrate some of the techniques that writers use when taking a stand and writing persuasively.

What have you heard about the civil rights era in the 1960s, Martin Luther King, Jr., Malcolm X, or other figures from that period?

Letter from the Birmingham Jail

Martin Luther King, Jr.

As founding president of the Southern Christian Leadership Conference, Dr. Martin Luther King, Jr. (1928–1968) led the nonviolent movement to desegregate the South. The efforts of King and his followers culminated in the Civil Rights Act of 1964 and the 1965 Voting Rights Act. After the passage of the Civil Rights Act, King received the Nobel Peace Prize, and, more recently, his birthday has been declared a national holiday. Dr. King's works include Stride toward Freedom *(1958), the story of the Montgomery Bus Boycott,* Why We Can't Wait *(1963), on the Birmingham Campaign, and* Where Do We Go from Here: Chaos or Community? *(1967), essays on the nuclear arms race and other problems of the late 1960s. He addressed the "Letter from the Birmingham Jail" to eight clergymen—four bishops, three ministers, and a rabbi—who had criticized him for resorting to civil disobedience in his fight against segregationist policies in the South. King worked for civil rights causes until his death at the hands of an assassin on April 4, 1968.*

My Dear Fellow Clergymen:

1   While confined here in the Birmingham city jail, I came across your recent statement calling my present activities "unwise and untimely." Seldom do I pause to answer criticism of my work and ideas. If I sought to answer all the criticisms that cross my desk, my secretaries would have little time for anything other than such correspondence in the course of the day, and I would have no time for constructive work. But since I feel that you are men of genuine good will and that your criticisms are sincerely set forth, I want to try to answer your statement in what I hope will be patient and reasonable terms.

2   I think I should indicate why I am here in Birmingham, since you have been influenced by the view that argues against "outsiders coming in." I have the honor of serving as president of the Southern Christian Leadership Conference, an organization operating in every southern state, with headquarters in Atlanta, Georgia. We have some eighty-five affiliated organizations across the South, and one of them is the Alabama Christian Movement for Human Rights. Frequently we share staff, educational, and financial resources with our affiliates. Several months ago the affiliate here in Birmingham asked us to be on call to engage in a nonviolent direct-action program if such were deemed necessary. We readily consented, and when the hour came we lived up to our promise. So I, along with several members of my staff, am here because I was invited here. I am here because I have organizational ties here.

But more basically, I am in Birmingham because injustice is here. Just as the prophets of the eighth century B.C. left their villages and carried their "thus saith the Lord" far beyond the boundaries of their home towns, and just as the Apostle Paul left his village of Tarsus and carried the gospel of Jesus Christ to the far corners of the Greco-Roman world, so am I compelled to carry the gospel of freedom beyond my own home town. Like Paul, I must constantly respond to the Macedonian call for aid.

Moreover, I am cognizant of the interrelatedness of all communities and states. I cannot sit idly by in Atlanta and not be concerned about what happens in Birmingham. Injustice anywhere is a threat to justice everywhere. We are caught in an inescapable network of mutuality, tied in a single garment of destiny. Whatever affects one directly, affects all indirectly. Never again can we afford to live with the narrow, provincial "outside agitator" idea. Anyone who lives inside the United States can never be considered an outsider anywhere within its bounds.

You deplore the demonstrations taking place in Birmingham. But your statement, I am sorry to say, fails to express a similar concern for the conditions that brought about the demonstrations. I am sure that none of you would want to rest content with the superficial kind of social analysis that deals merely with effects and does not grapple with underlying causes. It is unfortunate that demonstrations are taking place in Birmingham, but it is even more unfortunate that the city's white power structure left the Negro community with no alternative. . . .

You may well ask: "Why direct action? Why sit-ins, marches, and so forth? Isn't negotiation a better path?" You are quite right in calling for negotiation. Indeed, this is the very purpose of direct action. Nonviolent direct action seeks to create such a crisis and foster such a tension that a community that has constantly refused to negotiate is forced to confront the issue. It seeks so to dramatize the issue that it can no longer be ignored. My citing the creation of tension as part of the work of the nonviolent-resister may sound rather shocking. But I must confess that I am not afraid of the word "tension." I have earnestly opposed violent tension, but there is a type of constructive, nonviolent tension that is necessary for growth. Just as Socrates[1] felt that it was necessary to create a tension in the mind so that individuals could rise from the bondage of myths and half-truths to the unfettered realm of creative analysis and objective appraisal, so must we see the need for nonviolent gadflies to create the kind of tension in society that will help men rise from the dark depths of prejudice and racism to the majestic heights of understanding and brotherhood.

The purpose of our direct-action program is to create a situation so crisis-packed that it will inevitably open the door to negotiation. I therefore concur with you in your call for negotiation. Too long has our beloved Southland been bogged down in a tragic effort to live in monologue rather than dialogue.

---

[1] Greek philosopher (470–399 B.C.E.) whose outspoken criticism of the government in Athens led to his imprisonment and eventual death.

8   One of the basic points in your statement is that the action that I and my associates have taken in Birmingham is untimely. Some have asked: "Why didn't you give the new city administration time to act?" The only answer that I can give to this query is that the new Birmingham administration must be prodded about as much as the outgoing one, before it will act. . . . My friends, I must say to you that we have not made a single gain in civil rights without determined legal and nonviolent pressure. Lamentably, it is an historical fact that privileged groups seldom give up their privileges voluntarily. Individuals may see the moral light and voluntarily give up their unjust posture; but, as Reinhold Niebuhr[2] has reminded us, groups tend to be more immoral than individuals.

9   We know through painful experience that freedom is never voluntarily given by the oppressor; it must be demanded by the oppressed. Frankly, I have yet to engage in a direct-action campaign that was "well timed" in the view of those who have not suffered unduly from the disease of segregation. For years now I have heard the word "Wait!" It rings in the ear of every Negro with piercing familiarity. This "Wait" has almost always meant "Never." We must come to see, with one of our distinguished jurists, that "justice too long delayed is justice denied."

10   We have waited for more than 340 years for our constitutional and God-given rights. The nations of Asia and Africa are moving with jet-like speed toward gaining political independence, but we still creep at horse-and-buggy pace toward gaining a cup of coffee at a lunch counter. Perhaps it is easy for those who have never felt the stinging darts of segregation to say, "Wait." But when you have seen vicious mobs lynch your mothers and fathers at will and drown your sisters and brothers at whim; when you have seen hate-filled policemen curse, kick, and even kill your black brothers and sisters; when you see the vast majority of your twenty million Negro brothers smothering in an airtight cage of poverty in the midst of an affluent society; when you suddenly find your tongue twisted and your speech stammering as you seek to explain to your six-year-old daughter why she can't go to the public amusement park that has just been advertised on television, and see tears welling up in her eyes when she is told that Funtown is closed to colored children, and see ominous clouds of inferiority beginning to form in her little mental sky, and see her beginning to distort her personality by developing an unconscious bitterness toward white people; when you have to concoct an answer for a five-year-old son who is asking: "Daddy, why do white people treat colored people so mean?"; when you take a cross-country drive and find it necessary to sleep night after night in the uncomfortable corners of your automobile because no motel will accept you; when you are humiliated day in and day out by nagging signs reading "white" and "colored"; when your first name becomes "nigger," your middle name becomes "boy" (however old you are), and your last name becomes "John," and your wife and mother are never given the respected title "Mrs."; when you are harried by day and haunted by night by the fact that you are a Negro, living constantly at tiptoe stance, never quite knowing what to expect next, and are plagued with inner fears and outer resentments; when you are forever fighting a degenerating sense of "nobodiness"—then

---

[2] American theologian, 1892–1971.

you will understand why we find it difficult to wait. There comes a time when the cup of endurance runs over, and men are no longer willing to be plunged into the abyss of despair. I hope, sirs, you can understand our legitimate and unavoidable impatience.

You express a great deal of anxiety over our willingness to break laws. This is certainly a legitimate concern. Since we so diligently urge people to obey the Supreme Court's decision of 1954 outlawing segregation in the public schools, at first glance it may seem rather paradoxical for us consciously to break laws. One may well ask: "How can you advocate breaking some laws and obeying others?" The answer lies in the fact that there are two types of laws: just and unjust. I would be the first to advocate obeying just laws. One has not only a legal but a moral responsibility to obey just laws. Conversely, one has a moral responsibility to disobey unjust laws. I would agree with St. Augustine that "an unjust law is no law at all."

Now, what is the difference between the two? How does one determine whether a law is just or unjust? A just law is a man-made code that squares with the moral law or the law of God. An unjust law is a code that is out of harmony with the moral law. To put it in the terms of St. Thomas Aquinas: An unjust law is a human law that is not rooted in eternal law and natural law. Any law that uplifts human personality is just. Any law that degrades human personality is unjust. All segregation statutes are unjust because segregation distorts the soul and damages the personality. It gives the segregator a false sense of superiority and the segregated a false sense of inferiority. Segregation, to use the terminology of the Jewish philosopher Martin Buber,[3] substitutes an "I-it" relationship for an "I-thou" relationship and ends up relegating persons to the status of things. Hence segregation is not only politically, economically, and sociologically unsound, it is morally wrong and sinful. Paul Tillich has said that sin is separation. Is not segregation an existential expression of man's tragic separation, his awful estrangement, his terrible sinfulness? Thus it is that I can urge men to obey the 1954 decision of the Supreme Court, for it is morally right; and I can urge them to disobey segregation ordinances, for they are morally wrong.

Let us consider a more concrete example of just and unjust laws. An unjust law is a code that a numerical or power majority group compels a minority group to obey but does not make binding on itself. This is *difference* made legal. By the same token, a just law is a code that a majority compels a minority to follow and that it is willing to follow itself. This is *sameness* made legal.

Let me give another explanation. A law is unjust if it is inflicted on a minority that, as a result of being denied the right to vote, had no part in enacting or devising the law. Who can say that the legislature of Alabama, which set up that state's segregation laws, was democratically elected? Throughout Alabama all sorts of devious methods are used to prevent Negroes from becoming registered voters, and there are some counties in which, even though Negroes constitute a majority of the population, not a single Negro is registered. Can any law enacted under such circumstances be considered democratically structured? . . .

---

[3] Israeli philosopher and theologian (1878–1965) associated with religious existentialism.

Letter from the Birmingham Jail   Martin Luther King, Jr.   **243**

15   I hope you are able to see the distinction I am trying to point out. In no sense do I advocate evading or defying the law, as would the rabid segregationist. That would lead to anarchy. One who breaks an unjust law must do so openly, lovingly, and with a willingness to accept the penalty. I submit that an individual who breaks a law that conscience tells him is unjust, and who willingly accepts the penalty of imprisonment in order to arouse the conscience of the community over its injustice, is in reality expressing the highest respect for law.

16   Of course, there is nothing new about this kind of civil disobedience. It was evidenced sublimely in the refusal of Shadrach, Meshach, and Abednego[4] to obey the laws of Nebuchadnezzar, on the ground that a higher moral law was at stake. It was practiced superbly by the early Christians, who were willing to face hungry lions and the excruciating pain of chopping blocks rather than submit to certain unjust laws of the Roman Empire. To a degree, academic freedom is a reality today because Socrates practiced civil disobedience. In our own nation, the Boston Tea Party represented a massive act of civil disobedience.

17   We should never forget that everything Adolf Hitler did in Germany was "legal" and everything the Hungarian freedom fighters did in Hungary was "illegal." It was "illegal" to aid and comfort a Jew in Hitler's Germany. Even so, I am sure that, had I lived in Germany at the time, I would have aided and comforted my Jewish brothers. If today I lived in a Communist country where certain principles dear to the Christian faith are suppressed, I would openly advocate disobeying that country's antireligious laws.

18   I must make two honest confessions to you, my Christian and Jewish brothers. First, I must confess that over the past few years I have been gravely disappointed with the white moderate. I have almost reached the regrettable conclusion that the Negro's great stumbling block in his stride toward freedom is not the White Citizen's Councilor or the Ku Klux Klanner, but the white moderate, who is more devoted to "order" than to justice; who prefers a negative peace which is the absence of tension to a positive peace which is the presence of justice; who constantly says: "I agree with you in the goal you seek, but I cannot agree with your methods of direct action"; who paternalistically believes he can set the timetable for another man's freedom; who lives by a mythical concept of time and who constantly advises the Negro to wait for a "more convenient season." Shallow understanding from people of good will is more frustrating than absolute misunderstanding from people of ill will. Lukewarm acceptance is much more bewildering than outright rejection. . . .

19   You speak of our activity in Birmingham as extreme. At first I was rather disappointed that fellow clergymen would see my nonviolent efforts as those of an extremist. I began thinking about the fact that I stand in the middle of two opposing forces in the Negro community. One is a force of complacency, made up in part of Negroes who, as a result of long years of oppression, are so drained of self-respect and a sense of "somebodiness" that they have adjusted to segregation; and in part of a few middle-class Negroes who, because of a degree of academic and economic security and because in some ways they profit by segregation, have become insensitive to the problems of the

---

[4] The three Hebrew prophets in *The Book of Daniel* who emerged from the "fiery furnace" unharmed.

masses. The other force is one of bitterness and hatred, and it comes perilously close to advocating violence. It is expressed in the various black nationalist groups that are springing up across the nation, the largest and best-known being Elijah Muhammad's Muslim movement. Nourished by the Negro's frustration over the continued existence of racial discrimination, this movement is made up of people who have lost faith in America, who have absolutely repudiated Christianity, and who have concluded that the white man is an incorrigible "devil."[5]

20 I have tried to stand between these two forces, saying that we need emulate neither the "do-nothingism" of the complacent nor the hatred and despair of the black nationalist. For there is the more excellent way of love and nonviolent protest. I am grateful to God that, through the influence of the Negro church, the way of nonviolence became an integral part of our struggle.

21 If this philosophy had not emerged, by now many streets of the South would, I am convinced, be flowing with blood. And I am further convinced that if our white brothers dismiss as "rabble-rousers" and "outside agitators" those of us who employ nonviolent direct action, and if they refuse to support our nonviolent efforts, millions of Negroes will, out of frustration and despair, seek solace and security in black nationalist ideologies—a development that would inevitably lead to a frightening racial nightmare.

22 Oppressed people cannot remain oppressed forever. The yearning for freedom eventually manifests itself, and that is what has happened to the American Negro. Something within has reminded him of his birthright of freedom, and something without has reminded him that it can be gained. Consciously or unconsciously, he has been caught up by the *Zeitgeist*,[6] and with his black brothers of Africa and his brown and yellow brothers of Asia, South America, and the Caribbean, the United States Negro is moving with a sense of great urgency toward the promised land of racial justice. If one recognizes this vital urge that has engulfed the Negro community, one should readily understand why public demonstrations are taking place. The Negro has many pent-up resentments and latent frustrations, and he must release them. So let him march; let him make prayer pilgrimages to the city hall; let him go on freedom rides—and try to understand why he must do so. If his repressed emotions are not released in nonviolent ways, they will seek expression through violence; this is not a threat but a fact of history. So I have not said to my people: "Get rid of your discontent." Rather, I have tried to say that this normal and healthy discontent can be channeled into the creative outlet of nonviolent direct action. And now this approach is being termed extremist.

23 But though I was initially disappointed at being categorized as an extremist, as I continued to think about the matter I gradually gained a measure of satisfaction from the label. Was not Jesus an extremist for love: "Love your enemies, bless them that curse you, do good to them that hate you, and pray for them which despitefully use you, and persecute you." Was not Amos an extremist for justice: "Let justice roll down like waters

---

[5] King refers to the Black Muslim movement. Malcolm X, an eloquent spokesman for the Muslims, originally accepted Elijah Muhammad's teaching that, among other things, the white man was the devil incarnate.

[6] German for the "spirit of the age"—the way of thinking that is characteristic of a particular era.

and righteousness like an ever-flowing stream." Was not Paul an extremist for the Christian gospel: "I bear in my body the marks of the Lord Jesus." Was not Martin Luther[7] an extremist: "Here I stand; I cannot do otherwise, so help me God." And John Bunyan: "I will stay in jail to the end of my days before I make a butchery of my conscience." And Abraham Lincoln: "This nation cannot survive half slave and half free." And Thomas Jefferson: "We hold these truths to be self-evident, that all men are created equal . . ." So the question is not whether we will be extremists, but what kind of extremists we will be. Will we be extremists for hate or for love? Will we be extremists for the preservation of injustice or for the extension of justice? In that dramatic scene on Calvary's hill three men were crucified. We must never forget that all three were crucified for the same crime—the crime of extremism. Two were extremists for immorality, and thus fell below their environment. The other, Jesus Christ, was an extremist for love, truth and goodness, and thereby rose above his environment. Perhaps the South, the nation and the world are in dire need of creative extremists. . . .

24   I came to Birmingham with the hope that the white religious leadership of this community would see the justice of our cause and, with deep moral concern, would serve as the channel through which our just grievances could reach the power structure. I had hoped that each of you would understand. But again I have been disappointed.

25   I have heard numerous southern religious leaders admonish their worshipers to comply with a desegregation decision because it is the law, but I have longed to hear white ministers declare: "Follow this decree because integration is morally right and because the Negro is your brother." In the midst of blatant injustices inflicted upon the Negro, I have watched white churchmen stand on the sideline and mouth pious irrelevancies and sanctimonious trivialities. In the midst of a mighty struggle to rid our nation of racial and economic injustice, I have heard many ministers say: "Those are social issues, with which the gospel has no real concern." And I have watched many churches commit themselves to a completely other-worldly religion, which makes a strange, unbiblical distinction between body and soul, between the sacred and the secular.

26   I have traveled the length and breadth of Alabama, Mississippi and all the other southern states. On sweltering summer days and crisp autumn mornings I have looked at the South's beautiful churches with their lofty spires pointing heavenward. I have beheld the impressive outlines of her massive religious education buildings. Over and over I have found myself asking: "What kind of people worship here? Who is their God? Where were their voices when the lips of Governor Barnett dripped with words of interposition and nullification? Where were they when Governor Wallace gave a clarion call for defiance and hatred? Where were their voices of support when bruised and weary Negro men and women decided to rise from the dark dungeons of complacency to the bright hills of creative protest?"

27   Yes, these questions are still in my mind. In deep disappointment I have wept over the laxity of the church. But be assured that my tears have been tears of love. There can

---

[7] Martin Luther's protests against the Catholic Church started the Protestant movement in Europe.

be no deep disappointment where there is not deep love. Yes, I love the church. How could I do otherwise? I am in the rather unique position of being the son, the grandson, and the great-grandson of preachers. Yes, I see the church as the body of Christ. But, oh! How we have blemished and scarred that body through social neglect and through fear of being nonconformists.

There was a time when the church was very powerful—in the time when the early Christians rejoiced at being deemed worthy to suffer for what they believed. In those days the church was not merely a thermometer that recorded the ideas and principles of popular opinion; it was a thermostat that transformed the mores of society. Whenever the early Christians entered a town, the people in power became disturbed and immediately sought to convict the Christians for being "disturbers of the peace" and "outside agitators." But the Christians pressed on, in the conviction that they were "a colony of heaven," called to obey God rather than man. Small in number, they were big in commitment. They were too God-intoxicated to be "astronomically intimidated." By their effort and example they brought an end to such ancient evils as infanticide and gladiatorial contests. 28

Things are different now. So often the contemporary church is a weak, ineffectual voice with an uncertain sound. So often it is an archdefender of the status quo. Far from being disturbed by the presence of the church, the power structure of the average community is consoled by the church's silent—and often even vocal—sanction of things as they are. 29

But the judgment of God is upon the church as never before. If today's church does not recapture the sacrificial spirit of the early church, it will lose its authenticity, forfeit the loyalty of millions, and be dismissed as an irrelevant social club with no meaning for the twentieth century. Every day I meet young people whose disappointment with the church has turned into outright disgust. . . . 30

I hope the church as a whole will meet the challenge of this decisive hour. But even if the church does not come to the aid of justice, I have no despair about the future. I have no fear about the outcome of our struggle in Birmingham, even if our motives are at present misunderstood. We will reach the goal of freedom in Birmingham and all over the nation, because the goal of America is freedom. Abused and scorned though we may be, our destiny is tied up with America's destiny. Before the pilgrims landed at Plymouth, we were here. Before the pen of Jefferson etched the majestic words of the Declaration of Independence across the pages of history, we were here. For more than two centuries our forebears labored in this country without wages; they made cotton king; they built the homes of their masters while suffering gross injustice and shameful humiliation—and yet out of a bottomless vitality they continued to thrive and develop. If the inexpressible cruelties of slavery could not stop us, the opposition we now face will surely fail. We will win our freedom because the sacred heritage of our nation and the eternal will of God are embodied in our echoing demands. 31

Before closing I feel impelled to mention one other point in your statement that has troubled me profoundly. You warmly commended the Birmingham police force for keeping "order" and "preventing violence." I doubt that you would have so warmly 32 commended the police force if you had seen its dogs sinking their teeth into unarmed, nonviolent Negroes. I doubt that you would so quickly commend the policemen if you were to observe their ugly and inhumane treatment of Negroes here in the city jail; if you were to watch them push and curse old Negro women and young Negro girls; if you were to see them slap and kick old Negro men and young boys; if you were to observe them, as they did on two occasions, refuse to give us food because we wanted to sing our grace together. I cannot join you in your praise of the Birmingham police department. . . .

33   I wish you had commended the Negro sit-inners and demonstrators of Birmingham for their sublime courage, their willingness to suffer and their amazing discipline in the midst of great provocation. One day the South will recognize its real heroes. They will be the James Merediths, with the noble sense of purpose that enables them to face jeering and hostile mobs, and with the agonizing loneliness that characterizes the life of the pioneer. They will be old, oppressed, battered Negro women, symbolized in a seventy-two-year-old woman in Montgomery, Alabama, who rose up with a sense of dignity and with her people decided not to ride segregated buses, and who responded with ungrammatical profundity to one who inquired about her weariness: "My feets is tired, but my soul is at rest." They will be the young high school and college students, the young ministers of the gospel and a host of their elders, courageously and nonviolently sitting in at lunch counters and willingly going to jail for conscience's sake. One day the South will know that when these disinherited children of God sat down at lunch counters, they were in reality standing up for what is best in the American dream and for the most sacred values in our Judaeo-Christian heritage, thereby bringing our nation back to those great wells of democracy which were dug deep by the founding fathers in their formulation of the Constitution and the Declaration of Independence.

34   Never before have I written so long a letter. I'm afraid it is much too long to take your precious time. I can assure you that it would have been much shorter if I had been writing from a comfortable desk, but what else can one do when he is alone in a narrow jail cell, other than write long letters, think long thoughts, and pray long prayers?

35   If I have said anything in this letter that overstates the truth and indicates an unreasonable impatience, I beg you to forgive me. If I have said anything that understates the truth and indicates my having a patience that allows me to settle for anything less than brotherhood, I beg God to forgive me.

36   I hope this letter finds you strong in the faith. I also hope that circumstances will soon make it possible for me to meet each of you, not as an integrationist or a civil rights leader but as a fellow clergyman and a Christian brother. Let us all hope that the dark clouds of racial prejudice will soon pass away and the deep fog of misunderstanding will be lifted from our fear-drenched communities, and in some not too distant tomorrow the radiant stars of love and brotherhood will shine over our great nation with all their scintillating beauty.

Yours for the cause of Peace and Brotherhood,
MARTIN LUTHER KING, JR.

RESPONDING TO THE READING

FREEWRITING

Practice 8d. Based on what you have just read about segregation in the South, describe the situation blacks faced during the time period when Dr. King wrote his "Letter from the Birmingham Jail."

BUILDING YOUR VOCABULARY

affiliated (2)	ominous (10)	clarion (26)
deemed (2)	estrangement (12)	interposition (26)
agitator (4)	existential (12)	nullification (26)
cognizant (4)	relegating (12)	laxity (27)
interrelatedness (4)	terminology (12)	nonconformists (27)
mutuality (4)	anarchy (15)	gladiatorial (28)
grapple (5)	rabid (15)	infanticide (28)
appraisal (6)	paternalistically (18)	intimidated (28)
gadflies (6)	repudiated (19)	mores (28)
lamentably (8)	emulate (20)	archdefender (29)
prodded (8)	blatant (25)	forfeit (30)
query (8)	irrelevancies (25)	provocation (33)
concoct (10)	pious (25)	scintillating (36)
harried (10)	sanctimonious (25)	

QUESTIONS FOR DISCUSSION

1. Who was King's audience? Which of his arguments do you think were the most convincing for them?
2. Which of the issues King raises might apply to the country as a whole as well as to the community of Birmingham, Alabama?
3. King argues that the black community has been as patient as it can be in the struggle for equality. What evidence does he offer in support of his position? Do you find it convincing?
4. How does King distinguish between just and unjust laws (paragraphs 12–15)? Do you agree with his distinction? Why or why not?
5. State in your own words the purpose of nonviolent direct action (paragraphs 6 and 7). Might other situations be appropriate for this method of protest? Explain your response.
6. Why does King consider the white moderate a greater "stumbling block" to freedom than more open racists like the members of the White Citizens Council or the Ku Klux Klan (paragraph 18)?
7. What does King mean when he accuses the church of being an "archdefender of the status quo" (paragraph 29)? Is his statement accurate today? Are you aware of churches that work actively for social change?

TOPICS FOR WRITING

Topic 1. Write a paper arguing whether certain circumstances justify breaking a law. Consider, as does King, which laws, if any, one might break and why you think such an act would be justified.

Topic 2. Write a paper in which you identify a situation that you consider unjust and explain why it is unjust. Then propose solutions for changing this situation. As you discuss solutions, explain how they will make a difference.

Topic 3. If you belong to a church, temple, or mosque, write a letter to its religious leader evaluating what the church is doing for the community's homeless, disadvantaged, working poor, or other people in need. You may rely on your own knowledge, but also interview ministers, priests, rabbis, or members of the congregation to find out what they do and how effective their work has been.

TAKING A STAND: AN ANALYSIS OF "LETTER FROM THE BIRMINGHAM JAIL"

The writing techniques discussed earlier in this chapter for evaluating a topic will be useful as you write essays that take a stand. When writers take a position on a subject, they identify an unfair situation or a position that they feel needs changing. To defend their position, they make a rational, at times personal, appeal to the reader. Additional considerations for presenting rational, emotional, and moral appeals include a clear purpose and audience, a debatable thesis, a reasonable approach to the topic, an appeal to emotions, an appeal to moral values, and, as always, a clear organization.

CHARACTERISTICS OF PERSUADING

A Clear Purpose and Audience

The purpose of persuasive essays is often to convince the reader to take a particular stand on an issue or to take action to remedy a situation. In his "Letter from the Birmingham Jail," Martin Luther King, Jr.'s immediate purpose is to defend himself against the accusations that the sit-ins and marches he organized in an effort to integrate public facilities in Birmingham, Alabama, were "unwise and untimely." King addresses his letter to the four bishops, three ministers, and one rabbi who made the statement, but his answers have had a much wider audience. The letter was published in 1963 in a collection of King's essays entitled *Why We Can't Wait*. In the intervening 30 years, "Letter from the Birmingham Jail" has become standard reading in many high school and college classes.

A Debatable Thesis

For a topic to be suitable for an essay that takes a stand, it must be "debatable"; this means it must be possible for someone to take an opposing position on the issue.

For example, an essay arguing that funding for programs targeting children and adults with disabilities should be increased might have this thesis: "The amount this state budgets for services to the disabled should be increased." This thesis is debatable because a writer who opposes this solution could take this position: "The amount this state budgets for services to the disabled should *not* be increased." Taxpayers or groups that compete for funds might take this second position.

The following examples will help you distinguish between the thesis for a persuasive essay and thesis statements used for other writing strategies. Debatable thesis statements have a check (✓) beside them.

_____ Topic 1A: My family wastes a lot of electricity.

This thesis lends itself to an explanation of how the writer's family wastes electricity. The writer might also discuss solutions to this problem.

___✓___ Topic 1B: Because landfill sites are filling up, recycling of paper and glassware should be mandatory.

This thesis is debatable because it can be reversed: Someone else might argue that recycling should *not* be mandatory.

_____ Topic 2A: Interracial couples experience racism from several sources.

This thesis leads to an analysis of problems faced by interracial couples.

___✓___ Topic 2B: Nonviolent protest is an important, effective technique for fighting racism.

This position is debatable because one could also argue, as some people have, that nonviolent protest is *not* an effective technique for combating racism.

FOR PRACTICE

Practice 8e. Identify the thesis statements listed here that are debatable and, consequently, suitable for a paper that takes a stand. For statements that are *not* debatable, note the writing strategy you would use to develop them. The first one is done for you.

_____ 1. Some businesses work to defeat gun control for several reasons.
I would explain why certain businesses support the quick sale of handguns.

_____ 2. Laws should provide much stricter regulations for the use of firearms.

_____ 3. The United States has accumulated the most advanced weapons system the world has ever seen.

_____ 4. Teen suicide can be prevented if we learn to read the signs.

_____ 5. AIDS, often called the modern plague, has an obscure beginning and a tragic history.

_____ 6. Several important reasons justify why school lunch programs should not be cut from the federal budget.

A Reasonable Approach to the Topic

Even though writers have strong feelings about their topics, they must avoid lecturing their readers or relying on unsupported assumptions to make their case. If you consider your own experience, the reasons for taking such precautions become clear. In all probability, you are not convinced by parents', bosses', teachers', or other authority figures' arguments unless they offer evidence to support their claims. Similarly, a writer who appears demanding (you better listen to me) or pompous (you're foolish not to believe me) rarely makes the reader receptive to his or her position. A much more effective approach involves explaining the experience or knowledge that motivated a writer to take a particular stand. Writers may also make rational, moral, and emotional appeals to their readers. Dr. Martin Luther King, Jr.'s argument in "Letter from the Birmingham Jail" illustrates masterful use of these techniques.

A Reasonable Tone. To write persuasively, an author, although convinced of his or her position, must maintain an overall tone of reasonableness. A self-righteous or narrow-minded approach may intimidate an audience, but it won't convince them. In the opening of the letter he wrote from the Birmingham jail, King establishes such a rational, measured tone.

> My Dear Fellow Clergymen:
>
> While confined here in the Birmingham city jail, I came across your recent statement calling my present activities "unwise and untimely." Seldom do I pause to answer criticism of my work and ideas. If I sought to answer all the criticisms that cross my desk, my secretaries would have little time for anything other than such correspondence in the course of the day, and I would have no time for constructive work. But since I feel that you are men of genuine good will and that your criticisms are sincerely set forth, I want to try to answer your statement in what I hope will be patient and reasonable terms.

King acknowledges that his critics are "men of genuine good will" whose "criticisms are sincerely set forth," and he promises to be "patient and reasonable" in his response. He thereby establishes himself as someone who respectfully disagrees with his opponents and will remain reasonable in his rebuttal of their arguments.

A Clear Position. Readers need to know exactly what position the writer will defend and how that position will be supported. King makes it clear that his letter is an answer to a "recent statement" signed by several clergymen who assert that his nonviolent protests are "unwise and untimely." His letter answers each of their objections in turn, and in the process, it presents his own positions on the issues they raise.

Opposing Points of View. Writers of persuasive material often introduce opposing arguments and offer their own objections or counterarguments. In so doing, they anticipate objections that their readers may share. The tactic also shows that the writer examined the issue from several perspectives before reaching a reasonable conclusion. In his letter from jail, King presents and then refutes each of his opponents' arguments against nonviolent protest. A few of his rebuttals are illustrated in the following discussion of evidence.

Several Kinds of Evidence. Support for ideas is always an important element in an essay, but because persuasive essays try to convince the reader to change a position or to take action on a particular issue, solid evidence is literally the heart of persuasive writing. Facts, case studies, personal experience, and the opinions of witnesses or authorities provide convincing support. King uses each of these sources of evidence. He uses facts to counter his opponents' accusation that he is an "outsider" who has come to Birmingham to make trouble:

> I think I should indicate why I am here in Birmingham, since you have been in- fluenced by the view that argues against "outsiders coming in." I have the honor of serving as president of the Southern Christian Leadership Conference, an organiza- tion operating in every southern state, with headquarters in Atlanta, Georgia. We have some eighty-five affiliated organizations across the South, and one of them is the Alabama Christian Movement for Human Rights. Frequently we share staff, educational, and financial resources with our affiliates. Several months ago the affiliate here in Birmingham asked us to be on call to engage in a nonviolent direct- action program if such were deemed necessary. We readily consented, and when the hour came we lived up to our promise. So I, along with several members of my staff, am here because I was invited here. I am here because I have organizational ties here.

Next, King explains the biblical authority for his actions in Birmingham, and cites biblical precedent. Because his audience consists of four bishops, three minis- ters, and a rabbi, the Bible is completely appropriate as an "authority" for his actions, one that his clerical readers respect.

> But more basically, I am in Birmingham because injustice is here. Just as the prophets of the eighth century B.C. left their villages and carried their "thus saith the Lord" far beyond the boundaries of their home towns, and just as the Apostle Paul left his village of Tarsus and carried the gospel of Jesus Christ to the far corners of the Greco-Roman world, so am I compelled to carry the gospel of freedom beyond my own home town. Like Paul, I must constantly respond to the Macedonian call for aid.

An Appeal to Emotions

Although it should be used sparingly, an appeal to readers' emotions can some- times be quite effective. In some of the most persuasive writing in the English lan- guage, King makes an emotional appeal to his readers when he gives examples of the injustices suffered by black Americans and mentions the feeling of "nobodi- ness" that results from such treatment.

> We have waited for more than 340 years for our constitutional and God-given rights. The nations of Asia and Africa are moving with jetlike speed toward gain- ing political independence, but we still creep at horse-and-buggy pace toward gaining a cup of coffee at a lunch counter. Perhaps it is easy for those who have never felt the stinging darts of segregation to say, "Wait." But when you have

seen vicious mobs lynch your mothers and fathers at will and drown your sisters and brothers at whim; when you have seen hate-filled policemen curse, kick, and even kill your black brothers and sisters; when you see the vast majority of your twenty million Negro brothers smothering in an airtight cage of poverty in the midst of an affluent society; when you suddenly find your tongue twisted and your speech stammering as you seek to explain to your six-year-old daughter why she can't go to the public amusement park that has just been advertised on television, and see tears welling up in her eyes when she is told that Funtown is closed to colored children, and see ominous clouds of inferiority beginning to form in her little mental sky, and see her beginning to distort her personality by developing an unconscious bitterness toward white people; when you have to concoct an answer for a five-year-old son who is asking: "Daddy, why do white people treat colored people so mean?"; when you take a cross-country drive and find it necessary to sleep night after night in the uncomfortable corners of your automobile because no motel will accept you; when you are humiliated day in and day out by nagging signs reading "white" and "colored"; when your first name becomes "nigger," your middle name becomes "boy" (however old you are), and your last name becomes "John," and your wife and mother are never given the respected title "Mrs."; when you are harried by day and haunted by night by the fact that you are a Negro, living constantly at tiptoe stance, never quite knowing what to expect next, and are plagued with inner fears and outer resentments; when you are forever fighting a degenerating sense of "nobodiness"—then you will understand why we find it difficult to wait. There comes a time when the cup of endurance runs over, and men are no longer willing to be plunged into the abyss of despair. I hope, sirs, you can understand our legitimate and unavoidable impatience.

An Appeal to Moral Values
In "Letter from the Birmingham Jail," King uses the clergymen's own moral principles and the religious foundations on which their churches are based to criticize their position.

I have heard numerous southern religious leaders admonish their worshipers to comply with a desegregation decision because it is the law, but I have longed to hear white ministers declare: "Follow this decree because integration is morally right and because the Negro is your brother." In the midst of blatant injustices inflicted upon the Negro, I have watched white churchmen stand on the sideline and mouth pious irrelevancies and sanctimonious trivialities. In the midst of a mighty struggle to rid our nation of racial and economic injustice, I have heard many ministers say: "Those are social issues, with which the gospel has no real concern." And I have watched many churches commit themselves to a completely other-worldly religion, which makes a strange, unbiblical distinction between body and soul, between the sacred and secular.

I have traveled the length and breadth of Alabama, Mississippi, and all the other southern states. On sweltering summer days and crisp autumn mornings I have looked at the South's beautiful churches with their lofty spires pointing heavenward. I have beheld the impressive outlines of her massive religious education buildings. Over and over I have found myself asking: "What kind of people worship here? Who is their God?" . . .

. . . So often the contemporary church is a weak, ineffectual voice with an uncertain sound. So often it is an archdefender of the status quo. Far from being disturbed by the presence of the *church,* the power structure of the average community is consoled by the church's silent—and often even vocal—sanction of things as they are.

But the judgment of God is upon the church as never before. If today's church does not recapture the sacrificial spirit of the early church, it will lose its authenticity, forfeit the loyalty of millions, and be dismissed as an irrelevant social club with no meaning for the twentieth century.

As far as King is concerned, the white churches have betrayed their moral trust by their passive acceptance of overtly racist practices.

A Clear Organization

Persuasive essays have several possible patterns for organization, some of which are illustrated in the discussion of the writing process that appears later in this chapter. Generally, writers who use persuasive techniques acknowledge and rebut at least a few opposing arguments. King wrote "Letter from the Birmingham Jail" as a rebuttal to criticisms of his decision to organize nonviolent demonstrations. In his letter, he responds carefully to each of his critics' objections.

You may well ask: "Why direct action? Why sit-ins, marches, and so forth? Isn't negotiation a better path?" You are quite right in calling for negotiation. Indeed, this is the very purpose of direct action. Nonviolent direct action seeks to create such a crisis and foster such a tension that a community that has constantly refused to negotiate is forced to confront the issue. It seeks so to dramatize the issue that it can no longer be ignored. My citing the creation of tension as part of the work of the nonviolent resister may sound rather shocking. But I must confess that I am not afraid of the word "tension." I have earnestly opposed violent tension, but there is a type of constructive, nonviolent tension that is necessary for growth. Just as Socrates felt that it was necessary to create a tension in the mind so that individuals could rise from the bondage of myths and half-truths to the unfettered realm of creative analysis and objective appraisal, so must we see the need for nonviolent gadflies to create the kind of tension in society that will help men rise from the dark depths of prejudice and racism to the majestic heights of understanding and brotherhood.

In this excerpt, King answers his opponents' questions, explains his own position, notes a historical parallel to Socrates, and reaffirms his own moral goal.

THE WRITING PROCESS: TAKING A STAND

Essays that ask a reader to listen to the writer's side of an issue also require that the writer clearly express his or her conviction about the subject. Because commitment to a topic and a clearly stated position are essential for the success of essays that take a stand, the following discussion emphasizes the beginning stages of the writing process and pays attention to possible ways of organizing ideas.

DEVELOPING A TOPIC

To achieve the high degree of commitment to your position necessary for writers of essays that take a stand on an issue, it is imperative that you choose a topic that evokes strong feelings for you. If you have difficulty finding a topic you genuinely care about, ask yourself the following questions:

What are a few of the problems you are aware of in your neighborhood?

What can you and your neighbors do to solve them?

In reading the local newspaper lately, have you been able to identify issues in your community or the world that interest or involve you personally?

What can students, teachers, administrators, or other professionals do to solve a campus issue that you feel is not being properly addressed?

Imagine that you have been promoted to an important management position where you work. What would you change, how would you make your changes, and what would be the result?

Once you have chosen a topic, use the following questions to help clarify your position:

What is my topic? Why have I chosen it? What convictions about it do I hold?

Does my approach to this topic come from personal experience, or am I writing about a situation I feel strongly about but that does not affect me personally?

What is my purpose for writing this paper?

DEVELOPING IDEAS

As you begin gathering information for your essay, consider interviewing people who have some experience or expertise related to your topic. They can provide insights, details, examples, and solutions that might offer valuable support for your position. As always, you need to introduce comments and ideas from your sources with phrases like "According to [name of authority] . . . ." The following questions will help you fill out lists of ideas, draw an idea wheel, and conduct an interview:

Why do you feel strongly about this situation?

Who is affected by this prejudice or problem? How are they affected?

What examples illustrate serious consequences of this problem?

What are possible causes? Are some more important than others? Why do you think so?

How can the difficult or harmful situation you are writing about be changed?

Who can effect these changes?

ORGANIZING IDEAS

Two organizational patterns presented in earlier chapters—chronological and order of emphasis or importance—also inform essays based on argument. In addition, most essays that take a stand devote some time to the presentation and refutation of opposing views. The number of opposing arguments you present determines which of the following organizational patterns is most appropriate for your paper.

Presenting opposing arguments first

   I. Introduction
      A. Clarify the situation or problem
         1. Thesis states the position you will defend
  II. Body paragraphs
      A. Opposing argument
         1. Rebuttal and support
      B. Opposing argument
         1. Rebuttal and support
      C. Your argument
         1. Support
      D. Your argument
         1. Support
 III. Conclusion

Presenting your arguments first

   I. Introduction
      A. Clarify the situation or problem
         1. Thesis states the position you will defend
  II. Body paragraphs
      A. Your argument
         1. Support
      B. Your argument
         1. Support
      C. Your argument
         1. Support
      D. Opposing argument
         1. Rebuttal and support
 III. Conclusion

Presenting opposing arguments throughout

   I. Introduction
      A. Clarify the situation or problem
         1. Thesis states the position you will defend
  II. Body paragraphs
      A. Opposing argument
         1. Rebuttal and support
      B. Opposing argument
         1. Rebuttal and support

C. Opposing argument
   1. Rebuttal and support
D. Opposing argument
   1. Rebuttal and support
III. Conclusion

SHARING AND REVISING

Checklist

- ❏ Is the essay's thesis debatable?
- ❏ Is the position and purpose of the essay clearly stated in the introduction?
- ❏ Is the writer's position consistent throughout the paper?
- ❏ Does the essay acknowledge opposing views?
- ❏ Are rebuttals to opposing arguments reasonable and well supported?
- ❏ Are any discussions unduly brief or unsupported? What additional support might the writer add to these paragraphs?
- ❏ Has the writer corrected spelling and sentence errors?

Student Writing: Taking a Stand

Internet Censorship Will Accomplish Nothing

The Internet has become one of the greatest and most controversial tools in people's lives. Any business, government organization, group, or person can put up a site on the World Wide Web, and share information, conduct business, or simply talk about what they do all day. Users who search the Net can check the latest sports scores, get help with homework, and buy flowers for their mothers, all by sitting in front of a computer. But there is another side to the Internet. Since anyone can put up a site, everything people can think of is on the Internet, including anti-Semitic diatribe, White Supremacist rants, and sites depicting explicitly sexual or violent acts that no parent would want his or her children to see. This last category of Internet sites has drawn a great deal of negative attention to the Web. As Senator James Exon noted, "the worst, most vile, most perverse pornography is only a few 'click, click, clicks' away from any child on the Internet" (qtd. in Barron).

The availability of undesirable material explains why parents, children's advocacy groups, and some legislators favor various forms of Internet censorship. The censorship takes many forms, including laws prohibiting transmission of "indecent" material and policies that force public schools and libraries to install filtering software to censor Internet content on their computers. A number of problems make Internet censorship unworkable and undesirable. For one thing, censorship of any kind makes the Internet less useful for the average person who seeks information. Moreover, censorship has not been an effective solution to blocking children's access to pornography, and no one has been able to show that access to offensive Internet sites has a negative effect on children's behavior. Some critics argue that Internet censorship shifts the responsibility of raising children from parents to the censoring agency. Free-speech advocates also point out that Internet censorship, like censorship in general, presents a challenge to Americans' right to free speech (Newell 129).

One of parents' biggest objections to a free Internet is children's easy access to sexually explicit and other inappropriate material. To demonstrate how easy it is to access such sites, Blaise Cronin used the search engine, Excite, and typed in common, seemingly wholesome words, then counted the number of sites out of the first ten listed that had a link to a pornographic site. Seven sites for "animal," one site for "farmyard," seven for "body," nine for "girls," and eight for "boys," led not to children playing happily at a farm, but to sites featuring carnal "bestiality." But this author fails to acknowledge that even Internet censorship won't eliminate children's access to sexual and violent material because complete and thorough censorship is impossible. The Internet contains an immense quantity of material that cannot be rated fast enough even by the most diligent censors. Also, Internet sites that contain sexual and violent material might pass through crude filtering systems and still be accessible to children. Another point is that Internet censorship will not be entirely useful because the items that people want censored—sexually graphic material and other inappropriate material— are openly available to children in a number of places other than the Internet, including most bookstores, catalogs at the mall, libraries, and even at home (Sagall). Richard Sagall, editor for Pediatrics for Parents, remembers a childhood friend whose "respectable father" thought he had hidden his copies of Playboy, but his son managed to find them anyway. After a certain age, children are curious about their bodies and are able to imagine sexual adventures. They are bound to look for whatever information they can find to corroborate their fantasies. No amount of censorship can control this quest. Perhaps the larger question is whether pornography that children might discover on the Internet causes them any measurable harm.

As it turns out, no studies have been published that offer evidence linking aberrant behavior in children to their viewing pornography on the Internet or anywhere else. In fact, sociologist Michael Males argues that in his experience, none of the behavioral problems displayed by children he has worked with are connected to Internet use or to any other media. Males argues that during the 1990s when Internet access became common in many households, statistics of the time do not support critics' argument that Internet use "is sweeping youth to savagery." He notes that on the contrary, suicides, drunk driving, violent crimes, rapes and other sex offenses among juveniles declined during the 1990s. Even teenage pregnancy rates, figures that some might think would increase because of the supposed bad influence of the Internet, went down as well. Although there are other factors such as demographic changes, better tracking in schools, and intervention programs that might explain the decline, Internet use has had no measurable negative effect on the behavior of young Internet users. Groups interested in curbing deviant behavior will have little or no impact if they focus solely on blocking reprehensible material currently available on the Internet. Instead, they would do well to look at research such as the 1991 study of teenage sex offenders, which finds that even though many of the boys surveyed had been exposed to pornography, "the primary causes of sexual offenses among these adolescent boys were their own histories of physical and sexual abuse" (Heins 42). This study corroborates the testimony of William Stayton, a Baptist minister, psychologist, and expert witness for the ACLU who stated that "explicit sex information and even pornography do not themselves cause psychological harm to minors of any age" (qtd. in Heins 41). It is likely that proponents of Internet censorship will discover that their efforts change no one's behavior, largely because they are looking at the wrong cause.

A powerful argument against Internet censorship is that it moves the responsibility of raising children and informing them of sexuality from parents to an anonymous person or panel that would decide what other people's children can and cannot see. As Perry Aftab, a lawyer who works on cases of Internet censorship, argues, "I don't think it's an Internet issue. It's a parenting issue" (qtd. in Minderbrook). Parents have various filtering systems to prevent their children from seeing material they deem unsuitable. The use of filtering software on the family PC makes some sense because parents have the right to monitor their own children. But as one critic argues, Internet blocking, like any other censorship, should never replace what is really needed—parental guidance (Doyle 129). Parents should, of course, take an active role in their children's lives, and that includes overseeing what they view online. They should sit down with their children and discuss guidelines about what material is appropriate for them to see and what is not. Also, parents should help their children learn to think critically and to decide for themselves what information is useful to them. In this way, parents can help children protect themselves and "make good judgments about the information they encounter" (Doyle 130). As pediatrician Richard J. Sagall points out, parents can use the variety of information available on the Internet to teach their children about the "real world," and for better or worse, pornography is part of the world we live in.

Parents who do rely on the various filtering software programs or rating systems to block unwanted information may discover that these systems are not always effective, and they can unintentionally block the legitimate information their children are seeking. A number of blocking systems are available—filtering software and rating systems among them—but all such systems inevitably filter out useful information as well as the occasional pornographic site. This problem surfaced in some of the schools and libraries across the country that have been forced to use filtering software in an effort to restrict access to inappropriate Web sites. However, argues Michael Males, a sociology professor at UC Santa

Cruz, most software of this type cannot distinguish "good" sites from "bad" ones, with the result that students have been denied access to information at "CNN, USA Today, scholarship information [sites], and the Middlesex, Connecticut Web site" because these sites contain the word "sex" or other terms that might appear on pornographic or violent sites as well. Such systems have, says Michael Schuyler, "what is called 'dynamic filtering,' where they analyze any Web page for 'bad words' and allow access only if they are not found." As a result, "inadvertent filtering" is nearly impossible to prevent (Schuyler). The problem has to do with the way most filtering software search for particular words but have no means of analyzing the context in which those words appear. Such indiscriminate blocking explains how a scholarship Web site gets blocked because an online application includes a category marked "sex."

In addition to software programs, rating systems have become a popular way of blocking access to objectionable material, but here again, far more legitimate information than violent or pornographic Web sites disappear from view. In some cases, Web publishers use RSACi (Recreational Software Advisory Boards) or SafeSurf to rate their own sites for profanity, vulgar language, and other information inappropriate for children. In other instances, volunteers comb the Web for indecent material and rate sites using a program called "Family Search" (Heins 43). Rating systems also have serious problems with a nearly universal blockage of Web sites—"between 90 and 99 percent of responsive Web sites," notes Marjorie Heins, even when using innocuous words such as "American Red Cross, Museum of Modern Art, National Zoo, or Dr. Seuss" (43). This system carries an insurmountable practical problem as well; it is not possible to provide a thorough oversight of the millions of Web sites available for viewing on the Internet. Heins sees other more insidious problems with imposed rating systems like "Family Search." She has found that the ratings imposed by this group have much to do with the values and politics of the beholders. Such programs, Heins discovered, "tend to block sites that contain controversial points of view or what is simply controversial information" (44). This kind of oversight amounts to a censorship of information in general, and strays from the original problem of children's exposure to indecent material.

This leads to what is perhaps the most serious argument against censorship of the Internet—its infringement on the First Amendment right to free speech. According to the First Amendment, the government cannot censor something just because it seems "bad or dangerous" to some people. Regulation of unsavory Internet material is especially difficult because even if it were possible to agree on what is "bad or dangerous," pornography itself is difficult to define. Opponents of pornography on the Internet have argued that exposure to such material can lead to " 'immoral' and risky behavior" (Heins 42). Not only have these challenges been unable to demonstrate this result, they have had little connection to recognized constitutional limits on speech such as "slander, invasion of privacy, or the direct incitement of imminent violent acts" (42). Marjorie

Heins mentions the Communications Decency Act passed by Congress in 1996 as an example of an Internet censorship law that infringed on Americans' right to free speech. This act made it illegal to send underage people "indecent" subject matter over the Internet (38). The Supreme Court found the act unconstitutional because it failed to define important terms, such as "indecent." Also, supporters offered no proof that the Internet material was "dangerous" in any way. According to the Supreme Court, "The interest in encouraging freedom of expression in a democratic society outweighs any theoretical but unproven benefit of censorship" (qtd. in Doyle 129). Hopefully, the Court will have the last word on Internet censorship.

Even though the Internet provides easy access to material that we may deem unsuitable for our children, anything that leads to wide-sweeping censorship of the Internet is not a real solution. Not only would it render a useful tool useless, censorship of the Net would take away the rights of many people. The larger sociological argument is that parents should not try to hide the darker side of society from their children because they will have to confront it sooner or later. We should have faith that children can learn to judge this material for themselves, and we might take former President John F. Kennedy's words to heart when he asserted "We are not afraid to entrust the American people with unpleasant facts, foreign ideas, alien philosophies and competitive values. . . . For a nation that is afraid to let its people judge the truth and falsehood in an open market is a nation that is afraid of its people" (qtd. in Doyle 130).

Works Cited

Barron, Christina. "Internet Rights and Wrongs." Europe 363 (1997): 10–11. Master-FILE Premier. CD-ROM. EBSCO Publishing. 28 April, 2001.

Cronin, Blaise. "Whatever Happened to Common Sense?" Library Journal 125.14 (2000): S1.

Doyle, Robert P. "Libraries and the First Amendment." Illinois Libraries 81.3 (1999): 127–30.

Heins, Marjorie. "Screening out Sex: Kids, Computers, and the New Censors." American Prospect 39 July/August 1998: 38–44.

Males Michael. "Mythology and Internet Filtering." Teacher Librarian 28.2 (2000): 16–18. MasterFILE Premier. CD-ROM. EBSCO Publishing. 19 April, 2001_http://ehostvgw5.epnet.com_.

Minderbrook, Terence. "She Fights for Your (Internet) Rights." New Amsterdam News 89.20 (1998): 22. MasterFILE Premier. CD-ROM. EBSCO Publishing. 22 April, 2001.

Newell, Christopher G. "The Internet School Filtering Act: The Next Possible Challenge in the Development of Free Speech and the Internet." Journal of Law & Education 28.1 (1999): 129–38.

Sagall, Richard J. "Internet Censorship." Pediatrics for Parents 16.5 (1995): 10.

Schuyler, Michael. "When Does Filtering Turn into Censorship?" <u>Computers in Libraries</u> 17.5 (1997): 34–36. MasterFILE Premier. CD-ROM. EBSCO Publishing. 28 April, 2001.

—Linda Lee

QUESTIONS FOR DISCUSSION

1. Identify the techniques for persuasive writing that Lee uses in "Internet Censorship Will Accomplish Nothing."
2. Which of Lee's arguments do you find most convincing? Which seem least convincing? Explain your evaluation of her arguments.

Writing about Poetry

RESPONDING TO POETRY

This section of *We Are America* includes poems that will give you practice reading and writing about poetry. The form of poetry and the language used in poems may be quite different from writing you are used to reading. Understanding the basic form of a poem and something about the special language poets frequently use can help you interpret poetry. The devices discussed here can appear in short stories, novels, and drama as well.

POETIC FORM

Consider how the shape of a poem differs from prose paragraphs that are familiar to you. For one thing, poets usually break their poems into stanzas—a series of lines set off from the rest of the poem by a space before and after the stanza. Poets also use rhyme to connect lines and ideas. Study the shape of this poem by Gwendolyn Brooks.

We Real Cool

Gwendolyn Brooks[1]

The Pool Players.
Seven at the Golden Shovel.

1   We real cool. We
    Left school. We

    Lurk late. We
    Strike straight. We

5   Sing sin. We
    Thin gin. We

    Jazz June. We
    Die soon.

Brooks provides the setting in the first two lines of her poem. Her stanzas consist of two lines; each word at the end of a sentence rhymes with another word that ends a sentence. The subject of the sentences in the poem is "We," but what is unusual about the form of Brooks's poem is that she puts that subject at the end of every line. By splitting the subject from the rest of the sentence, Brooks emphasizes the word *We* and suggests that the pool players have exaggerated ideas about themselves, even as they list their limited self-definitions.

In addition, the line breaks produce "broken" sentences, a visual image of the broken lives captured in this brief poem.

---

[1] Gwendolyn Brooks was born in Topeka, Kansas, and grew up in Chicago. She was awarded a Pulitzer Prize in 1950 for her second book of poetry, *Annie Allen*. She was the first African American to receive a Pulitzer Prize.

POETIC VOICE

A poem's "voice" or point of view helps shape its meaning. That is true of the poem "We Real Cool." For the most part, Brooks's poem is written in the special slang of the seven pool players at the bar or pool hall called the "Golden Shovel." The first seven sentences capture their voices and their ideas about themselves. The last sentence of the poem, the eighth sentence, is different from the others. "We / die soon" is written in the poet's voice. In showing the fatal consequence of living on the edge, Brooks ends her poem with a warning for young people who choose to live this way.

FIGURES OF SPEECH

Figures of speech are important tools that poets and other writers use to give additional meaning to their words and phrases. Figurative language extends the meaning of words much beyond their literal or dictionary definitions.

One of the most famous examples of figurative language is Robert Burns's comparison between a woman and a rose: "My Luve's like a red, red rose." At first, a woman doesn't seem to have anything in common with a rose, but the poet's comparison, called a **simile** because it uses the word *like* or *as,* gives us an image or picture of her natural beauty more vividly than if he had simply said, "My love is very, very beautiful."

Writers sometimes make comparisons without using the words *like* or *as.* If Burns had chosen to make his comparison using a **metaphor** instead of a simile, he would have said, "My love is a red, red rose." Metaphors aren't always stated this directly, however. In the poem "Inheritance" (pages 271–272), Gary Soto uses a metaphor comparing the speaker's grandfather to a camel: "when the parakeet rang its bell / Grandfather moved his camel head and scolded, 'Shaddup.'" The metaphor gathers the image of the boy's grandfather in the first two lines of the poem as grandfather "chewed frijoles like a camel, / His large jaw churning." Later in the poem the boy describes his grandfather as a "work-worn camel," an image that adds sympathy to our perception of the man who, in his grandson's eyes, has taken on the mannerisms and hard labor of a camel.

Another figure of speech that appears often in poetry is **personification**. This poetic device allows writers to describe inanimate objects as though they had human characteristics. In several lines from "Inheritance," for example, Soto uses personification to give a lifelike appearance to inanimate objects. The speaker of the poem tells us:

> In the kitchen, the washer shivered a load of whites
> Plates rattled, black tea rolled its knuckles in a sauce pan.
> . . . the telephone rang its loud threats.

In the first line, Soto's description of the washer shivering through a load of clothes gives the machine distinctly human characteristics as if it were cold or afraid. The tea boiling "in a sauce pan" also takes on human attributes in the metaphor "the black tea rolled its knuckles." The ringing telephone makes "its loud threats," an image that compares the telephone's insistent ringing to a human voice.

The seventeenth-century poet John Donne used personification in a slightly different way. In one poem, Donne speaks directly to death as though he were addressing another person:

> Death, be not proud, though some have callèd thee
> Mighty and dreadful, for thou art not so

In this way, Donne is able to treat death like an ordinary being who isn't as powerful as he thinks he is. The device also allows the poet to challenge death directly and to deny that it has power over him.

Writers also use words as **symbols** to give them meaning beyond their usual definitions. To use a familiar example, the flag of the United States is a symbol. It stands for a number of things. The nation's history is symbolized in the stars and stripes on the flag. For many people it also embodies the ideal of individual rights, freedom and justice for all, and even the democratic process itself.

The huge ocean liner *Titanic* is another example of an object invested with symbolic meaning. The ship has come to symbolize the folly of human vanity and the belief that nothing can get in the way of human achievement. The builders of the *Titanic* thought they could construct a ship so large and so well designed that it could not be sunk. On its maiden voyage in the icy North Atlantic, the ship struck an iceberg and sank in a matter of hours. In a poem about the *Titanic* written by the English poet Thomas Hardy, sea-worms crawl "dumb" and "indifferent" over mirrors that once reflected the expensive decorations on the ship and the splendor of her aristocratic passengers. Meanwhile, "moon-eyed fish" gaze at the gilded fixtures they've found and wonder what these symbols of "vain-gloriousness" or excessive pride are doing at the bottom of the sea. Hardy's images establish the *Titanic* as a symbol of human vanity.

When writers use **verbal irony**, they are reversing the literal meaning of words. In "We Real Cool," for example, Brooks's broken phrases and her picture of the lives of these young pool-playing dropouts carries the opposite picture of what the boys mean by being "cool." The poem shows that living such a self-destructive life is anything but cool.

Once you are aware that poems use language in these special ways, you can read, understand, and respond to poetry in much the same way you would a piece of nonfiction writing. In fact, the techniques for active reading discussed in this chapter can help you read, understand, and respond to poems. Suggestions for using these techniques are listed here.

1. Preview the poem. Read it through quickly, without stopping to puzzle over words or phrasing you don't understand. Previewing this way gives you some idea about what is going on in the poem and makes it seem less overwhelming.
2. Read the poem a second time with more deliberation, look up words that you don't understand in a dictionary, underline important words and phrases, and

write questions in the margin about sections that don't make sense to you. Also, write down your thoughts about images or ideas in the poem.

3. To help you understand what you have read, try restating the poem in your own words.

4. Watch for figures of speech such as similes, metaphors, personification, symbols, or verbal irony. Ask yourself how these devices contribute to the overall effect and meaning of the poem.

5. Finally, use your own background, knowledge, and life experience to respond to the poem. Because reading any literature demands a personal response, your reading of a poem may be quite different from other people's responses.

QUESTIONS FOR DISCUSSION

1. What do you think Brooks's purpose was for writing "We Real Cool" (page 266)? How well does the poem achieve her purpose?

2. Describe the most likely audience for "We Real Cool." What effect might the poem have on that audience?

TOPICS FOR WRITING

Topic 1. Write an interpretation of Brooks's poem "We Real Cool." Include an evaluation of strengths or weaknesses in the poem.

Topic 2. Locate another of Brooks's poems and write a short analysis of the purpose and effectiveness of that poem.

WRITING BEFORE READING

What are your earliest memories of your father, mother, or guardian? Describe those memories in detail.

My Papa's Waltz

Theodore Roethke

Theodore Roethke (1908–1963) is one of the most important American poets of the twentieth century. In 1954, he won the Pulitzer Prize for poetry for the collection of poems titled The Waking. *Another collection,* Words for the Wind, *won the National Book Award and the Bollingen Prize in 1958. He is most appreciated for his ability to translate deep fears and strong emotions into raw, exacting detail.*

1   The whiskey on your breath
    Could make a small boy dizzy;
    But I hung on like death:
    Such waltzing was not easy.

5   We romped until the pans
    Slid from the kitchen shelf;
    My mother's countenance
    Could not unfrown itself.

    The hand that held my wrist
10 Was battered on one knuckle;
    At every step you missed
    My right ear scraped a buckle.

    You beat time on my head
    With a palm caked hard by dirt,
15 Then waltzed me off to bed
    Still clinging to your shirt.

RESPONDING TO THE READING

FREEWRITING

Practice 9a. Freewrite about what the little boy in "My Papa's Waltz" felt about his father. How do those feelings compare with your own feelings about a father or another older man who is important in your life?

BUILDING YOUR VOCABULARY

romped (5)   countenance (7)

QUESTIONS FOR DISCUSSION

1. Who is the "I" in "My Papa's Waltz"?
2. What details does Roethke's poem give us about the waltzing father? What impression of the father do those details create?
3. What opinion does the little boy's mother have of Papa's waltz? What details in the poem convey her attitude?
4. The speaker in the poem says that waltzing with Papa "was not easy." What made "dancing" with Papa so difficult?

TOPICS FOR WRITING

Topic 1. Summarize what happens in Roethke's poem "My Papa's Waltz". How does his poetry change the basic description of the action?

Topic 2. Identify two topic ideas that you find in "My Papa's Waltz." Write a short essay using experiences and observations from your own life to illustrate these ideas.

Topic 3. Write an essay in which you explain what Roethke's poem is about and how the poet conveys the emotion and meaning of the experience.

WRITING BEFORE READING

Think of an older adult you were close to as a child. What pictures come to mind as you think of this person? Are there particular physical details, a way of speaking, or habits that would help you describe him or her to someone else?

Inheritance

Gary Soto

Gary Soto is the author of several collections of poems, including Black Hair *(1985),* A Fire in My Hands *(1990),* Neighborhood Odes *(1992),* Canto Familiar *(1995), and* Junior College *(1996). He has written several collections of short stories and over fifteen books, including novels for young adults and children's picture books. Soto's poem "Inheritance" appears in the volume of his poetry titled* A Natural Man *(1999).*

1   Retired, my grandfather chewed his frijoles[1] like a camel,
     His large jaw churning,
     His tortilla a napkin at the edge of his plate.
     He ate alone, or nearly alone,
5   A parakeet the size of a swollen thumb
     Glancing in a mirror. When the parakeet rang its bell,
     Grandfather moved his camel head and scolded, "Shaddup."

     The bird was not his,
     But grandmother's, hall shuffler in pink slippers,
10   Whipper of rugs and work clothes,
     Beautician dying her hair black on shadow-cold mornings.

     Nights, grandfather sat in his recliner
     With the thorn-sharp doily on his neck.
     He sat while the TV shuffled light in his face
15   And the radio plugged his ears with mariachis.[2]

---

[1] Beans.
[2] Mexican band playing traditional music.

In the kitchen, the washer shivered a load of whites,
Plates rattled, black tea rolled its knuckles in a sauce pan.
When the telephone rang its loud threats,
He turned his camel head and shouted, "Shaddup!"
20   He wanted the peace of a green lawn, lost at dusk,
And a summer burst of tomatoes and squash on whiskery vines.
He believed in water, water of morning,
And of night, sprinklers sighing on the curb strip.
He knew how summer heat suckled trees and lawns.
25   This worried him. How it all could dry up,
Life included, dry up in the time you turned your back
And flicked a grain from under a fingernail.

Grandfather rose late,
The day already sobbing heat in the garden.
30   He sliced a lemon and in the bathroom
Rubbed its sweet acids under his arms,
The scent that would follow him through the day.
The squeezed lemon collapsed into a frown,
And he was ready. Ready for what? He ate
35   And drank coffee, his mouth pleated on each deep sip.
He studied his roses, the wicked queens of his garden,
And raked puckered oranges into a herd
Of croquet balls. "Keep things green, mijo."
He repeated to me of life.
40   In the flower bed, water surged into the volcanic peaks
Of ant hills, the silt as fine as gold.
Grandfather was a simple man, a work-worn camel
With a busy jaw. Our inheritance was a late afternoon
With my small hand under his, the garden hose splashing
45   For the good of the living.

RESPONDING TO THE READING

FREEWRITING

Practice 9b. Freewrite about the details that Soto uses to depict the two sides of his grandfather in this poem.

BUILDING YOUR VOCABULARY

Inheritance (title)   mariachis (15)   mijo (38)

QUESTIONS FOR DISCUSSION

1. In the first stanza of his poem, Soto compares his grandfather to a camel. How does this description affect our view of his grandfather? What might the comparison mean in the last lines of the poem?

2. Some of the images in "Inheritance" give human qualities to things in grandfather's life. For example, Soto describes tea boiling on the stove as rolling "its knuckles." The telephone "rang its loud threats." Why do you think the poet made these objects human in this way? How might these descriptions clarify the grandfather's relationship to things in his world?

3. What concerns does Soto's grandfather have about his garden? How does his attitude toward the plants in his garden differ from his feelings toward the objects in his house?

4. Find lines in Soto's poem that connect his grandfather's garden to ideas about life. Put the "message" of these thoughts about the garden and life in your own words.

5. What is Soto's final picture of the small boy and his grandfather? What importance might that memory hold for him?

TOPICS FOR WRITING

Topic 1. Write a one-page summary of what Soto's poem is about.

Topic 2. Write an essay in which you explain what the images in "Inheritance" convey about the poet's grandfather and his world.

Topic 3. What do your consider your "inheritance" from your parents, grandparents, extended family, or guardian? Write an essay illustrating the elements of that inheritance.

Topic 4. Write your own poem describing a person you are close to. Use details that capture the special relationship you have with him or her.

WRITING BEFORE READING

Choose a time that you performed hard work or were paid for especially difficult work. What made you satisfied or dissatisfied with the job you did?

Short-Order Cook

Jim Daniels

Jim Daniels is a professor and director of Carnegie Mellon's Creative Writing Program. He is also the author of sixteen books. A working-class poet, Daniels grew up in Detroit's blue-collar neighborhoods and worked at the Ford Motors assembly plant before earning a master's degree from Bowling Green University in 1980. His seven books of poetry include Places/Everyone *(1985), winner of the Brittingham Prize for Poetry,* Punching Out *(1990),* Blessing the House *(1997),* Blue Jesus *(2000), and* Night with Drive-By Shooting Stars *(2002). A book of short stories,* Detroit Tales, *was published in 2003. Daniels's poem "Short-Order Cook" originally appeared in* Places/Everyone.

1   An average joe comes in and orders
       30 cheeseburgers and 30 fries.
       I wait for him to pay before I start cooking.
       He pays—
5   he ain't no average joe.

       The grill is just big enough for 10 rows of 3.
       I slap the burgers down,
       throw two buckets of fries in the deep frier
       and they pop pop spit spit . . .
10   psss. . . .
       The counter girls laugh.
       I concentrate.
       It is the crucial point
       they are ready for the cheese.

15   My fingers shake as I tear off slices, toss
       them on the burgers/fries done/dump/
       refill buckets/burgers ready/flip
       into buns/beat that melting cheese/wrap
       burgers in plastic/into paper bags/fries done/
20   dump/fill 30 bags/bring them to the counter girls.
       I puff my chest out and bellow:
       "30 cheeseburgers, 30 fries."
       They look at me funny.
       I grab a handful of ice, toss it in my mouth,
25   do a little dance, and walk back to the grill.
       Pressure, responsibility, success
       30 cheeseburgers, 30 fries.

RESPONDING TO THE READING

FREEWRITING

Practice 9c. Characterize the attitude the short-order cook has toward his job. How does Daniels convey this attitude?

crucial (13)

QUESTIONS FOR DISCUSSION

1. What is your impression of the short-order cook? What details and images give you this impression?
2. Pick out the details in the "Short-Order Cook" that make the experience of cooking thirty burgers and thirty fries just right.
3. If you have had a retail job, have worked in a restaurant, or have done manual labor, compare your experience on the job to that of the short-order cook.
4. Explain what the speaker in the poem means when he says "Pressure, responsibility, success."

TOPICS FOR WRITING

Topic 1. Think of a job or assignment you have had that you found particularly rewarding. Explain in detail what made the task so satisfying.

Topic 2. If you have had a job you disliked, explain what might have been changed to make it a better job.

Topic 3. Interview members of your family or a few friends to find out what they liked or disliked about jobs they have had. Draw a few conclusions about what makes a job rewarding, and explain your findings in a short essay. You might ask yourself whether job satisfaction depends on the needs of the individual or whether there are certain characteristics that most good jobs seem to share.

Part III
Reading across Cultures

Family

The readings in this chapter explore the individual's experience of self in the context of family and the larger culture. Donald Hall remembers the "tender and tense" moments when he played baseball with his father in "Fathers Playing Catch with Sons." Hall speculates about what his father's chances of playing professionally might have been if he hadn't decided to get a full-time job because he needed to support a family. In "The Good Daughter," Caroline Hwang, the daughter of immigrants, writes about living between two cultures, American and Korean. Henry Louis Gates, Jr. remembers his mother's talent for straightening hair in the family's kitchen and describes his own mixed feelings about the practice. Barbara Ehrenreich's essay, "Oh, Those Family Values," questions whether we should rely on the family structure as the "moral foundation" of our lives, given the abusive behavior that takes place within it.

The kitchen that I'm speaking of is the very kinky bit of hair at the back of your head, where your neck meets your shirt collar. If there was ever a part of our African past that resisted assimilation, it was the kitchen.
—Henry Louis Gates, Jr.

I identify with Americans, but Americans do not identify with me.
—Caroline Hwang

Write about sacrifices a relative or friend has made for you. What were they? How did you feel at the time? How do you feel now?

Fathers Playing Catch with Sons

Donald Hall

Donald Hall is the author of over fifty books, including fifteen volumes of poetry, twenty-two collections of essays, textbooks, and children's books. His books of poetry include The One Day *(1988), a winner of the National Book Critics Circle Award, the* Los Angeles Times *Book Prize, and a Pulitzer Prize nomination; and* The Happy Man *(1986), which won the Lenore Marshall Poetry Prize. More recently, he published* Without: Poems *(1998), and* The Painted Bed *(2002). In addition to poetry, Hall has written books on poets, short stories, plays, and the autobiographical* Life Work *(1993). Hall has received two Guggenheim fellowships, the National Book Critics Circle Award (1988), the Robert Frost Silver medal awarded by the Poetry Society of America, and the Ruth Lilly Prize for poetry. Hall also received three nominations for the prestigious National Book Award. On June 13, 2006, he became the fourteenth U.S. Poet Laureate. In the following passage from his book* Fathers Playing Catch with Sons *(1985), Hall writes about his memories of his father and the guilt he feels for having changed his father's life.*

1   My father and I played catch as I grew up. Like so much else between fathers and sons, playing catch was tender and tense at the same time. He wanted to play with me. He wanted me to be good. He seemed to *demand* that I be good. I threw the ball into his catcher's mitt. Atta boy. Put her right there. I threw straight. Then I tried to put something on it; it flew twenty feet over his head. Or it banged into the sidewalk in front of him, breaking stitches and ricocheting off a pebble into the gutter of Greenway Street. Or it went wide to his right and lost itself in Mrs. Davis's bushes. Or it went wide to his left and rolled across the street while drivers swerved their cars.

2   I was wild. I was *wild.* I had to be wild for my father. What else could I be? Would you have wanted me to have *control*?

3   But I was, myself, the control on him. He had wanted to teach school, to coach and teach history at Cushing Academy in Ashburnham, Massachusetts, and he had done it for two years before he was married. The salary was minuscule and in the twenties people didn't get married until they had the money to live on. Since he wanted to marry my mother, he made the only decision he could make: he quit Cushing and went into the family business, and he hated business, and he wept when he fired people, and he wept when he was criticized, and his head shook at night, and he coughed from all the

cigarettes, and he couldn't sleep, and he almost died when an ulcer hemorrhaged when he was forty-two, and ten years later, at fifty-two, he died of lung cancer.

But the scene I remember—at night in the restaurant, after a happy, foolish day in the uniform of a Pittsburgh Pirate—happened when he was twenty-five and I was almost one-year-old. So I do not "remember" it at all. It simply rolls itself before my eyes with the intensity of a lost memory suddenly found again, more intense than the moment itself ever is.

It is 1929, July, a hot Saturday afternoon. At the ballpark near East Rock, in New Haven, Connecticut, just over the Hamden line, my father is playing semipro baseball. I don't know the names of the teams. My mother has brought me in a basket, and she sits under a tree, in the shade, and lets me crawl when I wake up.

My father is very young, very skinny. When he takes off his cap—the uniform is gray, the bill of the cap blue—his fine hair is parted in the middle. His face is very smooth. Though he is twenty-five, he could pass for twenty. He plays shortstop, and he is paid twenty-five dollars a game. I don't know where the money comes from. Do they pass the hat? They would never raise so much money. Do they charge admission? They must charge admission, or I am wrong that it was semipro and that he was paid. Or the whole thing is wrong, a memory I concocted. But of course the reality of 1929—and my mother and the basket and the shade and the heat—does not matter, not to the memory of the living nor to the bones of the dead nor even to the fragmentary images of broken light from that day which wander light-years away in unrecoverable space. What matters is the clear and fine knowledge of this day as it happens now, permanently and repeatedly, on a deep layer of the personal Troy.

There, where this Saturday afternoon of July in 1929 rehearses itself, my slim father performs brilliantly at shortstop. He dives for a low line drive and catches it backhand, somersaults, and stands up holding the ball. Sprinting into left field with his back to the plate, he catches a fly ball that almost drops for a Texas leaguer. He knocks down a ground ball, deep in the hole and nearly to third base, picks it up, and throws the man out at first with a peg as flat as the tape a runner breaks. When he comes up to bat, he feels lucky. The opposing pitcher is a sidearmer. He always hits side-armers. So he hits two doubles and a triple, drives in two runs and scores two runs, and his team wins 4 to 3. After the game a man approaches him, while he stands, sweating and tired, with my mother and me in the shade of the elm tree at the rising side of the field. The man is a baseball scout. He offers my father a contract to play baseball with the Baltimore Orioles, at that time a double-A minor league team. My father is grateful and gratified; he is proud to be offered the job, but he must refuse. After all, he has just started working at the dairy for his father. It wouldn't be possible to leave the job that had been such a decision to take. And besides, he adds, there is the baby.

My father didn't tell me he turned it down because of me. All he told me, or that I think he told me: he was playing semipro at twenty-five dollars a game; he had a good day in the field, catching a ball over his shoulder running away from the plate; he had a good day hitting, too, because he could always hit a side-armer. But he turned down the Baltimore Oriole offer. He couldn't leave the dairy then, and besides, he knew that he had just been lucky that day. He wasn't really that good.

9   But maybe he didn't even tell me that. My mother remembers nothing of this. Or rather she remembers that he played on the team for the dairy, against other businesses, and that she took me to the games when I was a baby. But she remembers nothing of semipro, of the afternoon with the side-armer, of the offered contract. Did I make it up? Did my father exaggerate? Men tell stories to their sons, loving and being loved.

10   I don't care.

11   Baseball is fathers and sons. Football is brothers beating each other up in the backyard, violent and superficial. Baseball is the generations, looping backward forever with a million apparitions of sticks and balls, cricket and rounders, and the games the Iroquois played in Connecticut before the English came. Baseball is fathers and sons playing catch, lazy and murderous, wild and controlled, the profound archaic song of birth, growth, age, and death. This diamond encloses what we are.

RESPONDING TO THE READING

FREEWRITING

Practice 10a. Without looking back at Hall's essay, write a brief summary of the scenes and ideas you remember.

Practice 10b. Write a few questions you have about Hall's essay to share with the class.

BUILDING YOUR VOCABULARY

minuscule (3)	concocted (6)	exaggerate (9)
hemorrhaged (3)	fragmentary (6)	apparitions (11)
intensity (4)	unrecoverable (6)	archaic (11)
semipro (5)	rehearses (7)	

QUESTIONS FOR DISCUSSION

1. What is the dominant impression of Hall's father? Which descriptions support this impression?
2. Briefly describe the relationship between father and son. What are the sources of tension between them?
3. Hall half remembers, half imagines, that his father made several sacrifices for his family. What were they? Why do you think he decided to make them? What would you have done in his place? Explain your choice.
4. Characterize the point of view Hall adopts in this essay. How does it differ from his mother's point of view? How do you explain this difference?

5. In paragraph 2 Hall says, "I was wild. I was *wild*. I had to be wild for my father. What else could I be? Would you have wanted me to have *control*?" What is he talking about? Who is he addressing as "you"?

6. Part of Hall's intention is to write about how memory works. He partly remembers and partly creates the past. How well does Hall really remember what happened (paragraphs 4, 5, 6, and 9)? Why isn't it important that he retell exactly what happened (paragraph 6)?

7. What is Hall's purpose in writing this reminiscence of his father? How is it similar to or different from Russell Baker's purpose in writing "Mother"?

TOPICS FOR WRITING

Topic 1. Briefly summarize the sacrifices Donald Hall's father made for his family. Explain what you would have done in his place. Be sure to explain why you would have made your decisions and the expected outcome of those decisions.

Topic 2. Think of a family member or friend who has just done something you consider unwise. Write this person a letter in which you briefly describe what he or she has done that you oppose. Then explain why you disagree with the decision. Finally, suggest what can be done to remedy the situation.

Topic 3. Do some freewriting about a time when a family member or friend made an important sacrifice. Use the steps in the writing process (pages 119–121) and the following questions to write about this sacrifice: What was the sacrifice? Who was it for? Was it worth making at the time? As you look back on it now, do you think you made a wise decision? Explain why or why not.

Topic 4. Donald Hall tells us that his recollection of his father's starring game in New Haven is not really a memory at all but an event that he has pieced together from what his parents have said and what he can imagine. Pick an event that stands out for you in your family history, such as a wedding, a baby naming, a vacation, etc. Interview at least two members of your family who were there during the event. Then write an essay recreating the event, taking into account other perceptions besides your own.

Topic 5. Write a long letter to Donald Hall in which you do *one* of the following: (a) summarize Hall's opinions of baseball, and explain the reasons you agree with his assessment, or (b) write a defense of football as more than "brothers beating each other up in the backyard, violent and superficial" (paragraph 11).

Topic 6. Identify the tone that Donald Hall and Russell Baker ("Mother," pages 108–112) use to describe their parents. Write an essay in which you compare the tone in each narrative and what that tone reveals about the writer's feelings for that parent and purpose for writing.

What images of the children of immigrants does the popular culture offer? Based on your own observations, how accurate are these images?

The Good Daughter

Caroline Hwang

Caroline Hwang has been a writer and editor for several magazines, including Mademoiselle, Glamour, *and* Redbook. *She holds a master's degree in fine arts from New York University. She is currently a senior editor at* Good Housekeeping *magazine and writes articles on fashion. Her first novel,* In Full Bloom, *was published in 2004. In this novel, the heroine, Ginger Lee, discovers that she must embrace her family and her Asian heritage before happiness can bloom. In her essay "The Good Daughter," which appeared in* Newsweek *in September 1998, Hwang records her struggles between the desire for independence, and her duty to her family and her Korean heritage.*

1   The moment I walked into the dry-cleaning store, I knew the woman behind the counter was from Korea, like my parents. To show her that we shared a heritage, and possibly get a fellow countryman's discount, I tilted my head forward, in shy imitation of a traditional bow.

2   "Name?" she asked, not noticing my attempted obeisance.

3   "Hwang," I answered.

4   "Hwang? Are you Chinese?"

5   Her question caught me off-guard. I was used to hearing such queries from non-Asians who think Asians all look alike, but never from one of my own people. Of course, the only Koreans I knew were my parents and their friends, people who've never asked me where I came from, since they knew better than I.

6   I ransacked my mind for the Korean words that would tell her who I was. It's always struck me as funny (in a mirthless sort of way) that I can more readily say "I am Korean" in Spanish, German and even Latin than I can in the language of my ancestry. In the end, I told her in English.

7   The dry-cleaning woman squinted as though trying to see past the glare of my strangeness, repeating my surname under her breath. "Oh, *Fxuang*," she said, doubling over with laughter. "You don't know how to speak your name."

8   I flinched. Perhaps I was particularly sensitive at the time, having just dropped out of graduate school. I had torn up my map for the future, the one that said not only where I was going but also who I was. My sense of identity was already disintegrating.

When I got home, I called my parents to ask why they had never bothered to correct   9
me. "Big deal," my mother said, sounding more flippant than I knew she intended. (Like
many people who learn English in a classroom, she uses idioms that don't always fit the
occasion.) "So what if you can't pronounce your name? You are American," she said.

Though I didn't challenge her explanation, it left me unsatisfied. The fact is, my cultural   10
identity is hardly that clear-cut.

My parents immigrated to this country 30 years ago, two years before I was born.   11
They told me often, while I was growing up, that, if I wanted to, I could be president
someday, that here my grasp would be as long as my reach.

To ensure that I reaped all the advantages of this country, my parents saw to it that   12
I became fully assimilated. So, like any American of my generation, I whiled away my
youth strolling malls and talking on the phone, rhapsodizing over Andrew McCarthy's
blue eyes or analyzing the meaning of a certain upperclassman's offer of a ride to the
Homecoming football game.

To my parents, I am all American, and the sacrifices they made in leaving Korea—   13
including my mispronounced name—pale in comparison to the opportunities those
sacrifices gave me. They do not see that I straddle two cultures, nor that I feel displaced
in the only country I know. I identify with Americans, but Americans do not identify with
me. I've never known what it's like to belong to a community—neither one at large, nor
of an extended family. I know more about Europe than the continent my ancestors
unmistakably come from. I sometimes wonder, as I did that day in the dry cleaner's, if
I would be a happier person had my parents stayed in Korea.

I first began to consider this thought around the time I decided to go to graduate   14
school. It had been a compromise: my parents wanted me to go to law school; I
wanted to skip the starched-collar track and be a writer—the hungrier the better. But
after 20-some years of following their wishes and meeting all of their expectations,
I couldn't bring myself to disobey or disappoint. A writing career is riskier than law,
I remember thinking. If I'm a failure and my life is a washout, then what does that
make my parents' lives?

I know that many of my friends had to choose between pleasing their parents and   15
being true to themselves. But for the children of immigrants, the choice seems more
complicated, a happy outcome impossible. By making the biggest move of their lives for
me, my parents indentured me to the largest debt imaginable—I owe them the fulfillment
of their hopes for me.

It tore me up inside to suppress my dream, but I went to school for a Ph.D. in   16
English literature, thinking I had found the perfect compromise. I would be able to
write at least about books while pursuing a graduate degree. Predictably, it didn't
work out. How could I labor for five years in a program I had no passion for? When
I finally left school, my parents were disappointed, but since it wasn't what they
wanted me to do, they weren't devastated. I, on the other hand, felt I was staring at
the bottom of the abyss. I had seen the flaw in my life of halfwayness, in my planned
life of compromises.

17   I hadn't thought about my love life, but I had a vague plan to make concessions there, too. Though they raised me as an American, my parents expect me to marry someone Korean and give them grandchildren who look like them. This didn't seem like such a huge request when I was 14, but now I don't know what I'm going to do. I've never been in love with someone I dated, or dated someone I loved. (Since I can't bring myself even to entertain the thought of marrying the non-Korean men I'm attracted to, I've been dating only those I know I can stay clearheaded about.) And as I near that age when the question of marriage stalks every relationship, I can't help but wonder if my parents' expectations are responsible for the lack of passion in my life.

18   My parents didn't want their daughter to be Korean, but they don't want her fully American, either. Children of immigrants are living paradoxes. We are the first generation and the last. We are in this country for its opportunities, yet filial duty binds us. When my parents boarded the plane, they knew they were embarking on a rough trip. I don't think they imagined the rocks in the path of their daughter who can't even pronounce her own name.

RESPONDING TO THE READING

FREEWRITING

Practice 10c. Freewrite about the "tone" or attitude Hwang adopts toward her subject. Locate passages in her essay that illustrate this tone.

BUILDING YOUR VOCABULARY

flippant (9)	indentured (15)	filial (18)
rhapsodizing (12)	devastated (16)	

QUESTIONS FOR DISCUSSION

1. What is the effect of Hwang's beginning her essay with the brief anecdote about her encounter with a Korean woman at the dry cleaner's? How does it set the tone for her relationship with the Korean culture? How does the woman's remark, "You don't know how to speak your name," anticipate what happens in the rest of Hwang's essay?
2. What examples in Hwang's essay support her comment: "I straddle two cultures. . . . I feel displaced in the only country I know."
3. Hwang says that she knew many friends who "had to choose between pleasing their parents and being true to themselves." What makes the choice especially complicated for children of immigrants? To what extent is this a universal experience?

TOPICS FOR WRITING

Topic 1. Write an essay in which you examine Hwang's purpose for writing her essay. Be sure to explain which of her examples and explanations support this purpose.

Topic 2. Compare the special pressures placed on immigrants or refugees, and the children of immigrants. Choose two or three of the following texts to gather support for your comparison: "The Good Daughter," "Complexion" (pages 350–356), "The Struggle to Be an All-American Girl" (pages 300–301), and "Pursuit of Happiness" (pages 358–360).

Topic 3. Focus on Elizabeth Wong's "The Struggle to Be an All-American Girl" (pages 300–301) and Caroline Hwang's "The Good Daughter." Write an essay in which you discuss similarities and differences you find in their attitudes toward American culture and their Asian heritage, or in compromises they have to make.

WRITING BEFORE READING

With the help of plastic surgery, people can alter the shape of their nose or obtain a "face lift" to smooth out wrinkles. Some women even undergo foot surgery to change the shape of their feet to conform to the shape of designer shoes. Do you think people have a right to make whatever changes they want, or do you see larger problems when people make permanent changes to their appearance?

In the Kitchen

Henry Louis Gates, Jr.

Henry Louis Gates is the W. E. B. Du Bois Professor of Humanities at Harvard and director of the Institute for Afro-American Research. He and his colleagues have gathered more than 40,000 fragments and texts for their Black Periodical Literature Project. He has written several books on critical theory and American culture, including The Signifyin(g) Monkey: Towards a Theory of Afro-American Literary Criticism *(1988), which earned the American Book Award, and* Loose Cannons: Notes on the Culture Wars *(1992). In all, Gates has written, coauthored, or edited 34 works of fiction and nonfiction, and over 100 articles, reviews, and essays for major publications. He was the recipient of a MacArthur Foundation fellowship in 1981. In his essay, "In the Kitchen," published in* The New Yorker *in 1994, Gates explores the memories of his mother's talent for straightening hair and the politics of assimilation that the "process" implies.*

We always had a gas stove in the kitchen, in our house in Piedmont, West Virginia, where I grew up. Never electric, though using electric became fashionable in Piedmont in the sixties, like using Crest toothpaste rather than Colgate, or watching Huntley and

Brinkley rather than Walter Cronkite. But not us: gas, Colgate, and good ole Walter Cronkite, come what may. We used gas partly out of loyalty to Big Mom, Mama's Mama, because she was mostly blind and still loved to cook, and could feel her way more easily with gas than with electric. But the most important thing about our gas-equipped kitchen was that Mama used to do hair there. The "hot comb" was a fine-toothed iron instrument with a long wooden handle and a pair of iron curlers that opened and closed like scissors. Mama would put it in the gas fire until it glowed. You could smell those prongs heating up.

2   I liked that smell. Not the smell so much, I guess, as what the smell meant for the shape of my day. There was an intimate warmth in the women's tones as they talked with my Mama, doing their hair. I knew what the women had been through to get their hair ready to be "done," because I would watch Mama do it to herself. How that kink could be transformed through grease and fire into that magnificent head of wavy hair was a miracle to me, and still is.

3   Mama would wash her hair over the sink, a towel wrapped around her shoulders, wearing just her slip and her white bra. (We had no shower—just a galvanized tub that we stored in the kitchen—until we moved down Rat Tail Road into Doc Wolverton's house, in 1954.) After she dried it, she would grease her scalp thoroughly with blue Bergamot hair grease, which came in a short, fat jar with a picture of a beautiful colored lady on it. It's important to grease your scalp real good, my Mama would explain, to keep from burning yourself. Of course, her hair would return to its natural kink almost as soon as the hot water and shampoo hit it. To me, it was another miracle how hair so "straight" would so quickly become kinky again the second it even approached some water.

4   My Mama had only a few "clients" whose heads she "did"—did, I think, because she enjoyed it, rather than for the few pennies it brought in. They would sit on one of our red plastic kitchen chairs, the kind with the shiny metal legs, and brace themselves for the process. Mama would stroke that red-hot iron—which by this time had been in the gas fire for half an hour or more—slowly but firmly through their hair, from scalp to strand's end. It made a scorching, crinkly sound, the hot iron did, as it burned its way through kink, leaving in its wake straight strands of hair, standing long and tall but drooping over at the ends, their shape like the top of a heavy willow tree. Slowly, steadily, Mama's hands would transform a round mound of Odetta kink into a darkened swamp of everglades. The Bergamot made the hair shiny; the heat of the hot iron gave it a brownish-red cast. Once all the hair was as straight as God allows kink to get, Mama would take the well-heated curling iron and twirl the straightened strands into more or less loosely wrapped curls. She claimed that she owed her skill as a hairdresser to the strength in her wrists, and as she worked her little finger would poke out, the way it did when she sipped tea. Mama was a southpaw, and wrote upside down and backward to produce the cleanest, roundest letters you've ever seen.

5   The "kitchen" she would all but remove from sight with a handheld pair of shears, bought just for this purpose. Now, the kitchen was the room in which we were sitting—the room where Mama did hair and washed clothes, and where we all took a bath in that

galvanized tub. But the word has another meaning, and the kitchen that I'm speaking of is the very kinky bit of hair at the back of your head, where your neck meets your shirt collar. If there was ever a part of our African past that resisted assimilation, it was the kitchen. No matter how hot the iron, no matter how powerful the chemical, no matter how stringent the mashed-potatoes-and-lye formula of a man's "process," neither God nor woman nor Sammy Davis, Jr., could straighten the kitchen. The kitchen was permanent, irredeemable, irresistible kink. Unassimilably African. No matter what you did, no matter how hard you tried, you couldn't de-kink a person's kitchen. So you trimmed it off as best you could.

When hair had begun to "turn," as they'd say—to return to its natural kinky glory— it was the kitchen that turned first (the kitchen around the back, and nappy edges at the temples). When the kitchen started creeping up the back of the neck, it was time to get your hair done again.   6

Sometimes, after dark, a man would come to have his hair done. It was Mr. Charlie Carroll. He was very light-complected and had a ruddy nose—it made me think of Edmund Gwenn, who played Kris Kringle in "Miracle on 34th Street." At first, Mama did him after my brother, Rocky, and I had gone to sleep. It was only later that we found out that he had come to our house so Mama could iron his hair—not with a hot comb or a curling iron but with our very own Proctor-Silex steam iron. For some reason I never understood, Mr. Charlie would conceal his Frederick Douglass-like mane under a big white Stetson hat. I never saw him take it off except when he came to our house, at night, to have his hair pressed. (Later, Daddy would tell us about Mr. Charlie's most prized piece of knowledge, something that the man would only confide after his hair had been pressed, as a token of intimacy, "Not many people know this," he'd say, in a tone of circumspection, "but George Washington was Abraham Lincoln's daddy." Nodding solemnly, he'd add the clincher: "A white man told me." Though he was in dead earnest, this became a humorous refrain around our house—"a white man told me"—which we used to punctuate especially preposterous assertions.)   7

My mother examined my daughters' kitchens whenever we went home to visit, in the early eighties. It became a game between us. I had told her not to do it, because I didn't like the politics it suggested—the notion of "good" and "bad" hair. "Good" hair was "straight," "bad" hair kinky. Even in the late sixties, at the height of Black Power, almost nobody could bring themselves to say "bad" for good and "good" for bad. People still said that hair like white people's hair was "good," even if they encapsulated it in a disclaimer, like "what we used to call 'good.'"   8

Maggie would be seated in her high chair, throwing food this way and that, and Mama would be cooing about how cute it all was, how I used to do just like Maggie was doing, and wondering whether her flinging her food with her left hand meant that she was going to be left-handed like Mama. When my daughter was just about covered with Chef Boyardee Spaghetti-O's, Mama would seize the opportunity: wiping her clean, she would tilt Maggie's head to one side and reach down the back of her neck. Sometimes Mama would even rub a curl between her fingers, just   9 to make sure that her bifocals had not deceived her. Then she'd sigh with satisfaction and relief: No kink . . . yet. Mama! I'd shout, pretending to be angry. Every once in a while, if no one was looking, I'd peek, too.

10   I say "yet" because most black babies are born with soft, silken hair. But after a few months it begins to turn, as inevitably as do the seasons or the leaves on a tree. People once thought baby oil would stop it. They were wrong.

11   Everybody I knew as a child wanted to have good hair. You could be as ugly as home-made sin dipped in misery and still be thought attractive if you had good hair. "Jesus moss," the girls at Camp Lee, Virginia, had called Daddy's naturally "good" hair during the war. I know that he played that thick head of hair for all it was worth, too.

12   My own hair was "not a bad grade," as barbers would tell me when they cut it for the first time. It was like a doctor reporting the results of the first full physical he has given you. Like "You're in good shape" or "Blood pressure's kind of high—better cut down on salt."

13   I spent most of my childhood and adolescence messing with my hair. I definitely wanted straight hair. Like Pop's. When I was about three, I tried to stick a wad of Bazooka bubble gum to that straight hair of his. I suppose what fixed that memory for me is the spanking I got for doing so: he turned me upside down, holding me by my feet, the better to paddle my behind. Little *nigger,* he had shouted, walloping away. I started to laugh about it two days later, when my behind stopped hurting.

14   When black people say "straight," of course, they don't usually mean literally straight—they're not describing hair like, say, Peggy Lipton's (she was the white girl on "The Mod Squad"), or like Mary's of Peter, Paul & Mary fame; black people call that "stringy" hair. No, "straight" just means not kinky, no matter what contours the curl may take. I would have done *anything* to have straight hair—and I used to try everything, short of getting a process.

15   Of the wide variety of techniques and methods I came to master in the challenging prestidigitation of the follicle, almost all had two things in common: a heavy grease and the application of pressure. It's not an accident that some of the biggest black-owned companies in the fifties and sixties made hair products. And I tried them all, in search of that certain silken touch, the one that would leave neither the hand nor the pillow sullied by grease.

16   I always wondered what Frederick Douglass put on *his* hair, or what Phillis Wheatley put on hers. Or why Wheatley has that rag on her head in the little engraving in the frontispiece of her book. One thing is for sure: you can bet that when Phillis Wheatley went to England and saw the Countess of Huntingdon she did not stop by the Queen's coiffeur on her way there. So many black people still get their hair straightened that it's a wonder we don't have a national holiday for Madame C. J. Walker, the woman who invented the process of straightening kinky hair. Call it Jheri-Kurled or call it "relaxed," it's still fried hair.

17   I used all the greases, from sea-blue Bergamot and creamy vanilla Duke (in its clear jar with the orange-white-and-green label) to the godfather of grease, the formidable Murray's. Now, Murray's was some *serious* grease. Whereas Bergamot was like oily jello,

and Duke was viscous and sickly sweet, Murray's was light brown and *hard*. Hard as lard and twice as greasy, Daddy used to say. Murray's came in an orange can with a press-on top. It was so hard that some people would put a match to the can, just to soften the stuff and make it more manageable. Then, in the late sixties, when Afros came into style, I used Afro Sheen. From Murray's to Duke to Afro Sheen: that was my progression in black consciousness.

We used to put hot towels or washrags over our Murray-coated heads, in order to melt the wax into the scalp and the follicles. Unfortunately, the wax also had the habit of running down your neck, ears, and forehead. Not to mention your pillowcase. Another problem was that if you put two palmfuls of Murray's on your head your hair turned white. (Duke did the same thing.) The challenge was to get rid of that white color. Because if you got rid of the white stuff you had a magnificent head of wavy hair. That was the beauty of it: Murray's was so hard that it froze your hair into the wavy style you brushed it into. It looked really good if you wore a part. A lot of guys had parts *cut* into their hair by a barber, either with the clippers or with a straightedge razor. Especially if you had kinky hair—then you'd generally wear a short razor cut, or what we called a Quo Vadis. | 18

We tried to be as innovative as possible. Everyone knew about using a stocking cap, because your father or your uncle wore one whenever something really big was about to happen, whether sacred or secular: a funeral or a dance, a wedding or a trip in which you confronted official white people. Any time you were trying to look really sharp, you wore a stocking cap in preparation. And if the event was really a big one, you made a new cap. You asked your mother for a pair of her hose, and cut it with scissors about six inches or so from the open end—the end with the elastic that goes up to the top of the thigh. Then you knotted the cut end, and it became a beehive shaped hat, with an elastic band that you pulled down low on your forehead and down around your neck in the back. To work well, the cap had to fit tightly and snugly, like a press. And it had to fit that tightly because it *was* a press: it pressed your hair with the force of the hose's elastic. If you greased your hair down real good, and left the stocking cap on long enough, voilà: you got a head of pressed-against-the-scalp waves. (You also got a ring around your forehead when you woke up, but it went away.) And then you could enjoy your concrete do. Swore we were bad, too, with all that grease and those flat heads. My brother and I would brush it out a bit in the mornings, so that it looked— well, "natural." Grown men still wear stocking caps—especially older men, who gener- ally keep their stocking caps in their top drawers, along with their cufflinks and their see-through silk socks, their "Maverick" ties, their silk handkerchiefs, and whatever else they prize the most. | 19

A Murrayed-down stocking cap was the respectable version of the process, which, by contrast, was most definitely not a cool thing to have unless you were an entertainer by trade. Zeke and Keith and Poochie and a few other stars of the high-school basketball team all used to get a process once or twice a year. It was expensive, and you had to go somewhere like Pittsburgh or D.C. or Uniontown—somewhere where there were enough colored people to support a trade. The guys would disappear, then reappear a day or | 20 two later, strutting like peacocks, their hair burned slightly red from the lye base. They'd also wear "rags"—cloths or handkerchiefs—around their heads when they slept or played basketball. Do-rags, they were called. But the result was straight hair, with just a hint of wave. No curl. Do-it-yourselfers took their chances at home with a concoction of mashed potatoes and lye.

21   The most famous process of all, however, outside of the process Malcolm X describes in his "Autobiography," and maybe the process of Sammy Davis, Jr., was Nat King Cole's process. Nat King Cole had patent-leather hair. That man's got the finest process money can buy, or so Daddy said the night we saw Cole's TV show on NBC. It was November 5, 1956. I remember the date because everyone came to our house to watch it and to celebrate one of Daddy's buddies' birthdays. Yeah, Uncle Joe chimed in, they can do shit to his hair that the average Negro can't even *think* about—secret shit.

22   Nat King Cole was *clean*. I've had an ongoing argument with a Nigerian friend about Nat King Cole for twenty years now. Not about whether he could sing—any fool knows that he could—but about whether or not he was a handkerchief head for wearing that patent-leather process.

23   Sammy Davis, Jr.'s process was the one I detested. It didn't look good on him. Worse still, he liked to have a fried strand dangling down the middle of his forehead, so he could shake it out from the crown when he sang. But Nat King Cole's hair was a thing unto itself, a beautifully sculpted work of art that he and he alone had the right to wear. The only difference between a process and a stocking cap, really, was taste; but Nat King Cole, unlike, say, Michael Jackson, looked *good* in his. His head looked like Valentino's head in the twenties, and some say it was Valentino the process was imitating. But Nat King Cole wore a process because it suited his face, his demeanor, his name, his style. He was as clean as he wanted to be.

24   I had forgotten all about that patent-leather look until one day in 1971, when I was sitting in an Arab restaurant on the island of Zanzibar surrounded by men in fezzes and white caftans, trying to learn how to eat curried goat and rice with the fingers of my right hand and feeling two million miles from home. All of a sudden, an old transistor radio sitting on top of a china cupboard stopped blaring out its Swahili music and started playing "Fly Me to the Moon," by Nat King Cole. The restaurant's din was not affected at all, but in my mind's eye I saw it: the King's magnificent sleek black tiara. I managed, barely, to blink back the tears.

RESPONDING TO THE READING

FREEWRITING

Practice 10d. Write about times when you have imitated a certain "look" in order to belong to a particular group or fit into a culture niche at work, at school, or in the neighborhood. Describe that look in detail, and explain what it meant to you.

assimilation (5)	encapsulated (8)	follicle (15)
irredeemable (5)	inevitable (10)	din (24)
preposterous (7)	prestidigitation (15)	

QUESTIONS FOR DISCUSSION

1. What are the two meanings of the title "In the Kitchen" in Gates's essay? What are the possible connections between the two senses of the word? How might the meanings be in opposition?
2. Identify the thesis that guides Gates's discussion of the process of straightening hair. Is there a deeper point he makes in the course of his essay? What passages make this point?
3. Discuss the various meanings of "good" and "bad" hair. What are Gates's feelings about these terms?
4. What might Gates's purpose and intended audience be for writing "In the Kitchen"? What phrases help you identify his purpose and audience?
5. "In the Kitchen" describes two of the favored methods of "processing" or straightening kinky hair that were popular when Gates was young. Identify other methods of development besides process analysis that the author uses in his essay.
6. How does Gates end his essay? What is the effect of this ending on the rest of his essay?
7. Gates mentions Malcolm X's description of the "process" of straightening kinky hair in *The Autobiography of Malcolm X*. Malcolm X eventually rejected the "process" as an inauthentic attempt to assimilate into a culture that rejected African Americans. Does Gates feel that some hairdos are more authentic than others? What hairdos seem to be considered authentic in various cultural groups today?

TOPICS FOR WRITING

Topic 1. Write an essay in which you explain Henry Louis Gates's tone or attitude toward the "process" that went on in his mother's kitchen. Analyze passages that convey his mixed feelings about hair straightening.

Topic 2. Analyze the view of African American history, both positive and negative, that Gates evokes in his essay about the "process" of straightening hair.

Topic 3. Write a paper in which you analyze the marriage customs, celebrations, or other traditional practices of your family. Try to focus on what makes your family's traditions unique.

Topic 4. Do some research to find biographical information about Nat King Cole and Sammy Davis, Jr. What besides their hairdos might explain Gates's preference for Nat King Cole over Sammy Davis, Jr.?

What "values" do you think families represent? Do you think families are generally true to these values? If not, in what ways might they contradict them?

Oh, Those Family Values

Barbara Ehrenreich

Barbara Ehrenreich was born in Butte, Montana in 1941 and is best known for her political essays and social criticism. She earned a B.A. from Reed College in 1963 and a Ph.D. in biology from Rockefeller University in 1968. Ehrenreich has worked as a columnist, editor, lecturer, and journalist whose work has appeared in the New York Times, Mother Jones, The Progressive, *and* Time *magazine. Her books include* The American Health Empire: Power, Profits, and Politics *(1970),* For Her Own Good: One Hundred Fifty Years of the Experts' Advice to Women *(1978),* The Hearts of Men: American Dreams and the Flight from Commitment *(1983),* Blood Rites: Origins and History of the Passions of War *(1997), and* Nickel and Dimed: On (Not) Getting by in America *(2001). Her latest book,* Bate and Switch *(2005), is a companion to* Nickel and Dimed. *In both books Ehrenreich discusses her attempts to survive first as a minimum-wage employee and then as a white-collar worker. Her numerous awards include a National Magazine Award in 1980 and a Guggenheim Fellowship in 1987. The following essay appeared in* Time *magazine on February 5, 1996.*

1   A disturbing subtext runs through our recent media fixations. Parents abuse sons—allegedly at least, in the Menendez case[1]—who in turn rise up and kill them. A husband torments a wife, who retaliates with a kitchen knife. Love turns into obsession, between the Simpsons anyway, and then perhaps into murderous rage: the family, in other words, becomes personal hell.

2   This accounts for at least part of our fascination with the Bobbits[2] and the Simpsons and the rest of them. We live in a culture that fetishizes the family as the ideal unit of human community, the perfect container for our lusts and loves. Politicians of both parties are aggressively "pro-family," even abortion-rights bumper stickers proudly link "pro-family" and "pro-choice." Only with the occasional celebrity crime do we allow ourselves to think the nearly unthinkable: that the family may not be the ideal and perfect living arrangement after all—that it can be a nest of pathology and a cradle of gruesome violence.

---

[1] Lyle and Erik Menendez murdered their parents on August 20, 1989. They were the subject of a high-profile trial from October 1995 through March 1996.

[2] John and Lorena Bobbitt made the news June 23, 1993, after Lorena cut off a piece of her husband's penis. John Bobbitt was accused of wife beating by several women, including Lorena.

It's a scary thought, because the family is at the same time our "haven in a heartless   3
world." Theoretically, and sometimes actually, the family nurtures warm, loving feelings,
uncontaminated by greed or power hunger. Within the family, and often only within the
family, individuals are loved "for themselves," whether or not they are infirm, inconti-
nent, infantile or eccentric. The strong (adults and especially males) lie down peaceably
with the small and weak.

But consider the matter of wife battery. We managed to dodge it in the Bobbitt case   4
and downplay it as a force in Tonya Harding's[3] life. Thanks to OJ.,[4] though, we're caught
up now in a mass consciousness-raising session, grimly absorbing the fact that in some
areas domestic violence sends as many women to emergency rooms as any other form
of illness, injury or assault.

Still, we shrink from the obvious inference: for a woman, home is, statistically   5
speaking, the most dangerous place to be. Her worst enemies and potential killers are
not strangers but lovers, husbands and those who claimed to love her once. Similarly,
for every child like Polly Klaas who is killed by a deranged criminal on parole, dozens are
abused and murdered by their own relatives. Home is all too often where the small and
weak fear to lie down and shut their eyes.

At some deep, queasy, Freudian level, we all know this. Even in the ostensibly   6
"functional," nonviolent family, where no one is killed or maimed, feelings are routinely
bruised and often twisted out of shape. There is the slap or put-down that violates a
child's shaky sense of self, the cold, distracted stare that drives a spouse to tears, the
little digs and rivalries. At best, the family teaches the finest things human beings can
learn from one another—generosity and love. But it is also, all too often, where we learn
nasty things like hate and rage and shame.

Americans act out their ambivalence about the family without ever owning up to it.   7
Millions adhere to creeds that are militantly "pro-family." But at the same time millions
flock to therapy groups that offer to heal the "inner child" from damage inflicted by
family life. Legions of women band together to revive the self-esteem they lost in
supposedly loving relationships and to learn to love a little less. We are all, it is often
said, "in recovery." And from what? Our families, in most cases.

There is a long and honorable tradition of "anti-family" thought. The French   8
philosopher Charles Fourier taught that the family was a barrier to human progress;
early feminists saw a degrading parallel between marriage and prostitution. More
recently, the renowned British anthropologist Edmund Leach stated that "far from being
the basis of the good society, the family, with its narrow privacy and tawdry secrets, is
the source of all discontents."

---

[3] Tonya Harding was a world-class figure skater in the early 1990s. She is best known for her role in the
attack on her competitor, Nancy Kerrigan, January 6, 1994, during a practice session for the championship
of the U.S. Figure Skating competition.
[4] Millions of Americans followed the lengthy criminal trial of O. J. Simpson, former football star, for the
murder of his estranged wife, Nicole Simpson, and Ronald Goldberg in 1994–1995.

Oh, Those Family Values   Barbara Ehrenreich   **295**

9   Communes proved harder to sustain than plain old couples, and the conservatism of the '80s crushed the last vestiges of life-style experimentation. Today even gays and lesbians are eager to get married and take up family life. Feminists have learned to couch their concerns as "family issues," and public figures would sooner advocate free cocaine on demand than criticize the family. Hence our unseemly interest in O.J. and Erik, Lyle and Lorena: they allow us, however gingerly, to break the silence on the hellish side of family life.

10   But the discussion needs to become a lot more open and forthright. We may be stuck with the family—at least until someone invents a sustainable alternative—but the family, with its deep, impacted tensions and longings, can hardly be expected to be the moral foundation of everything else. In fact, many families could use a lot more outside interference in the form of counseling and policing, and some are so dangerously dysfunctional that they ought to be encouraged to disband right away. Even healthy families need outside sources of moral guidance to keep the internal tensions from imploding—and this means, at the very least, a public philosophy of gender equality and concern for child welfare. When, instead, the larger culture aggrandizes wife beaters, degrades women or nods approvingly at child slappers, the family gets a little more dangerous for everyone, and so, inevitably, does the larger world.

RESPONDING TO THE READING

FREEWRITING

Practice 10e. Freewrite about both average and celebrity families whose stories make the news. What kinds of events seem to make families "newsworthy"?

QUESTIONS FOR DISCUSSION

1. What tone or attitude toward family values does Barbara Ehrenreich's title convey? Does the title prepare you for the argument that follows?
2. What is Ehrenreich's thesis, either stated or implied? What writing strategies does she use to defend her thesis?
3. How does Ehrenreich explain our interest in stories about families whose members are abusive, even murderous (paragraph 9)? Do you agree with her conclusion?
4. What does Ehrenreich hope we learn from her critique of the family?

TOPICS FOR WRITING

Topic 1. A writer once remarked that the family is the place where you can go, and "they have to take you in." Write a short essay in which you draw on your own experience, observations, or research to either support or challenge this statement.

Topic 2. Write an essay in which you explore whether families provide a "safe," nurturing environment or are dangerous places to be. Base your discussion on your own family or families of relatives, neighbors, and friends.

Topic 3. Ehrenreich makes several harsh criticisms of the family in her essay. Select at least one of her points and write a detailed response to that idea. Consider doing some research on the topic to gather additional information for your essay.

Getting an Education

The readings in this chapter explore several perspectives on getting an education. In "The Struggle to Be an All-American Girl," Elizabeth Wong describes how she felt about her life as a student in a Chinese school in Chinatown and in an American public school. Mike Rose explains what it was like to take high school courses designed for underachievers, then to struggle to meet the demands of college prep courses. In "An Open Letter to Black Parents: Send Your Children to the Libraries," Arthur Ashe draws attention to the need for African American students to prepare themselves for careers outside of sports and entertainment. Nathan Thornburgh takes a critical but hopeful look at the dropout rate in American high schools in "Dropout Nation." Langston Hughes finds common experiences and economic differences between himself and his white teacher and classmates in "Theme for English B."

As I learn from you,
I guess you learn from me—
although you're older—and white—
and somewhat more free.
    —Langston Hughes

Bullshit, of course, is everything you—
and the others—fear is beyond you:
books, essays, tests, academic
scrambling, complexity, scientific
reasoning, philosophical inquiry.
    —Mike Rose

Name a few events or activities that parents force their children to attend. Do you agree with this practice?

The Struggle to Be an All-American Girl

Elizabeth Wong

Elizabeth Wong began her writing life as a journalist, but she soon became an important playwright and screenwriter. Her play Kimchee and Chitlins *(1990) is a comedy about the Black boycott of Korean stores in New York City and the media's coverage of the event.* Letters to a Student Revolutionary *(1991), whose plot revolves around the massacre in Tiananmen Square, received the Playwright's Forum Award. Other plays by Wong include* China Doll *(1995), winner of several awards, including the Jane Chambers Playwriting Award. Wong was also a writer for the sitcom "All-American Girl," the first network program to cast an Asian American in the leading role. In addition to her active writing career, Wong teaches playwriting at the University of Southern California and the University of California, Santa Barbara. "The Struggle to Be an All-American Girl" (1980) is one of the many essays Wong wrote for the opinion/editorial section of the* Los Angeles Times.

1   It's still there; the Chinese school on Yale Street where my brother and I used to go. Despite the new coat of paint and the high wire fence, the school I knew ten years ago remains remarkably, stoically the same.

2   Every day at 5 PM, instead of playing with our fourth- and fifth-grade friends or sneaking out to the empty lot to hunt ghosts and animal bones, my brother and I had to go to Chinese school. No amount of kicking, screaming, or pleading could dissuade my mother, who was solidly determined to have us learn the language of our heritage.

3   Forcibly, she walked us the seven long, hilly blocks from our home to school, depositing our defiant, tearful faces before the stern principal. My only memory of him is that he swayed on his heels like a palm tree, and he always clasped his impatient, twitching hands behind his back. I recognized him as a repressed maniacal child killer, and knew that if we ever saw his hands, we'd be in big trouble.

4   We all sat in little chairs in an empty auditorium. The room smelled like Chinese medicine, an imported faraway mustiness. Like ancient mothballs or dusty closets. I hated that smell. I favored crisp new scents. Like the soft French perfume that my American teacher wore in public school.

5   There was a stage far to the right, flanked by an American flag and the flag of the Nationalist Republic of China, which was also red, white, and blue, but not as pretty.

6   Although the emphasis at the school was mainly language—speaking, reading, writing—the lessons always began with an exercise in politeness. With the entrance of the teacher, the best student would tap a bell and everyone would get up, kowtow, and chant, "*Sing sun ho,*" the phonetic for "How are you, teacher?"

Being ten years old, I had better things to learn than ideographs copied painstak-   7
ingly in lines that ran right to left from the tip of a *moc but,* a real ink pen that had to be
held in an awkward way if blotches were to be avoided. After all, I could do the multipli-
cation tables, name the satellites of Mars, and write reports on *Little Women* and *Black
Beauty.* Nancy Drew, my favorite book heroine, never spoke Chinese.

The language was a source of embarrassment. More times than not, I had tried to   8
dissociate myself from the nagging, loud voice that followed me wherever I wandered in
the nearby American supermarket outside Chinatown. The voice belonged to my grandmother, a fragile woman in her seventies, who could outshout the best of the street vendors. Her humor was raunchy, her Chinese rhythmless, patternless. It was quick, it was
loud, it was unbeautiful. It was not like the quiet, lilting romance of French or the gentle refinement of the American. South Chinese sounded pedestrian. Public.

In Chinatown, the comings and goings of hundreds of Chinese on their daily tasks   9
sounded chaotic and frenzied. I did not want to be thought of as mad, as talking gibberish.
When I spoke English, people nodded at me, smiled sweetly, said encouraging words.
Even the people in my culture would cluck and say that I'd do well in life. "My, doesn't
she move her lips fast," they'd say, meaning that I'd be able to keep up with the world
outside Chinatown.

My brother was even more fanatical than I about speaking English. He was espe-   10
cially hard on my mother, criticizing her, often cruelly, for her pidgin speech—smatterings
of Chinese scattered like chop suey in her conversation. "It's not 'What it is,' Mom," he'd
say in exasperation. "It's 'What *is,* what *is,* what *is!*'" Sometimes, Mom might leave out an
occasional "the" or "a," or perhaps a verb of being. He would stop her in mid-sentence: "Say
it again, Mom. Say it right." When he tripped over his own tongue, he'd blame it on her:
"See, Mom, it's all your fault. You set a bad example."

What infuriated my mother most was when my brother cornered her on her conso-   11
nants, especially *r.* My father had played a cruel joke on Mom by assigning her an
American name that her tongue wouldn't allow her to say. No matter how hard she tried,
"Ruth" always ended up "Luth" or "Roof."

After two years of writing with a *moc but* and reciting words with multiples of mean-   12
ings, I finally was granted a cultural divorce. I was permitted to stop Chinese school.

I thought of myself as multicultural. I preferred tacos to egg rolls; I enjoyed Cinco   13
de Mayo more than Chinese New Year. At last, I was one of you; I wasn't one of them.

Sadly, I still am.   14

RESPONDING TO THE READING

FREEWRITING

Practice 11a. Freewrite about a "cultural divorce" or rejection of values or
cultural practices that you have experienced.

Practice 11b. Freewrite about teachers you have had who are similar to either
the "child-killer" principal or the perfumed American teacher in Wong's essay.

stoically (1)	flanked (5)	dissociate (8)	exasperation (10)
dissuade (2)	kowtow (6)	lilting (8)	pidgin (10)
forcibly (3)	ideographs (7)	raunchy (8)	infuriated (11)

QUESTIONS FOR DISCUSSION

1. Examine Wong's portrait of her grandmother, and identify both sympathetic and critical descriptions of her. Is there anything about Wong's grandmother that might make her appealing for the reader?
2. Why does Wong write about her brother, with his "fanatical" insistence on speaking English? What does his perspective add to her depiction of the cultural separation between parents and children?
3. What does Wong gain and what does she lose in the process of becoming an American?
4. What does Wong mean when she says she was granted a "cultural divorce" (paragraph 12)? Do you think this was a positive separation? Why or why not?
5. What does Wong consider her identity now, if not strictly Chinese? How is it like or unlike your own?
6. How do you explain the sadness she expresses in the last line of her article? How does the last line change the story?
7. Wong's subjects for nonfiction and drama draw heavily on her Chinese-American heritage. How might "The Struggle to Be an All-American Girl" be read as a tribute to her Chinese heritage?

TOPICS FOR WRITING

Topic 1. Elizabeth Wong describes her hatred of the Chinese school that her mother forced her to attend in the hope of preserving the family's Chinese heritage in America. Write a paper in which you discuss the benefits or harm that children might experience when they are forced into an activity that they dislike. Some of the activities you might consider include taking music lessons, playing in organized sports such as Little League, and attending religious or language schools. To gather information for this paper, consider interviewing members of your family, friends, or students in other classes whose opinions you value.

Topic 2. We all enjoy feeling that we "belong" to certain groups as well as to the larger culture around us. But as Wong points out, assimilation may bring unforeseen costs. What, in your experience, are some of the costs of "belonging"? What are some of the advantages? Do some freewriting about your own experience and observations to gather information. You might also interview people to draw on their experiences.

Topic 3. Write an essay explaining the similarities and differences between Elizabeth Wong's early schooling and your own. Compare or contrast your teachers, your after-school activities, your parents' attitudes, your own struggles, or the atmosphere of the schools you attended with Wong's experiences. For a student sample of an essay using this topic, see "Becoming an American," pages 218–219.

Topic 4. In "The Struggle to Be an All-American Girl" and "In the Kitchen" (pages 287–292), Elizabeth Wong and Henry Louis Gates, Jr. write about the balance between cultural identity and assimilation into the "Anglo" culture. Write an essay in which you compare Wong's and Louis Gates's attempts to achieve this balance.

WRITING BEFORE READING

Describe your attitude toward school when you were in high school. What elements in your life—family, teachers, school environment, friends—contributed to your attitude?

I Just Wanna Be Average

Mike Rose

Mike Rose is a professor at the UCLA Graduate School of Education and Information Studies and a nationally recognized expert on language and literacy. He is a graduate of Loyola University, the University of Southern California, and UCLA. The son of Italian immigrants, Rose was raised in South Central Los Angeles. He recorded the experiences that would later influence his interest in literacy and remedial education in Lives on the Boundary: The Struggles and Achievements of America's Underprepared *(1989). In* Possible Lives: The Promises of Public Education in America *(1996), Rose writes about his four-year journey across the United States in search of effective teachers and teaching methods. His most recent work is* The Mind at Work: Valuing the Intelligence of the American Worker *(2004). He is also the author of a textbook for graduate students in education and has coauthored two other textbooks. Rose has received awards from the National Academy of Education, the National Council of Teachers of English, the Modern Language Association, the McDonnell Foundation, and the Guggenheim Foundation for his work on literacy and education.*

It took two buses to get to Our Lady of Mercy. The first started deep in South Los   1
Angeles and caught me at midpoint. The second drifted through neighborhoods with trees, parks, big lawns, and lots of flowers. The rides were long but were livened up by a group of South L.A. veterans whose parents also thought that Hope had set up shop in the west end of the county. There was Christy Biggars, who, at sixteen, was dealing and was, according to rumor, a pimp as well. There were Bill Cobb and Johnny Gonzales, grease-pencil artists extraordinaire, who left Nembutal-enhanced swirls of "Cobb" and "Johnny" on the corrugated walls of the bus. And then there was Tyrrell Wilson. Tyrrell was the

coolest kid I knew. He ran the dozens like a metric halfback, laid down a rap that out-rhymed and outpointed Cobb, whose rap was good but not great—the curse of a moderately soulful kid trapped in white skin. But it was Cobb who would sneak a radio onto the bus, and thus underwrote his patter with Little Richard, Fats Domino, Chuck Berry, the Coasters, and Ernie K. Doe's mother-in-law, an awful woman who was "sent from down below." And so it was that Christy and Cobb and Johnny G. and Tyrrell and I and assorted others picked up along the way passed our days in the back of the bus, a funny mix brought together by geography and parental desire.

2   Entrance to school brings with it forms and releases and assessments. Mercy relied on a series of tests, mostly the Stanford-Binet, for placement, and somehow the results of my tests got confused with those of another student named Rose. The other Rose apparently didn't do very well, for I was placed in the vocational tract, a euphemism for the bottom level. Neither I nor my parents realized what this meant. We had no sense that Business Math, Typing, and English-Level D were dead ends. The current spate of reports on the schools criticizes parents for not involving themselves in the education of their children. But how would someone like Tommy Rose, with his two years of Italian schooling, know what to ask? And what sort of pressure could an exhausted waitress apply? The error went undetected, and I remained in the vocational tract for two years. What a place.

3   My homeroom was supervised by Brother Dill, a troubled and unstable man who also taught freshman English. When his class drifted away from him, which was often, his voice would rise in paranoid accusations, and occasionally he would lose control and shake or smack us. I hadn't been there two months when one of his brisk, face-turning slaps had my glasses sliding down the aisle. Physical education was also pretty harsh. Our teacher was a stubby ex-lineman who had played old-time pro ball in the Midwest. He routinely had us grabbing our ankles to receive his stinging paddle across our butts. He did that, he said, to make men of us. "Rose," he bellowed on our first encounter; me standing geeky in line in my baggy shorts. "'Rose'? What the hell kind of name is that?"

4   "Italian, sir," I squeaked.

5   "Italian! Ho. Rose, do you know the sound a bag of shit makes when it hits the wall?"

6   "No, sir."

7   "Wop!"

8   Sophomore English was taught by Mr. Mitropetros. He was a large, bejeweled man who managed the parking lot at the Shrine Auditorium. He would crow and preen and list for us the stars he'd brushed against. We'd ask questions and glance knowingly and snicker, and all that fueled the poor guy to brag some more. Parking cars was his night job. He had little training in English, so his lesson plan for his day work had us reading the district's required text, *Julius Caesar*, aloud for the semester. We'd finish the play way before the twenty weeks was up, so he'd have us switch parts again and again and start again: Dave Snyder, the fastest guy at Mercy, muscling through Caesar to the breathless squeals of Calpurnia, as interpreted by Steve Fusco, a surfer who owned the school's most envied paneled wagon. Week ten and Dave and Steve would take on new

roles, as would we all, and render a water-logged Cassius and a Brutus that are beyond my powers of description.

Spanish I—taken in the second year—fell into the hands of a new recruit. Mr. Montez 9
was a tiny man, slight, five foot six at the most, soft-spoken and delicate. Spanish was a particularly rowdy class, and Mr. Montez was as prepared for it as a doily maker at a hammer throw. He would tap his pencil to a room in which Steve Fusco was propelling spitballs from his heavy lips, in which Mike Dweetz was taunting Billy Hawk, a half-Indian, half-Spanish, reed-thin, quietly explosive boy. The vocational tract at Our Lady of Mercy mixed kids traveling in from South L.A. with South Bay surfers and a few Slavs and Chicanos from the harbors of San Pedro. This was a dangerous miscellany: surfers and hodads and South-Central blacks all ablaze to the metronomic tapping of Hector Montez's pencil.

One day Billy lost it. Out of the corner of my eye I saw him strike out with his right 10
arm and catch Dweetz across the neck. Quick as a spasm, Dweetz was out of his seat, scattering desks, cracking Billy on the side of the head, right behind the eye. Snyder and Fusco and others broke it up, but the room felt hot and close and naked. Mr. Montez's tenuous authority was finally ripped to shreds, and I think everyone felt a little strange about that. The charade was over, and when it came down to it, I don't think any of the kids really wanted it to end this way. They had pushed and pushed and bullied their way into a freedom that both scared and embarrassed them.

Students will float to the mark you set. I and the others in the vocational classes 11
were bobbing in pretty shallow water. Vocational education has aimed at increasing the economic opportunities of students who do not do well in our schools. Some serious programs succeed in doing that, and through exceptional teachers—like Mr. Gross in *Horace's Compromise*—students learn to develop hypotheses and troubleshoot, reason through a problem, and communicate effectively—the true job skills. The vocational track, however, is most often a place for those who are just not making it, a dumping ground for the disaffected. There were a few teachers who worked hard at education; young Brother Slattery, for example, combined a stern voice with weekly quizzes to try to pass along to us a skeletal outline of world history. But mostly the teachers had no idea of how to engage the imaginations of us kids who were scuttling along at the bottom of the pond.

And the teachers would have needed some inventiveness, for none of us was 12
groomed for the classroom. It wasn't just that I didn't know things—didn't know how to simplify algebraic fractions, couldn't identify different kinds of clauses, bungled Spanish translations—but that I had developed various faulty and inadequate ways of doing algebra and making sense of Spanish. Worse yet, the years of defensive tuning out in elementary school had given me a way to escape quickly while seeming at least half alert. During my time in Voc. Ed., I developed further into a mediocre student and a somnam-bulant problem solver, and that affected the subjects I did have the wherewithal to han-dle: I detested Shakespeare; I got bored with history. My attention flitted here and there. I fooled around in class and read my books indifferently—the intellectual equivalent of playing with your food. I did what I had to do to get by, and I did it with half a mind.

13   But I did learn things about people and eventually came into my own socially. I liked the guys in Voc. Ed. Growing up where I did, I understood and admired physical prowess, and there was an abundance of muscle here. There was Davy Snyder, a sprinter and halfback of true quality. Dave's ability and his quick wit gave him a natural appeal, and he was welcome in any clique, though he always kept a little independent. He enjoyed acting the fool and could care less about studies, but he possessed a certain maturity and never caused the faculty much trouble. It was a testament to his independence that he included me among his friends—I eventually went out for track, but I was no jock. Owing to the Latin alphabet and a dearth of *Rs* and *Ss*, Snyder sat behind Rose, and we started exchanging one-liners and became friends.

14   There was Ted Richard, a much-touted Little League pitcher. He was chunky and had a baby face and came to Our Lady of Mercy as a seasoned street fighter. Ted was quick to laugh and he had a loud, jolly laugh, but when he got angry he'd smile a little smile, the kind that simply raises the corner of the mouth a quarter of an inch. For those who knew, it was an eerie signal. Those who didn't found themselves in big trouble, for Ted was very quick. He loved to carry on what we would come to call philosophical discussions: What is courage? Does God exist? He also loved words, enjoyed picking up big ones like *salubrious* and *equivocal* and using them in our conversations—laughing at himself as the word hit a chuckhole rolling off his tongue. Ted didn't do all that well in school—baseball and parties and testing the courage he'd speculated about took up his time. His textbooks were *Argosy* and *Field and Stream*, whatever newspapers he'd find on the bus stop—from the *Daily Worker* to pornography—conversations with uncles or hobos or businessmen he'd meet in a coffee shop, *The Old Man and the Sea*. With hindsight, I can see that Ted was developing into one of those rough-hewn intellectuals whose sources are a mix of the learned and the apocryphal, whose discussions are both assured and sad.

15   And then there was Ken Harvey. Ken was good-looking in a puffy way and had a full and oily ducktail and was a car enthusiast . . . a hodad. One day in religion class, he said the sentence that turned out to be one of the most memorable of the hundreds of thousands I heard in those Voc. Ed. years. We were talking about the parable of the talents, about achievement, working hard, doing the best you can do, blah-blah-blah, when the teacher called on the restive Ken Harvey for an opinion. Ken thought about it, but just for a second, and said (with studied, minimal affect), "I just wanna be average." That woke me up. Average?! Who wants to be average? Then the athletes chimed in with the clichés that make you want to laryngectomize them, and the exchange became a platitudinous melee. At the time, I thought Ken's assertion was stupid, and I wrote him off. But his sentence has stayed with me all these years, and I think I am finally coming to understand it.

16   Ken Harvey was gasping for air. School can be a tremendously disorienting place. No matter how bad the school, you're going to encounter notions that don't fit with the assumptions and beliefs that you grew up with—maybe you'll hear these dissonant notions from teachers, maybe from the other students, and maybe you'll read them. You'll also be thrown in with all kinds of kids from all kinds of backgrounds, and that can

be unsettling—this is especially true in places of rich ethnic and linguistic mix, like the L.A. basin. You'll see a handful of students far excel you in courses that sound exotic and that are only in the curriculum of the elite: French, physics, trigonometry. And all this is happening while you're trying to shape an identity, your body is changing, and your emotions are running wild. If you're a working-class kid in the vocational track, the options you'll have to deal with this will be constrained in certain ways: You're defined by your school as "slow"; you're placed in a curriculum that isn't designed to liberate you but to occupy you, or, if you're lucky, train you, though the training is for work the society does not esteem; other students are picking up the cues from your school and your curriculum and interacting with you in particular ways. If you're a kid like Ted Richard, you turn your back on all this and let your mind roam where it may. But youngsters like Ted are rare. What Ken and so many others do is protect themselves from such suffocating madness by taking on with a vengeance the identity implied in the vocational track. Reject the confusion and frustration by openly defining yourself as the Common Joe. Champion the average. Rely on your own good sense. Fuck this bullshit. Bullshit, of course, is everything you—and the others—fear is beyond you: books, essays, tests, academic scrambling, complexity, scientific reasoning, philosophical inquiry.

The tragedy is that you have to twist the knife in your own gray matter to make this defense work. You'll have to shut down, have to reject intellectual stimuli or diffuse them with sarcasm, have to cultivate stupidity, have to convert boredom from a malady into a way of confronting the world. Keep your vocabulary simple, act stoned when you're not or act more stoned than you are, flaunt ignorance, materialize your dreams. It is a powerful and effective defense—it neutralizes the insult and the frustration of being a vocational kid and, when perfected, it drives teachers up the wall, a delightful secondary effect. But like all strong magic, it exacts a price.   17

My own deliverance from the Voc. Ed. world began with sophomore biology. Every student, college prep to vocational, had to take biology, and unlike the other courses, the same person taught all sections. When teaching the vocational group, Brother Clint probably slowed down a bit or omitted a little of the fundamental biochemistry, but he used the same book and more or less the same syllabus across the board. If one class got tough, he could get tougher. He was young and powerful and very handsome, and looks and physical strength were high currency. No one gave him any trouble.   18

I was pretty bad at the dissecting table, but the lectures and the textbook were interesting: plastic overlays that, with each turned page, peeled away skin, then veins and muscle, then organs, down to the very bones that Brother Clint, pointer in hand, would tap out on our hanging skeleton. Dave Snyder was in big trouble, for the study of life—versus the living of it—was sticking in his craw. We worked out a code for our multiple-choice exams. He'd poke me in the back: once for the answer under *A*, twice for *B*, and so on; and when he'd hit the right one, I'd look up to the ceiling as though I were lost in thought. Poke: cytoplasm. Poke, poke: methane. Poke, poke, poke: William Harvey. Poke, poke, poke, poke: islets of Langerhans. This didn't work out perfectly, but Dave passed the course, and I mastered the dreamy look of a guy on a record jacket. And something else happened. Brother Clint puzzled over this Voc. Ed. kid who was racking   19 up 98s and 99s on his tests. He checked the school's records and discovered the error. He recommended that I begin my junior year in the College Prep program. According to all I've read since, such a shift, as one report put it, is virtually impossible. Kids at that level rarely cross tracks. The telling thing is how chancy both my placement into and exit from Voc. Ed. was; neither I nor my parents had anything to do with it. I lived in one world during spring semester, and when I came back to school in the fall, I was living in another.

20   Switching to College Prep was a mixed blessing. I was an erratic student. I was undisciplined. And I hadn't caught onto the rules of the game: Why work hard in a class that didn't grab my fancy? I was also hopelessly behind in math. Chemistry was hard; toying with my chemistry set years before hadn't prepared me for the chemist's equations. Fortunately, the priest who taught both chemistry and second-year algebra was also the school's athletic director. Membership on the track team covered me; I knew I wouldn't get lower than a C. U.S. History was taught pretty well and I did okay. But civics was taken over by a football coach who had trouble reading the textbook aloud—and reading aloud was the centerpiece of his pedagogy. College Prep at Mercy was certainly an improvement over the vocational program—at least it carried some status—but the social science curriculum was weak, and the mathematics and physical sciences were simply beyond me. I had a miserable quantitative background and ended up copying some assignments and finessing the rest as best I could. Let me try to explain how it feels to see again and again material you should once have learned but didn't.

21   You are given a problem. It requires you to simplify algebraic fractions or to multiply expressions containing square roots. You know this is pretty basic material because you've seen it for years. Once a teacher took some time with you, and you learned how to carry out these operations. Simple versions, anyway. But that was a year or two or more in the past, and these are more complex versions, and now you're not sure. And this, you keep telling yourself, is ninth- or even eighth-grade stuff.

22   Next it's a word problem. This is also old hat. The basic elements are as familiar as story characters: trains speeding so many miles per hour or shadows of buildings angling so many degrees. Maybe you know enough, have sat through enough explanations, to be able to begin setting up the problem: "If one train is going this fast . . ." or "This shadow is really one line of a triangle. . . ." Then: "Let's see . . ." "How did Jones do this?" "Hmmmm." "No." "No, that won't work." Your attention wavers. You wonder about other things: a football game, a dance, that cute new checker at the market. You try to focus on the problem again. You scribble on paper for a while, but the tension wins out and your attention flits elsewhere. You crumple the paper and begin daydreaming to ease the frustration.

23   The particulars will vary, but in essence this is what a number of students go through, especially those in so-called remedial classes. They open their textbooks and see once again the familiar and impenetrable formulas and diagrams and terms that have stumped them for years. There is no excitement here. *No* excitement. Regardless of what the teacher says, this is not a new challenge. There is, rather, embarrassment and frustration and, not surprisingly, some anger in being reminded once again of longstanding

inadequacies. No wonder so many students finally attribute their difficulties to something inborn, organic: "That part of my brain just doesn't work." Given the troubling histories many of these students have, it's miraculous that any of them can lift the shroud of hopelessness sufficiently to make deliverance from these classes possible.

Through this entire period, my father's health was deteriorating with cruel momentum. His arteriosclerosis progressed to the point where a simple nick on his shin wouldn't heal. Eventually it ulcerated and widened. Lou Minton would come by daily to change the dressing. We tried renting an oscillating bed—which we placed in the front room—to force blood through the constricted arteries in my father's legs. The bed hummed through the night, moving in place to ward off the inevitable. The ulcer continued to spread, and the doctors finally had to amputate. My grandfather had lost his leg in a stockyard accident. Now my father too was crippled. His convalescence was slow but steady, and the doctors placed him in the Santa Monica Rehabilitation Center, a sun-bleached building that opened out onto the warm spray of the Pacific. The place gave him some strength and some color and some training in walking with an artificial leg. He did pretty well for a year or so until he slipped and broke his hip. He was confined to a wheelchair after that, and the confinement contributed to the diminishing of his body and spirit.   24

I am holding a picture of him. He is sitting in his wheelchair and smiling at the camera. The smile appears forced, unsteady, seems to quaver, though it is frozen in silver nitrate. He is in his mid-sixties and looks eighty. Late in my junior year, he had a stroke and never came out of the resulting coma. After that, I would see him only in dreams, and to this day that is how I join him. Sometimes the dreams are sad and grisly and primal: my father lying in a bed soaked with his suppuration, holding me, rocking me. But sometimes the dreams bring him back to me healthy: him talking to me on an empty street, or buying some pictures to decorate our old house, or transformed somehow into someone strong and adept with tools and the physical.   25

Jack MacFarland couldn't have come into my life at a better time. My father was dead, and I had logged up too many years of scholastic indifference. Mr. MacFarland had a master's degree from Columbia and decided, at twenty-six, to find a little school and teach his heart out. He never took any credentialing courses, couldn't bear to, he said, so he had to find employment in a private system. He ended up at Our Lady of Mercy teaching five sections of senior English. He was a beatnik who was born too late. His teeth were stained, he tucked his sorry tie in between the third and fourth buttons of his shirt, and his pants were chronically wrinkled. At first, we couldn't believe this guy, thought he slept in his car. But within no time, he had us so startled with work that we didn't much worry about where he slept or if he slept at all. We wrote three or four essays a month. We read a book every two to three weeks, starting with the *Iliad* and ending up with Hemingway. He gave us a quiz on the reading every other day. He brought a prep school curriculum to Mercy High.   26

MacFarland's lectures were crafted, and as he delivered them he would pace the room jiggling a piece of chalk in his cupped hand, using it to scribble on the board the names of all the writers and philosophers and plays and novels he was weaving into his   27 discussion. He asked questions often, raised everything from Zeno's paradox to the repeated last line of Frost's "Stopping by Woods on a Snowy Evening." He slowly and carefully built up our knowledge of Western intellectual history—with facts, with connections, with speculations. We learned about Greek philosophy, about Dante, the Elizabethan world view, and Age of Reason, existentialism. He analyzed poems with us, had us reading sections from John Ciardi's *How Does a Poem Mean?*, making a potentially difficult book accessible with his own explanations. We gave oral reports on poems Ciardi didn't cover. We imitated the styles of Conrad, Hemingway, and *Time* magazine. We wrote and talked, wrote and talked. The man immersed us in language.

28   Even MacFarland's barbs were literary. If Jim Fitzsimmons, hungover and irritable, tried to smart-ass him, he'd rejoin with a flourish that would spark the indomitable Skip Madison—who'd lost his front teeth in a hapless tackle to flick his tongue through the gap and opine, "good chop," drawing out the single "o" in stinging indictment. Jack MacFarland, this tobacco-stained intellectual, brandished linguistic weapons of a kind I hadn't encountered before. Here was this *egghead,* for God's sake, keeping some pretty difficult people in line. And from what I heard, Mike Dweetz and Steve Fusco and all the notorious Voc. Ed. crowd settled down as well when MacFarland took the podium. Though a lot guys groused in the schoolyard, it just seemed that giving trouble to this particular teacher was a silly thing to do. Tomfoolery, not to mention assault, had no place in the world he was trying to create for us, and instinctively everyone knew that. If nothing else, we all recognized MacFarland's considerable intelligence and respected the hours he put into his work. It came to this: The troublemaker would look foolish rather than daring. Even Jim Fitzsimmons was reading *On the Road* and turning his incipient alcoholism to literary ends.

29   There were some lives that were already beyond Jack MacFarland's ministrations, but mine was not. I started reading again as I hadn't since elementary school. I would go into our gloomy little bedroom or sit at the dinner table while, on the television, Danny McShane was paralyzing Mr. Moto with the atomic drop, and work slowly back through *Heart of Darkness,* trying to catch the words in Conrad's sentences. I certainly was not MacFarland's best student; most of the other guys in College Prep, even my fellow slackers, had better backgrounds than I did. But I worked very hard, for MacFarland had hooked me. He tapped my old interest in reading and creating stories. He gave me a way to feel special by using my mind. And he provided a role model that wasn't shaped on physical prowess alone, and something inside me that I wasn't quite aware of responded to that. Jack MacFarland established a literacy club, to borrow a phrase of Frank Smith's, and invited me—invited all of us—to join.

30   There's been a good deal of research and speculation suggesting that the acknowledgment of school performance with extrinsic rewards—smiling faces, stars, numbers, grades—diminishes the intrinsic satisfaction children experience by engaging in reading or writing or problem solving. While it's certainly true that we've created an educational system that encourages our best and brightest to become cynical grade collectors and, in general, have developed an obsession with evaluation and assessment, I must tell you that venal though it may have been, I loved getting good grades from MacFarland. I now

know how subjective grades can be, but then they came tucked in the back of essays like bits of scientific data, some sort of spectroscopic readout that said, objectively and publicly, that I had made something of value. I suppose I'd been mediocre for too long and enjoyed a public redefinition. And I suppose the workings of my mind, such as they were, had been private for too long. My linguistic play moved into the world; like the intergalactic stories I told years before on Frank's berry-splattered truck bed, these papers with their circled, red B-pluses and A-minuses linked my mind to something outside it. I carried them around like a club emblem.

One day in the December of my senior year, Mr. MacFarland asked me where I was going to go to college. I hadn't thought much about it. Many of the students I teach today spent their last year in high school with a physics text in one hand and the Stanford catalog in the other, but I wasn't even aware of what "entrance requirements" were. My folks would say that they wanted me to go to college and be a doctor, but I don't know how seriously I ever took that; it seemed a sweet thing to say, a bit of supportive family chatter, like telling a gangly daughter she's graceful. The reality of higher education wasn't in my scheme of things: No one in the family had gone to college; only two of my uncles had completed high school. I figured I'd get a night job and go to the local junior college because I knew that Snyder and Company were going there to play ball. But I hadn't even prepared for that. When I finally said, "I don't know," MacFarland looked down at me—I was seated in his office—and said, "Listen, you can write." 31

My grades stank. I had A's in biology and a handful of B's in a few English and social science classes. All the rest were C's—or worse. MacFarland said I would do well in his class and laid down the law about doing well in the others. Still, the record for my first three years wouldn't have been acceptable to any four-year school. To nobody's surprise, I was turned down flat by USC and UCLA. But Jack MacFarland was on the case. He had received his bachelor's degree from Loyola University, so he made calls to old professors and talked to somebody in admissions and wrote me a strong letter. Loyola finally accepted me as a probationary student. I would be on trial for the first year, and if I did okay, I would be granted regular status. MacFarland also intervened to get me a loan, for I could never have afforded a private college without it. Four more years of religion classes and four more years of boys at one school, girls at another. But at least I was going to college. Amazing. 32

RESPONDING TO THE READING

FREEWRITING

Practice 11c. Freewrite about memories of students with whom you were friendly in high school. How do your friends compare with Rose's high school friends?

Practice 11d. What teachers, fellow students, or other adults encouraged you to stay in school?

euphemism (2)	rough-hewn (14)	arteriosclerosis (24)
spate (2)	apocryphal (14)	oscillating (24)
mediocre (12)	laryngectomize (15)	suppuration (25)
somnambulant (12)	platitudinous (15)	ministrations (29)
salubrious (14)	melee (15)	spectroscopic (30)
equivocal (14)	dissonant (16)	cynical (30)

THINKING ABOUT WORDS

Mike Rose's style of writing is unique because of the different levels of language he uses. For instance, to re-create the encounter with his physical education teacher, he chooses a combination of slang and four-letter words like the ones in these phrases: "across our butts," "What the hell kind of name," "standing geeky in line," and "a bag of shit." When he comments on his lack of preparation for the classroom, however, he uses more academic English: "teachers . . . needed some inventiveness," "bungled Spanish translations," "faulty and inadequate ways of doing algebra," and "a somnambulant problem solver."

FOR PRACTICE

Practice 11e. Select a paragraph from "I Just Wanna Be Average," and circle the words and phrases that seem unusual. Discuss what levels of language Rose uses and how those particular words serve to convey an idea or create an impression.

QUESTIONS FOR DISCUSSION

1. What does Rose think about the advice that parents need to get more involved "in the education of their children" (paragraph 2)? How does he convey his opinion of this advice? Do you agree with his assessment?
2. Rose describes Ted Richards, a friend from his days at Our Lady of Mercy High School, as someone who was becoming a "rough-hewn intellectual . . . whose discussions are both assured and sad." What does Rose find "sad" about Richards's discussions?
3. Aside from the occasional uninspiring instructor, what made it difficult for Rose to become interested in school?
4. In drawing conclusions about the educational system he experienced, Rose says, "Students will float to the mark you set." What does he mean by this statement? Can you think of examples where this has been true for you or for other students you know?

5. What does Rose think of the Voc. Ed. program at Mercy High? What is the effect of using the abbreviation "*Voc. Ed.*" in place of *Vocational Education?*
6. Rose says that many kids in the Voc. Ed. program protected themselves "by taking on with a vengeance the identity implied in the vocational track." Describe this "Voc. Ed. identity." Give a few examples of ways the students identified themselves as Voc. Ed. kids.
7. Discuss the title "I Just Wanna Be Average." What is the effect of replacing "want to" with "Wanna"? What does Rose think of the desire to be average? Do you agree with him?
8. This section of Mike Rose's *Lives on the Boundary* is a personal account of a period when he was in high school. How does Rose give his story a more universal meaning? Locate passages in "I Just Wanna Be Average" where Rose makes this connection for the reader.
9. What connections can you draw between Rose's personal experience in high school and the analysis of high school in Nathan Thornburgh's "Dropout Nation" (which is presented later in this chapter)?

TOPICS FOR WRITING

Topic 1. Mike Rose writes about his progress from Voc. Ed. to college prep classes. Write a paper in which you describe several stages in your own progress through school.

Topic 2. Rose admits that although some theorists say that grades and other rewards produce "cynical grade collectors," getting good grades from his English teacher meant a lot to him. Write a paper about what motivates or discourages you in English or in other classes you have taken.

Topic 3. The educational programs at Our Lady of Mercy included vocational education and college preparation classes. Write a paper in which you evaluate the kinds of courses students could take (college prep or otherwise) at your high school. Consider examining the material students were asked to learn or evaluating the quality of teaching in some courses.

Topic 4. Write an essay in which you examine the image of the intellectual, the thinker in this culture. Think of specific images or characters in film, on television, or in books you have read that contribute to this image.

WRITING BEFORE READING

Write about a time in your life when you struggled with fears, limitations, or misconceptions you had about yourself or your ability to succeed. What steps did you take to change the situation?

An Open Letter to Black Parents: Send Your Children to the Libraries

Arthur Ashe

Arthur Ashe (1943–1985) became a world-champion tennis player in a sport generally reserved for affluent whites. Ashe graduated from UCLA in 1966 with a degree in business administration. During his career in tennis, he won 51 titles, including the national intercollegiate competition in 1965, the first U.S. Open competition in 1968, the Davis Cup in 1968–1970 and 1981–1982, and the tournament in Wimbledon, England, in 1975. Ashe was the first African American male to win these titles and was elected to the Tennis Hall of Fame in 1985. Ashe used his recognition as a tennis champion to promote the cause of civil rights worldwide. He also founded numerous charitable organizations, including the National Junior Tennis League, the ABC Cities Tennis Program, the Athlete–Career Connection, and the Safe Passage Foundation. Ashe is the author of two books, A Hard Road to Glory *(1988), a three-volume history of African American athletes, and* Days of Grace: A Memoir *published in 1993. Illness and an early death in 1985 cut short his exceptional career. In "An Open Letter to Black Parents: Send Your Children to the Libraries," published in the* New York Times *in 1977, Ashe encourages African American athletes to make academics a priority in their lives.*

1   Since my sophomore year at UCLA, I have become convinced that we blacks spend too much time on the playing fields and too little time in the libraries. Consider these facts: for the major professional sports of hockey, football, basketball, baseball, golf, tennis and boxing, there are roughly only 3170 major league positions available (attributing 200 positions to golf, 200 to tennis and 100 to boxing). And the annual turnover is small.

2   There must be some way to assure that those who try but don't make it to pro sports don't wind up on street corners or in unemployment lines. Unfortunately, our most widely recognized role models are athletes and entertainers—"runnin" and "jumpin" and "singin" and "dancin."

3   Our greatest heroes of the century have been athletes—Jack Johnson, Joe Louis,[1] and Muhammad Ali. Racial and economic discrimination forced us to channel our energies into athletics and entertainment. These were the ways out of the ghetto, the ways to get that Cadillac, those regular shoes, that cashmere sport coat.

4   Somehow, parents must instill a desire for learning alongside the desire to be Walt Frazier.[2] Why not start by sending black professional athletes into high schools to explain the facts of life?

---

[1] Jack Johnson and Joe Louis were African American boxers who held world titles. Johnson won the world title in 1908; Louis became the world heavyweight champion in 1937 and held that title for eleven years, longer than any other fighter.

[2] Walt Frazier was an African American basketball player in the late 1960s and 1970s. The National Basketball Association named Frazier one of the fifty best players in U.S. basketball history.

I have often addressed high school audiences and my message is always the same: 5
"For every hour you spend on the athletic field, spend two in the library. Even if you make it as a pro athlete, your career will be over by the time you are 35. You will need that diploma."

Have these pro athletes explain what happens if you break a leg, get a sore arm, 6
have one bad year, or don't make the cut for five or six tournaments. Explain to them the star system, wherein for every star earning millions there are six or seven others making $15,000 or $20,000 or $30,000. Invite a bench-warmer or a guy who didn't make it. Ask him if he sleeps every night. Ask him whether he was graduated. Ask him what he would do if he became disabled tomorrow. Ask him where his old high school athletic buddies are.

We have been on the same roads—sports and entertainment—too long. We need to 7
pull over, fill up at the library and speed away to Congress and the Supreme Court, the unions and the business world.

I'll never forget how proud my grandmother was when I graduated from UCLA. 8
Never mind the Davis Cup. Never mind the Wimbledon title. To this day, she still doesn't know what those names mean. What mattered to her was that of her more than thirty children and grandchildren, I was the first to be graduated from college, and a famous college at that. Somehow, that made up for all those floors she scrubbed all those years.

RESPONDING TO THE READING

FREEWRITING

Practice 11f. Freewrite about athletes who are trying to help their community in some way.

Practice 11g. Record your thoughts about the way young people in general sometimes see themselves and their future in very narrow terms.

BUILDING YOUR VOCABULARY

attributing (1)   cashmere (3)

QUESTIONS FOR DISCUSSION

1. Who is the audience for "An Open Letter to Black Parents: Send Your Children to the Libraries"? Might there be more than one?
2. Identify Ashe's thesis. How well does he support his position? What suggestions would you make to extend Ashe's argument?

3. Ashe calls for greater involvement by parents and professional athletes to help young athletes make more informed decisions about their future. What other solutions can you think of to broaden people's thinking about themselves?
4. Examine the final paragraph of "An Open Letter to Black Parents: Send Your Children to the Libraries." What does the personal anecdote in that paragraph add to Ashe's argument?

TOPICS FOR WRITING

Topic 1. If you know about athletes who are promoting education and other issues that benefit young people, write about what they do and how successful they have been in pointing teens in the right direction.

Topic 2. Consult databases in your library and check Internet resources to find out about the trends in career opportunities for African Americans, another under-represented group, or women. What careers seem to have become less restricted? On the other hand, are there positions for which African Americans, Latinos, women, or others are not generally hired?

WRITING BEFORE READING

Approximately what percentage of students didn't graduate with your high school class? What do you remember about why they weren't able to graduate?

Dropout Nation

Nathan Thornburgh

Nathan Thornburgh is a regular contributor to Time *magazine. He wrote "Dropout Nation" for the April 17, 2006 issue of* Time. *In this article, Thornburgh focuses on a midwestern high school in Shelbyville, Indiana, in an effort to personalize the stories of dropouts from American high schools and to examine programs and policies that are designed to keep kids in school.*

1   It's lunchtime at Shelbyville High School, 30 miles southeast of Indianapolis, Ind., and more than 100 teenagers are buzzing over trays in the cafeteria. Like high schoolers every-where, they have arranged themselves by type: jocks, preps, cheerleaders, dorks, punks and gamers, all with tables of their own. But when they are finished chugging the milk and throwing Tater Tots at one another, they will drift out to their classes and slouch together through lessons on Edgar Allan Poe and Pythagoras. It's the promise of American public

education: no matter who you are or where you come from, you will be tugged gently along the path of learning, toward graduation and an open but hopeful future.

Shawn Sturgill, 18, had a clique of his own at Shelbyville High, a dozen or so friends who sat at the same long bench in the hallway outside the cafeteria. They were, Shawn says, an average crowd. Not too rich, not too poor; not bookish, but not slow. They rarely got into trouble. Mainly they sat around and talked about Camaros and the Indianapolis Colts. These days the bench is mostly empty. Of his dozen friends, Shawn says just one or two are still at Shelbyville High. If some cliques are defined by a common sport or a shared obsession with Yu-Gi-Oh! cards, Shawn's friends ended up being defined by their mutual destiny: nearly all of them became high school dropouts. | 2

Shawn's friends are not alone in their exodus. Of the 315 Shelbyville students who showed up for the first day of high school four years ago, only 215 are expected to graduate. The 100 others have simply melted away, dropping out in a slow, steady bleed that has left the town wondering how it could have let down so many of its kids. | 3

In today's data-happy era of accountability, testing and No Child Left Behind, here is the most astonishing statistic in the whole field of education: an increasing number of researchers are saying that nearly 1 out of 3 public high school students won't graduate, not just in Shelbyville but around the nation. For Latinos and African Americans, the rate approaches an alarming 50%. Virtually no community, small or large, rural or urban, has escaped the problem. | 4

There is a small but hardy band of researchers who insist the dropout rates don't quite approach those levels. They point to their pet surveys that suggest a rate of only 15% to 20%. The dispute is difficult to referee, particularly in the wake of decades of lax accounting by states and schools. But the majority of analysts and lawmakers have come to this consensus: the numbers have remained unchecked at approximately 30% through two decades of intense educational reform, and the magnitude of the problem has been consistently, and often willfully, ignored. | 5

That's starting to change. During his most recent State of the Union address, President George W. Bush promised more resources to help children stay in school, and Democrats promptly attacked him for lacking a specific plan. The Bill & Melinda Gates Foundation has trained its moneyed eye on the problem, funding "The Silent Epidemic," a study issued in March that has gained widespread attention both in Washington and in statehouses around the country. | 6

The attention comes against a backdrop of rising peril for dropouts. If their grandparents' generation could find a blue-collar niche and prosper, the latest group is immediately relegated to the most punishing sector of the economy, where whatever low-wage jobs haven't yet moved overseas are increasingly filled by even lower-wage immigrants. Dropping out of high school today is to your societal health what smoking is to your physical health, an indicator of a host of poor outcomes to follow, from low lifetime earnings to high incarceration rates to a high likelihood that your children will drop out of high school and start the cycle anew. | 7

8   Identifying the problem is just the first step. The next moves are being made by towns like Shelbyville, where a loose coalition of community leaders and school administrators have, for the first time, placed dropout prevention at the top of the agenda. Now they are gamely trying to identify why kids are leaving and looking for ways to reverse the tide. At the request of a former principal, a local factory promised to stop tempting dropouts with jobs. Superintendent David Adams is scouting vacant storefronts for a place to put a new alternative high school. And Shelbyville's Republican state representative, Luke Messer, sponsored a bill, signed into law by the Governor two weeks ago, that will give students alternatives to traditional high school while imposing tough penalties on those who try to leave early without getting permission from the school district or a judge.

9   Shelbyville, a town of almost 18,000 located on the outer fringe of the "doughnut" counties that ring Indianapolis, seems an unlikely battleground in the war on dropouts. Despite a few oddities—it's home to both the oldest living Hoosier and the world's tallest woman—it is an otherwise pleasantly unremarkable town. The capital is just a short drive away, but miles of rust-colored farmland, mainly cornfields waiting for seed, give the area a rural tinge. Most people live in single-family houses with yards and fences. Not many of them are very well off, but there's little acute poverty, as a gaggle of automotive and other factories has given the town a steady supply of well-paying jobs. Violent crime is rare, and the town is pervaded by a throwback decency. People wave at one another from their cars on Budd Street. They chitchat in the aisles of Mickey's T-Mart grocery store.

10   For years, Shelbyville had been comforted by its self-reported—and wildly inaccurate—graduation rate of up to 98%. The school district arrived at that number by using a commonly accepted statistical feint, counting any dropout who promises to take the GED test later on as a graduating student.

11   The GED trick is only one of many deployed by state and local governments around the country to disguise the real dropout rates. Houston, for example, had its notorious "leaver codes"—dozens of excuses, such as pregnancy and military service, that were often applied to students who were later reclassified as dropouts by outside auditors. The Federal Government has been similarly deceptive, producing rosy graduation-rate estimates—usually between 85% and 90%—by relying only on a couple of questions buried deep within the U.S. Census Bureau's Current Population Survey. The survey asks whether respondents have a diploma or GED. Critics say the census count severely underreports dropout numbers, in part because it doesn't include transients or prisoners, populations with a high proportion of dropouts.

12   In 2001, Jay Greene, a senior fellow at the Manhattan Institute, published a study that peeled back the layers of statistical legerdemain. Poring over raw education data, he asked himself a basic question: What percentage of kids who start at a high school finish? The answers led Greene and subsequent researchers around the country to place the national graduation rate at anywhere from 64% to 71%. It's a rate that most researchers say has remained fairly static since the 1970s, despite increased attention on the plight of public schools and a vigorous educational-reform movement.

Starting a year ago, the people of Shelbyville began to admit the scope of their problem by asking themselves the same simple questions about who was graduating. It helped that superintendent Adams was new to his job and that the high school's principal was too. They had a clean slate and little incentive to make excuses for the old way of doing things.

The Pushout

Sarah Miller, 28, was victim of those old ways. An intelligent but rebellious teenager with a turbulent home life, Sarah began falling behind in attendance and classwork her freshman year. Like many other 15-year-olds, she had a talent for making poor decisions. She and her friends would often skip out of school after lunch and cruise up and down Broadway. Teachers rarely stopped them, but school authorities knew what she and her friends were up to. One morning Sarah went to the school office to discuss getting back on track but got a surprise. One of the administrators asked her point-blank, "Why don't you just quit school?" "I was just a kid," says Sarah with a laugh. "It was like they said the magic words. So I told them, 'O.K.!' And I left."

Sarah never set foot in a high school again. She got her GED, but now she's too afraid to try community college, she says, because she doesn't want to look stupid. Although she has a house she owns with her husband and a fine job serving coffee, biscuits and small talk at Ole McDonald's Cafe in nearby Acton, Ind., Sarah is not without regret. "It would have been nice to have someone pushing me to stay," she says. "Who knows how things would have turned out?"

Researchers call students like Sarah "pushouts," not dropouts. Shelbyville High's new principal, Tom Zobel, says he's familiar with the mind-set. "Ten years ago," he says, "if we had a problem student, the plan was, 'O.K., let's figure out how to get rid of this kid.' Now we have to get them help."

But can educators really be faulted for the calculation, however cold, that certain kids are an unwise investment of their limited energies and resources? That question quickly leads to the much thornier issues of class and clout that shape the dropout crisis. The national statistics on the topic are blunt: according to the National Center for Education Statistics, kids from the lowest income quarter are more than six times as likely to drop out of high school as kids from the highest. And in Shelbyville, nearly every dropout I met voiced a similar complaint: teachers and principals treat the "rich kids" better. "The rich kids always knew how to be good kids," says Sarah in a more nuanced version of the same refrain. "So I guess it's natural the schools wanted to work with them more than with the rest of us." The poor kids, though, are exactly the ones who need the extra investment.

Shelbyville leaders hope to change the prevailing mentality. At a cavernous high school gym in nearby Columbus, I watched the boys' basketball sectional semifinal with Shelbyville mayor Scott Furgeson. The Shelbyville Golden Bears' 21-0 regular season record had turned the town's usual Hoosier hysteria into Hoosier histrionics. As his constituents cheered on the good kids—the lithe, clean-cut basketball players who were dominating Columbus North High School—Furgeson paused to think about the other kids. Before becoming mayor, he spent 22 years managing the local Pizza King franchise. Every year he had to hire up to 200 teenagers, many of them dropouts, just to keep 10 full-time positions staffed. Those teenagers, failing in life as they had failed at school, were often the children of people Furgeson had seen quit school when he was a student at Shelbyville High 25 years before. The dropout problem, he says, corrupts the community far beyond the halls of the high school. "I worry that we're creating a permanent underclass," he says.

19   John Bridgeland, CEO of the Washington-based public-policy firm Civic Enterprises, says it's that type of attitude shift, more than legislation, that is likely to lead to change. Messer's 2005 bill made Indiana one of six states in the past five years to raise its minimum dropout age to 18 from 16. (Twenty-three states still let kids drop out at the younger age without parental consent.) Bridgeland, who co-wrote the Gates Foundation—funded report, supports the age hike but warns that states can't legislate in a vacuum. "These laws have to be coupled with strong support from the school and the community," he says. Underlying that conviction is perhaps the most surprising finding of the Gates survey: just how few dropouts report being overwhelmed academically. Fully 88% said they had passing grades in high school. Asked to name the reasons they had left school, more respondents named boredom than struggles with course work.

The Restless One

20   Susan Swinehart, 17, was an honors student her freshman year. She also joined the yearbook staff and found that she loved selling the $300 full-page yearbook ads to local businesses like Rush Shelby Energy and Fat Daddy's restaurant. But the social cauldron of high school weighed on her. She didn't get along with the cheerleaders on the yearbook staff. And her avid interest in Stephen King novels and TV shows about forensics earned her a false reputation, she says, as a glum goth girl. So she started ditching class, barreling through the Indiana countryside alone in her Dodge Neon, blasting her favorite song, "The Ghost of You," by My Chemical Romance—a song, as she puts it, about missed opportunities and regret. "I'd rather regret something I did," she says, eyes welling with tears, "than regret something I didn't do." For her, sitting in a classroom biting her tongue and waiting to graduate when college wasn't necessarily in her future was a form of inaction. Working, saving money, starting her adult life—that was taking the initiative.

21   In cases like Susan's, American public education may be a victim of its own ambition. Rallying around the notion that every child should be prepared for higher education, schools follow a general-education model that marches students through an increasingly uniform curriculum, with admission to college as the goal. But what happens when a 17-year-old decides, rightly or wrongly, that her road in life doesn't pass through college? Then the college-prep exercise becomes a charade. At Shelbyville High School, as elsewhere, the general-education model became an all-or-nothing game that left far too many students with nothing.

Two months ago, Susan told her mother Kathy Roan that she was dropping out. "I 22 wanted to kill her," says Kathy. But Kathy had her own bitterness about Shelbyville High. Two decades earlier, she too had been angered by the indifference of the school. She dropped out as soon as she turned 16. On Feb. 22, Susan's mother went to school with her to sign her out of high school. That night Susan applied for more hours at the Taco Bell where she worked and promptly stayed for the 5 p.m.-to-2 a.m. shift. The other women on the graveyard shift gave her hell for quitting school. They were mostly dropouts themselves, says Susan, who reminded her that even at fast-food chains, anyone who wants to advance needs a diploma or GED. She had, they told her, just broken something that could not be easily put back together.

Susan says she will prove them wrong. She has started a Pennsylvania-based cor- 23 respondence course that both her mother and sister completed. For $985, it provides textbooks, online tests and teacher support via phone and e-mail. The rush to cash in on dropouts has made such correspondence courses and "virtual high schools" the Wild West of secondary education, a multimillion-dollar industry that can offer a valuable second chance but has suffered at times from poor oversight and a dizzying array of self-styled accrediting institutions, many of which aren't recognized by mainstream colleges.

There is, not surprisingly, partisan division over the dropout problem. Liberals say 24 dropouts are either a by-product of testing mania or an unavoidable result of public schools' being starved for funding. But more conservative reform advocates, like Marcus Winters, a senior research associate at the Manhattan Institute, disagree. "Spending more money just has not worked," he says. "We've doubled the amount we spend per pupil since the '70s, and the problem hasn't budged."

In Indiana, however, there is a bipartisan consensus about the state's latest 25 antidropout measure. Shelbyville representative Messer, former head of the Indiana Republican Party, is no stranger to partisan politics, but his strongest partner in pushing for the measure was a liberal Democrat named Stan Jones, who is now the state's com-missioner of higher education. The bill they championed had, fittingly, both carrot and stick. Students who drop out before age 18 could have their driver's license suspended or their work permit revoked unless their decision was first approved by a school or judge. But students who found the high school environment stifling could take classes at community colleges. The dual approach struck a chord, and both houses passed the bill unanimously.

Messer acknowledges that his law is no panacea. He's fond of saying he can't legis- 26 late away teenage mistakes. And indeed, Kentucky, Georgia and West Virginia have had similar laws on the books for a number of years, but critics say there's no proof that the laws have worked. Still, he says, "some kids are dropping out because it's easy and it's O.K. That is going to change."

On a national level, No Child Left Behind—the metric-heavy school reform that 27 President Bush would like to expand in public high schools—was designed to make schools accountable for their dropout rates. But it hasn't been carried out very seriously.

The Education Trust, an advocacy group for low-income and minority students, issued a scathing report in 2005 about how the Federal Government stood by while states handed in patently misleading graduation numbers: last year three states didn't submit any, and for many states, the figures were clearly inflated.

28   Secretary of Education Margaret Spellings tells TIME that much is being done to get better data on dropouts. She points to the National Governors Association resolution last year to set, for the first time, a common definition of a dropout that all states will use to report graduation rates to the Federal Government. But it's a nonbinding compact that five states, including Texas, California and Florida, didn't sign. And critics say the government is trying to slash funding for important support programs, including the Carl Perkins Act, which has funded vocational education across the country since 1984. Spellings says President Bush has proposed converting Perkins and other support programs like GEAR UP and Upward Bound into block grants for states to choose their own fixes. As long as states get results, says Spellings, "we're not going to prescribe particular programs or strategies like vocational education."

29   Superintendent Adams believes he has come up with the right prescription for Shelbyville. The high school has established a credit lab, a sort of open study hall that lets at-risk kids recover credit from classes that they have failed. The principal at the elementary school is trying to identify at-risk kids in first grade. In the middle school, students are taking high school-graduation pledges, promising to be onstage with a diploma along with the rest of their class.

30   The district will also continue to support the Blue River vocational school, where more than 300 juniors and seniors spend their afternoons learning trades from nursing to marketing to auto-body repair. And there is a plan to build an alternative high school, which Adams envisions as a low-key place where, if they want to, kids can eat a doughnut while instant-messaging friends during loosely structured study hall, so long as they get their work done at some point. "Too many kids, at their exit interviews, say, 'I'm just done with this process—50 minutes, bell, 50 minutes, bell," says principal Zobel. "With the alternative school, I could give them an option, another environment to be in."

The Comeback Kid

31   On the edge of Shelbyville's Old Town square, now a roundabout with a paved parking lot in the middle, there's a statue of one of central Indiana's most famous literary characters, a sort of Hoosier Huck Finn named Little Balser. The main character of The Bears of Blue River, a book for adolescents set in the woods of frontier-era Shelby County, Balser spends his days striking off into the wilderness, slaying countless bears (and even an Indian or two) and worrying his parents sick. He is the prototype of an American teenager, a combustible combination of independence and irresponsibility.

32   Ryan Tindle, 21, carried that legacy to its modern-day extreme. In middle school, he started ditching class, trying to escape a tough home life by ingratiating himself with older kids who played rough. So it was little surprise when he traveled the well-worn path of the troublemaker, dropping out of high school and promptly beating up an older

kid so severely that Ryan was sentenced to a year at Plainfield Juvenile Correctional Facility. Once inside, one of the few times he picked up a pencil, he used it to stab another inmate in the hand. He felt that he had to prove himself, he says, after witnessing weaker kids being assaulted at the facility. The attack earned him a stint in isolation in Cottage 13—"the cage"—and that, says Ryan, is where he got religion about schooling. "My family always thought I was going to be worthless," he says, "and for the first time, I saw they were right."

As soon as he was released, Ryan went back to Shelbyville High School and asked   33
to re-enroll. The Ryan Tindle that administrators knew, however, was nothing but grief. Wary administrators balked at letting him back in. He had to wait until a new principal arrived before he could convince the school that he was serious about his new leaf. But now he had to catch up quickly on a lot of lost years. "I went back with a fifth-grade education," he says. "That was the last time I had paid attention in school." In the end, it took him nearly two years of a grueling schedule to finish what he started. From 7 a.m. to 3 p.m., he sat in class at the high school, then took three hours of night school for basic reading and math. To everyone's amazement, he finished.

Ryan is working hard these days. He wakes up before 5 every morning to go to his   34
job at a car-parts factory, where he works on the line and earns less than $10 an hour. On Saturdays and Sundays, he trains new employees at the local Arby's. In all, he takes home about $23,000 a year. He would like to go to college someday, he says with a slightly embarrassed grin, to study criminology. He wants to be a cop. For now, however, graduation is reward enough. He pulls a laminated card out of his wallet. It's his Shelbyville High School diploma, miniaturized. "I'll always be able to look at that diploma and smile," he says. "It's the best thing I've ever done."

If Ryan's redemption seems remarkable, that's because it is. According to a 2005 re-   35
port from the Educational Testing Service, the company that runs the SATs, federal funding for second-chance programs, such as the night school Ryan attended, dropped from a high of $15 billion in the late 1970s to $3 billion last year. Yet the stakes in the struggle to get students to graduate are higher than ever: an estimated 67% of prison inmates nationwide are high school dropouts. A 2002 Northeastern University study found that nearly half of all dropouts ages 16 to 24 were unemployed.

Finding good work is only getting harder for dropouts in the era of the knowledge-   36
based economy and advanced manufacturing. Knauf Insulation is Shelbyville's largest employer, with more than 800 workers. Salaries start at $16.50 an hour, and the benefits at this German company are, well, positively European. In one of its factories along the Blue River, a row of mammoth 2400 degree furnaces spin the plant's secret recipe of sand, soda ash, borax and limestone into billions of billowy glass fibers, which will be cooled, packed and cut into battens of fiber-glass insulation. The workers running the furnaces are the last of a dying breed: people holding good jobs who never earned a high school diploma. Thirty years ago, the men came from as far away as the hills of Kentucky and proved themselves steady workers. Today they earn as much as $60,000 a year.

37   It's a fine life, but these days high school dropouts need not apply. Even a GED is not sufficient for a job here anymore. Take a tour of the factory floor, and the main reason is clear. Some workers—entry-level employees—stand at their stations and pluck irregular pieces of fiber glass from the line. It's mostly mindless labor, but the giant whirring belts and chomping insulation cutters are run by adjacent computer terminals called programmable-logic controllers. When the floor boss goes on a coffee break, it's the floor workers who must operate the controllers. In today's factories, no worker is more than a boss's coffee break away from needing at least some computing skills. And now more than ever, says Knauf president Bob Claxton, the company wants to invest in the continuing education of its workers so they can keep up with new technologies—an investment that might not be worth making if those workers lack high school basics.

38   But the firm's requirement of a high school diploma is as much about a mind-set as it is about a skill-set, says Claxton. A diploma "shows that these applicants had the discipline to gut out a tough process," he says. "They learned how to get along with people, some of whom they may not have liked so well, in order to achieve their goals." A GED, he says, doesn't prove they can do that.

39   Even the dropouts who do land factory jobs can find work tougher than they thought. A relative helped Christine Harden, 18, find work in a local car-parts factory four months after she dropped out of Shelbyville High. But she has to get up at 4:30 PM to make the first shift every day, and she says her back is killing her. "All my friends who are thinking about dropping out, I tell them, 'Don't do it,'" she says. "This is real life out here. It's not easy."

The Lone Holdout

40   I met Shawn Sturgill's parents in the living room of their ranch-style home around the corner from Shelbyville's cemetery. At age 15, Shawn's father Steve, with a child on the way, dropped out of high school and then spent more than a decade battling drug abuse. He was born again six years ago, he says, patting the thick wooden cross around his neck. He has been clean since and has a high-paying job burying fiber-optic cables. But his turnaround came too late to be a model for his three older children, two of whom dropped out of school.

41   Shelbyville schools are performing triage on Shawn's education. For much of the day, he is in credit lab, working at his own pace to recover classes he has failed. Every afternoon he goes to the Blue River school, where he is enrolled in auto-body-repair courses.

42   Shawn has a tough road ahead of him. Though he will attend his class's graduation ceremony to watch his peers get diplomas, he won't be on stage, at least not yet. Even the school's efforts to speed up his credit recovery haven't been enough, so he will have to return for a fifth year at Shelbyville High. It's no fun for a 19-year-old to be in high school. Shawn is already a big guy who doesn't like to draw attention to himself.

But Shawn's hopes are bolstered by his plan. Auto-body work is not just a passing 43
fancy for him—even when he's not at the vocational school, he is working on his Camaro,
which most recently needed a new bumper. His favorite TV show, of course, is "Pimp My
Ride." He wants to save for tuition at Lincoln Technical Institute in Indianapolis so he
can continue to develop his auto-sculpting skills. He rattles off the industry rates—car
painters make an hourly wage of $22, collision techs $17—and he wants to get there. So
he laughs it off every time somebody asks him in the hallway, "Hey, you're still in school?
I would have thought you'd drop out by now."

Shawn's friends who have dropped out are, for the most part, struggling. A couple 44
of them got their GED and are working in factories, but others are shuffling through menial jobs—one works at the car wash, another is washing dishes. A few, says Shawn,
aren't doing much of anything except playing video games at their parents' houses. But
Shawn says he is serious about not becoming a part of their dropout nation. "I've already
went and put 12 years into this thing," he says. "There's no use throwing it all away."

RESPONDING TO THE READING

FREEWRITING

Practice 11h. Freewrite about the most serious problems you see in high
schools today. Do you see any connection between those problems and the
persistent dropout rate (roughly 30%) in America's high schools?

BUILDING YOUR VOCABULARY

consensus (5)	legerdemain (12)	hysteria (18)	ingratiating (32)
relegated (7)	turbulent (14)	cauldron (20)	grueling (33)
gaggle (9)	nuanced (17)	panacea (26)	battens (36)
feint (10)	histrionics (18)	prototype (31)	triage (41)
notorious (11)			

QUESTIONS FOR DISCUSSION

1. Identify several solutions that schools like Shelbyville are using to slow the
   dropout rate in high school. Which do you think are most likely to keep kids in
   school?
2. Did you or teens you knew in high school drop out? Which of the reasons for
   teens dropping out of school that Thornburgh mentions are the most likely
   explanations for teens dropping out of your high school?
3. What might be other reasons, besides the ones Thornburgh discusses, why teens
   don't finish high school?
4. Based on your own experiences and observations, what opportunities are there
   for students who graduate from high school that might not be available for
   teens who don't obtain a diploma?

TOPICS FOR WRITING

Topic 1. Write a letter to a student who is thinking about dropping out of high school in which you present other alternatives the student should consider before dropping out of school altogether. Be sure to provide specific information to convince this student not to abandon his or her education.

Topic 2. Now that you're in college, what are your educational goals? Write an essay in which you explain how attending college will help you achieve these goals.

Topic 3. Write a report on your investigation into the current status of programs like vocational education (funded through the Carl Perkins Act), GEAR UP, and Upward Bound, programs mentioned in "Dropout Nation." Does Congress currently fund these programs? What seem to be the reasons for funding or cutting funding for these programs?

WRITING BEFORE READING

Describe relationships you have had with instructors—formal, personal, hostile, or indifferent. Use examples to illustrate the relationships you remember best. Share your responses with classmates.

If you are unfamiliar with poetry, consider reading the analysis of poetic form and meaning in Chapter 9 before reading "Theme for English B."

Theme for English B

Langston Hughes

James Mercer Langston Hughes was born in Joplin, Missouri, on February 1, 1902. He became an important figure during the Harlem Renaissance—a period in the 1920s when African American art, music, and literature flourished. He is the author of several volumes of poetry, an autobiography titled The Big Sea *(1940), and numerous critical essays, volumes of short stories, and plays. Hughes founded the Harlem Suitcase Theater in 1938 and encouraged dozens of African American writers, including Alice Walker and Amiri Baraka, to publish their work. "Theme for English B" is based on Hughes's experiences as a student at Columbia University, New York. Please note that the word* colored *is dated and no longer considered an acceptable term.*

The instructor said,

Go home and write
a page tonight.
And let that page come out of you—
5 *Then, it will be true.*

I wonder if it's that simple?
I am twenty-two, colored, born in Winston-Salem.
I went to school there, then Durham, then here
to this college on the hill above Harlem.
10 I am the only colored student in my class.
The steps from the hill lead down into Harlem,
through a park, then I cross St. Nicholas,
Eighth Avenue, Seventh, and I come to the Y,
the Harlem Branch Y, where I take the elevator
15 up to my room, sit down, and write this page:

It's not easy to know what is true for you or me
at twenty-two, my age. But I guess I'm what
I feel and see and hear, Harlem, I hear you:
hear you, hear me—we two—you, me, talk on this page.
20 (I hear New York, too.) Me—who?
Well, I like to eat, sleep, drink, and be in love.
I like to work, read, learn, and understand life.
I like a pipe for a Christmas present,
or records—Bessie,[1] bop, or Bach.
25 I guess being colored doesn't make me *not* like
the same things other folks like who are other races.
So will my page be colored that I write?
Being me, it will not be white.
But it will be
30 a part of you, instructor.
You are white—
yet a part of me, as I am a part of you.
That's American.
Sometimes perhaps you don't want to be a part of me.
35 Nor do I often want to be a part of you.
But we are, that's true!
As I learn from you,
I guess you learn from me—
although you're older—and white—
40 and somewhat more free.

This is my page for English B.

---

[1] Bessie Smith (1898–1937), influential blues singer of the Harlem Renaissance.

RESPONDING TO THE READING

FREEWRITING

Practice 11i. What perspective does Hughes offer on his relationship to his teacher? Freewrite about your relationships to teachers or classmates. Do those relationships contain elements of discomfort?

Practice 11j. Write a response of your own to the assignment Hughes and his classmates were given:

> *Go home and write*
> *a page tonight.*
> *And let that page come out of you—*
> *Then, it will be true.*

QUESTIONS FOR DISCUSSION

1. Describe the situation in Hughes's poem. Who is speaking? What do we know about him?
2. Why does Hughes ask whether it is "that simple" to complete the teacher's assignment? What makes the task complex?
3. Why do you think the teacher's assignment is written as a simple rhyme while Hughes's poem is in a more complex free verse?
4. Who is Hughes's audience? Is there more than one?
5. Summarize the walk Hughes takes from school to his home in Harlem. Why do you think he includes this walk in his poem?
6. What is the main point Hughes conveys in "Theme for English B"?
7. How well does his poem satisfy the teacher's assignment? Was that his main intent, or did he have an additional purpose?

TOPICS FOR WRITING

Topic 1. Write a paper describing your own relationship to school (either high school or college). You may wish to discuss how comfortable or uncomfortable you feel in particular classes with particular teachers or students. You could also focus on your relationship to students and teachers in sports, drama, or other school activities.

Topic 2. Write a paragraph or short essay giving reasons why you are going to college. Consider what experiences and people influenced your decision. Use details, examples, and explanations to explain your choice.

Topic 3. Reread your freewriting notes for Practice 11i. Then use the writing process to develop a more formal response to the teacher's assignment. If you are so moved, you might attach a poem that expresses the truth that "comes out of you."

Men and Women

The readings in this chapter examine relationships between the sexes and various images of men and women established by our environment and the culture. Scott Russell Sanders explains what men and women were expected to do when he was a child. In the selection "Why Boys Don't Play with Dolls," Katha Pollitt looks at ways that gender-specific toys and stereotypical boy/girl behavior have been accepted even by supposedly progressive parents. The authors of "Personal Politics: A Lesson in Straight Talk" and "Just Walk On By" write about their painful attempts to relate to others who view them as "different," even suspicious.

I was slow to understand the deep grievances of women. This was because, as a boy, I had envied them.
—Scott Russell Sanders

When someone describes the world and you are not in it, there is a moment of psychic disequilibrium, as if you looked into a mirror and saw nothing.
—Adrienne Rich (quoted in "Personal Politics: A Lesson in Straight Talk")

Who are the men or women who have been important in your life? Freewrite about the ways their appearance and behavior have shaped your ideas about what men or women are supposed to be.

The Men We Carry in Our Minds

Scott Russell Sanders

Scott Russell Sanders was born in Memphis, Tennessee, in 1945 and grew up in Ohio. A lover of science and literature, Sanders studied English and physics as an undergraduate at Brown University. He is currently Distinguished Professor of English at Indiana University, Bloomington, and director of the Wells Scholars program. He is the author of nineteen books, including novels, collections of short stories, children's books, and books of creative nonfiction. His nonfiction work includes Staying Put: Making a Home in a Restless World *(1993),* Hunting for Hope: A Father's Journeys *(1998), and his more recent work,* The Force of Spirit *(2000). He was awarded the John Burroughs Natural History Essay Award in 2000 and has received numerous other awards and fellowships for his nonfiction writing. Sanders's "The Men We Carry in Our Minds" was published in the essay collection* The Paradise of Bombs *(1987), which won an award for creative nonfiction. In this essay, Sanders examines the way childhood observations shaped his beliefs about men and women.*

1   The first men, besides my father, I remember seeing were black convicts and white guards, in the cottonfield across the road from our farm on the outskirts of Memphis. I must have been three or four. The prisoners wore dingy gray-and-black zebra suits, heavy as canvas, sodden with sweat. Hatless, stooped, they chopped weeds in the fierce heat, row after row, breathing the acrid dust of boll-weevil poison. The overseers wore dazzling white shirts and broad shadowy hats. The oiled barrels of their shotguns flashed in the sunlight. Their faces in memory are utterly blank. Of course those men, white and black, have become for me an emblem of racial hatred. But they have also come to stand for the twin poles of my early vision of manhood—the brute toiling animal and the boss.

2   When I was a boy, the men I knew labored with their bodies. They were marginal farmers, just scraping by, or welders, steelworkers, carpenters; they swept floors, dug ditches, mined coal, or drove trucks, their forearms ropy with muscle; they trained horses, stoked furnaces, built fires, stood on assembly lines wrestling parts onto cars and refrigerators. They got up before light, worked all day long whatever the weather, and when they came home at night they looked as though somebody had been whipping them. In the evenings and on weekends they worked on their own places, tilling gardens that were lumpy with clay, fixing broken-down cars, hammering on houses that were always too drafty, too leaky, too small.

3   The bodies of the men I knew were twisted and maimed in ways visible and invisible. The nails of their hands were black and split, the hands tattooed with scars. Some

had lost fingers. Heavy lifting had given many of them finicky backs and guts weak from hernias. Racing against conveyor belts had given them ulcers. Their ankles and knees ached from years of standing on concrete. Anyone who had worked for long around machines was hard of hearing. They squinted, and the skin of their faces was creased like the leather of old work gloves. There were times, studying them, when I dreaded growing up. Most of them coughed, from dust or cigarettes, and most of them drank cheap wine or whiskey, so their eyes looked bloodshot and bruised. The fathers of my friends always seemed older than the mothers. Men wore out sooner. Only women lived into old age.

As a boy I also knew another sort of men, who did not sweat and break down like mules. They were soldiers, and so far as I could tell they scarcely worked at all. During my early school years we lived on a military base, an arsenal in Ohio, and every day I saw GIs in the guardshacks, on the stoops of barracks, at the wheels of olive drab Chevrolets. The chief fact of their lives was boredom. Long after I left the Arsenal I came to recognize the sour smell the soldiers gave off as that of souls in limbo. They were all waiting—for wars, for transfers, for leaves, for promotions, for the end of their hitch—like so many braves waiting for the hunt to begin. Unlike the warriors of older tribes, however, they would have no say about when the battle would start or how it would be waged. Their waiting was broken only when they practiced for war. They fired guns at targets, drove tanks across the churned-up fields of the military reservation, set off bombs in the wrecks of old fighter planes. I knew this was all play. But I also felt certain that when the hour for killing arrived, they would kill. When the real shooting started, many of them would die. This was what soldiers were *for*, just as a hammer was for driving nails.

Warriors and toilers: those seemed, in my boyhood vision, to be the chief destinies for men. They weren't the only destinies, as I learned from having a few male teachers, from reading books, and from watching television. But the men on television—the politicians, the astronauts, the generals, the savvy lawyers, the philosophical doctors, the bosses who gave orders to both soldiers and laborers—seemed as removed and unreal to me as the figures in tapestries. I could no more imagine growing up to become one of these cool, potent creatures than I could imagine becoming a prince.

A nearer and more hopeful example was that of my father, who had escaped from a red-dirt farm to a tire factory, and from the assembly line to the front office. Eventually he dressed in a white shirt and tie. He carried himself as if he had been born to work with his mind. But his body, remembering the earlier years of slogging work, began to give out on him in his fifties, and it quit on him entirely before he turned sixty-five. Even such a partial escape from man's fate as he had accomplished did not seem possible for most of the boys I knew. They joined the Army, stood in line for jobs in the smoky plants, helped build highways. They were bound to work as their fathers had worked, killing themselves or preparing to kill others.

A scholarship enabled me not only to attend college, a rare enough feat in my circle, but even to study in a university meant for the children of the rich. Here I met for the first time young men who had assumed from birth that they would lead lives of comfort and power. And for the first time I met women who told me that men were guilty of

4

5

6

7

having kept all the joys and privileges of the rich for themselves. I was baffled. What privileges? What joys? I thought about the maimed, dismal lives of most of the men back home. What had they stolen from their wives and daughters? The right to go five days a week, twelve months a year, for thirty or forty years to a steel mill or coal mine? The right to drop bombs and die in war? The right to feel every leak in the roof, every gap in the fence, every cough in the engine, as a wound they must mend? The right to feel, when the lay-off comes or the plant shuts down, not only afraid but ashamed?

8   I was slow to understand the deep grievances of women. This was because, as a boy, I had envied them. Before college, the only people I had ever known who were interested in art or music or literature, the only ones who read books, the only ones who ever seemed to enjoy a sense of ease and grace were the mothers and daughters. Like the menfolk, they fretted about money, they scrimped and made do. But, when the pay stopped coming in, they were not the ones who had failed. Nor did they have to go to war, and that seemed to me a blessed fact. By comparison with the narrow, ironclad days of fathers, there was an expansiveness, I thought, in the days of mothers. They went to see neighbors, to shop in town, to run errands at school, at the library, at church. No doubt, had I looked harder at their lives, I would have envied them less. It was not my fate to become a woman, so it was easier for me to see the graces. Few of them held jobs outside the home and those who did filled thankless roles as clerks and waitresses. I didn't see, then, what a prison a house could be, since houses seemed to me brighter, handsomer places than any factory. I did not realize—because such things were never spoken of—how often women suffered from men's bullying. I did learn about the wretchedness of abandoned wives, single mothers, widows; but I also learned about the wretchedness of lone men. Even then I could see how exhausting it was for a mother to cater all day to the needs of young children. But if I had been asked, as a boy, to choose between tending a baby and tending a machine, I think I would have chosen the baby. (Having now tended both, I know I would choose the baby.)

9   So I was baffled when the women at college accused me and my sex of having cornered the world's pleasures. I think something like my bafflement has been felt by other boys (and by girls as well) who grew up in dirt-poor farm country, in mining country, in black ghettos, in Hispanic barrios, in the shadows of factories, in Third World nations—any place where the fate of men is as grim and bleak as the fate of women. Toilers and warriors, I realize now how ancient these identities are, how deep the tug they exert on men, the undertow of a thousand generations. The miseries I saw, as a boy, in the lives of nearly all men I continue to see in the lives of many—the body-breaking toil, the tedium, the call to be tough, the humiliating powerlessness, the battle for a living and for territory.

10   When the women I met at college thought about the joys and privileges of men, they did not carry in their minds the sort of men I had known in my childhood. They thought of their fathers, who were bankers, physicians, architects, stockbrokers, the big wheels of the big cities. These fathers rode the train to work or drove cars that cost more than any of my childhood houses. They were attended from morning to night by female helpers, wives and nurses and secretaries. They were never laid off, never short of cash

at month's end, never lined up for welfare. These fathers made decisions that mattered. They ran the world.

The daughters of such men wanted to share in this power, this glory. So did I. They yearned for a say over their future, for jobs worthy of their abilities, for the right to live at peace, unmolested, whole. Yes, I thought, yes yes. The difference between me and these daughters was that they saw me, because of my sex, as destined from birth to become like their fathers, and therefore as an enemy to their desires. But I knew better. I wasn't an enemy, in fact or in feeling. I was an ally. If I had known, then, how to tell them so, would they have believed me? Would they now? 11

RESPONDING TO THE READING

FREEWRITING

Practice 12a. Sanders says that boys where he grew up were likely to end up doing one of two things—"killing themselves or preparing to kill others." In your experience, are the choices open to young men limited to being laborers and soldiers, or do they have other choices as well?

Practice 12b. Apart from the laborers and toilers he knew as a child, Sanders gives his father as "a nearer and more hopeful example" of what was possible for men to do with their lives. What have the men or women in your family done with their lives? How did they choose their paths? Do you see yourself doing similar work?

BUILDING YOUR VOCABULARY

maimed (3)	tapestries (5)	ironclad (8)	baffled (9)
limbo (4)	slogging (6)	scrimped (8)	tedium (9)
potent (5)	grievances (8)	wretchedness (8)	

QUESTIONS FOR DISCUSSION

1. What were Sanders's initial ideas about the jobs that men are supposed to do? What observations shaped his ideas? In what ways have the men or women you observed in childhood helped you decide what you want or don't want to do with your life?
2. Why did Sanders think of soldiers as "souls in limbo"? How apt is his description of soldiers in paragraph 4, given the recent conflicts in Afghanistan and Iraq?
3. Sanders says he considers it something of an accomplishment that his father was able to make "a partial escape from man's fate." What does "fate" mean in this passage? What can you say about Sanders's own escape from "fate"?
4. Sanders says, "I was slow to understand the deep grievances of women." What made it difficult for him to comprehend the idea that men have kept certain privileges for themselves? What perspective does he have on women's complaints now?

5. Sanders's essay falls into two parts—paragraphs 1 through 6 and 7 through 11. What does he discuss in each of these sections? How well does Sanders make the two pieces of his essay cohere into a single argument or perspective?
6. At the end of his essay, Sanders questions whether women would have believed his sincerity if he had been able to explain himself to them and asks whether they would believe him now. Why do you think he ends his essay with these questions? How effective are they in pulling his essay together? What impact might they have on the reader?

TOPICS FOR WRITING

Topic 1. Write an essay in which you compare the role models you had when you were a child to the men who surrounded Sanders as he was growing up.

Topic 2. Sanders writes about the "toilers and warriors," and mothers whose identities, he now realizes, go back "a thousand generations." Write a paper in which you describe one or two people you know—male or female—who fill age-old roles. Use detailed descriptions as Sanders does when he describes the workers and soldiers of his childhood.

Topic 3. Sanders has received several creative nonfiction awards for his writing. Write an essay in which you analyze writing techniques that make his argument compelling for the reader. You might consider discussing the writer's control of point of view, tone, description, style of writing (images, word choices), or organization of ideas.

Topic 4. Do some research into current opportunities for working women in the United States. Write an essay in which you analyze both opportunities and barriers that remain for women in the workforce. Refer to the discussion of essay documentation (Chapters 15 and 16) as you gather information from sources.

WRITING BEFORE READING

Which toys or games are boys more likely to play with in your experience? What are girls' preferences in toys and games? Are there activities that both girls and boys enjoy?

Why Boys Don't Play with Dolls

Katha Pollitt

Katha Pollitt is a poet and journalist who has written essays and reviews for Mother Jones, The New Yorker, The New Republic, *and the* New York Times. *She has been a regular contributor to* The Nation *since 1980. Pollitt has won numerous awards for her poetry, including a National Book Critics Award for* Antarctic Traveler *(1983), a grant from the National Endowment for the Arts, and a Guggenheim Fellowship. Pollit is also the author of* Reasonable Creatures: Essays on Women and Feminism *(1995) and* Subject to Debate: Sense and Dissents on Women, Politics, and Culture *(2002), a collection of Pollitt's columns published in* The Nation *from 1994 through 2000. Her essay "Why Boys Don't Play with Dolls" first appeared in the* New York Times *on October 8, 1995.*

It's 28 years since the founding of NOW,[1] and boys still like trucks and girls still like dolls. Increasingly, we are told that the source of these robust preferences must lie outside society—in prenatal hormonal influences, brain chemistry, genes—and that feminism has reached its natural limits. What else could possibly explain the love of preschool girls for party dresses or the desire of toddler boys to own more guns than Mark from Michigan.[2]

True, recent studies claim to show small cognitive differences between the sexes: he gets around by orienting himself in space, she does it by remembering landmarks. Time will tell if any deserve the hoopla with which each is invariably greeted, over the protests of the researchers themselves. But even if the results hold up (and the history of such research is not encouraging), we don't need studies of sex-differentiated brain activity in reading, say, to understand why boys and girls still seem so unalike.

The feminist movement has done much for some women, and something for every woman, but it has hardly turned America into a playground free of sex roles. It hasn't even got women to stop dieting or men to stop interrupting them.

Instead of looking at kids to "prove" that differences in behavior by sex are innate, we can look at the ways we raise kids as an index to how unfinished the feminist revolution really is, and how tentatively it is embraced even by adults who fully expect their daughters to enter previously male-dominated professions and their sons to change diapers.

I'm at a children's birthday party. "I'm sorry," one mom silently mouths to the mother of the birthday girl, who has just torn open her present—Tropical Splash Barbie. Now, you can love Barbie or you can hate Barbie, and there are feminists in both camps. But *apologize* for Barbie? Inflict Barbie, against your own convictions, on the child of a friend you know will be none too pleased?

Every mother in that room had spent years becoming a person who had to be taken seriously, not least by herself. Even the most attractive, I'm willing to bet, had suffered over her body's failure to fit the impossible American ideal. Given all that, it seems crazy to transmit Barbie to the next generation. Yet to reject her is to say that what Barbie represents being—sexy, thin, stylish—is unimportant, which is obviously not true, and children know it's not true.

Women's looks matter terribly in this society, and so Barbie, however ambivalently, must be passed along. After all, there are worse toys. The Cut and Style Barbie styling

---

[1] The National Organization for Women. Founded in 1966, NOW works for "full equality for women in truly equal partnership with men."

[2] Mark Koernke, a former Michigan talk-show host and avid supporter of right-wing militia groups.

head, for example, a grotesque object intended to encourage "hair play." The grown-ups who give that probably apologize, too.

8   How happy would most parents be to have a child who flouted sex conventions? I know a lot of women, feminists, who complain in a comical, eyeball-rolling way about their sons' passion for sports: the ruined weekends, obnoxious coaches, macho values. But they would not think of discouraging their sons from participating in this activity they find so foolish. Or do they? Their husbands are sports fans, too, and they like their husbands a lot.

9   Could it be that even sports-resistant moms see athletics as part of manliness? That if their sons wanted to spend the weekend writing up their diaries, or reading, or baking, they'd find it disturbing? Too antisocial? Too lonely? Too gay?

10   Theories of innate differences in behavior are appealing. They let parents off the hook—no small recommendation in a culture that holds moms, and sometimes even dads, responsible for their children's every misstep on the road to bliss and success.

11   They allow grown-ups to take the path of least resistance to the dominant culture, which always requires less psychic effort, even if it means more actual work: just ask the working mother who comes home exhausted and nonetheless finds it easier to pick up her son's socks than make him do it himself. They let families buy for their children, without *too* much guilt, the unbelievably sexist junk that the kids, who have been watching commercials since birth, understandably crave.

12   But the thing the theories do most of all is tell adults that the *adult* world—in which moms and dads still play by many of the old rules even as they question and fidget and chafe against them—is the way it's supposed to be. A girl with a doll and a boy with a truck "explain" why men are from Mars and women are from Venus,[3] why wives do housework and husbands just don't understand.

13   The paradox is that the world of rigid and hierarchical sex roles evoked by determinist theories is already passing away. Three-year-olds may indeed insist that doctors are male and nurses female, even if their own mother is a physician. Six-year-olds know better. These days, something like half of all medical students are female, and male applications to nursing school are inching upward. When tomorrow's 3-year-olds play doctor, who's to say how they'll assign the roles?

14   With sex roles, as in every area of life, people aspire to what is possible, and conform to what is necessary. But these are not fixed, especially today. Biological determinism may reassure some adults about their present, but it is feminism, the ideology of flexible and converging sex roles, that fits our children's future. And the kids, somehow, know this.

15   That's why, if you look carefully, you'll find that for every kid who fits a stereotype, there's another who's breaking one down. Sometimes it's the same kid—the boy who skateboards *and* takes cooking in his after-school program; the girl who collects stuffed animals *and* A-pluses in science.

---

[3] Pollitt refers to the nonfiction book *Men Are from Mars, Women Are from Venus,* a popular discussion of differences between men and women.

Feminists are often accused of imposing their "agenda" on children. Isn't that what   16
adults always do, consciously and unconsciously? Kids aren't born religious, or polite,
or kind, or able to remember where they put their sneakers. Inculcating these behaviors,
and the values behind them, is a tremendous amount of work, involving many adults.
We don't have a choice, really, about *whether* we should give our children messages
about what it means to be male and female—they're bombarded with them from morning till night.

The question, as always, is what do we want those messages to be?   17

RESPONDING TO THE READING

FREEWRITING

Practice 12c. How might toys designed especially for girls or just for boys train
children for the roles they will assume as adults? What problems or limitations
might be connected with boy- and girl-toys?

Practice 12d. How fixed are male and female roles in your experience?

BUILDING YOUR VOCABULARY

hormonal (1)	ambivalently (7)	sexist (11)	hierarchical (13)
prenatal (1)	grotesque (7)	chafe (12)	paradox (13)
robust (1)	flouted (8)	fidget (12)	aspire (14)
cognitive (2)	innate (10)	determinist (13)	ideology (14)
hoopla (2)	nonetheless (11)	evoked (13)	inculcating (16)

QUESTIONS FOR DISCUSSION

1. Locate the thesis or main point of Pollitt's essay. Why do you think she places it
   where she does?
2. What is Pollitt's opinion of the argument that differences in the way boys and
   girls think and behave are "innate" or inborn? Do you agree with her?
3. What is Pollitt's opinion of current "feminists"? How well are feminists able to
   withstand social and media definitions of proper "male" and "female" behavior?
4. What does Pollitt mean when she says, "With sex roles, as in every area of life,
   people aspire to what is possible, and conform to what is necessary"? What
   might be the benefits and disadvantages to this way of thinking?
5. Pollitt argues that "the world of rigid and hierarchical sex roles . . . is already
   passing away." What evidence does she offer in support of this claim? Does your
   experience support her assertion that the old-style, fixed differences between
   men's and women's roles are disappearing?
6. Find portions of Pollitt's essay where she suggests what feminism means. How
   do her descriptions of feminism either match your own definition or challenge
   your ideas about feminism?

7. Both Katha Pollitt and Scott Russell Sanders examine forces that help shape the behavior of men and women and the roles they assume in the culture. What besides the parental short-sightedness that Pollitt observes might explain the rigid gender roles that Scott Russell Sanders remembers as a child?

TOPICS FOR WRITING

Topic 1. Katha Pollitt notes that commercial television has been pushing "unbelievable sexist junk" at children since they were born. Come up with a definition of "sexist" for yourself. Then watch a few hours of commercial television on a weekday or Saturday morning. Write a paper in which you examine the "sexist," nature of the commercials or the toys advertised on these programs. If you don't find anything sexist about the shows or the advertising, describe the behavior the station seems to be promoting.

Topic 2. Pollitt notes that "if you look carefully, you'll find that for every kid who fits a stereotype, there's another who's breaking one down." Apply this idea to adults you know and write a paper discussing the extent to which the behavior or careers of men and women you know are breaking down stereotypes.

Topic 3. Write a short paraphrase of Katha Pollitt's description of "the ideology of flexible and converging sex roles." Then write an essay in which you agree or disagree that this ideology "fits our children's future" based on the relative flexibility or inflexibility of gender roles. Your paragraphs should discuss why this ideology does or does not seem a plausible model for future roles of men and women in American culture.

WRITING BEFORE READING

Describe the people you know with whom you feel comfortable enough to have a private conversation. What qualities do they have that make you feel like confiding in them?

Personal Politics:
A Lesson in Straight Talk

Lindsy Van Gelder

Lindsy Van Gelder is a journalist and former contributing editor for Ms. *magazine. She has written two nonfiction books,* Are You Two Together? *(1991) about travels in Europe, and* The Girls Next Door: Into the Heart of Lesbian America *(1997), which she coauthored with her partner, Pamela Robin Brandt. The Girls Next Door* distills information gathered in over 200 interviews with *gay women around the United States. Gelder wrote "Personal Politics: A Lesson in Straight Talk" for the November 1987 issue of* Ms. *The essay advises straight people how to feel more at ease when first getting to know a gay woman.*

I'll begin at the beginning, when you and I first meet. Maybe we'll talk about our work or the weather. But my antennae are out, and if it's a particularly delicate situation (someone I'm interviewing, say, or another parent at school), I may even have a knot in my stomach. I haven't had a casual conversation in nearly a decade, because I know what's coming: any minute now we'll hit the topic that to most Americans seems innocuous, friendly, getting-to-know-you. *The Family.*

Are you married? "Not legally," I may answer, "but I've been in a relationship with Pamela since 1978." I've learned to say things like this in a perfectly natural tone of voice and to burble on a bit while you regain your composure. I've even started to refer to Pamela as my Life-Partner—even though I think it sounds like we run an insurance agency together—since I know that "lover," while an honorable term in the gay world, often falls upon straight ears as a synonym for someone I've had sex with a few times.

But unless you already have lesbian friends in your life (or you're gay yourself), chances are that you're incredibly uncomfortable. At worst, you think I'm saying something hostile—or dirty. Sometimes you think I'm confiding a deep secret. If by some fluke it takes a few conversations before we get to this point, you might even feel vaguely betrayed, as if you'd been getting to know me under false pretenses (although this can still coexist with the thought that I should have kept my "private life" private). If you're a man, you might tell me that you're "disappointed" or that I don't "seem the type," and expect me to be flattered. If you're a woman, your first thought might be to wonder if I'm coming on to you (by mentioning my long-term committed relationship?). If you're basically a nice, liberal person—a potential friend—your impulse will be to want to do the right thing. But maybe you're not sure what that is—so you quickly change the subject.

My straight friend Jane says I'm usually silly to tell the truth, especially to men. "He's really asking if you're available," she says. "So say yes, you're married." The problem with this, as Adrienne Rich has pointed out, is that whether you're dark-skinned or disabled or a lesbian, when someone "describes the world and you are not in it, there is a moment of psychic disequilibrium, as if you looked into a mirror and saw nothing." To collaborate and agree that there's no one in the mirror—that we *do not exist,* are not real—is what legions of closeted lesbians do, and it's a vicious cycle: how can a group of phantoms ever hope to change anything?

Lesbians have a serious visibility problem, which is one of the reasons you were surprised when you first met me. And it's not getting better, although "gays" have surfaced all over the map lately because of AIDS awareness. My own sense is that lesbians are even *less* visible than before—and if anything we've been subsumed. (How many times have you read that "homosexuals" are the major risk group?) Because of the times we live in, more of us also seem to be hiding who we are. For all the most sexist reasons, this is distressingly easy: a single man of a certain age might be presumed to be gay, especially if he has a roommate, but a woman is simply assumed to be saving her (underpaid) pennies and waiting for Mr. Right.

6   So what I would hope you would do, first of all, is to remember that any woman you meet might be a lesbian. By the same token, remember that any lesbian you meet probably wants to be treated pretty much like any other woman. When I mention Pamela, understand that she is as dear to me as any boyfriend or husband, and if you would have asked me about *him,* don't change the subject: ask about *her.*

7   But beyond that, I'm asking you not only for an awareness of the ways our lives are alike, but the ways they're different. Please don't feel that you have to pretend that my relationship is a clone of yours, exactly the same but with Veronica instead of Archie. Lesbians *do* exist in a context of discrimination, and like all minority groups, we have a culture of our own. Not only am I not offended if you've thought or even just wondered about this; I'm relieved.

8   After all, if we're going to be friends, isn't it because we're interested in each other's lives?

RESPONDING TO THE READING

FREEWRITING

Practice 12e. Describe your reaction to Lindsy Van Gelder's very personal appeal.

Practice 12f. How effective is this article in gaining your understanding?

BUILDING YOUR VOCABULARY

antennae (1)	coexist (3)	disequilibrium (4)	subsumed (5)
innocuous (1)	fluke (3)	legions (4)	context (7)
composure (2)	collaborate (4)	psychic (4)	discrimination (7)
synonym (2)			

QUESTIONS FOR DISCUSSION

1. Who is Van Gelder writing for? Who is the "you" she addresses?
2. What is her purpose in writing this piece? How well does she accomplish this purpose?
3. How does she organize her article? Suggest an alternate arrangement. Which do you feel is most effective and why?
4. How does the title relate to the point of Van Gelder's essay? Explain the meaning of "Straight Talk."

TOPICS FOR WRITING

Topic 1. Van Gelder quotes Adrienne Rich as saying that if someone "describes the world and you are not in it, there is a moment of psychic disequilibrium as if you looked into a mirror and saw nothing." Write a paper about a time when you felt left out in this profound way. When did this happen? How did it happen? How did you feel? Who or what made you feel this way? How did you handle the situation? How has your attitude toward the event changed?

Topic 2. Think about a time you felt misunderstood. Write a letter to the person who misunderstood you, explaining the points of misunderstanding and your own position as clearly as you can. You may wish to freewrite first about what you remember. Then choose the crucial events that need explaining and focus on them in your letter. Be sure to include a thesis that carries the main idea you want to communicate.

WRITING BEFORE READING

How safe would you feel walking in your neighborhood after dark? Do some freewriting about experiences or observations that have shaped your attitude about being out at night.

Just Walk On By: A Black Man Ponders His Power to Alter Public Space

Brent Staples

Brent Staples holds a Ph.D. in psychology from the University of Chicago and has been a contributing editor for the New York Times *since 1990. He also writes for the* Los Angeles Times *as well as other journals and newspapers. Staples's award-winning autobiography,* Parallel Time: Growing Up in Black and White *(1994), describes his life in Chester, Pennsylvania. This memoir received the Anisfield-Wolf Book Award and was nominated for the* Los Angeles Times *Book Prize. "Just Walk On By" was first published as "Black Men and Public Space" in the September 1986 issue of* Ms. *magazine.*

My first victim was a woman—white, well dressed, probably in her early twenties. I came upon her late one evening on a deserted street in Hyde Park, a relatively affluent neighborhood in an otherwise mean, impoverished section of Chicago. As I swung onto the avenue behind her, there seemed to be a discreet, uninflammatory distance between us. Not so. She cast back a worried glance. To her, the youngish black man—a broad six feet two inches with a beard and billowing hair, both hands shoved into the pockets of a bulky military jacket—seemed menacingly close. After a few more quick glimpses, she picked up her pace and was soon running in earnest. Within seconds she disappeared into a cross street.

That was more than a decade ago. I was 22 years old; a graduate student newly arrived at the University of Chicago. It was in the echo of that terrified woman's footfalls that I first began to know the unwieldy inheritance I'd come into—the ability to alter

1

2

public space in ugly ways. It was clear that she thought herself the quarry of a mugger, a rapist, or worse. Suffering a bout of insomnia, however, I was stalking sleep, not defenseless wayfarers. As a softy who is scarcely able to take a knife to a raw chicken—let alone hold it to a person's throat—I was surprised, embarrassed, and dismayed all at once. Her flight made me feel like an accomplice in tyranny. It also made it clear that I was indistinguishable from the muggers who occasionally seeped into the area from the surrounding ghetto. That first encounter, and those that followed, signified that a vast, unnerving gulf lay between nighttime pedestrians—particularly women—and me. And I soon gathered that being perceived as dangerous is a hazard in itself. I only needed to turn a corner into a dicey situation, or crowd some frightened, armed person in a foyer somewhere, or make an errant move after being pulled over by a policeman. Where fear and weapons meet—and they often do in urban America—there is always the possibility of death.

3   In that first year, my first away from my hometown, I was to become thoroughly familiar with the language of fear. At dark, shadowy intersections in Chicago, I could cross in front of a car stopped at a traffic light and elicit the *thunk, thunk, thunk, thunk* of the driver—black, white, male, or female—hammering down the door locks. On less traveled streets after dark, I grew accustomed to but never comfortable with people who crossed to the other side of the street rather than pass me. Then there were the standard unpleasantries with police, doormen, bouncers, cab drivers, and others whose business it is to screen out troublesome individuals *before* there is any nastiness.

4   I moved to New York nearly two years ago and I have remained an avid night walker. In Central Manhattan, the near-constant crowd cover minimizes tense one-on-one street encounters. Elsewhere—visiting friends in SoHo, where sidewalks are narrow and tightly spaced buildings shut out the sky—things can get very taut indeed.

5   Black men have a firm place in New York mugging literature. Norman Podhoretz in his famed (or infamous) 1963 essay, "My Negro Problem—And Ours," recalls growing up in terror of black males; they "were tougher than we were, more ruthless," he writes—and as an adult on the Upper West Side of Manhattan, he continues, he cannot constrain his nervousness when he meets black men on certain streets. Similarly, a decade later, the essayist and novelist Edward Hoagland extols a New York where once "Negro bitterness bore down mainly on other Negroes." Where some see mere panhandlers, Hoagland sees "a mugger who is clearly screwing up his nerve to do more than just *ask* for money." But Hoagland has "the New Yorker's quick-hunch posture for broken-field maneuvering," and the bad guy swerves away.

6   I often witness that "hunch posture" from women after dark on the warren-like streets of Brooklyn where I live. They seem to set their faces on neutral and, with their purse straps strung across their chests bandolier style, they forge ahead as though bracing themselves against being tackled. I understand, of course, that the danger they perceive is not a hallucination. Women are particularly vulnerable to street violence, and young black males are drastically overrepresented among the perpetrators of that violence. Yet these truths are no solace against the kind of alienation that comes of being ever the suspect, against being set apart, a fearsome entity with whom pedestrians avoid making eye contact.

It is not altogether clear to me how I reached the ripe old age of 22 without being conscious of the lethality nighttime pedestrians attributed to me. Perhaps it was because in Chester, Pennsylvania, the small, angry industrial town where I came of age in the 1960s, I was scarcely noticeable against a backdrop of gang warfare, street knifings, and murders. I grew up one of the good boys, had perhaps a half-dozen fist fights. In retrospect, my shyness of combat has clear sources.

Many things go into the making of a young thug. One of those things is the consummation of the male romance with the power to intimidate. An infant discovers that random flailings send the baby bottle flying out of the crib and crashing to the floor. Delighted, the joyful babe repeats those motions again and again, seeking to duplicate the feat. Just so, I recall the points at which some of my boyhood friends were finally seduced by the perception of themselves as tough guys. When a mark cowered and surrendered his money without resistance, myth and reality merged—and paid off. It is, after all, only manly to embrace the power to frighten and intimidate. We, as men, are not supposed to give an inch of our lane on the highway; we are to seize the fighter's edge in work and in play and even in love; we are to be valiant in the face of hostile forces.

Unfortunately, poor and powerless young men seem to take all this nonsense literally. As a boy, I saw countless tough guys locked away; I have since buried several, too. They were babies, really—a teenage cousin, a brother of 22, a childhood friend in his mid-twenties—all gone down in episodes of bravado played out in the streets. I came to doubt the virtues of intimidation early on. I chose, perhaps even unconsciously, to remain a shadow—timid, but a survivor.

The fearsomeness mistakenly attributed to me in public places often has a perilous flavor. The most frightening of these confusions occurred in the late 1970s and early 1980s when I worked as a journalist in Chicago. One day, rushing into the office of a magazine I was writing for with a deadline story in hand, I was mistaken for a burglar. The office manager called security and, with an ad hoc posse, pursued me through the labyrinthine halls, nearly to my editor's door. I had no way of proving who I was. I could only move briskly toward the company of someone who knew me.

Another time I was on assignment for a local paper and killing time before an interview. I entered a jewelry store on the city's affluent Near North Side. The proprietor excused herself and returned with an enormous red Doberman pinscher straining at the end of a leash. She stood, the dog extended toward me, silent to my questions, her eyes bulging nearly out of her head. I took a cursory look around, nodded, and bade her goodnight. Relatively speaking, however, I never fared as badly as another black male journalist. He went to nearby Waukegan, Illinois, a couple of summers ago to work on a story about a murderer who was born there. Mistaking the reporter for the killer, police hauled him from his car at gunpoint and but for his press credentials would probably have tried to book him. Such episodes are not uncommon. Black men trade tales like this all the time.

In "My Negro Problem—And Ours," Podhoretz writes that the hatred he feels for blacks makes itself known to him through a variety of avenues—one being his discomfort with that "special brand of paranoid touchiness" to which he says blacks are prone.

No doubt he is speaking here of black men. In time, I learned to smother the rage I felt at so often being taken for a criminal. Not to do so would surely have led to madness—via that special "paranoid touchiness" that so annoyed Podhoretz at the time he wrote the essay.

13 I began to take precautions to make myself less threatening. I move about with care, particularly late in the evening. I give a wide berth to nervous people on subway platforms during the wee hours, particularly when I have exchanged business clothes for jeans. If I happen to be entering a building behind some people who appear skittish, I may walk by, letting them clear the lobby before I return, so as not to seem to be following them. I have been calm and extremely congenial on those rare occasions when I've been pulled over by the police.

14 And on late-evening constitutionals along streets less traveled by, I employ what has proved to be an excellent tension-reducing measure: I whistle melodies from Beethoven and Vivaldi and the more popular classical composers. Even steely New Yorkers hunching toward nighttime destinations seem to relax, and occasionally they even join in the tune. Virtually everybody seems to sense that a mugger wouldn't be warbling bright, sunny selections from Vivaldi's *Four Seasons*. It is my equivalent of the cowbell that hikers wear when they know they are in bear country.

RESPONDING TO THE READING

FREEWRITING

Practice 12g. Freewrite about Staples's perspective as a "night walker." What point of view does he offer on the urban experience?

BUILDING YOUR VOCABULARY

affluent (1)	indistinguishable (2)	panhandlers (5)	intimidation (9)
billowing (1)	quarry (2)	bandolier (6)	ad hoc (10)
discreet (1)	unnerving (2)	warren-like (6)	labyrinthine (10)
impoverished (1)	unwieldy (2)	lethality (7)	perilous (10)
uninflammatory (1)	wayfarers (2)	retrospect (7)	paranoid (12)
accomplice (2)	avid (4)	consummation (8)	berth (13)
dicey (2)	taut (4)	flailings (8)	congenial (13)
errant (2)	maneuvering (5)	intimidate (8)	constitutionals (14)

QUESTIONS FOR DISCUSSION

1. How do people misjudge Brent Staples? How does his "unwieldy inheritance" affect their judgment?
2. What does this essay tell us about the author's education, personality, and origins? Why does Staples want the reader to know these things?

3. What, in Staples's estimation, causes young men to become "thugs"? Include an explanation of "the consummation of the male romance with the power to intimidate." What do you think of this and other explanations of why people use violence against others?
4. The details and word choice in Staples's essay give it an immediacy and vividness. Choose a few phrases and descriptions that caught your attention, and discuss how they contribute to the essay's realistic effect.
5. Examine Staples's tone or attitude toward those who fear him. Does his tone change in the course of the essay? If so, how do you explain this change?
6. What is Staples's purpose in writing this article? Who might be his intended audience? What evidence in the text illustrates his purpose and audience?
7. What solutions does Staples propose for dealing with public stereotyping? Does he seem resigned to the way people stereotyped him? Explain your answer.

TOPICS FOR WRITING

Topic 1. Brent Staples admits in his article that "the danger [women] perceive is not a hallucination." Write a paper advising women what precautions they should take to ensure their safety. Focus on two or three strategies that you consider most important, developing them in detail. You might consult your local police department for suggestions about what to do and how to judge the behavior of others. Check your suggestions to see that you have avoided stereotyping.

Topic 2. Write an essay in which you analyze in detail one or two times in your life when you felt threatened or uncomfortable. Your essay should make some point about these experiences. To support that point, you will need to explain, as Brent Staples does, why these things happened, what you felt at the time, any long-term effects on your behavior, and the larger social situation that may have produced these experiences.

Culture and Identity

CHAPTER

13

In a country with as much diversity among its people as the United States, most of us, at one time or another, have been caught between the rhythms of a culture or value system that we have known since birth and those of another culture to which we may have to adapt. In this chapter, you will read about the cross-cultural experiences of Mexican Americans, European Americans, and several immigrant groups. In "Complexion," Richard Rodriguez fights the image of the Mexican laborer as he struggles to forge a new identity as a student and intellectual. In "Pursuit of Happiness," Dympna Ugwu-Oju writes about ways she adheres to values in her Ibo culture even when those values conflict with her adopted American culture. In "America: The Multicultural Society," Ishmael Reed rejects the idea that North America can exist exclusively as a repository of Western civilization and offers an exuberant defense of our ethnic diversity. In the last reading in this chapter, "The New Immigrants: Up Close and Personal," Abigail McCarthy writes a defense of immigrants as "an achieving and hard-working lot."

At home I was quiet, so perhaps I seemed formal to my relations and other Spanish-speaking visitors to the house. But outside the house—my God!—I talked. Particularly in class or alone with my teachers, I chattered.
—Richard Rodriguez

Is that the kind of world we desire? A hum-drum homogeneous world of all brains but no heart, no fiction, no poetry; a world of robots with human attendants bereft of imagination, of culture? Or does North America deserve a more exciting destiny? To become a place where the cultures of the world crisscross. This is possible because the United States is unique in the world: The world is here.
—Ishmael Reed

Freewrite about situations that typically make people self-conscious and uncomfortable.

Complexion

Richard Rodriguez

Richard Rodriguez, whose parents emigrated from Mexico, distinguished himself as a student of English literature. He attended Stanford and Columbia universities, earned a Doctorate from the University of California at Berkeley, and received a fellowship to attend the Warburg Institute in London. Rodriguez is currently an editor for the Pacific News Service in San Francisco and writes for other national publications such as Harper's, U.S. News & World Report, *and the* Los Angeles Times. *His essays have also appeared in the* Wall Street Journal, The American Scholar, *and* Time *magazine. Rodriguez received a Peabody Award in 1997 and an Emmy for his* NewsHour *essays on American life. His other awards include the Frankel Medal from the National Endowment for the Humanities, and the International Journalism Award from the World Affairs Council of California. Rodriguez is the author of two BBC documentaries,* The King's Highway *(1999), and* Movements *(1999). He has written three books,* The Hunger of Memory: The Education of Richard Rodriguez *(1982),* Days of Obligation: An Argument with My Father *(1992), and* Brown: The Last Discovery of America *(2002), in which he rejects the black and white notions of race, offering instead the color brown as a more accurate description of the "melting pot" concept of the United States. In the following selection from* Hunger of Memory, *Rodriguez writes about his difficulties assimilating into Anglo-American culture.*

1   Visiting the East Coast or the gray capitals of Europe during the long months of winter, I often meet people at deluxe hotels who comment on my complexion. (In such hotels it appears nowadays a mark of leisure and wealth to have a complexion like mine.) Have I been skiing? In the Swiss Alps? Have I just returned from a Caribbean vacation? No. I say no softly but in a firm voice that intends to explain: My complexion is dark. (My skin is brown. More exactly, terra-cotta in sunlight, tawny in shade. I do not redden in sunlight. Instead, my skin becomes progressively dark; the sun singes the flesh.)

2   When I was a boy the white summer sun of Sacramento would darken me so, my T-shirt would seem bleached against my slender dark arms. My mother would see me come up the front steps. She'd wait for the screen door to slam at my back. "You look like a *negrito,*" she'd say, angry, sorry to be angry, frustrated almost to laughing, scorn. "You know how important looks are in this country. With *los gringos* looks are all that they judge on. But you! Look at you! You're so careless!" Then she'd start in all over again. "You won't be satisfied till you end up looking like *los pobres* who work in the fields, *los braceros.*"

(*Los braceros*: Those men who work with their *brazos,* their arms; Mexican nationals who were licensed to work for American farmers in the 1950s. They worked very hard for very little money, my father would tell me. And what money they earned they sent back to Mexico to support their families, my mother would add. *Los pobres*—the poor, the pitiful, the powerless ones. But paradoxically also powerful men. They were the men with brown-muscled arms I stared at in awe on Saturday mornings when they showed up downtown like gypsies to shop at Woolworth's or Penney's. On Monday nights they would gather hours early on the steps of the Memorial Auditorium for the wrestling matches. Passing by on my bicycle in summer, I would spy them there, clustered in small groups, talking—frightening and fascinating men—some wearing Texas *sombreros* and T-shirts which shone fluorescent in the twilight. I would sit forward in the back seat of our family's '48 Chevy to see them, working alongside Valley highways: dark men on an even horizon, loading a truck amid rows of straight green. Powerful, powerless men. Their fascinating darkness—like mine—to be feared.) 3

"You'll end up looking just like them." . . . 4

Dark skin was for my mother the most important symbol of a life of oppressive labor and poverty. But both my parents recognized other symbols as well. 5

My father noticed the feel of every hand he shook. (He'd smile sometimes—marvel more than scorn—remembering a man he'd met who had soft, uncalloused hands.) 6

My mother would grab a towel in the kitchen and rub my oily face sore when I came in from playing outside. "Clean the *graza* off of your face!" (*Greaser!*) 7

Symbols: When my older sister, then in high school, asked my mother if she could do light housework in the afternoons for a rich lady we knew, my mother was frightened by the idea. For several weeks she troubled over it before granting conditional permission: "Just remember, you're not a maid. I don't want you wearing a uniform." My father echoed the same warning. Walking with him past a hotel, I watched as he stared at a doorman dressed like a Beefeater. "How can anyone let himself be dressed up like that? Like a clown. Don't you ever get a job where you have to put on a uniform." In summertime neighbors would ask me if I wanted to earn extra money by mowing their lawns. Again and again my mother worried: "Why did they ask *you*? Can't you find anything better?" Inevitably, she'd relent. She knew I needed the money. But I was instructed to work after dinner. ("When the sun's not so hot.") Even then, I'd have to wear a hat. *Un sombrero de* baseball. 8

(*Sombrero.* Watching gray cowboy movies, I'd brood over the meaning of the broad-rimmed hat—that troubling symbol—which comically distinguished a Mexican cowboy from real cowboys.) 9

From my father came no warnings concerning the sun. His fear was of dark factory jobs. He remembered too well his first jobs when he came to this country, not intending to stay, just to earn money enough to sail on to Australia. (In Mexico he had heard too many stories of discrimination in *los Estados Unidos.* So it was Australia, that distant island-continent, that loomed in his imagination as his "America.") The work my father found in San Francisco was work for the unskilled. A factory job. Then a cannery job. (He'd remember the noise and the heat.) Then a job at a warehouse. (He'd remember the 10 dark stench of old urine.) At one place there were fistfights; at another a supervisor who hated Chinese and Mexicans. Nowhere a union.

11   His memory of himself in those years is held by those jobs. Never making money enough for passage to Australia; slowly giving up the plan of returning to school to resume his third-grade education—to become an engineer. My memory of him in those years, however, is lifted from photographs in the family album which show him on his honeymoon with my mother—the woman who had convinced him to stay in America. I have studied their photographs often, seeking to find in those figures some clear resemblance to the man and the woman I've known as my parents. But the youthful faces in the photos remain, behind dark glasses, shadowy figures anticipating my mother and father.

12   They are pictured on the grounds of the Coronado Hotel near San Diego, standing in the pale light of a winter afternoon. She is wearing slacks. Her hair falls seductively over one side of her face. He appears wearing a double-breasted suit, an unneeded raincoat draped over his arm. Another shows them standing together, solemnly staring ahead. Their shoulders barely are touching. There is to their pose an aristocratic formality, an elegant Latin hauteur.

13   The man in those pictures is the same man who was fascinated by Italian grand opera. I have never known just what my father saw in the spectacle, but he has told me that he would take my mother to the Opera House every Friday night—if he had money enough for orchestra seats. ("Why go to sit in the balcony?") On Sundays he'd don Italian silk scarves and a camel's hair coat to take his new wife to the polo matches in Golden Gate Park. But one weekend my father stopped going to the opera and polo matches. He would blame the change in his life on one job—a warehouse job, working for a large corporation which today advertises its products with the smiling faces of children. "They made me an old man before my time," he'd say to me many years later. Afterward, jobs got easier and cleaner. Eventually, in middle age, he got a job making false teeth. But his youth was spent at the warehouse. "Everything changed," his wife remembers. The dapper young man in the old photographs yielded to the man I saw after dinner: haggard, asleep on the sofa. During "The Ed Sullivan Show" on Sunday nights, when Roberta Peters or Licia Albanese would appear on the tiny blue screen, his head would jerk up alert. He'd sit forward while the notes of Puccini sounded before him ("Un bel dí").

14   By the time they had a family, my parents no longer dressed in very fine clothes. Those symbols of great wealth and the reality of their lives too noisily clashed. No longer did they try to fit themselves, like paper-doll figures, behind trappings so foreign to their actual lives. My father no longer wore silk scarves or expensive wool suits. He sold his tuxedo to a secondhand store for five dollars. My mother sold her rabbit fur coat to the wife of a Spanish radio station disc jockey. ("It looks better on you than it does on me," she kept telling the lady until the sale was completed.) I was six years old at the time, but I recall watching the transaction with complete understanding. The woman I knew as my mother was already physically unlike the woman in her honeymoon photos. My mother's hair was short. Her shoulders were thick from carrying children. Her fingers were swollen red, toughened by housecleaning. Already my mother would admit to foreseeing herself in her own mother, a woman grown old, bald and bowlegged, after a hard lifetime of working.

In their manner, both my parents continued to respect the symbols of what they considered to be upper-class life. Very early, they taught me the *propria* way of eating *como los ricos*. And I was carefully taught elaborate formulas of polite greeting and parting. The dark little boy would be invited by classmates to the rich houses on Forty-fourth and Forty-fifth streets. "How do you do?" or "I am very pleased to meet you," I would say, bowing slightly to the amused mothers of classmates. "Thank you very much for the dinner; it was very delicious." 15

I made an impression. I intended to make an impression, to be invited back. (I soon realized that the trick was to get the mother or father to notice me.) From those early days began my association with rich people, my fascination with their secret. My mother worried. She warned me not to come home expecting to have the things my friends possessed. But she needn't have said anything. When I went to the big houses, I remembered that I was, at best, a visitor to the world I saw there. For that reason, I was an especially watchful guest. I was my parents' child. Things most middle-class children wouldn't trouble to notice, I studied. Remembered to see: the starched black and white uniform worn by the maid who opened the door; the Mexican gardeners—their complexions as dark as my own. (One gardener's face, glassed by sweat, looked up to see me going inside.) 16

"Take Richard upstairs and show him your electric train," the mother said. But it was really the vast polished dining room table I'd come to appraise. Those nights when I was invited to stay for dinner, I'd notice that my friend's mother rang a small silver bell to tell the black woman when to bring in the food. The father, at his end of the table, ate while wearing his tie. When I was not required to speak, I'd skate the icy cut of crystal with my eye; my gaze would follow the golden threads etched onto the rim of china. With my mother's eyes I'd see my hostess's manicured nails and judge them to be marks of her leisure. Later, when my schoolmate's father would bid me goodnight, I would feel his soft fingers and palm when we shook hands. And turning to leave, I'd see my dark self, lit by chandelier light, in a tall hallway mirror. . . . 17

Throughout adolescence, I felt myself mysteriously marked. Nothing else about my appearance would concern me so much as the fact that my complexion was dark. My mother would say how sorry she was that there was not money enough to get braces to straighten my teeth. But I never bothered about my teeth. In three-way mirrors at department stores, I'd see my profile dramatically defined by a long nose, but it was really only the color of my skin that caught my attention. 18

I wasn't afraid that I would become a menial laborer because of my skin. Nor did my complexion make me feel especially vulnerable to racial abuse. (I didn't really consider my dark skin to be a racial characteristic. I would have been only too happy to look as Mexican as my light-skinned older brother.) Simply, I judged myself ugly. And, since the women in my family had been the ones who discussed it in such worried tones, I felt my dark skin made me unattractive to women. 19

Thirteen years old. Fourteen. In a grammar school art class, when the assignment was to draw a self-portrait, I tried and I tried but could not bring myself to shade in the face on the paper to anything like my actual tone. With disgust then I would come face to face with myself in mirrors. With disappointment I located myself in class 20 photographs—my dark face undefined by the camera which had clearly described the white faces of classmates. Or I'd see my dark wrist against my long-sleeved white shirt.

21   I grew divorced from my body. Insecure, overweight, listless. On hot summer days when my rubber-soled shoes soaked up the heat from the sidewalk, I kept my head down. Or walked in the shade. My mother didn't need anymore to tell me to watch out for the sun. I denied myself a sensational life. The normal, extraordinary, animal excitement of feeling my body alive—riding shirtless on a bicycle in the warm wind created by furious self-propelled motion—the sensations that first had excited in me a sense of my maleness, I denied. I was too ashamed of my body. I wanted to forget that I had a body because I had a brown body. I was grateful that none of my classmates ever mentioned the fact.

22   I continued to see the *braceros,* those men I resembled in one way and, in another way, didn't resemble at all. On the watery horizon of a Valley afternoon, I'd see them. And though I feared looking like them, it was with silent envy that I regarded them still. I envied them their physical lives, their freedom to violate the taboo of the sun. Closer to home I would notice the shirtless construction workers, the roofers, the sweating men tarring the street in front of the house. And I'd see the Mexican gardeners. I was unwilling to admit the attraction of their lives. I tried to deny it by looking away. But what was denied became strongly desired.

23   In high school physical education classes, I withdrew, in the regular company of five or six classmates, to a distant corner of a football field where we smoked and talked. Our company was composed of bodies too short or too tall, all graceless and all—except mine—pale. Our conversation was usually witty. (In fact we were intelligent.) If we referred to the athletic contests around us, it was with sarcasm. With savage scorn I'd refer to the "animals" playing football or baseball. It would have been important for me to have joined them. Or for me to have taken off my shirt, to have let the sun burn dark on my skin, and to have run barefoot on the warm wet grass. It would have been very important. Too important. It would have been too telling a gesture—to admit the desire for sensation, the body, my body.

24   Fifteen, sixteen. I was a teenager shy in the presence of girls. Never dated. Barely could talk to a girl without stammering. In high school I went to several dances, but I never managed to ask a girl to dance. So I stopped going. I cannot remember high school years now with the parade of typical images: bright drive-ins or gliding blue shadows of a Junior Prom. At home most weekend nights, I would pass evenings reading. Like those hidden, precocious adolescents who have no real-life sexual experiences, I read a great deal of romantic fiction. "You won't find it in your books," my brother would playfully taunt me as he prepared to go to a party by freezing the crest of the wave in his hair with sticky pomade. Through my reading, however, I developed a fabulous and sophisticated sexual imagination. At seventeen, I may not have known how to engage a girl in small talk, but I had read *Lady Chatterley's Lover.*

25   It annoyed me to hear my father's teasing: that I would never know what "real work" is; that my hands were so soft. I think I knew it was his way of admitting pleasure and pride in my academic success. But I didn't smile. My mother said she was glad her

children were getting their educations and would not be pushed around like *los pobres.*
I heard the remark ironically as a reminder of my separation from *los braceros.* At such times I suspected that education was making me effeminate. The odd thing, however, was that I did not judge my classmates so harshly. Nor did I consider my male teachers in high school effeminate. It was only myself I judged against some shadowy, mythical Mexican laborer—dark like me, yet very different.

Language was crucial. I knew that I had violated the ideal of the *macho* by becoming such a dedicated student of language and literature. *Machismo* was a word never exactly defined by the persons who used it. (It was best described in the "proper" behavior of men.) Women at home, nevertheless, would repeat the old Mexican dictum that a man should be *feo, fuerte, y formal.* "The three *F's,*" my mother called them, smiling slyly. *Feo* I took to mean not literally ugly so much as ruggedly handsome. (When my mother and her sisters spent a loud, laughing afternoon determining ideal male good looks, they finally settled on the actor Gilbert Roland, who was neither too pretty nor ugly but had looks "like a man.") *Fuerte,* "strong," seemed to mean not physical strength as much as inner strength, character. A dependable man is *fuerte. Fuerte* for that reason was a characteristic subsumed by the last of the three qualities, and the one I most often considered—*formal.* To be *formal* is to be steady. A man of responsibility, a good provider. Someone *formal* is also constant. A person to be relied upon in adversity. A sober man, a man of high seriousness.

I learned a great deal about being *formal* just by listening to the way my father and other male relatives of his generation spoke. A man was not silent necessarily. Nor was he limited in the tones he could sound. For example, he could tell a long, involved, humorous story and laugh at his own humor with high-pitched giggling. But a man was not talkative the way a woman could be. It was permitted a woman to be gossipy and chatty. (When one heard many voices in a room, it was usually women who were talking.) Men spoke much less rapidly. And often men spoke in monologues. (When one voice sounded in a crowded room, it was most often a man's voice one heard.) More important than any of this was the fact that a man never verbally revealed his emotions. Men did not speak about their unease in moments of crisis or danger. It was the woman who worried aloud when her husband got laid off from work. At times of illness or death in the family, a man was usually quiet, even silent. Women spoke up to voice prayers. In distress, women always sounded quick ejaculations to God or the Virgin; women prayed in clearly audible voices at a wake held in a funeral parlor. And on the subject of love, a woman was verbally expansive. She spoke of her yearning and delight. A married man, if he spoke publicly about love, usually did so with playful, mischievous irony. Younger, unmarried men more often were quiet. (The *macho* is a silent suitor. *Formal.*)

At home I was quiet, so perhaps I seemed *formal* to my relations and other Spanish-speaking visitors to the house. But outside the house—my God!—I talked. Particularly in class or alone with my teachers, I chattered. (Talking seemed to make teachers think I was bright.) I often was proud of my way with words. Though, on other occasions, for example, when I would hear my mother busily speaking to women, it would occur to me that my attachment to words made me like her. Her son. Not *formal* like my father. At such times I even suspected that my nostalgia for sounds—the noisy, intimate Spanish sounds of my past—was nothing more than effeminate yearning.

29   High school English teachers encouraged me to describe very personal feelings in words. Poems and short stories I wrote, expressing sorrow and loneliness, were awarded high grades. In my bedroom were books by poets and novelists—books that I loved—in which male writers published feelings the men in my family never revealed or acknowledged in words. And it seemed to me that there was something unmanly about my attachment to literature. Even today, when so much about the myth of the *macho* no longer concerns me, I cannot altogether evade such notions. Writing these pages, admitting my embarrassment or my guilt, admitting my sexual anxieties and my physical insecurity, I have not been able to forget that I am not being *formal.*

30   So be it.

RESPONDING TO THE READING

FREEWRITING

Practice 13a. Freewrite about a few passages from "Complexion" that fascinated or disturbed you in some way. Explain your choices.

Practice 13b. Freewrite for several pages about the ways in which Rodriguez's relationship to each of his parents was similar to or different from your relationship to your parents.

Practice 13c. How did Rodriguez's teachers encourage him? What kind of encouragement or discouragement have you received from teachers in your high school or college classes?

BUILDING YOUR VOCABULARY

terra-cotta (1)	hauteur (12)	audible (27)
tawny (1)	appraise (17)	irony (27)
uncalloused (6)	precocious (24)	mischievous (27)
stench (10)		

QUESTIONS FOR DISCUSSION

1. Write an outline of the scenes Rodriguez describes in "Complexion." Occasionally he leaves extra space between paragraphs to indicate breaks between sections in his essay. What is the effect of using these gaps in place of transitional phrases?
2. Which cultures clash in "Complexion"? How is Rodriguez both connected to and alienated from each?

3. How does Rodriguez's thinking reflect the values and concerns of his parents? How does he use them to measure himself?
4. What is Rodriguez's purpose for writing his observations? Is his attitude toward his experiences and observations humorous, critical, angry, informative, curious, bitter, or does some other emotion come to mind?
5. What writing strategy does Rodriguez use to convey his parents' disappointments in life? How effective is it?
6. What is your general impression of Richard Rodriguez? Which passages contributed to this impression?
7. Ask someone in your class who has a Catholic background to explain the term *confession*. In what way might "Complexion" be read as a "confession"?

TOPICS FOR WRITING

Topic 1. Rodriguez explains some of the uncertainties he has about himself and other people, particularly the *braceros*. Write a paper in which you illustrate one or two of the conflicts or contradictions in your own life. These may involve uneasy feelings about other people or doubts about yourself.

Topic 2. Rodriguez writes about his "association with rich people" and his fascination with their "secret." Examine several television shows and magazine advertisements to find characterizations or images of the rich. Write a paper in which you illustrate a few of the more frequent images of the rich that you find.

Topic 3. Rodriguez mentions characteristics of Latin *machismo* (*feo, fuerte,* and *formal*) as appealing to Hispanic women like his mother. Write a paper explaining some of the characteristics that you find most appealing in a partner. In writing your paper, be sure to give actual examples and explain *why* you find a particular behavior, attitude, or personality type appealing.

Topic 4. Conduct four or five interviews to discover how the people you select have been affected, either negatively or positively, by their parents. Find out how their parents affected their self-esteem, views of others, or attitudes toward work and school. Write an essay examining two or three important ways in which these people have been influenced by their parents.

Topic 5. Find two photographs of one or both of your parents or two photographs of your guardian taken several years apart. Analyze the differences you see. Discuss not only age differences but also changes in attitude, lifestyle, or values suggested by the photographs.

Topic 6. Rodriguez tells us that he says very little when he is at home, but is extremely talkative at school. Like Rodriguez, most of us have different personalities for different occasions. Write an essay in which you describe two different "faces" or "selves" you present to the world.

WRITING BEFORE READING

In what ways must you balance personal values with your activities at school or in the workplace?

Pursuit of Happiness

Dympna Ugwu-Oju

Dympna Ugwu-Oju teaches English at Madera Center Community College in central California. Her articles have appeared in national newspapers and magazines, including Newsweek *and the* New York Times. *Her autobiography,* What Will My Mother Say: A Tribal African Girl Comes of Age in America *(1995), describes her childhood during the civil war in Nigeria and her place in the patriarchal Ibo culture. She is currently waiting to publish her second book,* In the Eyes of God: A Biafran Story. *After obtaining her BA at Briarcliff College and a master's in Journalism from Syracuse University, Ugwu-Oju returned briefly to Nigeria and became the first Nigerian woman to hold a professional position in mass communication. "Pursuit of Happiness" was originally published in the* New York Times Magazine, *November 14, 1993.*

1   My best friend called me late on Saturday-night to tell me she was leaving her husband. It was completely unexpected, but yes, she was definitely leaving him. Her mind was made up—16 long years of marriage, 4 children—and she was leaving.

2   "Why? What Happened?" I asked on reflex. Something must have happened; why else would she be so resolute? It had to be something devastating.

3   "Nothing, really," she answered, "nothing I can put my finger on."

4   "Is he having an affair? Is he involved with someone else?" He didn't strike me as the cheating type, but why else would she be leaving?

5   "No, nothing like that." I was amazed at how calm she sounded.

6   "Did he beat you up?" I was not prepared yet to accept her dismissive attitude. Women don't end marriages for nothing. She just wasn't leveling.

7   "It's nothing in particular." She spoke haltingly, weighing every word. "All I know is that I've been very unhappy lately."

8   "Uhm, I'm listening," I nudged her, waiting for the litanies of abuse, of deprivation. But she said no more. "I just thought you should hear it from me," she added as we said our goodbyes.

9   I waited two days and called her back. I knew I had to tread very lightly. "Just tell me one thing and I'll leave you alone: Are *you* having an affair?" That wasn't the question I wanted to ask, but it popped out.

10   "No! Are you crazy? How could you even ask me that?" She laughed out loud. Then sensing my need to come to terms with her news, she said she'd call me back after her husband was asleep.

As I waited, I pondered the inquisition our friends would put me through. My friend   11
and I and both our husbands, like a majority of our friends, are Nigerians. While we've
lived in the United States for most of our adulthood and for all intents and purposes live
like Americans, we identify closely with our traditional Ibo culture. An Ibo woman is
born (educated if she is lucky), marries, procreates (a definite must, male children
preferably) and dies when her time comes, God rest her soul. Women of our generation,
educated and all, are expected to live through our husbands and children as our mothers and grandmothers did before us.

An Ibo woman has very little personal identity, even if she lives in the United States   12
and has success in her career. Our culture takes very little pride in a woman's accomplishment. At an Ibo gathering a woman is more likely to be asked whose wife or mother
she is before she is asked her name or what she does for a living. If the woman is
accomplished but unmarried, people will say, "But where is she going with all that
success?" Ibos cling to the adage that a woman is worth nothing unless she's married and
has children.

I am as guilty as any other Ibo woman living in the United States in perpetuating   13
this. Professionally, I am more successful than the majority of Ibo men I've met in this
country, yet when we gather for a party, usually to celebrate a marriage or birth, I join
the women in the kitchen to prepare food and serve the men. I remember to curtsy just
so before the older men, looking away to avoid meeting their eyes. I glow with pride
when other men tease my husband about his "good wife." I often lead the women in the
Ibo wedding song: "It is as it should be; give her the keys to her kitchen." At birth ceremonies, I start the chant: "Without a child, what would a woman be?" It is a song my
mother sang and one that every Ibo woman knows like her own name.

I know the rules and the consequences of breaking them. Our culture is unforgiving   14
of a stubborn woman. She always gets the maximum punishment—ostracism. "She thinks
she's smart; let's see if she can marry herself" is how mistreatment of a noncompliant
woman is justified.

To the surprise of my American friends, I've never had difficulty separating my Ibo   15
self from my professional and everyday American life. At work, I'm as assertive as any
American-born female. I raise my voice as loud as necessary to be heard in meetings. At
conferences where I present papers on "Women from the Third World," I make serious
arguments about the need for international intervention in countries where women are
deprived of all rights, where women are subjected to clitorectomies, where baby girls
are killed to make room for boys. Yet as easily as I switch from speaking English to Ibo, I
am content to slide into the role of the submissive and obedient wife. I never confuse my
two selves.

Hundreds of thousands of women from the third world and other traditional soci-   16
eties share my experience. We straddle two cultures, cultures that are often in opposition. Mainstream America, the culture we embrace in our professional lives, dictates
that we be assertive and independent—like men. Our traditional culture, dictated by
religion and years of socialization, demands that we be docile and content in our roles
as mothers and wives—careers or not.

17   But, suddenly, my best friend, steeped in the Ibo culture as much as I am, tells me she's leaving her husband—not for any offenses he's committed but because she is unhappy. I think of the question my mother and her mother would ask: "What on earth does she want?" She has everything any woman (Ibo woman, that is) would want: a professional husband (from a good family back home) with a good income, who allows her to pursue her own career; not one, not two, but *three* sons and a daughter; a huge house in the suburbs. And she tells me she's unhappy.

18   "Whoever told her a woman needs to be happy?" her mother would ask. Everyone knows that the happy part of a marriage is brief. After her first child, she is well on her way to fulfillment. This may sour a little if her first and second babies are girls. Her husband will drop subtle hints that he'll marry someone who can produce a son. But a good Ibo woman devises ways to hold his interest until she produces a son. My friend has three sons, and she's not happy?

19   "What about the children?" I heard her muffled sobs and sensed her struggle to regain composure. "They'll stay with their father," she said. She has no right to the children. That is the Ibo tradition, American laws or not. A woman departs from her husband's home as she came into it—empty-handed. She must refund the bride price her husband paid—plus interest—and may even have to refund the cost of the master's degree she obtained during the marriage.

20   My friend knows all that. And now she was going to leave without the children she had lived for, her guarantee of protection in her marriage. She had been lucky birthing three sons in a row, delighting her husband, winning praise in our community. Had she not consoled me when our first child was born female? "Don't worry, the next one will be a boy, you'll see." And when my second child was born male, had my friend not screamed louder than I with joy? Why would she now walk away from the secure future she had earned?

21   "How can you do this to yourself?" I lost all control. "Have you gone mad?" "I need to try to find happiness. I really thought that you, of all people, would understand," she said coldly, hanging up before I could reply.

22   Later, I realized what was going on with my friend. She thinks herself American. She has bought into America's concept of womanhood—personal satisfaction, no matter the cost. She wants to be happy. I wonder if she knows what she's getting into.

RESPONDING TO THE READING

FREEWRITING

Practice 13d. Dympna Ugwu-Oju remarks that her American friends are surprised that she has "ever had difficulty separating [her] Ibo self from [her] professional and everyday American life." Freewrite about how you balance different parts of your identity.

| resolute (2) | litanies (8) | ostracism (14) |
| dismissive (6) | inquisition (11) | noncompliant (14) |

QUESTIONS FOR DISCUSSION

1. How well does Ugwu-Oju's title, "Pursuit of Happiness," suit the focus of her essay?
2. Why does Ugwu-Oju incorporate quotations from the songs and sayings of her Ibo culture? What do these sayings tell her? What is the effect of including these quotations?
3. Ugwu-Oju begins and ends her essay with the story of her friend's divorce. How does this story act as a "frame" or context for the rest of her essay?
4. Why do you think the author's friend thought that she "of all people, would understand" why she decided to get a divorce? What information does Ugwu-Oju give the reader about herself that explains why she cannot support her friend's choice?
5. At the end of her essay, Ugwu-Oju says she understands her friend, a woman who plans to divorce her respectable Ibo husband and relinquish their four children to him. The author is convinced that her friend "has bought into America's concept of womanhood—personal satisfaction, no matter the cost. She wants to be happy. I wonder if she knows what she's getting into." How does this work as an ending to her essay? What does Ugwu-Oju leave unsaid?

TOPICS FOR WRITING

Topic 1. Write an essay in which you agree or disagree with Ugwu-Oju's definition of "America's concept of womanhood—personal satisfaction, no matter the cost." In your essay, show several reasons why "personal satisfaction" at any price is or is not of central importance to women in the United States. Be sure to support your topic ideas with detailed examples and explanations that connect those examples to your general points.

Topic 2. Select two or three of the ideas about women and the family in Ibo culture that Ugwu-Oju mentions, and write an essay in which you discuss how these attitudes conflict with values in the larger American culture. Use specific examples to develop ways the two cultures differ in their views of women.

WRITING BEFORE READING

How are various cultures or nationalities reflected in school programs, exhibitions, celebrations, or other events in your community? If you live in an area that doesn't have much ethnic or cultural diversity, write about individual differences in holiday celebrations, in behavior, or personal expression.

America: The Multinational Society

Ishmael Reed

Ishmael Reed was born in 1938 in Chattanooga, Tennessee, and grew up in Buffalo, New York. A novelist, poet, and essayist, Reed has published eleven novels, nine volumes of poetry, and six collections of essays. He has also edited several major anthologies of literature. Two of Reed's books were nominated for a National Book Award, and he has received numerous other honors and awards including a Guggenheim Foundation Award, the Lewis Michaux Literary Prize, and fellowships from the National Endowment of the Arts, the American Civil Liberties Union, and the California Arts Council. Reed has also distinguished himself as a songwriter, TV producer, publisher, and playwright. He has been a lecturer at University of California, Berkeley, for over twenty years and has also taught at Harvard, Yale, and Dartmouth. Reed's collections of essays include Multi-America: Essays on Cultural Wars and Cultural Peace *(1997),* Another Day at the Front: Dispatches from the Race War *(2003), and* Blues City: A Walk in Oakland *(2003). Reed currently publishes two e-zines,* Konch *and* Vines, *an international student anthology. In this essay from* Writin' Is Fightin': Thirty-Seven Years of Boxing on Paper *(1988), Reed argues for a broader meaning of the term* American.

At the annual Lower East Side Jewish Festival yesterday, a Chinese woman ate a pizza slice in front of Ty Thuan Duc's Vietnamese grocery store. Beside her a Spanish-speaking family patronized a cart with two signs: "Italian Ices" and "Kosher by Rabbi Alper." And after the pastrami ran out, everybody ate knishes.

(*New York Times,* 23 June 1983)

1   On the day before Memorial Day, 1983, a poet called me to describe a city he had just visited. He said that one section included mosques, built by the Islamic people who dwelled there. Attending his reading, he said, were large numbers of Hispanic people, forty thousand of whom lived in the same city. He was not talking about a fabled city located in some mysterious region of the world. The city he'd visited was Detroit.

2   A few months before, as I was leaving Houston, Texas, I heard it announced on the radio that Texas's largest minority was Mexican American, and though a foundation recently issued a report critical of bilingual education, the taped voice used to guide the passengers on the air trams connecting terminals in Dallas Airport is in both Spanish and English. If the trend continues, a day will come when it will be difficult to travel through some sections of the country without hearing commands in both English and Spanish; after all, for some western states, Spanish was the first written language and the Spanish style lives on in the western way of life.

3   Shortly after my Texas trip, I sat in an auditorium located on the campus of the University of Wisconsin at Milwaukee as a Yale professor—whose original work on the influence of African cultures upon those of the Americas has led to his ostracism from some monocultural intellectual circles—walked up and down the aisle, like an old-time

southern evangelist, dancing and drumming the top of the lectern, illustrating his points before some serious Afro-American intellectuals and artists who cheered and applauded his performance and his mastery of information. The professor was "white." After his lecture, he joined a group of Milwaukeeans in a conversation. All of the participants spoke Yoruban, though only the professor had ever traveled to Africa.

One of the artists told me that his paintings, which included African and Afro-American mythological symbols and imagery, were hanging in the local McDonald's restaurant. The next day I went to McDonald's and snapped pictures of smiling youngsters eating hamburgers below paintings that could grace the walls of any of the country's leading museums. The manager of the local McDonald's said, "I don't know what you boys are doing, but I like it," as he commissioned the local painters to exhibit in his restaurant. 4

Such blurring of cultural styles occurs in everyday life in the United States to a greater extent than anyone can imagine and is probably more prevalent than the sensational conflict between people of different backgrounds that is played up and often encouraged by the media. The result is what the Yale professor, Robert Thompson, referred to as a cultural bouillabaisse, yet members of the nation's present educational and cultural Elect still cling to the notion that the United States belongs to some vaguely defined entity they refer to as "Western civilization," by which they mean, presumably, a civilization created by the people of Europe, as if Europe can be viewed in monolithic terms. Is Beethoven's Ninth Symphony, which includes Turkish marches, a part of Western civilization, or the late nineteenth- and twentieth-century French paintings, whose creators were influenced by Japanese art? And what of the cubists, through whom the influence of African art changed modern painting, or the surrealists, who were so impressed with the art of the Pacific Northwest Indians that, in their map of North America, Alaska dwarfs the lower forty-eight in size? 5

Are the Russians, who are often criticized for their adoption of "Western" ways by Tsarist dissidents in exile, members of Western civilization? And what of the millions of Europeans who have black African and Asian ancestry, black Africans having occupied several countries for hundreds of years? Are these "Europeans" members of Western civilization, or the Hungarians, who originated across the Urals in a place called Greater Hungary, or the Irish, who came from the Iberian Peninsula? 6

Even the notion that North America is part of Western civilization because our "system of government" is derived from Europe is being challenged by Native American historians who say that the founding fathers, Benjamin Franklin especially, were actually influenced by the system of government that had been adopted by the Iroquois hundreds of years prior to the arrival of large numbers of Europeans. 7

Western civilization, then, becomes another confusing category like Third World, or Judeo-Christian culture, as man attempts to impose his small-screen view of political and cultural reality upon a complex world. Our most publicized novelist recently said that Western civilization was the greatest achievement of mankind, an attitude that flourishes on the street level as scribbles in public restrooms: "White Power," "Niggers and Spics Suck," or "Hitler was a prophet," the latter being the most telling, for wasn't Adolf Hitler the archetypal monoculturalist who, in his pigheaded 8 arrogance, believed that one way and one blood was so pure that it had to be protected from alien strains at all costs? Where did such an attitude, which has caused so much misery and depression in our national life, which has tainted even our noblest achievements, begin? An attitude that caused the incarceration of Japanese American citizens during World War II, the persecution of Chicanos and Chinese Americans, the near-extermination of the Indians, and the murder and lynchings of thousands of Afro-Americans.

9   Virtuous, hardworking, pious, even though they occasionally would wander off after some fancy clothes, or rendezvous in the woods with the town prostitute, the Puritans are idealized in our schoolbooks as "a hardy band" of no-nonsense patriarchs whose discipline razed the forest and brought order to the New World (a term that annoys Native American historians). Industrious, responsible, it was their "Yankee ingenuity" and practicality that created the work ethic. They were simple folk who produced a number of good poets, and they set the tone for the American writing style, of lean and spare lines, long before Hemingway. They worshiped in churches whose colors blended in with the New England snow, churches with simple structures and ornate lecterns.

10   The Puritans were a daring lot, but they had a mean streak. They hated the theater and banned Christmas. They punished people in a cruel and inhuman manner. They killed children who disobeyed their parents. When they came in contact with those whom they considered heathens or aliens, they behaved in such a bizarre and irrational manner that this chapter in the American history comes down to us as a late-movie horror film. They exterminated the Indians, who taught them how to survive in a world unknown to them, and their encounter with the calypso culture of Barbados resulted in what the tourist guide in Salem's Witches' House refers to as the Witchcraft Hysteria.

11   The Puritan legacy of hard work and meticulous accounting led to the establishment of a great industrial society; it is no wonder that the American industrial revolution began in Lowell, Massachusetts, but there was the other side, the strange and paranoid attitudes toward those different from the Elect.

12   The cultural attitudes of that early Elect continue to be voiced in everyday life in the United States: the president of a distinguished university, writing a letter to the *Times,* belittling the study of African civilizations; the television network that promoted its show on the Vatican art with the boast that this art represented "the finest achievements of the human spirit." A modern up-tempo state of complex rhythms that depends upon contacts with an international community can no longer behave as if it dwelled in a "Zion Wilderness" surrounded by beasts and pagans.

13   When I heard a schoolteacher warn the other night about the invasion of the American educational system by foreign curriculums, I wanted to yell at the television set, "Lady, they're already here." It has already begun because the world is here. The world has been arriving at these shores for at least ten thousand years from Europe, Africa, and Asia. In the late nineteenth and early twentieth centuries, large numbers of Europeans arrived, adding their cultures to those of the European, African, and Asian

settlers who were already here, and recently millions have been entering the country from South America and the Caribbean, making Yale Professor Bob Thompson's bouillabaisse richer and thicker.

One of our most visionary politicians said that he envisioned a time when the United States could become the brain of the world, by which he meant the repository of all of the latest advanced information systems. I thought of that remark when an enterprising poet friend of mine called to say that he had just sold a poem to a computer magazine and that the editors were delighted to get it because they didn't carry fiction or poetry. Is that the kind of world we desire? A humdrum homogenous world of all brains but no heart, no fiction, no poetry; a world of robots with human attendants bereft of imagination, of culture? Or does North America deserve a more exciting destiny? To become a place where the cultures of the world crisscross. This is possible because the United States is unique in the world. The world is here. 14

RESPONDING TO THE READING

FREEWRITING

Practice 13e. Look up the word *bouillabaisse* in a dictionary. Why do you think Reed prefers that term to the often-used *melting pot* as a description of American diversity?

BUILDING YOUR VOCABULARY

monocultural (3)	cubists (5)	archetypal (8)	ornate (9)
ostracism (3)	monolithic (5)	monoculturist (8)	razed (9)
Yoruban (3)	dissidents (6)	ingenuity (9)	meticulous (11)
bouillabaisse (5)	Tsarist (6)	lecterns (9)	

QUESTIONS FOR DISCUSSION

1. Write an outline of the main ideas in "America: The Multinational Society." What patterns does Reed use to organize his ideas? What are the strengths or drawbacks in this arrangement?
2. What have you learned in school about the "Puritan legacy"? How does your study of the Puritans compare with the information Reed provides about them in paragraphs 9, 10, and 11? What does Reed's discussion of the Puritans add to his argument?
3. What is Reed's position on the conflict between cultures portrayed in the media? What evidence does he offer as support for that position? Is it convincing?
4. Donald Kagan, president of Yale University, has argued that "It is necessary to place Western civilization and the culture to which it has given rise at the center of our studies, and we fail to do so at the peril of our students, country and the hopes for a democratic, liberal society." How might Reed respond to Kagan's concern?

TOPICS FOR WRITING

Topic 1. Reread Ishmael Reed's explanation of the term *American.* Then write your own definition of what it means to be an American.

Topic 2. Write a paper in which you discuss examples of Reed's notion that "The world is here."

Topic 3. Write an essay in which you analyze the "image" of American culture as reflected in recent newspapers. As you prepare to write your paper, collect several newspapers from your library, a computer database, or a newsstand. Find articles and advertisements that project images of the "American" way of life. Summarize the specific details you find; then group your examples carefully and draw your own conclusions about them before you begin writing.

Topic 4. Write an essay in which you present support for or opposition to one of Reed's statements about American history in paragraphs 7 through 10. Check several historical sources to find evidence for your position.

WRITING BEFORE READING

Describe stories about immigrants that have been in the media lately.

The New Immigrants

Abigail McCarthy

Abigail McCarthy (1915–2001) was the wife of former senator and presidential candidate Eugene McCarthy. A writer for Commonweal *from 1975 to 1999, McCarthy wrote over seventy articles, some of which were published in a biweekly column offering political and religious commentary. She is also the author of two novels and biographies of Eleanor Roosevelt and Saint Teresa of Avila. In 1972, she published her best-known work, a memoir entitled* Private Faces/Public Places. *McCarthy wrote "The New Immigrants" in 1998 for the April 24 issue of* Commonweal.

1   As with any surge in immigration, the current one—the second largest in this century—seems alarming to some experts. They fear that the children of these immigrants will develop into an underclass, cut off from the mainstream by academic failure and an inability to speak English. Nothing could be further from the truth.

2   A very interesting, recently published four-year study by sociologists Ruben Rumbaut of Michigan State University and Alejandro Portest of Princeton University indicates that, despite the doubts of some newcomers themselves, the future of these immigrants' children is bright. The study shows that the 13.7 million children of immigrants have higher grades and sharply lower dropout rates than other American

children. Although more than half have experienced discrimination, a larger majority said that the United States was the best country in which to live. Overwhelmingly they prefer English to the native languages of their parents. The study serves to assure us that the country is enriched by the latest immigrant wave.

Who are these immigrants? What countries did they leave? I gave little thought to that until I was thrown into intimate contact with many—first in the hospital, then in a rehabilitation center. They throng the field of health professionals—most still on the lowest rung of the career ladder, but a majority working toward fuller degrees. Clearly they fill a need in a country whose population swells as age advances. 3

Without exception, those I came to know were an achieving and hard-working lot. There was Freh, born in Ethiopia, fine-featured as most Ethiopians are, and a registered nurse. She had come as a child with her parents and was educated at the University of Southern Illinois. There were a veritable corps of licensed nursing assistants— soft-voiced and smiling Rhadika and Bilhibai from south India; Juliet, Lesford, and Linda from Jamaica; another Linda from Grenada; Clara from Sierra Leone; Charito from the Philippines; Pius and Christopher obviously from a Catholic missionary enclave in Cameroon; and from South Africa a gentle woman bearing a famous name, Nono Buthelezi, niece of the South African cabinet member who was once a rival of Mandela. 4

Like other immigrants in other times, some of the newcomers yearn for their countries of origin and plan to return. Nono speaks lyrically about the region around Durban and lists the flowers and fruit trees there like a litany. She and her husband alternate semesters—one goes to the university; the other works. When they finally graduate they will go back to South Africa. ("It is not so nice here," says Nono. "It is a hard place to raise children." To our shame, this is true of inner-city Washington. "And we can help our country.") Linda from Grenada and her husband also plan to return once they have their degrees. "It is nice at home, but not many jobs," Linda explains. "If we are educated, there are jobs for us." 5

On the other hand, many of these prospective citizens are enthusiastic about this country and the opportunities it offers them. Lesford tells of working three jobs and bringing up his three children alone after his wife left him. He is proud of his son in the Air Force and his other two children in school. He managed to buy a house in neighboring Prince George's County and to make a secure home for his children. But he hasn't stopped there. He gives a lot of time to helping others. He has a collection of musical instruments—some peculiar to the Caribbean—and on weekends gathers in children of less-fortunate friends to give them instrument lessons. He builds their self-esteem by finding places for them to perform—one of them entertaining the patients in the hospital where he works. In addition, he preaches in his small house church. He loves his adopted country and has only scorn for those who complain that they aren't given enough by our government. "I say to these American guys—you don't know—you just don't know!" 6

Pius from Cameroon, the most compassionate and kind of nurses, has taken to other American skills with alacrity. He reported a happy weekend working on the brakes of his car—"saved maybe $200," he says with satisfaction. He also spends many hours with his computer and has become an expert in computer graphics. He delights in 7 creating greeting cards for special occasions for his colleagues and patients. The only bachelor among the group, he says, "I'm looking, I'm looking." It goes without saying that when he finds the wife he seeks he will be a kind and responsible husband and father, and his family will be an example of "family values," albeit perhaps very different in aspect from the mental picture of those so quick to tout these values.

8   The new immigrants also have their dreams. Lesford rightly sees his life story as remarkable and has hopes of writing and publishing a book to inspire others. Juliet's dream is more modest. She was left behind in Jamaica when her mother and her mother's second family moved to this country and remembers her first thirteen years with her great-grandmother. That remarkable lady lived to be 111 and even as a centenarian gave Juliet a careful upbringing. "Because of her I love old people," says Juliet. "Some day I would like to have a house big enough to take in four or five older people and take care of them. I have worked in nursing homes and there are so many people who shouldn't be there but have nowhere else to go." As she awaits the fulfillment of this dream, Juliet has taken in her godmother, a former teacher of nursing who can no longer work. In turn, the godmother supervises Juliet's two sons and helps them with their manners and homework.

9   Some of these immigrants have survived harsh conditions that Americans might think of as causing lasting trauma. Families were often separated as one member or the other made the quota and worked to make a place here for the others. Clara speaks with pride of the self-possession of her youngest son who was left behind in Sierra Leone. When he was six and she sent for him, he made the journey here alone. (He refused to leave the plane until the attendants put his passport in his hand.) He has coped successfully with great changes in his life—getting to know the mother he had never seen and his stepfather, and going to a school where initially he did not know the language. The waiting and separation of his first years have left no lasting mark.

10   One of the nursing assistants had a far worse experience. Moved from family to family while she waited for her mother to send for her, she was attacked twice—once by the father in one household and once by the son in another. In still another she was beaten so badly by the woman of the house that her face bore marks for months. Mature now and caring for others, she speaks calmly of what she has endured. "You just hope and wait," she said.

11   Endurance, resilience, industry, good humor, and a cheery hopefulness—these were the marks of the new immigrants I came to know. Admittedly they worked in an environment where they were made to feel valuable members of a team—not always the case. ("At the first hospital where I worked," said Rhadika, "I was always a foreigner.") When welcomed they are quick to adapt to, and to love our common country, to which they bring a new energy.

RESPONDING TO THE READING

FREEWRITING

Practice 13f. Summarize the profile of immigrants that McCarthy's examples convey.

litany (5)   albeit (7)   centenarian (8)
alacrity (7)   tout (7)

QUESTIONS FOR DISCUSSION

1. What is McCarthy's purpose for writing "The New Immigrants"?
2. What strategies for writing does McCarthy rely on to support her position? Which of her discussions do you find most and/or least convincing? Explain your answer.
3. What is the effect of listing the names and origins of the twelve health care workers in paragraph 4? How does this list contribute to her argument?

TOPICS FOR WRITING

Topic 1. After reading "The New Immigrants" and "The Immigrants: How They Are Helping to Revitalize the U.S. Economy" (pages 183–189), write a paper discussing how the personal and statistical information in these articles completes the reader's picture of immigrants' contributions to this culture.

Topic 2. Conduct research to identify a controversial issue surrounding immigration. Write an essay in which you evaluate major arguments on each side of the controversy. You may wish to use information in "The Immigrants: How They Are Helping to Revitalize the U.S. Economy" (pages 183–189).

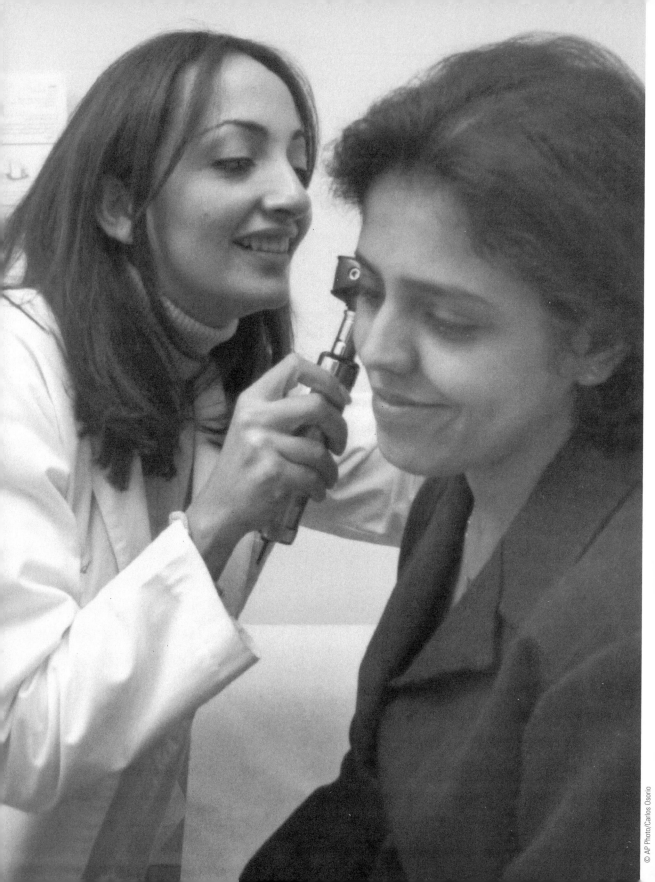

Examining
Stereotypes

CHAPTER
14

The authors whose work appears in this chapter
expose the psychology behind stereotypical notions
of particular groups of people and explore the
limitations that people who stereotype others place
on themselves. Robert L. Heilbroner discusses the
origin of a few stereotypes, examines problems
stereotypical thinking can cause, and suggests ways ·
to avoid stereotyping others. Judith Ortiz Cofer writes
a personal commentary on the media-created myths
about Latin women. Coauthors Laila Al-Marayati and
Semeen Issa address common misunderstandings
about Islam, particularly those concerning women
who wear head coverings.

*Stereotypes are a kind of gossip about
the world, a gossip that makes us
prejudge people before we ever lay
eyes on them.*
   —Robert L. Heilbroner

*My goal is to try to replace the old
stereotypes with a much more
interesting set of realities.*
   —Judith Ortiz Cofer

Do you consider yourself susceptible to stereotypical thinking? What examples can you think of that illustrate your open-mindedness or susceptibility to stereotypes?

Don't Let Stereotypes Warp Your Judgments

Robert L. Heilbroner

Robert L. Heilbroner (1919–2005) was born in New York City. He graduated from Harvard University in 1936 and attended classes at the New School for Social Research, where he studied with Adolph Lowe, one of the foremost economists of his day. He was professor of economics at the New School for Social Research for fifty years. Heilbroner is the author of over thirty books on economic theory and history, including The Worldly Philosophers *(1954), a best-selling economics textbook,* The Future as History *(1960),* The Nature and Logic of Capitalism *(1985),* The Crisis of Vision in Modern Economic Thought *(1995), and* The Economic Transformation of America since 1865 *(1997). In his essay "Don't Let Stereotypes Warp Your Judgments," published in* Think Magazine *in 1961, Heilbroner discusses the reasons why we cling to stereotypes and what we can do to change our stereotypical ways of thinking.*

1 Is a girl called Gloria apt to be better-looking than one called Bertha? Are criminals more likely to be dark than blond? Can you tell a good deal about someone's personality from hearing his voice briefly over the phone? Can a person's nationality be pretty accurately guessed from his photograph? Does the fact that someone wears glasses imply that he is intelligent?

2 The answer to all these questions is obviously, "No."

3 Yet, from all the evidence at hand, most of us believe these things. Ask any college boy if he'd rather take his chances with a Gloria or a Bertha, or ask a college girl if she'd rather blind-date a Richard or a Cuthbert. In fact, you don't have to ask: college students in questionnaires have revealed that names conjure up the same images in their minds as they do in yours—and for as little reason.

4 Look into the favorite suspects of persons who report "suspicious characters" and you will find a large percentage of them to be "swarthy" or "dark and foreign-looking"—despite the testimony of criminologists that criminals do *not* tend to be dark, foreign or "wild-eyed." Delve into the main asset of a telephone stock swindler and you will find it to be a marvelously confidence-inspiring telephone "personality." And whereas we all think we know what an Italian or a Swede looks like, it is the sad fact that when a group of Nebraska students sought to match faces and nationalities of 15 European countries, they were scored wrong in 93 percent of their identifications. Finally, for all the fact that horn-rimmed glasses have now become the standard television sign of an "intellectual," optometrists know that the main thing that distinguishes people with glasses is just bad eyes.

Stereotypes are a kind of gossip about the world, a gossip that makes us prejudge   5
people before we ever lay eyes on them. Hence it is not surprising that stereotypes have
something to do with the dark world of prejudice. Explore most prejudices (note that the
word means prejudgment) and you will find a cruel stereotype at the core of each one.

For it is the extraordinary fact that once we have typecast the world, we tend to see   6
people in terms of our standardized pictures. In another demonstration of the power of
stereotypes to affect our vision, a number of Columbia and Barnard students were shown
30 photographs of pretty but unidentified girls, and asked to rate each in terms of
"general liking," "intelligence," "beauty" and so on. Two months later, the same group were
shown the same photographs, this time with fictitious Irish, Italian, Jewish and "American"
names attached to the pictures. Right away the ratings changed. Faces which were now
seen as representing a national group went down in looks and still farther down in lika-
bility, while the "American" girls suddenly looked decidedly prettier and nicer.

Why is it that we stereotype the world in such irrational and harmful fashion? In   7
part, we begin to type-cast people in our childhood years. Early in life, as every parent
whose child has watched a TV Western knows, we learn to spot the Good Guys from the
Bad Guys. Some years ago, a social psychologist showed very clearly how powerful
these stereotypes of childhood vision are. He secretly asked the most popular youngsters in an elementary school to make errors in their morning gym exercises.
Afterwards, he asked the class if anyone had noticed any mistakes during gym period.
Oh, yes, said the children. But it was the *unpopular* members of the class—the "bad
guys"—they remembered as being out of step.

We not only grow up with standardized pictures forming inside of us, but as grown-   8
ups we are constantly having them thrust upon us. Some of them, like the half-joking,
half-serious stereotypes of mothers-in-law, or country yokels, or psychiatrists, are
dinned into us by the stock jokes we hear and repeat. In fact, without such stereotypes,
there would be a lot fewer jokes. Still other stereotypes are perpetuated by the advertisements we read, the movies we see, the books we read.

And finally, we tend to stereotype because it helps us make sense out of a highly   9
confusing world, a world which William James once described as "one great, blooming,
buzzing confusion." It is a curious fact that if we don't *know* what we're looking at, we
are often quite literally unable to *see* what we're looking at. People who recover their
sight after a lifetime of blindness actually cannot at first tell a triangle from a square.
A visitor to a factory sees only noisy chaos where the superintendent sees a perfectly
synchronized flow of work. As Walter Lippmann has said, "For the most part we do not
first see, and then define; we define first, and then we see."

Stereotypes are one way in which we "define" the world in order to see it. They   10
classify the infinite variety of human beings into a convenient handful of "types"
towards whom we learn to act in stereotyped fashion. Life would be a wearing process
if we had to start from scratch with each and every human contact. Stereotypes econo-
mize on our mental effort by covering up the blooming, buzzing confusion with big rec-
ognizable cutouts. They save us the "trouble" of finding out what the world is like—they
give it its accustomed look.

Don't Let Stereotypes Warp Your Judgments   Robert L. Heilbroner   **373**

11   Thus the trouble is that stereotypes make us mentally lazy. As S. I. Hayakawa, the authority on semantics, has written: "The danger of stereotypes lies not in their existence, but in the fact that they become for all people some of the time, and for some people all the time, *substitutes for observation.*" Worse yet, stereotypes get in the way of our judgment, even when we do observe the world. Someone who has formed rigid preconceptions of all Latins as "excitable," or all teenagers as "wild," doesn't alter his point of view when he meets a calm and deliberate Genoese, or a serious-minded high school student. He brushes them aside as "exceptions that prove the rule." And, of course, if he meets someone true to type, he stands triumphantly vindicated. "They're all like that," he proclaims, having encountered an excited Latin, an ill-behaved adolescent.

12   Hence, quite aside from the injustice which stereotypes do to others, they impoverish ourselves. A person who lumps the world into simple categories, who type-casts all labor leaders as "racketeers," all businessmen as "reactionaries," all Harvard men as "snobs," and all Frenchmen as "sexy," is in danger of becoming a stereotype himself. He loses his capacity to be himself—which is to say, to see the world in his own absolutely unique, inimitable and independent fashion.

13   Instead, he votes for the man who fits his standardized picture of what a candidate "should" look like or sound like, buys the goods that someone in his "situation" in life "should" own, lives the life that others define for him. The mark of the stereotypical person is that he never surprises us, that we do indeed have him "typed." And no one fits this strait-jacket so perfectly as someone whose opinions about *other people* are fixed and inflexible.

14   Impoverishing as they are, stereotypes are not easy to get rid of. The world we type-cast may be no better than a Grade B movie, but at least we know what to expect of our stock characters. When we let them act for themselves in the strangely unpredictable way that people do act, who knows but that many of our fondest convictions will be proved wrong?

15   Nor do we suddenly drop our standardized pictures for a blinding vision of the Truth. Sharp swings of ideas about people often just substitute one stereotype for another. The true process of change is a slow one that adds bits and pieces of reality to the pictures in our heads, until gradually they take on some of the blurriness of life itself. Little by little, we learn not that Jews and Negroes and Catholics and Puerto Ricans are "just like everybody else"—for that, too, is a stereotype—but that each and every one of them is unique, special, different and individual. Often we do not even know that we have let a stereotype lapse until we hear someone saying, "all so-and-so's are like such-and-such," and we hear ourselves saying, "Well—maybe."

16   Can we speed the process along? Of course we can.

17   First, we can become *aware* of the standardized pictures in our heads, in other people's heads, in the world around us.

18   Second, we can become suspicious of all judgments that we allow exceptions to "prove." There is no more chastening thought than that in the vast intellectual adventure of science, it takes but one tiny exception to topple a whole edifice of ideas.

Third, we can learn to be chary of generalizations about people. As F. Scott 19
Fitzgerald once wrote: "Begin with an individual, and before you know it you have created a type; begin with a type, and you find you have created—nothing."

Most of the time, when we type-cast the world, we are not in fact generalizing 20
about people at all. We are only revealing the embarrassing facts about the pictures that hang in the gallery of stereotypes in our own heads.

RESPONDING TO THE READING

FREEWRITING

Practice 14a. Freewrite about ways that Heilbroner's essay prompts you to reexamine your own assumptions about other people.

Practice 14b. Describe an instance when someone misjudged you because of a bias or stereotype.

BUILDING YOUR VOCABULARY

standardized (6)	synchronized (9)	chastening (18)
fictitious (6)	semantics (11)	topple (18)
type-cast (7)	racketeers (12)	edifice (18)
dinned (8)		

QUESTIONS FOR DISCUSSION

1. In the first six paragraphs of his essay, Heilbroner cites several surveys that illustrate college students' stereotypical images of people. Why do you think he chose this group to illustrate the pervasiveness of stereotyping?
2. In paragraph 5, Heilbroner defines *stereotypes* and *prejudice*. He expands his definition of *stereotypes* in paragraphs 9 and 10. How are the two terms related?
3. Summarize the causes of stereotyping according to Heilbroner. Which seem most important causes? Are there other causes he might have mentioned?
4. Heilbroner claims that "if we don't *know* what we're looking at, we are often quite literally unable to *see* what we're looking at." What does he mean by this comment? Why is this observation an important part of his argument?
5. According to Heilbroner, what are some of the effects of seeing people in terms of stereotypes? What is the most serious consequence of stereotyping others?
6. What does Heilbroner think can be done about our tendency to stereotype others? Are his suggestions reasonable? Can you add your own advice to his list?

TOPICS FOR WRITING

Topic 1. Heilbroner organizes the body of his essay into distinct groups of paragraphs, each with its own point. Take a few minutes to section off his essay for yourself. Then write a short summary of the main ideas in the essay. Your summary should contain no more than one sentence for each section.

Topic 2. In "Don't Let Stereotypes Warp Your Judgments," Robert Heilbroner describes stereotypes as "a kind of gossip about the world, a gossip that makes us prejudge people before we ever lay eyes on them." Write an essay in which you describe a time when you felt you were misunderstood because of a standardized or general idea people had about who you were or what you were supposed to be. Explain what, if anything, you did to change this mistaken view.

Topic 3. Write an essay about a time when you misjudged another person and later changed your mind about him or her.

Topic 4. The essays by Brent Staples (pages 343–346), Judith Ortiz Cofer (pages 376–380), Lindsy Van Gelder (pages 340–342), and Laila Al-Marayati and Semeen Issa (pages 381–384) address unpleasant stereotypes about African American males, Latinas, gay women, and Muslim women. Write an essay in which you explain how examples of stereotypical thinking from two of these essays illustrate Heilbroner's theory about the standardized thinking that produces such prejudices.

WRITING BEFORE READING

Describe a time when you felt insulted or offended in some way.

The Myth of the Latin Woman: I Just Met a Girl Named María

Judith Ortiz Cofer

Judith Ortiz Cofer was born in Puerto Rico in 1952 and grew up in New Jersey. She is Regents' and Franklin Professor of English and creative writing at the University of Georgia. Cofer has written fourteen books, including several novels, fiction for young adults, volumes of poetry, and collections of essays. Her novel, The Line of the Sun *(1989), was nominated for a Pulitzer Prize. Other works include* Woman in Front of the Sun: On Becoming A Writer *(2000),* The Meaning of Consuelo *(2003), and* Call Me Maria *(2004). The following selection is a shorter version of an essay that appeared in* The Latin Deli *(1993), an award-winning collection of poetry and prose. In "The Myth of the Latin Woman: I Just Met a Girl Named María," Cofer describes stereotypes associated with Latin women and examines the misconceptions about Hispanic culture on which they are based.*

On a bus trip to London from Oxford University where I was earning some graduate credits one summer, a young man, obviously fresh from a pub, spotted me and as if struck by inspiration went down on his knees in the aisle. With both hands over his heart he broke into an Irish tenor's rendition of "María" from *West Side Story*. My politely amused fellow passengers gave his lovely voice the round of gentle applause it deserved. Though I was not quite as amused, I managed my version of an English smile: no show of teeth, no extreme contortions of the facial muscles—I was at this time of my life practicing reserve and cool. Oh, that British control, how I coveted it. But "María" had followed me to London, reminding me of a prime fact of my life: you can leave the island, master the English language, and travel as far as you can, but if you are a Latina, especially one like me who so obviously belongs to Rita Moreno's gene pool, the island travels with you.

This is sometimes a very good thing—it may win you that extra minute of someone's attention. But with some people, the same things can make *you* an island—not a tropical paradise but an Alcatraz, a place nobody wants to visit. As a Puerto Rican girl living in the United States and wanting like most children to "belong," I resented the stereotype that my Hispanic appearance called forth from many people I met.

Growing up in a large urban center in New Jersey during the 1960s, I suffered from what I think of as "cultural schizophrenia." Our life was designed by my parents as a microcosm of their *casas* on the island. We spoke in Spanish, ate Puerto Rican food bought at the *bodega,* and practiced strict Catholicism at a church that allotted us a one-hour slot each week for mass, performed in Spanish by a Chinese priest trained as a missionary for Latin America.

As a girl I was kept under strict surveillance by my parents, since my virtue and modesty were, by their cultural equations, the same as their honor. As a teenager I was lectured constantly on how to behave as a proper *señorita*. But it was a conflicting message I received, since the Puerto Rican mothers also encouraged their daughters to look and act like women and to dress in clothes our Anglo friends and their mothers found too "mature" and flashy. The difference was, and is, cultural; yet I often felt humiliated when I appeared at an American friend's party wearing a dress more suitable to a semi-formal than to a playroom birthday celebration. At Puerto Rican festivities, neither the music nor the colors we wore could be too loud.

I remember Career Day in our high school, when teachers told us to come dressed as if for a job interview. It quickly became obvious that to the Puerto Rican girls "dressing up" meant wearing their mother's ornate jewelry and clothing, more appropriate (by mainstream standards) for the company Christmas party than as daily office attire. That morning I had agonized in front of my closet, trying to figure out what a "career girl" would wear. I knew how to dress for school (at the Catholic school I attended, we all wore uniforms), I knew how to dress for Sunday mass, and I knew what dresses to wear for parties at my relatives' homes. Though I do not recall the precise details of my Career Day outfit, it must have been a composite of these choices. But I remember a comment my friend (an Italian American) made in later years that coalesced my impressions of that day. She said that at the business school she was attending, the Puerto

Rican girls always stood out for wearing "everything at once." She meant, of course, too much jewelry, too many accessories. On that day at school we were simply made the negative models by the nuns, who were themselves not credible fashion experts to any of us. But it was painfully obvious to me that to the others, in their tailored skirts and silk blouses, we must have seemed "hopeless" and "vulgar." Though I now know that most adolescents feel out of step much of the time, I also know that for the Puerto Rican girls of my generation that sense was intensified. The way our teachers and classmates looked at us that day in school was just a taste of the cultural clash that awaited us in the real world, where prospective employers and men on the street would often misinterpret our tight skirts and jingling bracelets as a "come-on." ·

6   Mixed cultural signals have perpetuated certain stereotypes—for example, that of the Hispanic woman as the "hot tamale" or sexual firebrand. It is a one-dimensional view that the media have found easy to promote. In their special vocabulary, advertisers have designated "sizzling" and "smoldering" as the adjectives of choice for describing not only the foods but also the women of Latin America. From conversations in my house I recall hearing about the harassment that Puerto Rican women endured in factories where the "boss-men" talked to them as if sexual innuendo was all they understood, and worse, often gave them the choice of submitting to their advances or being fired.

7   It is custom, however, not chromosomes, that leads us to choose scarlet over pale pink. As young girls, it was our mothers who influenced our decisions about clothes and colors—mothers who had grown up on a tropical island where the natural environment was a riot of primary colors, where showing your skin was one way to keep cool as well as to look sexy. Most important of all, on the island, women perhaps felt freer to dress and move more provocatively since, in most cases, they were protected by the traditions, mores, and laws of a Spanish/Catholic system of morality and machismo whose main rule was *You may look at my sister, but if you touch her I will kill you.* The extended family and church structure could provide a young woman with a circle of safety in her small pueblo on the island; if a man "wronged" a girl, everyone would close in to save her family honor.

8   My mother has told me about dressing in her best party clothes on Saturday nights and going to the town's plaza to promenade with her girlfriends in front of the boys they liked. The males were thus given an opportunity to admire the women and to express their admiration in the form of *piropos:* erotically charged street poems they composed on the spot. (I have myself been subjected to a few *piropos* while visiting the island, and they can be outrageous, although custom dictates that they never cross into obscenity.) This ritual, as I understand it, also entails a show of studied indifference on the woman's part; if she is "decent," she must not acknowledge the man's impassioned words. So I do understand how things can be lost in translation. When a Puerto Rican girl dressed in her idea of what is attractive meets a man from the mainstream culture who has been trained to react to certain types of clothing as a sexual signal, a clash is likely to take place. I remember the boy who took me to my first formal dance leaning over to plant a sloppy, over-eager kiss painfully on my mouth; when I didn't respond with sufficient passion, he remarked resentfully, "I thought you Latin girls were supposed to mature early," as if I were expected to *ripen* like a fruit or vegetable, not just grow into womanhood like other girls.

It is surprising to my professional friends that even today some people, including those who should know better, still put others "in their place." It happened to me most recently during a stay at a classy metropolitan hotel favored by young professional couples for weddings. Late one evening after the theater, as I walked toward my room with a colleague (a woman with whom I was coordinating an arts program), a middle-aged man in a tuxedo, with a young girl in satin and lace on his arm, stepped directly into our path. With his champagne glass extended toward me, he exclaimed "Evita!"[1]

Our way blocked, my companion and I listened as the man half-recited, half-bellowed "Don't Cry for Me, Argentina." When he finished, the young girl said: "How about a round of applause for my daddy?" We complied, hoping this would bring the silly spectacle to a close. I was becoming aware that our little group was attracting the attention of the other guests. "Daddy" must have perceived this too, and he once more barred the way as we tried to walk past him. He began to shout-sing a ditty to the tune of "La Bamba"—except the lyrics were about a girl named María whose exploits rhymed with her name and gonorrhea. The girl kept saying "Oh, Daddy" and looking at me with pleading eyes. She wanted me to laugh along with the others. My companion and I stood silently waiting for the man to end his offensive song. When he finished, I looked not at him but at his daughter. I advised her calmly never to ask her father what he had done in the army. Then I walked between them and to my room. My friend complimented me on my cool handling of the situation, but I confessed that I had really wanted to push the jerk into the swimming pool. This same man—probably a corporate executive, well-educated, even worldly by most standards—would not have been likely to regale an Anglo woman with a dirty song in public. He might have checked his impulse by assuming that she could be somebody's wife or mother, or at least *somebody* who might take offense. But, to him, I was just an Evita or a María: merely a character in his cartoon-populated universe.

Another facet of the myth of the Latin woman in the United States is the menial, the domestic—María the housemaid or countergirl. It's true that work as domestics, as waitresses, and in factories is all that's available to women with little English and few skills. But the myth of the Hispanic menial—the funny maid, mispronouncing words and cooking up a spicy storm in a shiny California kitchen—has been perpetuated by the media in the same way that "Mammy" from *Gone with the Wind* became America's idea of the black woman for generations. Since I do not wear my diplomas around my neck for all to see, I have on occasion been sent to that "kitchen" where some think I obviously belong.

One incident has stayed with me, though I recognize it as a minor offense. My first public poetry reading took place in Miami, at a restaurant where a luncheon was being held before the event. I was nervous and excited as I walked in with notebook in hand. An older woman motioned me to her table, and thinking (foolish me) that she wanted me to autograph a copy of my newly published slender volume of verse, I went over. She ordered a cup of coffee from me, assuming that I was the waitress. (Easy enough to mistake my poems for menus, I suppose.) I know it wasn't an intentional act of cruelty. Yet of all the good things that happened later, I remember that scene most clearly,

---

[1] A musical about Eva Duarte de Perón, the former first lady of Argentina.

because it reminded me of what I had to overcome before anyone would take me seriously. In retrospect I understand that my anger gave my reading fire. In fact, I have almost always taken any doubt in my abilities as a challenge, the result most often being the satisfaction of winning a convert, of seeing the cold, appraising eyes warm to my words, the body language change, the smile that indicates I have opened some avenue for communication. So that day as I read, I looked directly at that woman. Her lowered eyes told me she was embarrassed at her faux pas, and when I willed her to look up at me, she graciously allowed me to punish her with my full attention. We shook hands at the end of the reading and I never saw her again. She has probably forgotten the entire incident, but maybe not.

13   Yet I am one of the lucky ones. There are thousands of Latinas without the privilege of an education or the entrees into society that I have. For them life is a constant struggle against the misconceptions perpetuated by the myth of the Latina. My goal is to try to replace the old stereotypes with a much more interesting set of realities. Every time I give a reading, I hope the stories I tell, the dreams and fears I examine in my work, can achieve some universal truth that will get my audience past the particulars of my skin color, my accent, or my clothes.

14   I once wrote a poem in which I called all Latinas "God's brown daughters." This poem is really a prayer of sorts, offered upward, but also, through the human-to-human channel of art, outward. It is a prayer for communication and for respect. In it, Latin women pray "in Spanish to an Anglo God/with a Jewish heritage," and they are "fervently hoping/that if not omnipotent,/at least He be bilingual."

RESPONDING TO THE READING

FREEWRITING

Practice 14c. Freewrite about media stereotypes that you remember about Asians, African Americans, women, white southerners, the elderly, or some other group of people.

Practice 14d. What problems might arise for people who are the targets of these stereotypical images?

BUILDING YOUR VOCABULARY

contortions (1)	surveillance (4)	innuendo (6)	menial (11)
coveted (1)	coalesced (5)	provocatively (7)	faux pas (12)

QUESTIONS FOR DISCUSSION

1. What does Judith Ortiz Cofer find disagreeable about having strangers sing "María" to her (paragraph 1)? Why does she include the description of a second man who insisted on singing to her (paragraph 10) and the woman who tried to order coffee from her (paragraph 12)? What do these three incidents represent for her?

2. Cofer says that she suffered from "cultural schizophrenia" as a Puerto Rican growing up in New Jersey. Explain what she means by this phrase, and give a few examples of the cultural contradictions she experienced.
3. What, according to Cofer, are the media-created stereotypes of the Latin woman? What is the truth behind these misinterpretations?
4. Why does Cofer give poetry readings? What does she hope to communicate to her audience?

TOPICS FOR WRITING

Topic 1. Using Judith Ortiz Cofer's essay as a model, write an essay analyzing the myths or stereotypes attached to a particular ethnic group. Explain what the stereotypes are, how they are perpetuated, and how damaging they might be.

Topic 2. Judith Ortiz Cofer objects to the media's representations of Latin women as "the menial, the domestic." Write a paper evaluating the media's portrayal of women, the elderly, or individuals belonging to a particular ethnic group. Use examples from television programs, commercials, news stories, political cartoons, comic strips, or movies to support your ideas.

Topic 3. Cofer and other writers in this book—such as Brent Staples (pages 343–346), Lindsy Van Gelder (pages 340–342), and Laila Al-Marayati and Semeen Issa (pages 381–384)—discuss the problems they encounter when they are confronted with other people's ideas of who they are. Write an essay in which you analyze the frustrations as well as the dangers that a few of these authors describe in their essays.

Topic 4. Describe how Cofer's experience of "cultural schizophrenia," being in the United States but living a Puerto Rican life, compares with the experience of mixed or confused identity expressed in two or three of the following essays: Elizabeth Wong's "The Struggle to Be an All-American Girl" (pages 300–301), Caroline Hwang's "The Good Daughter" (pages 284–286), Richard Rodriguez's "Complexion" (pages 350–356), or Dympna Ugwu-Oju's "Pursuit of Happiness" (pages 358–360).

WRITING BEFORE READING

What images do you have of Muslim women? What are the sources for these images?

Muslim Women: An Identity Reduced to a Burka

Laila Al-Marayati and Semeen Issa

Dr. Laila Al-Marayati is a physician and a spokesperson for the Muslim Women's League. An obstetrician-gynecologist, Al-Marayati is director of Women's Health at Northeast Valley Health Corporation and clinical professor at the USC School of Medicine. She is also a lecturer and a writer whose work addresses basic women's rights in Islam, reproductive health and sexuality, stereotyping of Muslims, and violence against women. She organized the Muslim Women's League's efforts to help rape survivors from the war in Bosnia in 1993, and in 1995 she was a member of the U.S. delegation to the UN Conference on Women in Beijing. Former president Bill Clinton appointed Al-Marayati to the nine-person U.S. Commission on International Religious Freedom (1999–2001), and she was a member of the State Department's Advisory Committee on Religious Freedom Abroad.

Semeen Issa is founder and current president of the Muslim Women's League. She also helped establish the first Muslim women's soccer team in Southern California and originated the first Muslim Girls Sports Camp. The purpose of the camp, says Issa, is to ensure that "the girls learn athletic skills without feeling hindered by their conservative attire." A teacher in Arcadia, California, Issa coauthored the following essay in response to misconceptions among non-Muslims in the United States regarding the "veil" that is sometimes worn by Muslim women. The article first appeared in the Los Angeles Times, *January 20, 2002.*

1   A few years ago, someone from the Feminist Majority Foundation called the Muslim Women's League to ask if she could "borrow a burka" for a photo shoot the organization was doing to draw attention to the plight of women in Afghanistan under the Taliban. When we told her that we didn't have one, and that none of our Afghan friends did either, she expressed surprise, as if she'd assumed that all Muslim women keep burkas in their closets in case a militant Islamist comes to dinner. She didn't seem to understand that her assumption was the equivalent of assuming that every Latino has a Mexican sombrero in his/her closet.

2   We don't mean to make light of the suffering of our sisters in Afghanistan, but the burka was—and is—not their major focus of concern. Their priorities are more basic, like feeding their children, becoming literate and living free from violence. Nevertheless, recent articles in the Western media suggest the burka means everything to Muslim women because they routinely express bewilderment at the fact that all Afghan women didn't cast off their burkas when the Taliban was defeated. The Western press' obsession with the dress of Muslim women is not surprising, however, since the press tends to view Muslims, in general, simplistically.

3   Headlines in the mainstream media have reduced Muslim female identity to an article of clothing—"the veil." One is hard-pressed to find an article, book or film about women in Islam that doesn't have "veil" in the title: "Behind the Veil," "Beyond the Veil," "At the Drop of a Veil" and more. The use of the term borders on the absurd: Perhaps next will come "What Color Is Your Veil?" or "Rebel Without a Veil" or "Whose Veil Is It, Anyway?"

4   The word "veil" does not even have a universal meaning. In some cultures, it refers to a face-covering known as *niqab;* in others, to a simple head scarf, known as *hijab.* Other manifestations of "the veil" include all-encompassing outer garments like the ankle-length *abaya* from the Persian Gulf states, the *chador* in Iran or the *burka* in Afghanistan.

Like the differences in our clothing from one region to another, Muslim women are diverse. Stereotypical assumptions about Muslim women are as inaccurate as the assumption that all American women are personified by the bikini-clad cast of "Baywatch." Anyone who has spent time interacting with Muslims knows that, despite numerous obstacles, Muslim women are active, assertive and engaged in society. In Qatar, women make up the majority of graduate-school students. The Iranian parliament has more women members than the U.S. Senate. Throughout the world, many Muslim women are educated and professionally trained; they participate in public debates, are often catalysts for reform and champions for their own rights. At the same time, there is no denying that in many Muslim countries, dress has been used as a tool to wield power over women. 5

What doesn't penetrate Western consciousness, however, is that forced uncovering is also a tool of oppression. During the reign of Shah Mohammad Reza Pahlavi in Iran, wearing the veil was prohibited. As an expression of their opposition to his repressive regime, women who supported the 1979 Islamic Revolution marched in the street clothed in *chadors*. Many of them did not expect to have this "dress code" institutionalized by those who led the revolution and then took power in the new government. 6

In Turkey, the secular regime considers the head scarf a symbol of extremist elements that want to overthrow the government. Accordingly, women who wear any type of head-covering are banned from public office, government jobs and academia, including graduate school. Turkish women who believe the head-covering is a religious obligation are unfairly forced to give up public life or opportunities for higher education and career advancement. 7

Dress should not bar Muslim women from exercising their Islam-guaranteed rights, like the right to be educated, to earn a living and to move about safely in society. Unfortunately, some governments impose a strict dress code along with other restrictions, like limiting education for women, to appear "authentically Islamic." Such laws, in fact, are inconsistent with Islam. Nevertheless, these associations lead to the general perception that "behind the veil" lurk other, more insidious examples of the repression of women, and that wearing the veil somehow causes the social ills that plague Muslim women around the world. 8

Many Muslim men and women alike are subjugated by despotic, dictatorial regimes. Their lot in life is worsened by extreme poverty and illiteracy, two conditions that are not caused by Islam but are sometimes exploited in the name of religion. Helping Muslim women overcome their misery is a major task. The reconstruction of Muslim Afghanistan will be a test case for the Afghan people and for the international community dedicated to making Afghan society work for everyone. To some, Islam is the root cause of the problems faced by women in Afghanistan. But what is truly at fault is a misguided, narrow interpretation of Islam designed to serve a rigid patriarchal system. 9

Traditional Muslim populations will be more receptive to change that is based on Islamic principles of justice, as expressed in the Koran, than they will be to change that abandons religion altogether or confines it to private life. Muslim scholars and leaders who emphasize Islamic principles that support women's rights to education, health care, 10 marriage and divorce, equal pay for equal work and participation in public life could fill the vacuum now occupied by those who impose a vision of Islam that infringes on the rights of women.

11 Given the opportunity, Muslim women, like women everywhere, will become educated, pursue careers, strive to do what is best for their families and contribute positively according to their abilities. How they dress is irrelevant. It should be obvious that the critical element Muslim women need is freedom, especially the freedom to make choices that enable them to be independent agents of positive change. Choosing to dress modestly, including wearing a head scarf, should be as respected as choosing not to cover. Accusations that modestly dressed Muslim women are caving in to male-dominated understandings of Islam neglect the reality that most Muslim women who cover by choice do so out of subservience to God, not to any human being.

12 The worth of a woman—any woman—should not be determined by the length of her skirt, but by the dedication, knowledge and skills she brings to the task at hand.

RESPONDING TO THE READING

FREEWRITING

Practice 14e. Do some freewriting about what you learned about Muslim women from "Muslim Women: An Identity Reduced to a Burka."

BUILDING YOUR VOCABULARY

equivalent (1)	obsession (2)	insidious (8)	subjugated (9)
bewilderment (2)	catalysts (5)	despotic (9)	subservience (11)

QUESTIONS FOR DISCUSSION

1. How does the opening anecdote or short narrative introduce the reader to the authors' tone and purpose for writing?
2. Why do Al-Marayati and Issa offer examples of political and educational opportunities afforded to Muslim women in some Arab countries (paragraph 5)? How do these examples and comparisons with American women contribute to their argument?
3. What complexities about Islam and Islamic countries do the authors convey to their readers? Select passages that illustrate these complexities.
4. What changes do the authors hope to effect by writing this essay? Identify portions of their argument that support their view.

TOPICS FOR WRITING

Topic 1. Write an essay in which you assume the point of view of a conservative Muslim who values modesty and believes that wearing head coverings and long dresses protects women's modesty. Use this perspective to evaluate styles of clothing and images of women in the United States that you see on the street and in the American media.

Topic 2. The authors of "Muslim Women: An Identity Reduced to a Burka" argue that "How [Muslim women] dress is irrelevant." However, a court case in Florida in 2003 determined that a Muslim woman was required to be photographed without her *burka,* a covering that completely shrouds the body, if she wished to obtain a driver's license. Try to think of other times when a head covering might be inappropriate. Then write an essay that explains how a woman's clothing might be relevant or irrelevant to what she does.

Topic 3. Issa and Al-Marayati argue that forced covering and uncovering have both been used to oppress women in Muslim countries. Write an essay exploring ways in which clothing restrictions have impeded women's activities and political advancement in other areas of the world besides the Middle East.

Topic 4. In February 2004, President Jacques Chirac of France approved a ban on head coverings in public schools, a move considered by some critics as a direct affront to conservative Muslim women. Chirac and members of the French parliament reasoned that any form of religious dress is a violation of the law requiring a separation of church and state. Write an essay in which you examine the politics behind dress requirements such as these. What, for example, might be the political motivations behind the French ban on head coverings, the prohibitions that Al-Marayati and Issa describe as law under the former shah Mohammad Reza Pahlavi of Iran, or other restrictions that still exist in Turkey? What is the U.S. policy toward head coverings, and what is the political thinking behind this policy?

Topic 5. Do some research to find other essays and personal statements that explore the meaning of the "veil" for Muslim women. Write an essay in which you analyze the stereotypes and realities of the "veil."

Part IV
Guidelines for Writing a Research Paper

Planning, Researching, and Writing a Research Paper

CHAPTER

15

Learning to do research and write an essay is a valuable part of any college experience. Not only is a research paper required in many college classes, but the process of writing a research paper helps you develop skills you may find useful in the workplace.

Chapter 15 offers a step-by-step process to help you use information from sources to write a research paper. The chapter includes a definition of the research paper, strategies for scheduling time and finding a topic, ways to locate information, and techniques for taking notes and for writing an essay using information gathered from sources. Chapter 16 includes a guide to writing a bibliography and citing sources in your essay using the Modern Language Association's standards for writing a research paper.[1] The techniques you learn in Part IV of this textbook can be applied to research projects in your English classes.

---

[1] Other styles for documentation include the Chicago style, generally used in the humanities; the APA style developed by the American Psychological Association; and the CBE style put together by the Council of Biology Editors and adopted by writers in the physical and life sciences.

WHAT IS THE VALUE OF DOING RESEARCH?

Writing a research paper teaches you to locate, evaluate, paraphrase, and incorporate the words and ideas of others into your own text. In general, research involves getting data and information to make a particular point or offer an observation about the subject you are investigating. In a history class, for example, you might decide to evaluate the U.S. government's policy toward a particular group of Native Americans. A communications teacher might ask you to analyze the role the media played in shaping public opinion of the 2003 war in Iraq, the 1992 riots in Los Angeles, or another well-publicized event. At work you might be asked to research and compare the features of two software programs; or, as a produce buyer for a supermarket, you might be asked to evaluate prices, appearance, and freshness of products carried by several suppliers. Your research might involve personal interviews or phone calls as well as the retrieval of printed and online information.

While writing research papers can be challenging, it is also rewarding because you are broadening your knowledge of a subject and are being challenged by what you read. The authorities you consult introduce issues, problems, controversies, and various points of view that may be new to you. In addition, you become something of an expert on your topic because you are gathering information that no one else in the class, including the teacher, is likely to have.

The skills you practiced in Chapter 2 will help you read sources carefully to determine which contain useful information for your paper, and you can apply what you learned in that chapter about writing summaries when you paraphrase ideas from these sources. You will also learn to take notes, outline the main ideas for your paper, and organize information you have gathered from several sources into an organized, coherent essay. When you incorporate ideas from several writers, you are also learning to distinguish between your language and the words, ideas, and phrasing from the sources you are using.

WHAT IS A RESEARCH PAPER?

Despite its importance, the idea of doing research and writing a paper based on the information gathered from sources is a terrifying prospect for many students. But research papers are not fundamentally different from other papers you write in college. You still must narrow your topic, gather information, use a thesis and topic sentences to organize your paper, provide transitions between ideas, offer detailed support and analysis of information, write a convincing conclusion, and revise your essay for coherence and sentence errors. Moreover, as you develop your ideas, you are using writing strategies (describing, defining, classifying, process analysis, causal analysis, comparison/contrast, evaluating, and taking a stand) that are familiar to you from your work in Part II of this textbook.

There are, however, a few differences between a research paper and other writing assignments. First, the research paper is often longer than papers you are used to writing. The second difference has to do with the source of support for your ideas. For a topic that does not require research, you can rely on your own experiences and observations for evidence, but when you write a research paper, you gather information from outside sources such as interviews, essays in magazines and newspapers, and chapters in books, as well as articles available on databases, CD-ROMs, and websites. In other words, a research paper relies on information provided by other writers rather than relying exclusively on students' own ideas, observations, and experiences.

A third difference between the usual college paper and the research paper is that you must give credit to the sources whose information you are borrowing. Even if you rewrite the author's ideas in your own words, you must identify the source of those ideas. Chapter 16 includes examples of the Modern Language Association's guide for citing sources both in the body of your paper and in a list of works cited.

PROBLEMS TO AVOID WHEN WRITING RESEARCH PAPERS

The following list contains common problems that students face when they try to incorporate information from sources into their own essays. A careful reading of this list may help you avoid these pitfalls when you write your research paper.

1. Avoid writing a research paper that is little more than a summary of one or two sources. Maintain control of the focus and organization of your paper to avoid copying the structure and summarizing the ideas of a single source. If you are having difficulty finding sources, perhaps your topic is too narrow or not much has been written about it. In this case, you may need help redirecting the topic.
2. Papers that string quotations and paraphrased material together in large, undigested chunks lack the organization and analysis of a coherent, readable research paper. To avoid this problem, use quotes sparingly, and never cite a passage without carefully explaining its connection to the points you want to make. Source material should be "sandwiched" between the general points you want to make and the explanations that connect the paraphrased or quoted information to your points.
3. Do not use exact wording or ideas paraphrased from sources without citing them correctly in your text. Put quotation marks around exact wording, and reference all source materials, even if ideas are paraphrased. (See pages 399–401 for a discussion of plagiarism.)
4. Improper documentation shows that you have not taken enough time to record bibliographic information from your sources. Refer to examples of documentation in Chapter 16 as you write bibliography cards and compile a list of works cited for your paper.

WHAT IS YOUR JOB AS A RESEARCHER AND WRITER?

Students often ask how much of their research paper should come from sources and how much they should add of their own opinion and wording. In general, the writer's job is to provide the focus for the essay, the transitions between sources and sections of the paper, and analysis that explains how information in the sources supports the paper's thesis or argument. Roughly 40 to 60 percent of the writing in a research paper represents the student's original ideas and wording; the rest of the paper consists of quotations and paraphrasing from sources. Source material provides support for ideas in the research paper, and these sources must be identified or "cited" both in the text and in a list of works cited.

A successful research paper cannot be written in the last few days before the assignment is due. To avoid putting off researching and writing the paper until you are unable meet the deadline for submitting it, allow plenty of time to find information, take notes, write, and revise the paper. The amount of time you need to complete a research paper of modest length, roughly five to eight pages, depends on the complexity of your topic, the number of sources your instructor requires, and the class schedule. In general, plan to spend an hour or more most days over a four- to six-week period, depending on the length of the assignment and the number of weeks in a school term. A good researcher must have patience and flexibility. It may take a week or two to schedule an important interview or to find the articles you need for your paper. The first library you try, and perhaps the second, may not have the book or article you want, but don't get discouraged—call around, and have a list of several sources in case you cannot locate one or two.

SAMPLE RESEARCH SCHEDULE

The sample schedule given here allows six weeks for your research paper; the timeline can be adjusted to accommodate quarter and semester projects of varying lengths.

Choose a topic for your research paper. Complete a research planning sheet to determine your topic and audience, and to develop the question(s) you would like your research paper to answer (e.g., What are current immigrations laws, and what has been their effect?). Visit the library, consult databases available to you, and search the Internet for sources. Use your research question to eliminate irrelevant source material.	Week 1
Schedule and conduct interviews if appropriate. Once you have located sources and collected information relevant to your topic, use note cards or a hypertext format to paraphrase and quote information you think you might be able to use in your essay. If you change your focus, modify your original research question, and develop a thesis and topic ideas to support it. Your instructor may schedule an in-class workshop to give you practice writing source notes.	Weeks 2–3

Develop an outline for the paper and organize your notes in stacks according to the topic you'll discuss in each paragraph or section of your essay.	Week 3
Write your draft and revise it. You may be asked to exchange drafts with classmates in a peer review workshop.	Weeks 4–5
Submit the final paper. Your instructor may ask you to include source notes, a bibliography, and drafts of the paper.	Week 6

The sample research schedule gives you an idea of how much time you will need for each stage of the research paper. It is very important to give yourself at least two weeks to search for information because it takes a while to locate sources or set up interviews, and you will need time to read, take notes, and analyze the material you gather.

STEPS TO WRITING A RESEARCH PAPER

What follows is a discussion of steps that will help you write a successful essay.

STEP 1: CHOOSING A TOPIC AND DEVELOPING A FOCUS FOR THE PAPER

Some instructors prefer to assign research topics, or they may give you a choice of topics. In these cases, the teacher either determines or narrows the subject of your paper for you. In the instance where you need to make some choices about the subject of your paper, there are a few things to keep in mind.

Find a subject that means something to you because you will be working with it for a month or more. Try to avoid broad subjects or subjects that have been overused as research topics, such as capital punishment, gun control, or abortion unless you can focus on a particular event, a new law, or a recent discovery that will help you limit the scope of your research.

If you are having difficulty thinking of a subject, freewrite about issues that you might like to investigate, and ask your instructor for ideas about possible subjects that are within the scope of the assignment. If the assignment is to develop a topic of your own, the following questions might help you choose a manageable subject.

1. What are your hobbies, career goals, or special skills?
2. Is there a subject that interests you or that you already know something about?
3. What social problems, community issues, arts, sports, travel destinations, films, or other entertainment are important to you?
4. Have you written a paper whose subject might become a topic for research?
5. What interesting subjects have come up in your classes lately?
6. Has there been a story on the news that you would like to explore?

Once you settle on a subject, spend about an hour writing everything you know or have heard about it. Pick a few of the topics you came up with and use them to focus your initial search for information.

Coming up with a manageable topic helps you avoid the seemingly impossible task of sorting through dozens if not hundreds of sources, all of which seem relevant to a topic that is too broad to provide adequate direction for your research. If you do find yourself starting with a fairly broad topic, try to ask yourself questions to help you narrow the topic until you have something you can actually write about in the required number of pages. You might, for example, ask yourself, What questions do I want this paper to answer? What are possible ways I might discuss this topic? What aspect of this topic seems most interesting?

Here are a few examples of general ideas that became narrower, more focused topics.

Broad Topic	Better Focus	Strong Focus
Cultural traditions	Tradition in the Hmong community	Significance of quilt-making in the Hmong community
Censorship	Internet censorship	Reasons why material on the Internet should not be censored
History of body art	Tatooing in America	Tatooing—a legitimate form of self-expression

Once you have found a topic that you think might be narrow enough, start checking indices and databases. If your initial search shows that little has been written on your topic, try a slightly different approach, or go back to your list of possible topics and try again. You might also ask your instructor or a librarian to help you develop a new approach to the topic. It is normal to feel unsure about a topic at the beginning of this process, but you will gain confidence once you begin finding information you can use.

STEP 2: LOCATING SOURCES

In your experience as a student writer, you may have written a paper using notes you took during an interview. If so, you have experience with the most difficult part of research—gathering, sorting, and organizing information from a source. For your research project you will probably need to consult books, magazines or journal articles, and newspapers, as well as electronic sources such as CD-ROM databases, and articles or web pages published on the Internet. Videotapes, lecture notes, pamphlets, letters, or flyers distributed by an organization or agency may also provide valuable information.

Kinds of Sources

Witnesses. There are usually people around you who know something about your subject and are willing to be interviewed. If, for example, you are interested in explaining the value of having competitive sports on your college campus, you might interview the basketball coach, a few of the players, or fans who come to watch the games. If you want to write about the importance of recycling, you could interview a county employee who works in waste management. Perhaps a family member is a volunteer for the local AIDS foundation and could give you some of the information you need to write a paper about the origin, transmission, or progress of that disease.

Your Experience and Observations. If you have knowledge about your subject, you can include it in your paper. For instance, if you are writing a paper about the problems single parents may face and you have personal knowledge of those problems, consider including your observations as additional support for ideas you develop in the essay.

Authorities. These are generally experts who have conducted research themselves and whose work may provide reputable material for your topic. Information gathered from interviews, scholarly journals, books, and databases can provide important support for your essay.

Sources in Libraries. Before you attempt to find sources, go to your campus library or to one of the larger libraries in your area, and talk to a librarian. Librarians are undoubtedly the most important contacts you can make while writing a research paper because they are experts at locating sources. Before asking a librarian for help, narrow your topic as much as you can, and develop several questions that you want your paper to answer.

If your library has a computerized index, ask a librarian to help you locate books or articles on your topic. Many libraries subscribe to national newspaper and magazine indices like InfoTrac® College Edition or NEWSBANK. These programs can help you locate information quickly.

If you have found a source you would like to see but are having difficulty locating it in your library, ask about interlibrary loan, how it works, what, if anything, the service costs, and the time it usually takes to get materials.

Using the Internet. The Internet can be a valuable resource for students writing research papers. However, many of the sources you find on websites are unreliable because of the bias of their information or the lack of credible support for their arguments. To give you a variety of research experience, your instructor may ask you to use a mixture of sources—print as well as database and Internet sources—in your essay. In general, check the credentials of any author—a university affiliation and publication in a journal or magazine recognized in the author's field are signs of legitimacy, although not necessarily readability.

STEP 3: TAKING NOTES ON SOURCES

Once you have determined which sources are most likely to provide you with useable information for your paper, the next step is to paraphrase and quote material in a form that you will be able to use when you draft your paper. Be extremely careful to put quotation marks around any phrases taken directly from your source. Ideas that are not placed in quotes must be paraphrased by rewriting the author's ideas and phrasing in your own words. Both direct quotations as well as paraphrased versions of the writer's ideas must be documented properly in your text. What follows is an example of a paraphrased version of source material taken from an article entitled "Internet Censorship."

Original Text	Student's Paraphrase
It is important to remember that there's nothing available on the Internet that isn't available other places. Pornography, sexually explicit material, "dirty talk," and everything else those in favor of censoring the Internet fear is available in many local bookstores, through catalogs, and from other sources. Some of the material those in favor of censoring the Internet want to restrict are available in local libraries (Sagall 10).	Internet censorship will not be entirely useful because the items that people want censored—sexually graphic material in particular—are openly available to children in a number of places other than the Internet, including most bookstores, catalogs of various kinds, libraries, and even at home (Sagall 10).

Notice how paraphrasing condenses and focuses the information in the source. Moreover, if your source notes are well thought out and carefully written, you are actually writing the paper as you take notes. When you are ready to write a draft of your essay, you can arrange your note cards in stacks representing paragraphs or sections of your essay, and, with the addition of transitions and explanations, you can incorporate what you have written on the note cards into your research paper. The information in parentheses refers to the author of the article and the page number of the original text. This notation helps the reader find the full reference to the source on the essay's Works Cited page.

Keeping a Bibliography

Writing accurate, detailed bibliography cards makes it easier to cite sources properly. Use 3 × 5 cards or a hypertext format to record bibliographical information. The information you need will vary according to the type of source and how much information is available, but in general you will list the name of the author, the title of the article (in quotation marks), the title of the book, database, or website title or sponsor (underlined), publication information (city where published and publication company if the source is a book), and the date of publication. Write a separate bibliography card for each source. You will use the information on these cards when you write the list of works cited, a list of sources you actually use in your essay. This list appears on the last page of your research paper.

Sample Bibliography Card

Heins, Marjorie. "Screening Out Sex: Kids, Computers, and the New Censors." American Prospect. 39 Jul./Aug. 1998: 38–44.

See Chapter 16 for sample references for various kinds of source material to include on your bibliography cards.

Recording Information from Sources on Note Cards

Perhaps the most effective way to get control of source material is to write paraphrased information from your sources on note cards. Even students who are resistant to using note cards discover that this technique makes it easier to write their research paper than any other way of organizing information.

A systematic approach to recording information can save writers a lot of time and many hours of anxiety. To determine what information belongs on your note cards, evaluate each source for its relevance to your topic. Ask yourself whether the information will help you develop some aspect of your research question. If it doesn't, go on to the next source.

To keep track of what information came from which source, write the author's last name or abbreviated title at the top of each note card. If it takes more than one note card to record the information you need, number the cards and continue the author or title heading. Also, jot down the page number of the text where you got the information if page numbers are available. This information will go directly into the in-text citation as you write your paper—for example, "(Bannister 4)." See the discussion of how to document sources in your text in Chapter 16, page 410.

Restate or paraphrase the writer's ideas in your own words most of the time. Use exact wording occasionally, but try not to copy extensive passages from your sources. If you do, you are simply postponing the hard work of paraphrasing until you draft the essay. Paraphrasing also allows you to condense lengthy material, and it guarantees that you have understood the ideas in the source.

If you find direct quotations you would like to use in your paper, copy them carefully and put them in quotation marks. You must distinguish between your words and ideas, and those of your source to avoid unintentional plagiarism. Plagiarized work (papers that contain words or ideas that are "kidnapped" from the source) usually receive an F. See page 400 for examples of plagiarism.

In some instances, you may wish to add your own responses, questions, or ideas for using information recorded on your note cards. These comments can sometimes make it easier to organize ideas into paragraphs as you prepare to write a draft of your essay.

Sample Note Cards

Heins (card 1)
Those who would like to censor the Internet in the hope of protecting children from overtly sexual images or messages are unable to show the connection between viewing explicit sexual information and sexual behavior. A study conducted in 1991 showed that "juvenile sex offenders" interviewed for the study had usually looked at pornographic pictures at one time or another.

> Heins (card 2)
> The study found that a much more likely cause of sexual offenses among teenage boys "were their own histories of physical and sexual abuse" (Heins 42).
> *Heins shows that censoring pornography is not likely to affect adolescents' sexual behavior.*

Notice that the student carefully paraphrased the ideas in her source and put quotation marks around phrases taken word for word from the author. She also included a note to herself about Heins's argument to help her place the material in the paper she will eventually write. When she writes her research paper, she must cite the source whenever she paraphrases this author's ideas or quotes directly from the text. Her in-text citations will include the author's last name and the page number where she found the information.

STEP 4: DRAFTING THE ESSAY

Write a **sentence outline** of the thesis and topic ideas for your essay. If you are having trouble connecting ideas, ask yourself, "What am I trying to say?" Then try writing a list of things that you might include in your essay based on information you have gathered from sources.

Sample Outline

The outline that follows presents a possible arrangement of paragraphs for the student paper on Internet censorship that appears in Chapter 8. The essay answers the question, What are some of the problems associated with censoring pornography on the Internet?

1. Some writers argue that Internet censorship protects children's innocence and prevents them from seeing things that might cause them to be sexually active or even sexually abusive.
2. Critics of Internet pornography see filtering systems and other software programs as the way to accomplish censorship.
3. Censorship raises questions about First Amendment rights to free speech.
4. No one has been able to show a connection between viewing pornography and sexual behavior, or even that censoring devices are effective in blocking offending sites.

The student's ideas for the outline lead to other questions about Internet censorship that needed more research. After rearranging ideas, the student refocused her essay to explore the idea that attempts to censor pornographic material on the Internet cause more problems than they solve. She wrote her thesis for the essay after drafting the main points of her body paragraphs.

I. Thesis: It isn't possible to completely block children's access to pornography, nor does research show that children's exposure to pornographic material on

Internet sites has a negative effect on their behavior. Censoring the Internet also takes away parents' responsibility and, more importantly, challenges Americans' right to free speech.

A. Parents object to the ease with which children can access pornographic sites on the Internet.
   1. They propose installing filtering systems and other software programs to censor such sites.
   2. Blocking systems are not always effective, and they can block legitimate information in the process.
B. No studies have been able to show that viewing pornography produces aberrant behavior.
C. Internet censorship takes responsibility for raising children from the parents and gives it to an anonymous group who decide what other people's children should see.
D. Worst of all, Internet censorship infringes on the right to free speech.

Once you have an outline, **sort** your note cards into stacks representing topic ideas. At this point you may need to gather more source material or step back and reorganize the paper based on new information.

Methods for Drafting Your Paper

You may want to write your first full draft by using the "fast draft" method. This involves writing the paper quickly, following your outline, and noting where sources would go. Then go back and fill in the source material and citations carefully. A second method is to write the paper section by section, carefully integrating sources and citations into your paper. You can also use a combination of the "fast" and "slow" methods of writing a draft. You might, for example, begin writing very quickly just to get ideas on paper. Once you get a little ways into the paper, you might start writing more slowly as you carefully work citations and analysis into your text.

Make sure you have cited sources in your text, and include a list of the works you cite in the paper. Find out from your teacher whether he or she requires a full bibliography of all works consulted or whether a list of works cited is all you need for the assignment.

How to Avoid Plagiarism

Plagiarism involves using the words or ideas of another as though they were your own work.

The most blatant kinds of plagiarism occur when a friend writes a paper for another friend's assignment or when a student purchases an essay from one of the writing services available at cost through the Internet. These are serious cases of plagiarism and may result in a student being dropped from a class, put on probation at his or her college, or expelled from school.

The more common kind of plagiarism is often unintentional and usually occurs when students don't take notes carefully or fail to distinguish their own words and ideas from those in their sources. What follows are two examples of plagiarism that are probably unintentional but will still result in an unacceptable paper. Both examples are taken from an essay about censorship and the Internet entitled "When Does Filtering Turn into Censorship?" Compare the original wording in the source in the left-hand column with the passage as it appears in the student's essay.

Original Text	**Plagiarized Text**
There is . . . the problem of inadvertent filtering, where search words that are otherwise legitimate ("breast," is an example) are filtered regardless of intent. Some of the filtering systems have what is called "dynamic" filtering, where they analyze any Web page for "bad words" and allow access only if they are not found.	Software filtering systems have the problem of inadvertent filtering, where legitimate search words, like "breast" for example, are filtered out no matter what the intent. Other filtering systems have a more "dynamic" way of filtering, and they analyze Web pages for "bad words," allowing access only if they are not found.

This example illustrates several problems. Although a few words have been changed and others are rearranged, the text is copied from the source rather than paraphrased. Moreover, exact wording does not appear in quotations, and the author is not given credit for his ideas or wording. Even if the author's name appeared in parentheses with a page reference, the passage would still be plagiarized because the writer is passing off borrowed words and phrasing as her own.

Another kind of plagiarism cites the source of information but fails to enclose wording from the original text in quotation marks. The passage in this example is from Richard J. Sagall's article, "Internet Censorship."

Original Text	**Plagiarized Text**
What parents can and should do is talk with their children about this type of material. It's the parents' responsibility to educate their children about the real world, and pornography is a part of the real world. Protecting children from pornography by trying to deny them access to it doesn't work. Talking with your children about pornography, the "sick" people they may encounter, and helping them learn how to deal with these situations is the best way to protect them (Sagall 10).	Parents can and should talk to their children about pornographic material. It is the parents' responsibility to educate their children about the "real" world, and that includes pornography. It does not work to deny children access to it thinking to protect them. The best way to protect children from pornography is to talk to them about it and the "sick" people they might meet, and to help them learn how to deal with such situations (Sagall 10).

Even though the author's name and a page reference appear in the student's paper, this passage is plagiarized because the student copied the information nearly word for word from the original text and placed it in the paper as though the words were the student's own writing. Enclosing exact wording in quotation marks gives proper credit to the source. However, as in the first example, a larger problem shows up—the student is not paraphrasing the text and, therefore, does not demonstrate a clear understanding of the material he or she is using. Staying this close to the original wording suggests a lack of control over the research material.

STEP 5: REVISE THE PAPER AND SUBMIT IT FOR GRADING

This is one of the most important steps in writing a research paper or any other essay. Like other essays you write, a well-written research paper is not produced in the first or even the second draft. That's why it is important to follow your schedule as closely as possible and leave at least two weeks to write and revise your paper. As you revise, ask yourself what you need to include in order to help the reader make sense of your discussion.

The following checklist will help you think about what to look for when revising. The checklist is also useful for peer review workshops in the classroom or in a computer forum.

Checklist for Revising Research Papers

- ❏ Does the opening catch the reader's attention?
- ❏ Does the thesis anticipate the topic ideas developed in the paper?
- ❏ Do topic sentences support the thesis and connect to paragraphs that precede them?
- ❏ Is each quotation and paraphrase properly cited both in the body of the paper and on the Works Cited page?
- ❏ Is the organizational pattern clear, or do some paragraphs seem out of order?
- ❏ Are quotations introduced with a lead-in (such as "According to . . ." or "A well-known scientist writes . . .") or attached to my writing at the end of a citation?
- ❏ Do transitions and explanations connect the topic ideas to evidence from sources?
- ❏ Is the essay free of sentence errors, mistakes in grammar, and spelling errors?

Documenting a Research Paper

As mentioned in Chapter 15, a research paper requires that you incorporate outside sources in the development of your essay. In the interests of courtesy and academic honesty, you must credit the sources whose ideas and wording you borrow by citing or naming the sources you use in the body of your essay.

The *MLA Handbook for the Writers of Research Papers* provides the format for documenting sources in your essay and in your list of works cited. The MLA style of documentation is used in disciplines of languages and literature. This format, in-text method of citing sources, requires that sources be named in your text, often in parentheses, and replaces the footnoting method of documentation.

Citing sources in the body of your essay makes for smoother reading, and this method of documentation is less likely to distract your reader from the flow of ideas in your paper.

Be aware that different disciplines have different methods of documentation—the American Psychological Association (APA) and the *Chicago Manual of Style* to name two. You can take comfort in the idea that once you learn the Modern Language Association's style of documentation, other methods of documentation should come fairly easily.

This chapter provides examples of citations that follow the MLA guidelines. You can use these examples as models for most of the sources you will use in your papers. If you do not find an example that approximates a source you are using, consult the *MLA Handbook for Writers of Research Papers,* a publication that should be available to you through your library. The Modern Language Association's web page, http://www.mla.org, can also provide you with the information you need.

A BIBLIOGRAPHY AND A LIST OF WORKS CITED

A Works Cited page contains a list of the sources you used to write your research paper. It appears as the last page of your essay, and it is always required when you write a research paper. A bibliography, on the other hand, is a complete list of the sources you consulted while doing research on your topic. Before submitting a research paper, ask your teacher if he or she requires you to submit a bibliography in addition to the list of works cited.

FORMAT FOR WORKS IN A LIST OF WORKS CITED OR BIBLIOGRAPHY

As the title suggests, the list of works cited includes all the sources that supply information for your paper. The list begins on a new page at the end of your research paper. Center the title, Works Cited, and number the page consecutively after the last page of your paper. The page number appears in the upper right-hand corner of the page roughly half an inch from the top and even with the right-hand margin.

Double-space the list of works cited and arrange your entries in alphabetical order by the author's last name. If the author's name is not available, use the first word of the title, excluding *A, An,* or *The*. This alphabetical listing should make it easy for your reader to find the sources you mention in your essay. Each new entry begins at the left-hand margin of your paper. Indent any additional or carryover lines half an inch from the left margin. Notice the punctuation and spacing in the following sample, and see if you can identify the pieces of information.

```
Fernández-Armesto, Felipe. Millennium: A History of
    the Last Thousand Years. New York: Touchstone, 1996.
```

In general, when you list a book on your bibliography cards and eventually on your Works Cited page, your entry has three parts: the author's name, the title of the book, and publication information. When citing most printed sources, include any of the following information the source provides in the order listed here: the author's name (last name first), the title of a chapter or section of a book in quotation marks (if given), the title of the book (underlined), the name of the editor or translator (if given), the book's edition, the number of the volume used (for multivolume works), the number of the series (for books published in a series), the place of publication (city), the name of the publisher, date of publication, and page numbers for the section or chapter of the book mentioned in your paper.

SAMPLE ENTRIES FOR BOOKS USING THE MLA STYLE

The entries in this chapter anticipate sources students are most likely to use in a research paper. Pay close attention to the placement of commas, periods, and colons. The parts of a standard bibliographical reference for a book are identified here, with an additional example. The MLA style uses conventional abbreviations for University Press (UP), and Press (P). Other commonly used abbreviations are explained after the entries in which they appear.

A BOOK WITH ONE TO THREE AUTHORS

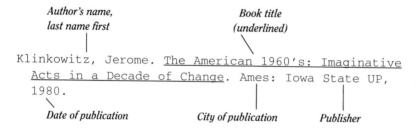

Barron, John and Anthony Paul. <u>Murder of a Gentle Land:
     The Untold Story of Communist Genocide in Cambodia</u>.
     New York: Reader's Digest P, 1977.

AN ANTHOLOGY OR COMPILATION

Pran, Dith, comp. <u>Children of Cambodia's Killing Fields:
     Memoirs by Survivors</u>. Ed. Kim DePaul. New Haven: Yale
     UP, 1997.

In this entry, *comp.* refers to "compiler"; *Ed.* is the abbreviation used for "editor." If the work has more than one editor, the abbreviation is *Eds.*

Boyer, Paul S., et al. <u>The Enduring Vision</u>. 4th ed. Vol. 2.
     Boston: Houghton Mifflin, 2000.

Et al. means "and others," indicating that this work has more than three authors. The abbreviation *ed.* identifies this as the fourth edition of the work. *Vol.* refers to the volume number in a multivolume work.

A WORK IN AN ANTHOLOGY WITH A TRANSLATOR, EDITOR, OR COMPILER

Jen, Gish. "The Water Faucet Vision." <u>Charlie Chan Is
     Dead: An Anthology of Contemporary Asian American
     Fiction</u>. Ed. Jessica Hagedorn. New York: Penguin,
     1993. 141-50.

For this entry, the title of the story is enclosed in quotation marks, and the title of the anthology is underlined. Page numbers indicate the location of the story in the anthology.

> Camus, Albert. "The Guest." Trans. Justin O'Brien. <u>Norton Anthology of World Masterpieces</u>. Ed. Maynard Mack. Expanded ed. Vol. 2. New York: Norton, 1995. 2253-62.

Here, *Trans.* stands for "translator" in works that have been translated into English from another language.

SEVERAL BOOKS BY A SINGLE AUTHOR

List works by the same author in alphabetical order by title. After listing the first work under the author's name, use hyphens followed by a period to indicate works by the same author.

> Ehrenreich, Barbara. <u>Fear of Falling: The Inner Life of the Middle Class</u>. New York: Random House, 1989.
>
> ---. <u>Nickel and Dimed: On (Not) Getting by in America</u>. New York: Henry Holt, 2001.

A CORPORATE AUTHOR

This category includes works published by an agency, foundation, committee, or association. Include information on authors or editors when available.

> National Cancer Institute. <u>Closing in on Cancer: Solving a 5000-Year-Old Mystery</u>. Washington: 1998.
>
> Bate, David V., and Robert B. Caton, eds. <u>A Citizen's Guide to Air Pollution</u>. 2nd ed. Vancouver: David Suzuki Foundation, 2002.
>
> Commission on Human Security. <u>Human Security Now: Protecting and Empowering People</u>. New York: Commission on Human Security, 2003.

When the corporate author and publisher are the same, the name appears twice.

SAMPLE ENTRIES FOR MAGAZINES, NEWSPAPERS, AND JOURNALS

Like the entries for books, bibliographic notes for articles in periodicals and scholarly journals also consist of three parts: the author's name, the title of the article and the name of the periodical, and publication information. A scholarly journal may have a volume and/or issue number. For most periodicals, include the date of publication and the page numbers on which the article appears.

ARTICLES IN A MONTHLY MAGAZINE

Betts, Katherine. "Body Language." <u>Vogue</u> Apr. 1994: 344–50.

ANONYMOUS ARTICLE (AUTHOR'S NAME OMITTED)

"Through the Eyes of Children: Bianca" <u>Time</u> 8 Aug. 1988: 49–50.

ARTICLES IN A SCHOLARLY JOURNAL

Quarcoopome, E. Nii. "Self-Decoration and Religious Power in Dangme Culture." <u>African Arts</u> 24.3 (1991): 56–66.

Because *African Arts* is a scholarly journal, the volume (24) and issue (3) numbers appear after the title of the journal. The date of publication appears in parentheses, and the page numbers of the article end the entry.

EDITORIALS PUBLISHED IN NEWSPAPERS

Macallair, Daniel. "Prisons: Power Nobody Dares Mess With: Guards Rake in $100,000 a Year and Political IOUs as They Battle Reform." Editorial. <u>Sacramento Bee</u>. 29 Feb. 2004. E1.

"Distorting the Intelligence." Editorial. <u>New York Times</u>. 17 Feb. 2004. A22.

DOCUMENTING OTHER SOURCES

INTERVIEWS

Interviews may be published, recorded, or conducted by the student-researcher.

Noujaim, Jehane. Interview with Terry Gross. <u>Fresh Air</u>. Natl. Public Radio. WHYY, Philadelphia. 20 May 2004.

Hoagland, John. Personal Interview. 26 Aug. 2004.

A LECTURE OR SPEECH

If you know the title of the lecture, include it in your reference.

Ford, Bonnie. "Seneca Falls Convention." History 18. Sacramento City College. 12 Mar. 1999.

A TELEVISION PROGRAM

In general, provide the following information where given: the title of the episode (in quotation marks), the title of the program (underlined), the title of the series without an underline (e.g., Frontline), the number of episodes (if part of a series), network name, local station, and broadcast date. You may wish to include the names of narrators, writers, directors, or performers. These are indicated by an abbreviated title (e.g., *narr.*, *writ.*, *dir.*, *perf.*) followed by the person's name.

> Jesus Factor: Examining George W. Bush's Personal
>   Religious Journey, Its Impact on His Political
>   Career and Presidency, and the Growing Influence
>   of America's Evangelical Christians. Narr. Will
>   Lyman. Writ. and Dir. Raney Aronson. Frontline.
>   WGBH, Boston. 29 April 2004.

> "The German Woman." Foyle's War. Writ. Anthony Horowitz.
>   Dir. Jeremy Silberston. Perf. Michael Kitchen, Anthony
>   Howell, Honeysuckle Weeks. 4 episodes. Masterpiece
>   Theatre. Introd. Russell Baker. PBS. WGBH, Boston.
>   6 June 2004.

A RADIO PROGRAM

> The MidEast: A Century of Conflict. Narr. Mike
>   Shuster. Morning Edition Natl. Public Radio.
>   30 Sept.-8 Oct. 2002.

A FILM

Films and video recordings include the title, the director, distributor, and the year the film was released. You may wish to include optional information, such as the names of the writer, performers, and producer.

> In America. Writ. Jim, Naomi, and Kirstin Sheridan.
>   Dir. Jim Sheridan. Perf. Samantha Morton and Paddy
>   Considine. Fox Searchlight, 2003.

> Equus. Screenplay by Peter Shaffer. Dir. Sidney Lumet.
>   Perf. Richard Burton, Peter Firth, Colin Blakely.
>   Videocassette. MGM/UA, 1977.

CITING ELECTRONIC SOURCES

Several things distinguish electronic sources from printed sources. When citing sources that were originally in printed form, include information about the original as well as the electronic source. The examples included here anticipate electronic sources students are most likely to use. For a more extensive sampling of electronic sources, consult the current edition of the *MLA Handbook for Writers of Research Papers.*

A BOOK ONLINE

For a book printed online, include as much of the following information as you have: the name of the author or the editor, translator, or compiler followed by *ed.*, *trans.*, or *comp.*, if no author is given; the title of the work (underlined); the name of the editor, translator, or compiler if applicable; publication information about the original text or information about the electronic publisher if there is no print version; date of Internet access (the date you retrieved the information); and the URL (Uniform Resource Locator—the Internet address) in angle brackets.

> Hill, Lynda Marion. <u>Social Rituals and the Verbal Art of Zora Neale Hurston</u>. Washington D.C.: Howard UP, 1996. 17 Apr. 2004 <http://www.questia.com/popularSearches/zora_neale_hurston.jsp>.

AN ARTICLE IN AN ONLINE JOURNAL, NEWSPAPER, OR MAGAZINE

When citing articles from online periodicals, include information available from the source in the following order: author, title (in quotation marks), title of periodical, volume or issue number, date of publication, pages for the article, date of access (date you downloaded the information), and the web address. As with many other Internet entries for online sources, the date that precedes the URL is the date the student accessed the source.

> Tuchman, Gary. "Kent State Forever Linked with Vietnam War Era." <u>CNN.com</u>. 4 May 2000. 18 Apr. 2004 <http://www.cnn.com/SPECIALS/views/y/2000/04/tuchman.kentstate.may4/>.

AN EDITORIAL PUBLISHED ONLINE

> Turley, Jonathan. "A Legal Tattoo Hullabaloo" Editorial. <u>Los Angeles Times</u>. 30 Sept. 2002. 10 Nov. 2002 <http://www.latimes.com/news/printedition/opinion/la-oe-turley30sep30.story>.

AN ONLINE MAGAZINE ARTICLE

> Lamb, Jack. "The Last of the Old-Time Cowboys?" <u>American Folk: People, Folklore, and Popular Culture</u>. 15 Mar. 1998. 25 May 2004 <http://www.americanfolk.com/stories/>.

AN ARTICLE FROM AN ONLINE SCHOLARLY JOURNAL

```
Cronin, Blaise. "Whatever Happened to Common Sense?"
    Library Journal. 125:14 (2000). 29 Apr. 2001
    <http://A:/hwwilson19.html>.
```

In the preceding entry, the online publication date was not given; April 29 is the date the student accessed the information.

A PROFESSIONAL, PERSONAL, OR ORGANIZATIONAL WEBSITE

```
Norton Anthology of English Literature: Norton
    Topics Online. WW Norton. 10 May 2004
    <http://www.wwnorton.com/nael/>.

Conachy, James. "Ten Years Since the Tiananmen Square
    Massacre: Political Lessons for the Working
    Class." 4 June 1999. World Socialist Website.
    20 May 2004. <http://www.wsws.org/articles/999/
    jun1999/tian-j04.shtml>.

Mehalek, Kyle. "Tiananmen Square Demonstrations and
    Massacre." Home page. 9 May 2002. 14 Apr. 2004
    <http://home.rochester.rr.com/kjmpage/tiananmen.htm>.
```

WORKS AVAILABLE ON A CD-ROM ELECTRONIC DATABASE

A Source from an Online Service

Check with libraries in your area and on campus to see whether they subscribe to an Internet service such as ProQuest, InfoTrac® College Edition, or EBSCOhost. The articles collected in these databases can provide valuable information for your paper.

```
Males, Michael. "Mythology and Internet Filtering."
    Teacher Librarian. 28:2 (2000). 16-18. MasterFILE
    Premier. CD-ROM. EBSCOhost. 19 Apr. 2001.
```

The following entry includes both the original publication information and the date of publication in the online service.

```
Tanouye, Erik. "Study Says Federal Programs Decrease
    Drug Use." Hearst Newspapers. 19 Sept. 1997.
    America Online. 3 Dec. 1997.
```

The next entry includes documentation from the original newspaper as well as the date of access from ProQuest and the service's web address in angle brackets.

```
"March One of Largest [Capitol] Mall Events." The
    Washington Post. 26 Apr. 2004 All. CD-ROM. UMI-ProQuest.
    17 May 2004 <http://proquest.umi.com/>.
```

CITING SOURCES IN YOUR TEXT

In addition to listing sources on the Works Cited page at the end of your essay, you must also refer to borrowed material in the text of your paper. The goal for in-text references is to work them into your paper so that they do not detract from your discussion.

The Modern Language Association has established guidelines for citing sources in your paper. A sampling of in-text citations for both print and online sources is listed in this section. Take note of the MLA standards for spacing and punctuating citations.

For most citations, you have the choice of either enclosing the author's last name and the page number (if one is given) in parentheses or referring to the author in your text with only the page number in parentheses. If the author's name is not available, use an abbreviated title. When a work has more than one author, both names appear in the reference, either in the text or in the parenthetical note.

A WORK BY ONE AUTHOR

Julie Caniglia points out that although Fakil Musafar claims to be "preserving rituals that are otherwise dying out," some critics question the motives of his "weekend shamanistic seminars and performances in trendy nightclubs" (31).

Although Fakil Musafar claims to be "preserving rituals that are otherwise dying out," some critics question the motives of his "weekend shamanistic seminars and performances in trendy nightclubs" (Caniglia 31).

The full reference for this source appears on the Works Cited page:

Caniglia, Julie. "Making Body Art." Utne Reader. Jan.-Feb. 1993: 30-32.

A WORK IN AN ANTHOLOGY

Gish Jen's short story is an excellent example of an author's use of first person point of view to develop characters (141-50).

The Works Cited page shows the full reference:

Jen, Gish. "The Water Faucet Vision." Charlie Chan Is Dead: An Anthology of Contemporary Asian American Fiction. Ed. Jessica Hagedorn. New York: Penguin, 1993. 141-50.

A WORK WITH MULTIPLE AUTHORS

When a work you are using has more than one but less than four authors, you may mention their names in the body of your paragraph or in parentheses.

For the Maisin women of Papua New Guinea, "tattooing is a secular ritual that marks the transition of girls into strong, sexually active, beautiful women" (Barker and Tietjen 226).

In their essay on ritualistic tattooing, anthropologists John Barker and Anne Marie Tietjen conclude that "tattooing is a secular ritual that marks the transition of girls into strong, sexually active, beautiful women" (226).

The full reference for this source appears in the list of works cited:

Barker, John, and Anne Marie Tietjen. "Women's Facial Tattooing among the Maisin of Oro Province, Papua New Guinea: The Changing Significance of an Ancient Custom." <u>Oceania</u>. March 1990: 217-34.

SOURCES IN AN ONLINE SERVICE

In the next two examples, the source is an online service that does not list an author and has no pagination. In the first example, an abbreviated title for "The Impact of the Los Angeles Riots on the Korean-American Community" appears in parentheses. The full title must be listed on the paper's Works Cited page. Information from the source is paraphrased rather than quoted word for word.

In the end, around 2,000 Korean-owned shops in South Central Los Angeles were destroyed and one third of the owners whose shops were destroyed never rebuilt ("The Impact").

The Works Cited page contains the following information for this online source:

"The Impact of the Los Angeles Riots on the Korean-American Community." <u>Asia Today</u>. 3 May 2002. AsiaSource.org. 6 Oct. 2003 <http://www.AsiaSource.org/news/at_mp)02.cfm?newsid=79441>.

A SOURCE FROM A CD-ROM DATABASE

Roughly half a million women packed Capitol Mall this week in a show of solidarity for women's rights ("March").

For this CD-ROM source, the full listing is as follows:

"March One of Largest [Capitol] Mall Events." <u>The Washington Post</u>. 26 Apr. 2004 All. CD-ROM. UMIProQuest. 17 May 2004 <http://proquest.umi.com/>.

A QUOTATION WITHIN A SOURCE

When you are quoting or paraphrasing material that your source has borrowed from another source, enclose in parentheses the abbreviation "qtd. in" for "quoted in" plus the name of the author or title of the source where you found the information.

```
As Senator James Exon noted, "The worst, most vile, most
perverse pornography is only a few 'click, click, clicks'
away from any child on the Internet" (qtd. in Barron).
```

The source appears in the list of works cited as follows:

```
Barron, Christina. "Internet Rights and Wrongs."
    Europe. 363 (1997): 10-11. MasterFILE Premier.
    CD-ROM. EBSCOhost. 28 April 2001.
```

BLOCKED QUOTATIONS

Citations that are taken word for word from a source and are more than four lines long are "blocked" and indented one inch from the left margin. Double-space these citations as you do the rest of the essay. The author's name may be part of the introduction to the quotation or included in the parenthetical note after the end punctuation.

```
The working life of a "salaryman" and small business
owners in Japan can be quite grueling. In his book, The
Japanese Way, Tadaka Lampkin explains:

    Many white-collar employees put in long hours each day,
    usually without additional compensation, invariably
    arriving at work 5 to 10 minutes before starting time
    and staying until the supervisor leaves. Stores and
    other small businesses also keep hours comparable to
    similar establishments elsewhere, including conven-
    ience stores (konbini) and many small, family-type
    stores, especially those near train stations, that
    are open late. (86)
```

Blocked quotations are not enclosed in quotation marks except to indicate material quoted by your source, as in the next example. Also, if you omit wording from the source, insert a series of periods or ellipsis dots, enclosed in brackets, in the space where the words were omitted.

```
In reality, Prince Sihanouk was a puppet of the Khmer
Rouge, a fact he was well aware of. In a candid
statement to journalist Oriana Fallaci in June, 1973,
Prince Sihanouk admitted:

    "The Khmer Rouge do not like me at all, and I know
    that. [...] I understand quite well that they only
```

tolerate me because without me they cannot prevail
over the peasants, and without the peasant, one can
make no revolution in Cambodia. [...] When they no
longer need me, they will spit me out like a cherry
pit." (qtd. in Barron 56)

Use blocked quotations sparingly. It is usually more effective to quote just what you need from the source and add your own explanations, transitions, and analysis to connect source material to your own discussion. Passages from sources that are loosely strung together indicate that the writer has not fully digested the material, and such papers have difficulty developing a larger, coherent argument.

ACCURATE USE OF QUOTATIONS AND PARAPHRASING

In addition to making sure you are not letting sources take over your paper, check to see that the quoted or paraphrased material actually supports the point you want to make. It is jarring to read quotations or paraphrasing that has no clear connection to the writer's discussion or that contradict other statements in the paragraph without the writer seeming to notice. The following passage illustrates a citation that is not clearly connected to the writer's argument.

Methadone is a widely used but controversial drug for
the treatment of heroin addiction. Although methadone
itself is highly addictive according to most research,
many physicians find it to be the safest and most
effective drug for heroin addicts. "The advantage of
methadone is that it is legal and cheap" (Swisher 10).

In this example, the writer has not connected the quotation from the source to her text, so the quotation "floats" without a lead-in attaching it to the student's line of argument. What is more problematic, the student has not shown that Swisher's statement that methadone is "legal and cheap" has any relevance to the point that the drug is safe and effective. These problems with the citation are corrected in the following paragraph.

Methadone is a widely used but controversial drug for
the treatment of heroin addiction. Although methadone
itself is highly addictive according to most research,
many physicians find it to be the most effective drug
for heroin addicts. Addicts are much more likely to
use methadone than drugs for any other maintenance
program because "it is legal and cheap" (Swisher 10).
Because methadone is legal, addicts don't have to
resort to criminal activities to get money to buy
the drug. Methadone is also inexpensive relative to
other treatments, so addicts are more likely to
take it.

CHANGING OR ADDING WORDS IN A QUOTATION

If you need to add words to a direct quotation when you insert it into your own sentence, put the added or changed material in brackets. This includes changes or additions of pronouns, punctuation, or tense.

> Michael Male, a sociology professor at UC Santa Cruz, argues that most software filtering programs cannot distinguish "good" sites from "bad" ones, with the result that students have been denied access to information at "CNN, USA Today, scholarship information [sites], and the Middlesex, Connecticut web site" because these sites contain the word "sex" or other terms that might appear on pornographic or violent sites as well.

The bibliographic information for this source appears in the list of works cited:

> Males, Michael. "Mythology and Internet Filtering." Teacher Librarian. 28:2 (2000). 16–18. MasterFILE Premier. CD-ROM. EBSCOhost. 19 Apr. 2001.

Part V
Editing Your Writing

Editing for Subject–Verb and Noun–Pronoun Agreement

CHAPTER 17

Writing clearly worded, grammatically correct sentences that are easy to read and understand is an important part of communicating ideas. If your reader has to stop several times in a paragraph to figure out what you meant to say, the words themselves have gotten in the way of the point you wanted to make. When you write for college classes or for employers, or as a manager or professional, the impression you make in your writing has just as much to do with the small things—the precise wording, sentence variety and complexity, and correct punctuation and spelling—as it does the larger elements such as focus, organization, and development of ideas. In addition, taking the time to correct sentence and grammar errors shows respect for your reader and indicates a commitment to the ideas you want to communicate.

Practices and explanations in Part V of this book will help you master basic skills you need to edit your sentences and to use a variety of sentence patterns. Additional exercises introduce sentence-combining techniques for adding variety to the way you write sentences. Other exercises give you practice writing correct sentences. Chapter 23 provides a handbook for grammar, spelling, punctuation, and capitalization.

As you complete the chapters in Part V, you should gain greater confidence in your ability to write correct, even powerful, sentences.

Whenever you write, connections between subjects and verbs, and those between the nouns and the pronouns that refer to them, must be clear to your reader. To give them that clarity, subjects and verbs, and nouns and pronouns, must agree in number. In other words, if a subject is singular, the verb must also be singular; if a noun is plural, any pronouns that refer to it must be plural as well. In this chapter you will practice making these elements in your sentences uniformly plural or singular.

MAKING VERBS AND SUBJECTS AGREE

To make clear connections between the subjects and verbs in your sentences, both words must agree in number. That means they must both be *either* plural *or* singular. If one is plural and the other singular, the result is an **agreement** error. Most subject–verb agreement errors occur because students either have difficulty writing the verb form that agrees with the subject of the sentence, or they cannot correctly identify the subject in the sentence. Explanations and practice exercises in this chapter will help clarify both of these common editing problems.

USING THIRD-PERSON SINGULAR VERBS

The verb form (he/she/it sees, hears, flies, etc.) often confuses students because it expresses a singular idea and has a singular subject, but it ends in the letter *s*. Many plural nouns in English end in *s* as well, but third-person-singular **verbs** also end in *s*.

Writers can avoid making many errors in subject–verb agreement by reviewing the verb forms in the present tense.

	Present Tense Singular		Present Tense Plural	
	Subject	*Verb*	*Subject*	*Verb*
1st person	I	live	we	live
2nd person	you	live	you	live
3rd person	he/she/it	lives	they	live
	Subject	*Verb*	*Subject*	*Verb*
1st person	I	have	we	have
2nd person	you	have	you	have
3rd person	he/she/it	has	they	have

Notice the *s* in the third-person singular form.

Study the following pairs of sentences. A check (✓) in front of the sentences indicates that they are written correctly.

_____ During Chinese New Year everyone express their appreciation of the family.

___✓___ During Chinese New Year everyone expresses his or her appreciation of the family.

_____ Back home, there is no loans or grants available for students.

_✓_ Back home, there are no loans or grants available for students.

_✓_ At a birthday party a child needs a fancy cake.

_____ At a birthday party a child need a fancy cake.

_____ In a World Series game there is a lot of anxious fans putting pressure on the players.

_✓_ In a World Series game there are a lot of anxious fans putting pressure on the players.

RULE TO REMEMBER	Verbs in the third-person present tense always end in *s*.

FOR PRACTICE

Practice 17a. In the following pairs of sentences, put a check (✓) next to the sentences in which the subjects and verbs agree in number (both the subject and verb are either plural or singular). The first pair is marked for you.

Planting

_✓_ Freida plants her garden every spring.
_____ Freida plant her garden every spring.

_____ She carefully tills the soil.
_____ She carefully till the soil.

_____ Keeping out bugs, aphids, and caterpillars requires a lot of work.
_____ Keeping out bugs, aphids, and caterpillars require a lot of work.

_____ When she is ready to plant the garden, her brother William help her.
_____ When she is ready to plant the garden, her brother William helps her.

_____ William sometimes mixes up the seeds.
_____ William sometimes mix up the seeds.

_____ When spring come, the flowers blooms in odd places.
_____ When spring comes, the flowers bloom in odd places.

Practice 17b. In this exercise, change the verbs in parentheses to their present tense, singular forms to make the sentences complete. The first one is written for you.

1. Sometimes a course __challenges__ a student, and the student __feels__ overwhelmed. (*to challenge, to feel*)

2. Perhaps the student _____ a clear understanding of the assignment. (*to lack*)

3. Absence also _____ in unfamiliarity with the instructor's lecture material. (*to result*)

4. When a student _____ confused about an assignment, it is best to ask the instructor for help. (*to get*)

5. Sometimes the homework for a class _____ too difficult, and a student _____ a little extra help. (*to seem, to need*)

6. A campus tutoring center or the help of another student often _____ the difference between passing or failing a course. (*to make*)

7. Often another student _____ notes for the days a fellow student has to miss. (*to take*)

8. An explanation from a student _____ in many cases more comprehensive than one from an instructor. (*to prove*)

9. A tutor provided by the Learning Center often _____ to clarify difficult concepts and instructions. (*to manage*)

10. At many colleges, tutoring assistance _____ beyond classroom instruction and _____ an important role in college success. (*to go, to play*)

Practice 17c. To practice making verbs and subjects agree in the present tense, rewrite the following sentences, changing the verbs from the past to the present tense. Try underlining the verbs and subjects first before changing the verbs to the present tense. You may need to change more than one verb in the sentence. The first sentence is done for you.

Trust Your Instincts

1. <u>Everyone</u> <u>had heard</u> of the idea that we should trust our intuition.

Corrected: <u>Everyone</u> <u>has heard</u> of the idea that we should trust our intuition.

2. Studies at UCLA, Harvard, and other institutions showed that we were correct in relying on intuition, especially in times of danger.

_____

_____

_____

3. It seemed that it wasn't just animals who sensed natural disasters, such as an impending tsunami. _____

_____

_____

4. Human beings had something like that feeling working for them as well.

_____

5. It usually took the form of being afraid in a particular situation or feeling uncomfortable when someone you didn't know approached.

6. Many of us distrusted that feeling and tried to shake it off, saying it was just our imagination. _____

7. But research demonstrated that those feelings about the car salesman who was just a little too nice, or our inexplicable suspicion that a co-worker was insincere, were often correct. _____

8. The experience of sensing that something was wrong could take many forms.

9. Some people felt that tingling sensation or "butterflies" in the stomach.

10. For other people, intuition came in the form of their heart beating so fast it seemed as if it might jump out of their chest.

11. Still others got the feeling of impending doom—the sensation that something bad was about to happen. _____

12. Whatever the signal, these signs weren't just hysterical fantasies.

_____

_____

_____

13. Researchers had found that such feelings were ways that our subconscious mind interpreted a situation based on our past experiences.

_____

_____

_____

14. As a result, we "feel" rather than "think" the message as it came from the subconscious. _____

_____

_____

15. We had to learn to trust these vague messages because our deeper instincts were probably trying to tell us something.

_____

_____

_____

Practice 17d. Change the underlined verbs in the following paragraph from the past to the present tense. Make sure they are written in the correct form (plural or singular) to agree with their subjects. Verbs in the first sentence are rewritten for you.

Just Say No and Mean It

          play   are

Women <u>played</u> a secondary role in a male-dominated world and <u>were</u> <u>taught</u> subservience to men. Rape <u>represented</u> the ultimate surrender of any remaining power, autonomy, and control. The surrender <u>was</u> not by choice but <u>was</u> usually made to ensure survival. By destroying a woman's feelings of personal power and self-worth, the rapist <u>hoped</u> to gain a sense of his own power and worth, and to take from the woman what he <u>did</u> not already <u>feel</u> in himself. Rape <u>occurred</u> any time a person <u>was</u> <u>forced</u> or coerced, physically or verbally, into sexual contact with another person. That assailant <u>was</u> often a friend, an acquaintance, an employer or fellow employee, or a husband. The fact of acquaintance rape <u>was</u> <u>ignored</u> or denied by most people. Even the women themselves <u>did</u> not <u>identify</u> their experiences as rape.

Practice 17e. Rewrite the verbs in the following essay in the present tense. This time they are not underlined, so you need to check the sentences carefully to find all the verbs and to make them agree in number with their subjects. The verb in the first sentence is rewritten for you. Use your own paper for this exercise.

Groupies

       are
There <u>were</u> many different groups on high school campuses. You could find them standing together in closed circles all over campus. The two groups most students wanted to join were the "cool" ones—the fashion group and the jock group. Everyone avoided the "nerd" group, the group that went to college and made something of themselves.

The fashion group thought they had it all. They dressed in name-brand clothes that their parents bought for them. These teens hung out together and talked about how everyone else dressed. Many people wanted to join this crowd. But it really wasn't worth it. Most of them were just snobs.

The most talked-about group were the jocks. They were completely unlike the fashion-conscious kids on campus. They wore sweats to school and didn't really care what they looked like. They knew it didn't matter how they looked; it was how they played the game that mattered.

The nerd group was not very popular. But they were the smartest people. They did not wear the cool clothes or play sports. Instead, they paid little attention to their clothes and studied all the time. Unlike the other two groups, they were not worried about trying to impress people. They were too busy thinking about the future.

PROBLEMS IDENTIFYING SUBJECTS

A Noun in a Prepositional Phrase Is Never the Subject in a Sentence
One kind of agreement error occurs when students confuse the noun in a prepositional phrase with the subject of the sentence. To understand this problem better, we will identify the prepositional phrases in the following sentences and examine their structure.

In the following sentences, the subjects are underlined once, the verbs twice. The troublesome prepositional phrases come between the subjects and verbs.

1. The <u>fans</u> at most games <u>are</u> really rowdy.
2. <u>Some</u> of the more boisterous people <u>throw</u> food.
3. <u>Others</u> in the crowd <u>yell</u> at the top of their lungs.

4. <u>Silence</u> during plays <u>is</u> not necessarily a good sign.
5. The <u>emotions</u> among enthusiastic fans <u>are</u> always <u>lying</u> just below the surface.

The first prepositional phrase in each of these sentences describes the noun that precedes it. In sentence 1, for example, *at most games* describes which *fans*. The prepositional phrase *of the more boisterous people* in sentence 2 describes the subject *Some*. In sentence 3, *in the crowd* refers to *Others*. Notice, too, that the prepositional phrases also contain nouns—*games, people,* and *crowd*. None of these nouns is the subject of the sentence in which it appears because the noun in a prepositional phrase is *never* the subject of a sentence.

Let's look at some of the prepositional phrases in the preceding sentences a little more closely. They are listed here:

at most games

of the more boisterous people

in the crowd

during plays

among enthusiastic fans

Each of these phrases follows a basic pattern:

Preposition	Adjective(s)	Noun
at	most	games
of	the more boisterous	people
in	the	crowd
during		plays
among	enthusiastic	fans

You can see from this list that a preposition and a noun appear in every prepositional phrase. Some prepositional phrases also contain adjectives—words that clarify or modify the noun in that phrase. In the prepositional phrase *at most games,* for example, the word *most* is an adjective because it tells us which *games*. In the same way, *the more boisterous* describes *people, the* refers to *crowd,* and *enthusiastic* modifies *fans*. Notice, however, that the prepositional phrase *during plays* contains no adjective; it's important to remember that not all prepositional phrases contain adjectives.

The following is a list of commonly used prepositions:

about	at	down	on	to
above	before	during	next	toward
across	behind	for	of	under
after	below	from	off	up
against	beneath	in	on	with
along	beside	inside	out	without
among	between	into	outside	
around	beyond	like	over	
as	by	near	through	

Rather than trying to memorize these prepositions, learn to recognize them as the short words that appear in the typical preposition–adjective–noun pattern of prepositional phrases. It is also helpful to know that prepositional phrases often indicate direction (for example, *around, to, toward,* and *through*) or location in time or space (for example, *under, behind, inside,* and *outside*).

RULE TO REMEMBER	The noun in a prepositional phrase is *never* the subject of the sentence.

Agreement errors sometimes occur when a prepositional phrase separates the subject and verb in a sentence, and the noun in the prepositional phrase is mistaken for the subject. To practice working with this sentence pattern, correct any agreement errors you find in the following exercises. If you have difficulty finding the subject of a sentence, try crossing out prepositional phrases.

FOR PRACTICE

Practice 17f. Read the following sentences carefully. Cross out any prepositional phrases you find. Then underline the subject in each sentence once and the verb twice. Three sentences are written incorrectly. Change the verbs in these sentences to agree with their subjects. The first sentence is done for you.

1. The <u>man</u> ~~of my dreams~~ <u>likes</u> to cook.
2. Several of the jugglers in town for the circus own parrots.
3. When students write regularly, freewriting about a topic get easier.
4. That clever Queen of Hearts tricked Alice.
5. The pizza from Sammy's Restaurant always disappears in a matter of minutes.
6. Films about a national disaster has become popular.
7. In front of the building down the block a gigantic pillar of yellow metal is sticking out of the grass.
8. The hours before dawn make me most uneasy.
9. Writing for a class assignment usually need editing.
10. The biggest problem for writers is that they don't write regularly.

Practice 17g. In the following sentences about sports fans, the subjects and verbs do not agree. Correct the sentences to make their subjects and verbs either plural or singular. If you are having trouble finding the subjects, try crossing out the prepositional phrases and underlining the subjects and verbs. The first sentence is done for you.

In the Crowd

1. During a baseball game, the <u>time</u> ~~between plays~~ <u>bore</u> even the most loyal fan.

Corrected: During a baseball game, the <u>time</u> between plays <u>bores</u> even the most loyal fan.

2. The benches beside the field is sometimes very uncomfortable. _____

_____

3. A sign of dissatisfaction are the "thumbs down" gesture. _____

_____

4. The crowd of spectators shout and hiss. _____

_____

5. The person next to you decide to yell every few minutes. _____

_____

6. The fans for the opposing teams sometimes heckles each other. _____

_____

7. There have even been occasions when boxes of popcorn comes flying through the air. _____

8. The moments after a bad play is the hardest to take. _____

_____

9. Sometimes the coach of a team get pretty angry about a bad play.

_____

10. The coaches from each team often acts out conflicts on the sidelines.

_____

Practice 17h. Create your own sentences using prepositional phrases. To make this task easier, you might focus on a single subject. Wherever possible, make your prepositional phrases modify the subjects of your sentences. Refer to the list of prepositions on page 424 as you write.

1. _____

_____

2. _____

_____

3. _____

_____

4. _____

_____

5. _____

_____

Singular Indefinite Pronouns

Indefinite pronouns used as subjects of sentences may cause errors in agreement. Some indefinite pronouns are always singular and take singular verbs. In the following sentences, the subjects are the indefinite pronouns *someone, everybody, each, everyone,* and *neither.* In each case, the verbs are singular to match these singular subjects.

> <u>Someone</u> <u>is listening</u> at the door.
>
> <u>Everybody</u> at this meeting <u>has</u> something to say.
>
> <u>Each</u> of Paula's answers <u>makes</u> sense to the other students.
>
> <u>Everyone</u> in the class <u>needs</u> to participate for this to be a lively discussion.
>
> <u>Neither</u> of Rodney's classes <u>requires</u> much homework.

RULE TO REMEMBER	When the following indefinite pronouns are used as subjects, they are *always* singular and take singular verbs.

anybody	everything
anyone	neither
anything	nobody
each	nothing
either	somebody
every	someone
everybody	something
everyone	

These words express singular ideas in English. Think of *anyone,* for example, as referring to *any one person,* and *each* as referring to *each individual answer.*

FOR PRACTICE

Practice 17i. Write the proper present tense verb form in the following sentences. The parenthetical verbs are listed in the order you will use them. Keep in mind that an *s* on the end of a verb in the third-person present tense makes the verb singular. You may need to refer to the preceding list of indefinite pronouns for help in choosing the proper verb form. The first sentence in this exercise is written as a sample.

Anthropology Class

1. Everyone in Ms. Rice's anthropology class __loves__ the subject. (*to love*)

2. Each of the students _____ seen an ancient skull of Cro-Magnon man. (*to have*)

3. Ms. Rice makes the lectures so vivid that nobody _____ bored. (*to get*)

4. The anthropology class is also interesting because someone always _____ an interesting question that _____ to a good discussion. (*to ask, to lead*)

5. Ms. Rice makes the whole class feel so comfortable that nobody _____ afraid to ask questions. (*to be*)

6. In addition, each of the two books for the course _____ several fascinating articles about major debates between anthropologists. (*to include*)

7. Either of the two books _____ enough information to keep me reading for several years. (*to have*)

8. Neither textbook _____ information that _____ commonly known. (*to contain, to be*)

9. Each of the chapters _____ detailed examples of the subjects it _____. (*to include, to cover*)

10. Anybody who _____ to take anthropology _____ to enroll in Ms. Rice's class. (*to plan, to need*)

Variable Indefinite Pronouns

A few indefinite pronouns, such as *all, any, most, none, some,* and *part,* can be singular or plural. Whether they are plural or singular depends on the noun in the prepositional phrase that follows them.

> *subject*　　　　　　　*verb*
> Some of the dollars never get to the bank.

> *subject*　　　　　　　*verb*
> Some of the money never gets to the bank.

In the first sentence, *some* refers to a number of dollars; in this case, *some* could also be expressed as a specific number (three dollars, six dollars, fifty dollars, and so forth) and is, therefore, a plural or count noun. In the second sentence, *some* refers to an amount of money, something you cannot count. In this case, *some* is a singular noun.

> *subject*　　　　　*verb*
> All of the burgers were eaten by Glenn.

> *subject*　　　*verb*
> All of the food was eaten by Glenn.

In the first sentence, *all* refers to a specific number of burgers—three or four, for instance—and is therefore a countable noun. In the second sentence, *all* refers to an amount of food that cannot be counted or quantified. Because the amount is uncountable, *all* is a singular noun.

> **RULE TO REMEMBER** When *all, any, most, none,* or *some* refer to how many (the number of X), use a plural verb. When these words refer to the amount of something, they take a singular verb.

FOR PRACTICE

Practice 17j. Write the correct form of the verb in parentheses. Reread the explanations just given if you have difficulty. Use the present tense throughout.

1. Most of the students here _____ serious about their studies. (*to be*)

2. Any of the vitamins you want _____ available without a prescription. (*to be*)

3. Any of the medication for heart disease _____ to be prescribed by a doctor. (*to need*)

4. Some of the houses in rural areas _____ from $20,000 to $50,000. (*to cost*)

5. Most of the property in the city _____ for $75,000 to $100,000. (*to sell*)

6. None of the land _____ for sale at the moment. (*to be*)

7. Realtors are angry because all the building permits _____ been issued for the year, and none _____ presently available for new construction. (*to have, to be*)

8. All members of the City Council _____ against proposals to increase the number of building permits. (*to vote*)

9. Any attempt to change their minds _____ in defeat. (*to end*)

10. Some contractors _____ defeat and _____ forward to next year's building season. (*to accept, to look*)

Subjects Joined by *either/or, neither/nor, not only/but also*

When sentences contain subjects joined by these word pairs, the verb in the sentence will be plural or singular depending on the subject closest to it.

        subject   *subject*   *verb*
1. <u>Either</u> "Rapunzel" <u>or</u> "The Fairy Prince" <u>is required</u> reading for my folklore class.

           subject   *subject* *verb*
2. <u>Neither</u> an evil stepmother <u>nor</u> wicked sisters <u>have</u> much chance of being liked.

           subject   *subject*   *verb*
3. <u>Neither</u> wicked sisters <u>nor</u> an evil stepmother <u>has</u> much chance of being liked.

Making Verbs and Subjects Agree   **429**

When one of the word pairs *either/or, neither/nor,* or *not only/but also* joins parts of a compound subject, the verb agrees with the subject closest to the verb.

FOR PRACTICE

Practice 17k. Write the correct form of the verb in parentheses in the space provided. Be sure the verb you write is plural or singular to match the subject. The first sentence is done for you.

Fairy Tales

1. Fairy tales usually _____take_____ place in magical towers, palaces, or castles. (*to take*)

2. Most fairy tales _____ about princes, kings, queens, and princesses. (*to be*)

3. Either the prince or king in the tale _____ the beautiful female. (*to marry*)

4. Sometimes characters metamorphose in fairy tales, and either the princess or the prince _____ into a bird or frog. (*to turn*)

5. Leprechauns and elves also _____ the woods in fairy tales. (*to inhabit*)

6. But neither the wise old leprechaun nor the bands of elves _____ much more than a supporting role in most stories. (*to have*)

7. They exist mainly to assist the real hero or heroine of the story because neither the princess nor her admirers ever _____ from their adventures without help. (*to return*)

8. Help from elves and leprechauns _____ necessary because heroes or heroines face difficult challenges. (*to be*)

9. Jealous siblings or a stepparent often _____ conflict for the main character in these tales. (*to create*)

10. Such conflicts or some horrible obstacle often _____ poison or magic. (*to involve*)

MAKING NOUNS AND PRONOUNS AGREE

Like subjects and verbs, pronouns and the nouns they refer to (called **antecedents**) must agree in number. If the noun is plural, the pronoun must also be plural; if the noun is singular, any pronoun that refers to it must be singular as well.

In the sentences that follow, arrows connect pronouns to their antecedents.

1. In many older films, male characters have a cigarette in their hands in most of the scenes.
   Are the noun and pronoun singular or plural? _____

2. In many older films, the male lead has a cigarette in his hand in most of the scenes.
   Are the noun and pronoun singular or plural? _____

RULE TO REMEMBER   A pronoun must agree with its antecedent.

FOR PRACTICE

Practice 17l. Write the correct pronoun in the blanks. Your choices are listed in parentheses at the end of the sentence.

The Changing Image of Smokers

1. Whereas cigarettes once gave a movie character sex appeal, _____ are now smoked mostly by villains. (*it* or *they*)

2. In most of the spy thrillers, enemy agents smoke _____ cigarettes in full view of rival American agents. (*his/her* or *their*)

3. No self-respecting U.S. agent would dare smoke in front of _____ enemy. (*his/her* or *their*)

4. Even the antihero in most mass-market movies refuses to take a cigarette if _____ is offered one. (*he/she* or *they*)

5. In some films, a character who has obvious mental problems smokes _____ favorite cigarettes during tense moments. (*his/her* or *their*)

6. This pressure to change the image of the movie hero comes from the movement in our culture to eliminate smoking and to see _____ as characteristic of only the most despicable characters. (*it* or *them*)

7. Although it is true that smoking does pose health hazards, nobody should lose completely _____ right to smoke. (*his/her* or *their*)

8. Smoking in the movies influences an individual almost as much as do smokers in _____ immediate environment. (*his/her* or *their*)

Making Nouns and Pronouns Agree   **431**

9. If a person smokes in public, _____ (*he/she* or *they*) may influence others, especially young people who look to _____ (*him/her* or *them*) for guidance.

10. Many communities, in fact, have imposed restrictions on smoking within _____ (*its* or *their*) public areas.

Practice 17m. In the following sentences about working, nouns and pronouns do not always agree in number. Locate any agreement errors in these sentences, and make both the nouns and the pronouns that refer to them uniformly singular or plural. Two possible corrections are given for the first sentence.

Working

1. If someone really wants to do something well, they must work hard.

Corrected: If someone really wants to do something well, he or she must work hard.

Corrected: If individuals really want to do something well, they must work hard.

2. A person can gain self-respect, regardless of what their job is, by working hard.

_____

_____

_____

3. When a new employee is hired, it is important that they be shown around and helped with the tasks they don't understand. _____

_____

_____

4. Even the most seasoned worker needs help from their fellow workers once in a while. _____

_____

_____

5. Anyone who has been asked to work with a self-absorbed coworker knows how unpleasant they can be. _____

_____

_____

6. If someone decides to quit their job, they must take full responsibility for that decision. _____

_____

_____

7. A car salesperson has to keep their quota of sales. If they don't, they will not get much of a commission at the end of the month. _____

_____

8. Real estate agents, who work under similar pressure, push themselves to sell as many houses as they can. _____

_____

9. Salespeople sometimes quit because he or she finds the competition too stressful. He or she may discover that the money doesn't compensate for the amount of pressure they face. _____

_____

10. When an advertiser puts an ad on television, they always make working in fast-food restaurants seem better than it really is. _____

_____

> For online practice with subject–verb agreement, log on to "The Blue Book of Grammar and Punctuation" (http://www.grammarbook.com), and click on "Grammar Rules" then "Subject and Verb Agreement." Additional explanations and exercises are at OWL (http://owl.english.purdue.edu/); add handouts/esl/eslsubverb.html to the URL. Then click on "Exercises" at the bottom of the page.

WRITING PRACTICE

Practice 17n. Write two paragraphs about a major change that has taken place in your life in the past year or two. In the first paragraph, describe what your life was like before the change; in the second paragraph, discuss what is happening now as a result of the change. Be sure to proofread your paragraphs carefully and correct any agreement errors you find.

Combining Sentences: Coordinating Conjunctions and Other Connecting Words

Part of effective proofreading means making sure that ideas in your sentences are connected logically. To help you make those connections, this chapter introduces you to independent clauses—the basic units of thought in any sentence. Practice exercises in this chapter ask you to use coordinating conjunctions and transitional words called conjunctive adverbs that you can use to link clauses logically in sentences.

> For an online introduction to sentence variety, log on to http://owl.english.purdue.edu and add handouts/general/gl_sentvar.html to the URL.

CONNECTING INDEPENDENT CLAUSES

A clause contains a subject and a complete verb. Only two types of clauses occur in English—independent clauses and dependent clauses.

The first clause we will discuss is the **independent** clause, sometimes called a **main clause.** We call this clause independent because it could be written by itself as a sentence.

COORDINATING CONJUNCTIONS

Coordinating conjunctions are commonly used to join ideas in independent clauses. Clauses joined by coordinating conjunctions are called **compound sentences.**

Here are two independent clauses written as sentences.

I waved to Melissa. She didn't see me.

These two sentences can be rewritten as a compound sentence, two independent clauses joined by a comma and the coordinating conjunction *but.* To emphasize this pattern, the independent clauses in the sample sentence are enclosed in brackets, and the coordinating conjunction is circled.

independent clause	*coordinating conjunction*	*independent clause*
[I waved to Melissa,]	(but)	[she didn't see me.]

Here is a list of coordinating conjunctions, their function, and samples of how they may be used. The explanations in brackets clarify the meaning of each coordinating conjunction. Use this list to make logical connections between short, choppy sentences in your own writing.

List of Coordinating Conjunctions

for—shows a reason or cause
> I am going back to school part-time, for [because, for this reason] I expect to get a better job with a college education.

and—adds the ideas together
> My starting salary is $6.50 an hour, and [plus, in addition] I will get a raise every three months.

nor—the least common coordinating conjunction; keeps the second independent clause negative
> I was not content to work for $5.25 an hour, nor [he or she wasn't either] was my boss willing to raise my salary.

but—shows a contrast or makes an exception
> I actually liked the work at the gas station, but [even so] I think my time is worth more than minimum wage.

or—gives a choice or alternative
> Last month I told my boss at Rick's Chevron to give me a raise, or [as an alternative] I would look for another job.

yet—like *but,* draws a strong contrast

> My current job as a dishwasher and cook at a Chinese restaurant keeps me in the kitchen most of the time, yet [in spite of this] I get to talk to customers occasionally.

so—shows a consequence or result.

> My old boss would not give in, so [as a result] I looked for and got a new job.

One good way to remember these seven coordinating conjunctions is by memorizing the word formed by the first letter in each:

RULE TO REMEMBER | For And Nor But Or Yet So = FANBOYS

FOR PRACTICE

Practice 18a. Complete this exercise by underlining verbs twice and subjects once, and by circling the words that join the two independent clauses. The first sentence is done for you.

Knowing When to Quit

1. At seventeen I started working at a gas station, (for) I wanted to earn enough money to buy a car.
2. I actually liked the work at the gas station, but I soon realized that my time is worth more than the amount of money I was paid.
3. After a few months, I was no longer content to work for $6.25 an hour, nor was my boss willing to raise my salary.
4. He would not give in, so I looked for and got a new job.
5. My current job as dishwasher and cook at a Chinese restaurant keeps me in the kitchen most of the time, yet I get to talk to customers occasionally.
6. My starting salary is $7.80 an hour, and I will get a raise every three months.
7. I am going back to school part-time, for I will be able to compete for better jobs with a college education.
8. Several of my peers at the restaurant dislike restaurant work, yet they aren't willing to go back to school to get a degree.
9. My ambitions include managing my own restaurant, so I take business classes.
10. By working in the restaurant business while attending college, I will gain experience, and I will earn enough money to pay my tuition.
11. My boss is very flexible and lets me work nights and go to school during the day, or I can work the lunch shift and attend school in the evening.
12. It will take time to achieve my objective of managing my own restaurant, but with education and experience I will reach my goal.

Practice 18b. Add commas and coordinating conjunctions to the following sentences. Be sure that the conjunction you choose links the ideas in the two clauses logically; refer to the list of coordinating conjunctions if necessary. In some sentences, several conjunctions may work logically. The first sentence has been completed for you.

On the Spot

1. It was a muggy Monday morning, _____and_____ I was in no mood to work.

2. My math teacher was busily going over the homework assignment _____ I just sat in my seat thinking about how good it would feel to be in bed.

3. Suddenly she called on me to answer_____ I could feel my heart pounding.

4. My hand began to shake from nervousness _____ I was really scared.

5. At the time a few things were going through my mind: I could tell her that I had done the work _____ I didn't understand it _____ I could just refuse to do the work.

6. The work was absolutely no problem _____ I had done my homework in thirty minutes.

7. At this point I was going through real emotional turmoil. I knew what was right _____ I didn't know exactly how to act on it.

8. I had to do something _____ I quickly considered how disappointed my teacher would be if I refused to do the problems.

9. Then it occurred to me that it would not hurt me to share my knowledge with the class _____ I took a deep breath and began to answer the question correctly.

10. In spite of my anxiety, this experience was good _____ I was able to return to my desk with the feeling that I had contributed something valuable to the class _____ I hadn't betrayed my own intelligence.

Practice 18c. Add your own independent clauses to complete the following compound sentences. The first one is done as a sample. Notice that commas precede the coordinating conjunctions.

Worried about School

1. I used to dread the first day in a new school, for <u>I was worried that I would not be able to find my classes or find any of my old friends.</u>

2. I tried and tried to get to bed early the night before my first day at school, but

_____

_____

3. I would lie awake wondering what would happen if I could not find my classes,

and _____

_____

4. By the time morning finally came, I was always a wreck, yet _____

_____

_____

5. Once I got to school, I usually felt better, for _____

_____

6. Then, too, as soon as I got my schedule, I bought my new books, and

_____

_____

7. Now that I am in college, I have a little more confidence about that opening

day of school, so _____

_____

8. I realize that my fears about school were unfounded, for _____

_____

9. _____, so I guess

it's worth the anxiety it causes me to start the new term.

10. Several of my old friends are attending my college, and _____

_____

_____

Practice 18d. Write five sentences in which you connect two independent clauses with a comma and coordinating conjunction. Use your own paper for this exercise.

TRANSITIONAL WORDS (CONJUNCTIVE ADVERBS)

In Chapter 4 you saw how transitional words and phrases add coherence to paragraphs by showing logical connections between ideas. Some of these transitions (also called **conjunctive adverbs**) are used in combination with a semicolon to join two independent clauses. The following sentence illustrates this pattern. The clauses are enclosed in brackets, and the transitional word is circled for you.

[For years, women have been working in police departments as secretaries and dispatchers]; (however), [they are no longer satisfied with these roles.]

Common transitions and the logical connection they express are listed here:

To add ideas:	use *also, besides, furthermore, moreover, in fact, in addition*
To order ideas in time:	use *finally, hence, then*
To emphasize:	use *certainly, actually*
To show contrast:	use *however, nevertheless*
To show similarity:	use *similarly*
To draw conclusions or show results:	use *consequently, therefore, thus, then, of course, as a result, unfortunately*

FOR PRACTICE

Practice 18e. Complete the following sentences by adding a transitional word to connect the two independent clauses. Notice that a semicolon precedes the transition and a comma follows the transition. The first sentence is completed for you.

Campus Events

1. Juan Ortega finds campus events to be an important part of his college life; <u>in fact,</u> he attends every cultural event and guest lecture that he can.

2. Juan's chemistry teacher encourages the class to attend cultural events; _____, she occasionally lets him leave class to participate in such activities.

3. She definitely appreciates Juan's interest in such events; _____, Juan must agree to make up any classwork he might miss.

4. Before noon on days when there are interesting events on campus, Juan waits by the fountain at the center of campus; _____, he can catch his girl-friend Judy as she comes from class.

5. Ti Lee, a friend of Juan's, likes to attend these events with his friend; _____, he sometimes has to leave campus before a performance begins.

6. Poetry readings and loud music bore Judy; _____, she sometimes leaves these events early.

7. Ti Lee and Juan play soccer together on the school's team; _____, they have the best team in the district.

8. Judy sometimes practices soccer with them; _____, she is better at the game than they are.

9. Judy, Ti Lee, and Juan all play chess on the coffeehouse patio; _____, they are planning a campus chess tournament.

10. Judy is the chairperson of the organizing committee; _____, she controls the scheduling for many campus events.

Practice 18f. Use a transition to connect the following pairs of sentences. The first two are joined for you.

Women in Law Enforcement

1. Female friends usually support women who want to become police officers. Family members may find it more difficult to accept an aunt, sister, or daughter as a police officer.

Combined: Female friends usually support women who want to become police officers; however, family members may find it more difficult to accept an aunt, sister, or daughter as a police officer.

2. Executives view women as fragile and helpless. They are unwilling to employ women as police officers. _____

_____

3. Women who are hired are not always given the same treatment as male officers. These women are expected to perform at least as well as the men who shun them.

_____

_____

4. Some officers refuse to be paired with a female. Male officers may stop eating at coffee shops or restaurants where female officers congregate.

_____

_____

5. The Equal Employment Opportunity Act of 1972 forced police departments to hire women as officers. Women continue to be underrepresented.

_____

_____

6. Training programs for female police officers sometimes ignore the martial arts. Women officers are forced to avoid potentially dangerous situations.

_____

_____

7. Parents are likely to discourage women from entering such a dangerous profession. They think that their sons are capable of handling conflicts, even violence. _____

_____

8. Studies have shown that women officers are just as effective as men. There is no logical reason not to hire them. _____

_____

9. In some cases, female officers have been able to break up fights or avoid violence in situations where a male officer could expect a confrontation. Such situations suggest that women can contribute a great deal to a police department.

_____

_____

10. Women officers are particularly effective in cases of domestic violence. When the department receives calls about suspected child abuse, the chief is likely to send women to investigate. _____

_____

Practice 18g. Complete the following sentences by adding a clause that works logically with the rest of the sentence. The first one has been completed for you.

Television

1. Some writers have called excessive television viewing "addictive" behavior; furthermore, <u>they argue that watching television impairs our ability to think and reason.</u>

2. It is true that, as a nation, we watch many hours of television a week; consequently, _____

_____

3. It is not clear that watching five hours of television a day is as harmful as taking drugs; certainly, _____

_____

4. I have never known anyone who stayed home from work to watch television; however, _____

_____

5. _____

_____;

consequently, television can draw the whole family together.

6. Some elderly or severely disabled people cannot go to a movie or nice restaurant for entertainment; therefore, _____

_____

7. The television can help non-English speakers learn language skills; however,

_____

_____

8. Television has often been used as a babysitter; consequently, _____

_____

_____

9. Television has played an important role in the creation of the "global village";
moreover, _____

_____

10. For better or worse, most American households contain at least one television
set; thus, _____

_____

WRITING PRACTICE

Practice 18h. Use the sentence patterns you practiced in this chapter to write a
paragraph on one of the following topics. Use coordinating conjunctions and transitional phrases (conjunctive adverbs) in at least five sentences. When you have
finished, circle the punctuation and coordinating conjunctions that join each
independent clause.

1. Describe one or two unusual or frustrating experiences that happened to you
   during the first few weeks of this term.
2. Write about a time when you were under tremendous pressure. Be sure to
   write in enough detail to recreate the experience for your reader.
3. Discuss an event in your life that you found particularly rewarding.

Combining Sentences: Subordinating Conjunctions and Relative Pronouns

CHAPTER
19

In this chapter, you will work with the second kind of clause found in English sentences—the dependent or subordinate clause. Like a sentence, a clause has a subject and a complete verb. Any clause that begins with a subordinating conjunction is a **subordinate** or **dependent clause** because it cannot stand by itself as a sentence. Instead, it can be attached to an independent clause or rewritten as an independent sentence. The exercises in this chapter give you practice using subordinating conjunctions and relative pronouns to make logical connections between the clauses in sentences.

For an online introduction to sentence variety, log on to http://owl.english.purdue.edu and add handouts/general/gl_sentvar.html to the URL.

CONNECTING DEPENDENT AND INDEPENDENT CLAUSES

Read the following sentence carefully. Can you find the coordinating conjunction?

A big city can seem like an impersonal place, for it takes a long time to meet new friends.

Now read this second sentence. Notice that like the preceding sentence, it has two clauses.

A big city can seem like an impersonal place *because* it takes a long time to meet new friends.

In the second sentence, the word *because* is a **subordinating conjunction.** It makes the clause *it takes a long time to meet new friends* state the reason why *a big city can seem like an impersonal place.*

Here is a list of frequently used subordinating conjunctions and ways they can link clauses.

SUBORDINATING CONJUNCTIONS

as, because	show a reason or cause
although, even if, even though, rather than	denote a contrast or exception
in order that, so that	indicate a consequence or result
as if, if, provided that, unless, whether	state a condition
where, wherever	show location
after, before, since, once, until, when(ever), while	denote a sequence in time

PATTERNS OF SUBORDINATION

The two patterns for combining dependent and independent clauses are explained in this section. The order of the elements in the first pattern is *independent clause, conjunction, dependent clause.* The order in the second pattern is *conjunction, dependent clause, independent clause.* Both patterns are correct, but notice that the idea in the second clause receives the most emphasis because it is the last thing the reader sees. Keep this notion of emphasis in mind when you choose one pattern over the other.

The following two sentences illustrate the first pattern for combining dependent and independent clauses—*independent clause + subordinating conjunction + dependent clause.* Clauses are enclosed in brackets, and the subordinating conjunctions are circled for you.

independent clause   *subordinating conjunction*   *dependent clause*

[Not everyone is friendly]   [(when) you first move to a big city.]

independent clause   *subordinating conjunction*   *dependent clause*

[A big city can be an impersonal place]   [(because) it takes a long time to meet new friends.]

The conjunctions in these two sentences provide the logical connection between the clauses. In the first sentence, *when* tells us that moving to a big city is the time that *not everyone is friendly*. In the second sentence, *because* gives the reason why *a big city can be an impersonal place*.

Notice that when a dependent clause follows a main clause, as in the preceding sentences, it is usually *not* preceded by a comma. This pattern differs from the punctuation with *for, and, nor, but, or, yet,* and *so* where commas precede these coordinating conjunctions. Consult Chapter 18 for a discussion of how to punctuate clauses linked by coordinating conjunctions.

The two sentences shown next illustrate the second pattern for combining a dependent and an independent clause—*subordinating conjunction + dependent clause + independent clause*. In this pattern, the dependent clause *precedes* rather than follows the independent clause, as the following samples show. The clauses in these sentences are enclosed in brackets, and the subordinating conjunctions are circled for you.

subordinating conjunction   *dependent clause*   *independent clause*

[(When) I was a little girl in Hong Kong,]   [I went to a fish market with my mom every Sunday morning.]

subordinating conjunction   *dependent clause*   *independent clause*

[(Once) my mother found this market,]   [she never went anywhere else for our fish.]

The subordinating conjunctions *when* and *once* are words that connect the dependent and independent clauses by showing how the two relate to each other in time. In the first sentence, *when* connects a time in the writer's life (her childhood in Hong Kong) to a specific activity (the Sunday morning trip to the fish market with her mother). In the second sentence, *once* shows how one event follows another in time: first mother found the fish market; after that she never went anywhere else to shop for fish.

Notice, too, that the dependent clauses, *when I was a little girl in Hong Kong* and *once my mother found this market,* precede their independent clauses. In this sentence pattern, a comma follows the dependent clause.

FOR PRACTICE

Practice 19a. Put brackets around the clauses in the following sentences, and circle the subordinating conjunctions. Add punctuation if the dependent clause comes first in the sentence. The first one is done for you.

The Dangers of MySpace.com

1. [MySpace is a website on the Internet] [(where) everyone, teenagers in particular, can meet new people and share information about everything from popular music to personal problems.]
2. In the last few years, MySpace has become the most visited site on the Internet although it also poses dangers, especially for young girls.
3. Before MySpace became so popular teens were more likely to gather at the mall to exchange news and just "hang out" together.
4. Although teens still find malls attractive places to meet their friends MySpace has several features that malls can't offer.
5. MySpace may be luring teens away from the malls since MySpace offers teens and young adults access to a much larger, worldwide community.
6. Anyone who registers on MySpace can obtain a personal web space where users can post photographs or upload videos to personalize their pages.
7. However, MySpace has generated much criticism because the Internet site has its share of stalkers.
8. Although MySpace claims to restrict use to teens fourteen and older, there is nothing to stop a pre-teen from pretending to be older and registering as a member.
9. While their young sons and daughters are captivated by this website parents worry about the safety of their children.
10. Parents, as well as teachers, are concerned because a growing number of police reports link violent crimes with MySpace.
11. Because of its popularity and relatively easy access MySpace does, without a doubt, attract its share of unsavory characters.
12. A few professionals caution parents against forbidding their teens to use MySpace because, in their view, it may serve an important function in the development of a young person's identity.

Practice 19b. Fill in an appropriate subordinating conjunction to link the clauses in the sentences listed here. Make sure that the word you choose makes sense in the sentence as a whole. You may wish to consult the list of subordinating conjunctions on page 444. Be sure to add commas where you need them. The first sentence is completed for you.

One Teacher's Story

1. In the early 1980s, teaching positions were cut in the school district where I worked _____because_____ enrollment had dropped.

2. _____ several hundred teachers, young and old, had assembled in the gym each of us picked a number to determine which classes we could have and how often we could teach.

3. That year we got our classes by lottery _____ I suspected that the real reason they used a lottery in assigning classes was to encourage some of us to retire.

4. _____ I managed to stay in the district three more tough, miserable years, I sometimes wonder how I did it.

5. For those three years I worked as a relief teacher _____ teachers who didn't like their assignments could be excused from a class.

6. _____ the sun came up in the morning, I was getting ready for my early morning physical education class.

7. Most children were cooperative and behaved nicely _____ one horrible morning.

8. _____ the class left for their second period, I noticed a child hanging around the entrance to the classroom.

9. I had the feeling she was watching for somebody _____ she kept peering around the corner into the class.

10. I learned the reason for my caution _____ later that day she punched a little boy in the stomach.

11. I decided that afternoon to give the school district my notice and quit _____ they could find a replacement.

12. Ten other teachers either retired or asked for transfer _____ the district would hire tougher administrators and put more money into resources for the teaching staff.

Practice 19c. In the following sentences, the dependent clauses are supplied for you. Add your own ideas in a main clause that completes the sentence. The first sentence is completed for you.

1. When I enrolled at City College, <u>my goal was to graduate and become</u>

<u>an accountant</u>.

2. Once I took a computer class, _____

_____

3. Even though I was bored with math in high school, _____

_____

4. _____ because

I want to make my parents proud of me.

5. Since I live with my parents, _____

_____.

6. When I got my first job, _____

_____.

7. _____ although

I am worth more than minimum wage.

8. If I continue going to school, _____

_____

Practice 19d. To practice connecting clauses logically, combine the following sentences. As you write your sentences, think about which idea you want to subordinate and which is most appropriate for the main clause. Add commas as you need them. The first pair is combined for you.

Why Have a Cell Phone?

1. The concept of the cell phone has been around since 1947.
   The technology and a viable cellular system are relatively new.
   Combined: <u>Although</u> the concept of the cell phone has been around since 1947, the technology and viable cellular systems are relatively new.
2. Initially, mobile phones were designed for use as "car phones."
   They were mainly used in police vehicles.
3. Researchers soon realized that a system of small "cells" could increase the number of possible users.
   The FCC would release radio frequencies for the commercial use of cell phones.
4. In the last few years, cell phones have become a fact of life.
   There may be a few holdouts who reject the technology.
5. Cell phones became widely used.
   They have served many functions, from the trivial to the significant.
6. A father may use his cell phone.
   He wants to find out what the family would like to have for dinner.
7. He hangs up after getting the information.
   He can swing by the market to assemble the makings of the meal.
8. Recycled cell phones can make emergency calls.
   These phones have often been donated.
   Someone is in trouble.

9. Nowadays, cellular phones have numerous special features.
   Their owners may choose to use those features or not.
10. They are too far from a transmission source.
    Cell phone users can connect to the Internet, send text messages to their friends, and even photograph their favorite sunset.
11. A person may never have used a cell phone.
    It takes just a few minutes to learn how to use the basic features.
12. It is also true.
    Cell phones can be disruptive in meetings and in the classroom.
    Users remember to turn them off.

Practice 19e. Use your own paper for this exercise. Write a paragraph on one of the topics listed here. At least five sentences should combine dependent and independent clauses. Try to use both of the two possible patterns discussed in this chapter. Be sure to punctuate your sentences correctly. When you have finished writing, go back over your paragraph and put brackets around independent and dependent clauses. Then circle the subordinating conjunctions.

1. a difficult parting
2. shopping for a special occasion
3. an offensive advertisement
4. a favorite television program
5. your least favorite member of the family

RELATIVE PRONOUNS

When writers need to clarify an idea or identify a person more precisely, they use a **relative clause.** The relative clause in the following sentence is placed in brackets.

> My uncle, [who raises hogs for a living,] taught me the care and feeding of these misunderstood animals.

Notice that the relative clause *who raises hogs for a living* interrupts the independent clause *my uncle taught me the care and feeding of these misunderstood animals.* The relative pronoun, *who,* refers to *uncle;* the clause *who raises hogs for a living* says something about what this *uncle* does. In addition, because *who* refers to *uncle,* it is singular; that means the verb *raises* must be singular as well to agree with *uncle,* the singular subject of the sentence.

RULE TO REMEMBER   Relative clauses modify nouns. The verbs in these clauses agree with the noun that the clause modifies.

The three common relative pronouns are *who, that,* and *which.* In this special kind of dependent clause, *who, that,* and *which* are the subjects of the clauses in which they appear. Here again, the verbs in these clauses agree in number with the noun the clause modifies. The arrows in the following sentences illustrate how *that* and *which* are connected to the nouns they modify.

My uncle has almost two hundred hogs and pigs [that are waiting to be sold.]

He has to mend the fences, [which the hogs love to charge,] at least once a month.

FOR PRACTICE

Practice 19f. Complete the relative clauses in the following sentences. The first one is completed for you.

Raising Hogs

1. The hogs that __my uncle raises__ are some of the most interesting animals I have ever seen.

2. My hog-raising uncle, who _____ _____, showed me what hogs do to keep warm.

3. When it gets cold, which _____ _____, hogs lie on top of one another to keep warm.

4. Most human beings, who _____ _____, could never be so close together for that long.

5. If the temperature dips below freezing, which _____ _____, we light a fire to keep them warm.

DEFINITION AND NONDEFINITION CLAUSES

The following sentences and explanations illustrate the use of relative pronouns in definition and nondefinition clauses. The relative clauses are enclosed in brackets.

People [who marry in their teens] often divorce in their twenties.

In this sentence, the relative clause *who marry in their teens* defines which people often divorce in their twenties. Notice that no commas are used to separate this definition clause from the rest of the sentence. Here is the same sentence *without* the relative clause:

People often divorce in their twenties.

This second sentence has a completely different meaning from the first. It says that people in general get divorced in their twenties, but the author really wanted to refer only to a certain group of people—those *who marry in their teens*. Therefore, the relative clause defines or restricts the meaning of *people*. Without it, the original point of the sentence is lost.

FOR PRACTICE

Practice 19g. Combine each pair of sentences into a single sentence by changing the second sentence to a *who, which,* or *that* clause. Make sure *who* refers to people and *which* refers to things. *That* may refer to people or things. Write the relative clause so it *defines* the meaning of the noun it modifies. Punctuate the sentence correctly. The first sentence is done for you.

Hope for the Future

1. Immigrants are often hoping for a better life. Immigrants come to the United States.

Combined: Immigrants who come to the United States are often hoping for a better life.

2. Many people fled from the war in Southeast Asia. They came to the United States during the 1970s. _____

_____

3. Soldiers went from house to house. These soldiers were looking for new recruits. _____

_____

4. People kept listening for the sound of bombs. The bombs exploded in the distance. _____

_____

5. The constant bombardment became a signal for people to leave. It drove people crazy. _____

_____

NONDEFINITION CLAUSES

In the next sample sentence, the relative clause (in brackets) does not define the meaning of the noun it modifies.

> My sons, [who are three and four years of age,] are having a terrible time getting along with one another.

Definition and Nondefinition Clauses   **451**

The relative clause *who are three and four years of age* refers to *my sons* but does not define or restrict that term. For that reason, commas are used to separate it from the rest of the sentence.

Here is the same sentence written without the relative clause.

My sons are having a terrible time getting along with one another.

In this sentence and in the prior sample that included a relative clause, the writer makes the point that the sons are having trouble getting along. The author used the relative clause *who are three and four years of age* to make an additional comment, but *my sons* is a term that is specific enough to convey the meaning of the sentence without further elaboration.

RULE TO REMEMBER | A relative clause that *does not* define or limit the noun it modifies *is* set off by commas.

FOR PRACTICE

Practice 19h. Combine each pair of sentences into a single sentence. Use one of the relative pronouns—*who, that,* or *which*—to make one of the sentences a relative clause. Add commas to separate the relative clause if it does not define or limit the noun it modifies. Make sure *who* refers to people and *which* refers to things. *That* may refer to people or things. The first sentence is done for you.

1. Education is only for the very rich. Education is very important in our country.

Combined: Education, which is very important in our country, is only for the very rich.

2. Government officials punished anyone trying to leave the country. They did not want anyone to escape. _____

_____

_____

3. My cousins decided to leave anyway. They had very little hope for a happy life.

_____

_____

_____

4. Friends and neighbors kept quiet about their plan. They supported their efforts.

_____

_____

_____

5. The boat trip was long and arduous. It took several weeks.

_____

_____

_____

Distinguishing Clauses That Define from Nondefining Clauses

To become more familiar with clauses that define and those that do not, study the following sentences and the explanations that follow them. Relative clauses are enclosed in brackets.

My uncle John, [who is wearing a clown costume,] is visiting from France.

When a noun-subject is already defined by modifying words, as in *my uncle John,* the relative clause that follows it is *not* essential to its meaning and is, therefore, set off by commas.

In the next sentence, the relative clause *is* essential to the meaning of the noun it modifies.

The man *who is wearing the clown costume* is my uncle John.

Because the reader does not know which man the writer means, the relative clause is essential for defining *man.* Consequently, *no* commas are used.

Occasionally relative clauses may be definition or nondefinition clauses, depending on the writer's meaning. The following sentences illustrate this possibility. Again, relative clauses are placed in brackets.

Older students, [who have a reason for being in school,] tend to work very hard.

In the preceding sentence, the writer includes commas; consequently, the relative clause does not define only those older students *who have a reason for being in school.* Instead, the writer implies that *all* older students *have a reason for being in school.* Compare this sentence about older students with the next one:

Older students who have a reason for being in school tend to work very hard.

This writer does not assume that all older students *have a reason for being in school.* Instead, the focus is on a particular group of older students—those *who have a reason for being in school.*

Practice 19i. In the following sentences, enclose the relative clauses in brackets and add commas when the clauses *do not* define the noun to which they refer.

War

1. The combat soldier who knows what war is like has a much better idea of how frightening, chaotic, and horrifying it is.
2. Men and women who are soldiers cannot really be trained for actual combat.
3. Sometimes soldiers who become nervous during combat will shoot at anything that moves just to relieve the tension.
4. In any ground war, invading soldiers who are keyed up from battle can mistake ordinary citizens for the enemy.
5. Fighter pilots who are not involved in the ground war can make mistakes too.
6. Fog, rain, or snow which are common weather conditions in some countries can hide the bomber's target.
7. Bombings of civilian targets that have military significance are inevitable in war.
8. To confuse matters even more, schools and hospitals which are ordinarily reserved for civilian use may provide temporary shelter for militia or other combatants.
9. One thing is certain; men and women who live in a village or city inside a war zone must leave that place or risk death.
10. Every war is a human tragedy that both sides share, regardless of who might be declared the "winner."

Practice 19j. Combine the following sentences. Use definition and nondefinition clauses as appropriate, adding punctuation as needed. The first group is combined for you, and the relative clause is enclosed in brackets.

1. Immigrants may come to this country as refugees.
   Usually they can't choose the part of the country where they'll live.
   Combined: Immigrants [who come to this country as refugees] usually can't choose the part of the country where they'll live.
2. These new arrivals may end up living in cities.
   They drive their own cabs, work in hotels, and eventually manage their own businesses.
3. Many immigrants come from cultures that value independence.
   They are often too proud to rely on public assistance.
4. Immigrants' jobs vary just as much as those of other people.
   Other people may have been here a few years longer.

5. Sometimes immigrants settle in the Midwest on farmland.
   The midwestern farmland often resembles land in their home countries.
6. Urban-dwelling immigrants may find it difficult to get work.
   They have little farming experience.
7. Farmers are often looking for additional workers.
   They may need help with the harvest.
8. They learn quickly.
   They can grow their own food on small truck farms.
9. The immigrants learn to appreciate the rural way of life.
   They get used to the work.
10. Farmers and immigrants are slowly becoming familiar with each other's culture.
    Initially, they know little about one another.

Practice 19k. Write a paragraph describing an activity with which you are familiar. Use definition and nondefinition clauses in at least five of your sentences.

The following chart is a reminder of the connections you can make using the conjunctions and relative pronouns you have studied thus far. Use them to complete the next exercise.

WORDS THAT SHOW CONNECTION

Relationship	Coordinating Conjunctions	Subordinating Conjunctions	Relative Pronouns	Conjunctive Adverbs
To modify persons			who, whom	
To modify things			that, which	
To add ideas	and			moreover
To compare		as		
To contrast	but, yet, nor	although, even though		nevertheless
To show cause or result	so, for	because, in order that, so that		consequently, therefore
To show choice	or			
To show condition		as if, if, provided that, unless		
To show location		where, wherever		
To show sequence in time		after, before, since, until, when, while		

Practice 19l. Use coordinating or subordinating conjunctions, or relative pronouns, to combine the following sentences. Add commas where needed. The first one is done for you.

Childhood in Germany

1. My great-grandmother's name was Wanda Schmit.
   She was a child living in Germany.
   World War II broke out in 1939.
   Combined: [My great-grandmother, Wanda Schmit, was a child living in Germany] [(when) World War II broke out in 1939.]
2. Her father held an important post in Hamburg.
   He was sent to the front immediately.
   He was a mechanical engineer.
3. Wanda was only eight years old.
   She was caught in the major seaboard city of Hamburg.
   The city had strategic importance.
4. Most of the men in the city were sent into battle.
   The women, including mothers, were assigned to factories and offices.
5. Schools and churches were not really prepared for their task.
   They assumed the task of caring for the thousands of children left alone eight to ten hours a day.
6. Hamburg was a major port.
   It became a target for Allied bombs.
   Germany began its fourth year of war.
7. Food quickly became scarce.
   The bombings and transference of supplies to the soldiers left severe shortages.
8. The city's occupants were mostly women and children.
   They often found themselves running to protective shelters and cellars for cover.
9. The bombing attacks were aimed at the German industries in Hamburg.
   They increased in the last years of the war.
   The children had to be moved to the farmlands of Southern Germany.
10. Today Hamburg is a thriving city.
    It was once devastated by war.

WRITING PRACTICE

Practice 19m. Write a paragraph on one of the topics listed here. The paragraph should contain a variety of conjunctions and relative pronouns that link ideas in your sentences. When you are finished, check to make sure you have punctuated correctly; then circle the conjunctions and relative pronouns you used.

1. soap operas
2. winning a lottery
3. something unique about you
4. a song that stays with you

Correcting Fragments and Run-on Sentences

CHAPTER

20

Now that you have an understanding of how clauses form sentences, you are ready to examine one of the common errors students make when writing sentences. As we have seen, independent clauses and complete sentences must have a subject and complete verb, and be able to stand alone as an independent unit. In this chapter, you will identify and correct four kinds of fragments: fragments missing a subject, fragments that add ideas, infinitive and *-ing* fragments, and dependent-clause fragments. You will also practice recognizing and correcting another common error—run-on sentences.

For an online discussion of sentence fragments, go to http://owl.english.purdue.edu and add handouts/grammar/g_frag.html. For practice identifying and correcting fragments, click "fragment exercises" at the bottom of the page.

IDENTIFYING FRAGMENTS

A **fragment** is a group of words that is written as though it were a complete sentence, but it is *not* a sentence because of one or more of the following reasons:

1. It is missing a subject.
2. It is really a phrase meant to add ideas.
3. It is an infinitive or *-ing* phrase.
4. It is a dependent clause.

CORRECTING FRAGMENTS WITH SUBJECTS OMITTED

One common kind of fragment is a group of words written as if it were a sentence but missing a subject. Read the following examples carefully. Put a check (✓) in front of the word groups that omit the subject.

_____ Poppies bloom in early spring.
_____ But rarely appear in summer.

_____ Wintering robins enjoy nesting in my neighbor's trees.
_____ But seldom come to mine.

_____ Autumn winds soon stripped the trees.
_____ And left random piles of red and yellow leaves.

The second word group in each of these pairs is a fragment. Even though the subjects for these fragments appear in the sentences that precede them, every sentence must have its own subject. To correct the fragments, we must either join them to the sentences or add pronoun subjects. Study the corrections for the first example. Write two sample corrections for each of the other examples.

Poppies bloom in early spring but rarely appear in summer.

Poppies bloom in early spring. But they rarely appear in summer.

Wintering robins enjoy nesting in my neighbor's trees. But seldom come to mine.

1. _____

_____

2. _____

_____

Autumn winds soon stripped the trees. And left random piles of red and yellow leaves.

1. _____

_____

2. _____

_____

Practice 20a. Some of the following word groups are fragments because a subject is missing. Correct any fragments you find by either adding a subject or joining the fragment to a complete sentence.

Companions

1. Animals can be very important to us. And sometimes are lifelong, loyal companions. _____

_____

2. Dogs, in particular, remain loyal to their masters. Drawn to their every word.

_____

_____

_____

3. My first dog, Sheena, seemed to sympathize with my pain. And acted mournful and sad when I was sick or upset. _____

_____

_____

4. One day Sheena jumped the fence and was gone. Or maybe squeezed through an opening in the gate in the backyard. _____

_____

_____

5. I still think about that dog from time to time. And have never quite recovered from the loss. _____

_____

_____

Practice 20b. Some of the word groups listed next are fragments because a subject is missing. Correct any fragments you find by either adding a subject or joining the fragment to a complete sentence. The first one is corrected for you.

Who's Getting Married?

1. Today, men and women in the United States marry at an older age than they did twenty years ago. And have good reasons for doing so.

Correcting Fragments with Subjects Omitted   **459**

Corrected: Today, men and women in the United States marry at an older age than they did twenty years ago and have good reasons for doing so.

Corrected: Today, men and women in the United States marry at an older age than they did twenty years ago. And they have good reasons for doing so.

2. Fear of being laid off can have a lot to do with people's decision to wait. As well as worry about not being able to pay their bills. _____

_____

_____

3. Some men are reluctant to marry without first having a steady job. And may decide to wait until they are financially secure. _____

_____

_____

4. Some people in their twenties and thirties are afraid that getting married means losing their freedom. Or worse, giving up all control over their lives. _____

_____

_____

5. Many couples can't decide whether to get married. But find an alternative in living together. _____

_____

_____

6. Occasionally, they even raise children together. And never get married. _____

_____

_____

RULE TO REMEMBER | A group of words that is missing a subject is a fragment. To correct these fragments, add the missing subject or attach them to a complete sentence.

CORRECTING ADDED-IDEA FRAGMENTS

In added-idea fragments both a verb and a subject are missing. What follows are examples of words that are often used to add ideas. When they appear by themselves in phrases, they create fragments.

especially	such as
like	including
for example	for instance
also	along with

Put a check (✓) in front of the groups of words listed here that add ideas but lack a subject and verb. Correct these fragments by attaching them to complete sentences or adding a verb and subject. The first example is corrected for you.

1. ____ Finding a job can be difficult. ✓ ____ Especially without much work experience.

   Corrected: Finding a job can be difficult, especially without much work experience. OR

   Finding a job can be difficult. That is especially true if you don't have much work experience.

2. ____ You may, however, have valuable contacts who are willing to help you. ____ For example, among relatives and friends.

3. ____ A well-written résumé can make a difference. ____ Along with an attention-getting cover letter.

4. ____ It is important to list other work you have done. ____ Such as volunteer work for your school or for religious institutions.

5. ____ Political work and jobs you do for your community count as well. ____ Including work you might have done to register voters or to remove litter from highways.

6. ____ Most young people don't think much about owning their own business. ____ Like everyone else.

7. ____ When jobs are hard to find, however, the idea of starting up a business can become attractive to people in their twenties. ____ Even to students.

8. ____ Financing can be difficult, and it is easy to overlook an expense. ____ Including important ones like utilities and insurance.

9. ____ It is important to think twice about hiring employees as well. ____ Especially relatives and friends.

10. ____ In spite of the headaches, there are tremendous rewards for making a business work. ____ For example, a decent income and job satisfaction.

FOR PRACTICE

Practice 20c. Correct any fragments you find in the following paragraph by either adding a subject and verb, or joining the fragment to a complete sentence. Use your own paper to rewrite the paragraph.

When I was growing up in Vietnam, I had a lot of responsibilities. My parents got up at 3 A.M. to work in the rice fields and expected me to watch the children. For example, my two younger sisters and baby cousin. I had to get them up in the morning, help them get dressed, and feed them breakfast. It was difficult watching so many children. Especially the baby. My little cousin could make my life miserable. He loved throwing things around the room. Including the food I prepared for his breakfast. My sisters helped me as much as they could, but they had their own chores to take care of. Like most little kids.

CORRECTING INFINITIVE AND -*ING* FRAGMENTS

Fragments are also created when the writer uses an infinitive—a verb form like *to be, to seek,* or *to stammer*—in place of a complete verb. Another kind of fragment occurs when writers use an *-ing* verb form without a helping verb. Samples of each kind of fragment are discussed here.

INFINITIVE FRAGMENTS

Look at these two example fragments:

> Daniel studied hard. *To be* the foremost sky diver in northern Utah.

> Felicia, a hot dog vendor, *to run* after a nonpaying customer.

Two ways of correcting these fragments are as follows:

1. Connect the fragment to the complete sentence. You may need to change a few words.

   > Daniel studied hard to be the foremost sky diver in northern Utah.

   > Felicia, a hot dog vendor, ran after a nonpaying customer.

2. Rewrite the fragment so it can stand on its own.

   > Daniel studied hard. He wants to be the foremost sky diver in northern Utah.

   > Felicia, a hot dog vendor, had to run after a nonpaying customer.

-*ING* FRAGMENTS

Now let's look at another pair of fragments:

> *Living* by herself. My grandmother often complains of boredom.

> The robins that live in the tree next door insist on going to sleep when the sun goes down. And *leaving* their nest early in the morning.

To correct these fragments, do one of the following:

1. Add the fragment to the sentence that precedes it.

   > Living by herself, my grandmother often complains of boredom.

   > The robins that live in the tree next door insist on going to sleep when the sun goes down and leaving their nest early in the morning.

2. Rewrite the verb in the past, present, or future tense, and add a subject. You can make other changes for clarity or sentence variety.

My grandmother lives by herself. She often complains of boredom. OR

Because my grandmother lives by herself, she often complains of boredom.

The robins that live in the tree next door insist on going to sleep when the sun goes down. They leave their nest early in the morning. OR

The robins that live in the tree next door insist on going to sleep when the sun goes down, and they leave their nest early in the morning.

FOR PRACTICE

Practice 20d. Most of the following items are either infinitive or *-ing* fragments. Correct any fragments you find. The first example is corrected for you.

The World of Reading

1. Most people who like to read have the same goal. To find the time to read books they enjoy.

Corrected: Most people who like to read have the same goal, to find the time to read books they enjoy. OR

Most people who like to read have the same goal. They want to find the time to read books they enjoy.

2. A reader can go anywhere in the world. Traveling to the most remote areas of the globe. _____

_____

_____

3. The world becomes literally an open book for the reader. Wishing to go to the lush rainforests of Brazil, the savannas of Central Africa, or the Himalayas.

_____

_____

4. There are tales from the Maori of New Zealand or the nomads of North Africa. To fascinate the reader interested in human culture. _____

_____

_____

5. The story of Lucy, one of the oldest humanlike creatures in the world, awaits as well. To tempt the reader to study anthropology. _____

_____

_____

6. Of course other worlds besides travel and anthropology may stir the human imagination. _____

_____

_____

7. Readers can also find plenty of books about space travel, politics, gardening, cooking, and many more subjects. To provide enough material for a lifetime of reading. _____

_____

_____

8. There are novels as well. Introducing the reader to the suffering, the joys, and the triumph of the human experience. _____

_____

_____

9. Tolstoy's *The Death of Ivan Ilyich* is one classic story. Depicting a man who undergoes a spiritual awakening just before his death. _____

_____

_____

10. Chinua Achebe tells the story of one Nigerian man's struggle. First to become a hero in his own culture, then to free himself and his people from British colonialism. _____

_____

_____

RULE TO REMEMBER | To correct infinitive fragments, (1) rewrite the infinitive in the past, present, or future tense, or (2) add a conjugated verb to the sentence.
To correct *-ing* fragments, (1) change the *-ing* form to the past, present, or future tense, or (2) keep the *-ing* verb and add a helping verb to make it complete.

CORRECTING DEPENDENT-CLAUSE FRAGMENTS

A **dependent-clause fragment** results from writing a dependent or relative clause as though it were a separate sentence. You should not be discouraged if you find dependent-clause fragments in your writing. They are positive signs that you are trying to make your sentences more complex and varied.

Practice correcting fragments in the following exercises, and look for them in your own writing. The following examples illustrate how fragments are created when a relative clause or a dependent clause is written as though it were a complete sentence. The fragments are underlined for you.

> Last night I saw Sara. <u>Who hasn't spoken to me in ten years</u>.
>
> <u>After Barley went home</u>. Wanda started having a great time.

To correct these fragments:

1. Attach them to the independent clauses to which they logically belong.

    > Last night I saw Sara, who hasn't spoken to me in ten years.
    > After Barley went home, Wanda started having a great time.

2. Omit the subordinating conjunction.

    > Barley went home. Wanda started having a great time.

    You can join these shorter sentences in a different way:

    > Barley went home; then Wanda started having a great time.

3. Add or change words to complete the sentence.

    > Last night I saw Sara. She hasn't spoken to me in ten years.

    You can join these shorter sentences in a different way:

    > When I saw Sara last night, she hadn't spoken to me in ten years.

> **RULE TO REMEMBER**
>
> Correct a dependent-clause fragment by (1) joining it to an independent clause, (2) omitting the relative pronoun (or subordinating conjunction) to create an independent clause, or (3) adding words that complete the clause.

FOR PRACTICE

Practice 20e. Use any of the three methods just listed to rewrite fragments you find in the following sentences. A few sentences are correct.

America the Beautiful

1. The United States has some of the most spectacular scenery in the world.

Partly because so much land has been preserved in state and national parks.

_____

_____

2. Yosemite National Park, for example, has magnificent vistas with El Capitan and Yosemite Falls in the background. _____

_____

_____

3. Before the tragic fire that burned thousands of acres of forest. Yellowstone was the most popular of the national parks. _____

_____

_____

4. Old Faithful still gushes. Despite the blackened landscape you can still see in some parts of the park. _____

_____

_____

5. The peace and quiet in any of these parks is indeed a national treasure. That even the most skeptical visitors can't help but appreciate. _____

_____

_____

6. And don't forget about the wildlife. _____

_____

_____

7. If you are camping and especially lucky. You may see an eagle or hear a coyote.

_____

_____

8. Before you are really ready to get up. You are likely to hear raucous blue jays scolding each other in the branches above your tent. _____

_____

_____

9. In late afternoon, you will see small herds of elk. Wherever they find a meadow with a stream and their favorite bushes and trees. _____

_____

_____

10. Provided that we manage our national parks wisely. They will provide a home for these and other animals for centuries to come. _____

_____

_____

Practice 20f. Read the following essays carefully. Then choose one of them and rewrite it, correcting any dependent-word, *-ing,* and infinitive fragments you find.

A Place I Call Home

As I was turning onto Sunset Drive. I felt as if I was also turning back the hands of time to a time when I was safe and free of worry, so carefree and so innocent. At that moment I forgot. That I was twenty years old, engaged, struggling to pay the rent, worrying about my GPA, and most of all worrying about how to pay the bills. I decided to leave the present for the moment. In order to sit back and take a ride down memory lane.

Suddenly I had this incredible feeling. That the street knew me. It was as if the street were wrapping itself around me and giving me a welcome-home hug. I stood on the sidewalk, stunned and happy. Realizing how much I had missed playing childhood games, laughing and running in the vacant lot on the corner, and riding my bike all over the neighborhood. When I finally left Sunset Drive in the late afternoon. I had collected dozens of happy scenes from my childhood. To carry with me and to reassure me in future troubled times.

Problems with Mass Transit

Currently, the mass-transit system in this city leaves much to be desired. For one thing, when I called the bus company for information on my bus route. I had to stay on the line for seven minutes before I got information I needed about the bus schedule. In another instance, requesting a schedule by mail. I called and left my name and address. Which the recorded message instructed me to do. Several weeks passed without my receiving any information. As if my message had been ignored. After a second request, I received a map. But still no schedule. I finally had to pretend. That I had a rotary phone in order to speak with an operator.

Because of the frustrations I suffered with the automated information system, I thought the bus drivers might be better sources of information. To my disappointment. This is not what I found. Instead, the drivers were insensitive and their information misleading. For instance, one day when I was getting off the train to take the #94 bus. To my surprise I saw the #94 at the stop earlier than the scheduled time. The driver informed me that the bus was indeed #94 but failed to tell me its direction. As a result, I ended up on the other side of town and had to come all the way back. Just to get to the point where I had started. The worst of it was. That I had to pay for another ticket to go in the opposite direction. Because the driver refused to give me a transfer for the ride back.

CORRECTING RUN-ON SENTENCES

Run-ons are incorrectly written sentences in which independent clauses are put together with a comma or no punctuation at all. Run-on sentences are also called **fused sentences** or **comma splices.** As you begin taking risks with your writing, you may see an increase in run-on sentences. Don't be discouraged; the fact that you are writing run-ons is a sign that you are connecting ideas in new ways.

> For an online explanation of run-ons, comma splices, and fused sentences, see http://owl.english.purdue.edu and add handouts/grammar/g_sentpr.html to the URL. For an explanation of these errors and for quizzes, go to "The Guide to Grammar and Writing" at http://grammar.ccc.commnet.edu/grammar/runons.htm.

Study the following reasons why you might be mistaking run-ons for correct sentences; then try correcting your own run-ons in some of the ways suggested.

MISUSE OF TRANSITIONS

If you are using a lot of run-on constructions, you may be misusing transitional words and expressions like *however, besides, therefore,* and *then.* Here is an example:

> Jason usually gets to class early **as a result** he gets involved in some stimulating conversations.

Like the other transitional phrases listed in the discussion in Chapter 4, *as a result,* when used within a sentence, is preceded by a semicolon. It may also begin a new sentence, in which case it is followed by a comma.

> Jason usually gets to class early; **as a result,** he gets involved in some stimulating conversations.

> Jason usually gets to class early. **As a result,** he gets involved in some stimulating conversations.

CONNECTING IDEAS

Some run-on constructions may result from the fact that you are trying to suggest connections between closely related ideas.

> Rhonda enjoys her history class, the teacher encourages class discussion.

To solve this problem, you can suggest a logical or sequential connection by using a semicolon to join the two independent clauses:

> Rhonda enjoys her history class; the teacher encourages class discussion.

In this case, the semicolon indicates that the second clause explains why Rhonda enjoys her history class. The following corrected sentences express that causal relationship more explicitly by using conjunctions to join the clauses.

> Rhonda enjoys her history class, **for** the teacher encourages class discussion.

> Rhonda enjoys her history class **because** the teacher encourages class discussion.

SHOWING CONTRAST OR OPPOSITION

Finally, run-ons may be appearing in your writing because you are trying to show a contrast or opposition between ideas.

> Lucilla broke her leg last week, she continues to attend class.

A conjunction or transition can express this opposition:

> Lucilla broke her leg last week, **yet** she continues to attend class.
>
> Lucilla broke her leg last week; **however,** she continues to attend class.
>
> **Although** Lucilla broke her leg last week, she continues to attend class.

RULE TO REMEMBER

A run-on sentence can be corrected by using one of the following patterns:
1. independent clause + comma + coordinating conjunction + independent clause
2. dependent clause + comma + independent clause
3. independent clause + dependent clause (no comma)
4. independent clause + semicolon + independent clause
5. sentence + period + sentence + period

Complete the next exercises to practice spotting run-on sentences when you revise your own writing.

FOR PRACTICE

Practice 20g. Correct any run-on sentences you find in this exercise. Pay attention to the logical connections you make as you revise. The first sentence is corrected for you.

Cartoon Violence

1. On weekend mornings, children can have a little violence with their breakfast the robotic heroes of *Mighty Morphin' Power Rangers* and *X-Men* demonstrate how to blow up evil robots and destroy invaders from space.

   Corrected: On weekend mornings, children can have a little violence with their breakfast _∧ ^{as} the robotic heroes of *Mighty Morphin' Power Rangers* and *X-Men* demonstrate how to blow up evil robots and destroy invaders from space.

2. Other cartoon programs, such as *Superman,* offer shallow versions of men and women, some cartoon characters are little more than gender stereotypes.

3. To be heroic, men must be muscular, women must be big-breasted, skinny, and seductive.

4. Cartoons are teaching little boys to be warriors while little girls are learning to be sexy.

5. The characters on programs like *X-Men* have become as familiar to children as the names of members of their own families, they discuss the exploits of Wolverine, Gambit, and Rogue and have favorites with whom they identify.
6. Most cartoon characters fight continually they rarely exchange words with their enemies.
7. In these cartoons, children learn that situations can be solved with violence, no one is required to negotiate or compromise with anyone believed to be evil.
8. The popularity of the Power Rangers and their imitators has a sinister side to it, it means that more and more children are finding that violence itself can be a source of entertainment.
9. There is some debate among child psychologists about the effects of cartoon violence on children a direct connection may be difficult to prove.
10. Certainly teachers can tell which children are most likely to act out in class usually they are the ones watching these cartoons and other programming at least three hours a day.

Practice 20h. Make logical connections between ideas in any run-on sentences you find in this exercise. Use any of the sentence patterns you have studied to make your revisions. Some sentences are correct.

Toys and Children's Play

1. Many of the toys manufactured today do not challenge children's imaginations they are merely imitations of what kids have seen in cartoons.
2. Children learn to mimic their favorite cartoon heroes, they simply re-enact episodes they have seen on *Mighty Morphin' Power Rangers* or *X-Men*.
3. Fewer and fewer children play with building blocks or Legos® to create a house or small town they rarely think of building a space ship or igloo out of cardboard boxes.
4. In the old days, parents helped their children build forts and houses out of wood or papier-mâché today, dolls and robots come with their own town houses and space stations.
5. Teachers are complaining about their pupils' behavior they contend that children are imitating the violence they see in cartoons.
6. The Power Rangers, for example, solve problems by hitting and kicking, so the child concludes that problems are best solved by force.
7. Little boys are now fighting over little girls, this degree of sexual rivalry is new in elementary classrooms.
8. Cartoon mania is affecting performance in other ways as well. In today's crowded classrooms, teachers spend much of their time just getting the children to calm down.
9. Not much learning can take place in a room full of Power Rangers and robotic warriors teachers are convinced that parents must help.
10. There are many things parents can do to influence their child's behavior they can regulate hours for watching television, for one thing.

11. Parents can ask to see their child's homework assignments, that way they can be sure he or she is doing schoolwork.
12. In addition, parents can spend more time with their children so that they can help with school projects.

Practice 20i. Correct any fragments or run-on sentences you find in the following essay. Some sentences are correct.

Stereotypes Are All Alike

People use stereotypes to simplify their lives. Stereotypical thinking allows people to make assumptions about each other. Without spending much time on the effort. I know from personal experience that like many generalizations, stereotypes are rarely based on fact.

When I was younger. I was often asked if, like other Latinos, I was an immigrant. My father moved the family from New Mexico three years ago. To open up an art gallery in Southern California. We have lived all over the Southwest. Without having traveled outside the United States. Nevertheless, I am frequently asked to prove my citizenship. Especially when interviewing for a job. My first job was at a fast-food restaurant when I went for an interview, the manager who had spoken with me seemed pleased with my application. And acted as though he wanted to hire me. I was surprised when he asked to see my green card. Thinking that he had read my application more carefully. It was his turn to be surprised when I told him I was born in the United States, I have lived here all my life. Why would he think otherwise? Since I speak English as well as most people do.

Which brings me to my next point. People often assume that I speak broken English. Or have a lot of difficulty understanding the language. I was once in a bookstore in a small town in California, the cashier said to me, "Gee you speak English real good." After I got over my anger at the silliness of that comment. I was genuinely puzzled. I have gone to elementary school, high school, and now college in this country. Like many people who were born here. Anyone listening who pays the slightest attention to the way I talk. Knows at once that I speak English like a "native." That's because I *am* a native, of course.

My favorite insulting stereotype is the guessing game "What part of Mexico are you from?" Sometimes in the course of a conversation before a math class or in a passing exchange with someone I have met once or twice. The assumption that I am from Mexico surfaces. Often the speaker will have visited a city or an archeological site. And want to see if I was born anywhere near there. Mexico is a wonderful country, my ancestors were Mexican when states that now form the Southwest were part of Mexico. There's nothing wrong with being born in Mexico, however, not everyone who looks Latino was. I have had friends from Costa Rica, Argentina, and Columbia tell me about similar experiences. For some reason people expect anyone who is vaguely Latino looking. To be from Mexico. Asians suffer from a similar kind of stereotyping. A close friend of mine from Hawaii is frequently asked if she is from another country. Such as China, Japan, Korea, the Philippines, or some other Pacific Rim country.

For most people, making generalizations about the people they meet who may be different from themselves. Is a simple matter of convenience. Such stereotypes are often little more than distracting embarrassments for the person about whom the generalization is made.

WRITING PRACTICE

Practice 20j. Write one or two paragraphs on the following topics. As you revise, make sure that you have used a variety of sentence patterns and that clauses are combined correctly.

1. Describe the sort of imaginative play you did as a child.
2. Write your observations about how television influences children or adults you know.
3. Describe one or two unusual or frustrating experiences that happened to you during the first few weeks on a new job.
4. Summarize the plot of a novel you have read or a movie you have seen.

Making Logical Connections

By using a variety of sentence patterns, you can increase your ability to express your thoughts in complex ways. You will also make your writing more interesting to read. In this chapter, you will practice combining ideas using several sentence patterns. You will also learn techniques for checking your sentences to ensure that they are correctly written.

> For a discussion of sentence-combining skills and quizzes to test your ability to write effective sentences, see "Guide to Grammar and Writing" at http://grammar.ccc.commnet.edu/grammar/combining_skills.htm.

PHRASES IN A SERIES

Unlike a clause, a **phrase** lacks a complete verb, a subject, or both. In Chapter 17 you studied one kind of phrase—the prepositional phrase. These and other phrases may be connected in a series as long as all items in the series have the same form; that is, they are all prepositional phrases, *-ing* phrases, and so on. In the explanation and exercises that follow, you will practice combining such phrases correctly.

COMBINING PHRASES

The prepositional phrases in the following sentences describe the objects on Tina's hat:

> Tina decorated her hat with a peacock feather.
>
> She decorated her hat with a small pearl pin.
>
> She decorated her hat with a tiny Chinese dragon.

We can combine these sentences and write a more interesting, less monotonous sentence by joining the prepositional phrases.

> Tina decorated her hat with a peacock feather, a small pearl pin, and a tiny Chinese dragon.

Similarly, subjects, other nouns in a sentence, adjective phrases, and verb phrases may be combined to form a single sentence.

FOR PRACTICE

Practice 21a. Combine each of the following groups of sentences into a single sentence. The first is done as a sample.

1. Sal sent a letter of complaint to his congressman.

He sent a copy to his senator.

He sent a copy to the president.

Combined: Sal sent letters of complaint to his congressman, his senator, and the president.

2. When my son first began playing baseball, he had a nasty temper.

My son also had difficulty losing gracefully.

My son sometimes screamed at other children.

_____

_____

3. Beverly wanted enough money to live on.

Beverly wanted a house to live in.

Beverly wanted a modest car to drive.

_____

_____

4. The raging gorilla made the zoo a noisy place.

The squawking macaws made the zoo a noisy place.

The roaring lions made the zoo a noisy place.

_____

_____

5. My elderly aunt eats peaches in summer.

She eats boysenberries in fall.

She eats red apples in winter.

_____

_____

6. Heavy rain made the trip to Kansas a nightmare for Dorothy.

Violent tornadoes also made the trip a nightmare.

A high wind made the trip a nightmare.

_____

_____

7. Dean is devoted to his family.

He is devoted to the kids whose team he coaches.

He is devoted to his friends on the Internet.

_____

_____

8. Unemployment is sometimes linked to divorce.

It may also help explain why children are failing in school.

Unemployment may contribute to delinquency.

_____

_____

CREATING PHRASES AND CLAUSES

When joining shorter sentences, you can use a combination of phrases and clauses to create a more complex sentence. In the following example, several sentences are combined to make a single description.

My friend Switzer is devoted to exercise.

He insists on jogging in the morning before work.

He insists on working out at noon.

He insists on playing racquetball or tennis at night.

Combined: My friend Switzer, who is devoted to exercise, insists on jogging in the morning before work, working out at the gym at noon, and playing racquetball or tennis at night.

FOR PRACTICE

Practice 21b. Form a single sentence by joining the following groups of sentences. The first group is combined for you.

The Poor in Honduras

1. Honduras is a small country in Central America.

Its economy is based on agriculture.

It has a small industrial base.

Lumber is the leading industry.

Combined: Honduras, a small country in Central America, has an economy based on agriculture, with lumber as the leading industry. OR

Honduras is a small country in Central America whose economy is based on agriculture and whose major industry is lumber.

2. Most Hondurans speak Spanish.

Some speak a little English.

Indian dialects are spoken near the Guatemalan border.

_____

_____

3. Mountains cover most of Honduras.

The mountains make communication difficult.

_____

_____

4. The villagers live in mountain valleys.

The villagers live in relative isolation.

_____

_____

5. People in the Agwan Valley live in cardboard houses.

Their income is meager.

They eat whatever they can scratch out of the soil.

_____

_____

6. In Honduras, diseases are rampant.

They are often deadly.

Medical care is difficult to find, especially in rural areas.

_____

_____

7. Devoted Hondurans minister to their families' needs.

They treat illnesses with home remedies.

They share the little food they have.

_____

_____

8. In the last decade, the poverty in Honduras has increased among farmers.

The poverty has spread to some members of the middle class.

The poverty has even affected some professionals.

_____

_____

CORRECTING ILLOGICALLY JOINED SENTENCES

When you combine phrases, you achieve greater sentence variety and usually make your writing more interesting to read. It is important, however, to check the phrases being combined to ensure that they all have the same form. Such correctly combined phrases are considered to be **parallel.**

For an online explanation of parallel form and supporting quizzes, go to http://grammar.ccc.commnet.edu/grammar/parallelism.htm.

Study this example:

I caught Greg in a moment of weakness as he was watching television, munching corn nuts, and ignored his homework.

Underline any phrases that don't seem to fit in the sentence. The following break-down of the phrases in this sentence will clarify its structure:

I caught Greg in a moment of weakness as he was

watching television
munching corn nuts

and

ignored his homework

Notice that the last three ideas in the sentence are written in a series; all three must work logically with the helping verb *was* for the phrases to be parallel. *Was watching television* and *was munching corn nuts* make sense, but *was ignored his homework* does not. That is because it does not fit the pattern of the *-ing* ending established by the other two verb phrases. Phrases written in a series like this express a close connection between like ideas. If one of the forms is incorrect, that connection is lost or confused.

To clarify the relationship between the ideas in this sentence, we can rewrite it in one of several ways. Here are two possible corrections:

I caught Greg in a moment of weakness as he was watching television, munching on corn nuts, and *ignoring* his homework.

I caught Greg in a moment of weakness as he was watching television and munching on corn nuts; *he had ignored his homework*.

In the first sentence, the verb *ignored* is changed to match the pattern in the other two verb phrases. The second sentence links *watching* and *munching* and puts *ignored* in a clause by itself.

RULE TO REMEMBER | All phrases connected in a series must be written in the same form.

FOR PRACTICE

Practice 21c. Identify any forms in the following sentences that are not parallel. Rewrite them to fit logically with the rest of the sentence. You can add, delete, or change words as necessary. Some sentences are correct. In the first sentence, the correction is highlighted for you.

Hiding Well

1. My friend George is a master at deceiving people about his reading difficulties, at pretending he understands what he reads, and convince his teachers he knows more than he does.

Corrected: My friend George is a master at deceiving people about his reading difficulties, at pretending he understands what he reads, and **at convincing** his teachers he knows more than he does.

2. To cover up, he coaxes his friends and classmates to do his homework, type his papers, but not learning anything himself. _____

_____

_____

3. If he is asked to read aloud in class, he makes elaborate excuses, has a sudden and serious coughing fit, or fallen over his seat in a dead faint. _____

_____

_____

4. His teachers have gotten the message and no longer call on him to read.

_____

_____

5. If he goes to a party or dines out, George has to cover up his ignorance of many vocabulary words. _____

_____

_____

6. Sometimes he simply acts as though he is not interested in the conversation or having too much fun to be bothered. _____

_____

_____

7. Occasionally he slips and misinterprets what someone has asked and responding to a completely different question. _____

_____

_____

8. I have seen the time when such exchanges have become quite heated, feathers have gotten ruffled, and George to leave early. _____

_____

_____

9. There's a great deal about George that I appreciate—his love of sports and his devotion to friends are just two of them. _____

_____

_____

10. But for his own sake, George should think about getting into a reading program, start off slowly at first, and improving his reading skills gradually.

_____

_____

CONNECTING OTHER VERB PHRASES CORRECTLY

Writers use other phrases created from verb forms to add meaning to or modify the subjects in a sentence. Consider the following examples.

> Denise took a chemistry test at eight o'clock this morning.

To clarify the condition Denise was in when she took the test, the author of the sentence might add a verb phrase.

> Exhausted from studying, Denise took a chemistry test at eight o'clock this morning.

> Denise, exhausted from studying, took a chemistry test at eight o'clock this morning.

The -*ing* verb form (the present participle) is also used in verb phrases that modify nouns.

> While studying for an algebra test, Jackson gained a new understanding of the word *stressed*.

The infinitive form of a verb is the final kind of verb phrase that can be used to modify a noun.

> To get a good grade on his psychology test, Kenji reviewed his notes.

FOR PRACTICE

> *Practice 21d.* Use any of the three kinds of phrases illustrated earlier and combine the following groups of sentences. First write the second sentence as a verb

phrase (use an infinitive, an *-ing* form, or an *-ed* form); then combine it with the first sentence. Two sample groups are combined for you.

> Jason tried to start his car but discovered it had a dead battery.
>
> Jason <u>was running</u> late this morning.
>
> ↓
>
> Combined: <u>Running</u> late this morning, Jason tried to start his car but discovered it had a dead battery.

Notice that the subject and helping verb must be dropped to connect these ideas in one sentence.

> Jason took a taxicab to his mechanic's shop.
>
> He <u>intended</u> to get his money back for the battery.
>
> ↓
>
> Combined: <u>Intending</u> to get his money back for the battery, Jason took a taxicab to his mechanic's shop.

In this example, *intended* changes to *intending* to create a logical combination with *Jason took a taxicab to his mechanic's shop.*

My Dad

1. My dad was a very jolly in his later years.

He resembled Santa Claus.

_____

_____

2. My dad was a sawyer.

He worked in sawmills most of his life.

_____

_____

3. He worked long hours through the week.

He often came home after we had gone to bed.

_____

_____

4. He liked to spend as much time with us as he could.

He sacrificed his time during the week.

He wanted to make sure he had the weekend off.

_____

_____

5. He tried to make up for the time he couldn't be with us.

He would leave little treats each morning before he left for work.

_____

_____

6. He would fly the airplane he bought with a few of his buddies.

He went between mill towns.

_____

_____

7. My family used his plane to go shopping sometimes.

We were living miles from any large towns.

_____

_____

8. My dad would pile us into his plane and take off for Montana or the Southwest.

He wanted to go on vacation.

_____

_____

9. He also flew us to the Oregon coast in the summer.

He wanted to enjoy a different kind of scenery.

_____

_____

10. I now realize that his memory lives on in my heart.

I was saddened by his death three years ago.

_____

_____

CONNECTING DANGLING MODIFIERS

A verb phrase that is illogically connected to the main clause creates a **dangling modifier.**

> For an online explanation of misplaced modifiers, see http://grammar.ccc
> .commnet.edu/grammar/modifiers.htm.

In the following example, the first sentence makes a logical connection between the ideas in its verb phrase and those in the main or independent clause. The second sentence does not. Arrows indicate connections between the subjects and the introductory verb phrases.

To become more muscular, John started lifting weights every morning.

To become more muscular, weights were lifted every morning.

Both sentences begin with the phrase *To become more muscular.* In the first sentence, this phrase modifies *John,* thereby clarifying the fact that he started lifting weights to become more muscular. In the second sentence, however, the phrase modifies the noun *weights.* Because it does not make sense to say that weights want to become more muscular, the second sentence is an example of an illogical or dangling modifier.

Dangling or illogical phrases may appear at the end of a sentence as well as at the beginning:

Devita's parents were careful not to wake her while sleeping so soundly.

In this case, the subject of the sentence, *parents,* is the subject of both *were careful not to wake her* and *while sleeping so soundly.* This dangling modifier creates the illogical situation of having Devita's parents be asleep at the same time they are trying not to waken their daughter. Here is a corrected version of this dangling modifier:

Devita's parents were careful not to wake her while she was sleeping so soundly.

RULE TO REMEMBER	Verb phrases placed at the beginning or end of a sentence must have a logical connection to the subject in the independent clause.

When you find dangling modifiers in your writing, use one of two easy ways to fix them. To use the first method, create a dependent clause. This solution gives the phrase a subject and complete verb, and clarifies its connection to the independent clause. Consider the following example:

After dropping his backpack, **Lamar's books** went tumbling down the stairs. (dangling modifier)

To correct this error, give the phrase a subject to make it a dependent clause and to keep the emphasis in the main clause on the falling books.

After **Lamar** dropped his backpack, his books went tumbling down the stairs.

To use the second method, create a new subject and verb for the main clause.

After dropping his backpack, **Lamar watched** his books go tumbling down the stairs.

This time the subject *Lamar's books* has been changed to *Lamar,* and the verb *watched* has been added. With these changes the subject now works logically with both the phrase at the beginning of the sentence and the independent clause.

Notice that these methods of correcting illogical modifiers change the meaning and emphasis in the sentence. Be aware of these subtle changes in meaning as you revise your own writing.

FOR PRACTICE

Practice 21e. In the following sentences, some modifying phrases are written illogically. Rewrite sentences that contain errors. More than one answer may be correct. The first one is rewritten for you.

Ancient Writing

1. Before inventing written language, ideas could only be expressed verbally. (dangling modifier)

Corrected: Before inventing written language, humans could express ideas only verbally.

2. As a result, knowledge was difficult to transmit, learning only by word of mouth. _____

_____

_____

3. Some ancient peoples developed pictographs, word pictures of animals and other objects, to convey ideas. _____

_____

_____

4. Unable to decode these complex pictures with certainty, the paintings may represent anything from religious ceremonies to complex hunting techniques.

_____

_____

_____

5. Painted in caves, on canyon walls, or on pottery, the people who designed this art may have wanted simply to record a hunt. _____

_____

_____

6. Seven archaic cultures developed hieroglyphic or cuneiform writing whose symbols formed words, not pictures. _____

_____

_____

7. After inventing the first language systems, exact accounting records, histories, and religious beliefs soon appeared in the form of signs and symbols.

_____

_____

_____

8. Archeologists have deciphered all but a few ancient languages, involving detailed research. _____

_____

_____

WRITING PRACTICE

Practice 21f. Describe an activity that happens repeatedly in your life or a dream that keeps recurring. Use the techniques for connecting ideas that you have learned in this and previous chapters to vary the patterns of the sentences you write.

Consistency of Person and Tense

Consistency in your use of pronouns and tense is important for establishing a clear point of view in any paper you write. Losing this consistency results in confusing shifts in point of view (from *I* to *he,* for example) and tense (from past to present or from present to past). This chapter gives you practice recognizing and correcting inconsistencies of person and tense.

For an online explanation with supporting quizzes, see "Guide to Grammar and Writing" at http://grammar.ccc.commnet.edu/grammar/consistency.htm.

CONSISTENCY OF PERSON

The review of pronoun forms in this section will help you identify the point of view in any piece of writing and recognize when a writer has shifted from that point of view.

PRONOUNS

Pronoun Form	Singular	Plural
first person	I	we
second person	you	you
third person	he/she/it	they

When drafting a paper, writers sometimes use the pronouns *I, we, you,* and *they* at random. Such random use of pronouns is referred to as a **pronoun shift**. These shifts are confusing because they make it difficult for readers to tell what point of view the writer wants to use. An author must decide whether to adopt a personal point of view (using the first person, *I*), to write objectively (using *he/she/it/they*), or to address the reader directly (using *you*). These distinctions are not inflexible, however. The writer may, for example, use his or her own experience to illustrate a point in an otherwise objective paper.

The following sentences illustrate the confusion that occurs when the point of view or "voice" is not used consistently in a paragraph.

> Despite the efforts of the American Cancer Society and the American Lung Association, we Americans continue to smoke. I am more likely to be a smoker if I am a teenager, but you should not forget that the middle-aged and elderly also keep lighting up.

The writer of this paragraph will communicate ideas more clearly if she chooses a single point of view. The following is one possible revision:

> Despite the efforts of the American Cancer Society and the American Lung Association, many Americans continue to smoke. Americans are more likely to smoke if they are teenagers, but it should not be forgotten that the middle-aged and elderly also keep lighting up.

In this revision, the point of view is objective because it uses the third person (*he/she/it/they*) throughout. Here is a second revision:

> Despite the efforts of the American Cancer Society and the American Lung Association, we Americans continue to smoke. We are more likely to be smokers if we are teenagers, but we should not forget that as middle-aged and elderly adults, we also keep lighting up.

This second revision uses the first-person plural pronoun *we* to make a more personal appeal to the reader.

No single point of view will be appropriate all the time. Sometimes it is best to write about something using your own voice (*I*). On other occasions, you will want to be more objective about what you write. The important thing is to avoid confusing shifts among points of view. The best way to avoid that problem is to decide what point of view you will use before you begin writing.

FOR PRACTICE

Practice 22a. The following sentences form a single paragraph. They have been separated for ease in correcting. Read all of them before deciding which point of view to use. Change any pronouns that are not consistent with your choice.

Memories of Uncle Hugh and Aunt Florence

1. Years ago, before they sold their land to a developer whose company leveled their farmhouse, you could visit my great-aunt and -uncle.
2. To us, their house was like a grand palace, and my uncle was a nobleman who could have been driven about in a limousine.
3. Actually, Uncle Hugh was a humble man, a man who would take me into the fields to pick strawberries, who would help you fill your bucket to the brim.
4. Then, too, my great-aunt Florence was as fine a woman as I have ever known.
5. I remember her playful sense of humor most of all, and one could not imagine a more patient teacher.
6. When I was four and one's fingers barely reached the keys, Aunt Florence gave me my first lesson on her grand piano that sat in her living room.
7. The cold, ivory keys came alive when she played them, and people could hear the sounds of a musical waterfall throughout the house.
8. It is important to remember these kindhearted people for the rest of one's life.

Practice 22b. Decide whether the following paragraphs should be written from a personal point of view (*I*), an objective point of view (*he/she/it/they*), or as a direct address to the reader (*you*). Change pronouns that are not consistent with the point of view you have chosen. More than one choice is possible; what matters is that you use the pronouns consistently.

Autocross Racing

You can learn to race at the autocross school in town. Taught by experts, the courses teach a driver that autocross racing is fun but challenging. After a single lesson, you can tell that autocross involves much more than showing off hot cars. Much skill is required to drive the course safely and effectively.

Autocross itself is a miniature racecourse marked by little orange cones. A large parking lot usually provides a good site for the course. You are put into two groups for "run" purposes. Engine size, type of tires, and the make and year of your car determine drivers' class designations. One by one, the drivers in each group take three laps: one is for practice, and two are timed. Our ultimate goal is to turn in the fastest time in your class.

The differences between an autocross race and normal, everyday driving make them like night and day. When driving normally, for example, one turns a corner by letting up on the gas, stepping on your brakes, turning the wheel, and accelerating out of the turn. In autocross, on the other hand, the driver must approach the corner with one foot on the gas, then take the foot off the gas while braking hard and fast. Instead of waiting to come out of the turn, you punch the gas pedal and accelerate around the corner. In short, the driver attacks the course and controls it with his car.

CONSISTENCY OF TENSE

Like consistency of person, consistency of tense is important for the coherence and readability of your papers. The examples here illustrate this point. Study the underlined verbs in the following sentences:

> The student who studies is like the squirrel who prepares for winter. When the cold weather hit, or the teacher gave a test, both the squirrel and the student are ready.

The writer of these sentences shifts from the present tense (*studies, is, prepares*) to the past tense (*hit, gave*) and back to the present tense (*are*). The reader is bound to be confused because what begins as a lesson about the importance of keeping up with one's studies becomes a description of a past event. In this revised version, notice how much easier it is to understand the comparison.

> The student who studies is like the squirrel who prepares for winter. When the cold weather hits, or the teacher gives a test, both the squirrel and the student are ready.

Like consistency of person, consistency of tense is important to ensure that the sequence of events is clear to the reader. For ensuring such consistency, the writer must decide which tense—past, present, or future—controls each paragraph. An author recounting the events that led to the decision to become a machinist will write in the past tense. A writer wishing to describe the most impressive displays at the Smithsonian Institute in Washington, D.C., may choose the present tense in order to make the experience vivid and immediate for the audience. The writer may refer to something that happened before or after the basic tense of the paragraph but will return to that basic tense immediately after the reference.

Use the following exercises to practice proofreading for consistency of tense.

FOR PRACTICE

Practice 22c. Study the following paragraphs. Look for clues that will help you decide whether to use the past, present, or future as the basic tense. Change verbs as needed to make them consistent with the basic tense.

Brother's Power

My older brother used to bully me unmercifully when we were children. He knows that as his younger sister, I worship him, and he can get me to do whatever he wants. I do exactly what he told me to do until the day he made me beat up a boy he doesn't like. At first I refuse to do what he asks, but eventually, in a fit of rage at my brother, I run over and punch my brother's rival in the nose. That day I swore I would never do my brother's bidding again.

Raising Money

Several ways are available for volunteer or nonprofit organizations to raise money. Auctions and bake sales were important sources of income for church organizations and groups like the Girl Scouts. Telephone and mail solicitation work best for large, national organizations, although these activities return cash only a small percentage of the time. It was expensive to use the mail, too, even though community organizations can mail letters and announcements for free. Of course, the costs of printing letters and fliers must be budgeted. Someone had to volunteer to stuff envelopes, as well.

Practice 22d. Decide the most appropriate tense for the following paragraphs. Then change any verbs you find that shift from that tense.

Roommate

I had a close friend who tried and succeeded in ruining our friendship. After meeting in January, I enjoyed Ruth's company every time we are together. We study together in coffee shops, go clothes shopping, and rode our bikes in the park. After a few months of this acquaintance, we move in together, thinking we will get along just fine. We have so many goals in common. We are both in school, we were practical, and we both agree about most political issues.

Living together is fine at first, until Ruth began hiding important things by lying. I told her there were certain things I will not tolerate as her roommate, but she ignores me. She tells me that she has plenty of money in the bank, and she didn't. She also tells me what a good line of credit she had, and that wasn't true. The first time she lied, I overlooked it, but when she continued, I become frustrated. Then our friendship became worse because I felt I can no longer trust her. We talked about what had happened and where things went wrong and agree that the best thing to do was move away from each other.

WRITING PRACTICE

Practice 22e. Write a paragraph or short essay on one of the following topics. When you edit your paper, check for consistency of person and tense.

1. Write a short essay describing the driving styles of several people you know.
2. Think of a time when you were little and you stood up for yourself. Compare that event with a more recent example of standing up for yourself or something you believe in. Explain similarities or differences between the two events.
3. Write a short paper in which you compare your initial impression of someone with a later opinion of that person.

Sentence Types, Grammar, and Mechanics

CHAPTER
23

This chapter summarizes some of the basic rules covering kinds of sentences, grammar, and the mechanics of a sentence. These fundamentals include rules for verb forms and techniques for identifying subjects and verbs; for using commas, semicolons, colons, and apostrophes; and for correcting spelling and capitalization. Refer to this chapter when you need help proofreading your papers.

KINDS OF SENTENCES

Different sentence types express a range of ideas. Knowledge of the types of English sentences gives you the flexibility you need to convey different ideas. If, for example, you want to describe several characteristics of your subject, a series of phrases or clauses separated by commas probably works best. Here's a sample of a sentence that uses a series of phrases:

> The Beatles recorded "Revolution 9" as a mixture of strange, orchestrated noises, random spoken words, and musical phases played backward.

To clarify important characteristics of a person or situation, adding a clause with *who* or *that* may be the best choice:

> Tiger Woods, who showed tremendous talent as a young golfer, grew up dreaming of becoming the best golfer in the world.

What follows is a discussion of the four kinds of English sentences. Although there are countless ways to write these four patterns, each construction is based on a particular combination of independent and dependent clauses. Both kinds of clauses contain a subject and a complete verb. A dependent clause, however, "depends" on an independent clause for its meaning and cannot form a complete sentence by itself.

SIMPLE SENTENCE

A simple sentence contains one independent clause.

> Immigrants sometimes seek political asylum in the United States.
>
> Joseph Conrad, a native of Poland, wrote some of the most complex fiction in the English language.

COMPOUND SENTENCE

A compound sentence has two or more independent clauses joined by *and, or, nor, for, yet,* or *so.*

independent　　　　　　　　　　　*independent*
[Great writers sometimes had short, tragic lives,] but [their fiction remains as a tribute to their vision.]

independent
[Nowadays people can make their dreams of traveling in space a little more real,] for

independent
[they can buy expensive tickets to visit a space station or to land on the moon.]

COMPLEX SENTENCE

A complex sentence has one independent clause and at least one dependent clause.

independent

[People from other countries usually expect to improve their economic and educa-

dependent

tional opportunities] [when they immigrate to the United States.]

independent   *dependent (relative clause)*

[Some of the residents] [who lived in areas devastated by Hurricane Katrina]

independent (continued, split by dependent clause)

[have returned and plan to rebuild their homes.]

COMPOUND-COMPLEX SENTENCE

A compound-complex sentence has at least two independent clauses and one dependent clause.

independent   *dependent*

[I know a couple] [who wants to get married on the moon,] but

independent

[of course neither one of them is an astronaut.]

independent

[Lewis and Clark saw a peaceful future for Jefferson's America,] for

independent   *dependent*

[they envisioned a time] [when Europeans and native peoples would live side by
side in peace and harmony.]

RECOGNIZING VERBS

THE PRESENT TENSE

The **subject** and **verb** are the two basic parts of every sentence you will ever write. The subject tells who or what you are writing about. The verb is the heartbeat of the sentence—it provides action or says something about the subject. It may describe what the subject is doing, what it is like, or what is said about it. Locating verbs in sentences usually makes it easier to find the subject.

Study the following sentences about waking up in the morning. The verbs are underlined twice.

At 7 A.M. my alarm clock buzzes me awake.

I poke my nose out of the covers into the freezing air.

I pour myself out of my nice, warm bed while my teeth chatter like castanets.

Outside, the rain <u>pounds</u> against my window.

Inside, my breath <u>forms</u> clouds before my face.

In the sentences you just read, the words identified as verbs are alike in that they are in the **present tense**, they provide the action in the sentence, and they tell us what the subject is doing.

CHECKING FOR VERBS

The **verb** helps anchor a sentence in time. When we refer to the tense of a written verb, we literally mean the "time" in which it is written—past, present, or future. If you aren't sure whether or not a word is the verb in the sentence, use the following test to see if it can be written in the past, present, and future tenses.

THE VERB TEST

To find the verb in the sentence *Sometimes dirty water floods my grandmother's bathroom floor,* try changing the tense of any words that you think might be the verb. If, for example, you think that the action in the sentence is the flooding, then try putting the word *floods* in the past, present, and future tenses:

Today dirty water *floods* her bathroom floor.

Yesterday dirty water *flooded* her bathroom floor.

Tomorrow dirty water *will flood* her bathroom floor.

Because you can write *flood* in these three tenses and have the sentences make sense, *flood* is indeed the verb you were seeking.

If you have trouble finding the verb in the sentence *Luckily, I know something about plumbing,* use this test on words you think might be verbs. Let's say that you think the word *luckily* sounds like a verb, and you write something like this:

Today I *luckily* I know something about plumbing.

Yesterday I *luckilied* I know something about plumbing.

Tomorrow I *will luckily* I know something about plumbing.

The fact that these sentences don't make sense tells you that the word *luckily* is *not* a verb because it cannot change tense, so you must keep looking. (*Luckily* is actually an adverb used as an introductory word to modify the sentence.)

Perhaps the next word you check in this sentence about plumbing is *know.* This time the test looks like this:

Today I *know* something about plumbing.

Yesterday I *knew* something about plumbing.

Tomorrow I *will know* something about plumbing.

The test shows that *know* is a word that can change tense; therefore, it is a verb.

Try this test whenever you are not sure whether a particular word in a sentence is a verb. It may not work for you in every instance, but it is generally a good guide.

VERB FORMS IN THE PRESENT TENSE

The following table illustrates the possible forms of three regular verbs—*grow, run,* and *wait*—written in the present tense. The *s* on the end of the third-person singular form is underlined for you.

			Present Tense Singular		Present Tense Plural	
			Subject	*Verb*	*Subject*	*Verb*
grow	1st person		I	grow	we	grow
	2nd person		you	grow	you	grow
	3rd person		he/she/it	grow<u>s</u>	they	grow
			Subject	*Verb*	*Subject*	*Verb*
run	1st person		I	run	we	run
	2nd person		you	run	you	run
	3rd person		he/she/it	run<u>s</u>	they	run
			Subject	*Verb*	*Subject*	*Verb*
wait	1st person		I	wait	we	wait
	2nd person		you	wait	you	wait
	3rd person		he/she/it	wait<u>s</u>	they	wait

The verb *be* is irregular in the present tense. That means that the base or core of the word changes forms. The verb *be* is conjugated below with the *s* in the third-person singular form underlined for you.

			Present Tense Singular		Present Tense Plural	
			Subject	*Verb*	*Subject*	*Verb*
be	1st person		I	am	we	are
	2nd person		you	are	you	are
	3rd person		he/she/it	i<u>s</u>	they	are

The third-person singular form—*he, she,* or *it*—in the present tense often gives students trouble because it ends in *s,* even though it is singular.

RULE TO REMEMBER | Verbs written in the third person, present tense (the *he/she/it* form) always end in *s.*

THE PAST TENSE

Most past tense verbs in English end in *-ed*. The underlined verbs in the following sentences are written in the **past tense.**

> At seven years of age, I <u>asked</u> my parents to let me take horseback riding lessons.
>
> My instructor <u>started</u> me on "Cocoa," a little Shetland pony.
>
> At first Cocoa <u>seemed</u> nervous, and I just <u>wanted</u> to go home.
>
> She definitely <u>challenged</u> me.
>
> After about two months, I <u>wanted</u> a bigger horse, a "real" horse.

IRREGULAR VERBS

Irregular verbs change form in the past tense and must be memorized. The following chart lists the present and past tense forms of common irregular verbs. The past participles are used with helping verbs.

Infinitive	Past Tense	Past Participle
become	became	become
begin	began	begun
bite	bit	bitten, bit
blow	blew	blown
break	broke	broken
bring	brought	brought
buy	bought	bought
catch	caught	caught
choose	chose	chosen
come	came	come
do	did	done
draw	drew	drawn
drink	drank	drunk
drive	drove	driven
eat	ate	eaten
fall	fell	fallen
find	found	found
fly	flew	flown
forget	forgot	forgotten
freeze	froze	frozen
get	got	got, gotten
give	gave	given
go	went	gone
grow	grew	grown
hear	heard	heard
hide	hid	hidden
hold	held	held
keep	kept	kept

Infinitive	Past Tense	Past Participle
know	knew	known
lay	laid	laid
lead	led	led
leave	left	left
lie	lay	lain
lose	lost	lost
pay	paid	paid
prove	proved	proved, proven
ride	rode	ridden
ring	rang	rung
rise	rose	risen
run	ran	run
say	said	said
see	saw	seen
shake	shook	shaken
sing	sang, sung	sung
sink	sank, sunk	sunk
sit	sat	sat
speak	spoke	spoken
stand	stood	stood
steal	stole	stolen
swim	swam	swum
take	took	taken
tear	tore	torn
throw	threw	thrown
wear	wore	worn
write	wrote	written

THE FUTURE TENSE

The verbs that are underlined here are written in the **future tense.** These verbs describe what the subject will be doing or will be like in the future.

I can tell this <u>will be</u> another bad day for Raphael.

He <u>will</u> not <u>get</u> to work on time.

He <u>will reach</u> the highway during rush hour.

He <u>will</u> probably <u>be</u> at least an hour late for work.

Notice that words like *not* and *probably* may come between the helping verb *will* and the verb. (See page 501 for more work with helping verbs.)

Verb Forms in the Future Tense

The future tense uses the helping verb *will* and the base form of a verb (the infinitive without the word *to*). When the verb is negative, *will* may be written as *won't*. Following are some sample sentences.

The activities I will do tomorrow won't be much different than the things I do every day.

I'm going to bed so late that I probably won't hear my alarm tomorrow morning.

I will still be half-asleep when I take my morning shower and probably won't remember where I put the shampoo.

IDENTIFYING VERBS AND SUBJECTS

What follows is a review of verbs and subjects as they appear in several sentence patterns. These patterns include:

- clauses with multiple verbs and subjects
- clauses with linking verbs and auxiliary verbs
- commands
- questions
- sentences with introductory phrases

Read these three sentences carefully. The verbs are underlined twice.

In my younger years I did a lot of irresponsible things.

My older brothers got me into a lot of trouble.

My mother blamed me for everything.

Let's explore the relationship between the subject and the verb in these sentences.

In my younger years, I did a lot of irresponsible things.
  [*Who* or *what* did a lot of irresponsible things?]

My older brothers got me into a lot of trouble.
  [*Who* or *what* got me into trouble?]

My mother blamed me for everything.
  [*Who* or *what* blamed me for everything?]

FINDING THE VERB AND SUBJECT

Use the following questions to help you locate first the verb and then the subject in a sentence:

1. Which word can change tense in the sentence?
   (See the discussion of verb tense in "The Verb Test" on page 494.)

2. Who or what does the verb describe or refer to?

RULE TO REMEMBER | The subject of a sentence is the *who* or *what* doing the action, being described, or being talked about.

PRONOUNS

A pronoun as well as a noun can be the subject of a sentence. Study the following sentences; the subjects are underlined.

> It isn't difficult to find Selena on a rainy day.
>
> You are likely to see her walking along at a brisk clip, smiling and enjoying the rain.
>
> She wears an old felt hat and a light raincoat on such occasions.

MULTIPLE SUBJECTS

When two nouns are used as the subject of a sentence, they form a **compound subject**. The compound subjects in the sentences below are underlined once; the verbs are underlined twice.

> At fourteen or fifteen years of age, the teenage boy or girl grows extremely restless.
>
> Parents and teachers are no longer respected authorities.
>
> Family and friends often look at these teenagers suspiciously.

FORMING SENTENCES WITH MULTIPLE SUBJECTS

You may find in your own writing that you can combine several short, choppy sentences by creating one longer sentence with a multiple subject. This technique is illustrated in the following examples. The subjects are underlined for you.

> Janet performs well on the trapeze. Algernon does too.

It is easy to combine these two short sentences to make one smooth sentence by combining the subjects.

> Janet and Algernon perform well on the trapeze.

Notice that the third-person singular verb *performs* becomes the plural *perform* in the rewritten sentence, the word *and* joins the subjects of the new sentence, and there is no comma in front of *and*. Let's add a third sentence and combine it with the first two.

> Janet and Algernon perform well on the trapeze. Charla performs with them.

Here are the three sentences combined:

> Janet, Algernon, and Charla perform well on the trapeze.

Notice that we've added commas to separate the subjects because commas are used to separate *three* items in a series (see the first Rule to Remember under the Commas heading on page 503). The comma preceding the third item is optional, but once you begin using it, use it throughout your paper.

MULTIPLE VERBS

When two verbs in a sentence have the same subject, they form a **compound verb**. The compound verb in the sentence below is underlined twice, the subject once.

> The <u>businessman</u> <u>yanked</u> the tie off his neck and <u>stuffed</u> it into his shirt pocket.

The student who wrote this sentence wanted to describe *two* actions that the man (the subject) performed: first he *yanked the tie off his neck;* then he *stuffed it into his shirt pocket.*

Forming Sentences with Multiple Verbs

Carefully read the following sentences. The verbs are underlined twice for you.

> I <u>run</u> to my bicycle. I <u>jump</u> over the handlebars.

We can combine these short sentences to make one longer sentence in the following way:

> I <u>run</u> to my bicycle and <u>jump</u> over the handlebars.

Notice that the second *I* is omitted in the rewritten sentence, the word *and* joins the two parts of the new sentence, and there is no comma in front of *and.* Let's add a third sentence and combine it with the first two.

> I <u>run</u> to my bicycle and <u>jump</u> over the handlebars. I <u>hit</u> the seat hard.

Here are the three sentences combined:

> I <u>run</u> to my bicycle, <u>jump</u> over the handlebars, and <u>hit</u> the seat hard.

Notice that the *I* in the third sentence has been omitted in the new sentence and that commas separate the verb phrases because there are *three* items in a series.

LINKING VERBS

So far you have been working with verbs that show movement or action in the sentence. The underlined verbs in the following sentences are different from verbs like *crouches, growls, jumps,* or *rips* because they show a state or condition rather than an action.

> My father <u>is</u> old-fashioned.
> My mother and brother <u>are</u> ill.
> My aunt <u>is</u> angry.

In the first sentence, the verb *is* links the subject *father* with the adjective phrase *old-fashioned.* What words are linked by *are* in the second sentence and *is* in the third sentence?

The verb *be,* and other verbs like *become, feel, turn, look, seem, smell, appear, taste,* and *sound* are **linking verbs.** That means they link or join the subject of a sentence to a word or group of words that describe it.

The linking verbs in the following sentences are underlined twice, and subjects are underlined once. The word or words that describe the subject are placed in brackets. You will see that the descriptive words, usually called **subject complements,** always answer a question about the subject. These descriptive words are called *complements* because they complete the meaning of the subject.

complement   *complement*
It is [the Fourth of July, 1989,] and I look [beautiful.]
What day is it?   *the Fourth of July*

How do I look?   *beautiful*

complement
Today is [my wedding day.]
What day is it?   *my wedding day*

complement   *complement*
My dress is [a peach color] and looks [like an April garden.]
What color is my dress?   *peach color*

What does it look like?   *like an April garden*

AUXILIARY OR HELPING VERBS

Compare the verbs in the following pairs of sentences. In the second sentence in each pair, helping verbs have been added, and the main verb has been changed to its *-ing* form. This *-ing* form is called the **present participle**.

A giant bulldog crouches on the sidewalk.

A giant bulldog is crouching on the sidewalk.

I wear regular glasses.

I am wearing regular glasses.

Marlease watches the man at the bus stop.

Holden is watching the man at the bus stop.

The word *is*, a form of the verb *be*, serves as a helping verb in the sense that it "helps" to complete the verb.

Other common helping verbs in English are forms of *have* and *do*. The following list illustrates how these verbs might combine with the verb *see: have seen, had seen, will have seen; have been seen, had been seen, will have been seen;* and *do see, does see, did see.*

Other auxiliary verbs like *will* and *been; could* and *can; would* and *should;* and *may, might,* and *must* are also used frequently. These verbs do not change form as do the verbs *have, be,* and *do.*

VERBS AND SUBJECTS IN COMMANDS

Examine the following sentences carefully. They are written in the imperative or command form. The verbs in these sentences are underlined twice.

Don't give up.

Never take your freedom lightly.

Go to the window and look at the sunshine.

The subject in an imperative sentence is *you*—the person spoken to. If we wanted to indicate the subject for these sentences, we could write it after the sentence, as in the following examples:

Don't give up. (you)

Never take your freedom lightly. (you)

Go to the window and look at the sunshine. (you)

It probably seems impolite to your ears, as it does to most English speakers, to say "You come to the window." That's why sentences like these give the listener a command without including the subject. The subject, then, is implied but not stated.

VERBS AND SUBJECTS IN QUESTIONS

Compare these pairs of sentences. Subjects and verbs are underlined for you.

I became an actor.

Why did I become an actor?

I was afraid of the elephant's feet.

Was I afraid of the elephant's feet?

I will do something after graduation.

What will I do after graduation?

Notice that the subject and verb change positions when the sentences are rewritten as questions. In the case of the examples with *did I become* and *will I do,* the subject comes between the two parts of the verb.

DIFFERENTIATING VERBS AND SUBJECTS FROM INTRODUCTORY WORDS AND PHRASES

Many sentences in English begin with introductory phrases. Usually these phrases simply add information. When the adverb *here* or *there* begins a sentence or a clause within a sentence, it is important not to mistake these adverbs for the subject of the sentence.

Study the following sentences. Some begin with introductory phrases; others illustrate the placement of verbs and subjects in clauses that begin with *here* or *there.* The verbs and subjects in these sentences are underlined for you.

Here we are on San Fernando Road, not too far from Los Angeles.

In the mid-1920s, my great-grandfather brought his family to this place.

There were very few cars on the streets then.

In fact, there were no streets to speak of.

For many years, streets were made of dirt or gravel, rather than asphalt.

PUNCTUATION

COMMAS

This section summarizes seven of the basic rules for using commas. Several examples follow each rule. Most of these rules will be familiar to you if you have worked through the chapters in Part V.

RULE TO REMEMBER Commas are used to separate three items in a series.

Tina decorated her hat with a peacock feather, a small pearl pin, and a tiny Chinese dragon.

Janet, Algernon, and Charla perform well on the trapeze.

I caught Greg in a moment of weakness as he was watching television, munching corn nuts, and ignoring his homework.

RULE TO REMEMBER Commas are used after introductory words and phrases.

In the mid-1920s, my great-grandfather brought his family to Los Angeles.

Slowly but surely, cities began pulling up the old streetcar tracks.

Exhausted from her studying, Denise took a chemistry test at 8 A.M.

RULE TO REMEMBER A comma precedes a coordinating conjunction.

I waved to Melissa, but she didn't see me.

I am going back to school part-time, for I expect to get a better job with a college education.

It was a muggy Monday morning, and I was in no mood to work.

RULE TO REMEMBER A comma follows an introductory dependent clause.

When I worked for the Department of Parks and Recreation, I had the opportunity to play Santa Claus.

Although the children always told me they had been good, they acted like animals.

Because I had studied Sears' catalogs, I knew about all the latest toys.

Commas separate nondefinition relative clauses—clauses that do not define the noun they modify.

My Uncle John, who is wearing a clown costume, is visiting from France.

The combat soldier, who knows what war is like, has a good idea of how frightening, chaotic, and horrifying it is.

The economy, which suffered from stagnation and inflation, was weakened during Carter's administration.

RULE TO REMEMBER Commas are used to set off noun modifiers of more than one word. These modifiers are appositives.

Max Mosley, a cousin of mine, has taken up skydiving.

William Brown, the local dentist in Knox Grove, has difficulty keeping his patients.

Julie looked warily at the painting, a blotchy and dreary thing.

A diseased tree, the elm was removed last winter.

RULE TO REMEMBER Commas are used to punctuate dates and addresses.

I live at 4932 Winchester Street, Chicago, Illinois.

The prime minister of England lives at 10 Downing Street, London, England.

January 16, 1991, marked the beginning of the Persian Gulf War.

SEMICOLONS

The semicolon is sometimes characterized as a "weak period" because, like a period, it separates independent clauses. With a semicolon, readers don't pause quite as long as they would if the writer had used a period. Here are a few rules for using semicolons correctly.

RULE TO REMEMBER Semicolons separate independent clauses.

The Kurdish people are suffering severe hardships; let's hope aid comes quickly.

Rhonda enjoys her history class; the teacher encourages class discussion.

Most cartoon characters fight continually; they rarely exchange words with their enemies.

For years, women have been working in police departments as secretaries and dispatchers; however, they are no longer satisfied with these roles.

It is very difficult to carry fifteen credit hours and work at the same time; nevertheless, some people manage to do it.

Alejandro did well on his entrance exams; consequently, he was accepted to the University of Arizona with a full scholarship.

COLONS

There are two things I love to eat at the movies: popcorn and licorice.

If you are having a picnic this Sunday, be sure to invite the following people: Samantha, Bernie, and George.

Take several things with you when you go fishing: a rod, a reel, and a good book.

Unable to vote herself, my grandmother arranged to get several votes for her candidates: she told her husband and two sons how to vote.

APOSTROPHES

I can't see you very clearly. (*can + not = can't*)

I haven't got my glasses handy. (*have + not = haven't*)

I'm sure you will understand why I didn't recognize you. (*I + am = I'm; did + not = didn't*)

Wilmington's bicycle has beautiful chrome.

Fiona fed Martha's chipmunk while she was away.

A men's support group meets on Wednesday nights.

Note: Make a word like man plural first, then add the apostrophe *s*. When a plural noun ends in *s*, add just an apostrophe to show possession.

The students' trip to Mexico took six months to plan.

SPELLING

Some writers find it difficult to spell English words correctly because they are not always spelled quite like they sound. Words often follow the spelling conventions of the numerous languages that have given English its highly diverse vocabulary. This diversity accounts for the richness of English as well as its sometimes-quirky spelling.

One way to approach problems you have with spelling is to keep a list of words you commonly misspell. Make sentences with those words, and try to memorize a few each week. In addition, if you increase the amount of reading you do, spelling gets easier because you are seeing words in print rather than just hearing them.

BASIC SPELLING RULES

RULE TO REMEMBER | Use *i* before *e* except after *c* or when sounded like *ay* as in *neighbor* and *weigh*.

Most words in English follow this rule. Here are lists of words that follow each of the three parts of the jingle:

i before *e:* bel*ie*ve, ch*ie*f, fr*ie*nd, gr*ie*ve, th*ie*f
except after *c:* c*ei*ling, dec*ei*t, perc*ei*ve, rec*ei*pt
or when sounded like *ay* as in *neighbor* and *weigh:* *ei*ght, fr*ei*ght, v*ei*n, w*ei*ght

As with so many rules in English, this one has some exceptions. Here are a few of the words that break this rule: *either, neither, height, seize, society, their,* and *weird.*

RULE TO REMEMBER | When a word ends with a silent *e*, drop it when adding an ending that begins with a vowel like *-able*, *-ion*, or *-ing*.

The *-ing* ending is one of the most common endings in English, so remember this rule when you add these endings to words. Here are a few examples.

adore + able = adorable

vacate + ion = vacation

care + ing = caring

leave + ing = leaving

write + ing = writing

fly + es = flies

hurry + es = hurries

marry + es = marries

family + es = families

study + es = studies

worry + ed = worried

Keep the *y* when it follows a vowel or when the word ends in *-ing*.

pray + s = prays

study + ing = studying

worry + ing = worrying

COMMONLY CONFUSED WORDS

Some spelling mistakes occur because writers confuse a word with others that either look or sound like the word they are trying to spell. In the following lists of look-alike and sound-alike words, these frequently confused words are defined for you and put into sample sentences. Create your own sentences with words that give you trouble.

a
: Use *a* before a word that begins with a consonant.
  I have *a* bad habit.

an
: Use *an* before a word that begins with a vowel or vowel sound.
  Joe has *an* empty cup.

a lot
: *A lot* expresses a quantity of things. *A lot* is **never** spelled as one word.
  I have *a lot* of trouble with Zenobia.

allot
: *Allot* means to distribute a certain amount of something.
  Ms. Jones *allotted* five minutes for each presentation.

accept
: *Accept* means to receive or agree to.
  I *accept* your apology.

except
: *Except* means to exclude.
  I have taken all the requirements *except* chemistry.

already
: *Already* indicates something that has happened before the moment of speaking.
  Your paper is *already* three days late.

all ready	*All ready* means prepared. The entire class is *all ready* for the quiz.
buy	*Buy* means to purchase. I *buy* my coats in the off-season.
by	*By* is a preposition that can mean authorship or direction. *Lincoln* was written *by* Gore Vidal. Stop *by* the house on your way home.
have	*Have* is a verb. I *have* more bills than I need. *Have* is most often confused with the preposition *of* in combination with the helping verb *should*. Victor should *have* phoned me. (**not** "should *of*")
of	*Of* is a preposition. Adrian's heart is full *of* love.
its	*Its* is a possessive pronoun. The cat loves *its* new toy.
it's	*It's* is the contraction of *it + is*. *It's* a shame to have rainy weather on the weekend.
knew	*Knew* is the past tense of *know*. Regina *knew* six female athletes.
new	Something *new* has never existed before or is strange. The latest software programs are completely *new* to me.
lie	*Lie* means to recline (as well as to tell an untruth). I like to *lie* in the sun during the early hours of the morning.
lay	*Lay* means to settle or put something down. Help John *lay* this problem to rest. *Lay* the matches on the sink.
loose	*Loose* means the opposite of tight. The string is too *loose* to hold the papers in place. *Loose* also means free or unbound. Prometheus broke *loose* from his chains.
lose	*Lose* has the sound *ooze* in it. It means to misplace something. Why do I always *lose* my keys in the morning? *Lose* is also the opposite of winning. I don't like to gamble because I am afraid I might *lose*.
passed	*Passed* is the past tense form of the verb *to pass*. Maria *passed* the bar exam.
past	*Past* can be used as an adjective. Don't judge Mai on her *past* performance. (modifies *performance*) *Past* can also be a noun. Everett is living in the *past*. (The article *the* precedes a noun.)

	Past can also be a preposition.
	Aaron lives *past* the stadium. (indicates direction)
principal	The best way to remember this word is to think of the principal as your *pal*—the last three letters in *principal*.
	Ms. Weinstock was the *principal* of my high school.
	Principal also means first in rank.
	Sara is the *principal* actor in her theater company.
principle	A *principle* refers to a truth, rule, or standard.
	Gwendolyn tries to live by her *principles*.
set	*To set* something down refers to the act of placing an object on a surface.
	Please *set* the fan near the window.
sit	*Sit* means to be seated.
	How can Howard *sit* so long in one place?
their	*Their* is a possessive pronoun.
	In *their* earliest months, babies are very awkward.
there	*There* refers to a particular place.
	My brother and his wife live in Florida, but I have never been *there*.
they're	*They're* is a contraction of *they + are*.
	They're too busy to see friends at the moment.
quiet	*Quiet* means to have very little sound.
	Abigail is the *quiet* type.
quit	*Quit* means to give up.
	I *quit* my job after the boss hired his nephew.
quite	*Quite* can mean entirely or truly.
	This grading system isn't *quite* fair.
you	*You* is a subject pronoun.
	You are doing well in this class.
your	*Your* is a possessive pronoun.
	Your book fell off the desk.
you're	*You're* is a contraction of *you + are*.
	You're awfully nice.

CAPITALIZATION

The rules for capitalization are fewer, but they are important for achieving overall correctness in your writing. The basic rules for capitalization are listed here with examples to illustrate their use. Capitalize the following words:

1. The first word in a sentence, including sentences that are quoted

   My garden is full of flowers. Jamie said, "My garden is full of flowers."

2. The names of countries and languages
   Madagascar, Bolivia, Tagalog, English
3. The names of nationalities and religions
   American, Vietnamese, Islam
4. People's names
   Bob Marley, Titian, Ghengis Khan, Cher
5. The names of particular courses of instruction
   Aeronautics 3, Biology 1
6. The days of the week, names of the months, and holidays
   Friday, June, New Year's Day, Rosh Hashanah
7. The names of streets, cities, and specific places
   Broadway, Lafayette Drive, Oakland, Lake Tahoe, Wrigley Field
8. The names of major unrepeatable events and historical periods
   the Civil War, Bastille Day, the Harlem Renaissance
9. The titles of books, plays, television shows, magazines, and documents
   Love Medicine, Joe Turner's Come and Gone, The Simpsons, The Atlantic Monthly, the Bill of Rights

Writers sometimes make mistakes with capitalization by capitalizing words that do not require it. The most frequent errors in capitalization are listed here.

1. Seasons of the year are *not* capitalized.
   spring, summer, fall, winter
2. General names of courses are *not* capitalized.
   math, humanities, biology
3. If, however, the course is also the name of a language, it is capitalized.
   French, Latin, Japanese
4. General place names are *not* capitalized.
   the mountains, a lake back home
5. Occupations are *not* capitalized.
   teacher, policeman, podiatrist

As a general rule, words must be very specific to be capitalized.

Appendix

APPENDIX A

PRELIMINARY QUESTIONS FOR WRITING

1. What subject do I want to write about?
2. Who am I writing for and why did I choose this audience?
3. What is the main idea I want to communicate to my audience?

APPENDIX B

QUESTIONS FOR EXPANDING IDEAS

1. *Who? What?* Could I add information to better explain the persons, objects, or ideas in my paper?
2. *Where? When?* Could I write more about the place or time of my topic?
3. *Why?* Which causes or results could I write about? (Try asking this question several times to help you explore your topic as thoroughly as you can. If something didn't happen that you expected, try asking "Why not?")
4. *How?* What details, examples, or explanations can I add to show how something works? How is another object, event, or idea similar to or different from my subject?

APPENDIX C

QUESTIONS FOR PEER REVIEW

Questions for Discussing Paragraphs

1. What did you like about the paragraph?
2. Does it have a beginning that helps you focus on the subject?
3. Would you like more information about any of the general ideas? If so, which one(s)?
4. Did you have difficulty following the writer's ideas or reading some of the sentences? Explain.
5. Does the paragraph come to a logical end?

Questions for Discussing Essays

1. What did you like about the essay?
2. Does the opening paragraph get you interested in the subject? Explain why or why not.
3. Does the introduction include the main point of the paper—its *thesis*—either stated or implied? Write the thesis.
4. Would you like more information about any of the general ideas? If so, which one(s)?
5. Were there paragraphs that seemed off the topic and unrelated to the thesis?
6. Did you have difficulty following the writer's ideas or reading any of the sentences? Explain.
7. Does the essay come to a logical conclusion? What is it?
8. Would you like to ask the writer any questions about the topic, or do you have additional points you would like to make about the essay?

APPENDIX D

WORDS THAT SHOW CONNECTION

Relationship	Coordinating Conjunctions	Subordinating Conjunctions	Relative Pronouns	Conjunctive Adverbs
To modify persons			who, whom	
To modify things			that, which	
To add ideas	and			moreover
To compare		as		
To contrast	but, yet, nor	although, even though		nevertheless
To show cause or result	so, for	because, in order that, so that		consequently, therefore
To show choice	or			
To show condition		as if, if, provided that, unless		
To show location		where, wherever		
To show sequence in time		after, before, since, until, when, while		

Credits

PHOTO CREDITS

All part openers
© Jamie Tanaka Photography

Chapter 6
Courtesy of Tracy Albano and Karen Anderson Maiden

Chapter 7
© Jeff Greenberg/PhotoEdit

Chapter 8
Courtesy of D.C. Public Library

Chapter 9
© Rose DiBiasi/Photographers Direct

Chapter 10
© Tony Metaxas/Asia Images/Getty Images

Chapter 11
© Li-Hua Lan/Syracuse Newspapers/The Image Works

Chapter 12
© Gary Conner/Index Stock Imagery

Chapter 13
© Randi Sidman-Moore/Masterfile

Chapter 14
© AP Photo/Carlos Osorio

Index

D

Dangling modifiers, 482–484
Daniels, Jim
    "Short-Order Cook," 273–274
Davis, Norma, 7
    "Can You Go Home Again?",
      216–217
Definition clauses, 450–456
Definitions, 137–148
    causal analysis in, 144–145
    characteristics of, 142–145
    comparison in, 144
    contrasts in, 144
    description in, 143
    developing a topic, 145
    developing ideas, 145
    examples in, 143
    explanations in, 143–144
    patterns of organization in,
      145–146
    in process analysis, 175
    sharing and revising, 146
Dependent clauses, 443–449
Dependent-clause fragments,
    465–467
Description, 90, 123–136
    audience for, 131
    characteristics of, 118, 127–130
    in definitions, 143
    developing a topic, 130–131
    developing ideas, 131–132
    for evaluation, 229
    explanations in, 129–130
    in narrative, 117–118
    patterns of organization in, 133
    revisions, 133
    transitional words and phrases, 129
Descriptive words, 501
Details in compare and contrast, 211
Development of ideas. *See* Ideas,
    development of
Development of topics. *See* Topics,
    development of
Dictionaries, 23
Dominant impression, 118, 128
Donne, John, 268
"Don't Let Stereotypes Warp Your
    Judgments" (Heilbroner),
    372–375
"Dropout Nation" (Thornburgh),
    316–325

E

Editing, 52–53
    connecting dependent and
      independent clauses, 444–456
    connecting independent clauses,
      435–442

noun-pronoun agreement,
    430–433
    subject-verb agreement, 418–430
Education, readings on, 299–328
Ehrenreich, Barbara
    "Oh, Those Family Values,"
      294–296
Elbow, Peter, 5
Electronic sources, citation of,
    407–409, 411
"Emergency Room" (Morales),
    146–148
Emotions, appeal to, 253–254
Emphatic order, 50–51, 93, 159, 174,
    195–196, 229–230, 256
Essays
    audience for, 36–38
    body paragraphs, 29, 81
    coherence in, 92–96
    conclusions, 29, 81, 100–101
    developing a topic (*See* Topics,
      development of)
    developing ideas (*See* Ideas,
      development of)
    fast drafts, 51–52
    introductions, 29, 81, 96–100
    outlines, 47–48
    paragraphs (*See* Paragraphs)
    patterns of organization (*See*
      Organization, patterns of)
    peer review, 53–55
    revision of (*See* Revision)
    structure of, 29–32
    thesis, 29, 43–47, 81–89
    titles of, 102–103
    topic sentences, 44–47
    transitional words and phrases,
      94–96, 116–117
    unity of, 81–89
Evaluation, 90, 222
    characteristics of, 226–230
    compare and contrast in, 229
    criteria for, 227–229, 231–232
    description in, 229
    developing a topic, 230
    developing ideas, 230–231
    narrative in, 229
    patterns of organization,
      229–230, 231
    points of view in, 226–227
    process analysis in, 229
    purpose in, 226–227
    sharing and revising, 232–233
Evidence in persuasion, 253
Examples in definitions, 143
Explanation
    characteristics of, 118
    in definitions, 143–144

in description, 129–130
in narrative, 117–118
in process analysis, 176

F

Family, readings on, 279–297
Farrell, Christopher
    "The Immigrants," 183–189
Fast drafts, 51–52
    in causal analysis, 196
    in narrative, 121
    in process analysis, 179
"Fathers Playing Catch with Sons"
    (Hall), 280–282
Ferguson, Norman
    "Garage," 133–134
Figures of speech, 267–269
    metaphors, 267
    personification, 267–268
    similes, 267
    symbols, 268
    verbal irony, 268
Films, citation of, 407
Finishing, 56
First person, 114–115, 128
First steps. *See* Getting started
Flashbacks, 116
Fragments
    added-idea, 460–462
    dependent-clause, 465–467
    infinitive, 462–464
    present participles, 462–464
    subjects omitted, 458–460
Freewriting, 5–6
Fused sentences. *See* Run-on
    sentences
Future tense, 497–498

G

Galbraith, John Kenneth, 5
"Garage" (Ferguson), 133–134
Gates, Henry Louis, Jr., 279
    "In the Kitchen," 287–292
Getting started
    freewriting, 5–6
    journals, 6–8
    strategies for, 8
"Getting through School" (Gilbert),
    60–61
Gilbert, Gary
    "Getting through School," 60–61
Godwin, Gail
    "The Watcher at the Gates," 18–20
Gonzales, Doug, 7, 33, 35–36, 37,
    42–43, 44, 52, 54–56, 95
    "Coping with Stress," 56–58
"Good Daughter, The" (Hwang),
    284–286

H

Hall, Donald
  "Fathers Playing Catch with
    Sons," 280–282
Harris, Tom, 165
  "How Urban Legends Work,"
    166–172
Heilbroner, Robert L., 371
  "Don't Let Stereotypes Warp Your
    Judgments," 372–375
Hewitt, Bill et al.
  "MySpace Nation," 222–225
"How Urban Legends Work" (Harris),
    166–172
Hughes, Langston, 299
  "Theme for English B," 326–327
Hwang, Caroline, 279
  "The Good Daughter," 284–286
"Hypocrisy" (Myers), 233–234

I

"I Just Wanna Be Average" (Rose),
    303–311
Ideas, development of, 38–43, 90–92
  asking yourself questions, 39
  in classification, 160
  in compare and contrast, 213
  in definitions, 145
  in description, 131–132
  in evaluation, 230–231
  idea wheels, 39–42, 178
  making a list of ideas, 42–43
  in narrative, 120–121
  in persuasion, 256
  in process analysis, 178–179
Ideas, organization of. See
    Organization, patterns of
Identity, readings on, 349–369
Illustration. See Description
"Immigrants, The" (Mandel and
    Farrell), 183–189
Imperatives, 501–502
"In the Kitchen" (Gates), 287–292
Indefinite pronouns, 427–429
Independent clauses, 435–438,
    443–449
Infinitives in fragments, 462–464
Information mapping, 193
-ing. See Present participles
"Inheritance" (Soto), 267–268, 271–272
Inn, Donald
  "The Art of Lion Dancing," 161–163
Internet. See Electronic sources
"Internet Censorship Will Accomplish
    Nothing" (Lee), 258–263
Interviews, citation of, 406
Introductions, 29, 81, 96–100
Introductory phrases, 502

Irony, 268
Irregular verbs, 496–497
Issa, Semeen
  "Muslim Women," 381–384

J

Jahnke, Art, 107
  "What Ever Happened to
    Friendship?", 149–154
Jamison, Shenice, 26–27
Journals
  citation of, 405–406, 410–411
  ideas for journal entries, 9
  sample journal entries, 6–8
"Just Walk On By" (Staples), 343–346

K

Kent, Misty
  "Americans' Obsession with
    Celebrities," 197–201
Keywords, 34, 60, 62–63
  in thesis statement, 83–85
King, Martin Luther, Jr.
  "Letter from the Birmingham
    Jail," 240–248
Krum, Dan
  "Relationships in My Life," 180–181

L

Lectures, citation of, 406
Lee, Linda
  "Internet Censorship Will
    Accomplish Nothing,"
    258–263
"Letter from the Birmingham Jail"
    (King), 240–248
Linking verbs, 500–501
Little, Sheryl
  "Love and War: An Evaluation of
    Dr. Zhivago" 234–236
Loeb, Paul Rogat
  "The Civil Rights Movement Was
    the Sum of Many People,"
    12–15
"Love and War: An Evaluation of
    Dr. Zhivago" (Little), 234–236
Luu, Wendy, 8

M

Magazines, citation of, 405–406
Main clauses. See Independent
    clauses
Mandel, Michael J.
  "The Immigrants," 183–189
Masuno, Sam
  "To Be Thankful," 122–123
McCarthy, Abigail
  "The New Immigrants," 366–368

Men and women, readings on, 331–347
"Men We Carry in Our Minds, The"
    (Sanders), 332–335
Metaphors, 267
Miller, Marjorie, 107
  "Border Culture," 137–141
*MLA Handbook for the Writers of
    Research Papers*, 402–414
Moral values, appeal to, 254–255
Morales, Ernesto
  "Emergency Room," 146–148
"Mother" (Baker), 108–112
Multiple subjects, 499
Multiple verbs, 500
"Muslim Women" (Al-Marayati and
    Issa), 381–384
"My Luve's like a red, red rose"
    (Burns), 267
"My Papa's Waltz" (Roethke), 269–270
Myers, Jamie
  "Hypocrisy," 233–234
"MySpace Nation" (Hewitt et al.),
    222–225
"Myth of the Latin Woman, The"
    (Cofer), 376–380

N

Narrative, 90, 108–123
  audience for, 115, 120
  characteristics of, 114–118
  conflicts in, 116
  description in, 117–118
  developing a topic, 119
  developing ideas, 120–121
  in evaluation, 229
  explanation in, 117–118
  fast drafts, 121
  patterns of organization in, 121
  in process analysis, 175
  purpose of, 115
  sharing and revising, 121
  transitional words and phrases in,
    116–117
"New Immigrants, The" (McCarthy),
    366–368
Newspapers, citation of, 405–406
Nondefinition clauses, 450–456
Noun-pronoun agreement, 430–433
Nuñez, Tony
  "Becoming an American," 218–219

O

"Oh, Those Family Values"
    (Ehrenreich), 294–296
"Open Letter to Black Parents, An"
    (Ashe), 314–315
Order-of-importance organization.
    See Emphatic order